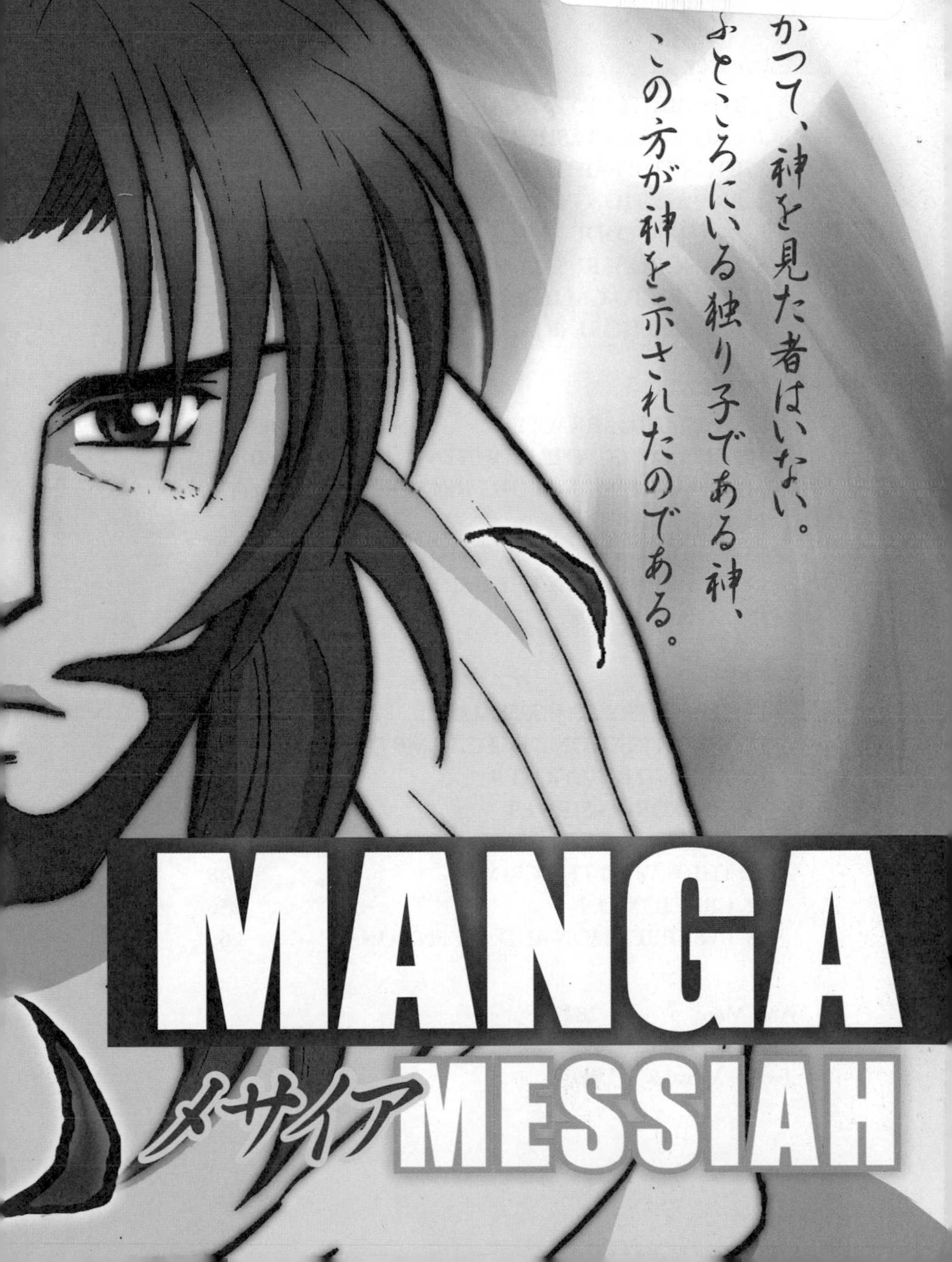
かつて、神を見た者はいない。
ふところにいる独り子である神、
この方が神を示されたのである。
MANGA
メサイア MESSIAH

Contents

Chapter

Chapter

Chapter

Chapter I

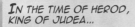

IN THE TIME OF HEROD, KING OF JUDEA...

NAZARETH, A TOWN IN GALILEE LOCATED ABOUT 60 MILES NORTH OF JERUSALEM...

YOSEF!!

YOU'VE BEEN WORKING SO HARD ALL DAY!

I'VE BROUGHT SOMETHING FOR YOU!

THANK YOU, MIRYAM!

MIRYAM WAS JUST A YOUNG TEENAGER ENGAGED TO A CARPENTER NAMED YOSEF...

YOU'VE WORKED ALL THE WAY UNTIL EVENING, YOSEF!

SEE? THERE ARE STARS IN THE SKY!

YES, THEY'RE BEAUTIFUL, MIRYAM...

WELL, WE'D BETTER GO HOME... GOOD NIGHT!

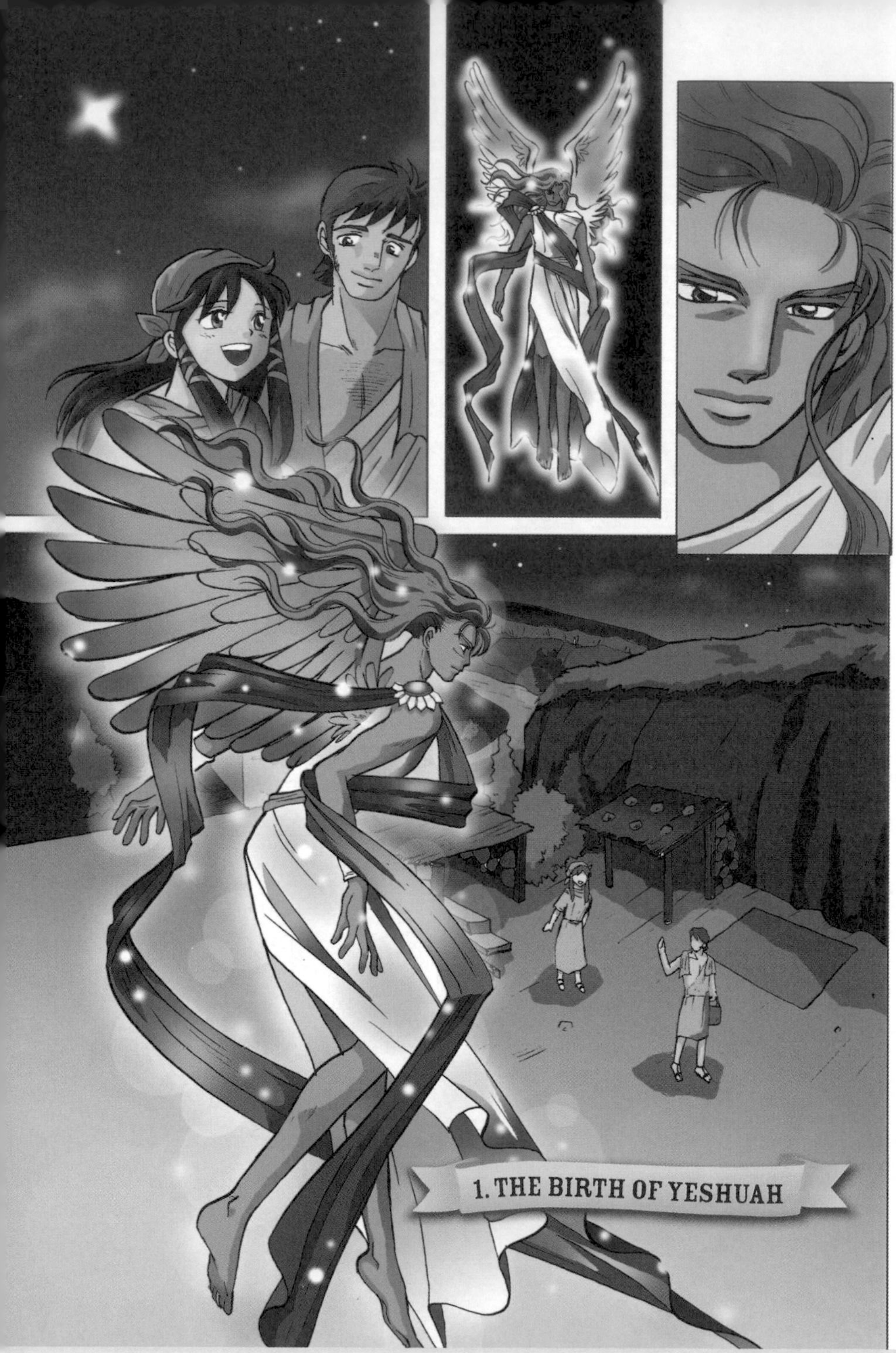
1. THE BIRTH OF YESHUAH

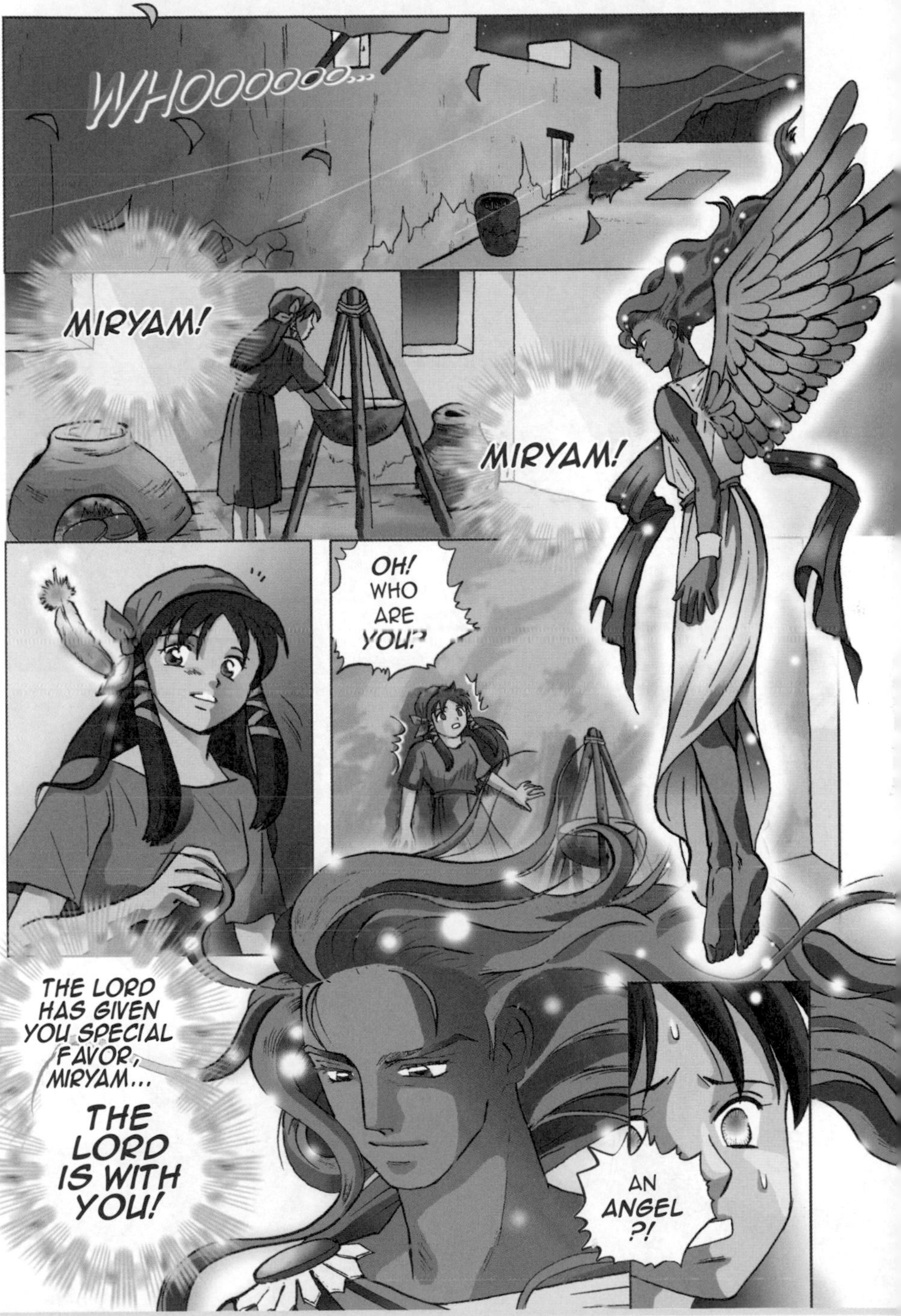
WHOOOOOO...
MIRYAM!
MIRYAM!
OH! WHO ARE YOU!?
THE LORD HAS GIVEN YOU SPECIAL FAVOR, MIRYAM...
THE LORD IS WITH YOU!
AN ANGEL ?!

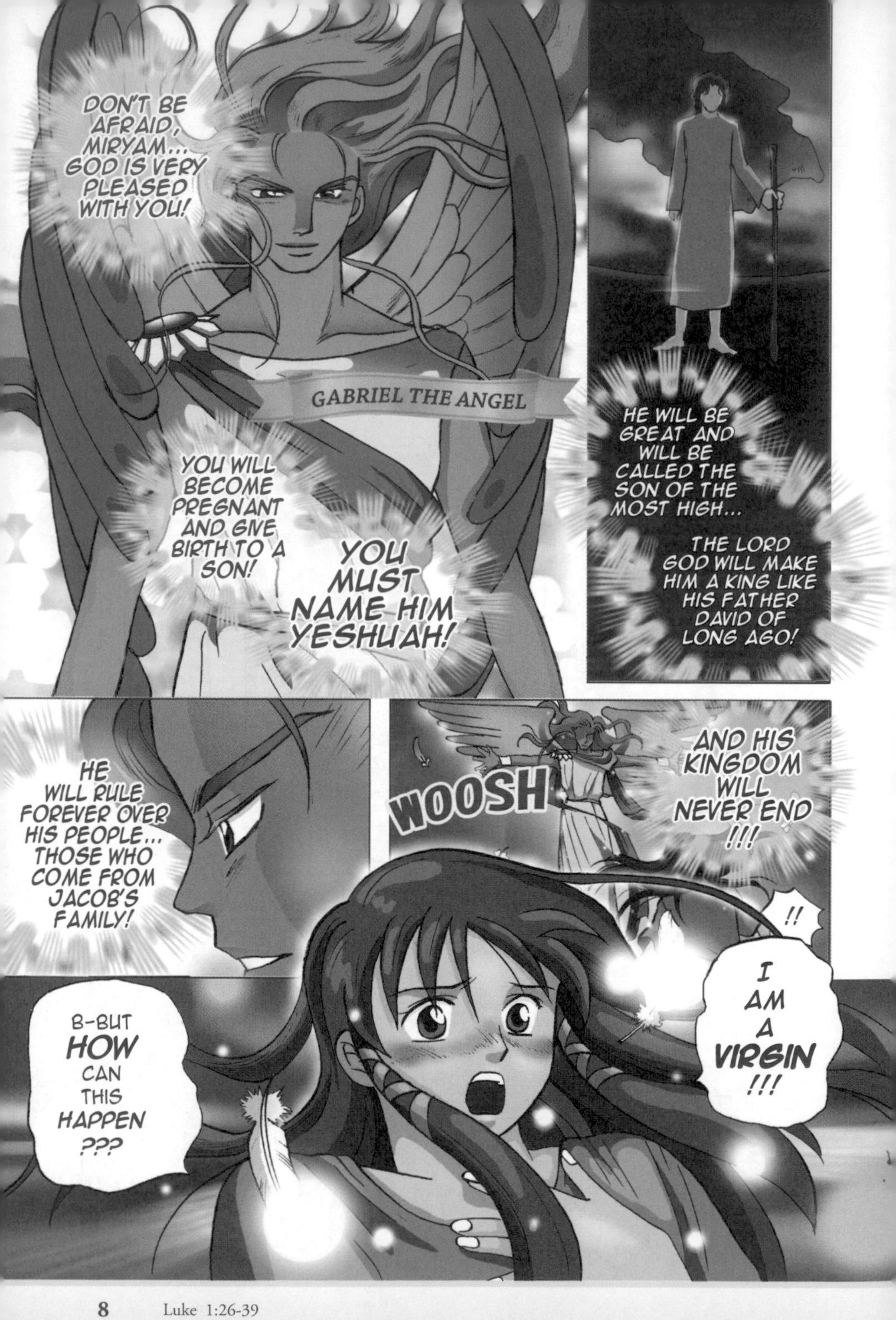
DON'T BE AFRAID, MIRYAM... GOD IS VERY PLEASED WITH YOU!
GABRIEL THE ANGEL
YOU WILL BECOME PREGNANT AND GIVE BIRTH TO A SON!
YOU MUST NAME HIM YESHUAH!
HE WILL BE GREAT AND WILL BE CALLED THE SON OF THE MOST HIGH...
THE LORD GOD WILL MAKE HIM A KING LIKE HIS FATHER DAVID OF LONG AGO!
HE WILL RULE FOREVER OVER HIS PEOPLE... THOSE WHO COME FROM JACOB'S FAMILY!
WOOSH
AND HIS KINGDOM WILL NEVER END !!!
!!
I AM A VIRGIN !!!
B-BUT HOW CAN THIS HAPPEN ???

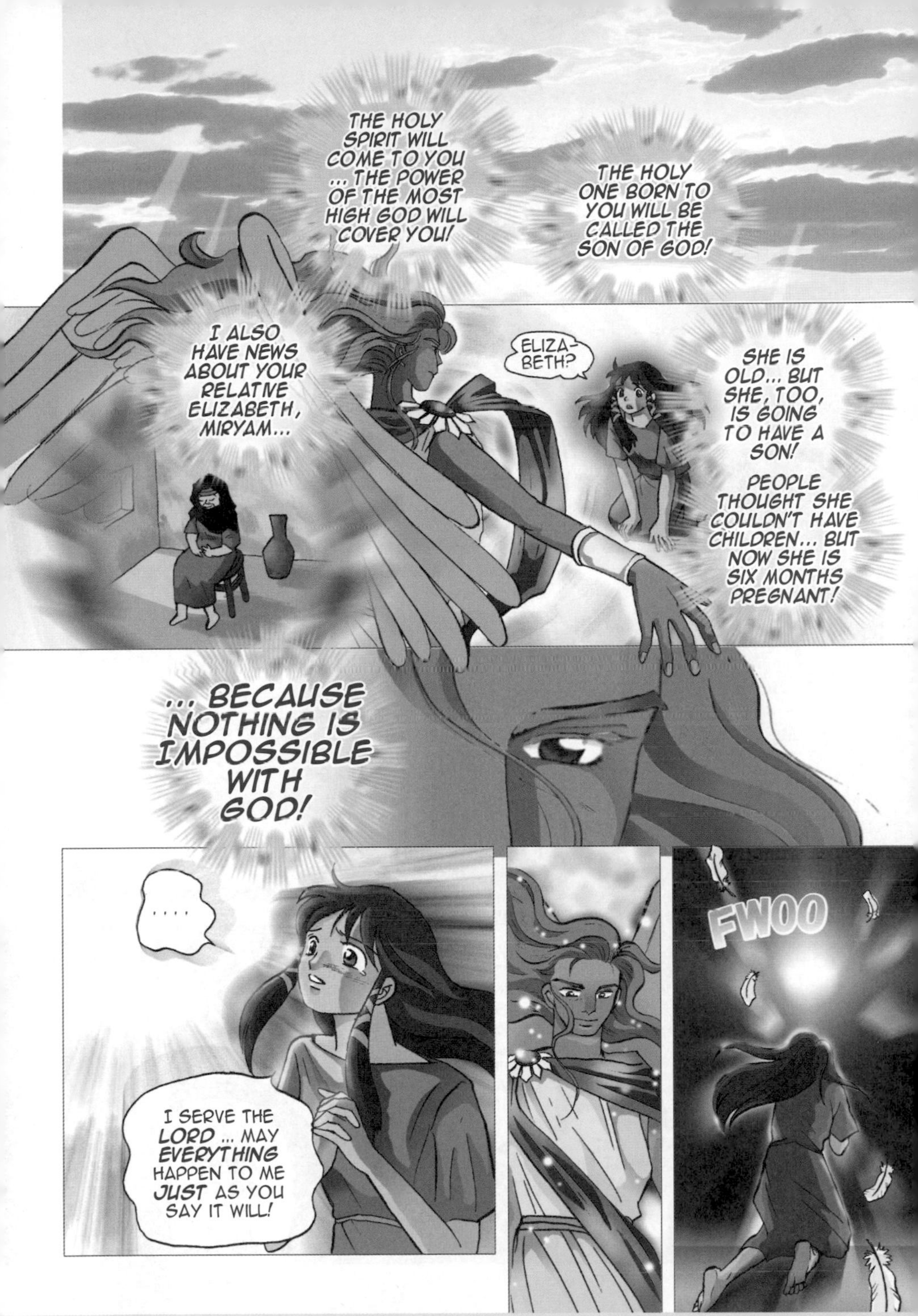
THE HOLY SPIRIT WILL COME TO YOU ... THE POWER OF THE MOST HIGH GOD WILL COVER YOU!
THE HOLY ONE BORN TO YOU WILL BE CALLED THE SON OF GOD!
I ALSO HAVE NEWS ABOUT YOUR RELATIVE ELIZABETH, MIRYAM...
ELIZA-BETH?
SHE IS OLD... BUT SHE, TOO, IS GOING TO HAVE A SON!
PEOPLE THOUGHT SHE COULDN'T HAVE CHILDREN... BUT NOW SHE IS SIX MONTHS PREGNANT!
... BECAUSE NOTHING IS IMPOSSIBLE WITH GOD!
....
I SERVE THE LORD ... MAY EVERYTHING HAPPEN TO ME JUST AS YOU SAY IT WILL!
FWOO

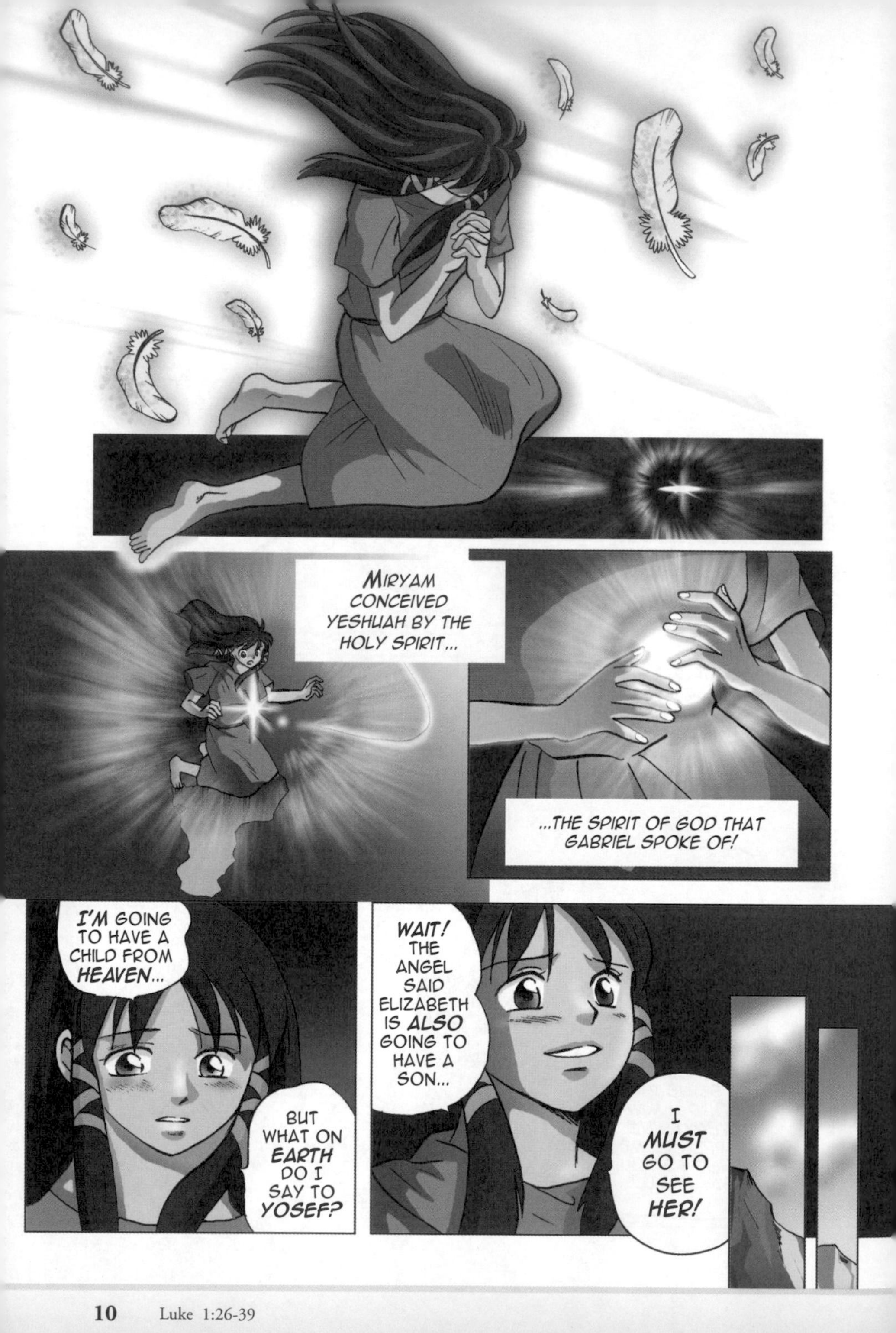
MIRYAM CONCEIVED YESHUAH BY THE HOLY SPIRIT...
...THE SPIRIT OF GOD THAT GABRIEL SPOKE OF!
I'M GOING TO HAVE A CHILD FROM HEAVEN...
BUT WHAT ON EARTH DO I SAY TO YOSEF?
WAIT! THE ANGEL SAID ELIZABETH IS ALSO GOING TO HAVE A SON...
I MUST GO TO SEE HER!

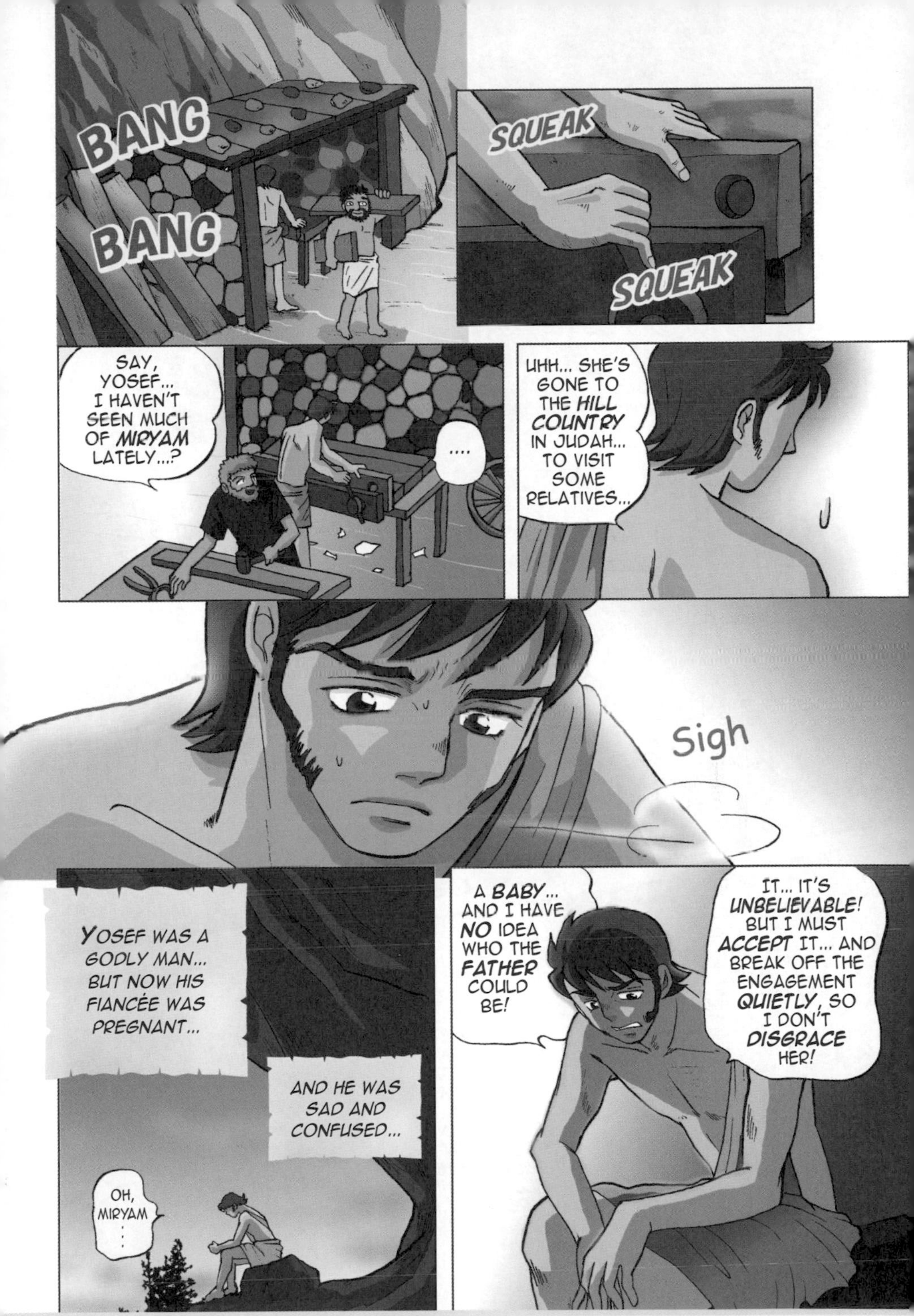
BANG
BANG
SQUEAK
SQUEAK
SAY, YOSEF... I HAVEN'T SEEN MUCH OF MIRYAM LATELY...?
....
UHH... SHE'S GONE TO THE HILL COUNTRY IN JUDAH... TO VISIT SOME RELATIVES...
Sigh
YOSEF WAS A GODLY MAN... BUT NOW HIS FIANCÉE WAS PREGNANT...
AND HE WAS SAD AND CONFUSED...
OH, MIRYAM . . .
A BABY... AND I HAVE NO IDEA WHO THE FATHER COULD BE!
IT... IT'S UNBELIEVABLE! BUT I MUST ACCEPT IT... AND BREAK OFF THE ENGAGEMENT QUIETLY, SO I DON'T DISGRACE HER!

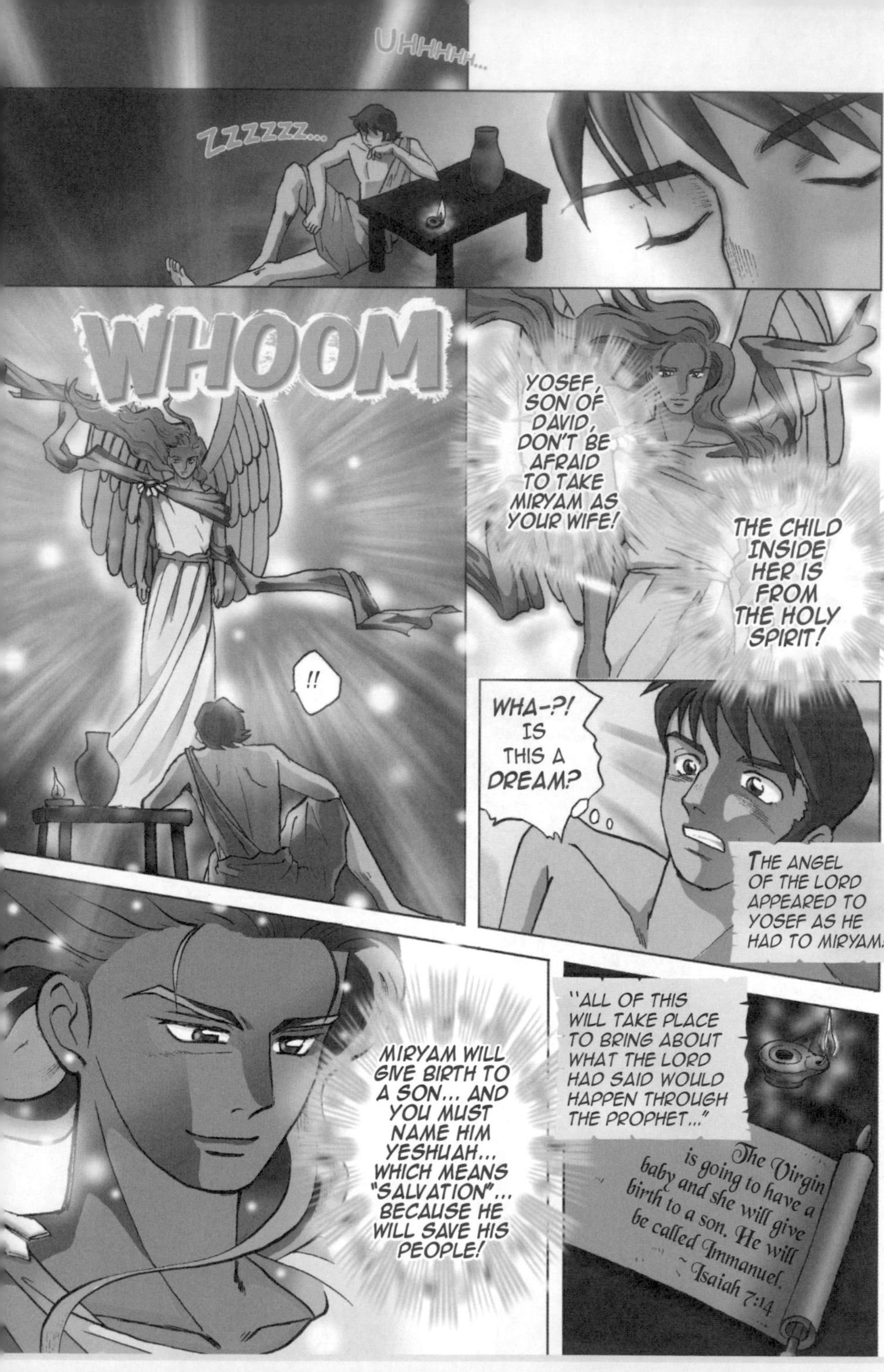
UHHHHH...
ZZZZZZ...
WHOOM
YOSEF, SON OF DAVID, DON'T BE AFRAID TO TAKE MIRYAM AS YOUR WIFE!
THE CHILD INSIDE HER IS FROM THE HOLY SPIRIT!
!!
WHA-?! IS THIS A DREAM?
THE ANGEL OF THE LORD APPEARED TO YOSEF AS HE HAD TO MIRYAM!
MIRYAM WILL GIVE BIRTH TO A SON... AND YOU MUST NAME HIM YESHUAH... WHICH MEANS "SALVATION"... BECAUSE HE WILL SAVE HIS PEOPLE!
"ALL OF THIS WILL TAKE PLACE TO BRING ABOUT WHAT THE LORD HAD SAID WOULD HAPPEN THROUGH THE PROPHET..."
The Virgin is going to have a baby and she will give birth to a son. He will be called Immanuel.
~ Isaiah 7:14

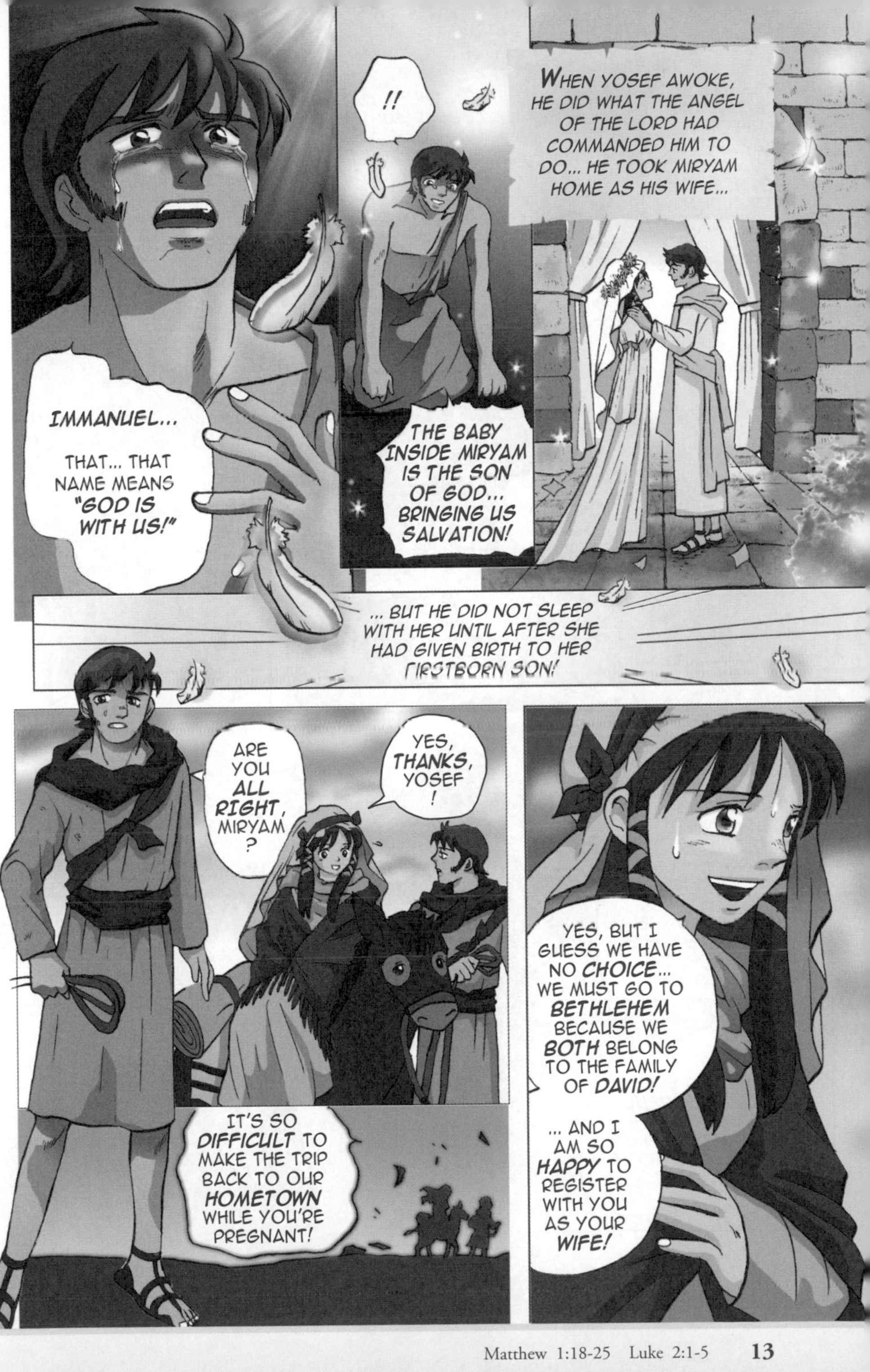
IMMANUEL... THAT... THAT NAME MEANS "GOD IS WITH US!"
!!
THE BABY INSIDE MIRYAM IS THE SON OF GOD... BRINGING US SALVATION!
WHEN YOSEF AWOKE, HE DID WHAT THE ANGEL OF THE LORD HAD COMMANDED HIM TO DO... HE TOOK MIRYAM HOME AS HIS WIFE...
... BUT HE DID NOT SLEEP WITH HER UNTIL AFTER SHE HAD GIVEN BIRTH TO HER FIRSTBORN SON!
ARE YOU ALL RIGHT, MIRYAM?
YES, THANKS, YOSEF!
IT'S SO DIFFICULT TO MAKE THE TRIP BACK TO OUR HOMETOWN WHILE YOU'RE PREGNANT!
YES, BUT I GUESS WE HAVE NO CHOICE... WE MUST GO TO BETHLEHEM BECAUSE WE BOTH BELONG TO THE FAMILY OF DAVID!
... AND I AM SO HAPPY TO REGISTER WITH YOU AS YOUR WIFE!

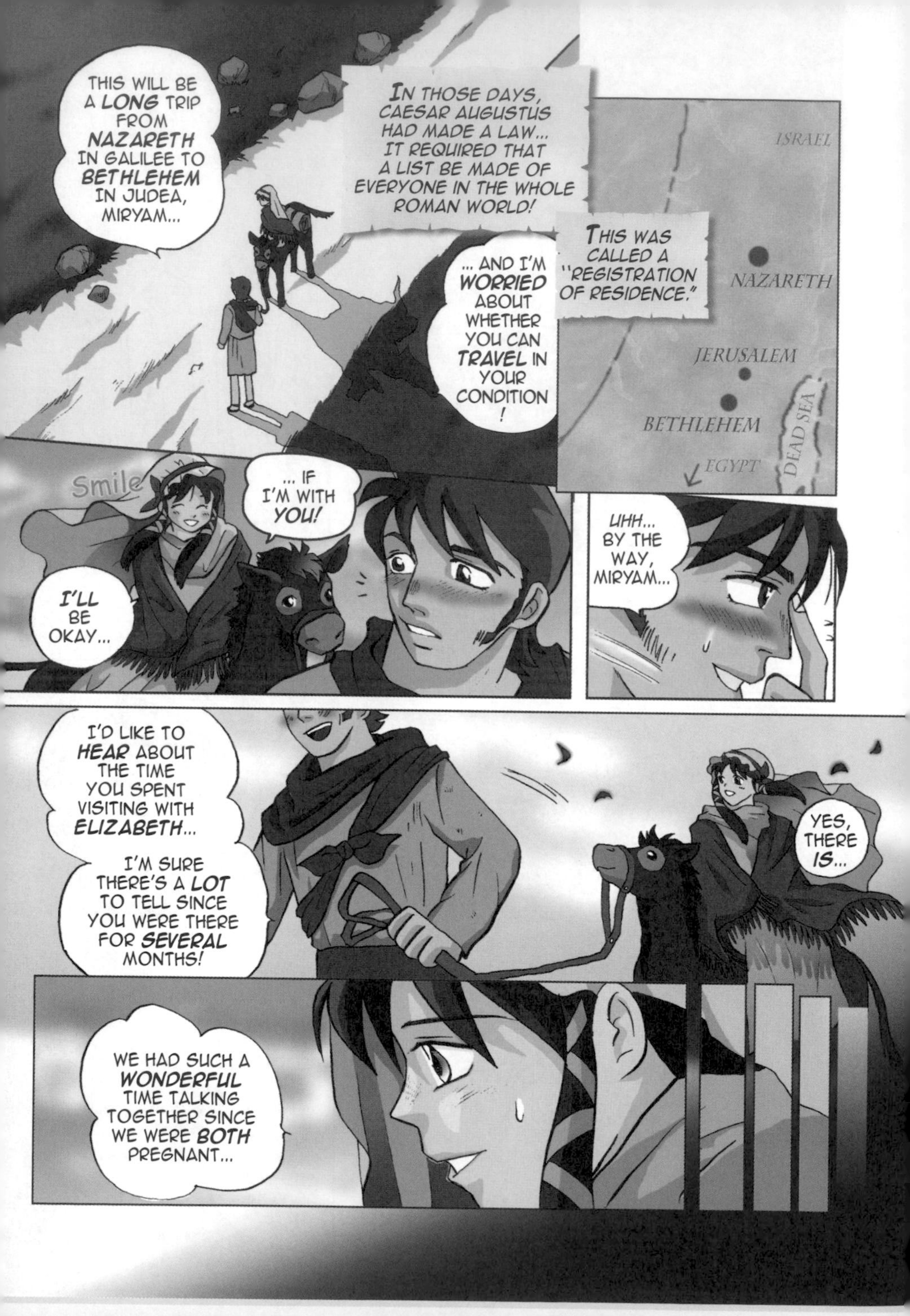
THIS WILL BE A LONG TRIP FROM NAZARETH IN GALILEE TO BETHLEHEM IN JUDEA, MIRYAM...
IN THOSE DAYS, CAESAR AUGUSTUS HAD MADE A LAW... IT REQUIRED THAT A LIST BE MADE OF EVERYONE IN THE WHOLE ROMAN WORLD!
... AND I'M WORRIED ABOUT WHETHER YOU CAN TRAVEL IN YOUR CONDITION!
THIS WAS CALLED A "REGISTRATION OF RESIDENCE."
ISRAEL
NAZARETH
JERUSALEM
BETHLEHEM
DEAD SEA
EGYPT
Smile
I'LL BE OKAY...
... IF I'M WITH YOU!
UHH... BY THE WAY, MIRYAM...
I'D LIKE TO HEAR ABOUT THE TIME YOU SPENT VISITING WITH ELIZABETH...
I'M SURE THERE'S A LOT TO TELL SINCE YOU WERE THERE FOR SEVERAL MONTHS!
YES, THERE IS...
WE HAD SUCH A WONDERFUL TIME TALKING TOGETHER SINCE WE WERE BOTH PREGNANT...

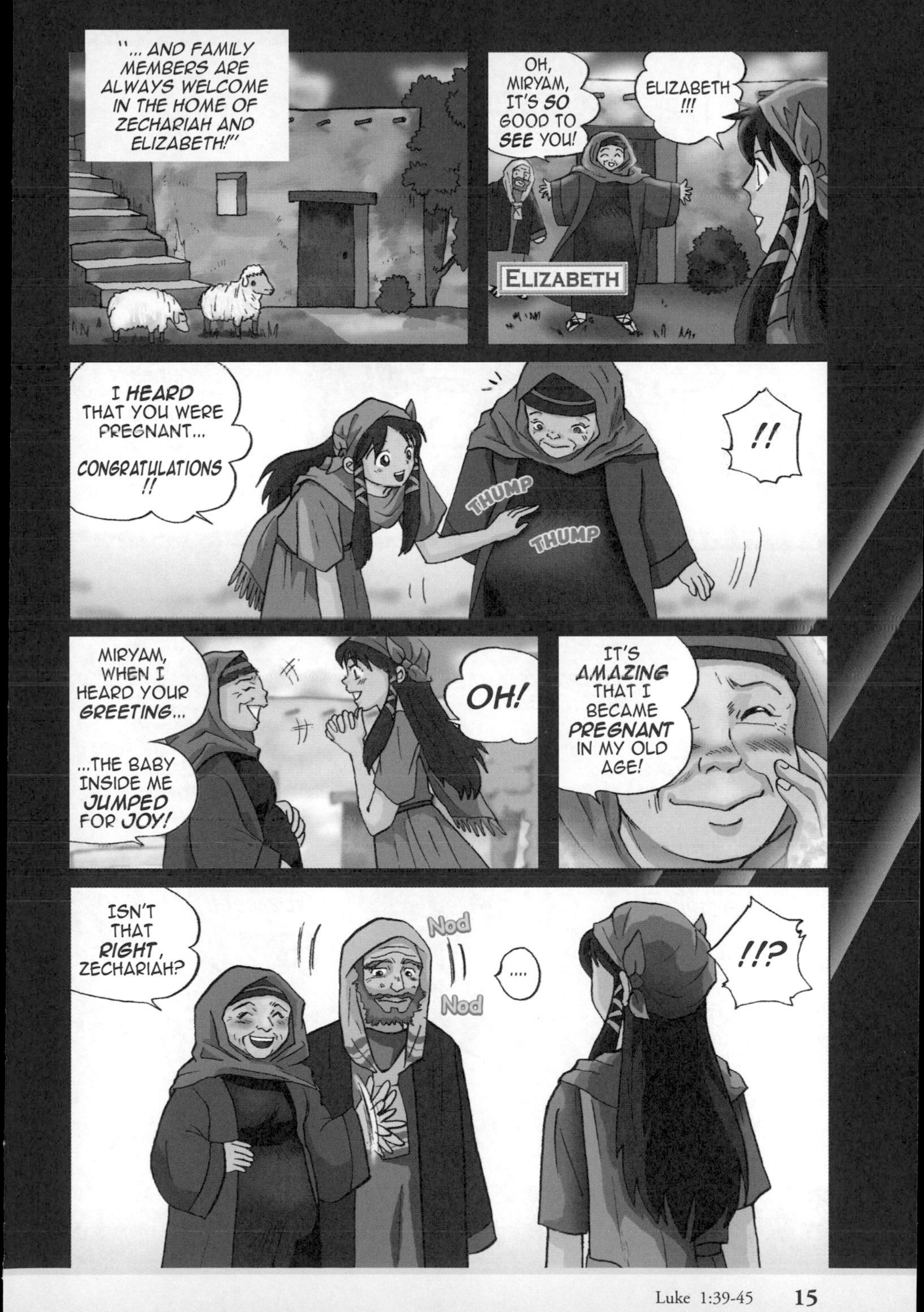
"... AND FAMILY MEMBERS ARE ALWAYS WELCOME IN THE HOME OF ZECHARIAH AND ELIZABETH!"
OH, MIRYAM, IT'S SO GOOD TO SEE YOU!
ELIZABETH !!!
ELIZABETH
I HEARD THAT YOU WERE PREGNANT...
CONGRATULATIONS !!
THUMP
THUMP
!!
MIRYAM, WHEN I HEARD YOUR GREETING...
...THE BABY INSIDE ME JUMPED FOR JOY!
OH!
IT'S AMAZING THAT I BECAME PREGNANT IN MY OLD AGE!
ISN'T THAT RIGHT, ZECHARIAH?
Nod
Nod
....
!!?

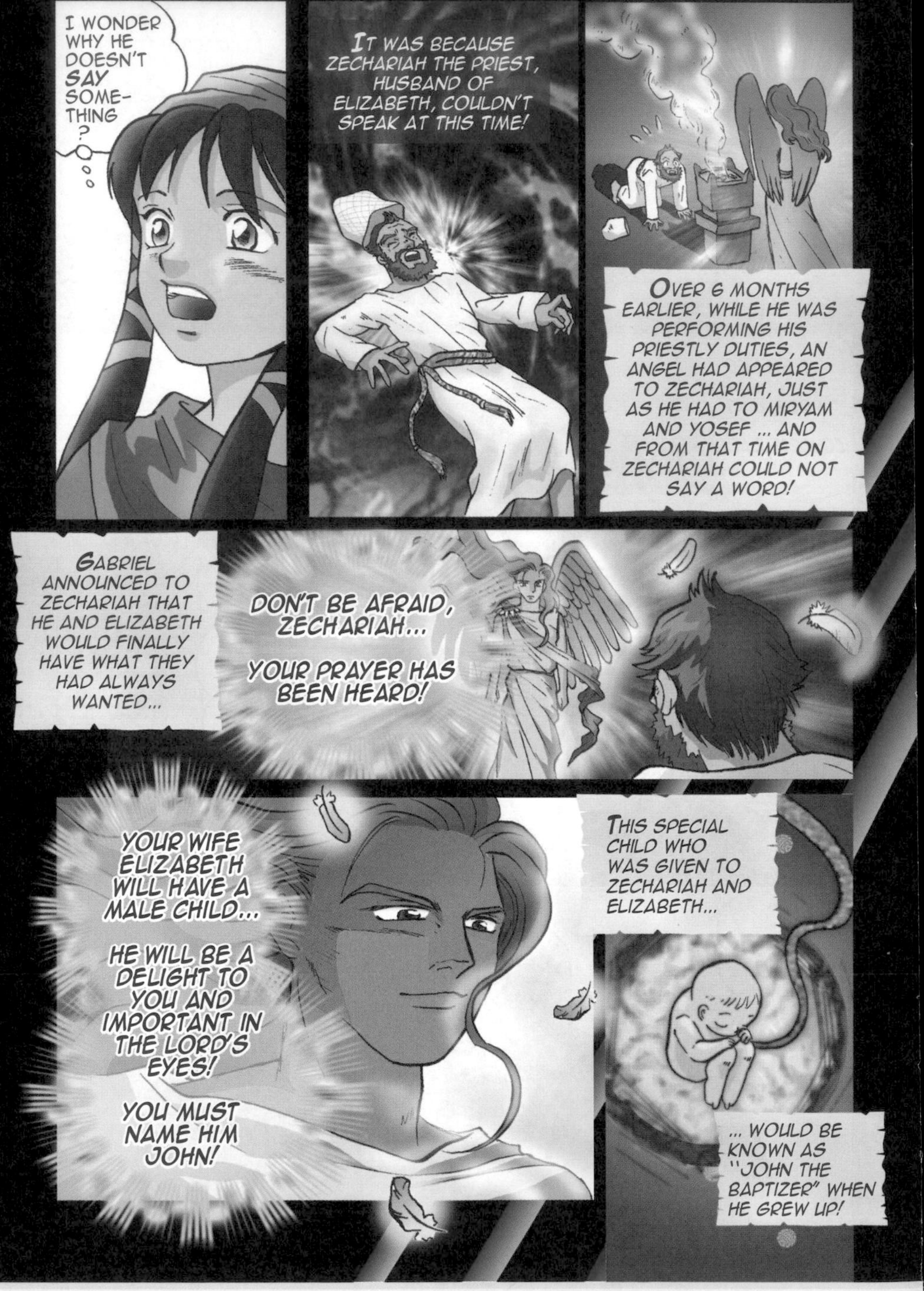
I WONDER WHY HE DOESN'T SAY SOME-THING?
IT WAS BECAUSE ZECHARIAH THE PRIEST, HUSBAND OF ELIZABETH, COULDN'T SPEAK AT THIS TIME!
OVER 6 MONTHS EARLIER, WHILE HE WAS PERFORMING HIS PRIESTLY DUTIES, AN ANGEL HAD APPEARED TO ZECHARIAH, JUST AS HE HAD TO MIRYAM AND YOSEF ... AND FROM THAT TIME ON ZECHARIAH COULD NOT SAY A WORD!
GABRIEL ANNOUNCED TO ZECHARIAH THAT HE AND ELIZABETH WOULD FINALLY HAVE WHAT THEY HAD ALWAYS WANTED...
DON'T BE AFRAID, ZECHARIAH...
YOUR PRAYER HAS BEEN HEARD!
YOUR WIFE ELIZABETH WILL HAVE A MALE CHILD...
HE WILL BE A DELIGHT TO YOU AND IMPORTANT IN THE LORD'S EYES!
YOU MUST NAME HIM JOHN!
THIS SPECIAL CHILD WHO WAS GIVEN TO ZECHARIAH AND ELIZABETH...
... WOULD BE KNOWN AS "JOHN THE BAPTIZER" WHEN HE GREW UP!

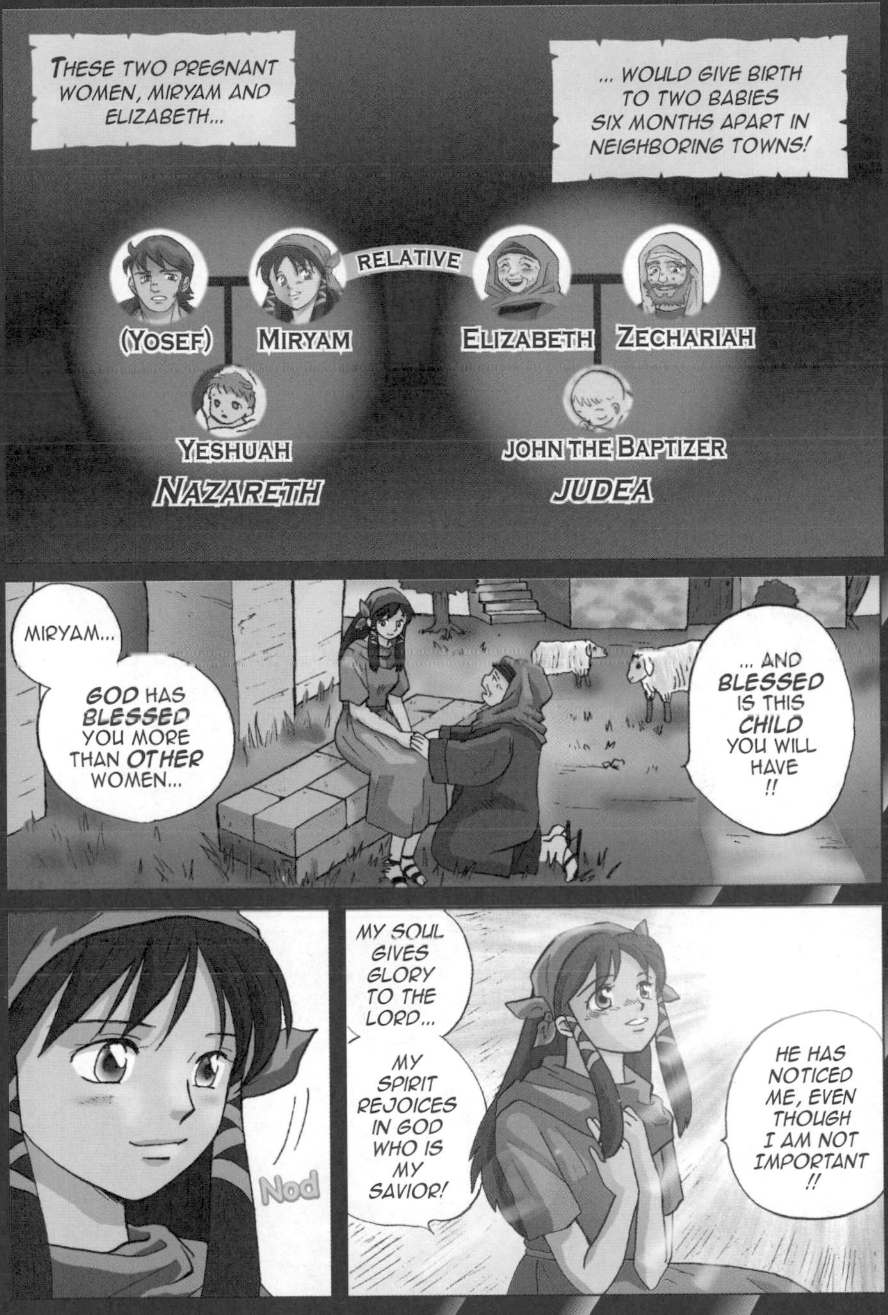
THESE TWO PREGNANT WOMEN, MIRYAM AND ELIZABETH...
... WOULD GIVE BIRTH TO TWO BABIES SIX MONTHS APART IN NEIGHBORING TOWNS!
RELATIVE
(YOSEF)
MIRYAM
ELIZABETH
ZECHARIAH
YESHUAH
JOHN THE BAPTIZER
NAZARETH
JUDEA
MIRYAM...
GOD HAS BLESSED YOU MORE THAN OTHER WOMEN...
... AND BLESSED IS THIS CHILD YOU WILL HAVE !!
Nod
MY SOUL GIVES GLORY TO THE LORD...
MY SPIRIT REJOICES IN GOD WHO IS MY SAVIOR!
HE HAS NOTICED ME, EVEN THOUGH I AM NOT IMPORTANT !!

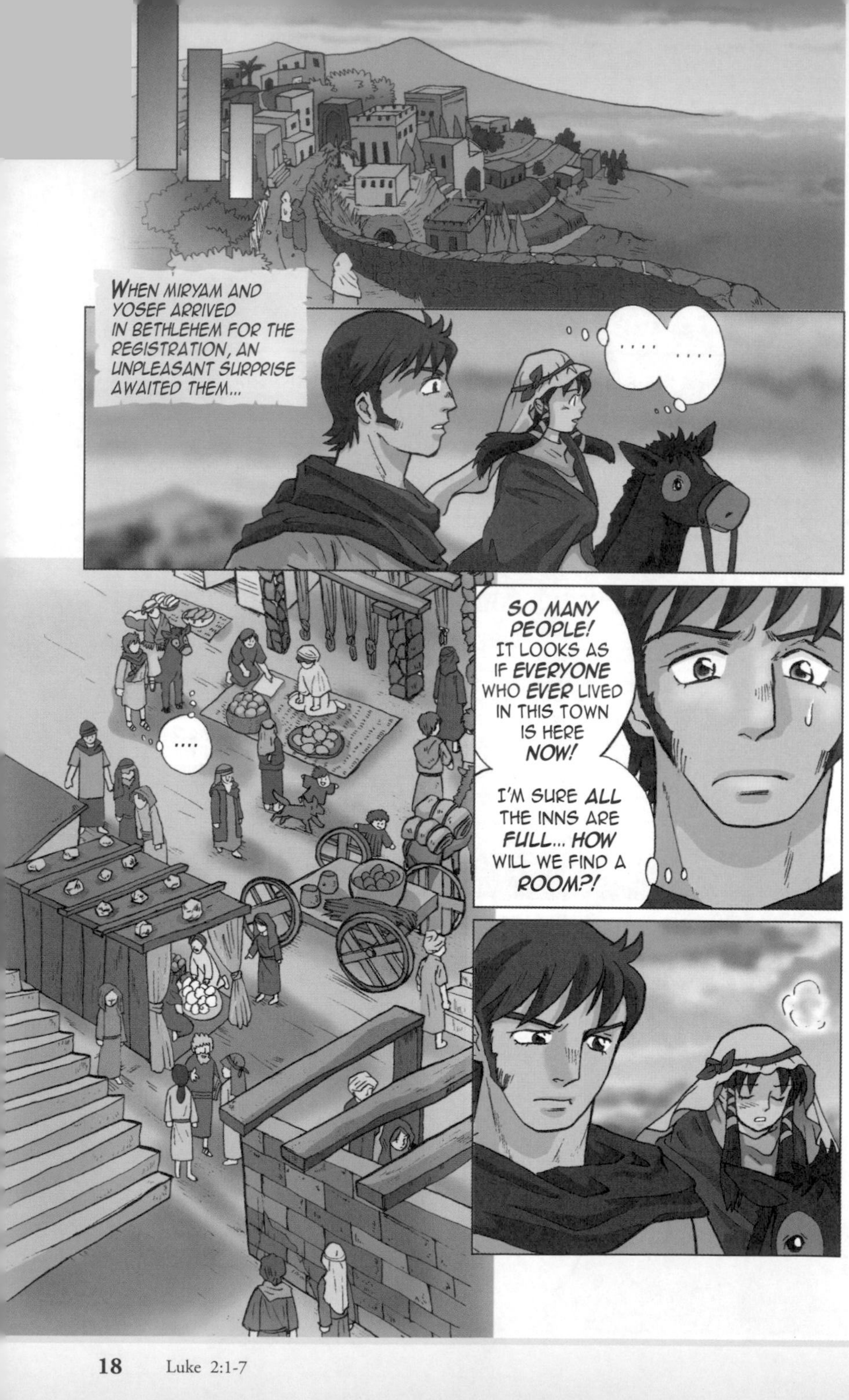
WHEN MIRYAM AND YOSEF ARRIVED IN BETHLEHEM FOR THE REGISTRATION, AN UNPLEASANT SURPRISE AWAITED THEM...
....
....
SO MANY PEOPLE! IT LOOKS AS IF EVERYONE WHO EVER LIVED IN THIS TOWN IS HERE NOW!
I'M SURE ALL THE INNS ARE FULL... HOW WILL WE FIND A ROOM?!

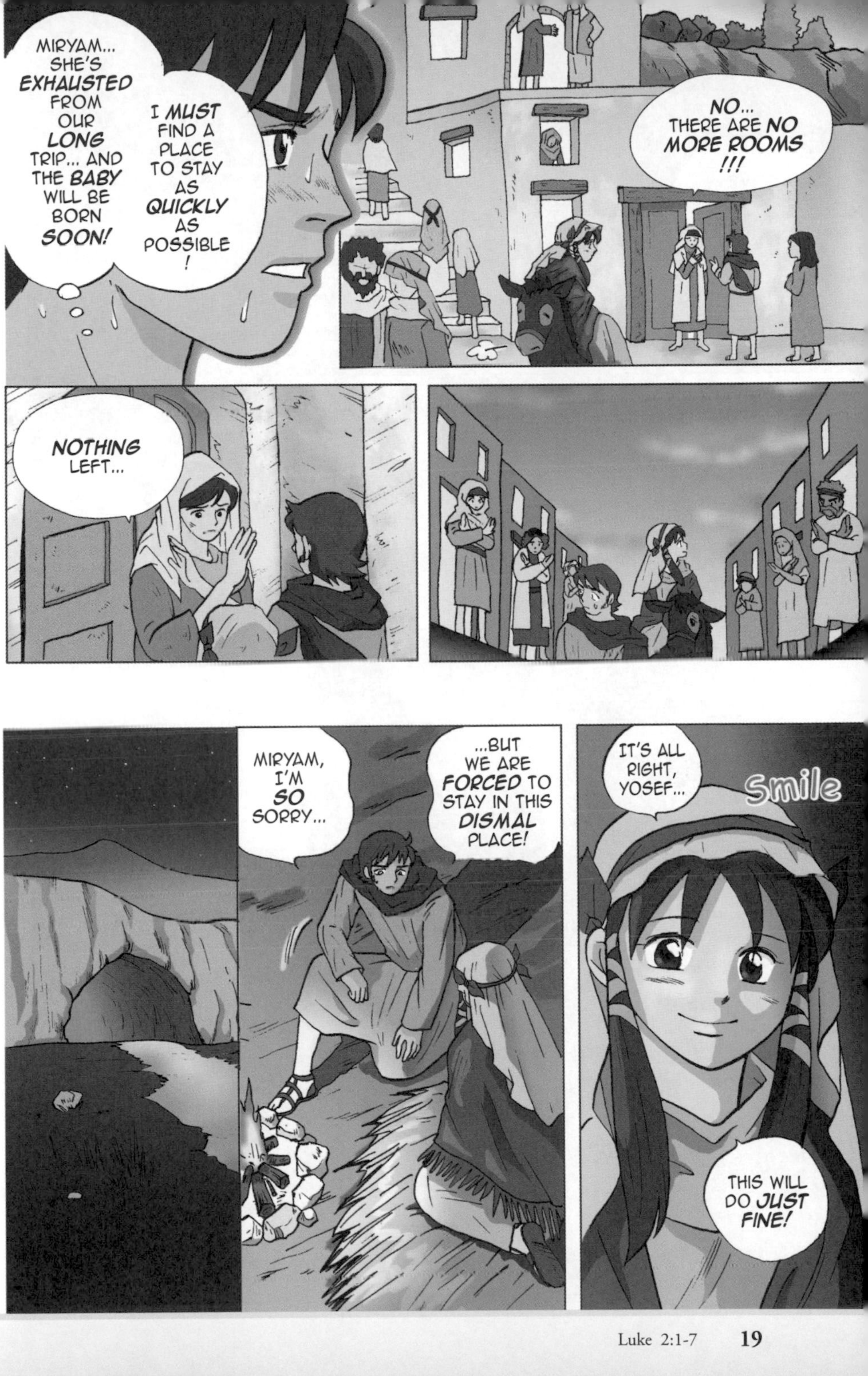
MIRYAM... SHE'S EXHAUSTED FROM OUR LONG TRIP... AND THE BABY WILL BE BORN SOON!
I MUST FIND A PLACE TO STAY AS QUICKLY AS POSSIBLE!
NO... THERE ARE NO MORE ROOMS!!!
NOTHING LEFT...
MIRYAM, I'M SO SORRY...
...BUT WE ARE FORCED TO STAY IN THIS DISMAL PLACE!
IT'S ALL RIGHT, YOSEF...
Smile
THIS WILL DO JUST FINE!

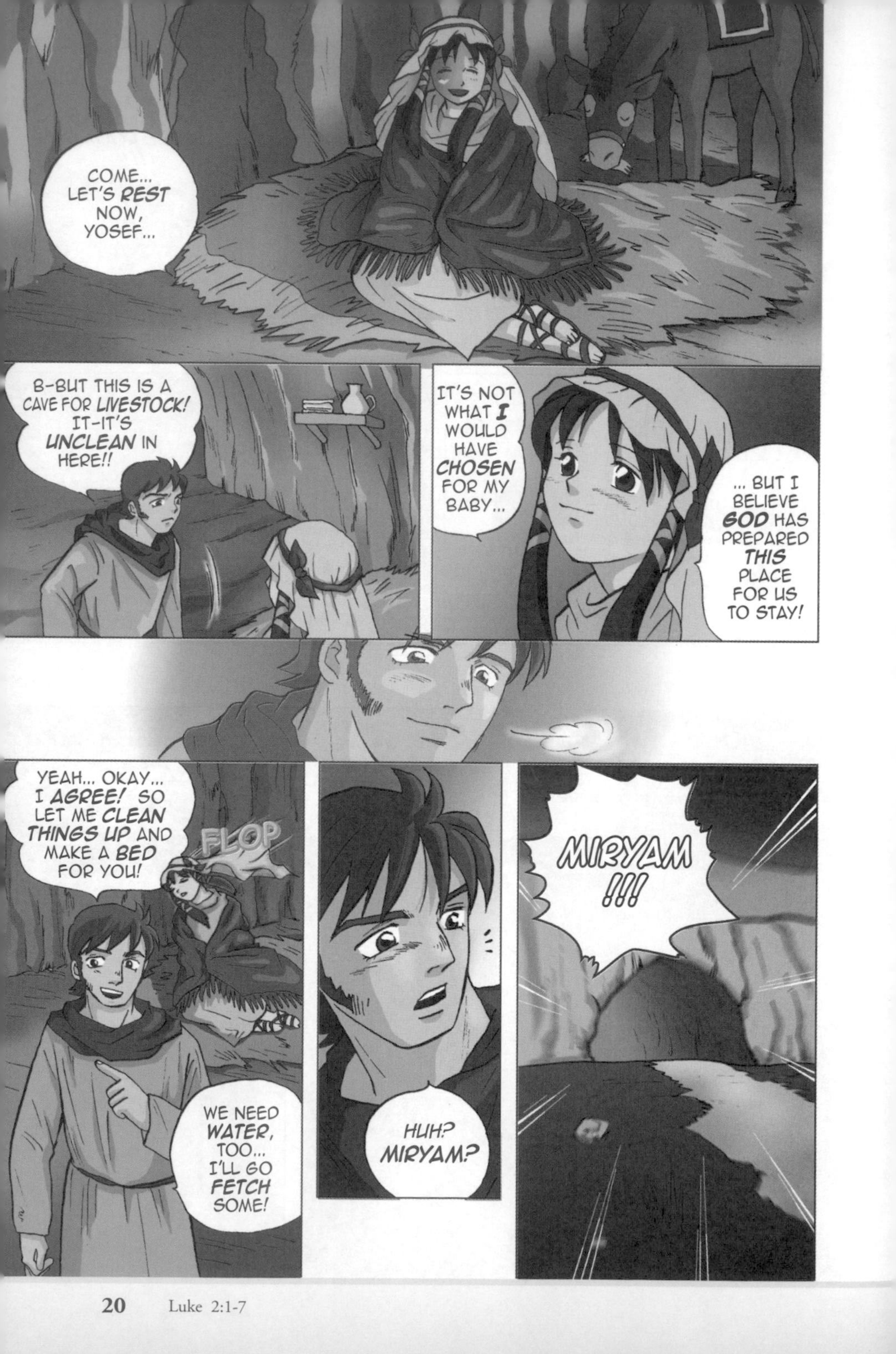
COME... LET'S REST NOW, YOSEF...
B-BUT THIS IS A CAVE FOR LIVESTOCK! IT-IT'S UNCLEAN IN HERE!!
IT'S NOT WHAT I WOULD HAVE CHOSEN FOR MY BABY...
... BUT I BELIEVE GOD HAS PREPARED THIS PLACE FOR US TO STAY!
YEAH... OKAY... I AGREE! SO LET ME CLEAN THINGS UP AND MAKE A BED FOR YOU!
FLOP
WE NEED WATER, TOO... I'LL GO FETCH SOME!
HUH? MIRYAM?
MIRYAM !!!

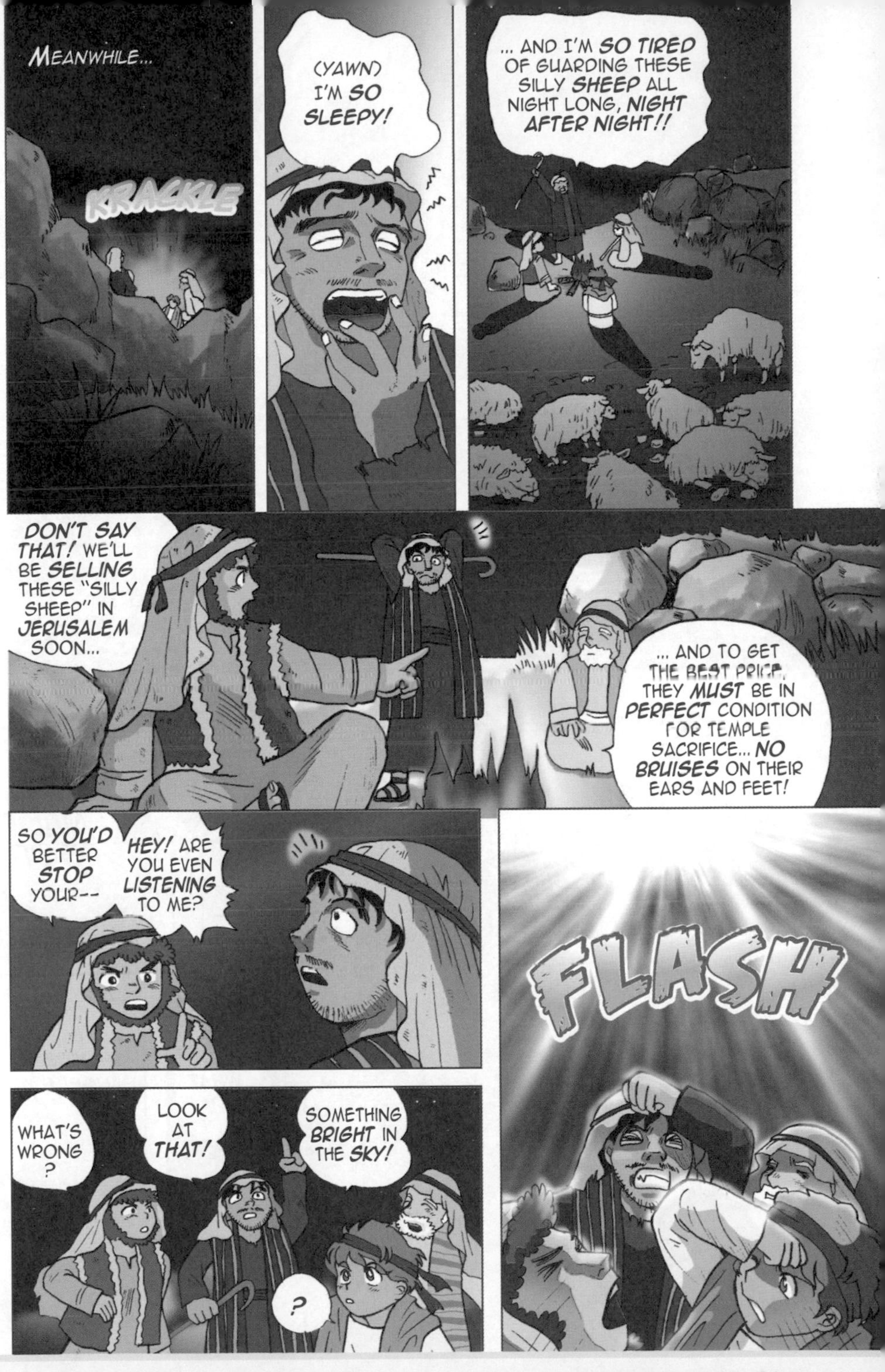
MEANWHILE...
KRACKLE
(YAWN) I'M SO SLEEPY!
... AND I'M SO TIRED OF GUARDING THESE SILLY SHEEP ALL NIGHT LONG, NIGHT AFTER NIGHT!!
DON'T SAY THAT! WE'LL BE SELLING THESE "SILLY SHEEP" IN JERUSALEM SOON...
... AND TO GET THE BEST PRICE, THEY MUST BE IN PERFECT CONDITION FOR TEMPLE SACRIFICE... NO BRUISES ON THEIR EARS AND FEET!
SO YOU'D BETTER STOP YOUR--
HEY! ARE YOU EVEN LISTENING TO ME?
WHAT'S WRONG ?
LOOK AT THAT!
SOMETHING BRIGHT IN THE SKY!
?
FLASH

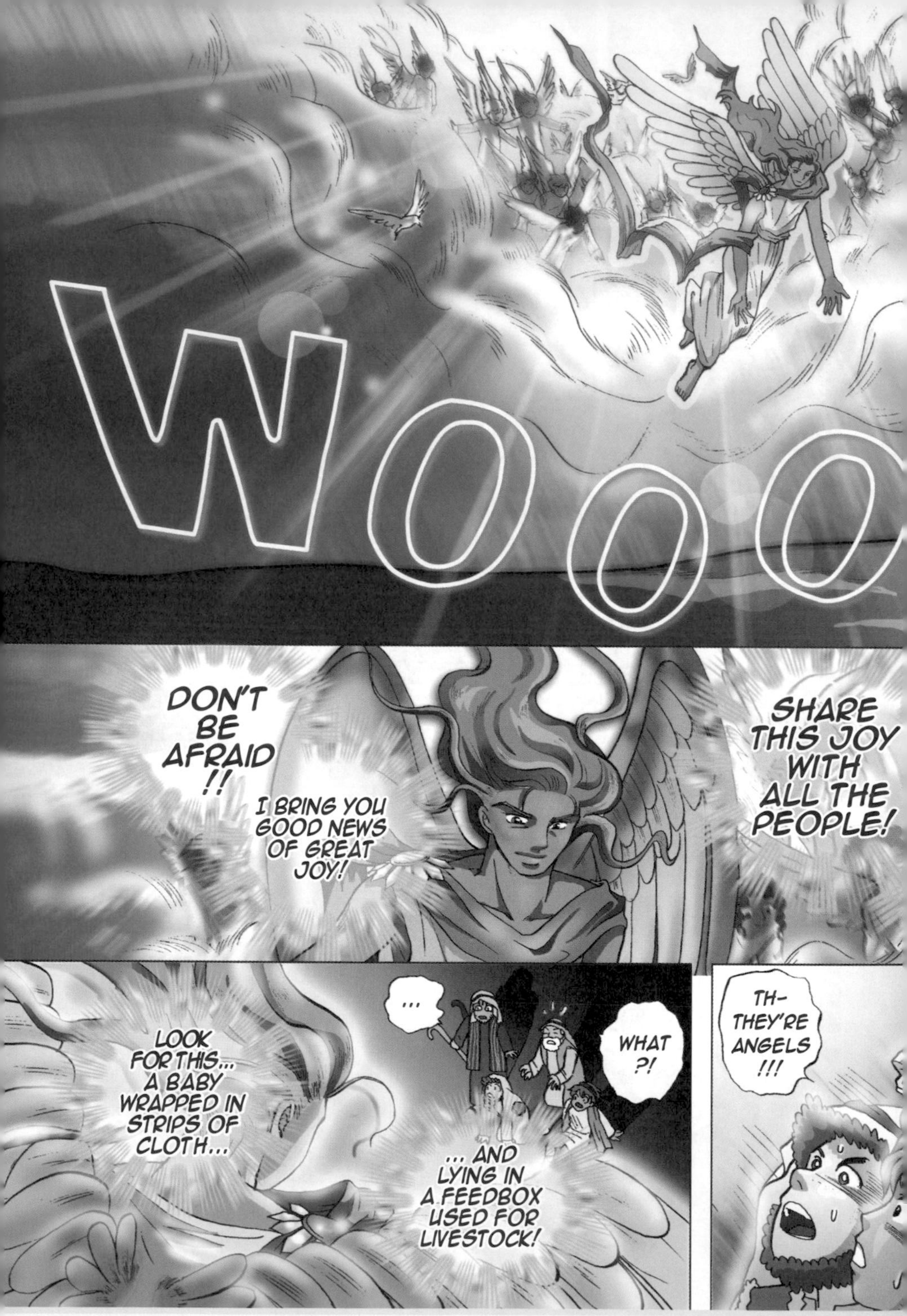
WOOO
DON'T BE AFRAID !!
I BRING YOU GOOD NEWS OF GREAT JOY!
SHARE THIS JOY WITH ALL THE PEOPLE!
LOOK FOR THIS... A BABY WRAPPED IN STRIPS OF CLOTH...
... AND LYING IN A FEEDBOX USED FOR LIVESTOCK!
...
WHAT ?!
TH- THEY'RE ANGELS !!!

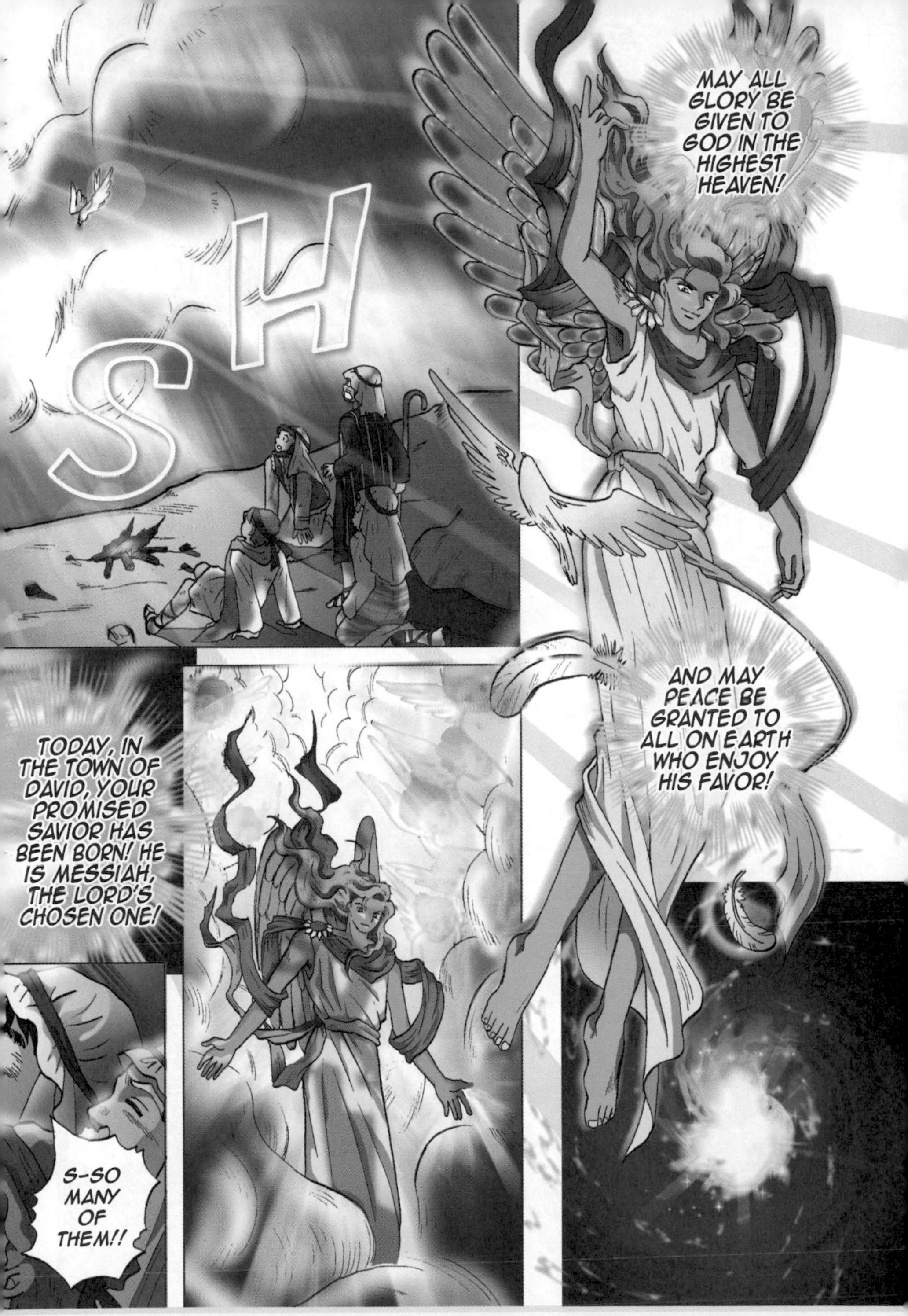
SH
MAY ALL GLORY BE GIVEN TO GOD IN THE HIGHEST HEAVEN!
TODAY, IN THE TOWN OF DAVID, YOUR PROMISED SAVIOR HAS BEEN BORN! HE IS MESSIAH, THE LORD'S CHOSEN ONE!
S-SO MANY OF THEM!!
AND MAY PEACE BE GRANTED TO ALL ON EARTH WHO ENJOY HIS FAVOR!

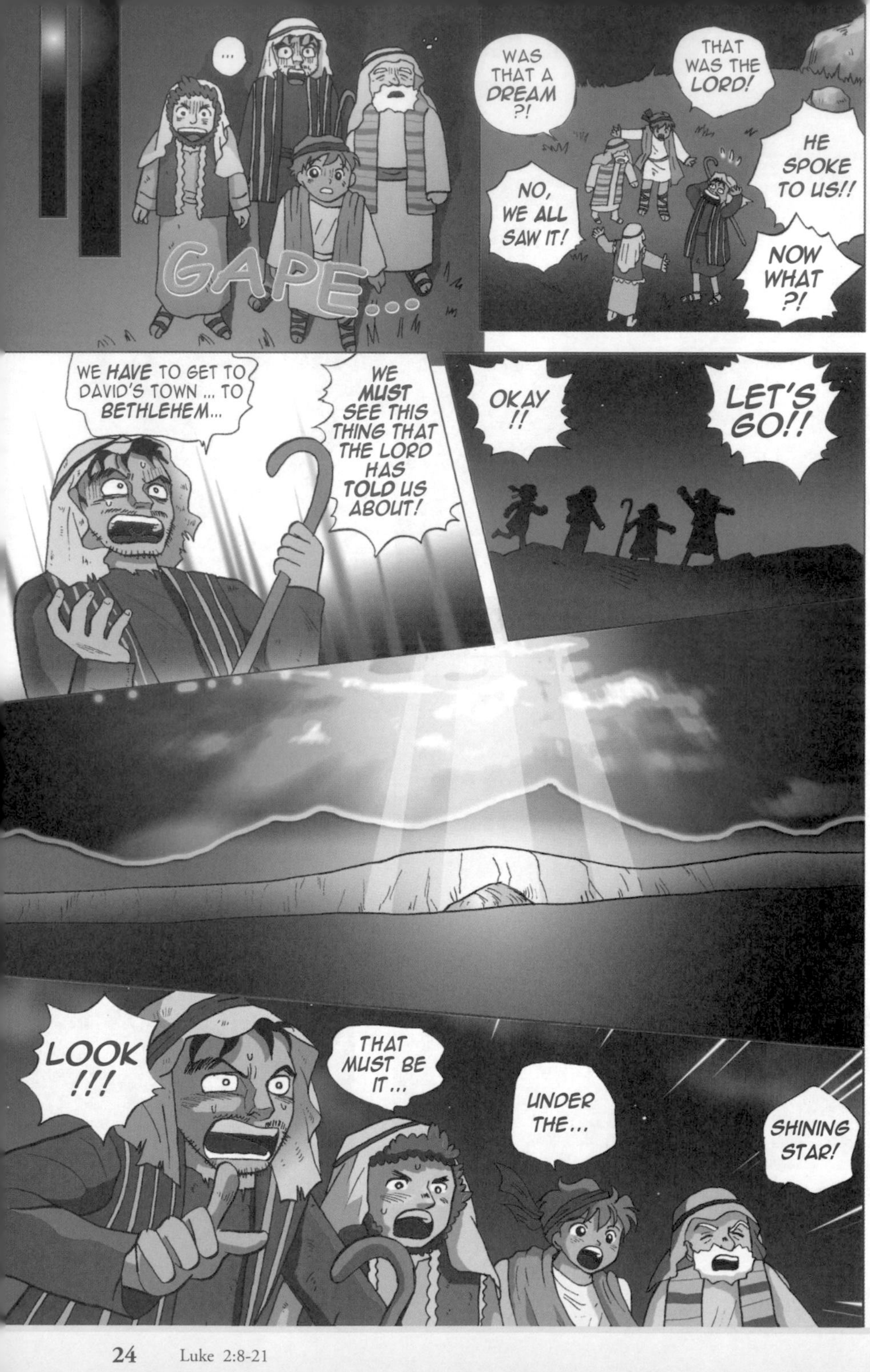
...
GAPE...
WAS THAT A DREAM ?!
THAT WAS THE LORD!
HE SPOKE TO US!!
NO, WE ALL SAW IT!
NOW WHAT ?!
WE HAVE TO GET TO DAVID'S TOWN ... TO BETHLEHEM...
WE MUST SEE THIS THING THAT THE LORD HAS TOLD US ABOUT!
LET'S GO!!
OKAY !!
LOOK !!!
THAT MUST BE IT ...
UNDER THE...
SHINING STAR!

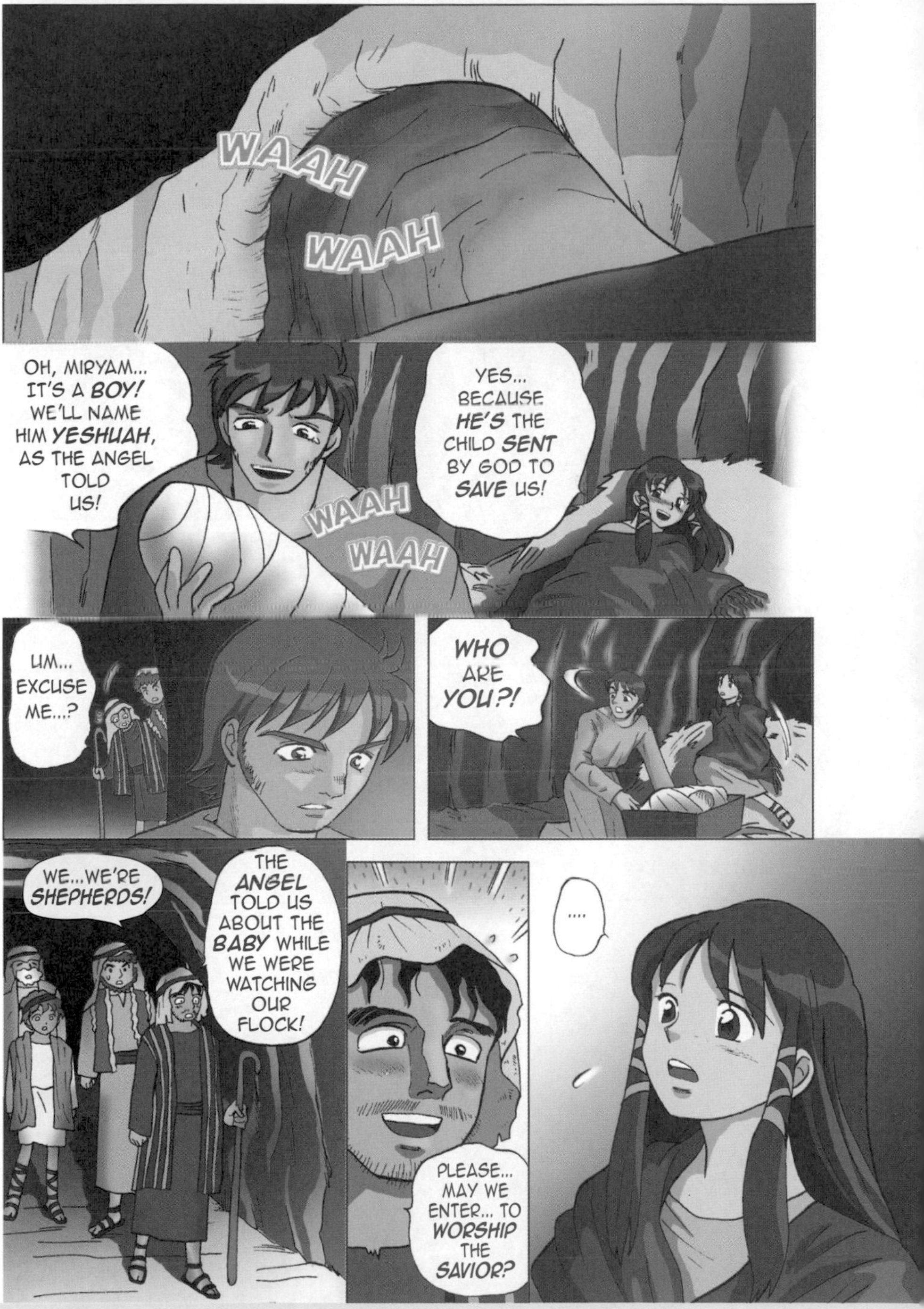
WAAH
WAAH
OH, MIRYAM... IT'S A BOY! WE'LL NAME HIM YESHUAH, AS THE ANGEL TOLD US!
YES... BECAUSE HE'S THE CHILD SENT BY GOD TO SAVE US!
WAAH
WAAH
UM... EXCUSE ME...?
WHO ARE YOU?!
WE...WE'RE SHEPHERDS!
THE ANGEL TOLD US ABOUT THE BABY WHILE WE WERE WATCHING OUR FLOCK!
....
PLEASE... MAY WE ENTER... TO WORSHIP THE SAVIOR?

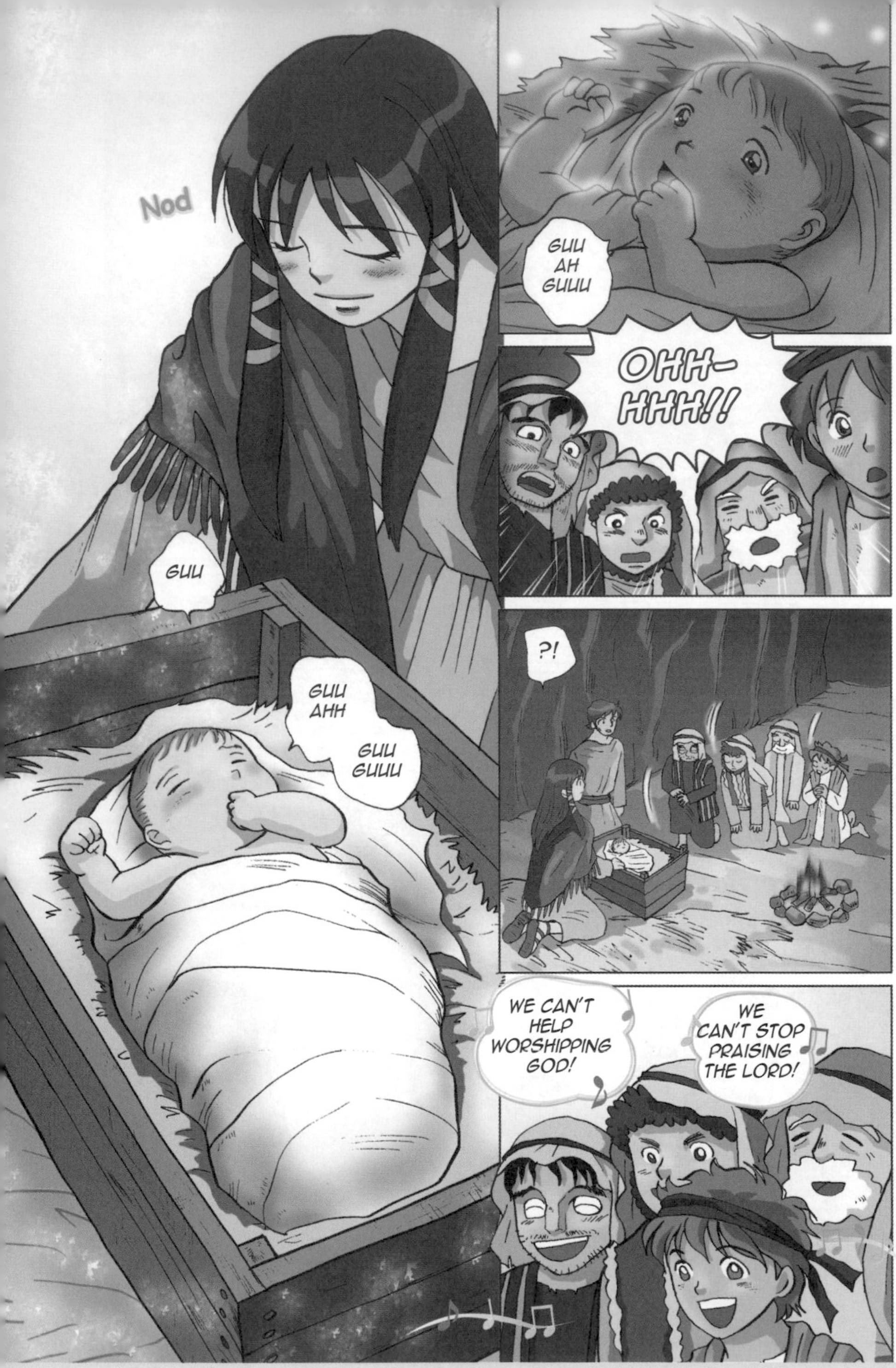
Nod
GUU
GUU AHH
GUU GUUU
GUU AH GUUU
OHH-HHH!!
?!
WE CAN'T HELP WORSHIPPING GOD!
WE CAN'T STOP PRAISING THE LORD!

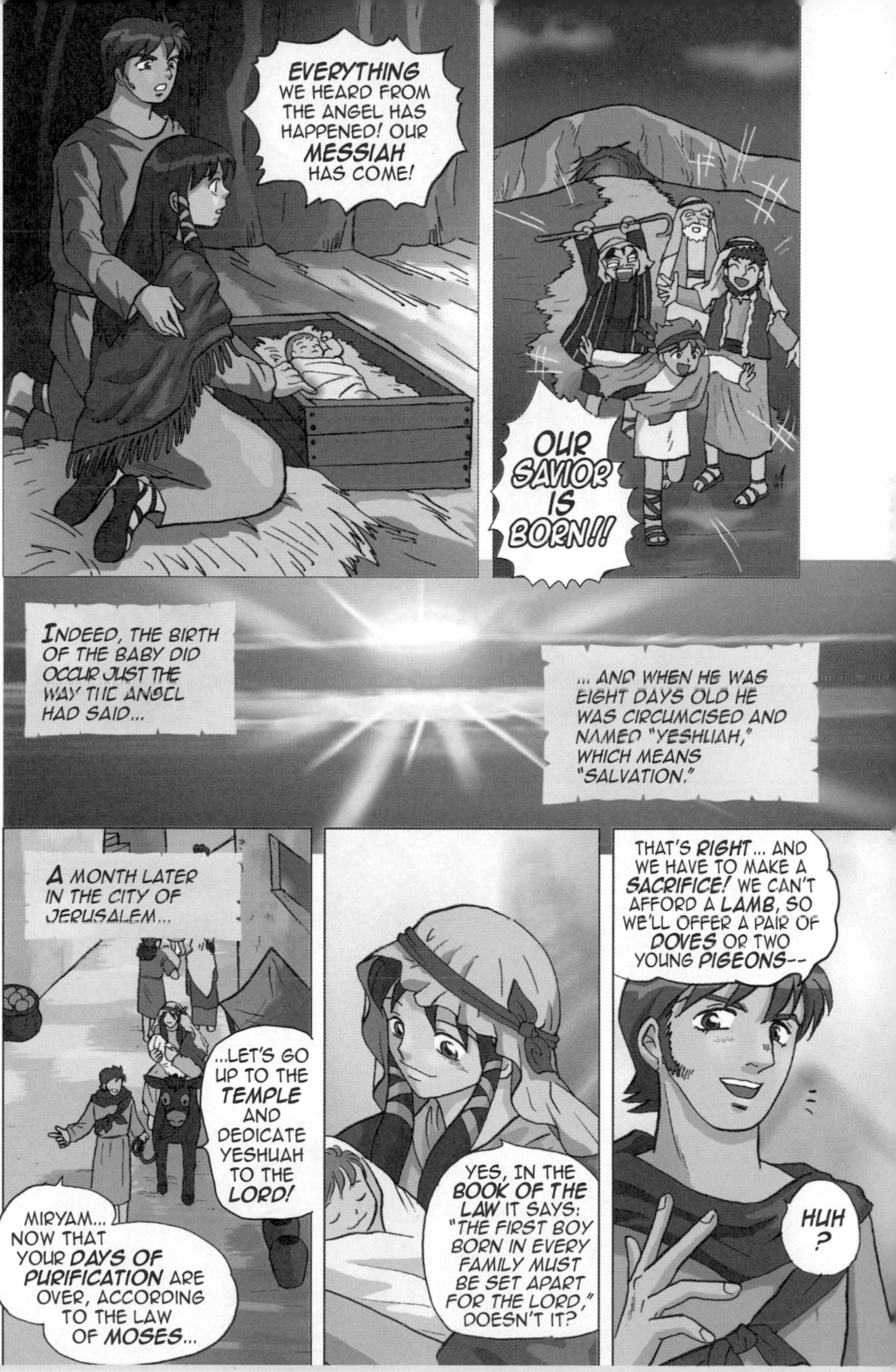
EVERYTHING WE HEARD FROM THE ANGEL HAS HAPPENED! OUR MESSIAH HAS COME!
OUR SAVIOR IS BORN!!
INDEED, THE BIRTH OF THE BABY DID OCCUR JUST THE WAY THE ANGEL HAD SAID...
... AND WHEN HE WAS EIGHT DAYS OLD HE WAS CIRCUMCISED AND NAMED "YESHUAH," WHICH MEANS "SALVATION."
A MONTH LATER IN THE CITY OF JERUSALEM...
MIRYAM... NOW THAT YOUR DAYS OF PURIFICATION ARE OVER, ACCORDING TO THE LAW OF MOSES...
...LET'S GO UP TO THE TEMPLE AND DEDICATE YESHUAH TO THE LORD!
YES, IN THE BOOK OF THE LAW IT SAYS: "THE FIRST BOY BORN IN EVERY FAMILY MUST BE SET APART FOR THE LORD," DOESN'T IT?
THAT'S RIGHT... AND WE HAVE TO MAKE A SACRIFICE! WE CAN'T AFFORD A LAMB, SO WE'LL OFFER A PAIR OF DOVES OR TWO YOUNG PIGEONS--
HUH?

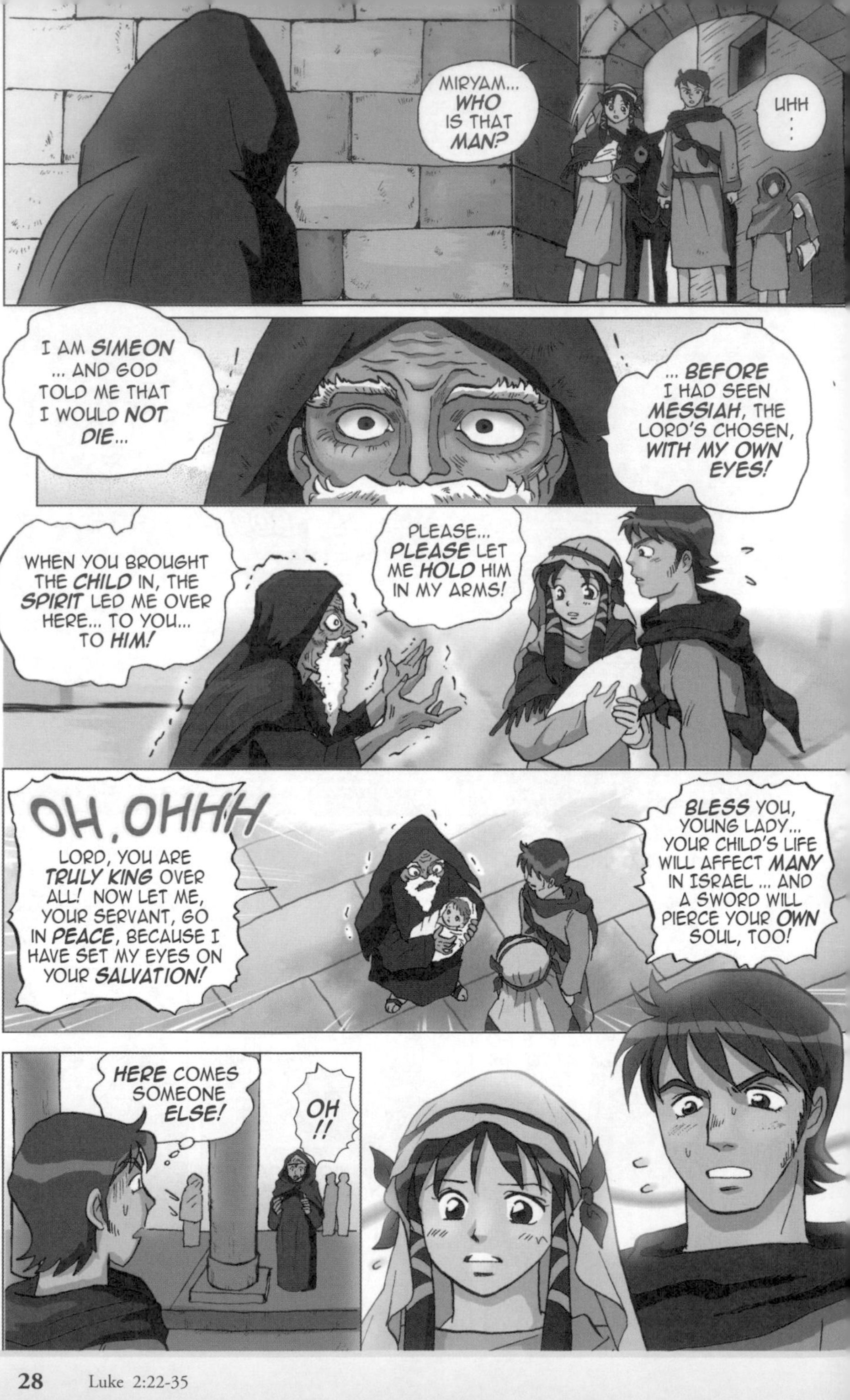
MIRYAM... WHO IS THAT MAN?
UHH . . .
I AM SIMEON ... AND GOD TOLD ME THAT I WOULD NOT DIE...
... BEFORE I HAD SEEN MESSIAH, THE LORD'S CHOSEN, WITH MY OWN EYES!
WHEN YOU BROUGHT THE CHILD IN, THE SPIRIT LED ME OVER HERE... TO YOU... TO HIM!
PLEASE... PLEASE LET ME HOLD HIM IN MY ARMS!
OH, OHHH
LORD, YOU ARE TRULY KING OVER ALL! NOW LET ME, YOUR SERVANT, GO IN PEACE, BECAUSE I HAVE SET MY EYES ON YOUR SALVATION!
BLESS YOU, YOUNG LADY... YOUR CHILD'S LIFE WILL AFFECT MANY IN ISRAEL ... AND A SWORD WILL PIERCE YOUR OWN SOUL, TOO!
HERE COMES SOMEONE ELSE!
OH !!

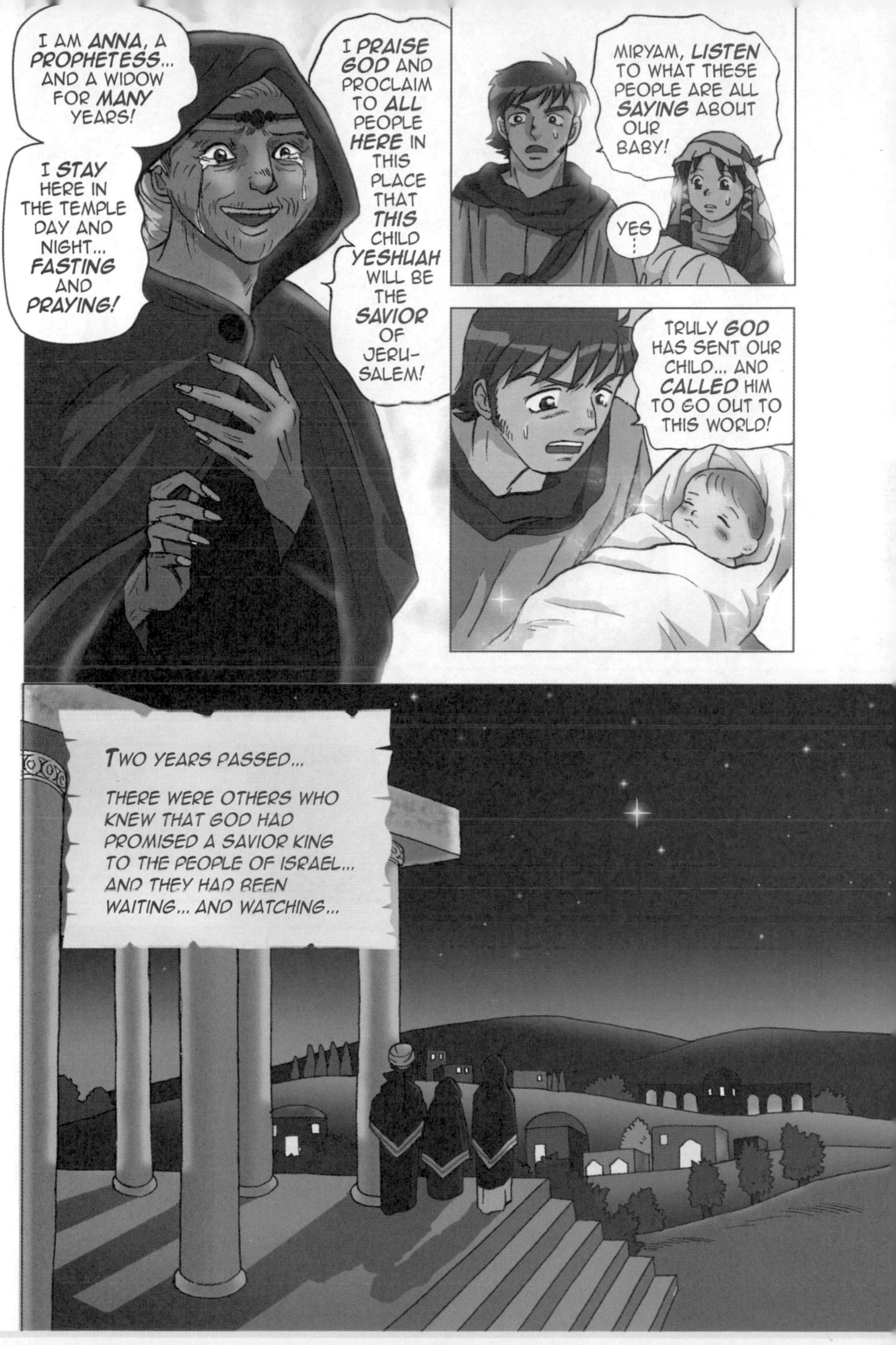
I AM ANNA, A PROPHETESS... AND A WIDOW FOR MANY YEARS!
I STAY HERE IN THE TEMPLE DAY AND NIGHT... FASTING AND PRAYING!
I PRAISE GOD AND PROCLAIM TO ALL PEOPLE HERE IN THIS PLACE THAT THIS CHILD YESHUAH WILL BE THE SAVIOR OF JERU-SALEM!
MIRYAM, LISTEN TO WHAT THESE PEOPLE ARE ALL SAYING ABOUT OUR BABY!
YES...
TRULY GOD HAS SENT OUR CHILD... AND CALLED HIM TO GO OUT TO THIS WORLD!
TWO YEARS PASSED...
THERE WERE OTHERS WHO KNEW THAT GOD HAD PROMISED A SAVIOR KING TO THE PEOPLE OF ISRAEL... AND THEY HAD BEEN WAITING... AND WATCHING...

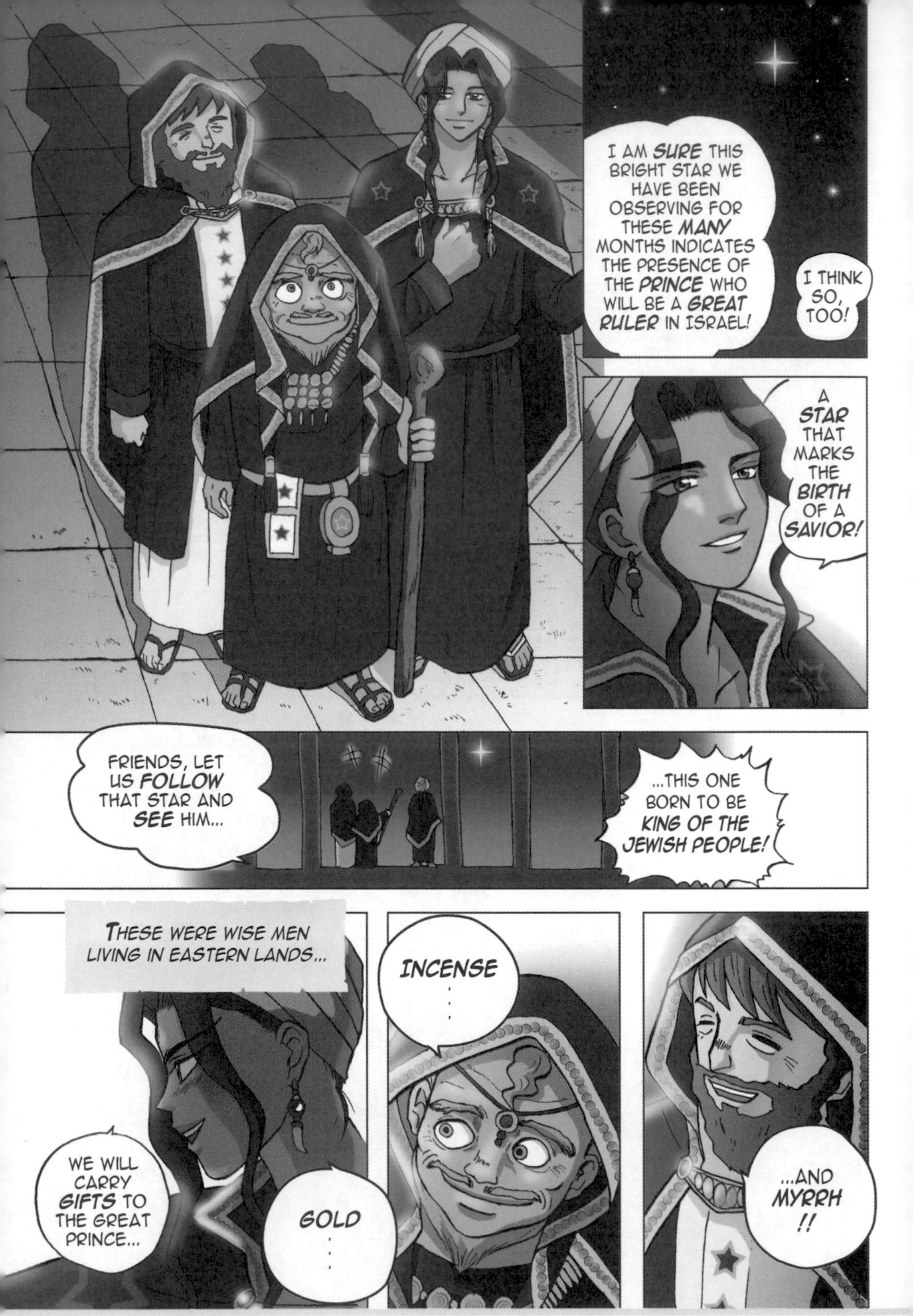
I AM SURE THIS BRIGHT STAR WE HAVE BEEN OBSERVING FOR THESE MANY MONTHS INDICATES THE PRESENCE OF THE PRINCE WHO WILL BE A GREAT RULER IN ISRAEL!
I THINK SO, TOO!
A STAR THAT MARKS THE BIRTH OF A SAVIOR!
FRIENDS, LET US FOLLOW THAT STAR AND SEE HIM...
...THIS ONE BORN TO BE KING OF THE JEWISH PEOPLE!
THESE WERE WISE MEN LIVING IN EASTERN LANDS...
WE WILL CARRY GIFTS TO THE GREAT PRINCE...
GOLD . . .
INCENSE . . .
...AND MYRRH !!

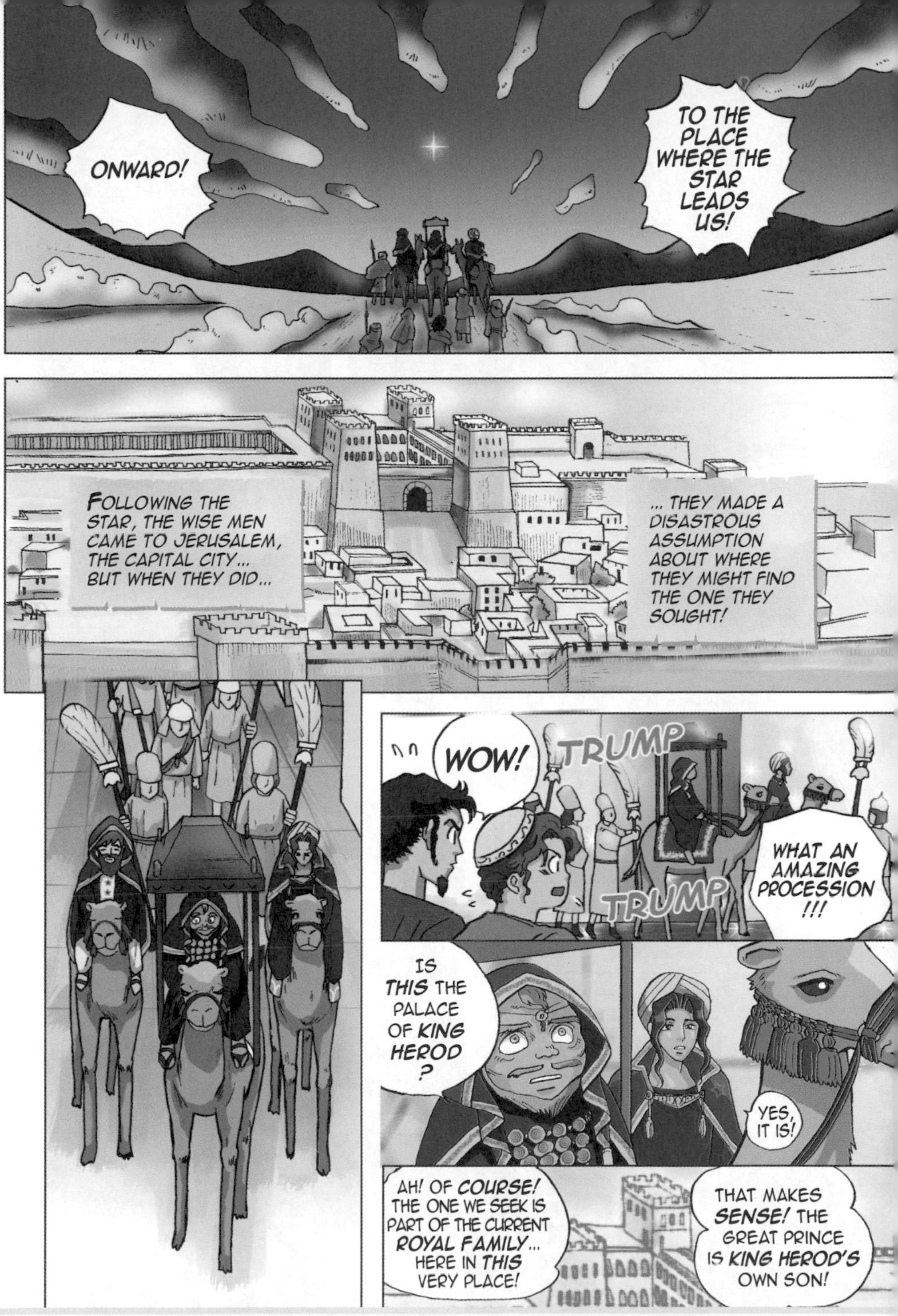
ONWARD!
TO THE PLACE WHERE THE STAR LEADS US!
FOLLOWING THE STAR, THE WISE MEN CAME TO JERUSALEM, THE CAPITAL CITY... BUT WHEN THEY DID...
... THEY MADE A DISASTROUS ASSUMPTION ABOUT WHERE THEY MIGHT FIND THE ONE THEY SOUGHT!
WOW!
TRUMP
WHAT AN AMAZING PROCESSION !!!
TRUMP
IS THIS THE PALACE OF KING HEROD ?
YES, IT IS!
AH! OF COURSE! THE ONE WE SEEK IS PART OF THE CURRENT ROYAL FAMILY... HERE IN THIS VERY PLACE!
THAT MAKES SENSE! THE GREAT PRINCE IS KING HEROD'S OWN SON!

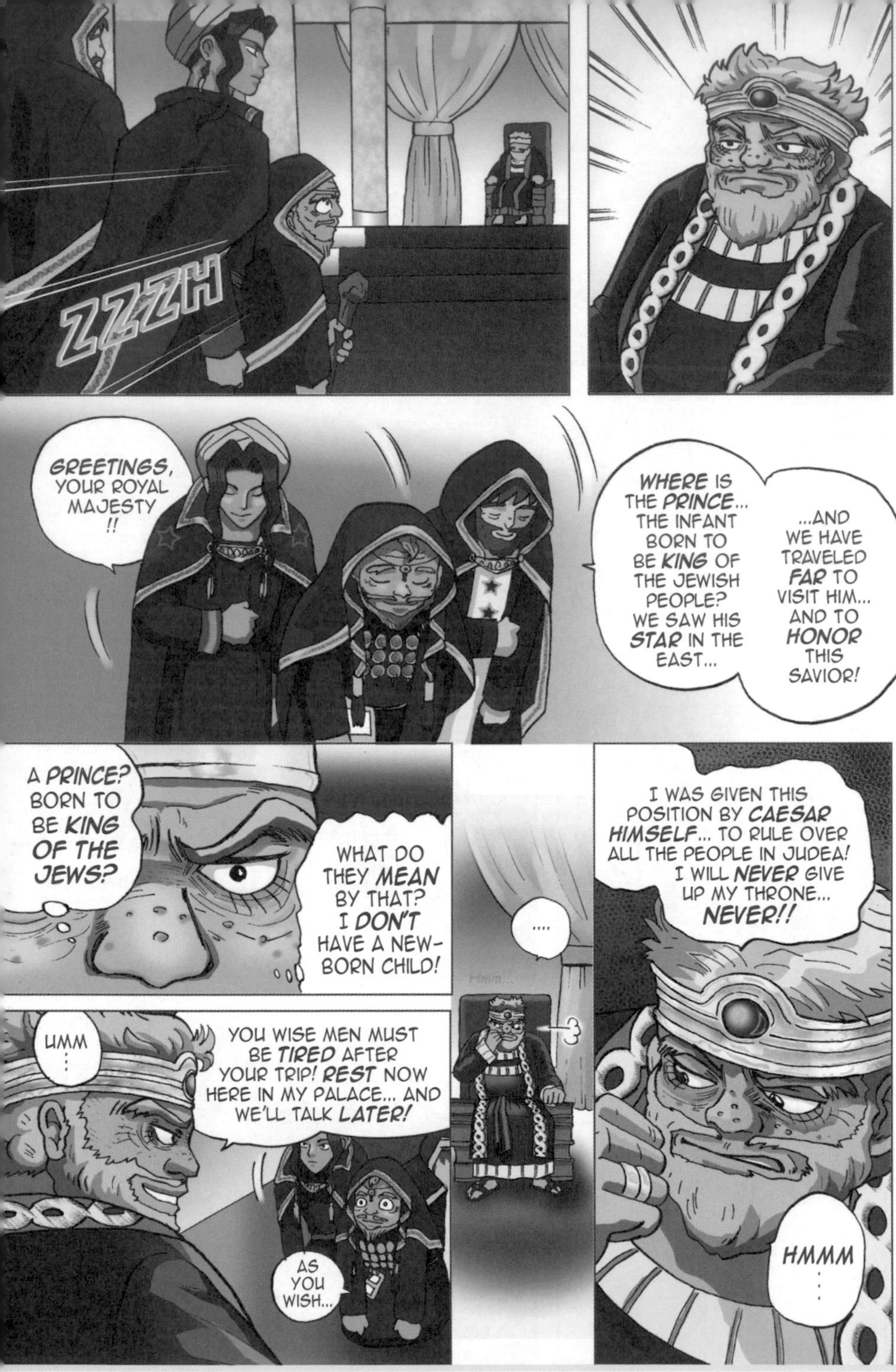
ZZZH
GREETINGS, YOUR ROYAL MAJESTY !!
WHERE IS THE PRINCE... THE INFANT BORN TO BE KING OF THE JEWISH PEOPLE? WE SAW HIS STAR IN THE EAST...
...AND WE HAVE TRAVELED FAR TO VISIT HIM... AND TO HONOR THIS SAVIOR!
A PRINCE? BORN TO BE KING OF THE JEWS?
WHAT DO THEY MEAN BY THAT? I DON'T HAVE A NEW-BORN CHILD!
....
I WAS GIVEN THIS POSITION BY CAESAR HIMSELF... TO RULE OVER ALL THE PEOPLE IN JUDEA! I WILL NEVER GIVE UP MY THRONE... NEVER!!
UMM ...
YOU WISE MEN MUST BE TIRED AFTER YOUR TRIP! REST NOW HERE IN MY PALACE... AND WE'LL TALK LATER!
AS YOU WISH...
HMMM ...

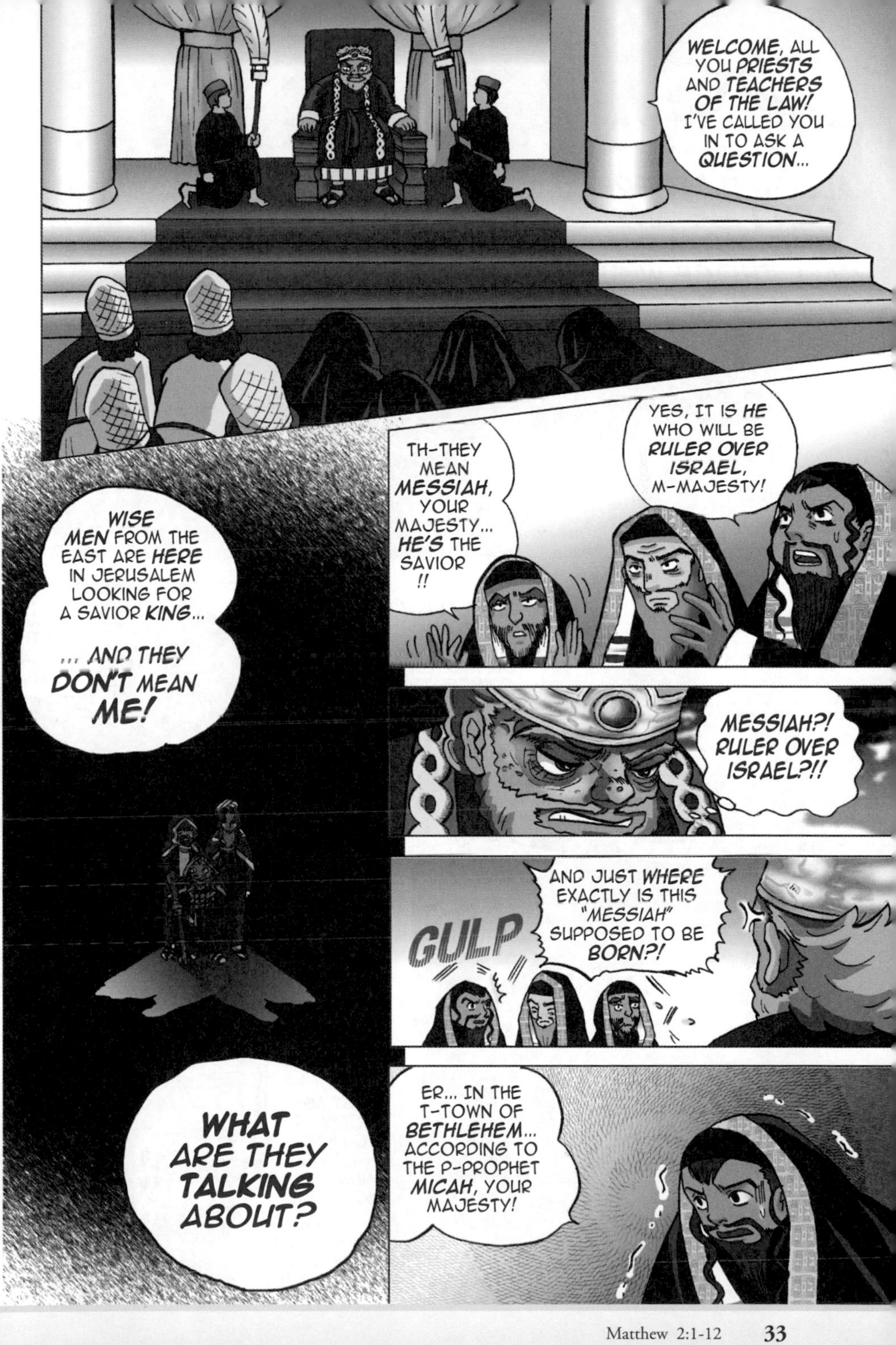
WELCOME, ALL YOU PRIESTS AND TEACHERS OF THE LAW! I'VE CALLED YOU IN TO ASK A QUESTION...
WISE MEN FROM THE EAST ARE HERE IN JERUSALEM LOOKING FOR A SAVIOR KING...
... AND THEY DON'T MEAN ME!
TH-THEY MEAN MESSIAH, YOUR MAJESTY... HE'S THE SAVIOR !!
YES, IT IS HE WHO WILL BE RULER OVER ISRAEL, M-MAJESTY!
MESSIAH?! RULER OVER ISRAEL?!!
AND JUST WHERE EXACTLY IS THIS "MESSIAH" SUPPOSED TO BE BORN?!
GULP
WHAT ARE THEY TALKING ABOUT?
ER... IN THE T-TOWN OF BETHLEHEM... ACCORDING TO THE P-PROPHET MICAH, YOUR MAJESTY!

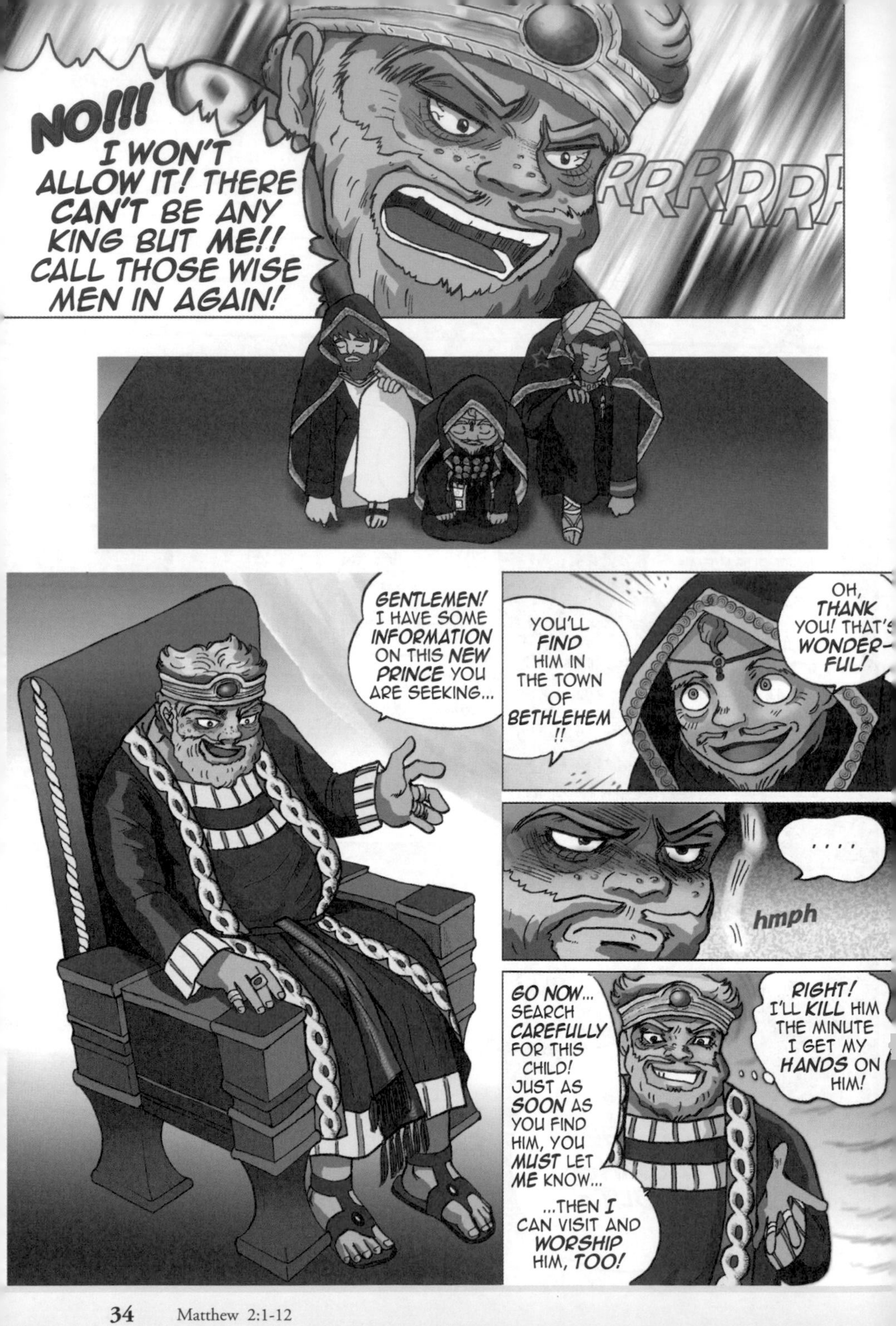
NO!!! I WON'T ALLOW IT! THERE CAN'T BE ANY KING BUT ME!! CALL THOSE WISE MEN IN AGAIN!
RRRRRR
GENTLEMEN! I HAVE SOME INFORMATION ON THIS NEW PRINCE YOU ARE SEEKING...
YOU'LL FIND HIM IN THE TOWN OF BETHLEHEM !!
OH, THANK YOU! THAT'S WONDERFUL!
....
hmph
GO NOW... SEARCH CAREFULLY FOR THIS CHILD! JUST AS SOON AS YOU FIND HIM, YOU MUST LET ME KNOW...
...THEN I CAN VISIT AND WORSHIP HIM, TOO!
RIGHT! I'LL KILL HIM THE MINUTE I GET MY HANDS ON HIM!

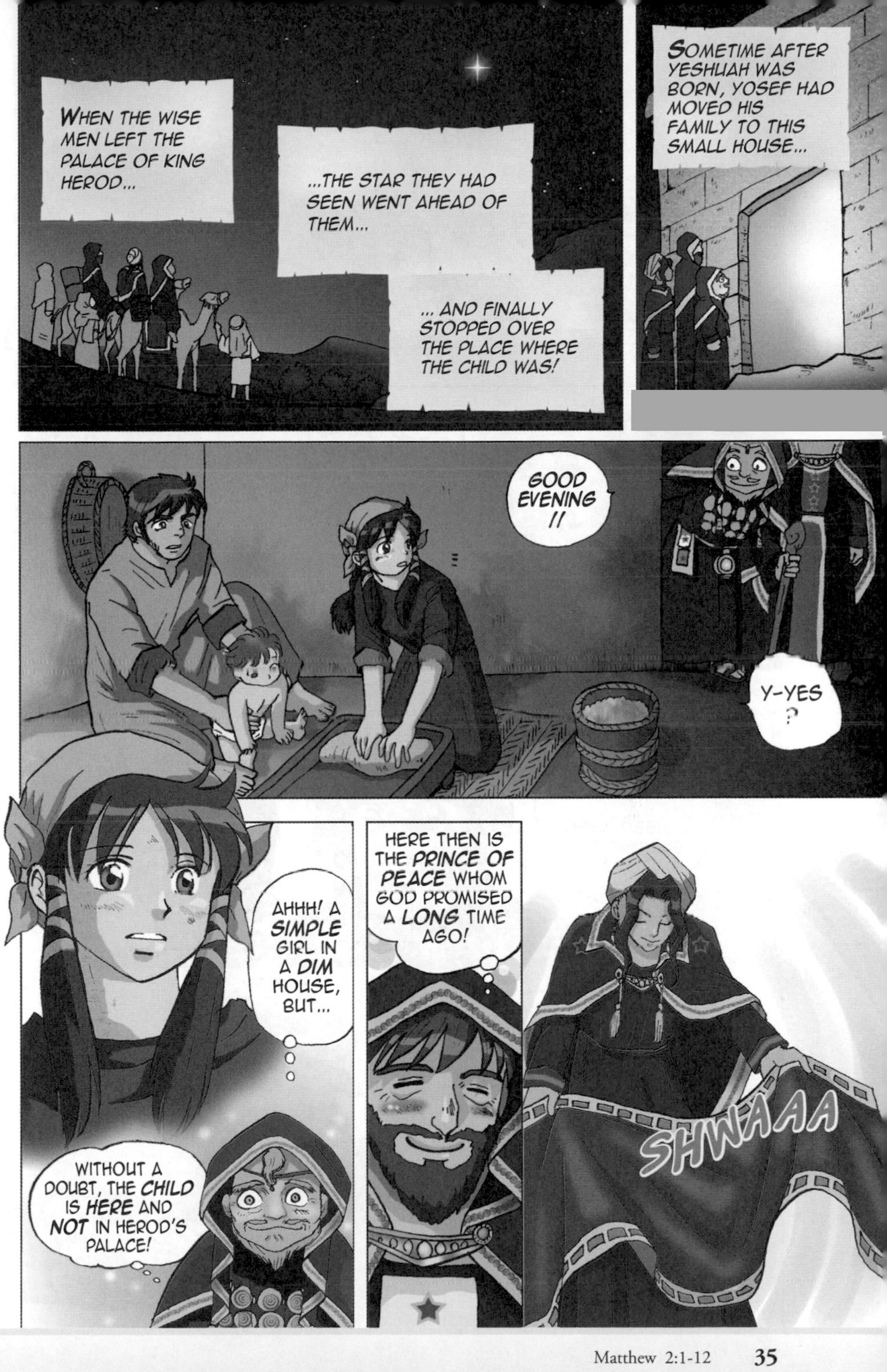

WHEN THE WISE MEN LEFT THE PALACE OF KING HEROD...
...THE STAR THEY HAD SEEN WENT AHEAD OF THEM...
... AND FINALLY STOPPED OVER THE PLACE WHERE THE CHILD WAS!
SOMETIME AFTER YESHUAH WAS BORN, YOSEF HAD MOVED HIS FAMILY TO THIS SMALL HOUSE...
GOOD EVENING !!
Y-YES ?
AHHH! A SIMPLE GIRL IN A DIM HOUSE, BUT...
WITHOUT A DOUBT, THE CHILD IS HERE AND NOT IN HEROD'S PALACE!
HERE THEN IS THE PRINCE OF PEACE WHOM GOD PROMISED A LONG TIME AGO!
SHWAAA

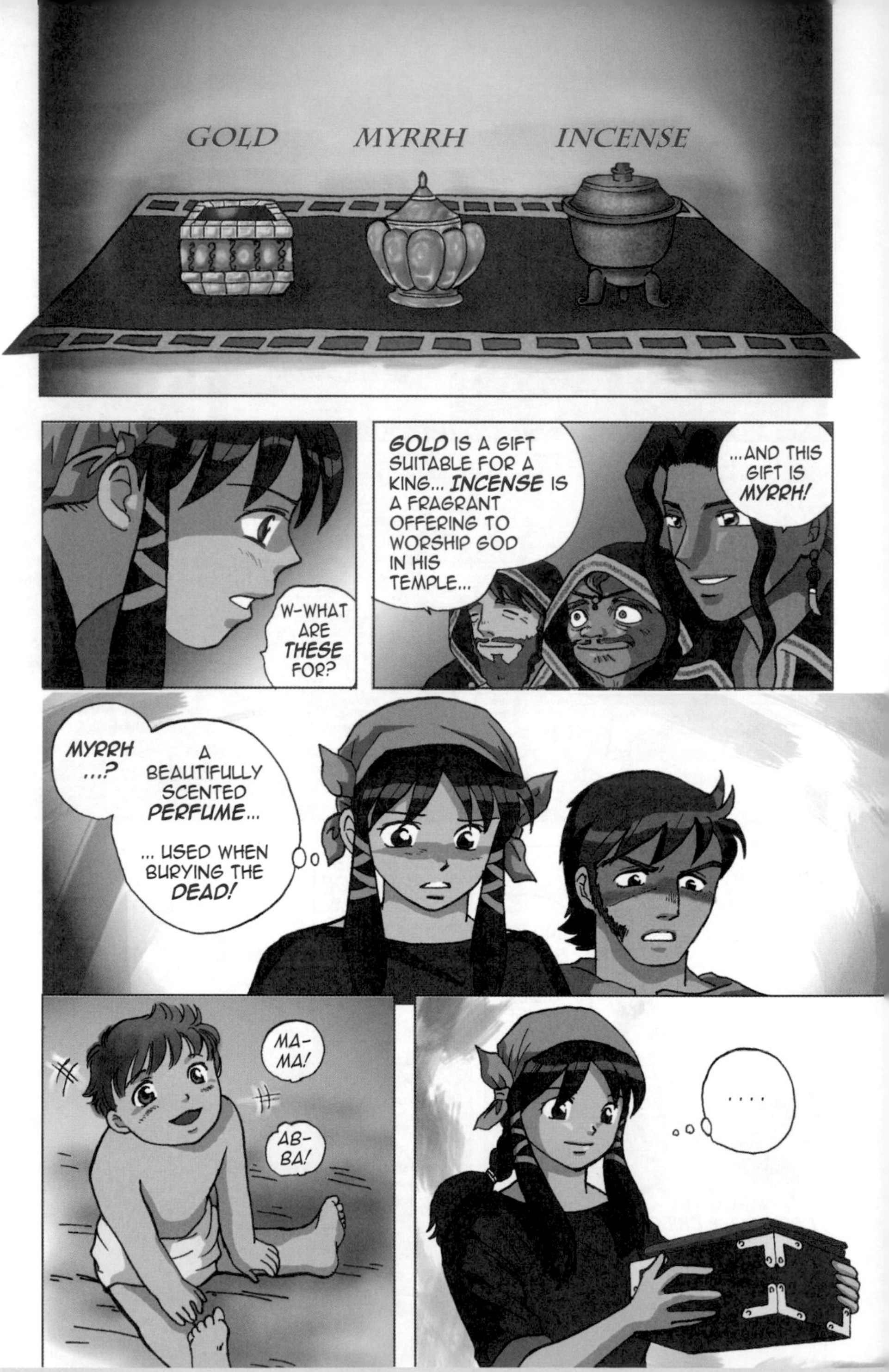
GOLD
MYRRH
INCENSE
W-WHAT ARE THESE FOR?
GOLD IS A GIFT SUITABLE FOR A KING... INCENSE IS A FRAGRANT OFFERING TO WORSHIP GOD IN HIS TEMPLE...
...AND THIS GIFT IS MYRRH!
MYRRH ...?
A BEAUTIFULLY SCENTED PERFUME...
... USED WHEN BURYING THE DEAD!
MA-MA!
AB-BA!
. . . .

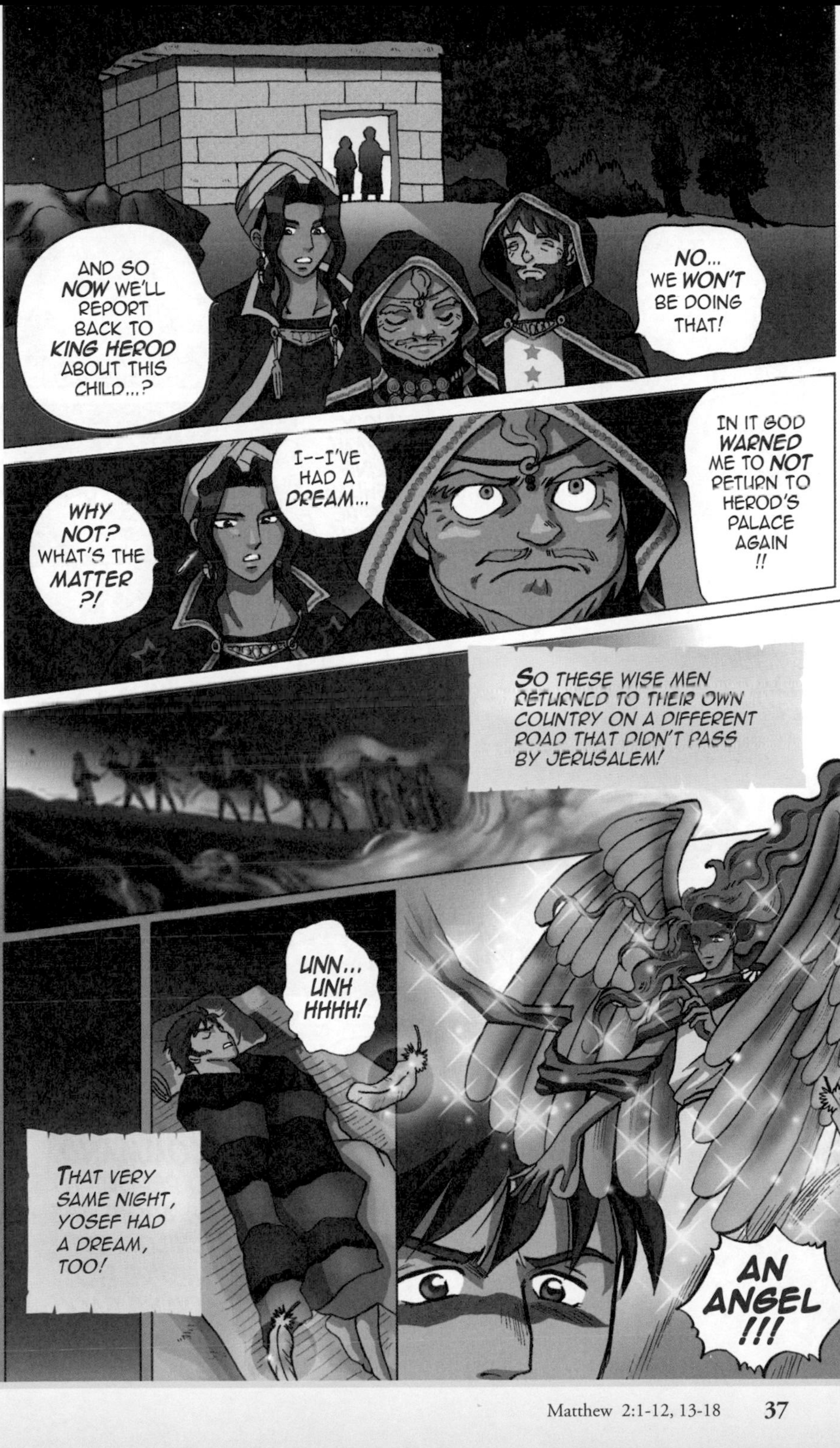
AND SO NOW WE'LL REPORT BACK TO KING HEROD ABOUT THIS CHILD...?
NO... WE WON'T BE DOING THAT!
WHY NOT? WHAT'S THE MATTER ?!
I--I'VE HAD A DREAM...
IN IT GOD WARNED ME TO NOT RETURN TO HEROD'S PALACE AGAIN !!
SO THESE WISE MEN RETURNED TO THEIR OWN COUNTRY ON A DIFFERENT ROAD THAT DIDN'T PASS BY JERUSALEM!
UNN... UNH HHHH!
THAT VERY SAME NIGHT, YOSEF HAD A DREAM, TOO!
AN ANGEL !!!

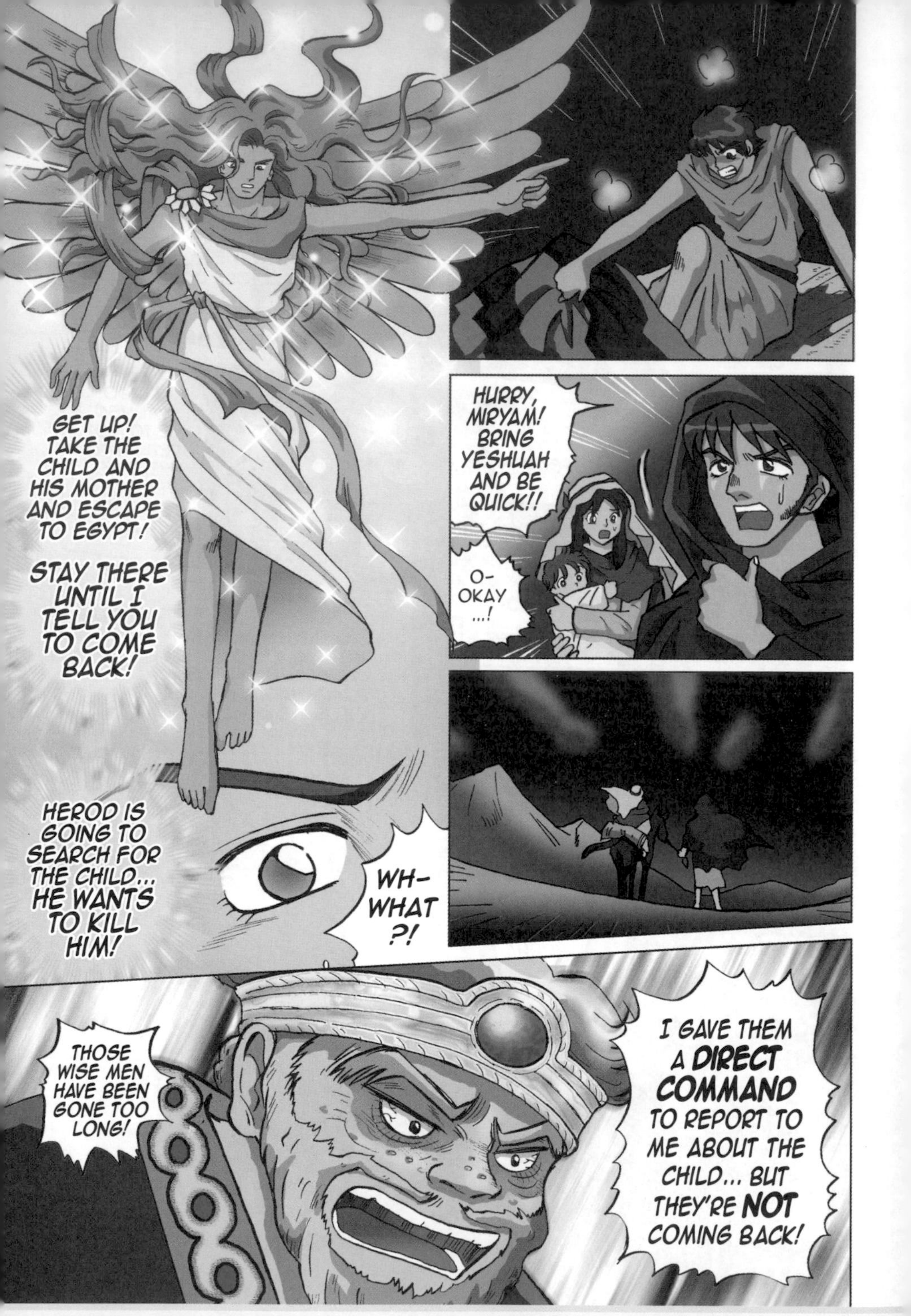
GET UP! TAKE THE CHILD AND HIS MOTHER AND ESCAPE TO EGYPT!
STAY THERE UNTIL I TELL YOU TO COME BACK!
HEROD IS GOING TO SEARCH FOR THE CHILD... HE WANTS TO KILL HIM!
WH- WHAT ?!
HURRY, MIRYAM! BRING YESHUAH AND BE QUICK!!
O- OKAY ...!
THOSE WISE MEN HAVE BEEN GONE TOO LONG!
I GAVE THEM A DIRECT COMMAND TO REPORT TO ME ABOUT THE CHILD... BUT THEY'RE NOT COMING BACK!

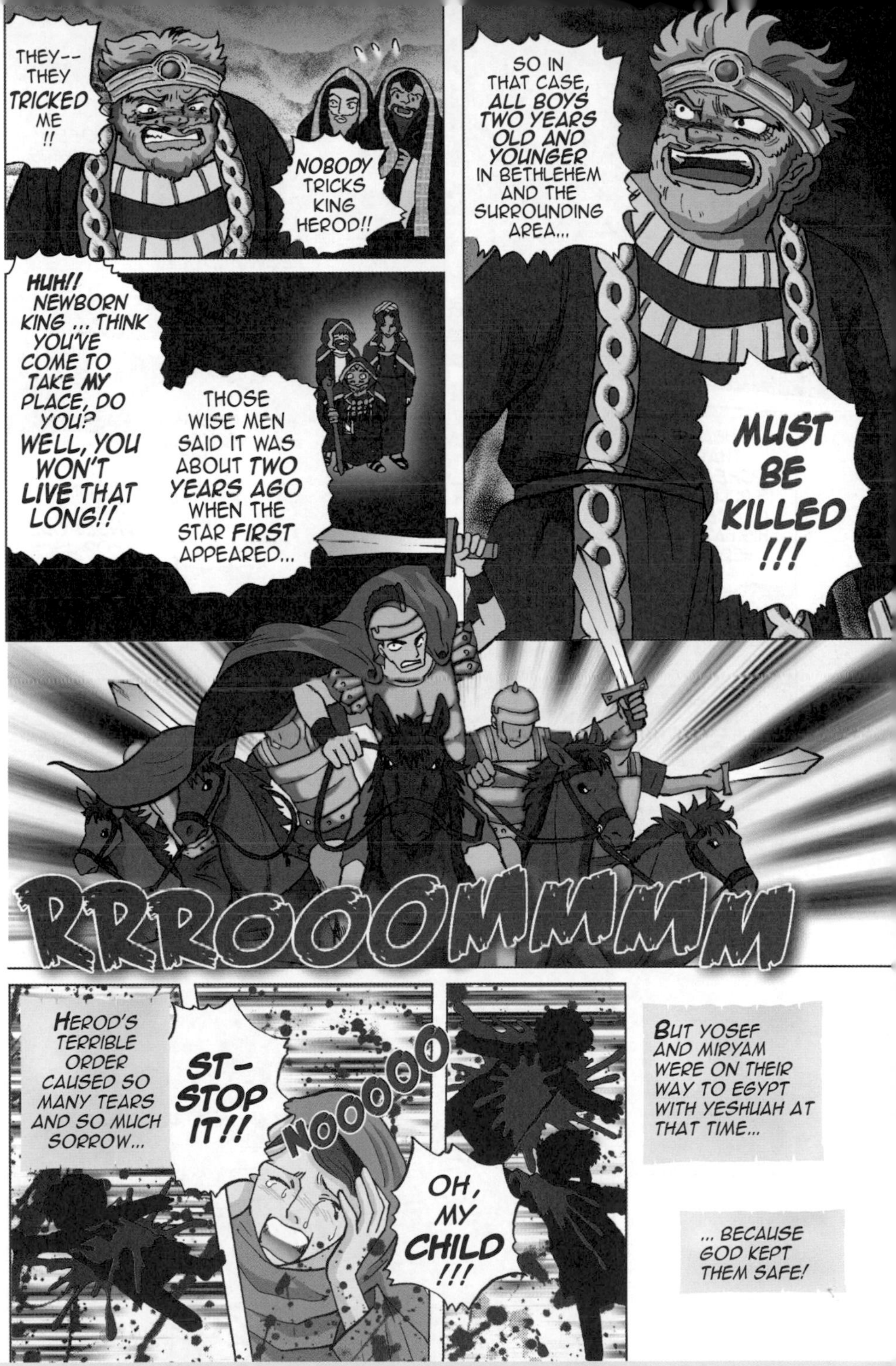
THEY-- THEY TRICKED ME !!
NOBODY TRICKS KING HEROD!!
HUH!! NEWBORN KING ... THINK YOU'VE COME TO TAKE MY PLACE, DO YOU? WELL, YOU WON'T LIVE THAT LONG!!
THOSE WISE MEN SAID IT WAS ABOUT TWO YEARS AGO WHEN THE STAR FIRST APPEARED...
SO IN THAT CASE, ALL BOYS TWO YEARS OLD AND YOUNGER IN BETHLEHEM AND THE SURROUNDING AREA...
MUST BE KILLED !!!
RRROOOMMMMM
HEROD'S TERRIBLE ORDER CAUSED SO MANY TEARS AND SO MUCH SORROW...
ST-STOP IT!!
NOOOOOO
OH, MY CHILD !!!
BUT YOSEF AND MIRYAM WERE ON THEIR WAY TO EGYPT WITH YESHUAH AT THAT TIME...
... BECAUSE GOD KEPT THEM SAFE!

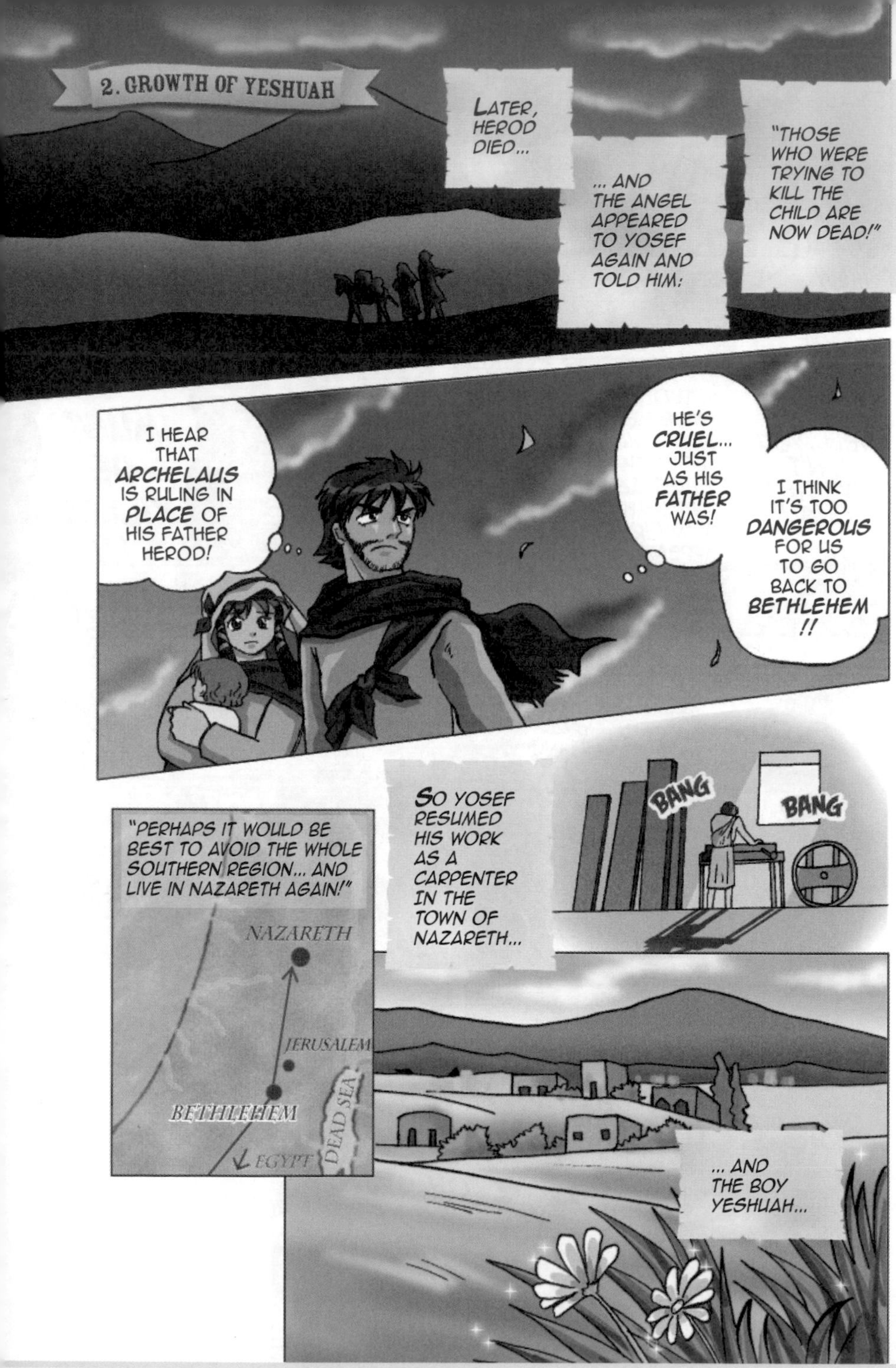
2. GROWTH OF YESHUAH
LATER, HEROD DIED...
... AND THE ANGEL APPEARED TO YOSEF AGAIN AND TOLD HIM:
"THOSE WHO WERE TRYING TO KILL THE CHILD ARE NOW DEAD!"
I HEAR THAT ARCHELAUS IS RULING IN PLACE OF HIS FATHER HEROD!
HE'S CRUEL... JUST AS HIS FATHER WAS!
I THINK IT'S TOO DANGEROUS FOR US TO GO BACK TO BETHLEHEM !!
"PERHAPS IT WOULD BE BEST TO AVOID THE WHOLE SOUTHERN REGION... AND LIVE IN NAZARETH AGAIN!"
NAZARETH
JERUSALEM
BETHLEHEM
DEAD SEA
EGYPT
SO YOSEF RESUMED HIS WORK AS A CARPENTER IN THE TOWN OF NAZARETH...
BANG
BANG
... AND THE BOY YESHUAH...

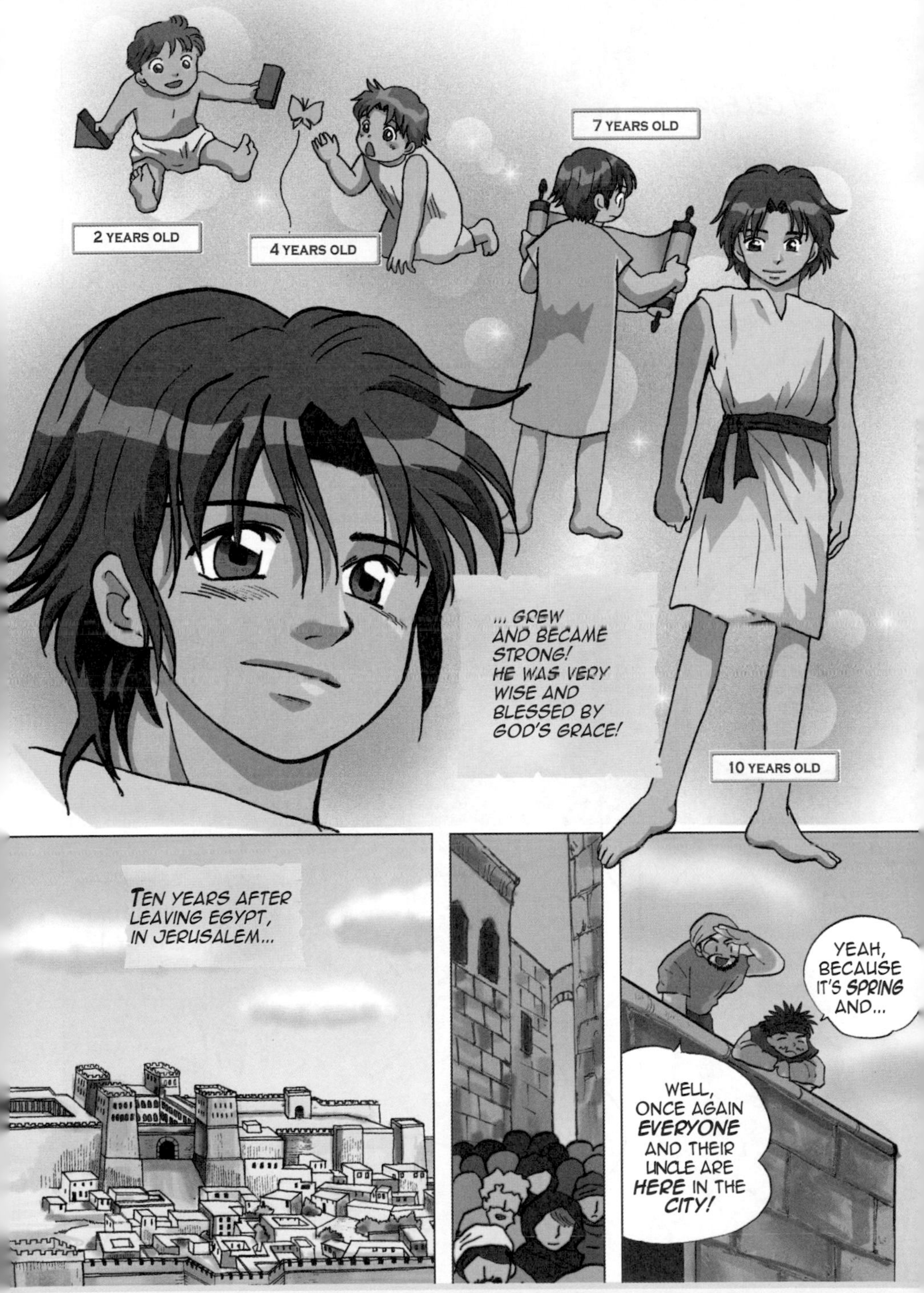
2 YEARS OLD
4 YEARS OLD
7 YEARS OLD
... GREW AND BECAME STRONG! HE WAS VERY WISE AND BLESSED BY GOD'S GRACE!
10 YEARS OLD
TEN YEARS AFTER LEAVING EGYPT, IN JERUSALEM...
YEAH, BECAUSE IT'S SPRING AND...
WELL, ONCE AGAIN EVERYONE AND THEIR UNCLE ARE HERE IN THE CITY!

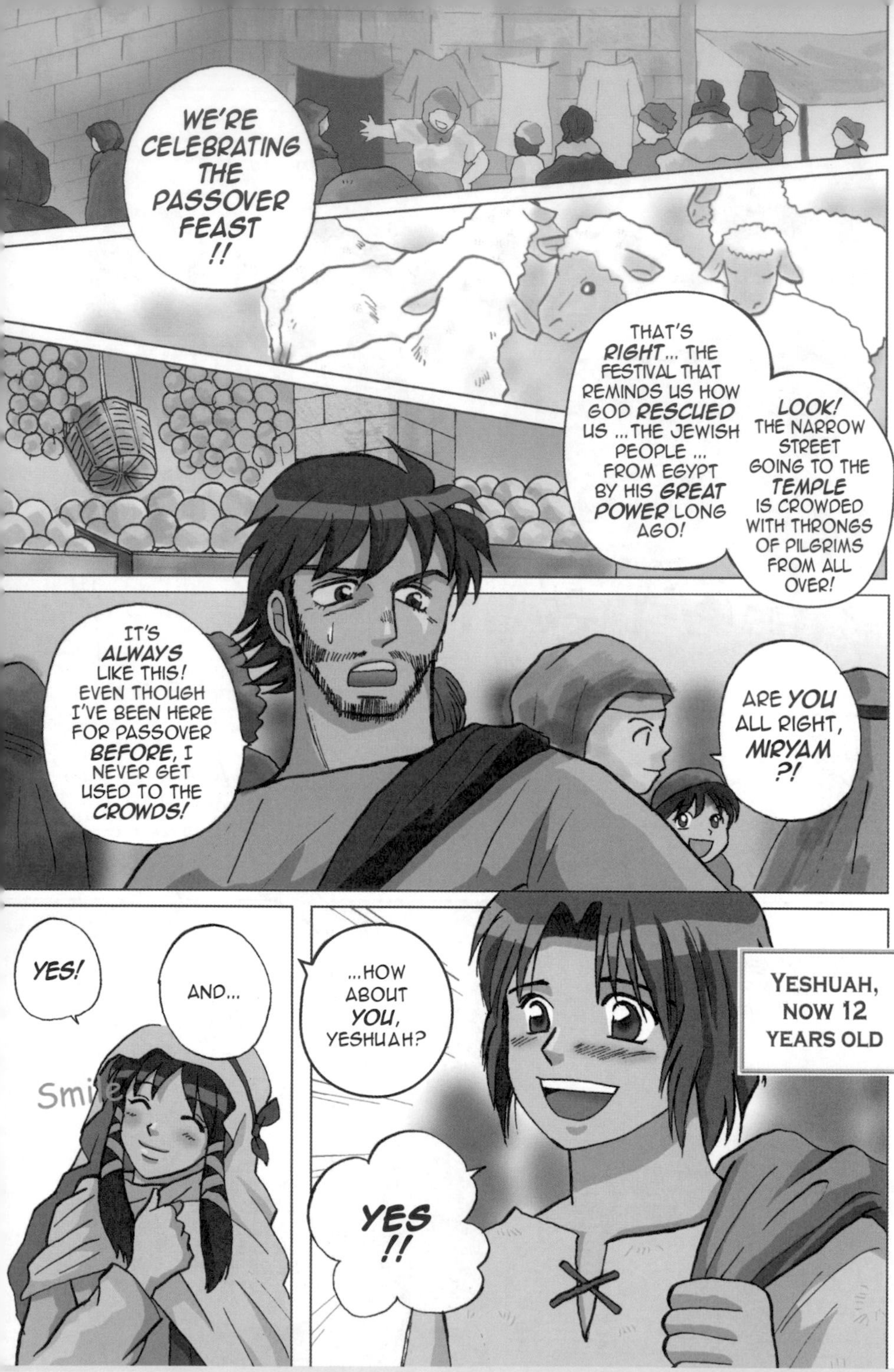
WE'RE CELEBRATING THE PASSOVER FEAST !!
THAT'S RIGHT... THE FESTIVAL THAT REMINDS US HOW GOD RESCUED US ...THE JEWISH PEOPLE ... FROM EGYPT BY HIS GREAT POWER LONG AGO!
LOOK! THE NARROW STREET GOING TO THE TEMPLE IS CROWDED WITH THRONGS OF PILGRIMS FROM ALL OVER!
IT'S ALWAYS LIKE THIS! EVEN THOUGH I'VE BEEN HERE FOR PASSOVER BEFORE, I NEVER GET USED TO THE CROWDS!
ARE YOU ALL RIGHT, MIRYAM ?!
YES!
AND...
Smile
...HOW ABOUT YOU, YESHUAH?
YESHUAH, NOW 12 YEARS OLD
YES !!

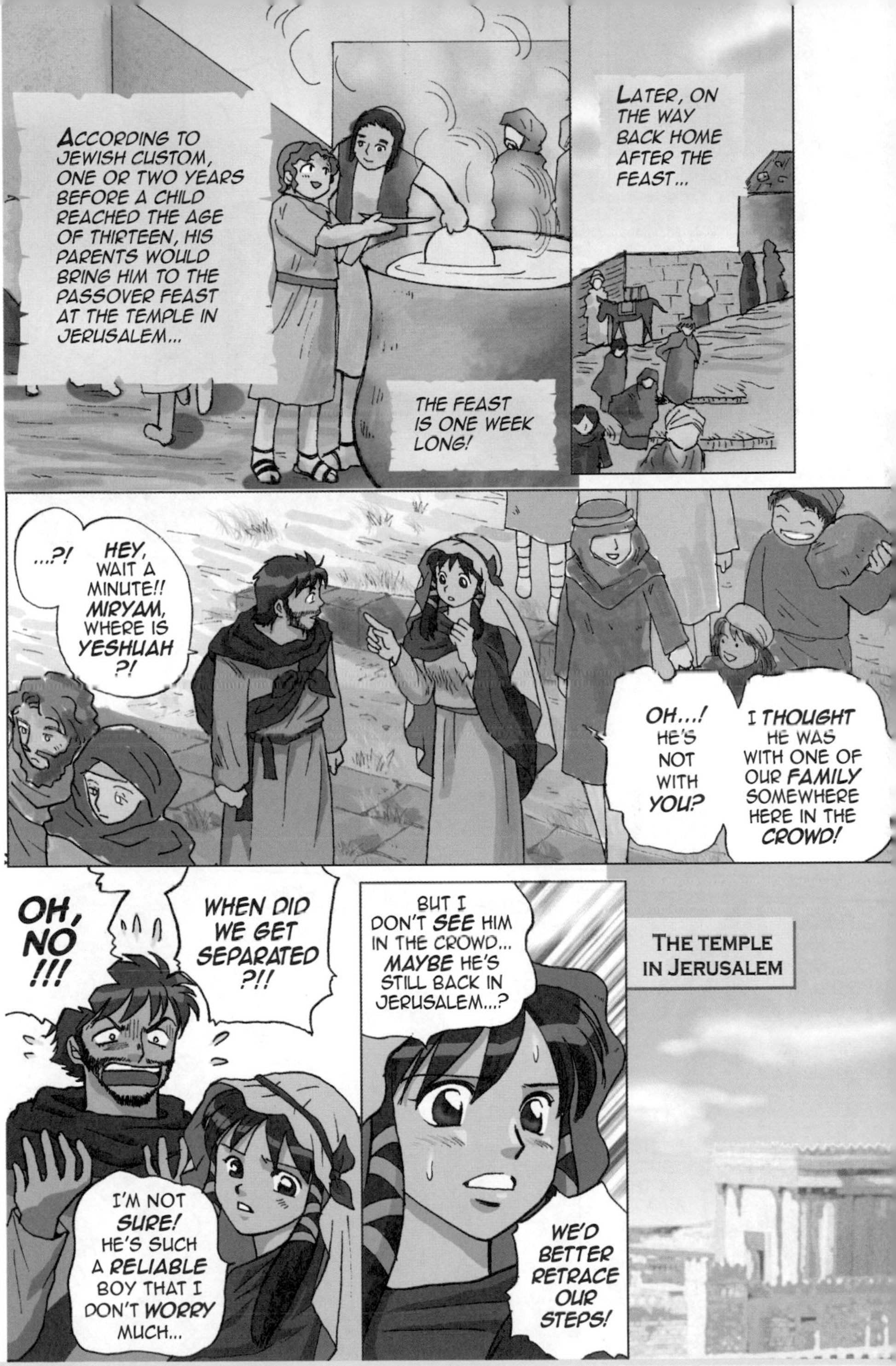
According to Jewish custom, one or two years before a child reached the age of thirteen, his parents would bring him to the Passover feast at the temple in Jerusalem...
The feast is one week long!
Later, on the way back home after the feast...
...?!
Hey, wait a minute!! Miryam, where is Yeshuah?!
Oh...! He's not with you?
I thought he was with one of our family somewhere here in the crowd!
Oh, no!!!
When did we get separated?!!
I'm not sure! He's such a reliable boy that I don't worry much...
But I don't see him in the crowd... Maybe he's still back in Jerusalem...?
We'd better retrace our steps!
The temple in Jerusalem

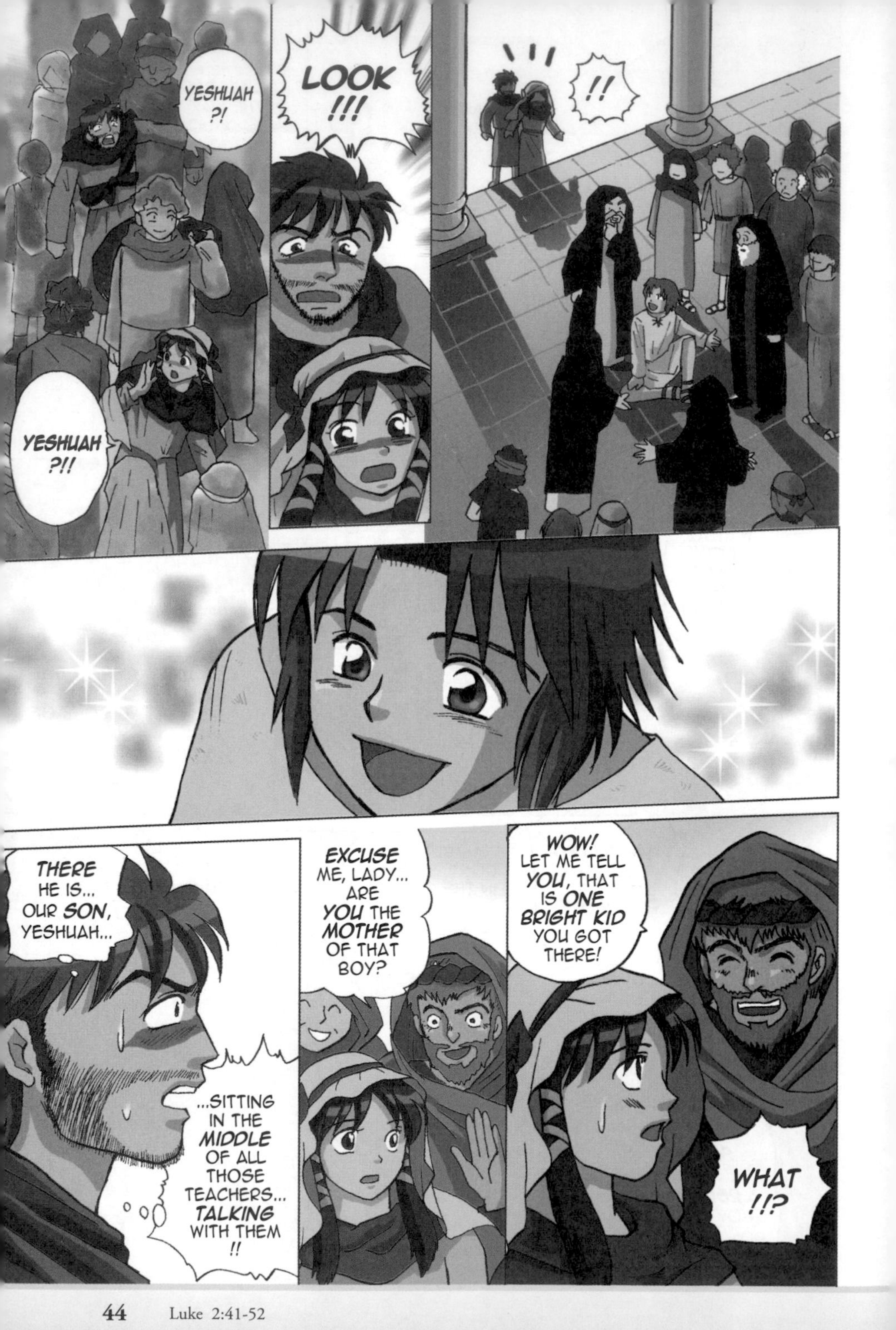
YESHUAH ?!
LOOK !!!
!!
YESHUAH ?!!
THERE HE IS... OUR SON, YESHUAH...
...SITTING IN THE MIDDLE OF ALL THOSE TEACHERS... TALKING WITH THEM !!
EXCUSE ME, LADY... ARE YOU THE MOTHER OF THAT BOY?
WOW! LET ME TELL YOU, THAT IS ONE BRIGHT KID YOU GOT THERE!
WHAT !!?

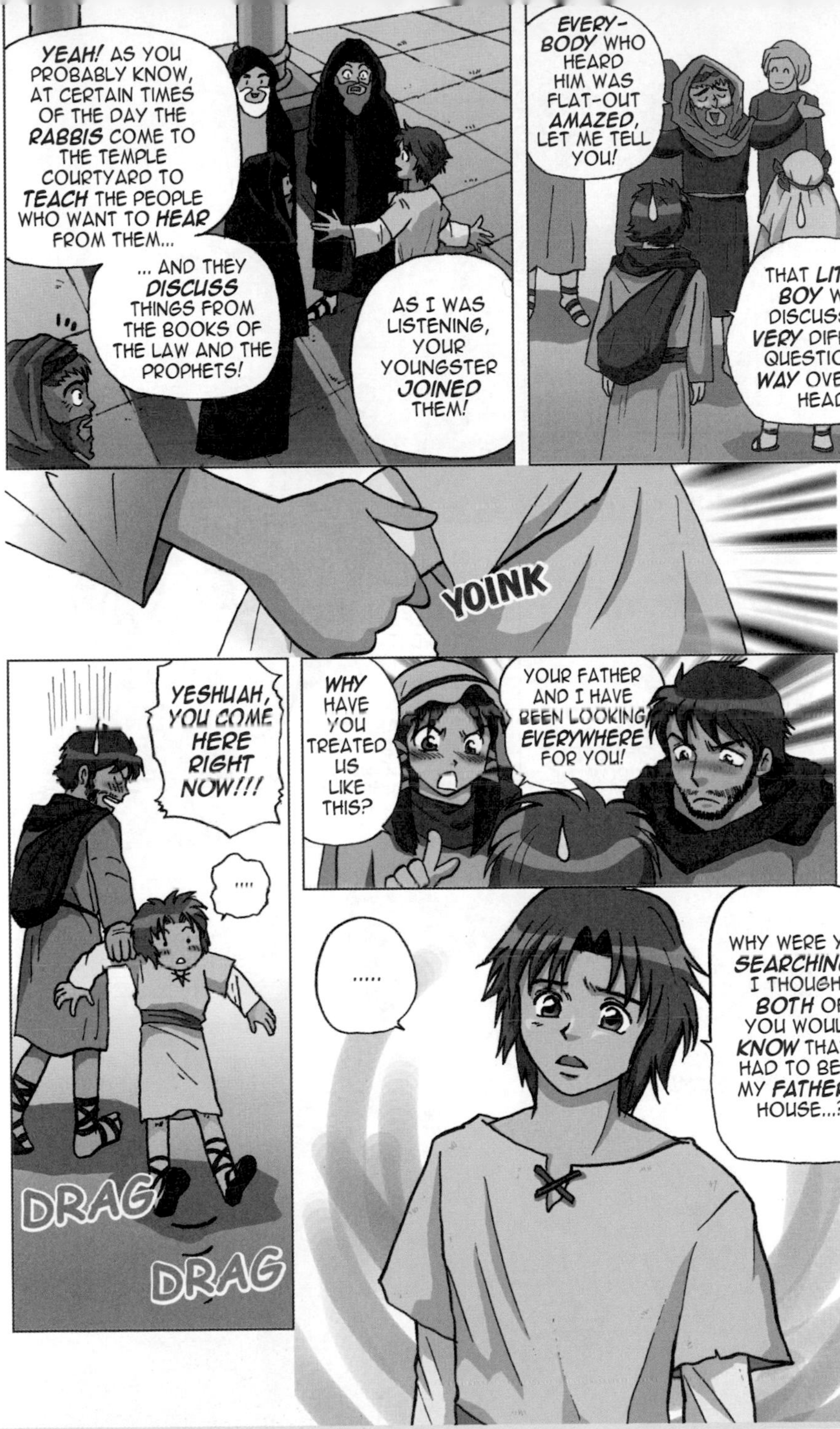
YEAH! AS YOU PROBABLY KNOW, AT CERTAIN TIMES OF THE DAY THE RABBIS COME TO THE TEMPLE COURTYARD TO TEACH THE PEOPLE WHO WANT TO HEAR FROM THEM...
... AND THEY DISCUSS THINGS FROM THE BOOKS OF THE LAW AND THE PROPHETS!
AS I WAS LISTENING, YOUR YOUNGSTER JOINED THEM!
EVERY-BODY WHO HEARD HIM WAS FLAT-OUT AMAZED, LET ME TELL YOU!
THAT LITTLE BOY WAS DISCUSSING VERY DIFFICULT QUESTIONS... WAY OVER MY HEAD!
YOINK
YESHUAH, YOU COME HERE RIGHT NOW!!!
....
DRAG
DRAG
WHY HAVE YOU TREATED US LIKE THIS?
YOUR FATHER AND I HAVE BEEN LOOKING EVERYWHERE FOR YOU!
.....
WHY WERE YOU SEARCHING? I THOUGHT BOTH OF YOU WOULD KNOW THAT I HAD TO BE IN MY FATHER'S HOUSE...?

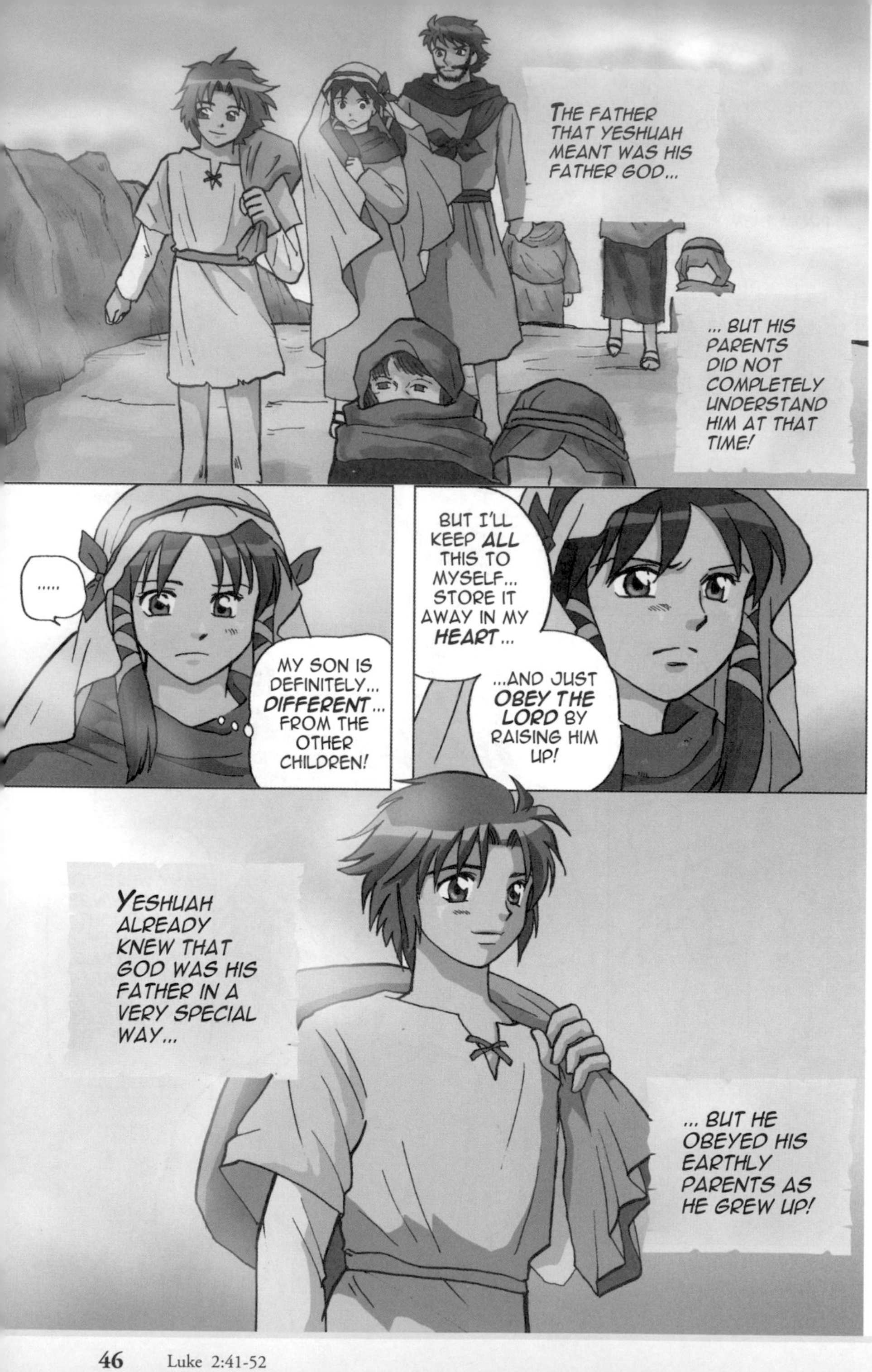
THE FATHER THAT YESHUAH MEANT WAS HIS FATHER GOD...
... BUT HIS PARENTS DID NOT COMPLETELY UNDERSTAND HIM AT THAT TIME!
.....
MY SON IS DEFINITELY... DIFFERENT... FROM THE OTHER CHILDREN!
BUT I'LL KEEP ALL THIS TO MYSELF... STORE IT AWAY IN MY HEART...
...AND JUST OBEY THE LORD BY RAISING HIM UP!
YESHUAH ALREADY KNEW THAT GOD WAS HIS FATHER IN A VERY SPECIAL WAY...
... BUT HE OBEYED HIS EARTHLY PARENTS AS HE GREW UP!

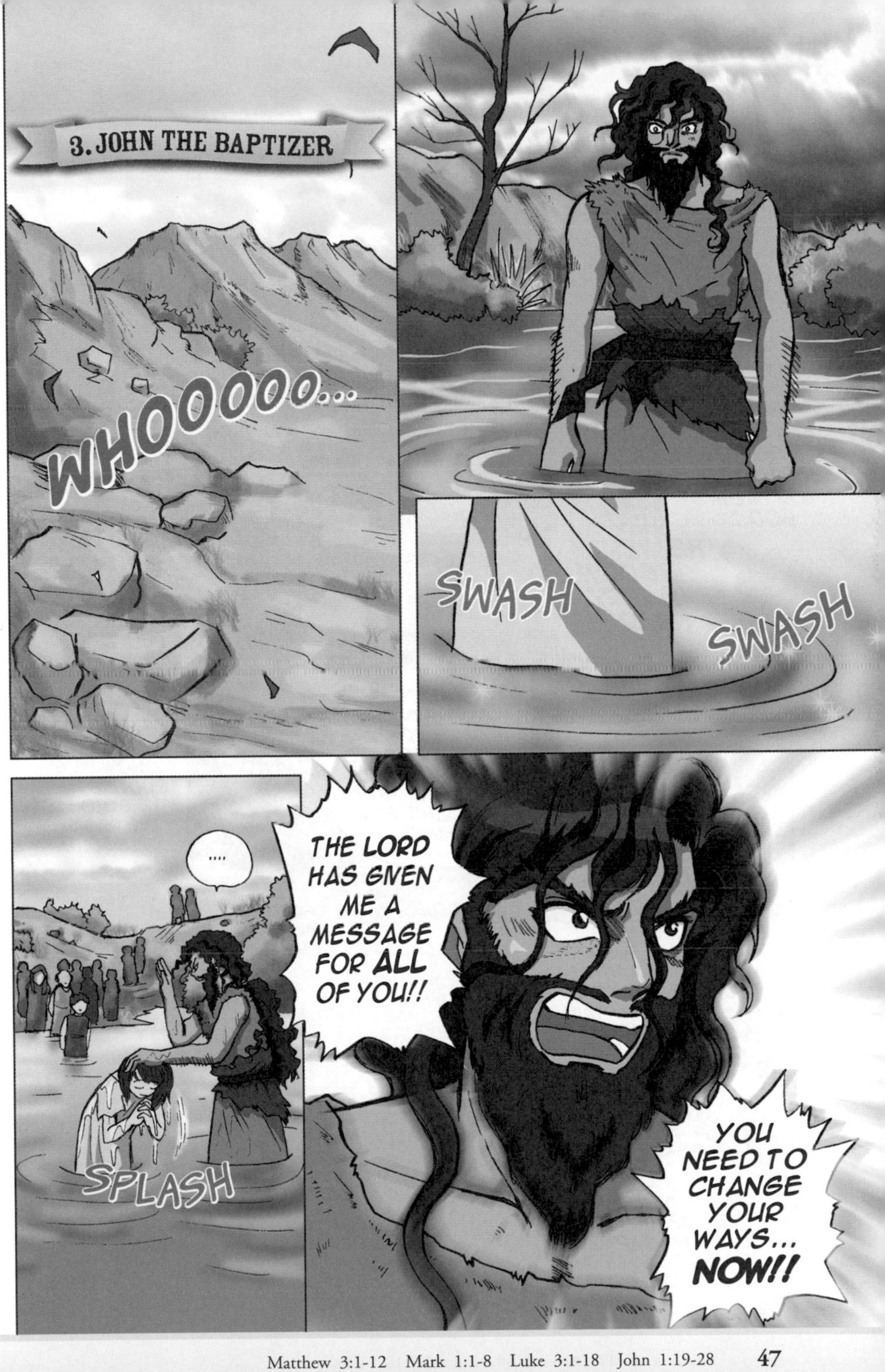
3. JOHN THE BAPTIZER
WHOOOOO...
SWASH
SWASH
....
SPLASH
THE LORD HAS GIVEN ME A MESSAGE FOR ALL OF YOU!!
YOU NEED TO CHANGE YOUR WAYS... NOW!!

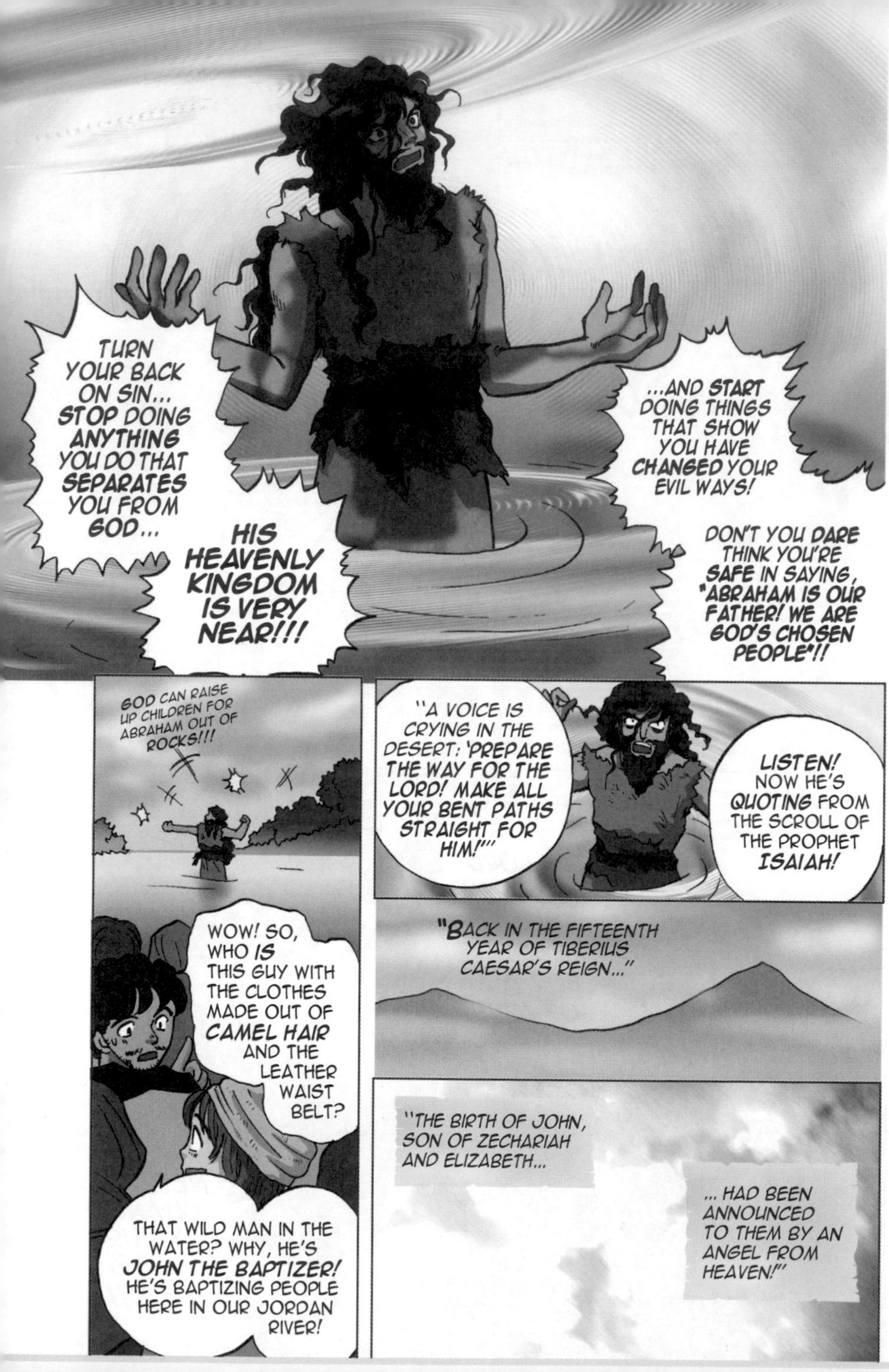

TURN YOUR BACK ON SIN... STOP DOING ANYTHING YOU DO THAT SEPARATES YOU FROM GOD...
HIS HEAVENLY KINGDOM IS VERY NEAR!!!
...AND START DOING THINGS THAT SHOW YOU HAVE CHANGED YOUR EVIL WAYS!
DON'T YOU DARE THINK YOU'RE SAFE IN SAYING, "ABRAHAM IS OUR FATHER! WE ARE GOD'S CHOSEN PEOPLE"!!
GOD CAN RAISE UP CHILDREN FOR ABRAHAM OUT OF ROCKS!!!
"A VOICE IS CRYING IN THE DESERT: 'PREPARE THE WAY FOR THE LORD! MAKE ALL YOUR BENT PATHS STRAIGHT FOR HIM!'"
LISTEN! NOW HE'S QUOTING FROM THE SCROLL OF THE PROPHET ISAIAH!
WOW! SO, WHO IS THIS GUY WITH THE CLOTHES MADE OUT OF CAMEL HAIR AND THE LEATHER WAIST BELT?
THAT WILD MAN IN THE WATER? WHY, HE'S JOHN THE BAPTIZER! HE'S BAPTIZING PEOPLE HERE IN OUR JORDAN RIVER!
"BACK IN THE FIFTEENTH YEAR OF TIBERIUS CAESAR'S REIGN..."
"THE BIRTH OF JOHN, SON OF ZECHARIAH AND ELIZABETH...
... HAD BEEN ANNOUNCED TO THEM BY AN ANGEL FROM HEAVEN!"

 Matthew 3:1-12 Mark 1:1-8 Luke 3:1-18 John 1:19-28

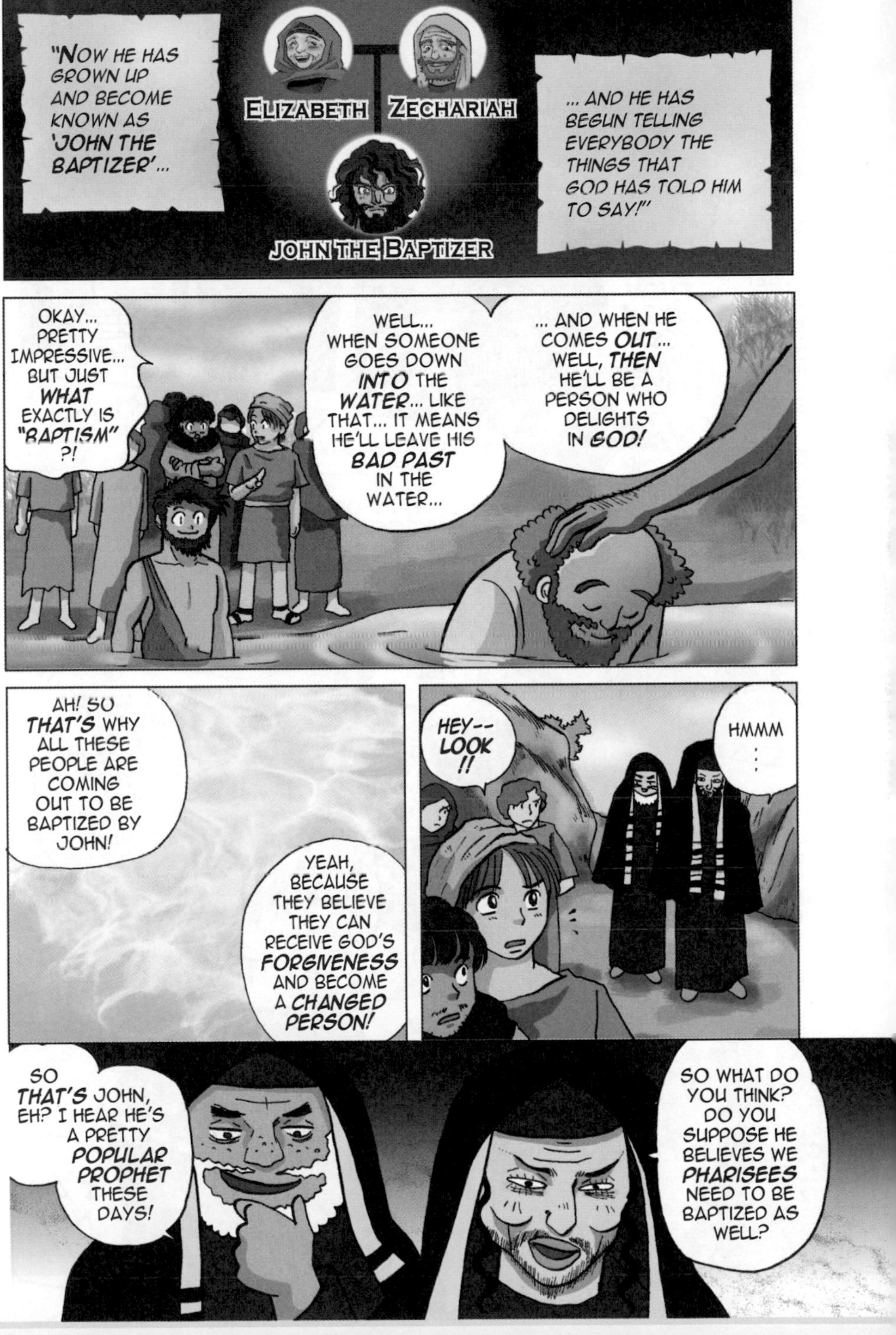
"NOW HE HAS GROWN UP AND BECOME KNOWN AS 'JOHN THE BAPTIZER'...
ELIZABETH
ZECHARIAH
JOHN THE BAPTIZER
... AND HE HAS BEGUN TELLING EVERYBODY THE THINGS THAT GOD HAS TOLD HIM TO SAY!"
OKAY... PRETTY IMPRESSIVE... BUT JUST WHAT EXACTLY IS "BAPTISM" ?!
WELL... WHEN SOMEONE GOES DOWN INTO THE WATER... LIKE THAT... IT MEANS HE'LL LEAVE HIS BAD PAST IN THE WATER...
... AND WHEN HE COMES OUT... WELL, THEN HE'LL BE A PERSON WHO DELIGHTS IN GOD!
AH! SO THAT'S WHY ALL THESE PEOPLE ARE COMING OUT TO BE BAPTIZED BY JOHN!
YEAH, BECAUSE THEY BELIEVE THEY CAN RECEIVE GOD'S FORGIVENESS AND BECOME A CHANGED PERSON!
HEY-- LOOK !!
HMMM . . .
SO THAT'S JOHN, EH? I HEAR HE'S A PRETTY POPULAR PROPHET THESE DAYS!
SO WHAT DO YOU THINK? DO YOU SUPPOSE HE BELIEVES WE PHARISEES NEED TO BE BAPTIZED AS WELL?

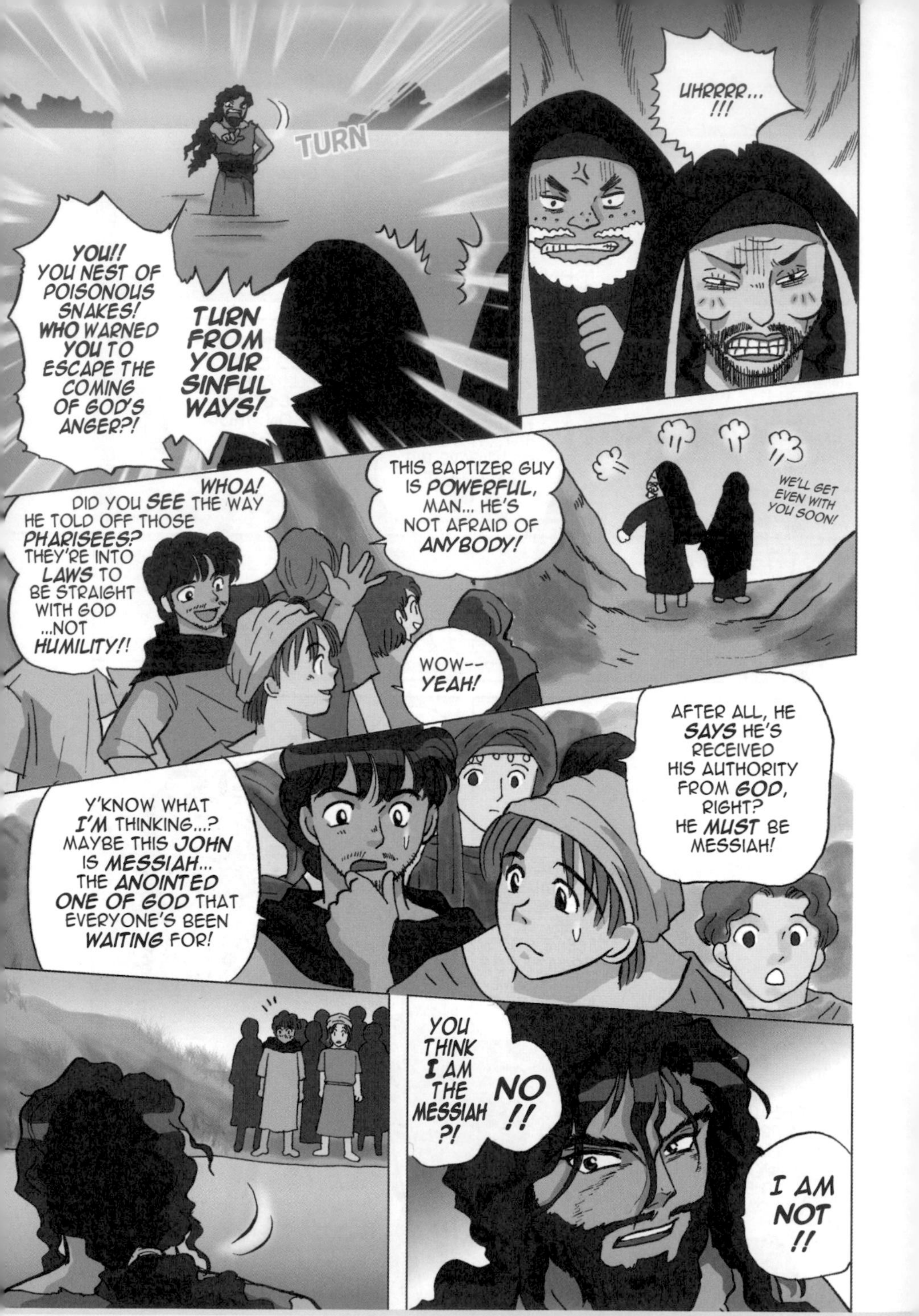
TURN
YOU!! YOU NEST OF POISONOUS SNAKES! WHO WARNED YOU TO ESCAPE THE COMING OF GOD'S ANGER?!
TURN FROM YOUR SINFUL WAYS!
UHRRRR... !!!
WHOA! DID YOU SEE THE WAY HE TOLD OFF THOSE PHARISEES? THEY'RE INTO LAWS TO BE STRAIGHT WITH GOD ...NOT HUMILITY!!
THIS BAPTIZER GUY IS POWERFUL, MAN... HE'S NOT AFRAID OF ANYBODY!
WOW-- YEAH!
WE'LL GET EVEN WITH YOU SOON!
Y'KNOW WHAT I'M THINKING...? MAYBE THIS JOHN IS MESSIAH... THE ANOINTED ONE OF GOD THAT EVERYONE'S BEEN WAITING FOR!
AFTER ALL, HE SAYS HE'S RECEIVED HIS AUTHORITY FROM GOD, RIGHT? HE MUST BE MESSIAH!
YOU THINK I AM THE MESSIAH ?!
NO !!
I AM NOT !!

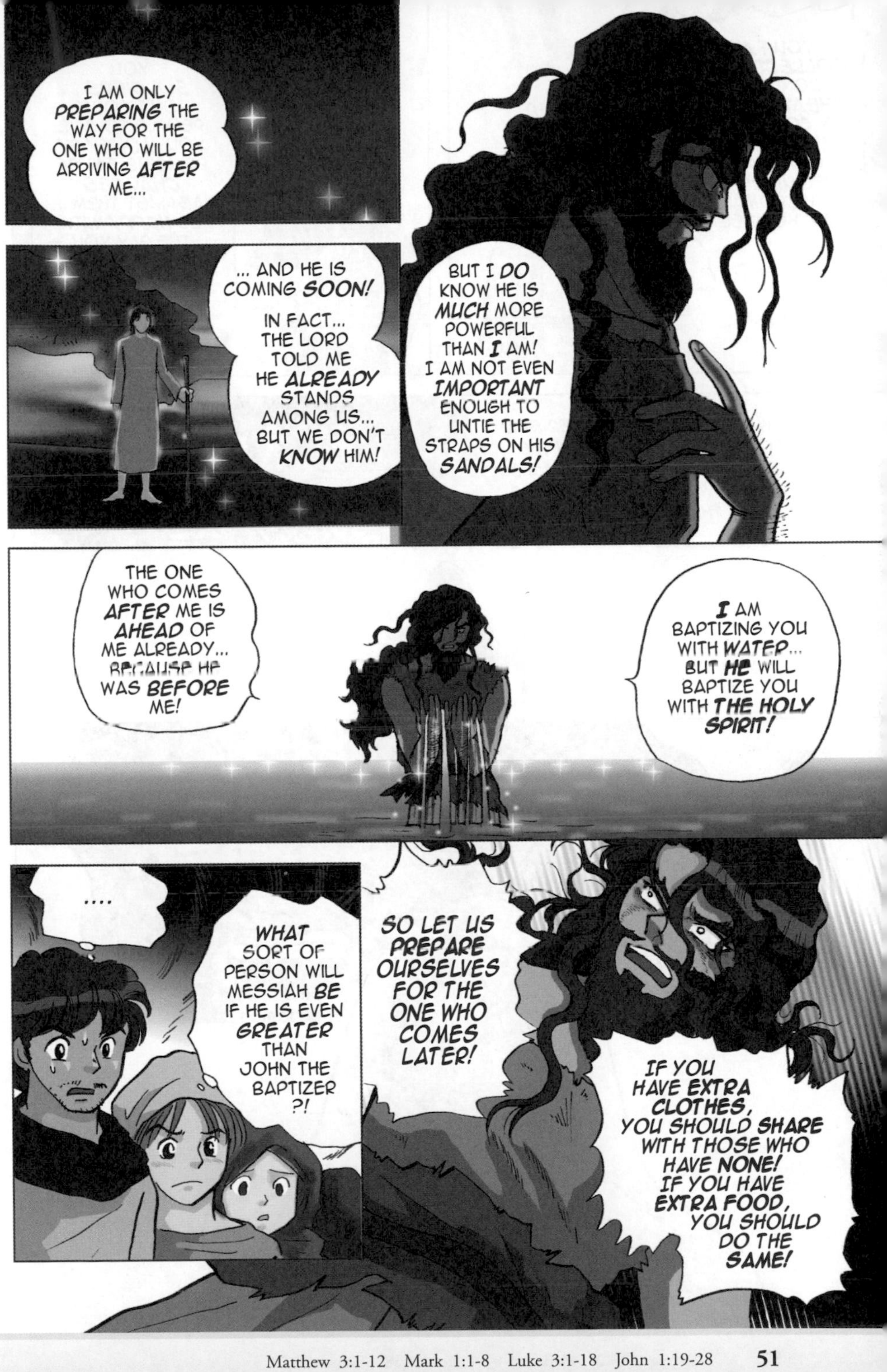

I AM ONLY PREPARING THE WAY FOR THE ONE WHO WILL BE ARRIVING AFTER ME...
... AND HE IS COMING SOON!
IN FACT... THE LORD TOLD ME HE ALREADY STANDS AMONG US... BUT WE DON'T KNOW HIM!
BUT I DO KNOW HE IS MUCH MORE POWERFUL THAN I AM! I AM NOT EVEN IMPORTANT ENOUGH TO UNTIE THE STRAPS ON HIS SANDALS!
THE ONE WHO COMES AFTER ME IS AHEAD OF ME ALREADY... BECAUSE HE WAS BEFORE ME!
I AM BAPTIZING YOU WITH WATER... BUT HE WILL BAPTIZE YOU WITH THE HOLY SPIRIT!
....
WHAT SORT OF PERSON WILL MESSIAH BE IF HE IS EVEN GREATER THAN JOHN THE BAPTIZER ?!
SO LET US PREPARE OURSELVES FOR THE ONE WHO COMES LATER!
IF YOU HAVE EXTRA CLOTHES, YOU SHOULD SHARE WITH THOSE WHO HAVE NONE! IF YOU HAVE EXTRA FOOD, YOU SHOULD DO THE SAME!

Matthew 3:1-12 Mark 1:1-8 Luke 3:1-18 John 1:19-28

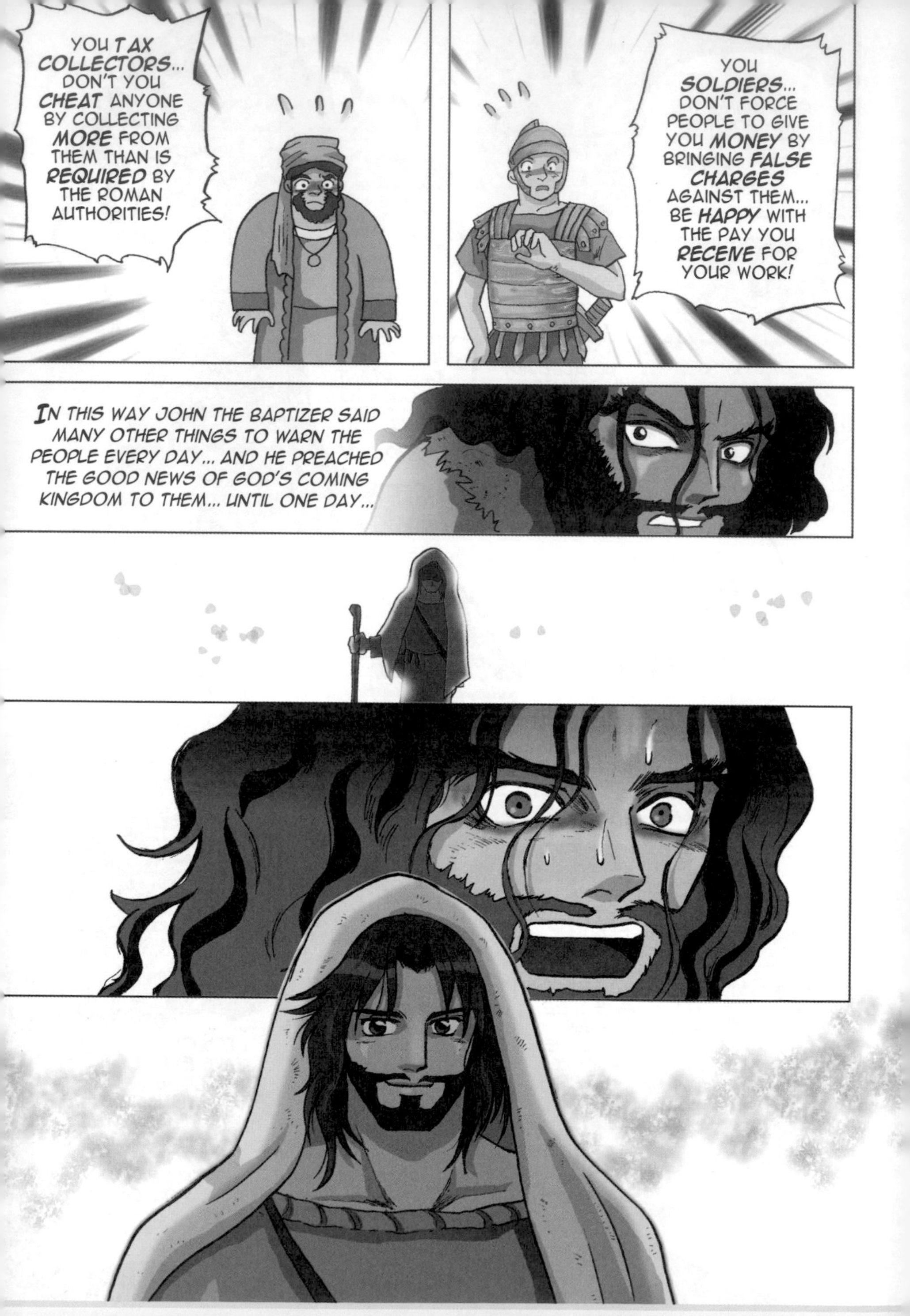
YOU TAX COLLECTORS... DON'T YOU CHEAT ANYONE BY COLLECTING MORE FROM THEM THAN IS REQUIRED BY THE ROMAN AUTHORITIES!
YOU SOLDIERS... DON'T FORCE PEOPLE TO GIVE YOU MONEY BY BRINGING FALSE CHARGES AGAINST THEM... BE HAPPY WITH THE PAY YOU RECEIVE FOR YOUR WORK!
IN THIS WAY JOHN THE BAPTIZER SAID MANY OTHER THINGS TO WARN THE PEOPLE EVERY DAY... AND HE PREACHED THE GOOD NEWS OF GOD'S COMING KINGDOM TO THEM... UNTIL ONE DAY...

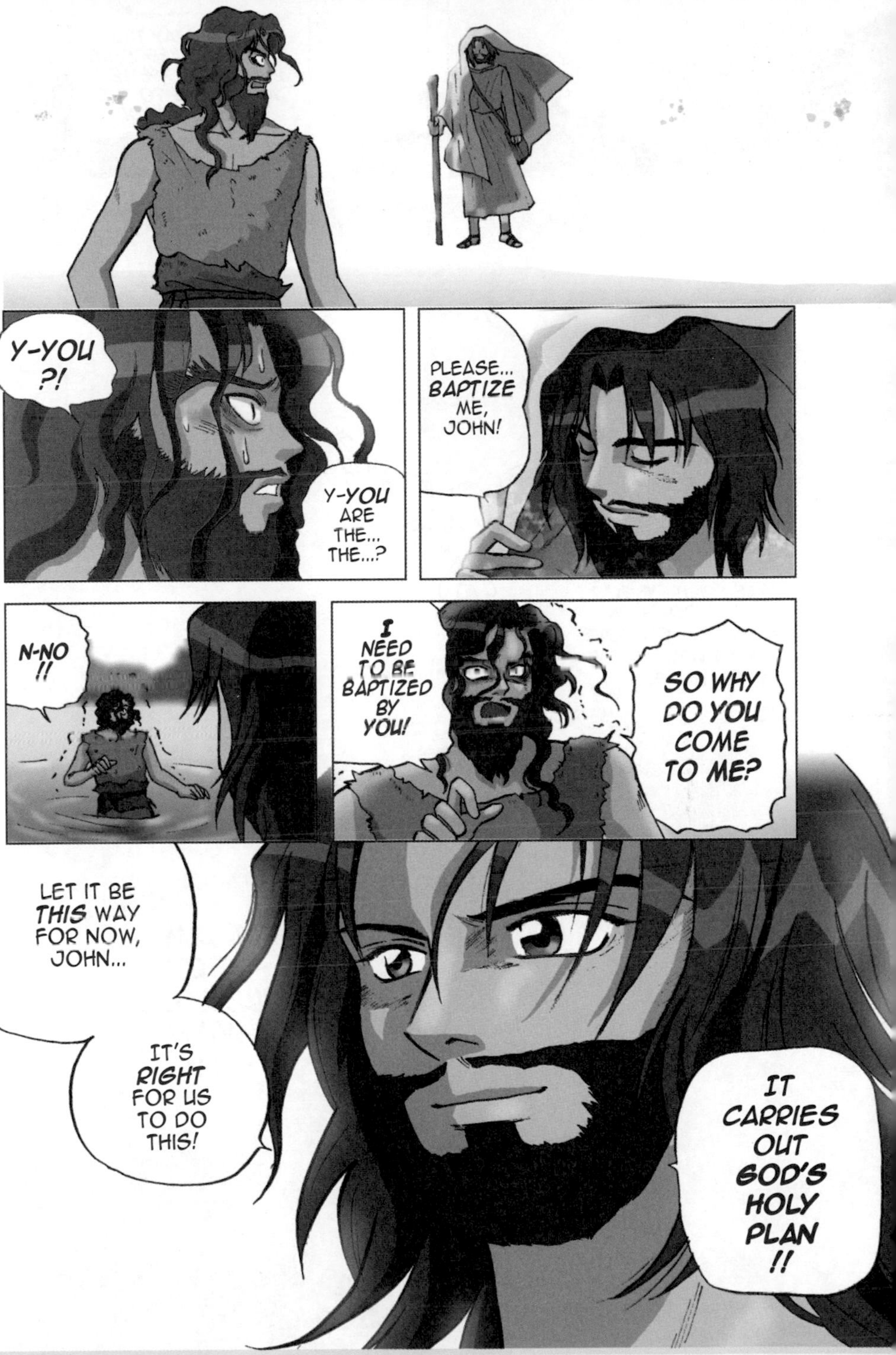
Y-YOU ?!
Y-YOU ARE THE... THE...?
PLEASE... BAPTIZE ME, JOHN!
N-NO !!
I NEED TO BE BAPTIZED BY YOU!
SO WHY DO YOU COME TO ME?
LET IT BE THIS WAY FOR NOW, JOHN...
IT'S RIGHT FOR US TO DO THIS!
IT CARRIES OUT GOD'S HOLY PLAN !!

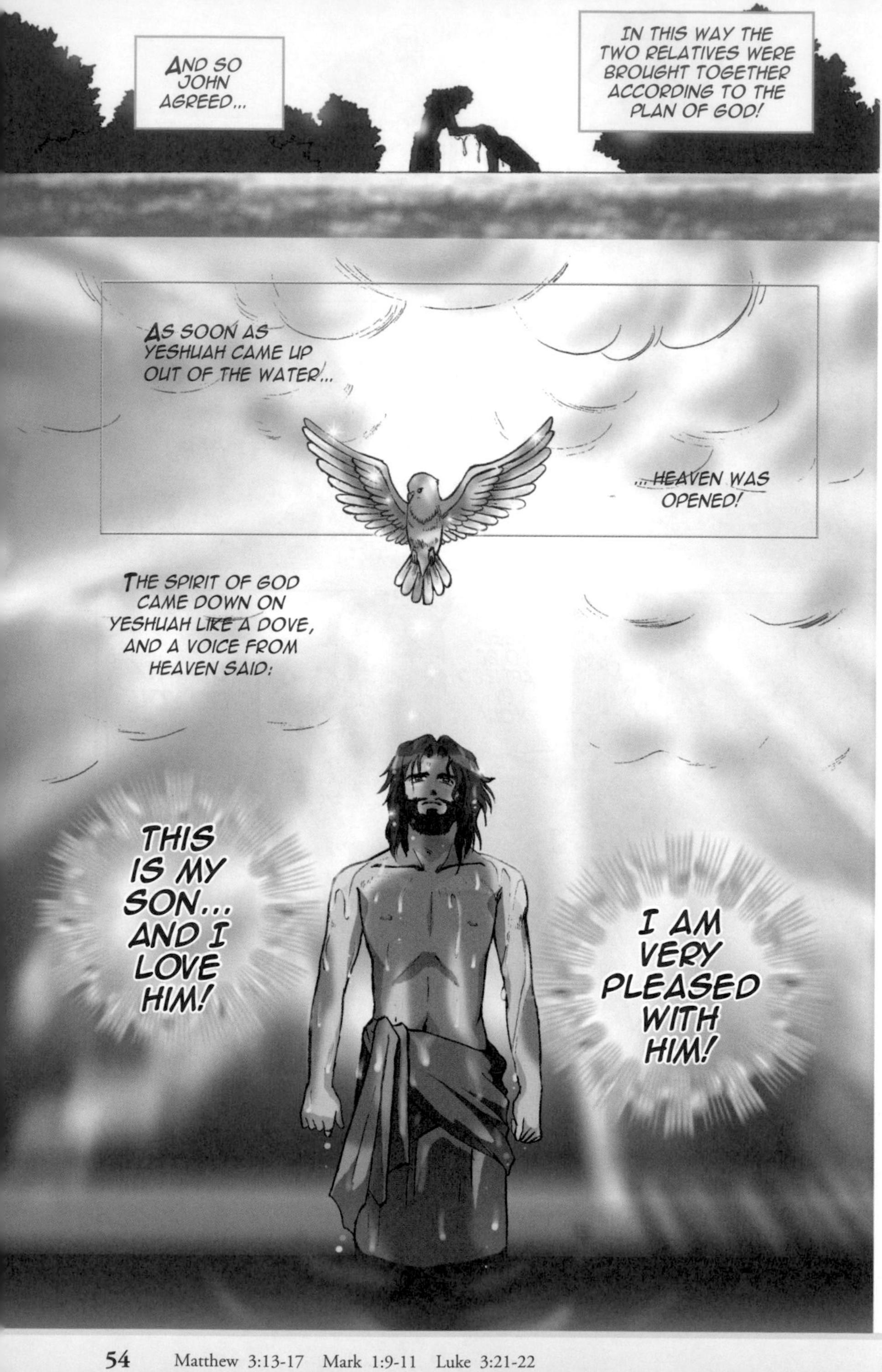
AND SO JOHN AGREED...
IN THIS WAY THE TWO RELATIVES WERE BROUGHT TOGETHER ACCORDING TO THE PLAN OF GOD!
AS SOON AS YESHUAH CAME UP OUT OF THE WATER...
...HEAVEN WAS OPENED!
THE SPIRIT OF GOD CAME DOWN ON YESHUAH LIKE A DOVE, AND A VOICE FROM HEAVEN SAID:
THIS IS MY SON... AND I LOVE HIM!
I AM VERY PLEASED WITH HIM!

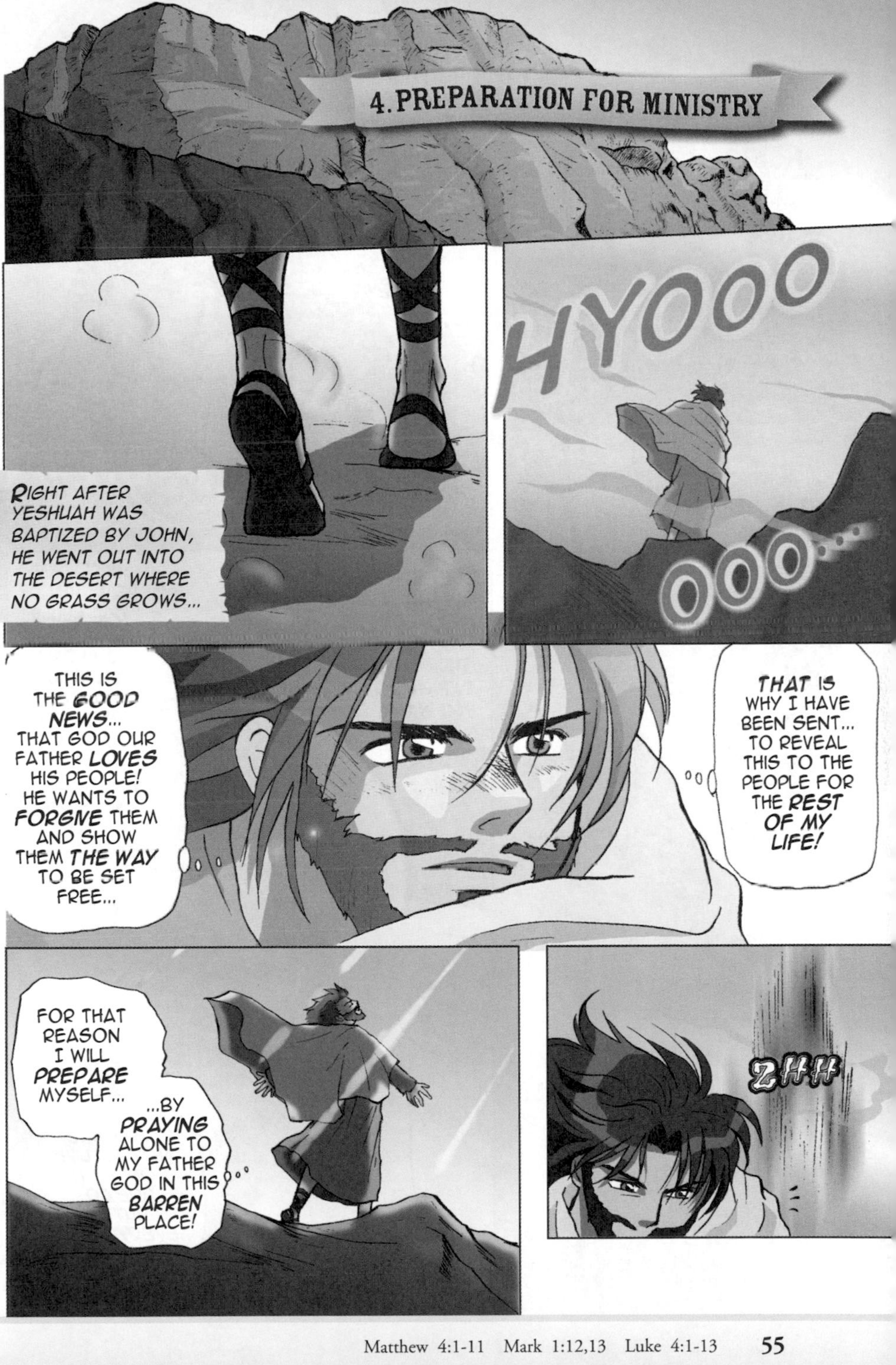
4. PREPARATION FOR MINISTRY
RIGHT AFTER YESHUAH WAS BAPTIZED BY JOHN, HE WENT OUT INTO THE DESERT WHERE NO GRASS GROWS...
HYOOO
OOO...
THIS IS THE GOOD NEWS... THAT GOD OUR FATHER LOVES HIS PEOPLE! HE WANTS TO FORGIVE THEM AND SHOW THEM THE WAY TO BE SET FREE...
THAT IS WHY I HAVE BEEN SENT... TO REVEAL THIS TO THE PEOPLE FOR THE REST OF MY LIFE!
FOR THAT REASON I WILL PREPARE MYSELF...
...BY PRAYING ALONE TO MY FATHER GOD IN THIS BARREN PLACE!
ZHH

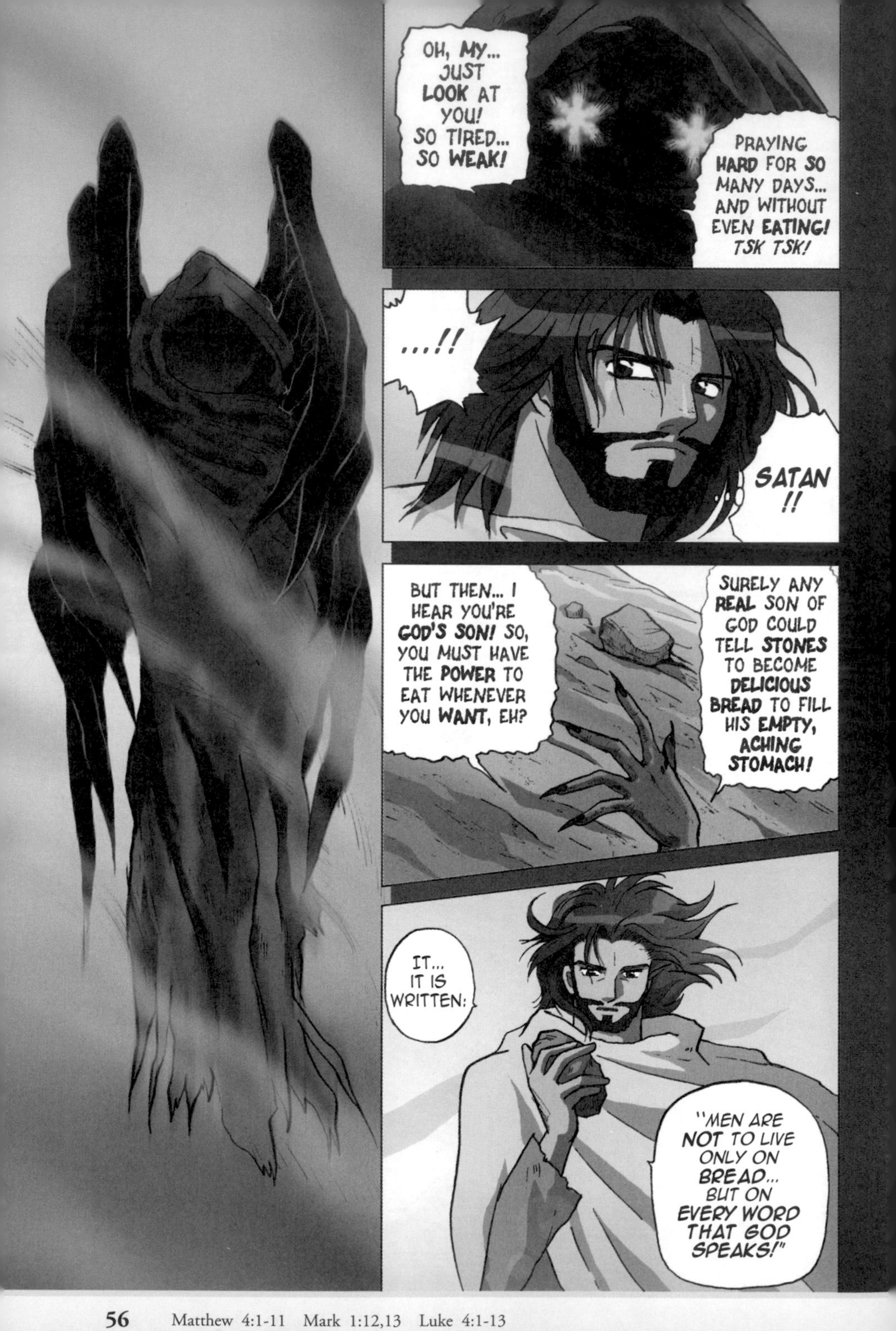
OH, MY... JUST LOOK AT YOU! SO TIRED... SO WEAK!
PRAYING HARD FOR SO MANY DAYS... AND WITHOUT EVEN EATING! TSK TSK!
...!!
SATAN !!
BUT THEN... I HEAR YOU'RE GOD'S SON! SO, YOU MUST HAVE THE POWER TO EAT WHENEVER YOU WANT, EH?
SURELY ANY REAL SON OF GOD COULD TELL STONES TO BECOME DELICIOUS BREAD TO FILL HIS EMPTY, ACHING STOMACH!
IT... IT IS WRITTEN:
"MEN ARE NOT TO LIVE ONLY ON BREAD... BUT ON EVERY WORD THAT GOD SPEAKS!"

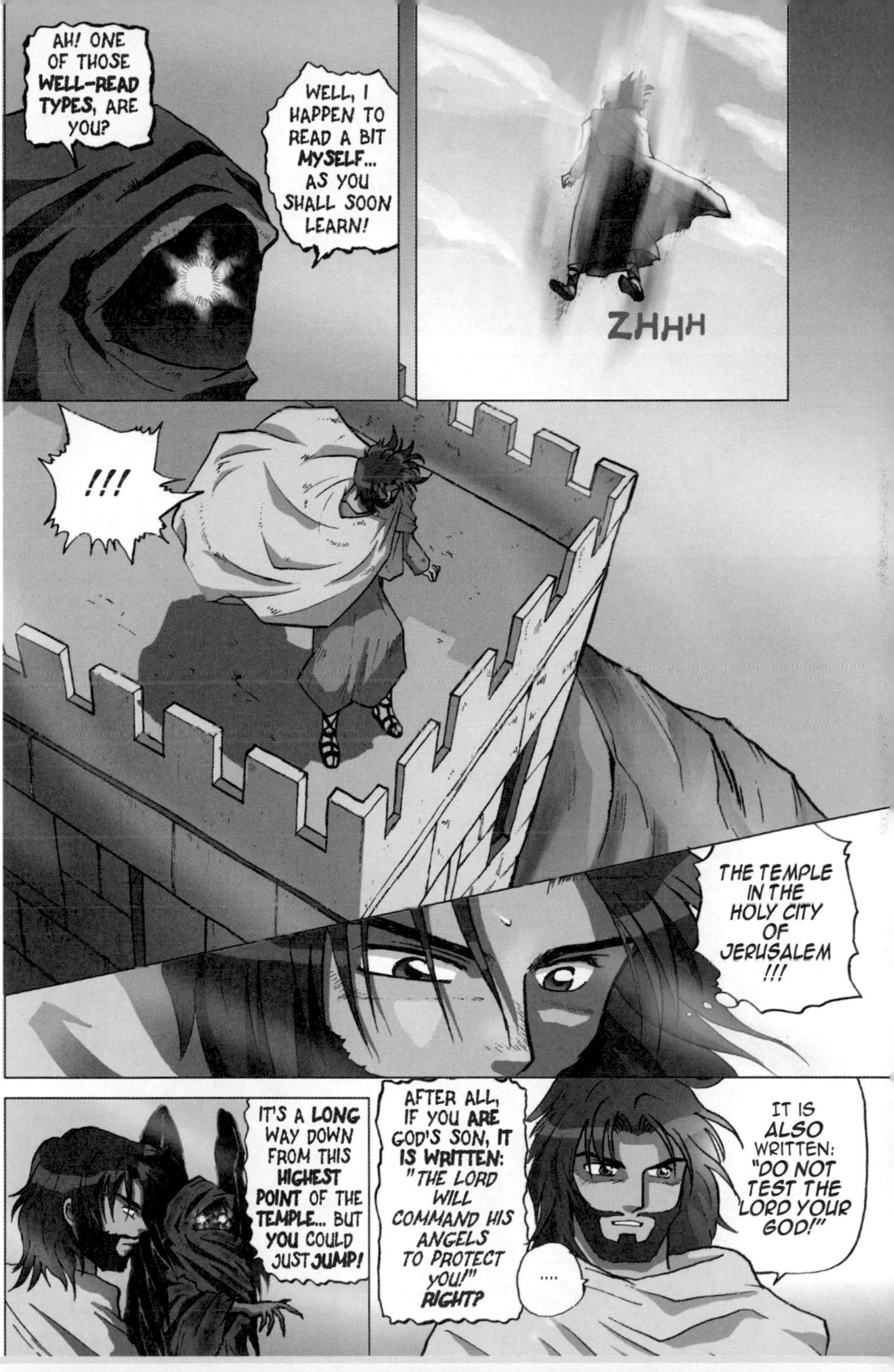

AH! ONE OF THOSE WELL-READ TYPES, ARE YOU?
WELL, I HAPPEN TO READ A BIT MYSELF... AS YOU SHALL SOON LEARN!
ZHHH
!!!
THE TEMPLE IN THE HOLY CITY OF JERUSALEM !!!
IT'S A LONG WAY DOWN FROM THIS HIGHEST POINT OF THE TEMPLE... BUT YOU COULD JUST JUMP!
AFTER ALL, IF YOU ARE GOD'S SON, IT IS WRITTEN: "THE LORD WILL COMMAND HIS ANGELS TO PROTECT YOU!" RIGHT?
....
IT IS ALSO WRITTEN: "DO NOT TEST THE LORD YOUR GOD!"

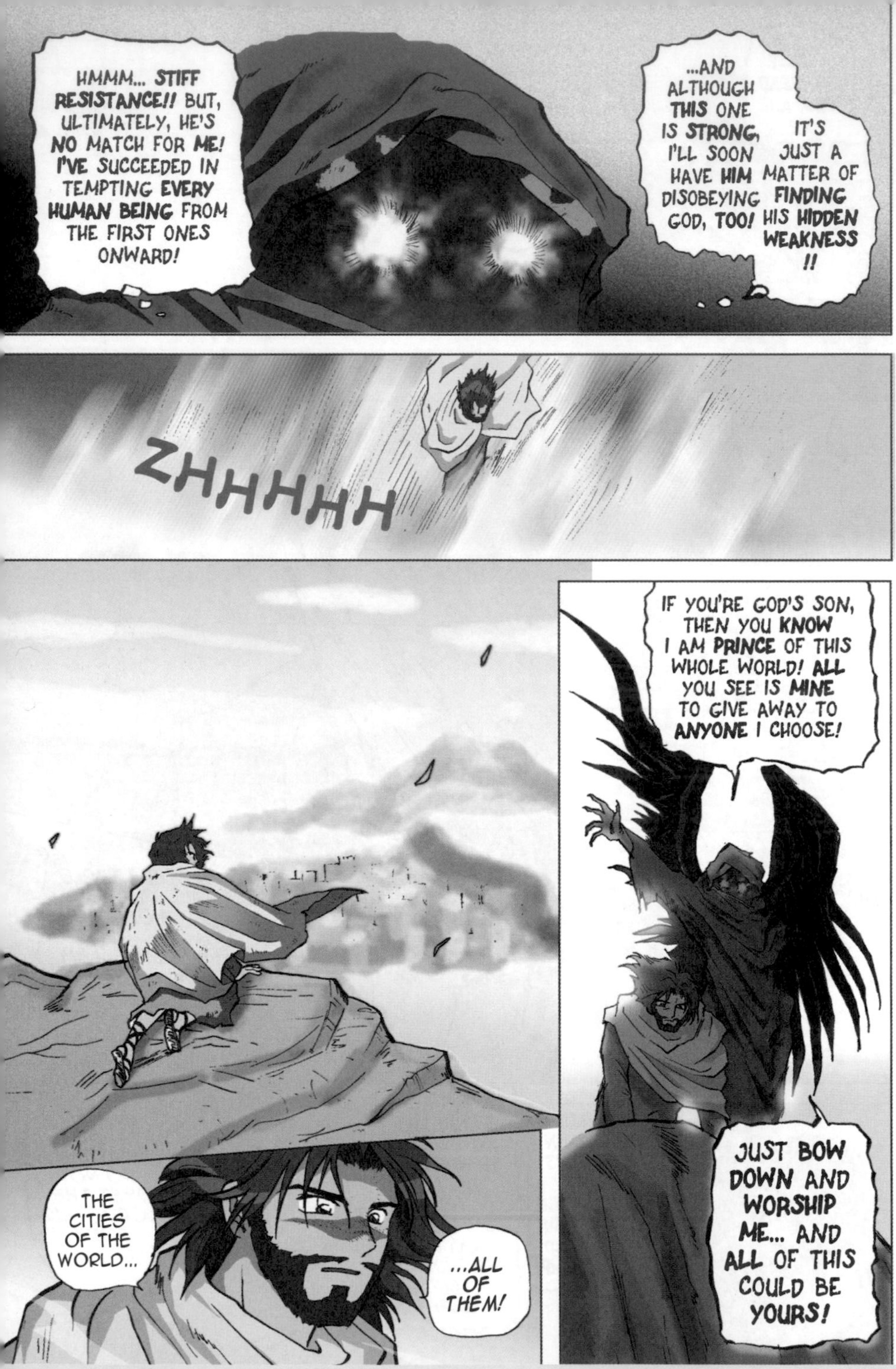
HMMM... STIFF RESISTANCE!! BUT, ULTIMATELY, HE'S NO MATCH FOR ME! I'VE SUCCEEDED IN TEMPTING EVERY HUMAN BEING FROM THE FIRST ONES ONWARD!
...AND ALTHOUGH THIS ONE IS STRONG, I'LL SOON HAVE HIM DISOBEYING GOD, TOO!
IT'S JUST A MATTER OF FINDING HIS HIDDEN WEAKNESS !!
ZHHHHH
IF YOU'RE GOD'S SON, THEN YOU KNOW I AM PRINCE OF THIS WHOLE WORLD! ALL YOU SEE IS MINE TO GIVE AWAY TO ANYONE I CHOOSE!
THE CITIES OF THE WORLD...
...ALL OF THEM!
JUST BOW DOWN AND WORSHIP ME... AND ALL OF THIS COULD BE YOURS!

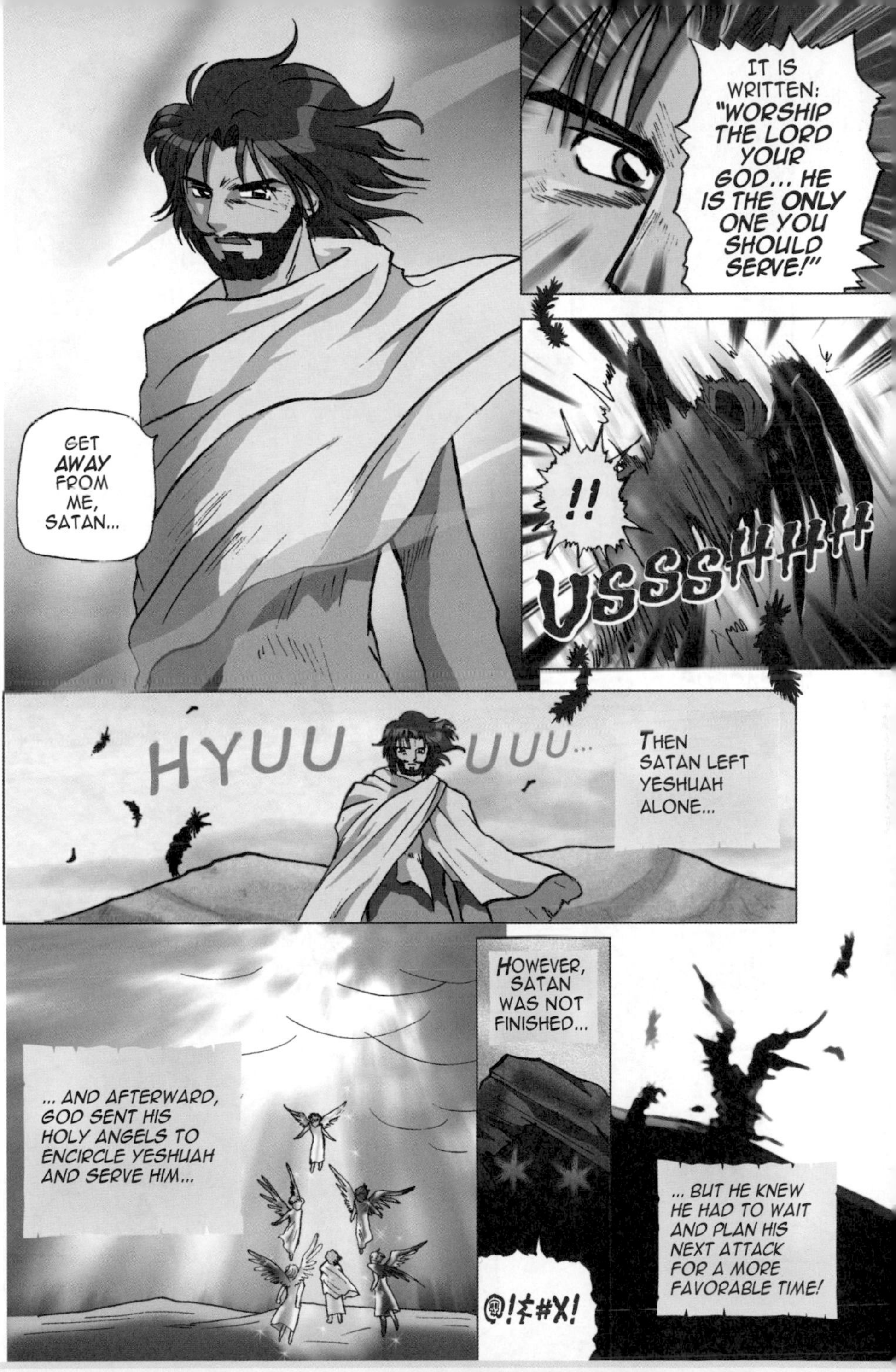
GET AWAY FROM ME, SATAN...
IT IS WRITTEN: "WORSHIP THE LORD YOUR GOD... HE IS THE ONLY ONE YOU SHOULD SERVE!"
!!
USSSHHHH
HYUU UUU...
THEN SATAN LEFT YESHUAH ALONE...
... AND AFTERWARD, GOD SENT HIS HOLY ANGELS TO ENCIRCLE YESHUAH AND SERVE HIM...
HOWEVER, SATAN WAS NOT FINISHED...
... BUT HE KNEW HE HAD TO WAIT AND PLAN HIS NEXT ATTACK FOR A MORE FAVORABLE TIME!
@!*#X!

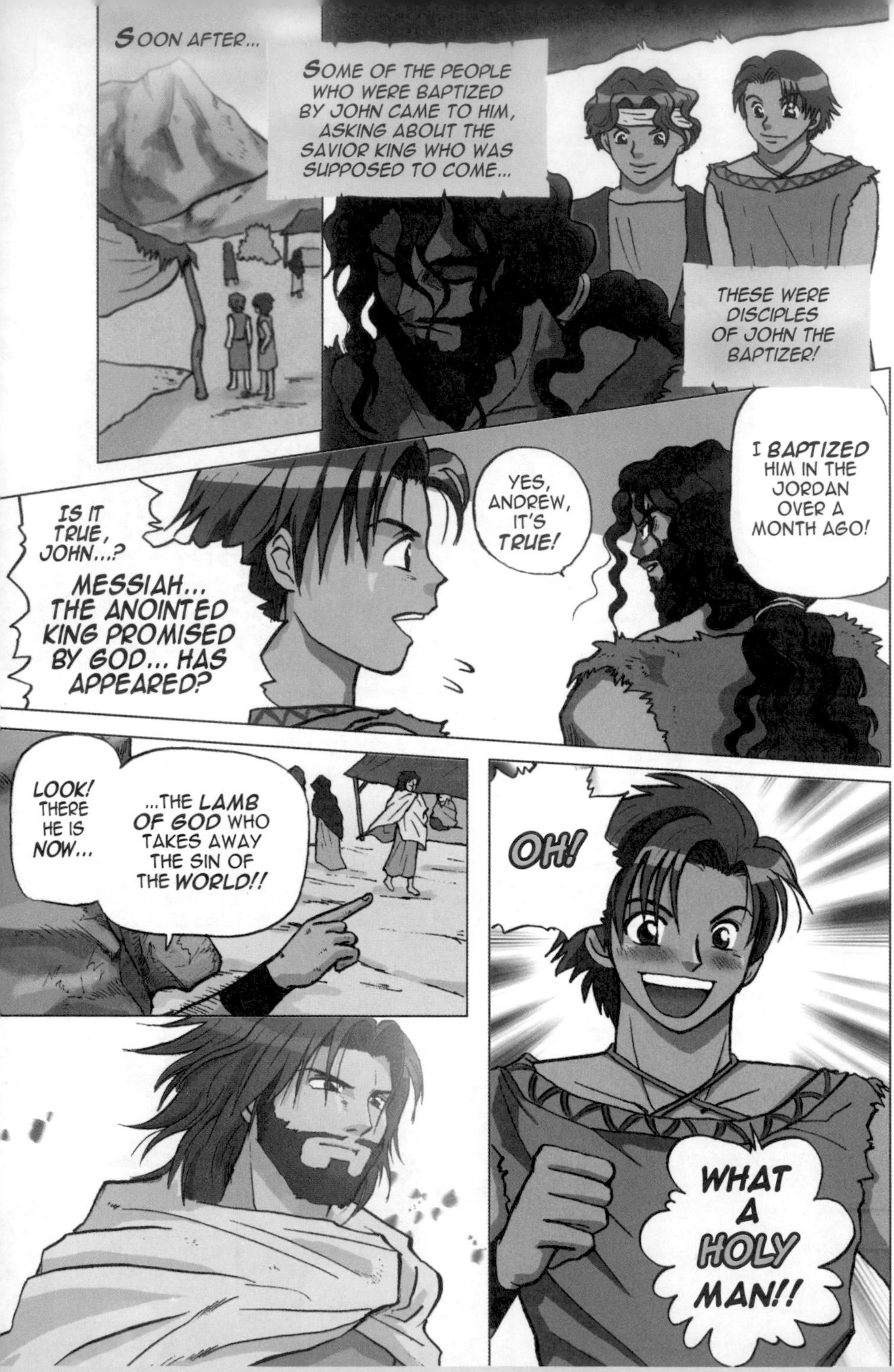
SOON AFTER...
SOME OF THE PEOPLE WHO WERE BAPTIZED BY JOHN CAME TO HIM, ASKING ABOUT THE SAVIOR KING WHO WAS SUPPOSED TO COME...
THESE WERE DISCIPLES OF JOHN THE BAPTIZER!
IS IT TRUE, JOHN...?
MESSIAH... THE ANOINTED KING PROMISED BY GOD... HAS APPEARED?
YES, ANDREW, IT'S TRUE!
I BAPTIZED HIM IN THE JORDAN OVER A MONTH AGO!
LOOK! THERE HE IS NOW...
...THE LAMB OF GOD WHO TAKES AWAY THE SIN OF THE WORLD!!
OH!
WHAT A HOLY MAN!!

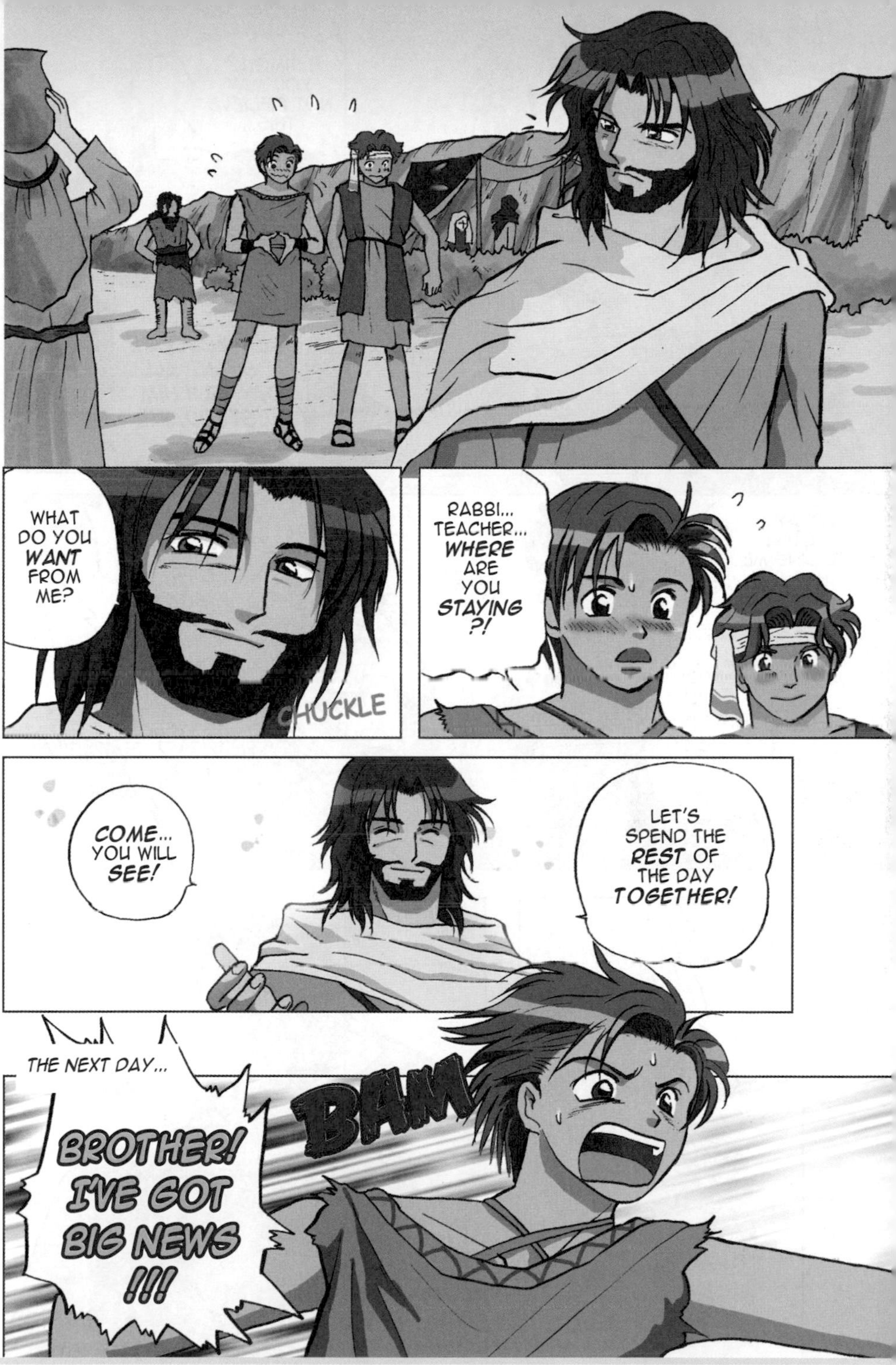
WHAT DO YOU WANT FROM ME?
CHUCKLE
RABBI... TEACHER... WHERE ARE YOU STAYING ?!
COME... YOU WILL SEE!
LET'S SPEND THE REST OF THE DAY TOGETHER!
THE NEXT DAY...
BAM
BROTHER! I'VE GOT BIG NEWS !!!

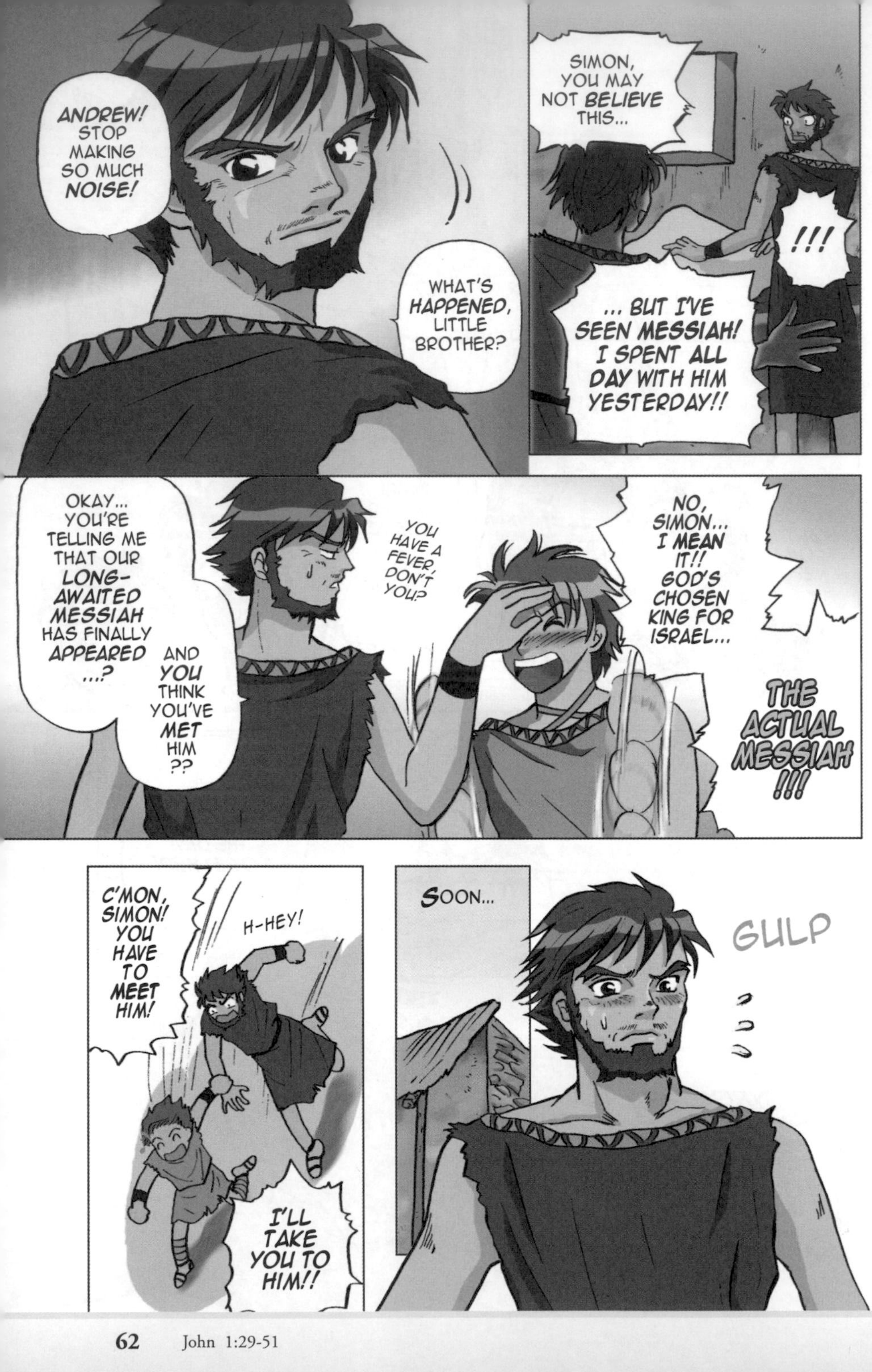
ANDREW! STOP MAKING SO MUCH NOISE!
WHAT'S HAPPENED, LITTLE BROTHER?
SIMON, YOU MAY NOT BELIEVE THIS...
!!!
... BUT I'VE SEEN MESSIAH! I SPENT ALL DAY WITH HIM YESTERDAY!!
OKAY... YOU'RE TELLING ME THAT OUR LONG-AWAITED MESSIAH HAS FINALLY APPEARED ...?
AND YOU THINK YOU'VE MET HIM ??
YOU HAVE A FEVER, DON'T YOU?
NO, SIMON... I MEAN IT!! GOD'S CHOSEN KING FOR ISRAEL...
THE ACTUAL MESSIAH !!!
C'MON, SIMON! YOU HAVE TO MEET HIM!
H-HEY!
I'LL TAKE YOU TO HIM!!
SOON...
GULP

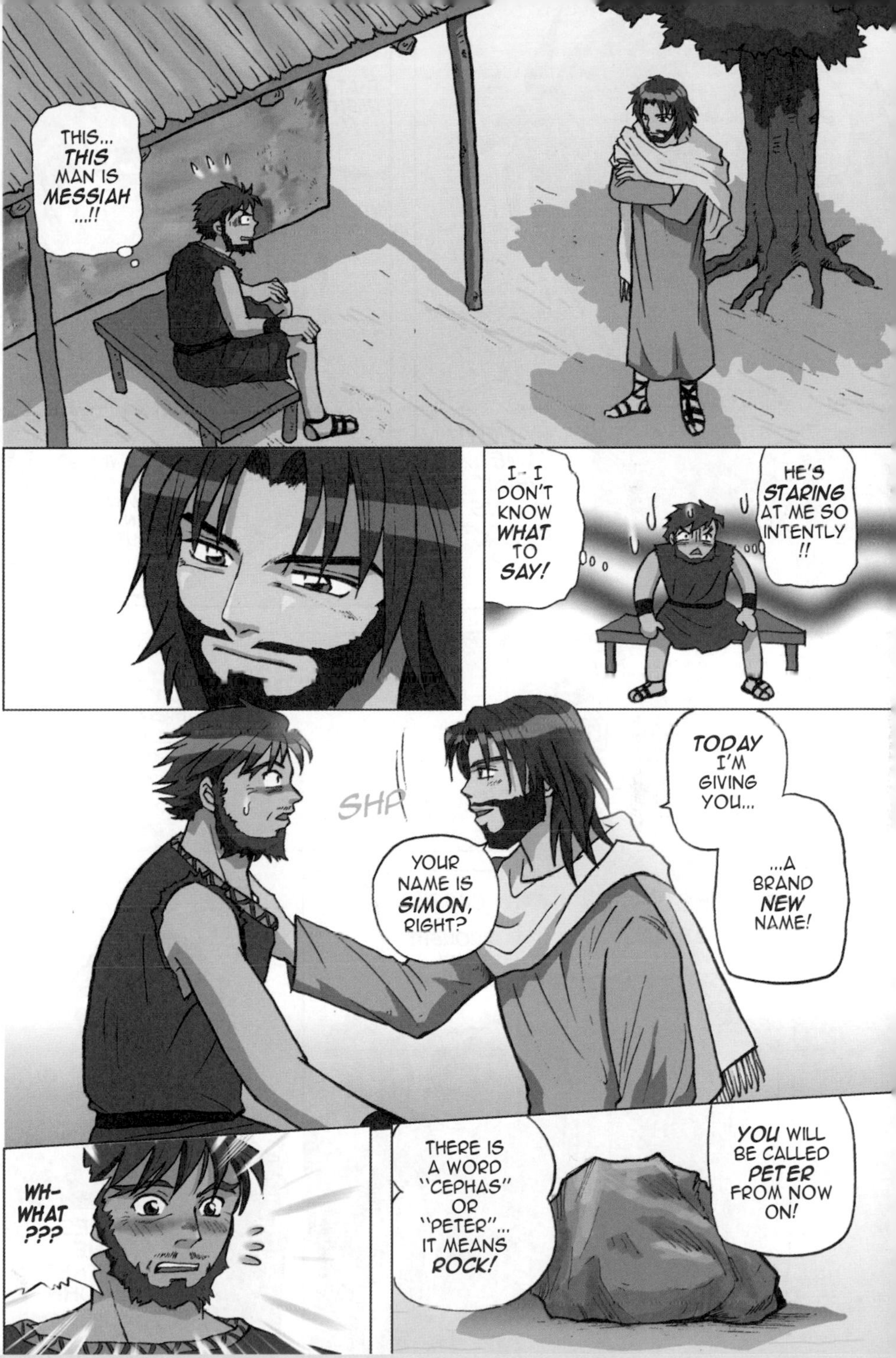
THIS... THIS MAN IS MESSIAH ...!!
HE'S STARING AT ME SO INTENTLY !!
I- I DON'T KNOW WHAT TO SAY!
TODAY I'M GIVING YOU...
SHP
YOUR NAME IS SIMON, RIGHT?
...A BRAND NEW NAME!
YOU WILL BE CALLED PETER FROM NOW ON!
THERE IS A WORD "CEPHAS" OR "PETER"... IT MEANS ROCK!
WH- WHAT ???

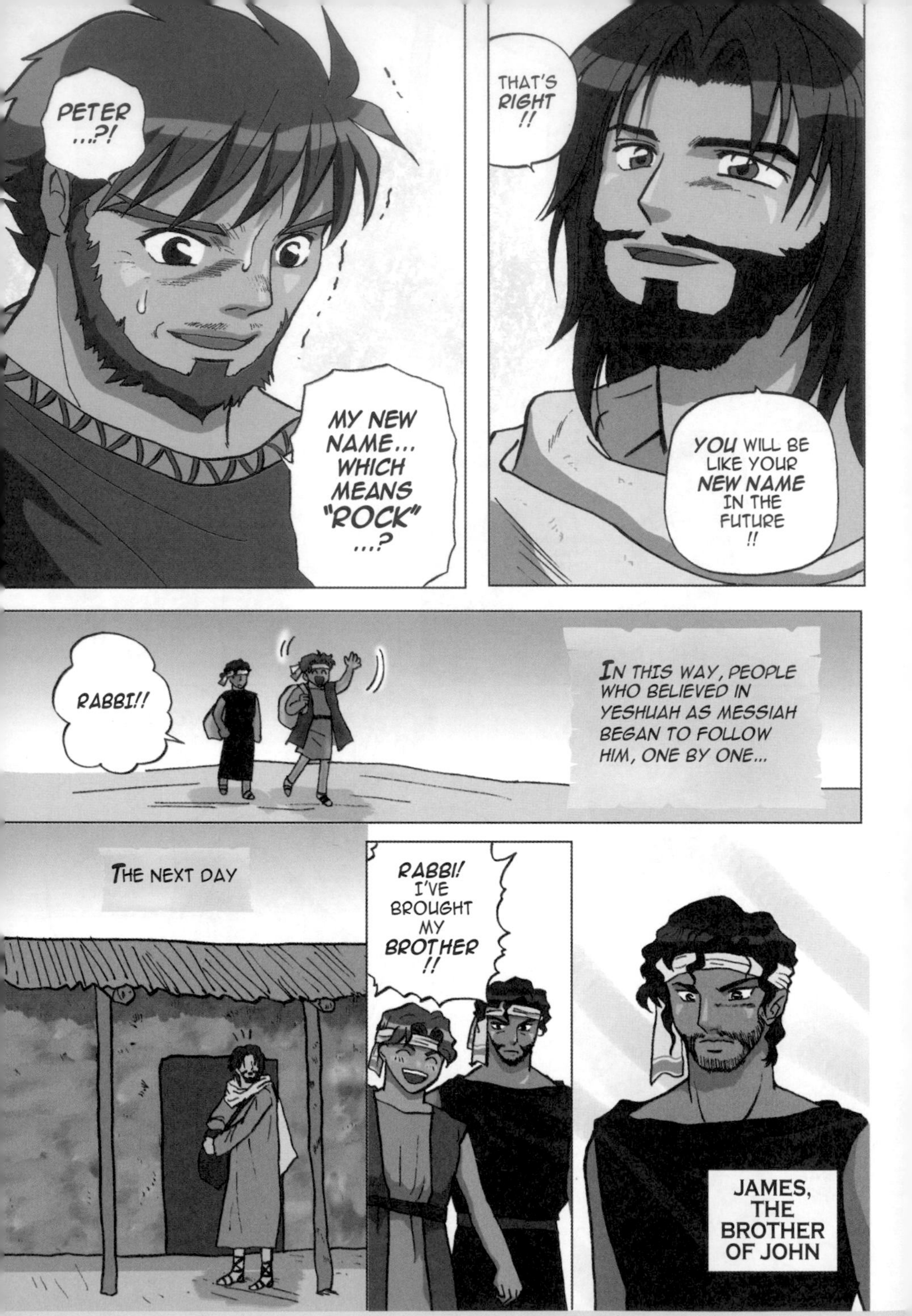
PETER ...?!
MY NEW NAME... WHICH MEANS "ROCK" ...?
THAT'S RIGHT !!
YOU WILL BE LIKE YOUR NEW NAME IN THE FUTURE !!
RABBI!!
IN THIS WAY, PEOPLE WHO BELIEVED IN YESHUAH AS MESSIAH BEGAN TO FOLLOW HIM, ONE BY ONE...
THE NEXT DAY
RABBI! I'VE BROUGHT MY BROTHER !!
JAMES, THE BROTHER OF JOHN

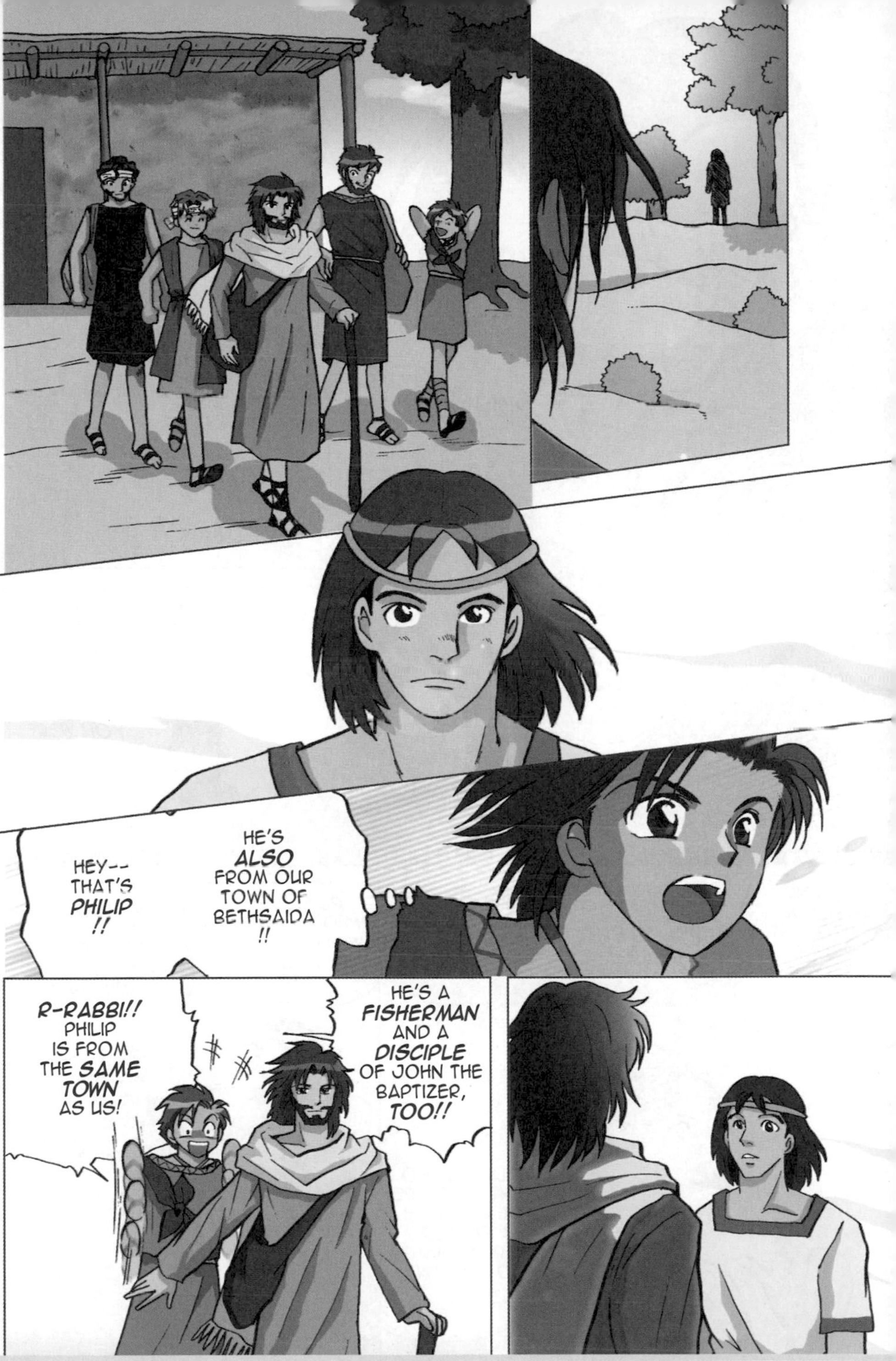
HEY--
THAT'S
PHILIP
!!
HE'S
ALSO
FROM OUR
TOWN OF
BETHSAIDA
!!
R-RABBI!!
PHILIP
IS FROM
THE SAME
TOWN
AS US!
HE'S A
FISHERMAN
AND A
DISCIPLE
OF JOHN THE
BAPTIZER,
TOO!!

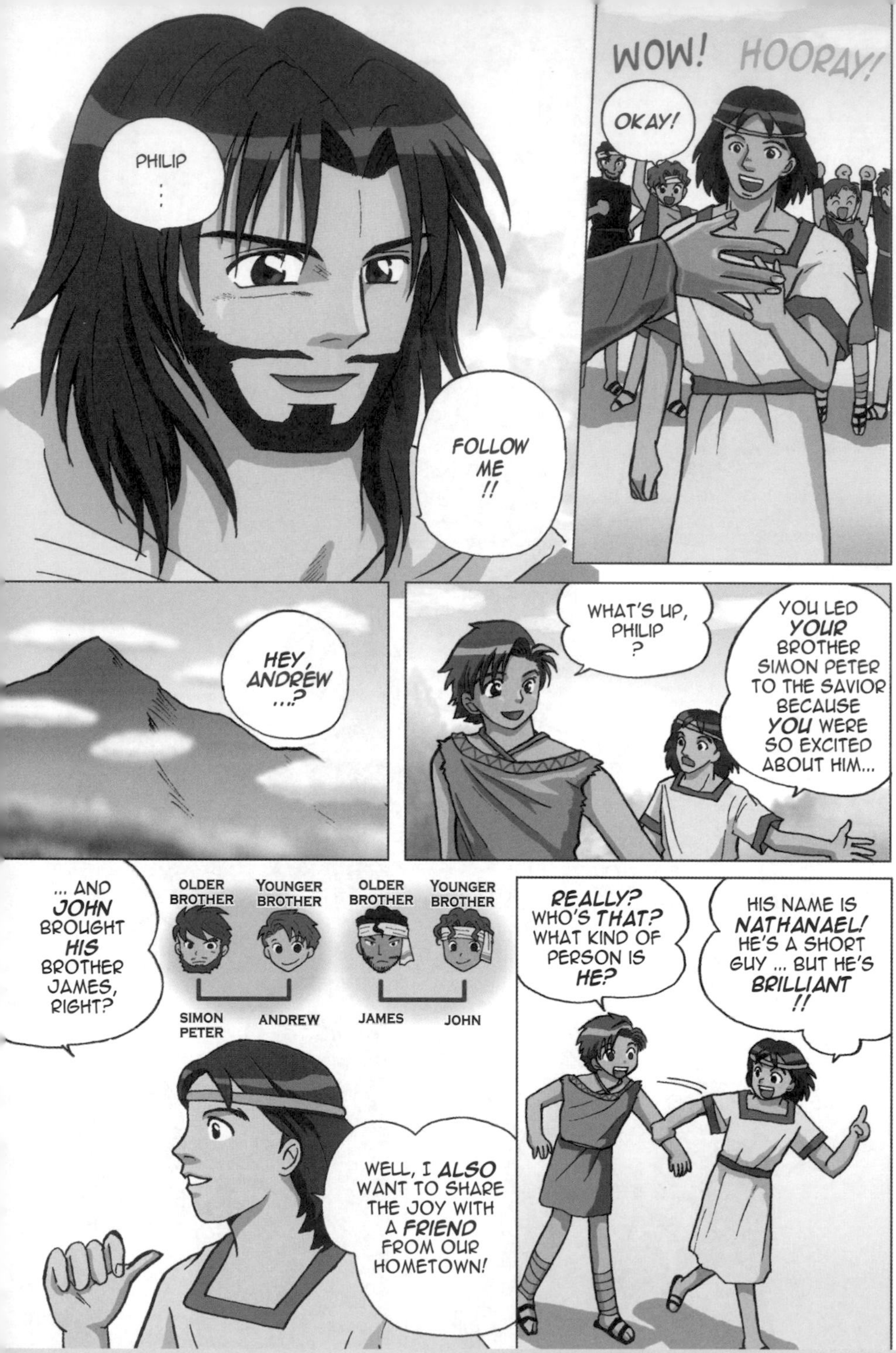
PHILIP
...
FOLLOW ME !!
WOW!
HOORAY!
OKAY!
HEY, ANDREW ...?
WHAT'S UP, PHILIP ?
YOU LED YOUR BROTHER SIMON PETER TO THE SAVIOR BECAUSE YOU WERE SO EXCITED ABOUT HIM...
... AND JOHN BROUGHT HIS BROTHER JAMES, RIGHT?
OLDER BROTHER
YOUNGER BROTHER
OLDER BROTHER
YOUNGER BROTHER
SIMON PETER
ANDREW
JAMES
JOHN
WELL, I ALSO WANT TO SHARE THE JOY WITH A FRIEND FROM OUR HOMETOWN!
REALLY? WHO'S THAT? WHAT KIND OF PERSON IS HE?
HIS NAME IS NATHANAEL! HE'S A SHORT GUY ... BUT HE'S BRILLIANT !!

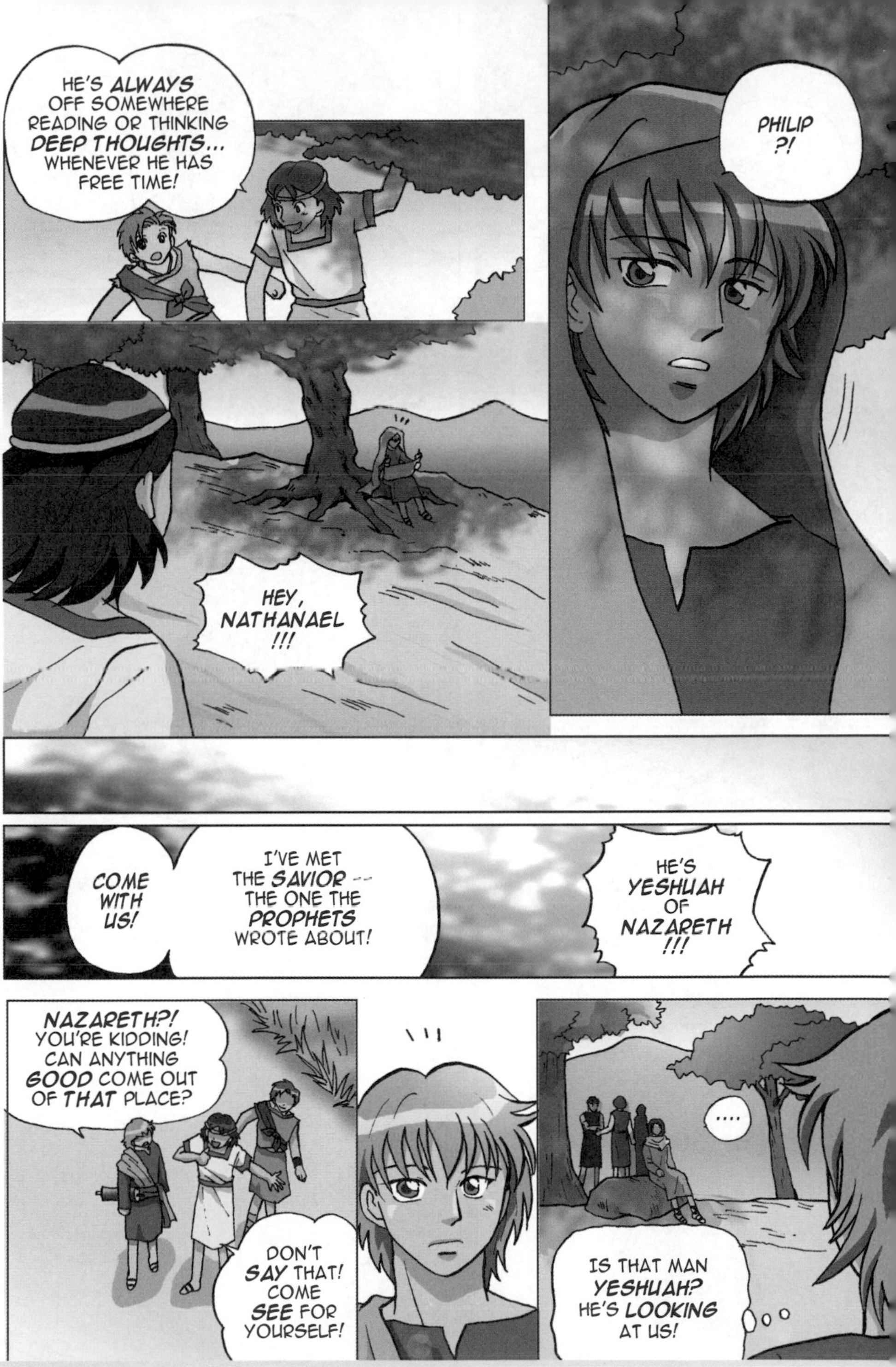
HE'S ALWAYS OFF SOMEWHERE READING OR THINKING DEEP THOUGHTS... WHENEVER HE HAS FREE TIME!
PHILIP ?!
HEY, NATHANAEL !!!
COME WITH US!
I'VE MET THE SAVIOR -- THE ONE THE PROPHETS WROTE ABOUT!
HE'S YESHUAH OF NAZARETH !!!
NAZARETH?! YOU'RE KIDDING! CAN ANYTHING GOOD COME OUT OF THAT PLACE?
DON'T SAY THAT! COME SEE FOR YOURSELF!
....
IS THAT MAN YESHUAH? HE'S LOOKING AT US!

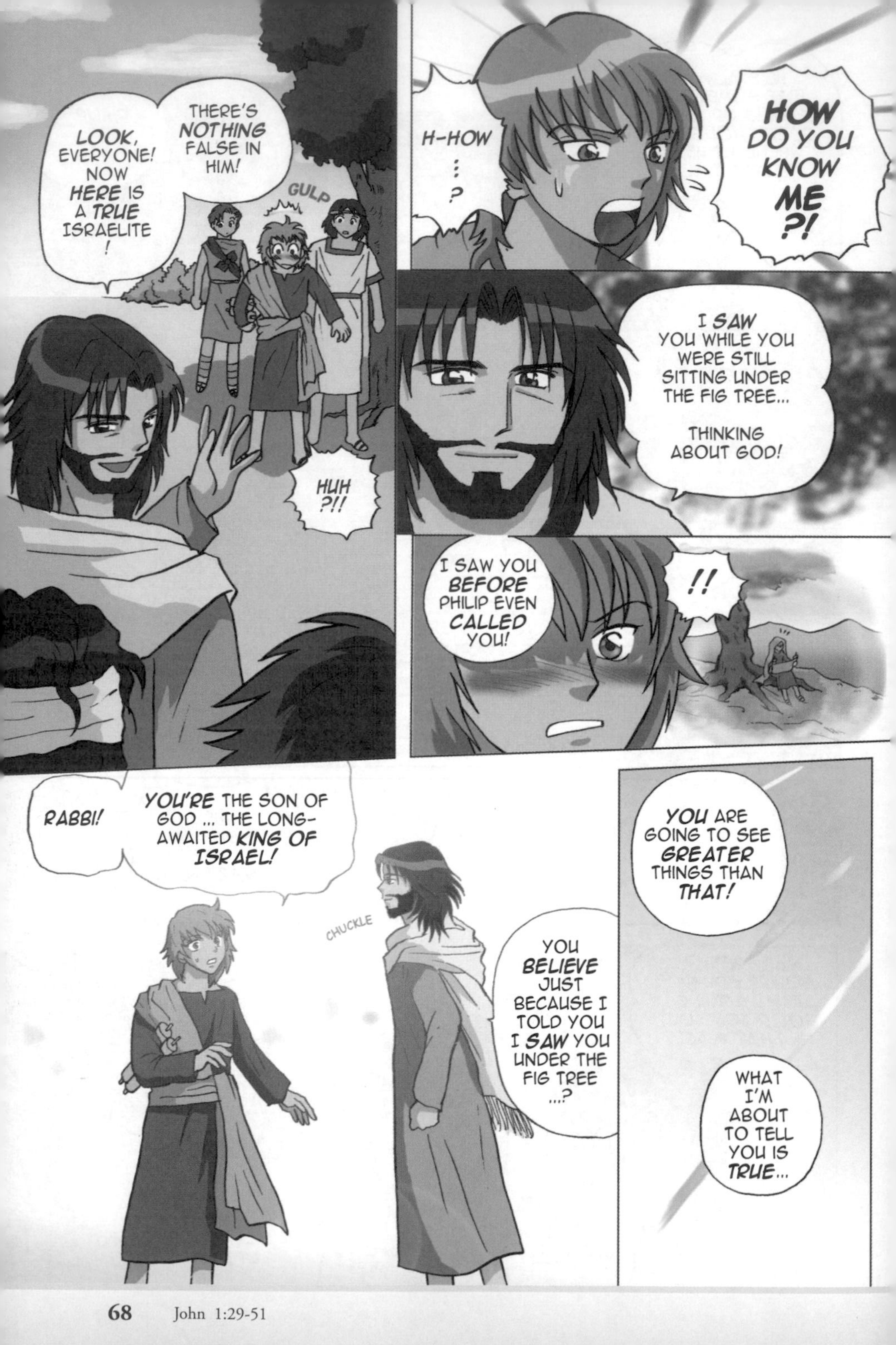

LOOK, EVERYONE! NOW HERE IS A TRUE ISRAELITE!
THERE'S NOTHING FALSE IN HIM!
GULP
HUH ?!!
H-HOW ...?
HOW DO YOU KNOW ME ?!
I SAW YOU WHILE YOU WERE STILL SITTING UNDER THE FIG TREE...
THINKING ABOUT GOD!
I SAW YOU BEFORE PHILIP EVEN CALLED YOU!
!!
RABBI!
YOU'RE THE SON OF GOD ... THE LONG-AWAITED KING OF ISRAEL!
CHUCKLE
YOU BELIEVE JUST BECAUSE I TOLD YOU I SAW YOU UNDER THE FIG TREE ...?
YOU ARE GOING TO SEE GREATER THINGS THAN THAT!
WHAT I'M ABOUT TO TELL YOU IS TRUE...

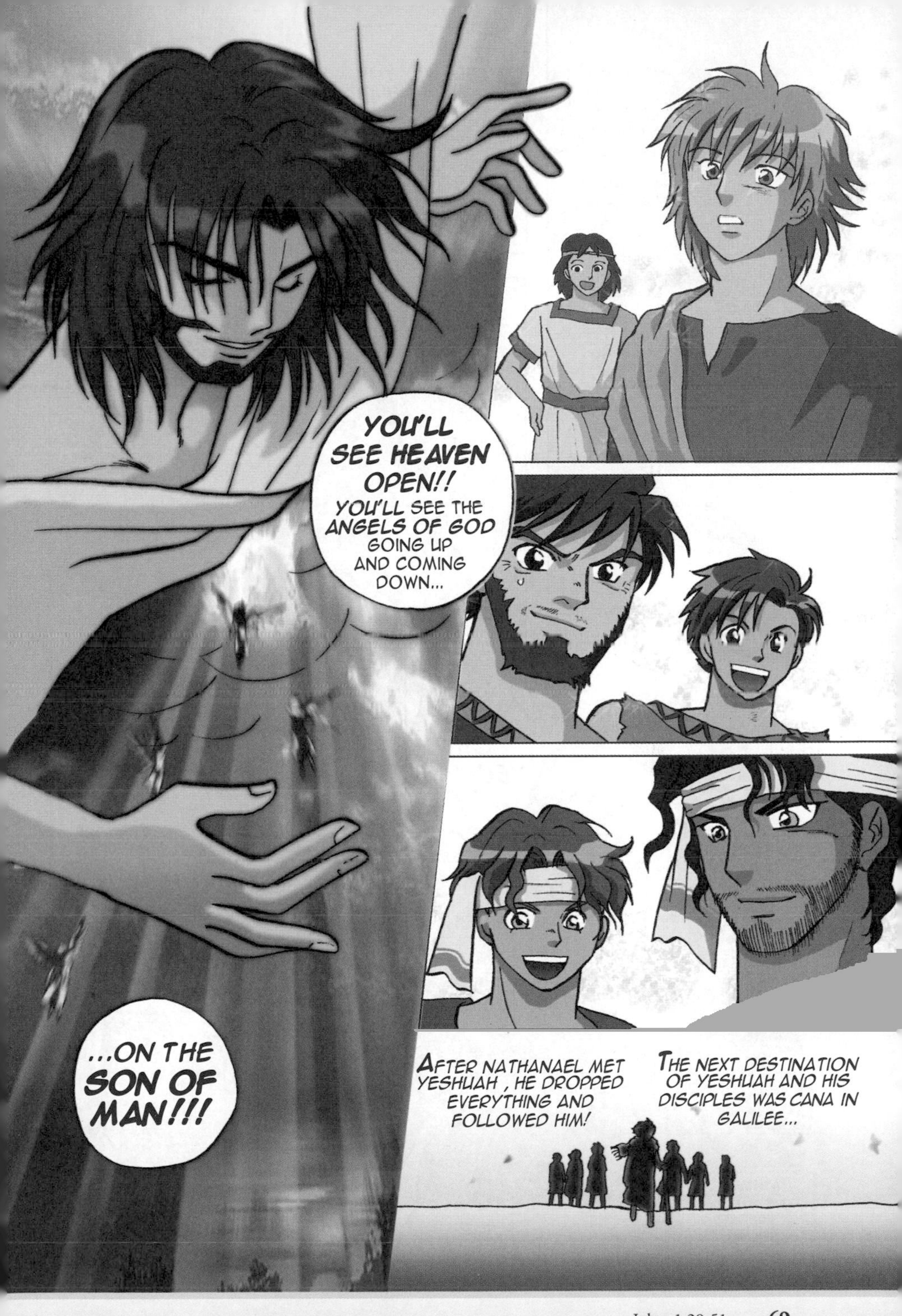
YOU'LL SEE HEAVEN OPEN!! YOU'LL SEE THE ANGELS OF GOD GOING UP AND COMING DOWN...
...ON THE SON OF MAN!!!
AFTER NATHANAEL MET YESHUAH , HE DROPPED EVERYTHING AND FOLLOWED HIM!
THE NEXT DESTINATION OF YESHUAH AND HIS DISCIPLES WAS CANA IN GALILEE...

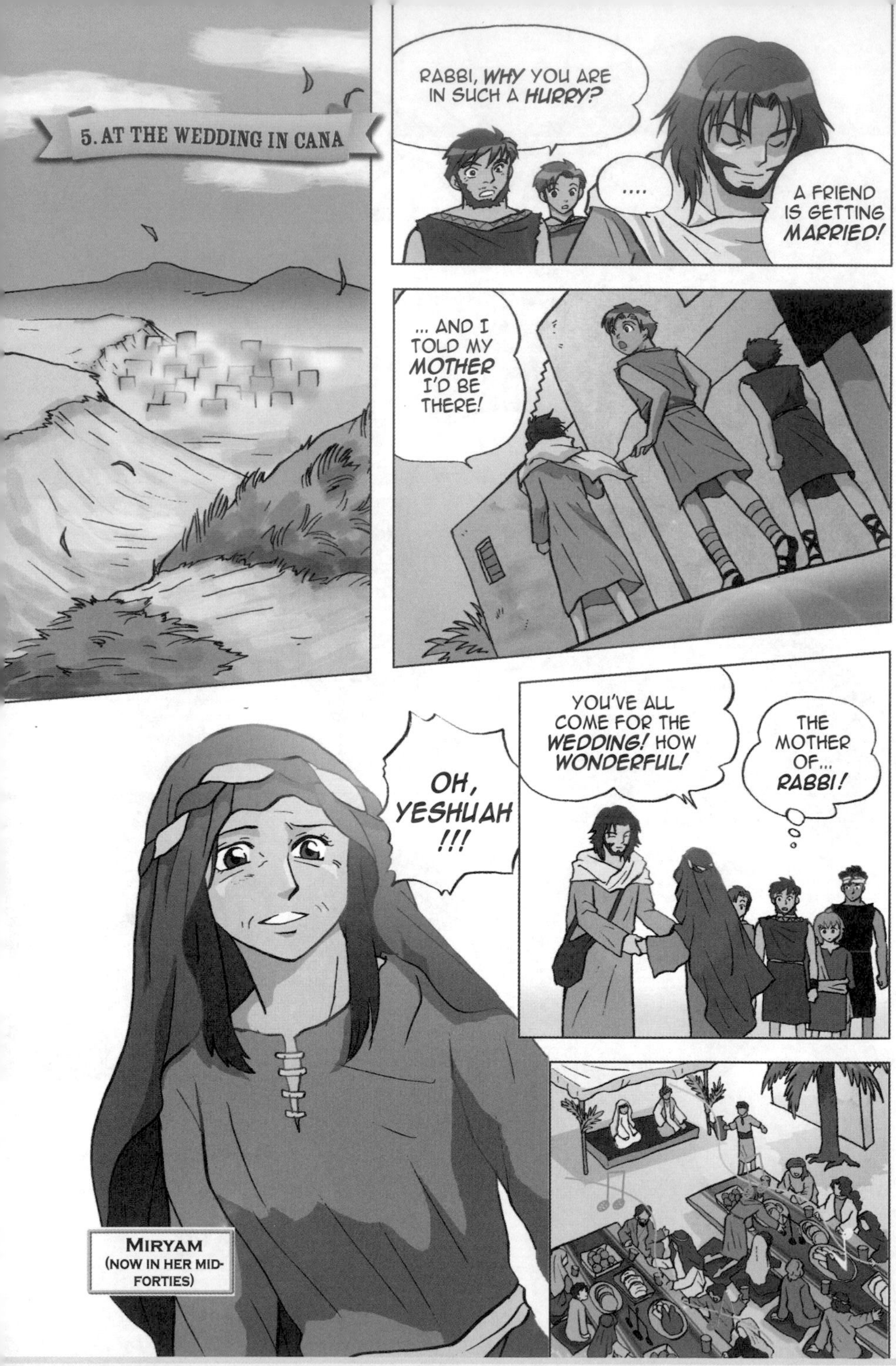
5. AT THE WEDDING IN CANA
RABBI, WHY YOU ARE IN SUCH A HURRY?
....
A FRIEND IS GETTING MARRIED!
... AND I TOLD MY MOTHER I'D BE THERE!
OH, YESHUAH !!!
YOU'VE ALL COME FOR THE WEDDING! HOW WONDERFUL!
THE MOTHER OF... RABBI!
MIRYAM (NOW IN HER MID-FORTIES)

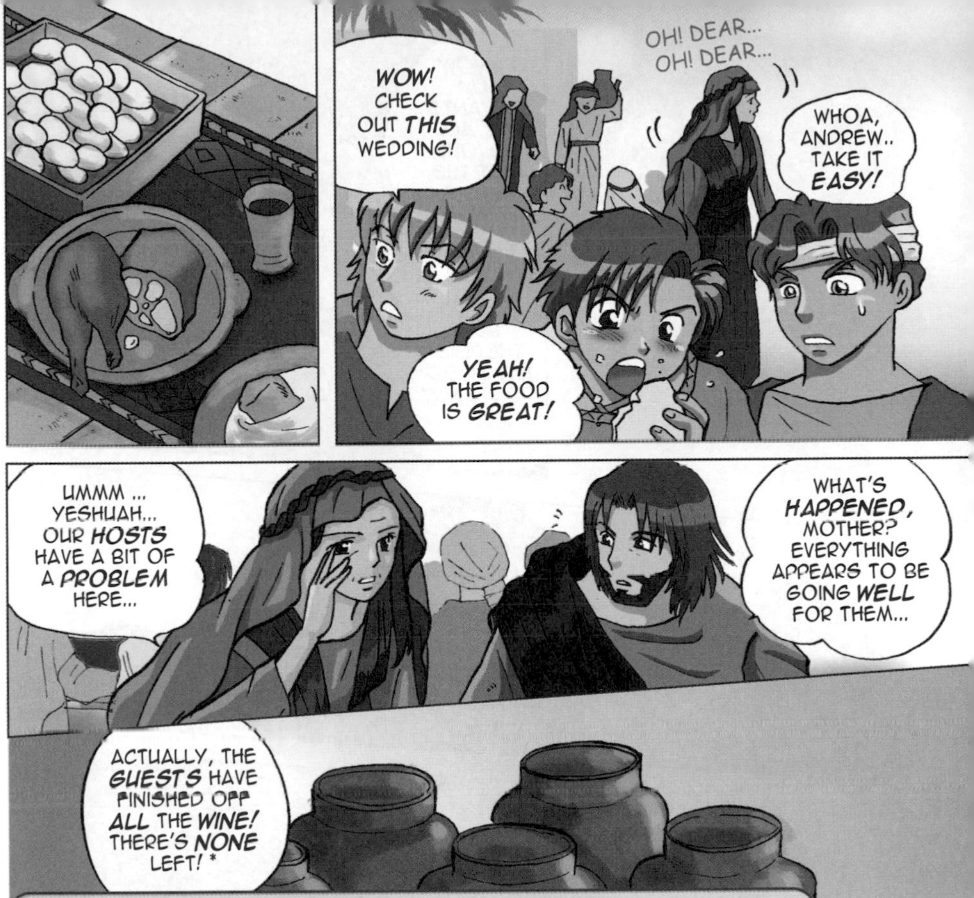
WOW! CHECK OUT THIS WEDDING!
YEAH! THE FOOD IS GREAT!
OH! DEAR... OH! DEAR...
WHOA, ANDREW.. TAKE IT EASY!
UMMM ... YESHUAH... OUR HOSTS HAVE A BIT OF A PROBLEM HERE...
WHAT'S HAPPENED, MOTHER? EVERYTHING APPEARS TO BE GOING WELL FOR THEM...
ACTUALLY, THE GUESTS HAVE FINISHED OFF ALL THE WINE! THERE'S NONE LEFT! *

* THIS WOULD HAVE BEEN A MAJOR SOCIAL EMBARRASSMENT FOR THE BRIDEGROOM AND HIS FAMILY. IN ADDITION, THERE WAS A STRONG ELEMENT OF RECIPROCITY ABOUT WEDDINGS IN ANCIENT MIDDLE EASTERN CULTURE. POSSIBLY THIS FAMILY WOULD HAVE BEEN INVOLVED IN A FINANCIAL LIABILITY FOR FAILING TO PROVIDE ADEQUATELY FOR THEIR GUESTS, SINCE IT WAS EVEN POSSIBLE, IN CERTAIN CIRCUMSTANCES, TO TAKE LEGAL ACTION AGAINST ANY MAN WHO FAILED TO PROVIDE AN APPROPRIATE WEDDING GIFT.

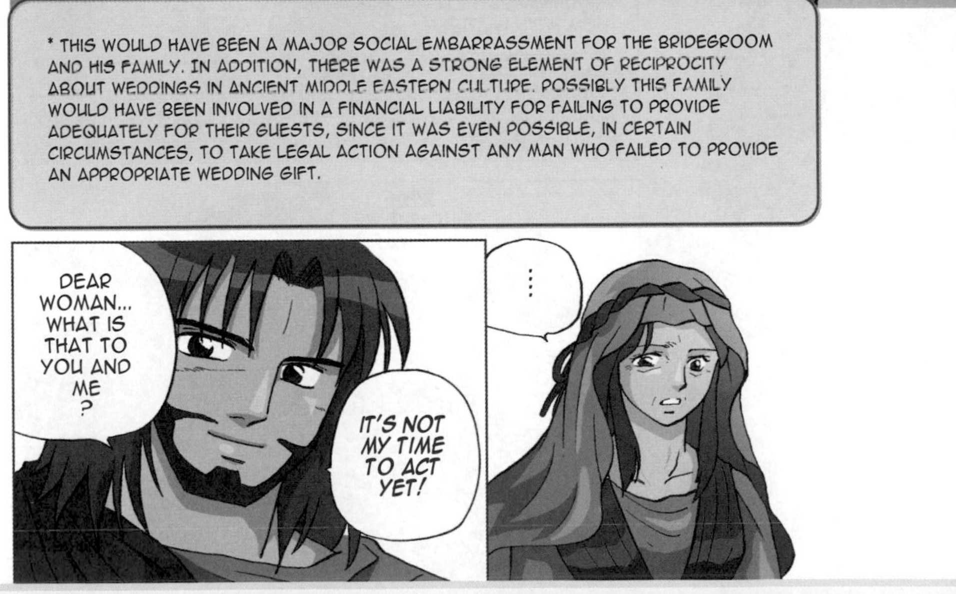
DEAR WOMAN... WHAT IS THAT TO YOU AND ME ?
IT'S NOT MY TIME TO ACT YET!
....

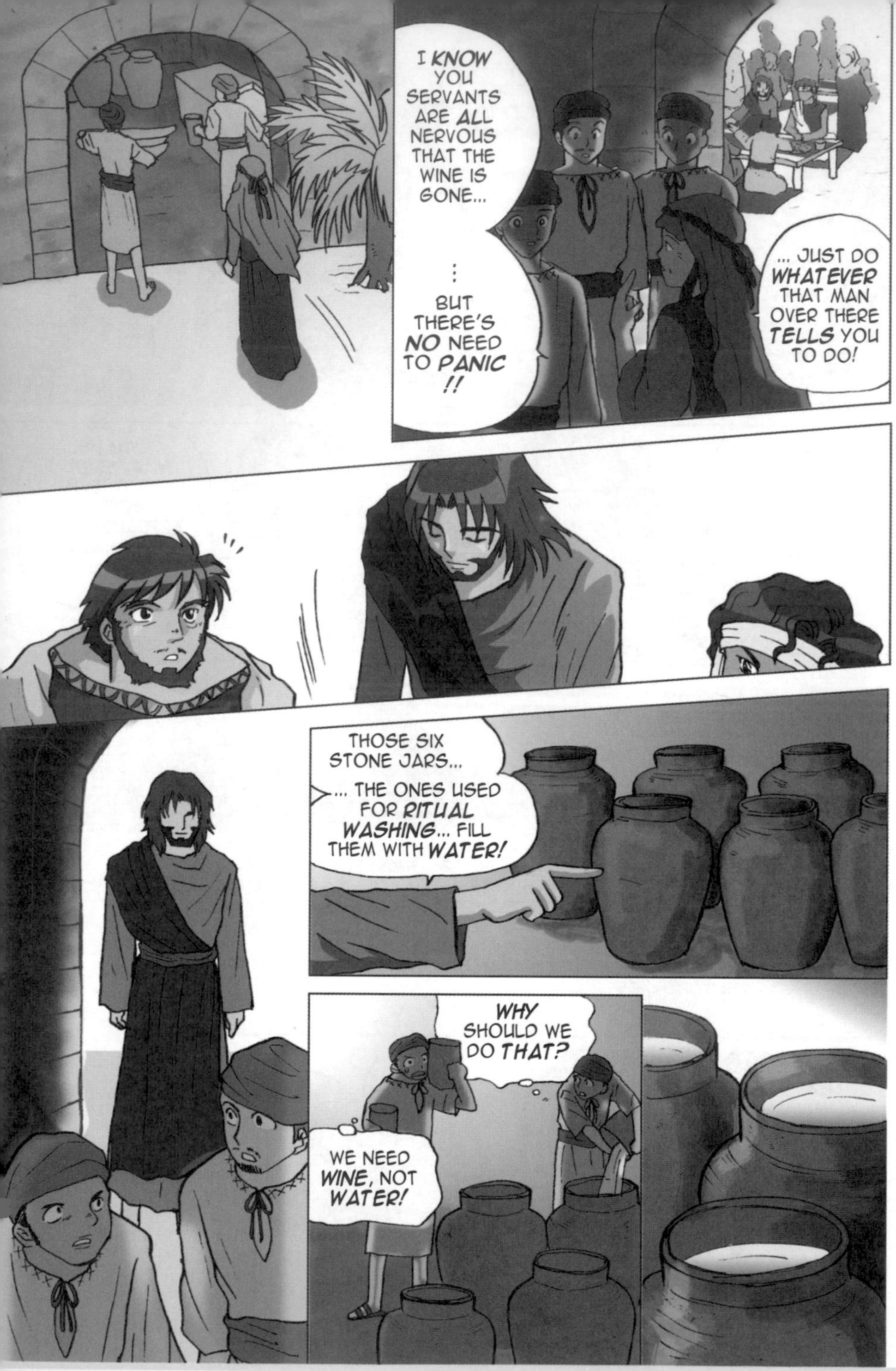
I KNOW YOU SERVANTS ARE ALL NERVOUS THAT THE WINE IS GONE...
... BUT THERE'S NO NEED TO PANIC !!
... JUST DO WHATEVER THAT MAN OVER THERE TELLS YOU TO DO!
THOSE SIX STONE JARS...
... THE ONES USED FOR RITUAL WASHING... FILL THEM WITH WATER!
WHY SHOULD WE DO THAT?
WE NEED WINE, NOT WATER!

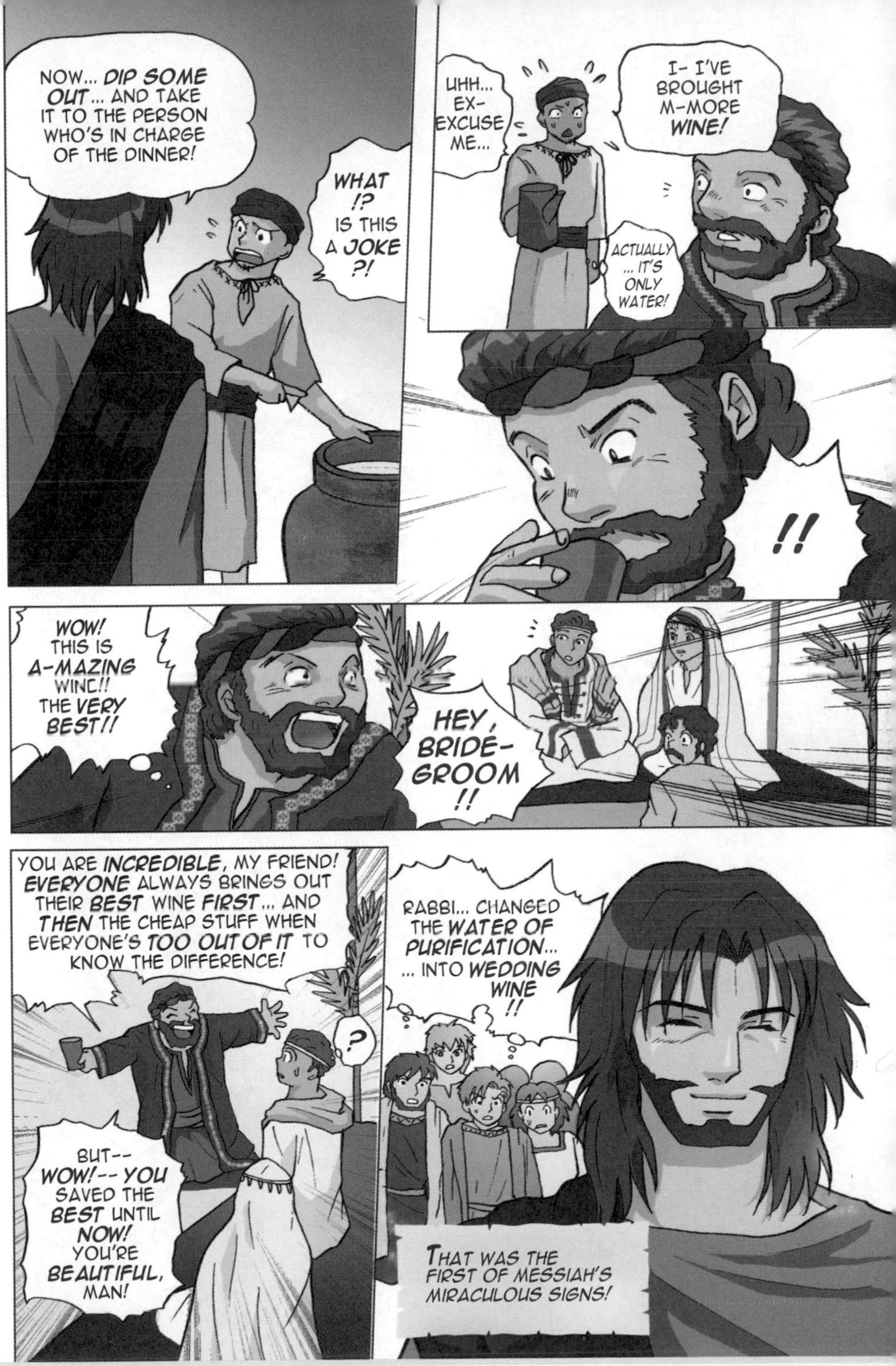
NOW... DIP SOME OUT... AND TAKE IT TO THE PERSON WHO'S IN CHARGE OF THE DINNER!
WHAT !? IS THIS A JOKE ?!
UHH... EX- EXCUSE ME...
I- I'VE BROUGHT M-MORE WINE!
ACTUALLY ... IT'S ONLY WATER!
!!
WOW! THIS IS A-MAZING WINE!! THE VERY BEST!!
HEY, BRIDE-GROOM !!
YOU ARE INCREDIBLE, MY FRIEND! EVERYONE ALWAYS BRINGS OUT THEIR BEST WINE FIRST... AND THEN THE CHEAP STUFF WHEN EVERYONE'S TOO OUT OF IT TO KNOW THE DIFFERENCE!
?
BUT-- WOW!-- YOU SAVED THE BEST UNTIL NOW! YOU'RE BEAUTIFUL, MAN!
RABBI... CHANGED THE WATER OF PURIFICATION... ... INTO WEDDING WINE !!
THAT WAS THE FIRST OF MESSIAH'S MIRACULOUS SIGNS!

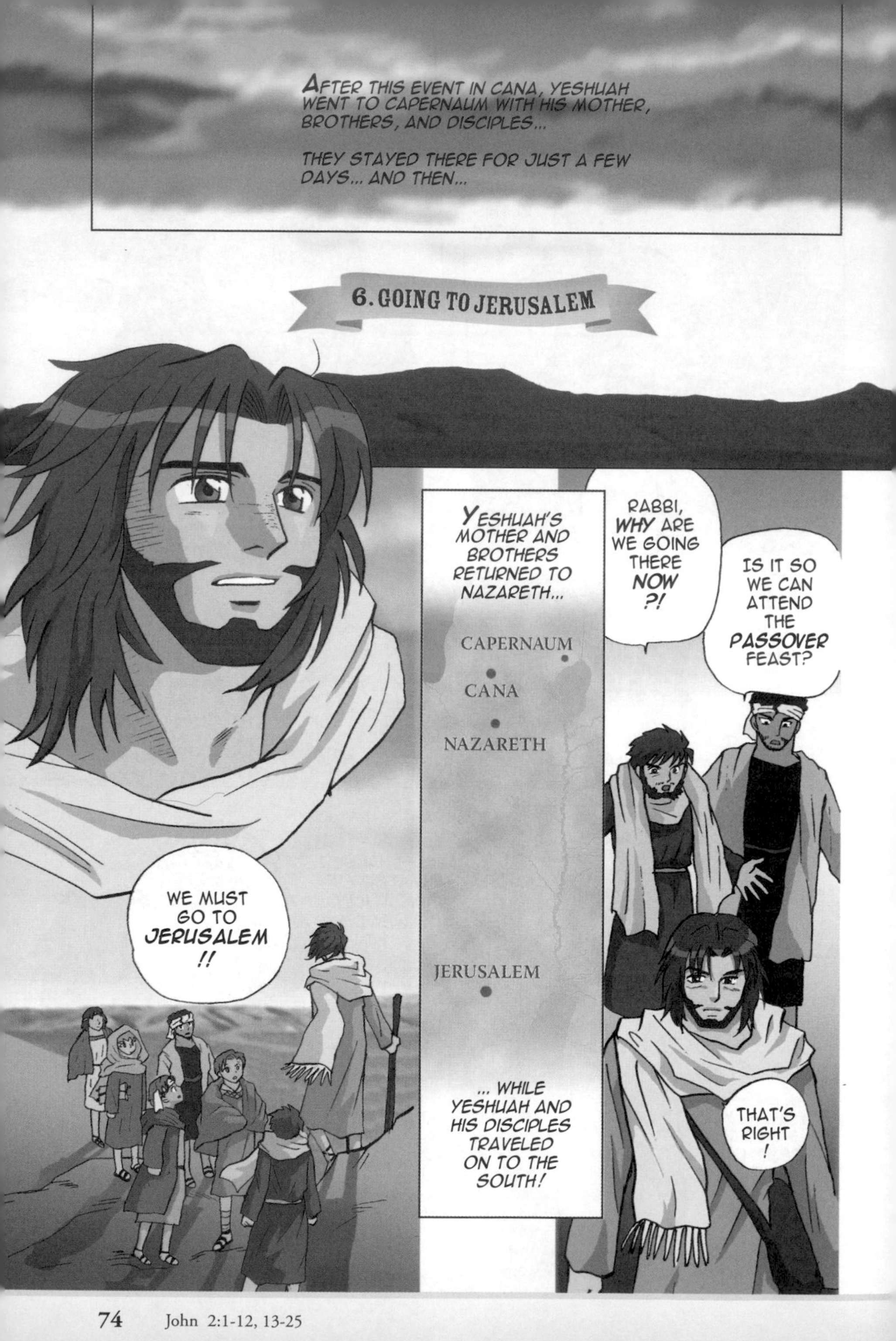

AFTER THIS EVENT IN CANA, YESHUAH WENT TO CAPERNAUM WITH HIS MOTHER, BROTHERS, AND DISCIPLES...
THEY STAYED THERE FOR JUST A FEW DAYS... AND THEN...
6. GOING TO JERUSALEM
WE MUST GO TO JERUSALEM !!
YESHUAH'S MOTHER AND BROTHERS RETURNED TO NAZARETH...
CAPERNAUM
CANA
NAZARETH
JERUSALEM
... WHILE YESHUAH AND HIS DISCIPLES TRAVELED ON TO THE SOUTH!
RABBI, WHY ARE WE GOING THERE NOW ?!
IS IT SO WE CAN ATTEND THE PASSOVER FEAST?
THAT'S RIGHT !

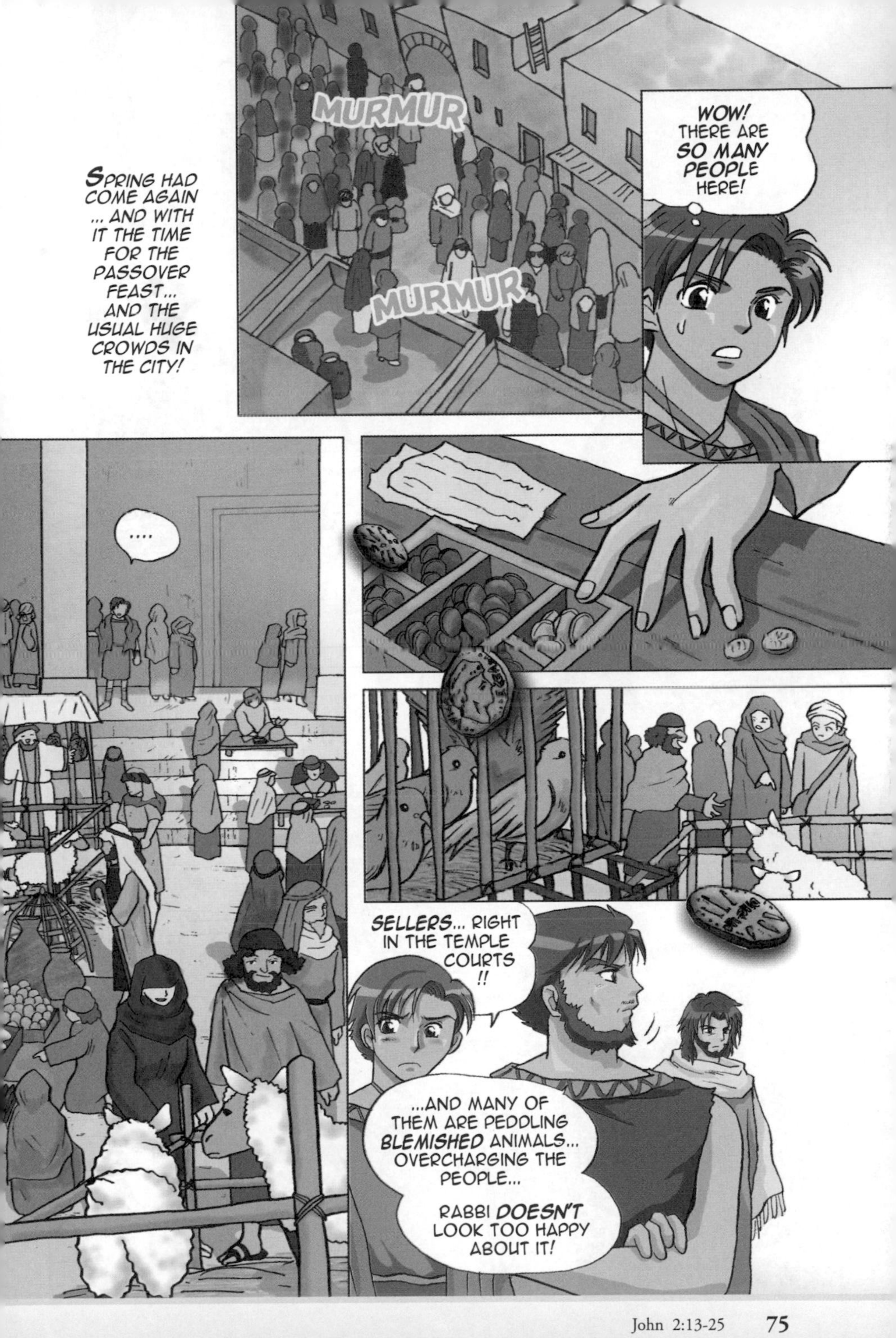
SPRING HAD COME AGAIN ... AND WITH IT THE TIME FOR THE PASSOVER FEAST... AND THE USUAL HUGE CROWDS IN THE CITY!
MURMUR
MURMUR
WOW! THERE ARE SO MANY PEOPLE HERE!
....
SELLERS... RIGHT IN THE TEMPLE COURTS !!
...AND MANY OF THEM ARE PEDDLING BLEMISHED ANIMALS... OVERCHARGING THE PEOPLE...
RABBI DOESN'T LOOK TOO HAPPY ABOUT IT!

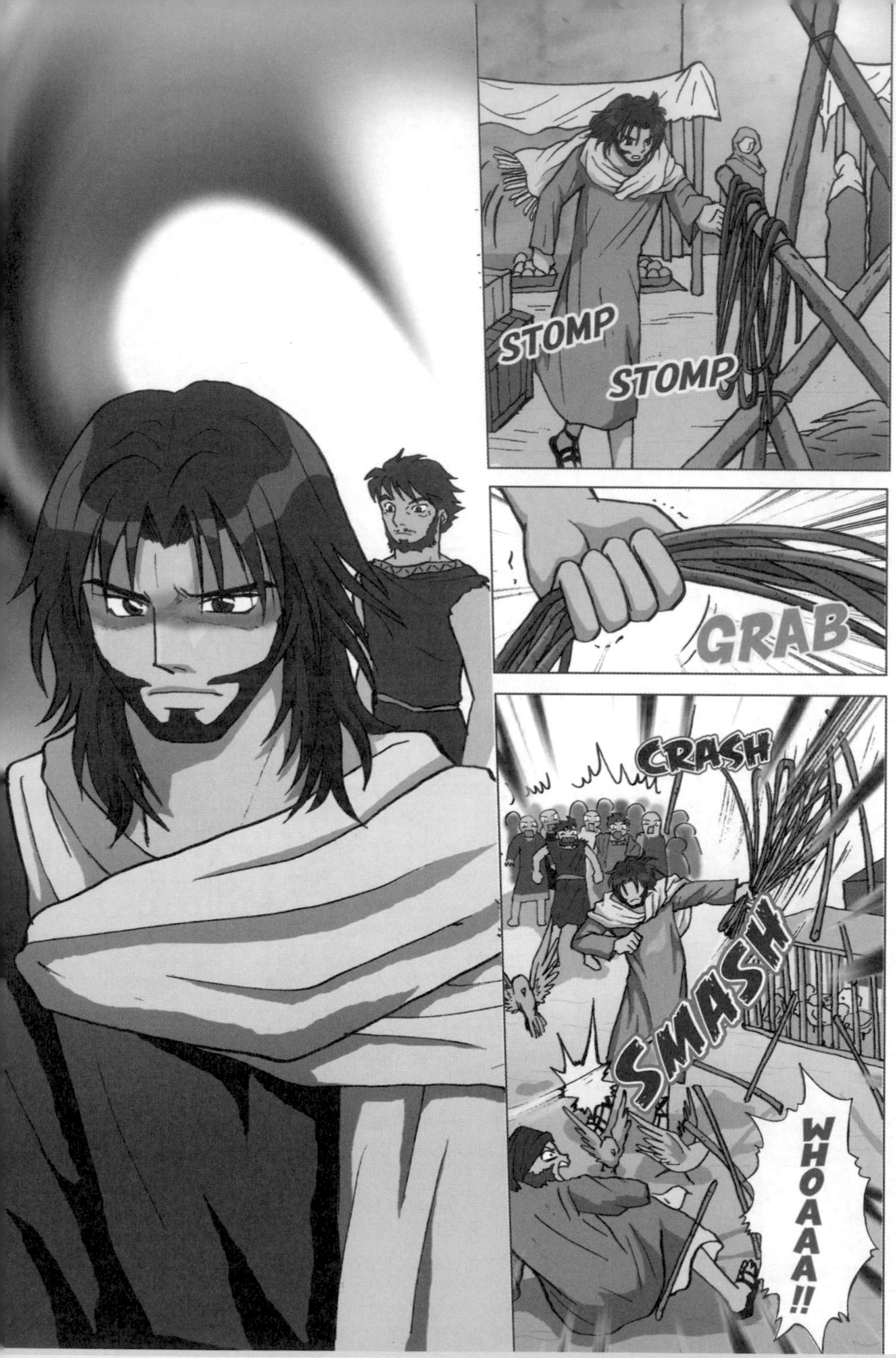
STOMP
STOMP
GRAB
CRASH
SMASH
WHOAAAA!!

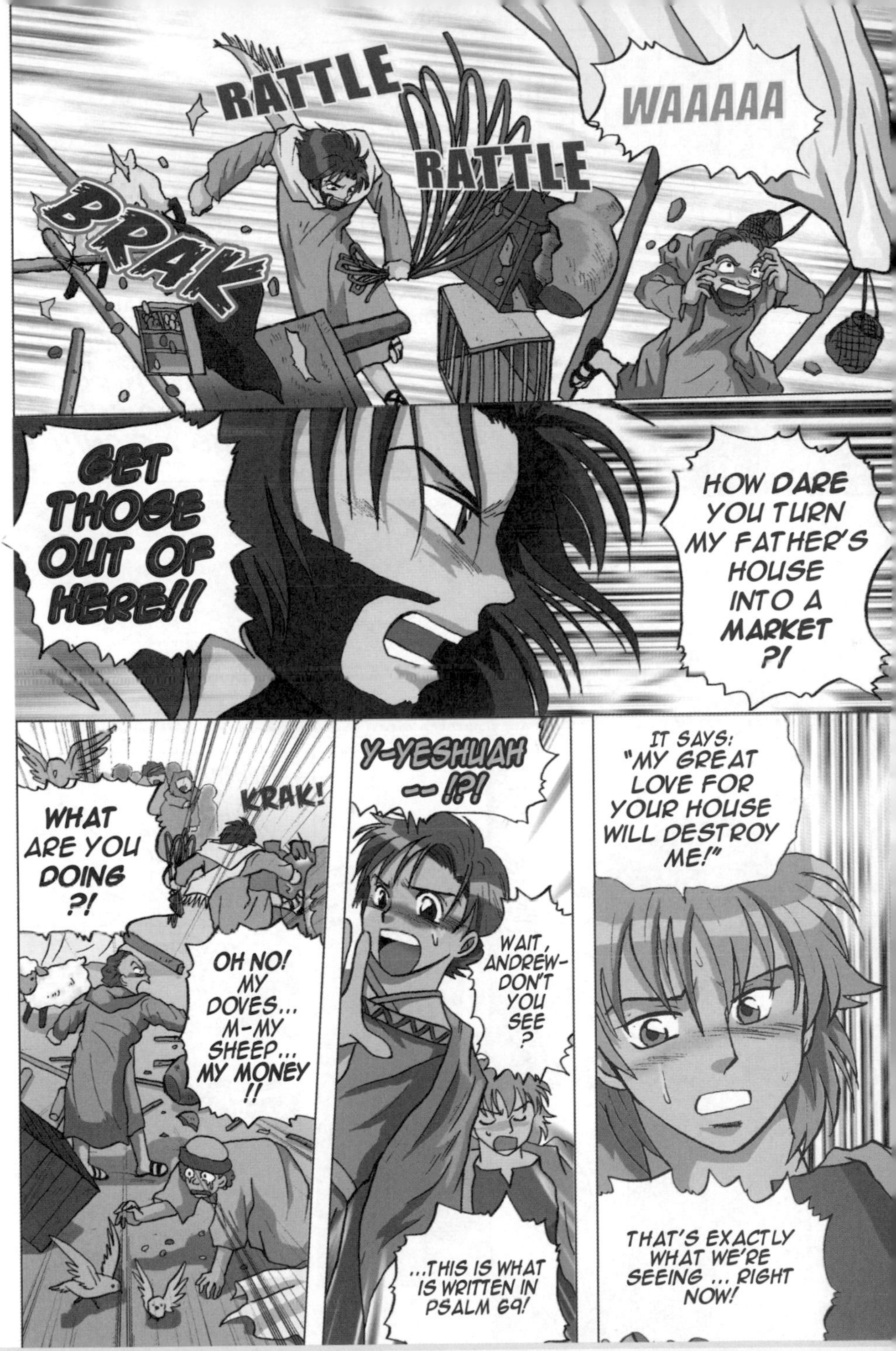
RATTLE
RATTLE
BRAK
WAAAAA
GET THOSE OUT OF HERE!!
HOW DARE YOU TURN MY FATHER'S HOUSE INTO A MARKET ?!
WHAT ARE YOU DOING ?!
KRAK!
OH NO! MY DOVES... M-MY SHEEP... MY MONEY !!
Y-YESHUAH --!?!
WAIT, ANDREW- DON'T YOU SEE ?
...THIS IS WHAT IS WRITTEN IN PSALM 69!
IT SAYS: "MY GREAT LOVE FOR YOUR HOUSE WILL DESTROY ME!"
THAT'S EXACTLY WHAT WE'RE SEEING ... RIGHT NOW!

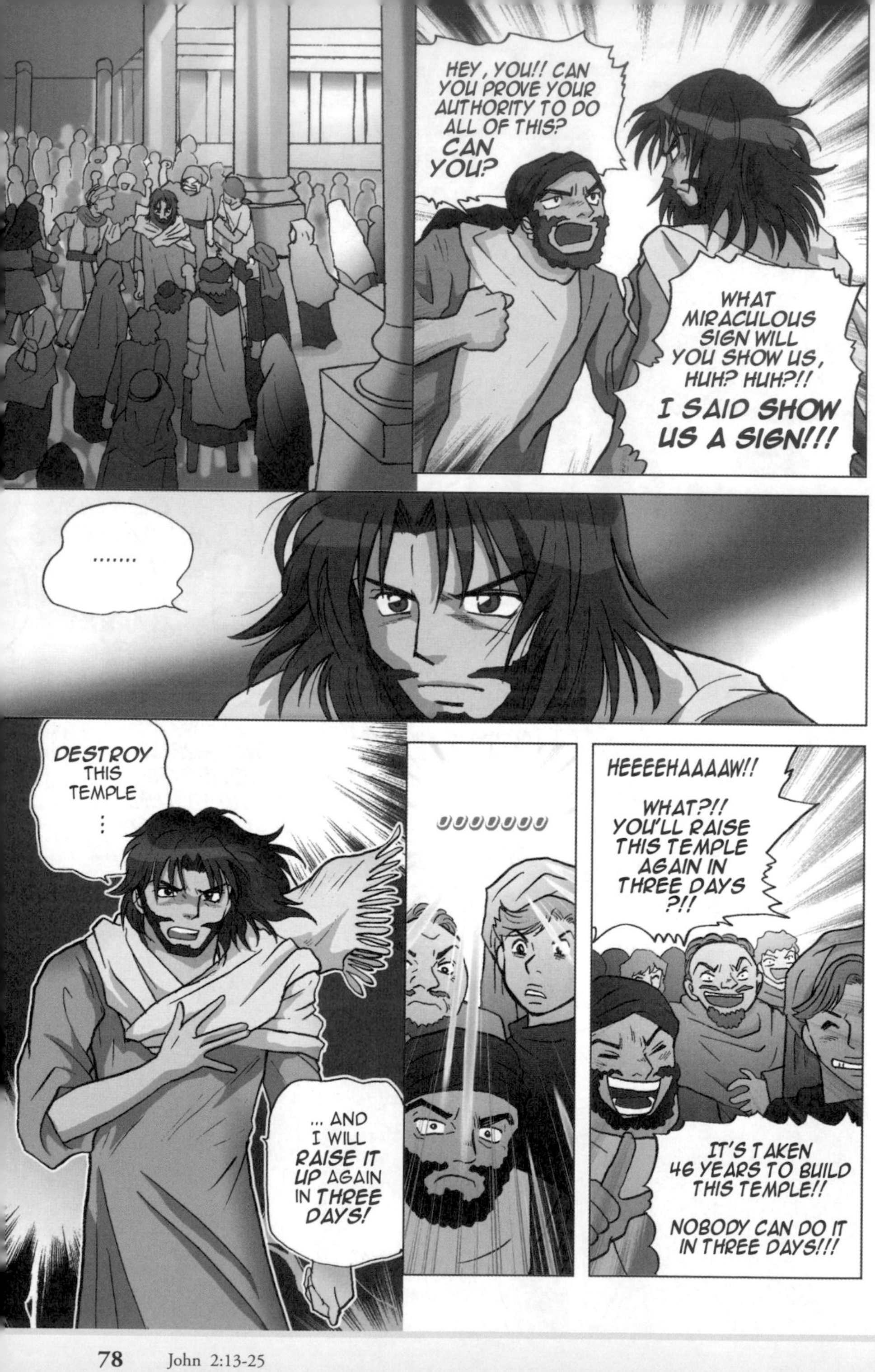
HEY, YOU!! CAN YOU PROVE YOUR AUTHORITY TO DO ALL OF THIS? CAN YOU?
WHAT MIRACULOUS SIGN WILL YOU SHOW US, HUH? HUH?!!
I SAID SHOW US A SIGN!!!
....
DESTROY THIS TEMPLE
:
... AND I WILL RAISE IT UP AGAIN IN THREE DAYS!
HEEEEHAAAAW!!
WHAT?!! YOU'LL RAISE THIS TEMPLE AGAIN IN THREE DAYS ?!!
IT'S TAKEN 46 YEARS TO BUILD THIS TEMPLE!!
NOBODY CAN DO IT IN THREE DAYS!!!

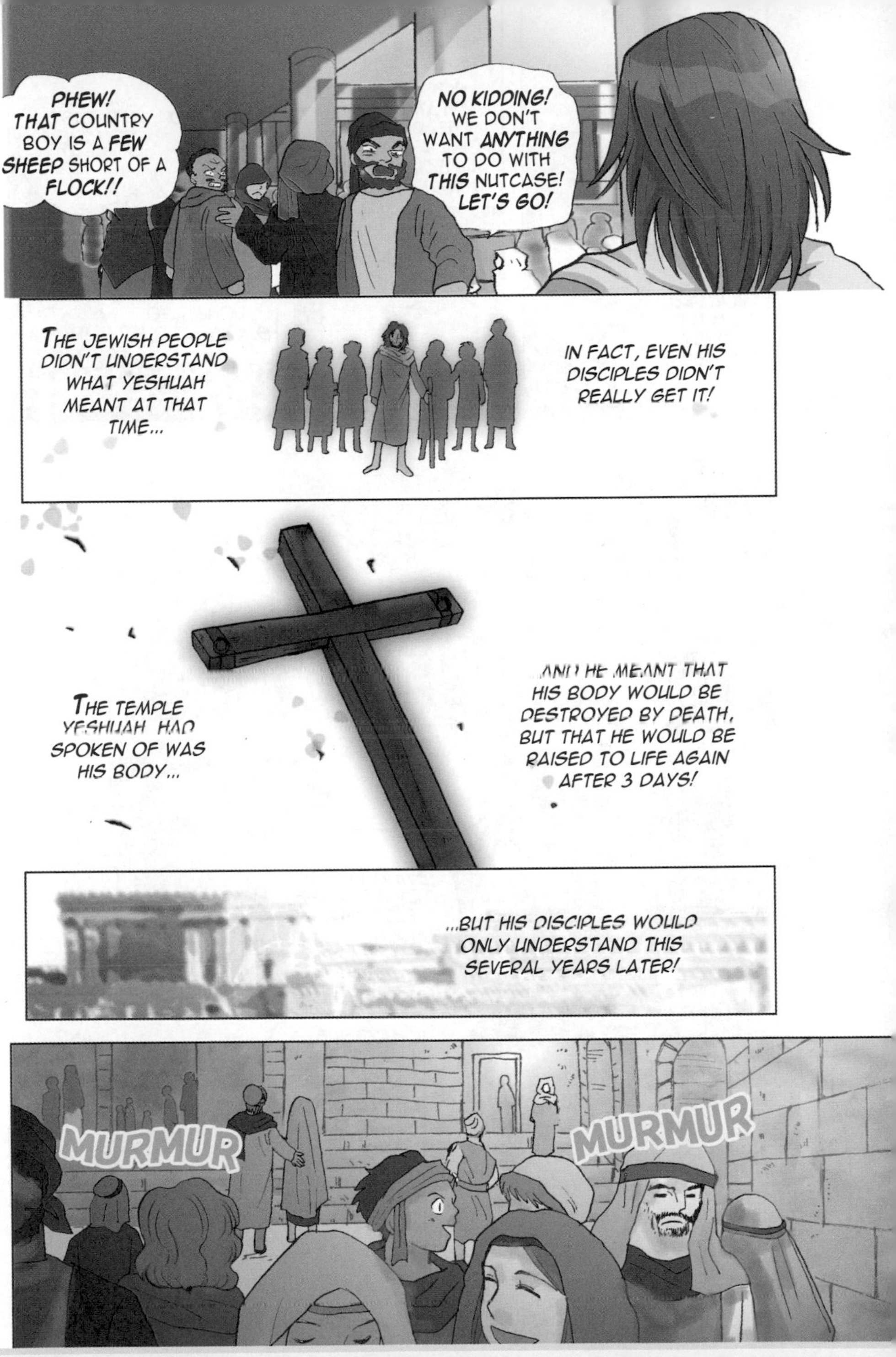
PHEW! THAT COUNTRY BOY IS A FEW SHEEP SHORT OF A FLOCK!!
NO KIDDING! WE DON'T WANT ANYTHING TO DO WITH THIS NUTCASE! LET'S GO!
THE JEWISH PEOPLE DIDN'T UNDERSTAND WHAT YESHUAH MEANT AT THAT TIME...
IN FACT, EVEN HIS DISCIPLES DIDN'T REALLY GET IT!
THE TEMPLE YESHUAH HAD SPOKEN OF WAS HIS BODY...
AND HE MEANT THAT HIS BODY WOULD BE DESTROYED BY DEATH, BUT THAT HE WOULD BE RAISED TO LIFE AGAIN AFTER 3 DAYS!
...BUT HIS DISCIPLES WOULD ONLY UNDERSTAND THIS SEVERAL YEARS LATER!
MURMUR
MURMUR

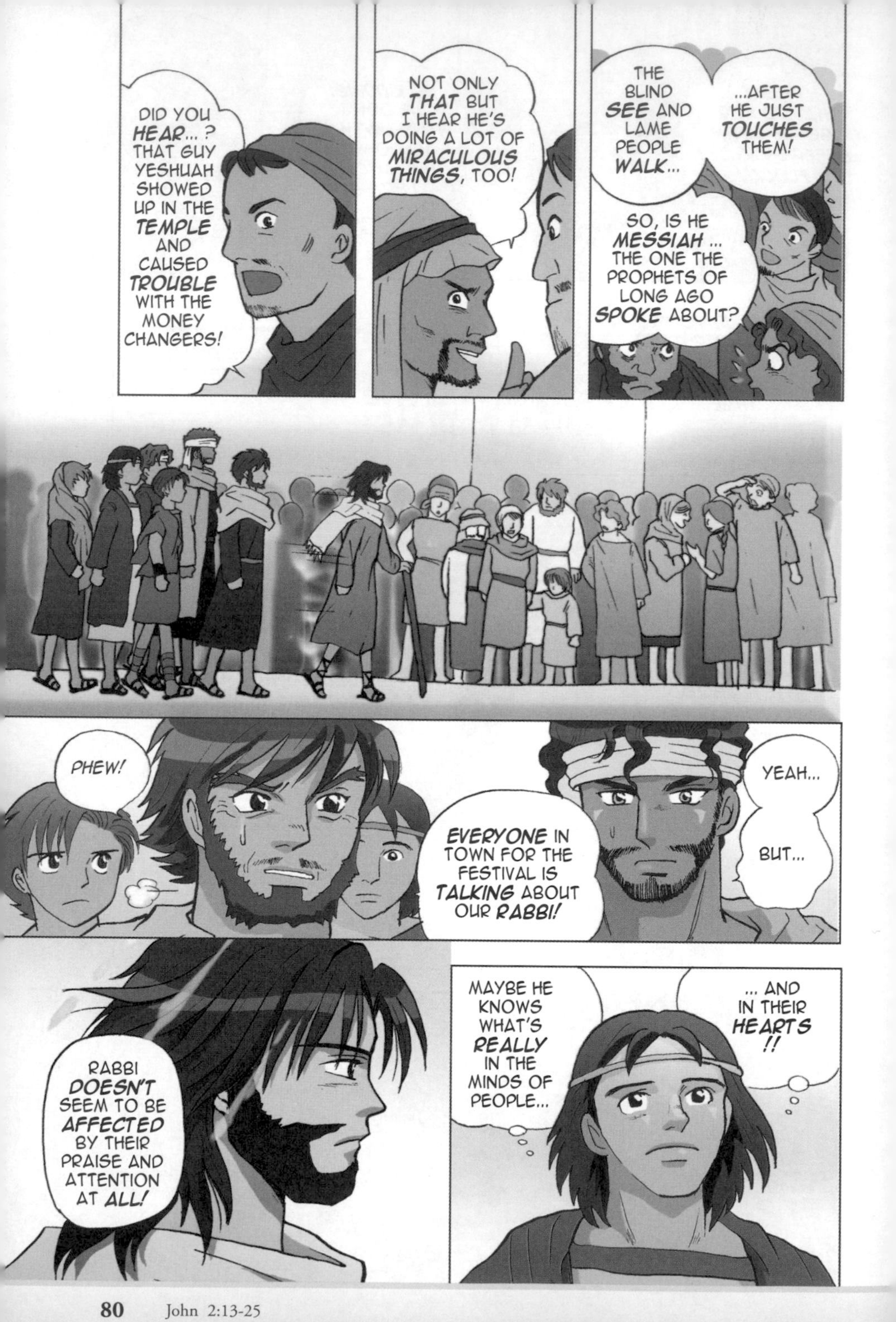
DID YOU HEAR... ? THAT GUY YESHUAH SHOWED UP IN THE TEMPLE AND CAUSED TROUBLE WITH THE MONEY CHANGERS!
NOT ONLY THAT BUT I HEAR HE'S DOING A LOT OF MIRACULOUS THINGS, TOO!
THE BLIND SEE AND LAME PEOPLE WALK...
...AFTER HE JUST TOUCHES THEM!
SO, IS HE MESSIAH ... THE ONE THE PROPHETS OF LONG AGO SPOKE ABOUT?
PHEW!
EVERYONE IN TOWN FOR THE FESTIVAL IS TALKING ABOUT OUR RABBI!
YEAH...
BUT...
RABBI DOESN'T SEEM TO BE AFFECTED BY THEIR PRAISE AND ATTENTION AT ALL!
MAYBE HE KNOWS WHAT'S REALLY IN THE MINDS OF PEOPLE...
... AND IN THEIR HEARTS !!

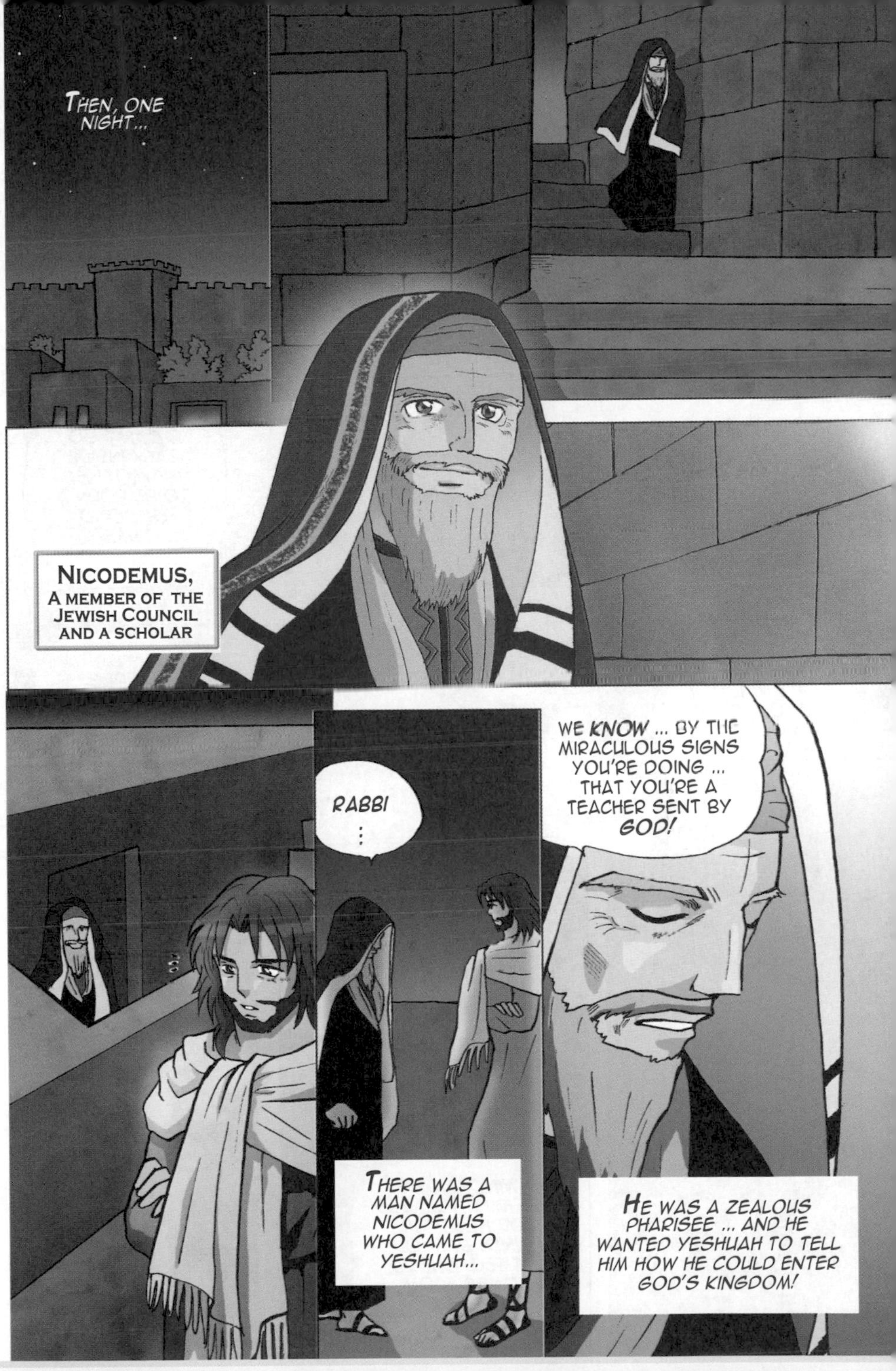
THEN, ONE NIGHT...
NICODEMUS, A MEMBER OF THE JEWISH COUNCIL AND A SCHOLAR
RABBI ...
WE KNOW ... BY THE MIRACULOUS SIGNS YOU'RE DOING ... THAT YOU'RE A TEACHER SENT BY GOD!
THERE WAS A MAN NAMED NICODEMUS WHO CAME TO YESHUAH...
HE WAS A ZEALOUS PHARISEE ... AND HE WANTED YESHUAH TO TELL HIM HOW HE COULD ENTER GOD'S KINGDOM!

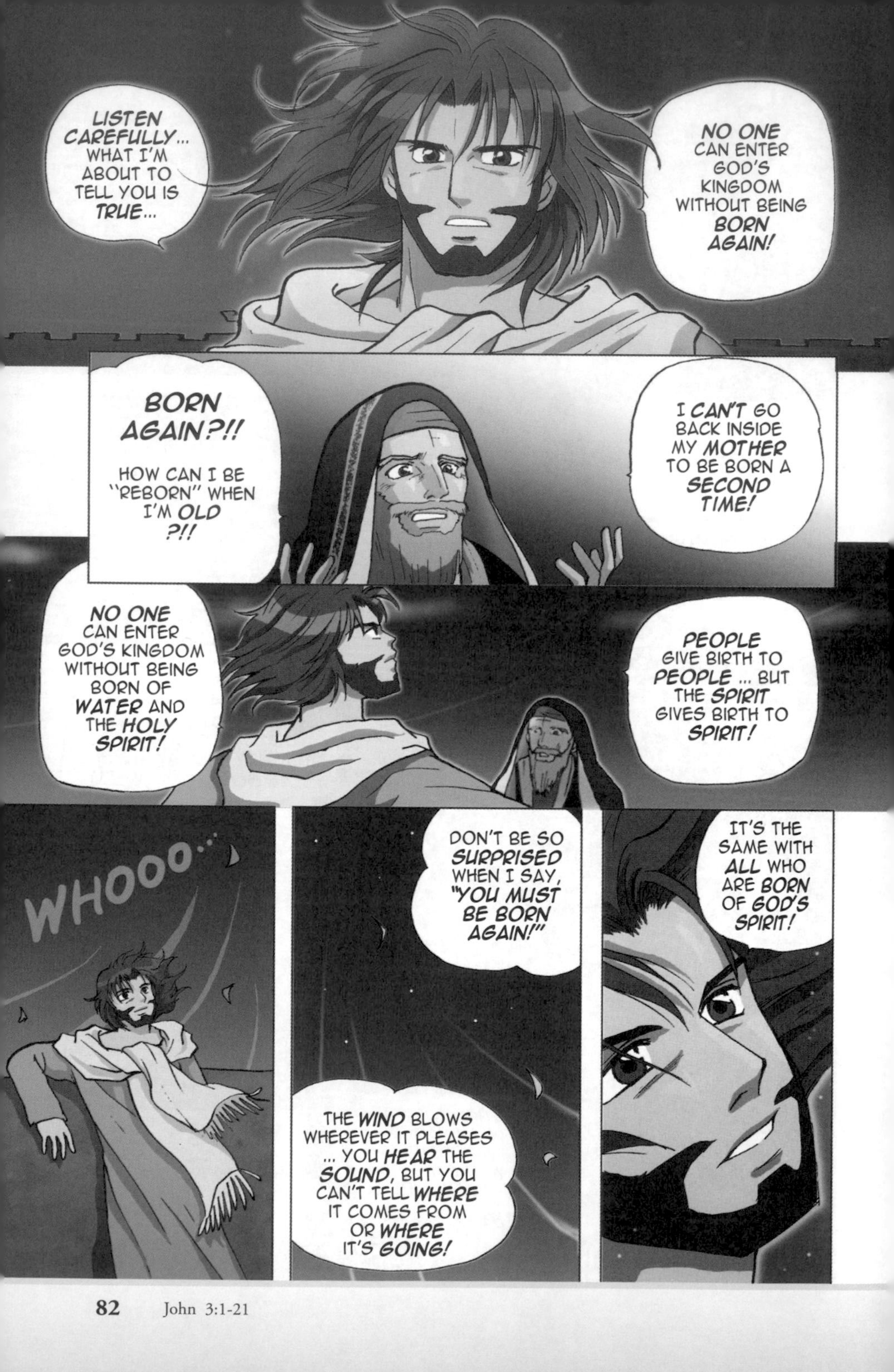

LISTEN CAREFULLY... WHAT I'M ABOUT TO TELL YOU IS TRUE...
NO ONE CAN ENTER GOD'S KINGDOM WITHOUT BEING BORN AGAIN!
BORN AGAIN?!! HOW CAN I BE "REBORN" WHEN I'M OLD ?!!
I CAN'T GO BACK INSIDE MY MOTHER TO BE BORN A SECOND TIME!
NO ONE CAN ENTER GOD'S KINGDOM WITHOUT BEING BORN OF WATER AND THE HOLY SPIRIT!
PEOPLE GIVE BIRTH TO PEOPLE ... BUT THE SPIRIT GIVES BIRTH TO SPIRIT!
WHOOO...
DON'T BE SO SURPRISED WHEN I SAY, "YOU MUST BE BORN AGAIN!"
THE WIND BLOWS WHEREVER IT PLEASES ... YOU HEAR THE SOUND, BUT YOU CAN'T TELL WHERE IT COMES FROM OR WHERE IT'S GOING!
IT'S THE SAME WITH ALL WHO ARE BORN OF GOD'S SPIRIT!

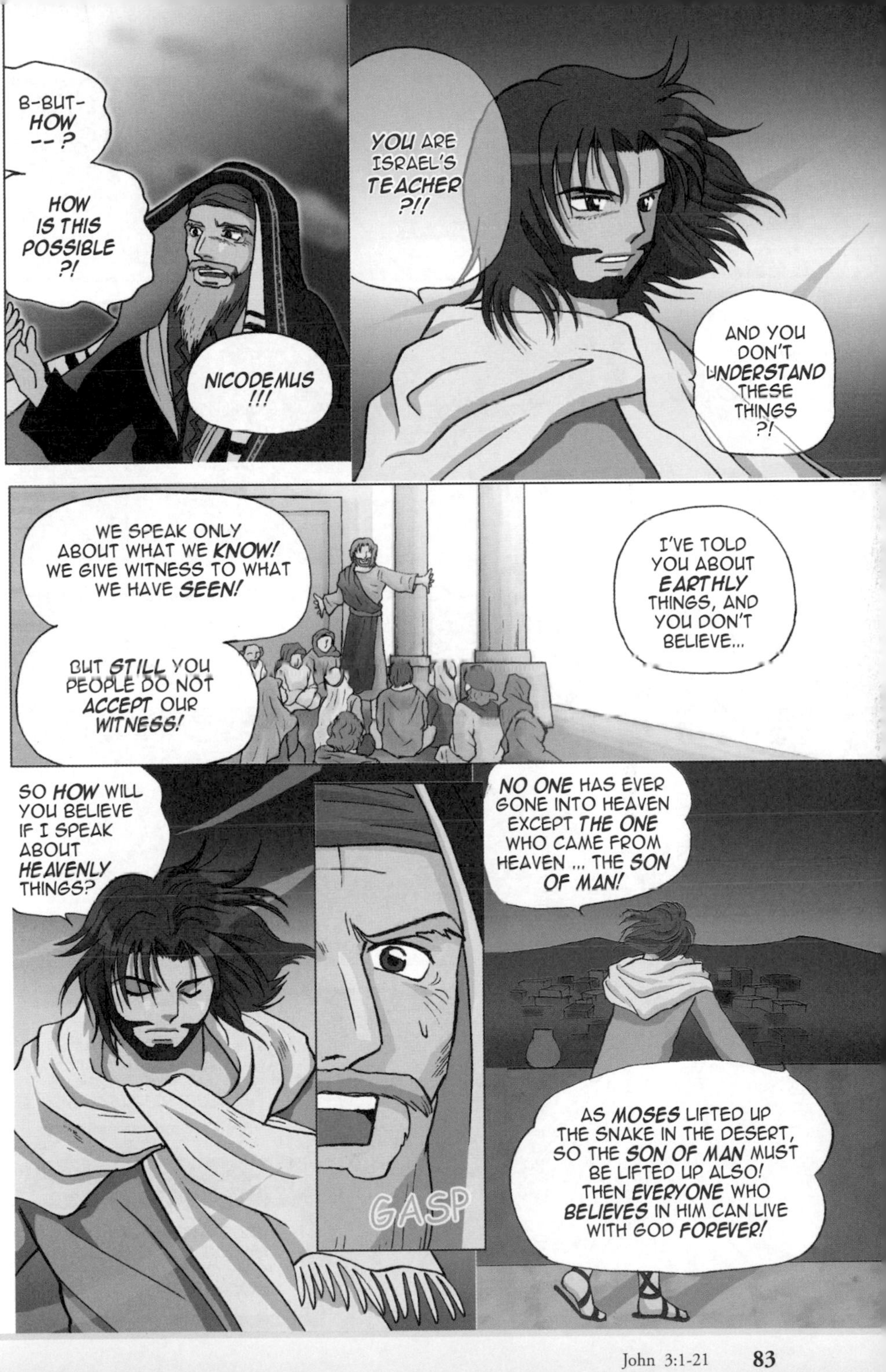

B-BUT-
HOW
-- ?
HOW
IS THIS
POSSIBLE
?!
NICODEMUS
!!!
YOU ARE
ISRAEL'S
TEACHER
?!!
AND YOU
DON'T
UNDERSTAND
THESE
THINGS
?!
WE SPEAK ONLY
ABOUT WHAT WE KNOW!
WE GIVE WITNESS TO WHAT
WE HAVE SEEN!
BUT STILL YOU
PEOPLE DO NOT
ACCEPT OUR
WITNESS!
I'VE TOLD
YOU ABOUT
EARTHLY
THINGS, AND
YOU DON'T
BELIEVE...
SO HOW WILL
YOU BELIEVE
IF I SPEAK
ABOUT
HEAVENLY
THINGS?
GASP
NO ONE HAS EVER
GONE INTO HEAVEN
EXCEPT THE ONE
WHO CAME FROM
HEAVEN ... THE SON
OF MAN!
AS MOSES LIFTED UP
THE SNAKE IN THE DESERT,
SO THE SON OF MAN MUST
BE LIFTED UP ALSO!
THEN EVERYONE WHO
BELIEVES IN HIM CAN LIVE
WITH GOD FOREVER!

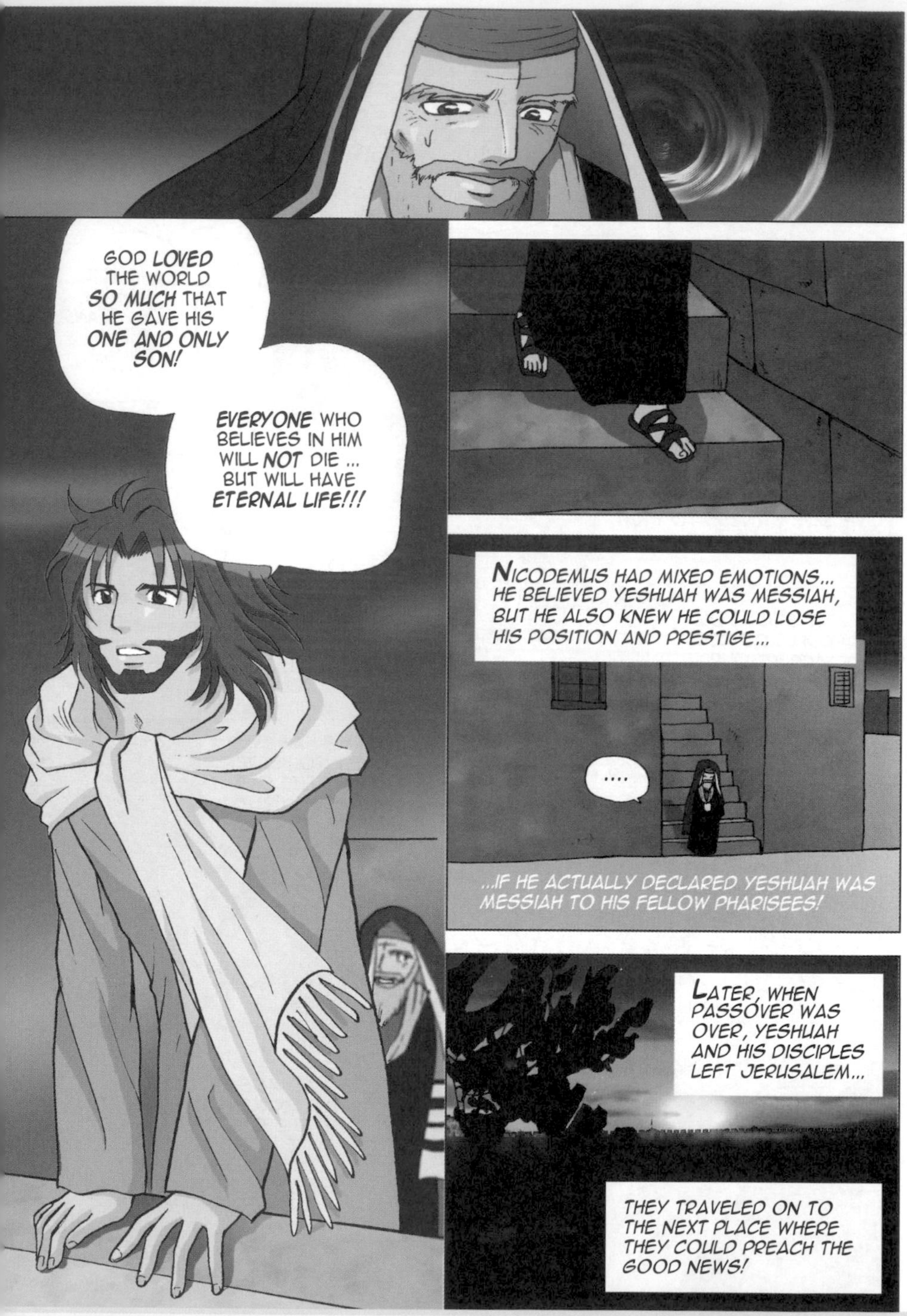
GOD LOVED THE WORLD SO MUCH THAT HE GAVE HIS ONE AND ONLY SON!
EVERYONE WHO BELIEVES IN HIM WILL NOT DIE ... BUT WILL HAVE ETERNAL LIFE!!!
NICODEMUS HAD MIXED EMOTIONS... HE BELIEVED YESHUAH WAS MESSIAH, BUT HE ALSO KNEW HE COULD LOSE HIS POSITION AND PRESTIGE...
....
...IF HE ACTUALLY DECLARED YESHUAH WAS MESSIAH TO HIS FELLOW PHARISEES!
LATER, WHEN PASSOVER WAS OVER, YESHUAH AND HIS DISCIPLES LEFT JERUSALEM...
THEY TRAVELED ON TO THE NEXT PLACE WHERE THEY COULD PREACH THE GOOD NEWS!

7. RETURN TO GALILEE

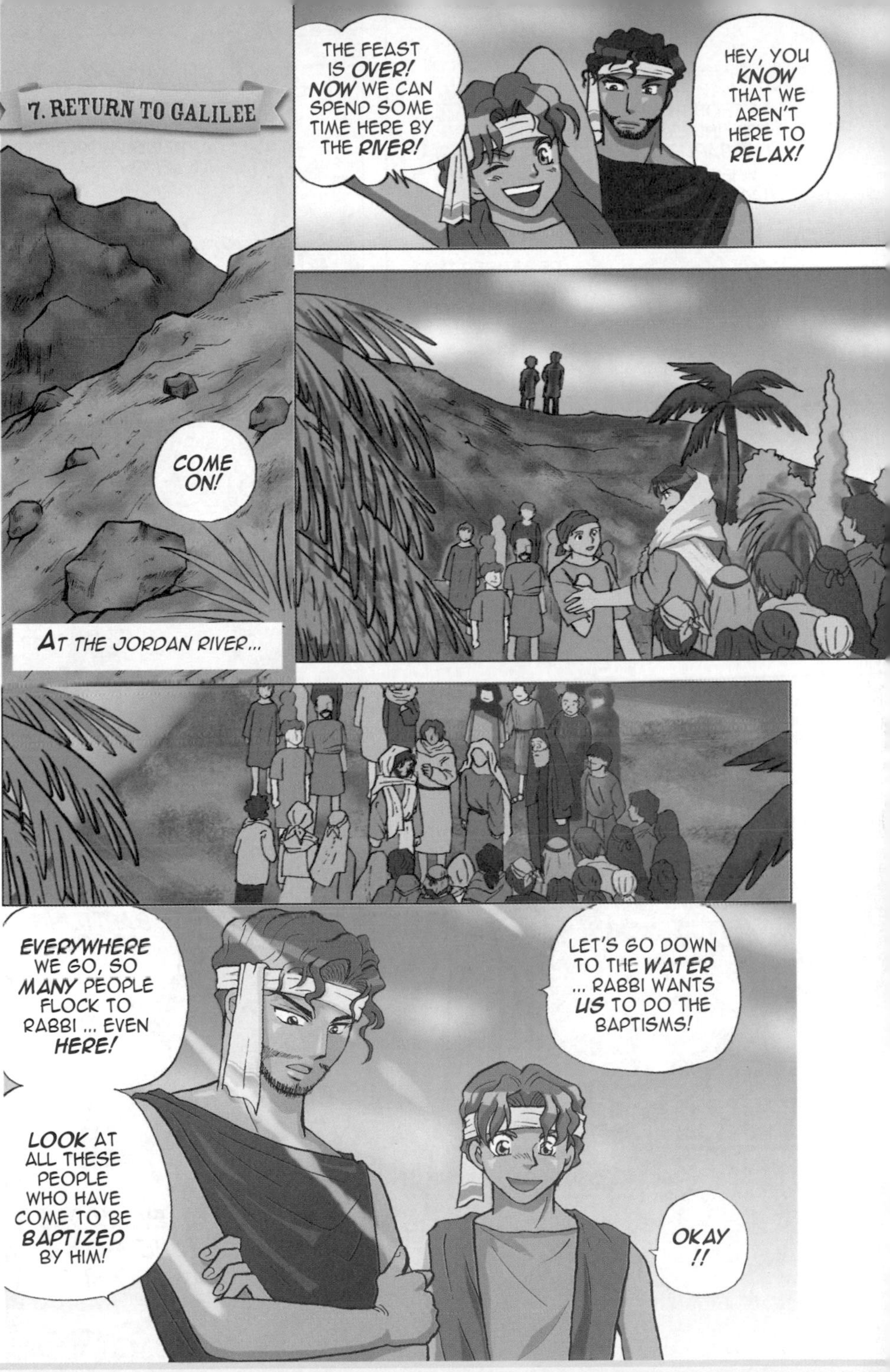

THE FEAST IS OVER! NOW WE CAN SPEND SOME TIME HERE BY THE RIVER!
HEY, YOU KNOW THAT WE AREN'T HERE TO RELAX!
COME ON!
AT THE JORDAN RIVER...
EVERYWHERE WE GO, SO MANY PEOPLE FLOCK TO RABBI ... EVEN HERE!
LOOK AT ALL THESE PEOPLE WHO HAVE COME TO BE BAPTIZED BY HIM!
LET'S GO DOWN TO THE WATER ... RABBI WANTS US TO DO THE BAPTISMS!
OKAY !!

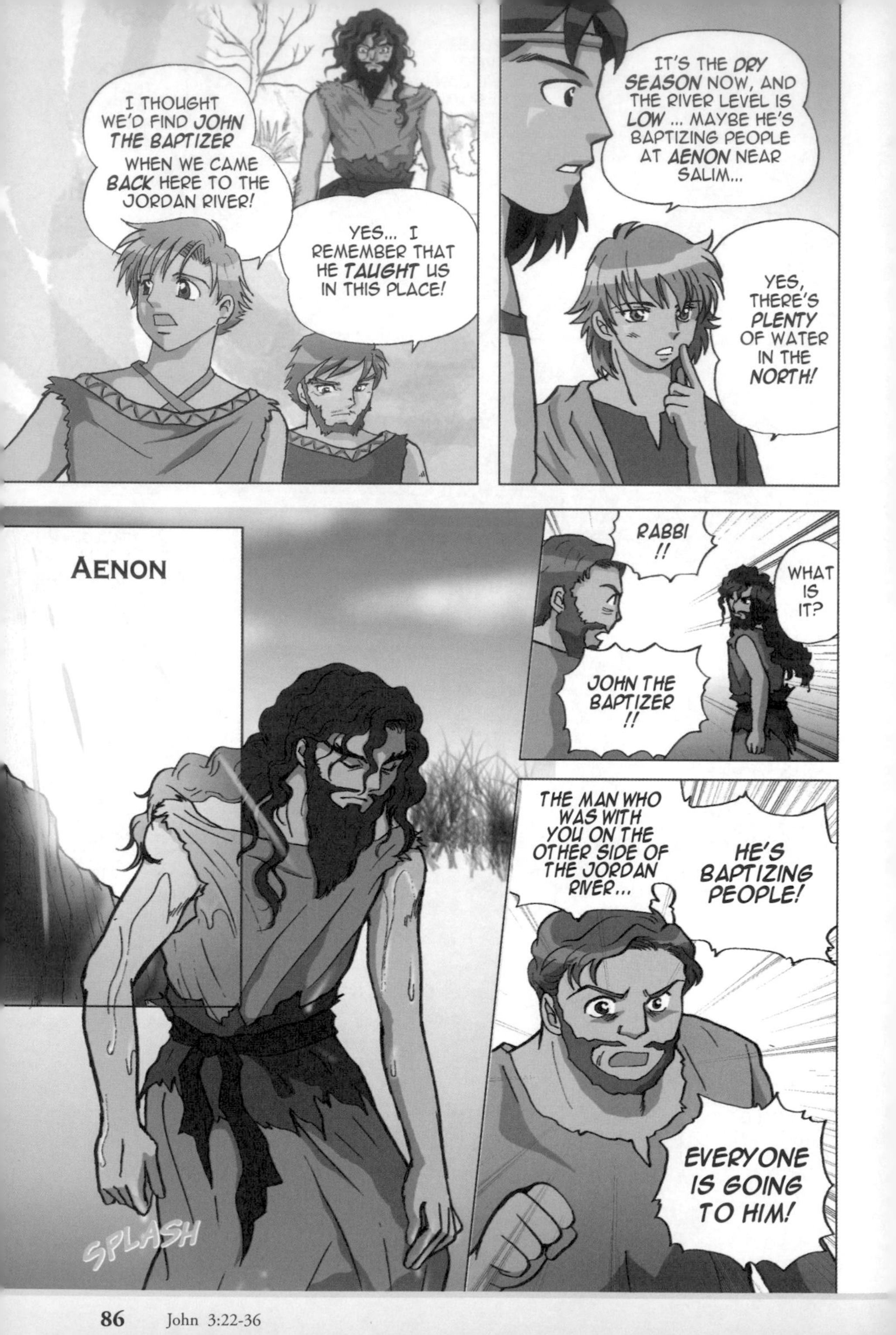

I THOUGHT WE'D FIND JOHN THE BAPTIZER WHEN WE CAME BACK HERE TO THE JORDAN RIVER!
YES... I REMEMBER THAT HE TAUGHT US IN THIS PLACE!
IT'S THE DRY SEASON NOW, AND THE RIVER LEVEL IS LOW ... MAYBE HE'S BAPTIZING PEOPLE AT AENON NEAR SALIM...
YES, THERE'S PLENTY OF WATER IN THE NORTH!
AENON
SPLASH
RABBI !!
WHAT IS IT?
JOHN THE BAPTIZER !!
THE MAN WHO WAS WITH YOU ON THE OTHER SIDE OF THE JORDAN RIVER...
HE'S BAPTIZING PEOPLE!
EVERYONE IS GOING TO HIM!

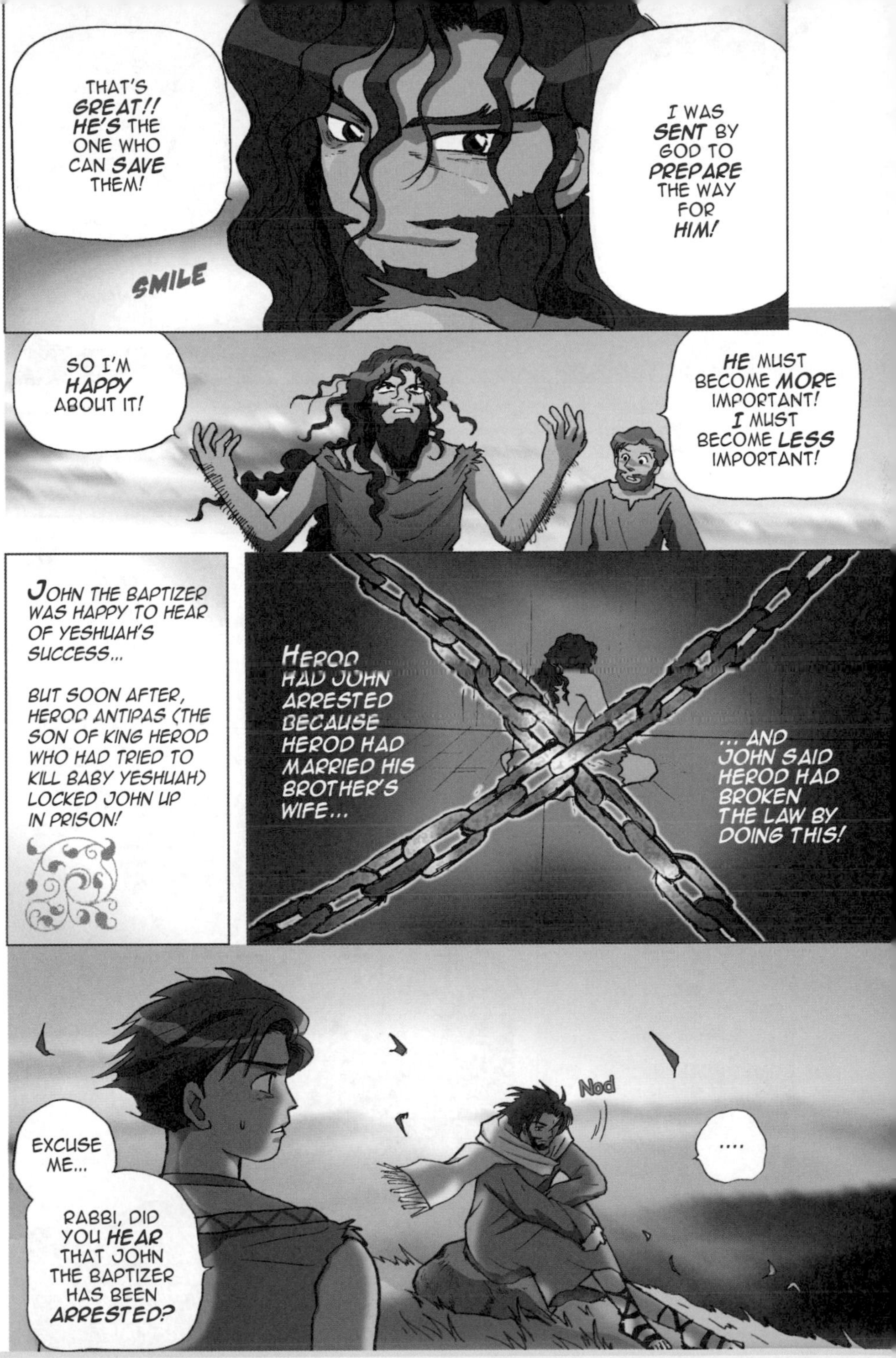
THAT'S GREAT!! HE'S THE ONE WHO CAN SAVE THEM!
I WAS SENT BY GOD TO PREPARE THE WAY FOR HIM!
SMILE
SO I'M HAPPY ABOUT IT!
HE MUST BECOME MORE IMPORTANT! I MUST BECOME LESS IMPORTANT!
JOHN THE BAPTIZER WAS HAPPY TO HEAR OF YESHUAH'S SUCCESS...
BUT SOON AFTER, HEROD ANTIPAS (THE SON OF KING HEROD WHO HAD TRIED TO KILL BABY YESHUAH) LOCKED JOHN UP IN PRISON!
HEROD HAD JOHN ARRESTED BECAUSE HEROD HAD MARRIED HIS BROTHER'S WIFE...
... AND JOHN SAID HEROD HAD BROKEN THE LAW BY DOING THIS!
EXCUSE ME...
RABBI, DID YOU HEAR THAT JOHN THE BAPTIZER HAS BEEN ARRESTED?
Nod
....

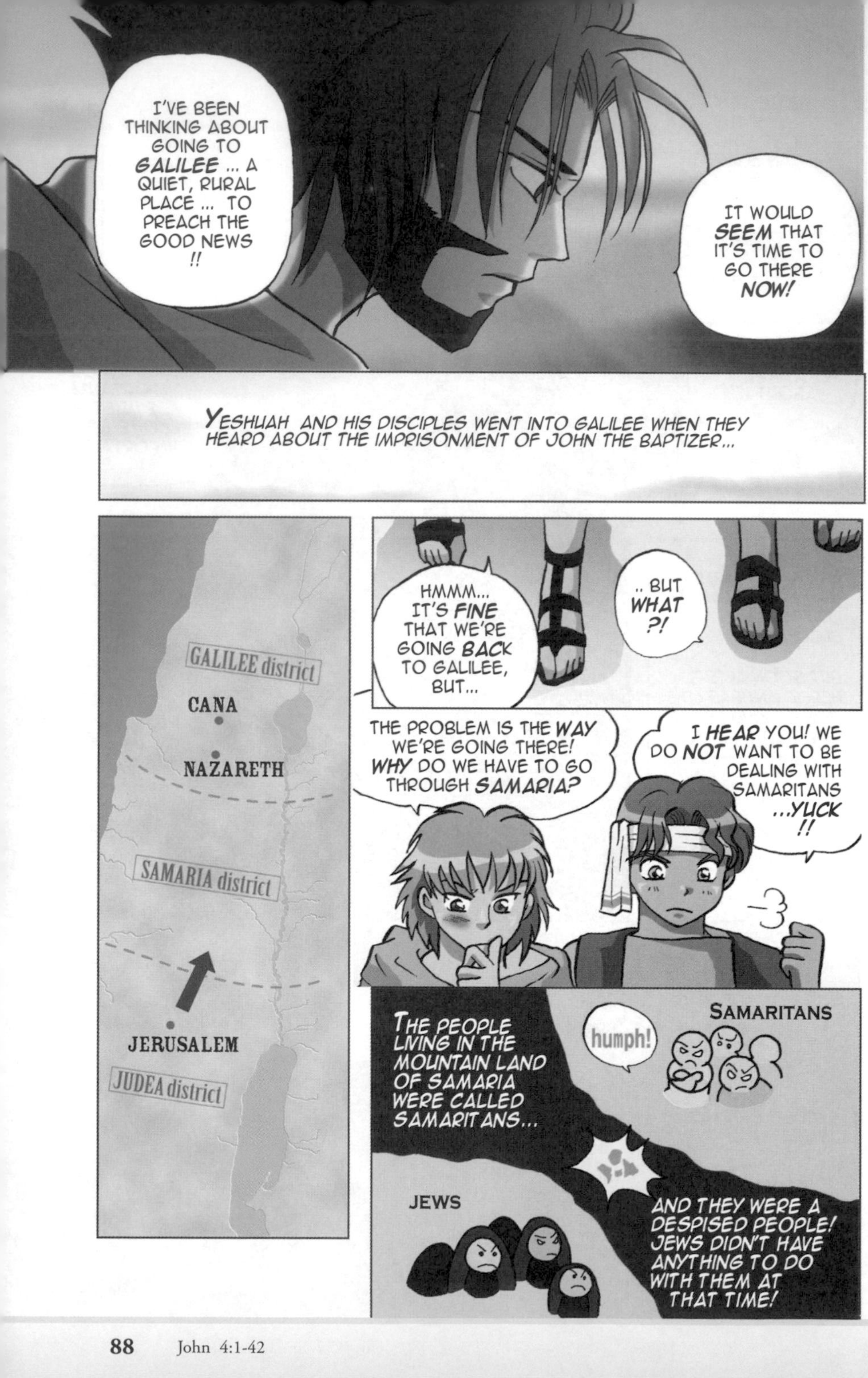
I'VE BEEN THINKING ABOUT GOING TO GALILEE ... A QUIET, RURAL PLACE ... TO PREACH THE GOOD NEWS !!
IT WOULD SEEM THAT IT'S TIME TO GO THERE NOW!
YESHUAH AND HIS DISCIPLES WENT INTO GALILEE WHEN THEY HEARD ABOUT THE IMPRISONMENT OF JOHN THE BAPTIZER...
GALILEE district
CANA
NAZARETH
SAMARIA district
JERUSALEM
JUDEA district
HMMM... IT'S FINE THAT WE'RE GOING BACK TO GALILEE, BUT...
.. BUT WHAT ?!
THE PROBLEM IS THE WAY WE'RE GOING THERE! WHY DO WE HAVE TO GO THROUGH SAMARIA?
I HEAR YOU! WE DO NOT WANT TO BE DEALING WITH SAMARITANS ...YUCK !!
THE PEOPLE LIVING IN THE MOUNTAIN LAND OF SAMARIA WERE CALLED SAMARITANS...
humph!
SAMARITANS
JEWS
AND THEY WERE A DESPISED PEOPLE! JEWS DIDN'T HAVE ANYTHING TO DO WITH THEM AT THAT TIME!

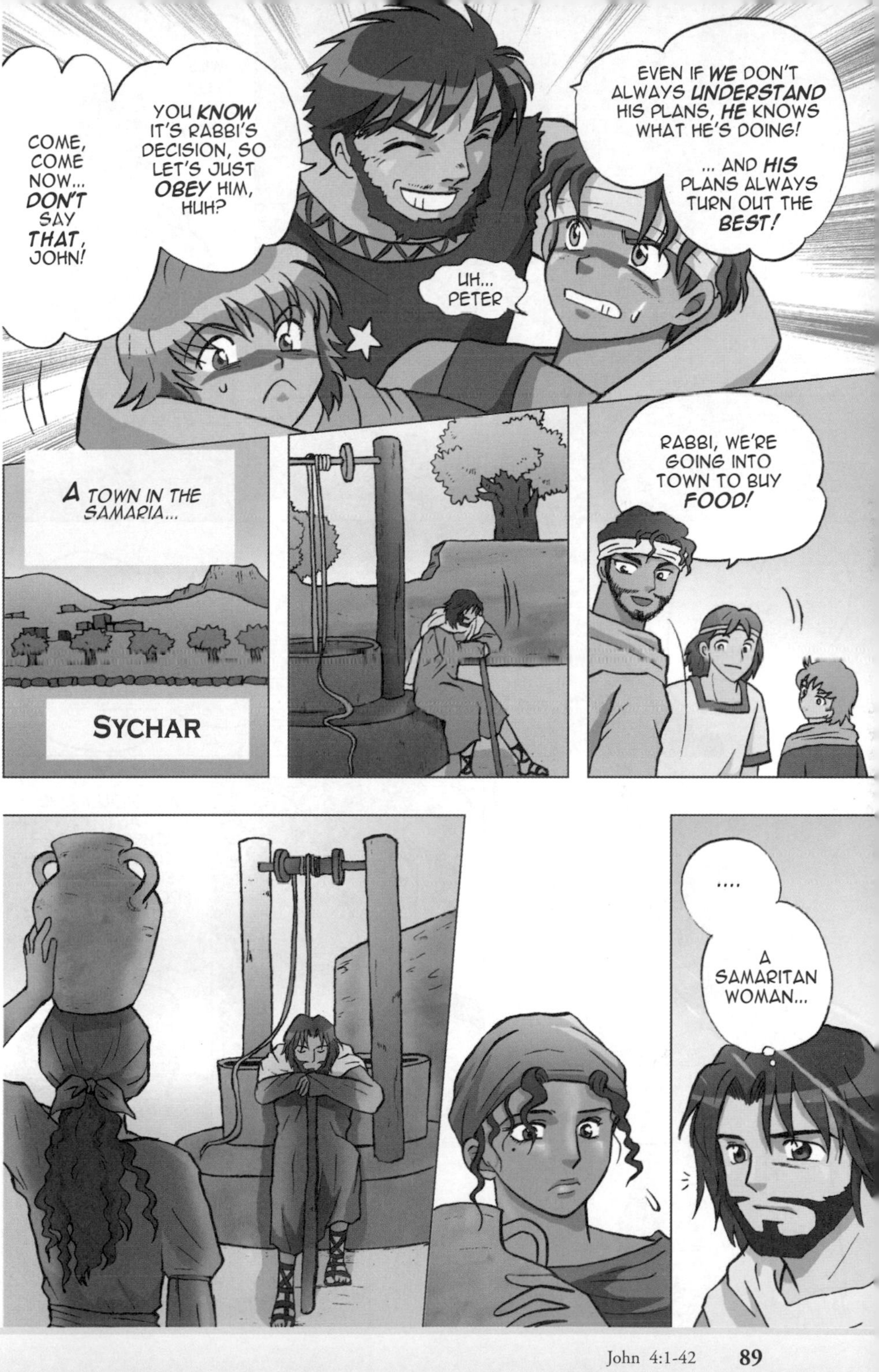
COME, COME NOW... DON'T SAY THAT, JOHN!
YOU KNOW IT'S RABBI'S DECISION, SO LET'S JUST OBEY HIM, HUH?
EVEN IF WE DON'T ALWAYS UNDERSTAND HIS PLANS, HE KNOWS WHAT HE'S DOING!
... AND HIS PLANS ALWAYS TURN OUT THE BEST!
UH... PETER
A TOWN IN THE SAMARIA...
SYCHAR
RABBI, WE'RE GOING INTO TOWN TO BUY FOOD!
....
A SAMARITAN WOMAN...

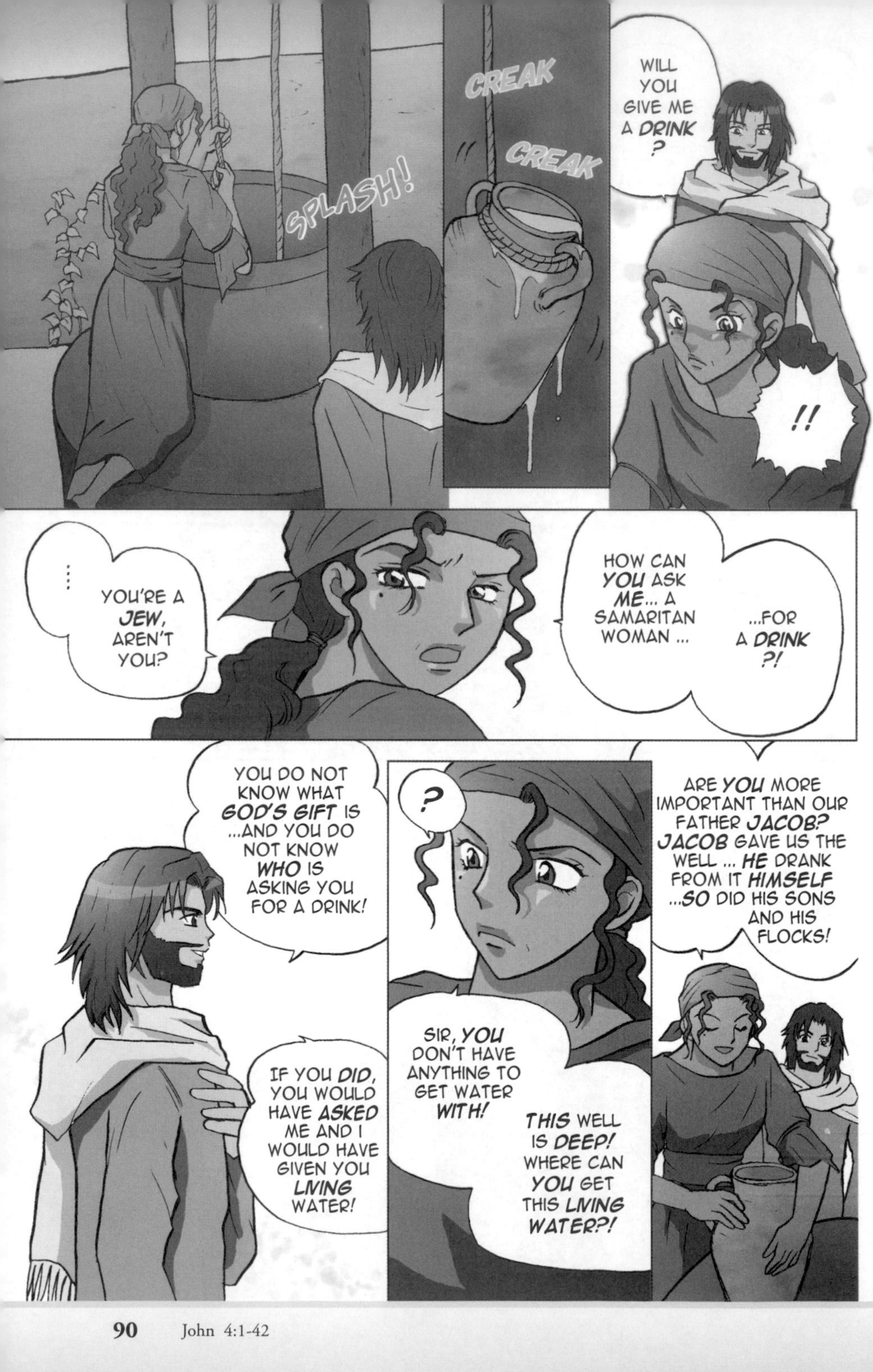
SPLASH!
CREAK
CREAK
WILL YOU GIVE ME A DRINK?
!!
...
YOU'RE A JEW, AREN'T YOU?
HOW CAN YOU ASK ME... A SAMARITAN WOMAN ...
...FOR A DRINK?!
YOU DO NOT KNOW WHAT GOD'S GIFT IS ...AND YOU DO NOT KNOW WHO IS ASKING YOU FOR A DRINK!
IF YOU DID, YOU WOULD HAVE ASKED ME AND I WOULD HAVE GIVEN YOU LIVING WATER!
?
SIR, YOU DON'T HAVE ANYTHING TO GET WATER WITH!
THIS WELL IS DEEP! WHERE CAN YOU GET THIS LIVING WATER?!
ARE YOU MORE IMPORTANT THAN OUR FATHER JACOB? JACOB GAVE US THE WELL ... HE DRANK FROM IT HIMSELF ...SO DID HIS SONS AND HIS FLOCKS!

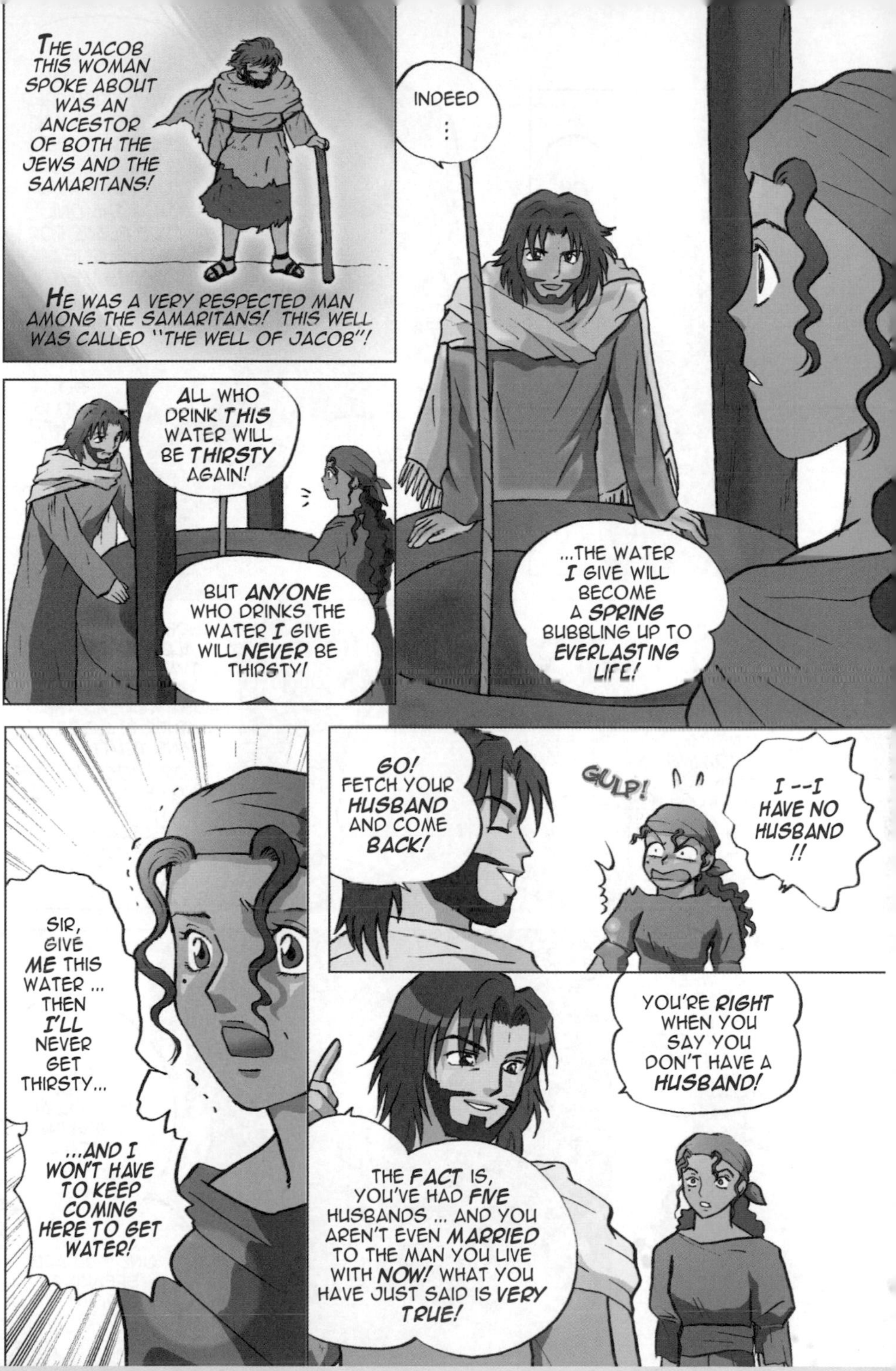

THE JACOB THIS WOMAN SPOKE ABOUT WAS AN ANCESTOR OF BOTH THE JEWS AND THE SAMARITANS!
HE WAS A VERY RESPECTED MAN AMONG THE SAMARITANS! THIS WELL WAS CALLED "THE WELL OF JACOB"!
INDEED ...
ALL WHO DRINK THIS WATER WILL BE THIRSTY AGAIN!
BUT ANYONE WHO DRINKS THE WATER I GIVE WILL NEVER BE THIRSTY!
...THE WATER I GIVE WILL BECOME A SPRING BUBBLING UP TO EVERLASTING LIFE!
SIR, GIVE ME THIS WATER ... THEN I'LL NEVER GET THIRSTY...
...AND I WON'T HAVE TO KEEP COMING HERE TO GET WATER!
GO! FETCH YOUR HUSBAND AND COME BACK!
GULP!
I --I HAVE NO HUSBAND !!
YOU'RE RIGHT WHEN YOU SAY YOU DON'T HAVE A HUSBAND!
THE FACT IS, YOU'VE HAD FIVE HUSBANDS ... AND YOU AREN'T EVEN MARRIED TO THE MAN YOU LIVE WITH NOW! WHAT YOU HAVE JUST SAID IS VERY TRUE!

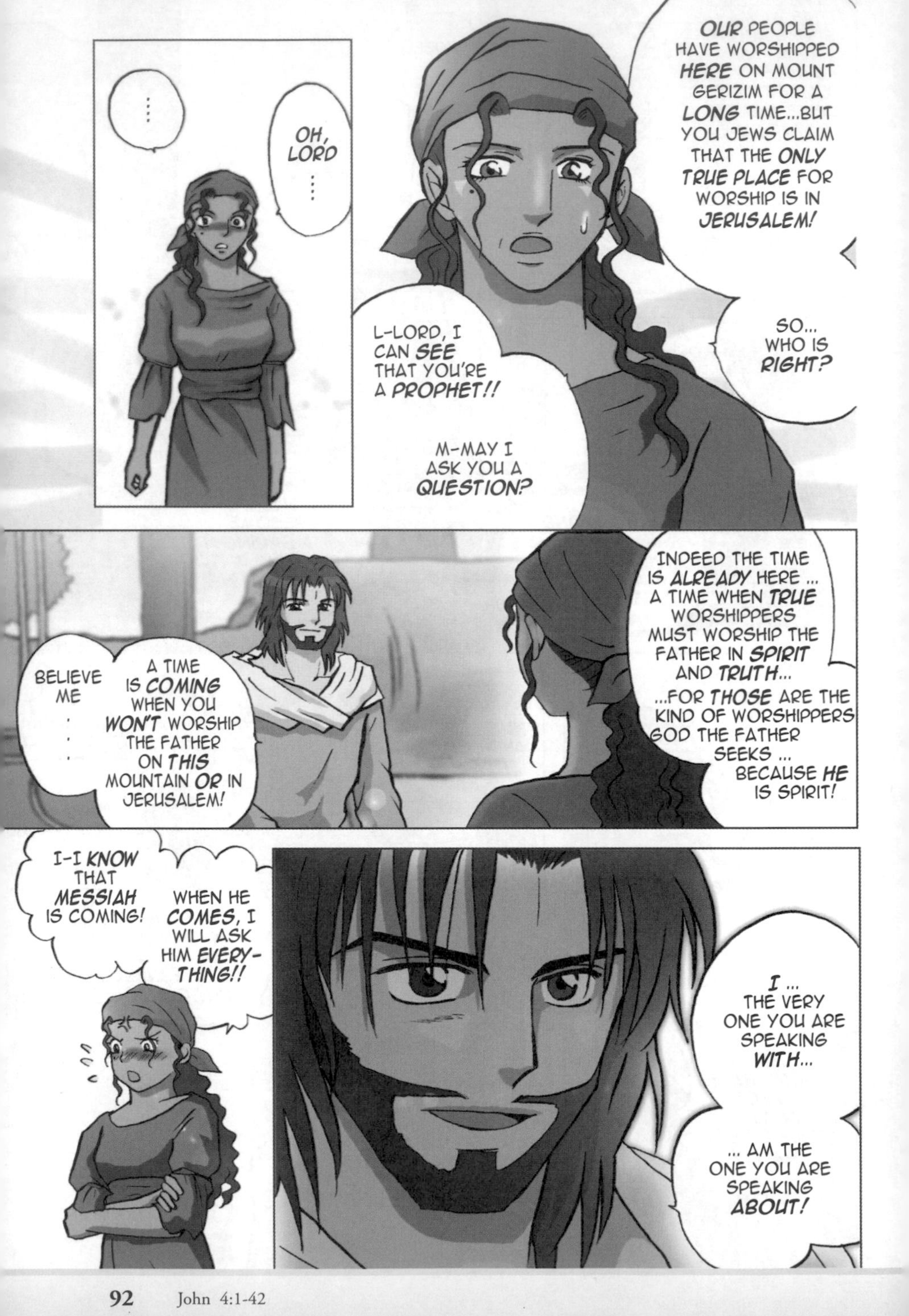

OH, LORD ....
....
OUR PEOPLE HAVE WORSHIPPED HERE ON MOUNT GERIZIM FOR A LONG TIME...BUT YOU JEWS CLAIM THAT THE ONLY TRUE PLACE FOR WORSHIP IS IN JERUSALEM!
L-LORD, I CAN SEE THAT YOU'RE A PROPHET!!
M-MAY I ASK YOU A QUESTION?
SO... WHO IS RIGHT?
BELIEVE ME . . .
A TIME IS COMING WHEN YOU WON'T WORSHIP THE FATHER ON THIS MOUNTAIN OR IN JERUSALEM!
INDEED THE TIME IS ALREADY HERE ... A TIME WHEN TRUE WORSHIPPERS MUST WORSHIP THE FATHER IN SPIRIT AND TRUTH...
...FOR THOSE ARE THE KIND OF WORSHIPPERS GOD THE FATHER SEEKS ... BECAUSE HE IS SPIRIT!
I-I KNOW THAT MESSIAH IS COMING!
WHEN HE COMES, I WILL ASK HIM EVERY-THING!!
I ... THE VERY ONE YOU ARE SPEAKING WITH...
... AM THE ONE YOU ARE SPEAKING ABOUT!

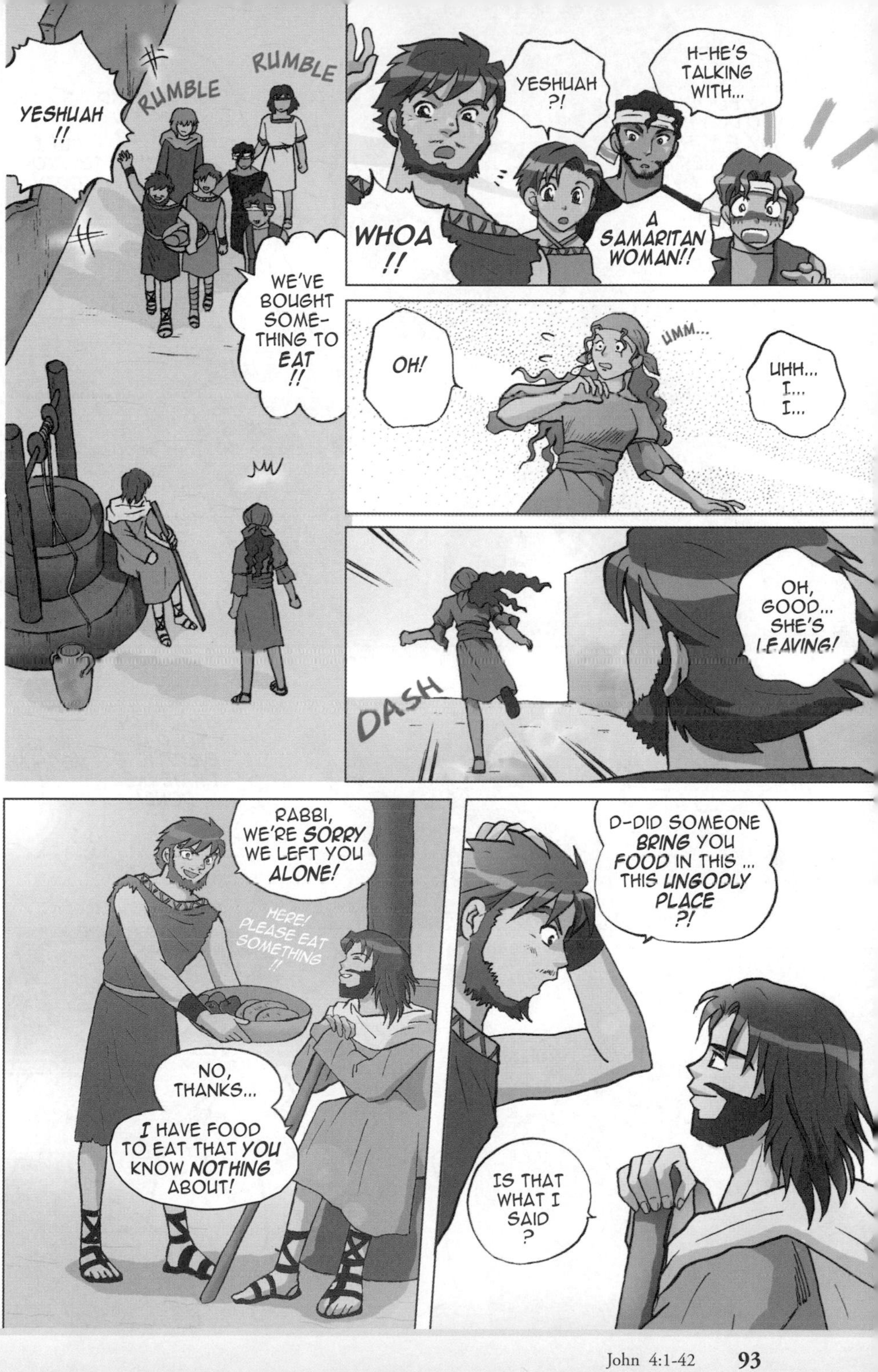
RUMBLE
RUMBLE
YESHUAH !!
WE'VE BOUGHT SOME-THING TO EAT !!
WHOA !!
YESHUAH ?!
H-HE'S TALKING WITH...
A SAMARITAN WOMAN!!
OH!
UMM...
UHH... I... I...
DASH
OH, GOOD... SHE'S LEAVING!
RABBI, WE'RE SORRY WE LEFT YOU ALONE!
HERE! PLEASE EAT SOMETHING !!
NO, THANKS...
I HAVE FOOD TO EAT THAT YOU KNOW NOTHING ABOUT!
D-DID SOMEONE BRING YOU FOOD IN THIS ... THIS UNGODLY PLACE ?!
IS THAT WHAT I SAID ?

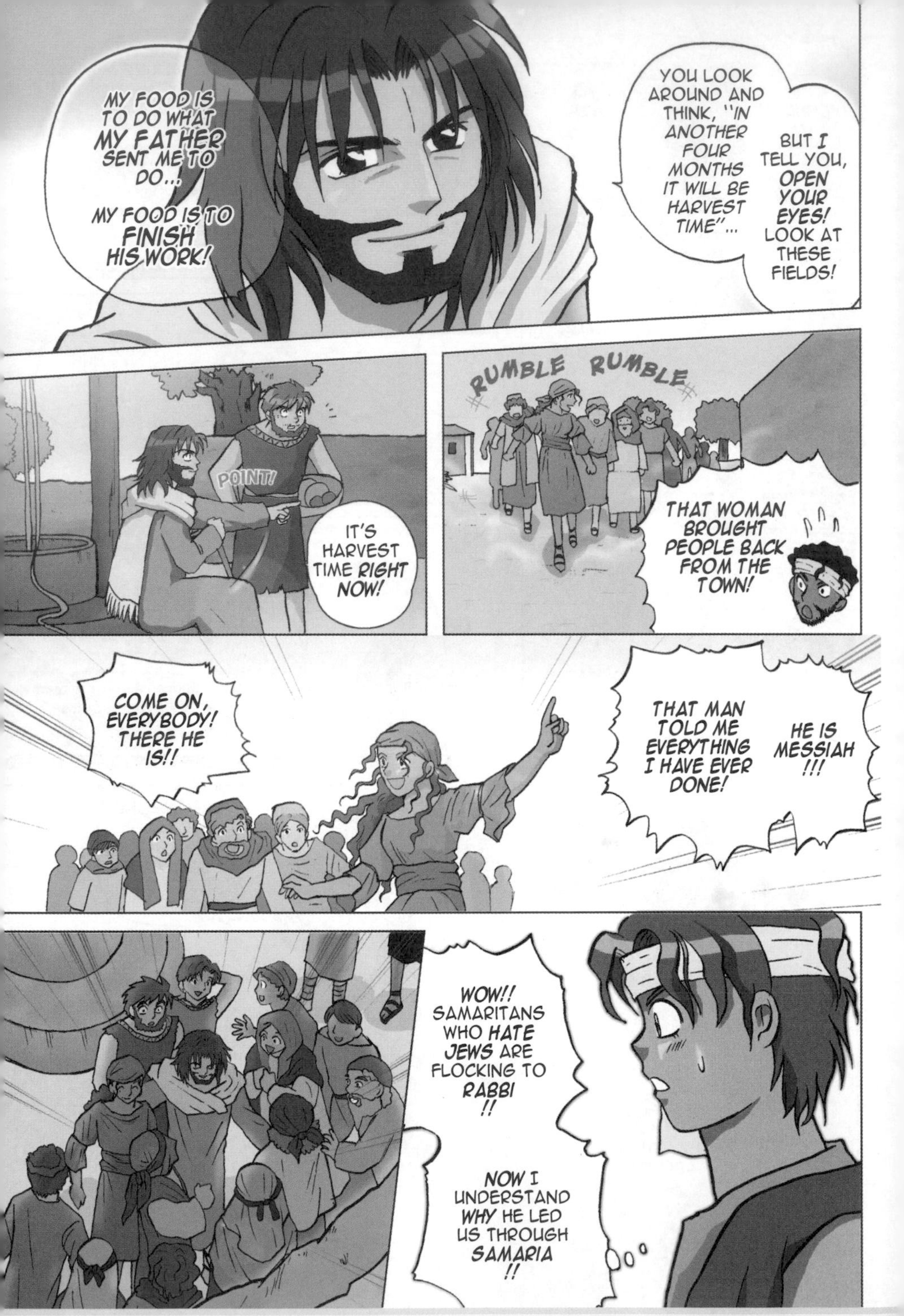
MY FOOD IS TO DO WHAT MY FATHER SENT ME TO DO...
MY FOOD IS TO FINISH HIS WORK!
YOU LOOK AROUND AND THINK, "IN ANOTHER FOUR MONTHS IT WILL BE HARVEST TIME"...
BUT I TELL YOU, OPEN YOUR EYES! LOOK AT THESE FIELDS!
POINT!
IT'S HARVEST TIME RIGHT NOW!
RUMBLE RUMBLE
THAT WOMAN BROUGHT PEOPLE BACK FROM THE TOWN!
COME ON, EVERYBODY! THERE HE IS!!
THAT MAN TOLD ME EVERYTHING I HAVE EVER DONE!
HE IS MESSIAH !!!
WOW!! SAMARITANS WHO HATE JEWS ARE FLOCKING TO RABBI !!
NOW I UNDERSTAND WHY HE LED US THROUGH SAMARIA !!

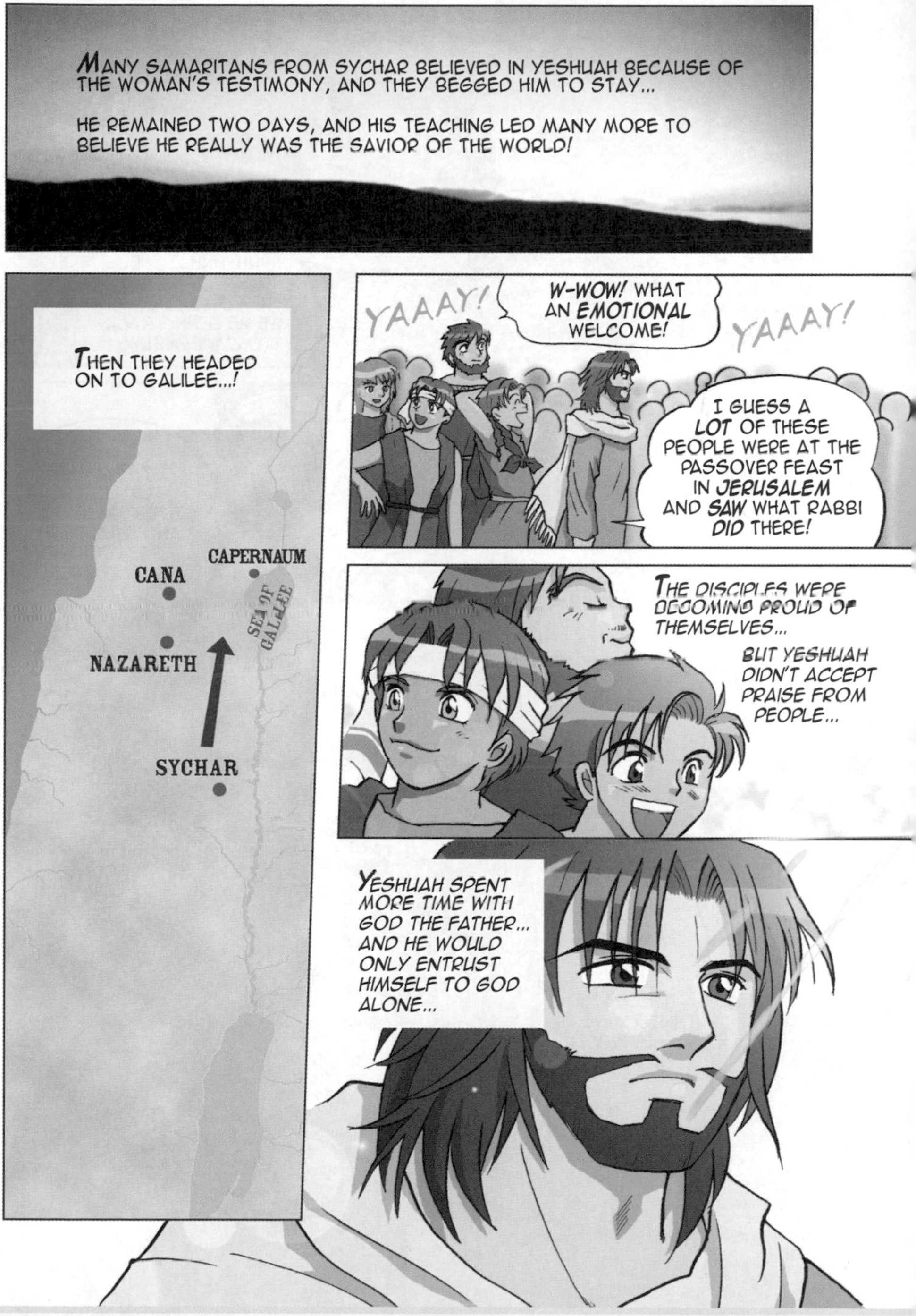
MANY SAMARITANS FROM SYCHAR BELIEVED IN YESHUAH BECAUSE OF THE WOMAN'S TESTIMONY, AND THEY BEGGED HIM TO STAY...
HE REMAINED TWO DAYS, AND HIS TEACHING LED MANY MORE TO BELIEVE HE REALLY WAS THE SAVIOR OF THE WORLD!
THEN THEY HEADED ON TO GALILEE...!
CANA
CAPERNAUM
SEA OF GALILEE
NAZARETH
SYCHAR
YAAAY!
W-WOW! WHAT AN EMOTIONAL WELCOME!
YAAAY!
I GUESS A LOT OF THESE PEOPLE WERE AT THE PASSOVER FEAST IN JERUSALEM AND SAW WHAT RABBI DID THERE!
THE DISCIPLES WERE BECOMING PROUD OF THEMSELVES...
BUT YESHUAH DIDN'T ACCEPT PRAISE FROM PEOPLE...
YESHUAH SPENT MORE TIME WITH GOD THE FATHER... AND HE WOULD ONLY ENTRUST HIMSELF TO GOD ALONE...

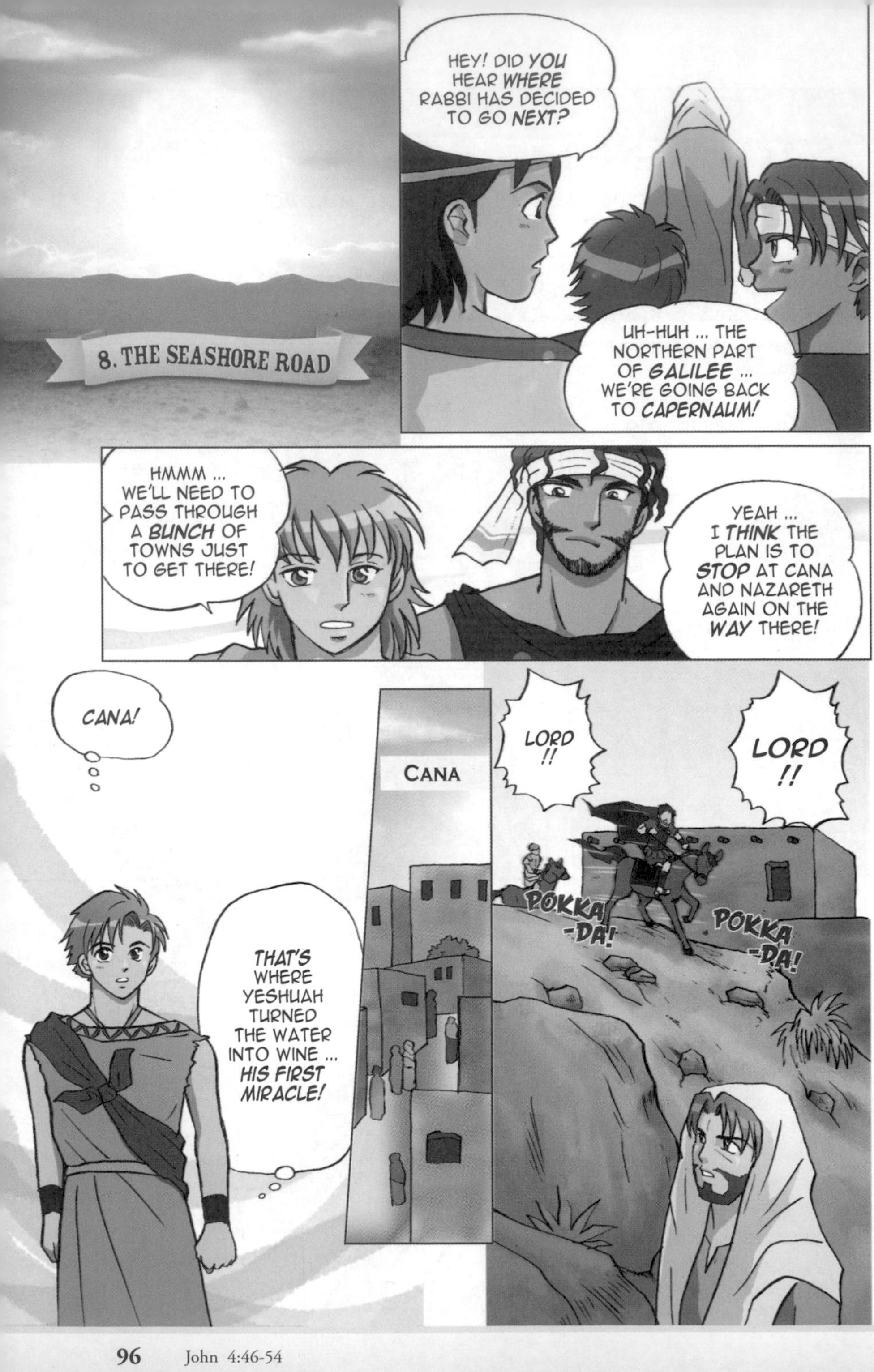
8. THE SEASHORE ROAD
HEY! DID YOU HEAR WHERE RABBI HAS DECIDED TO GO NEXT?
UH-HUH ... THE NORTHERN PART OF GALILEE ... WE'RE GOING BACK TO CAPERNAUM!
HMMM ... WE'LL NEED TO PASS THROUGH A BUNCH OF TOWNS JUST TO GET THERE!
YEAH ... I THINK THE PLAN IS TO STOP AT CANA AND NAZARETH AGAIN ON THE WAY THERE!
CANA!
THAT'S WHERE YESHUAH TURNED THE WATER INTO WINE ... HIS FIRST MIRACLE!
CANA
LORD !!
LORD !!
POKKA -DA!
POKKA -DA!

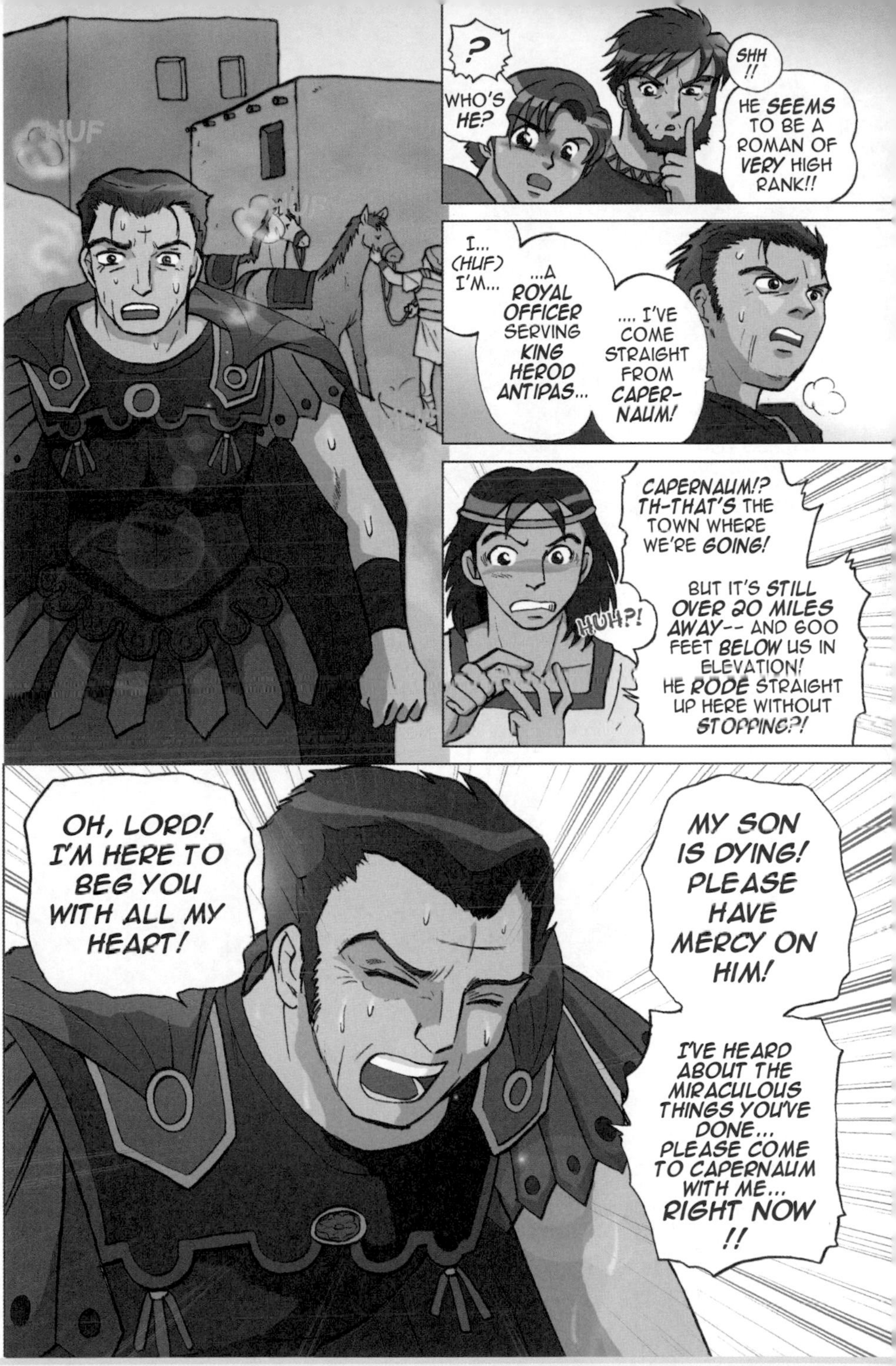
HUF
HUF
?
WHO'S HE?
SHH !!
HE SEEMS TO BE A ROMAN OF VERY HIGH RANK!!
I... (HUF) I'M...
...A ROYAL OFFICER SERVING KING HEROD ANTIPAS...
.... I'VE COME STRAIGHT FROM CAPER-NAUM!
CAPERNAUM!? TH-THAT'S THE TOWN WHERE WE'RE GOING!
HUH?!
BUT IT'S STILL OVER 20 MILES AWAY-- AND 600 FEET BELOW US IN ELEVATION! HE RODE STRAIGHT UP HERE WITHOUT STOPPING?!
OH, LORD! I'M HERE TO BEG YOU WITH ALL MY HEART!
MY SON IS DYING! PLEASE HAVE MERCY ON HIM!
I'VE HEARD ABOUT THE MIRACULOUS THINGS YOU'VE DONE... PLEASE COME TO CAPERNAUM WITH ME... RIGHT NOW !!

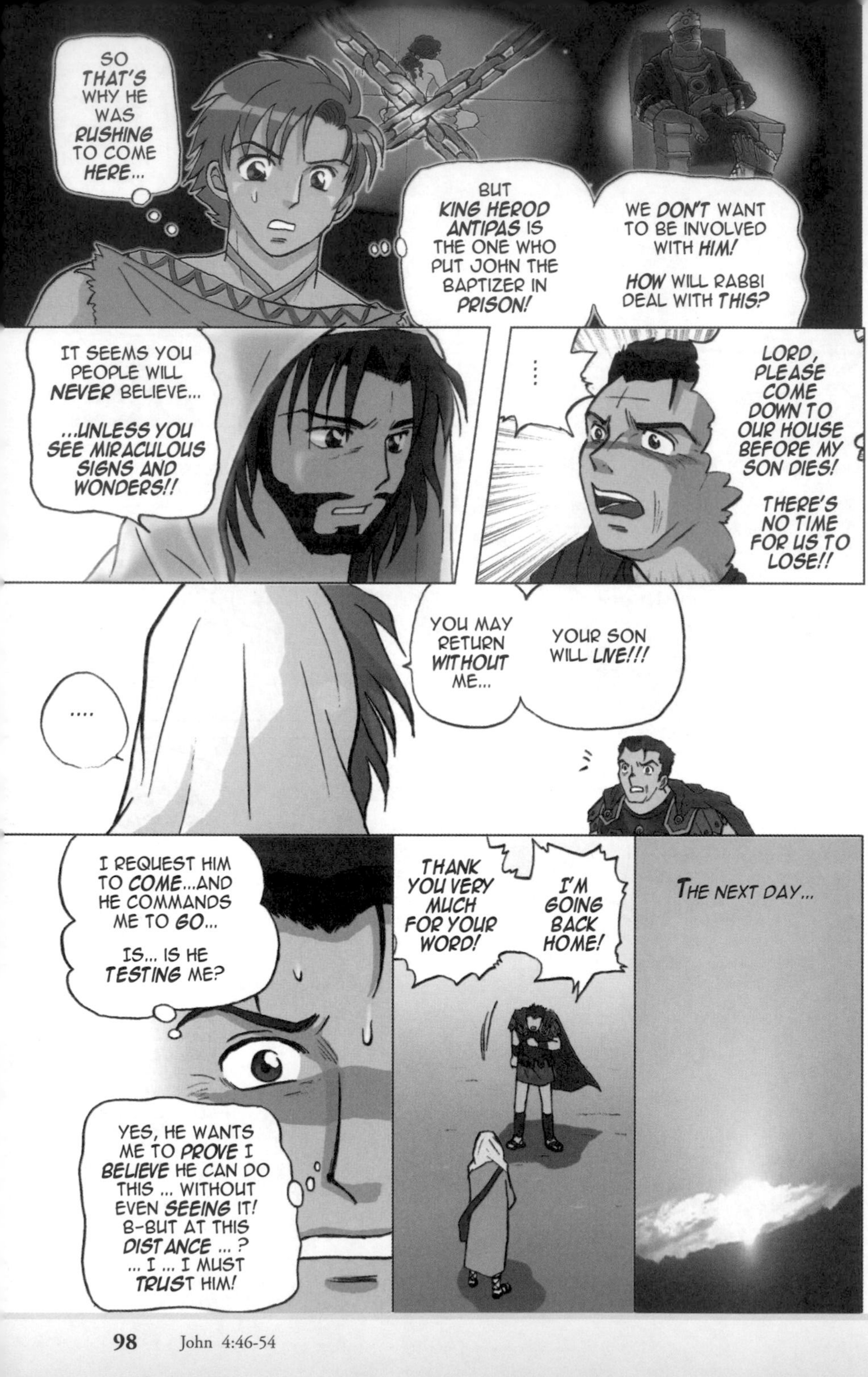
SO THAT'S WHY HE WAS RUSHING TO COME HERE...
BUT KING HEROD ANTIPAS IS THE ONE WHO PUT JOHN THE BAPTIZER IN PRISON!
WE DON'T WANT TO BE INVOLVED WITH HIM! HOW WILL RABBI DEAL WITH THIS?
IT SEEMS YOU PEOPLE WILL NEVER BELIEVE... ...UNLESS YOU SEE MIRACULOUS SIGNS AND WONDERS!!
...
LORD, PLEASE COME DOWN TO OUR HOUSE BEFORE MY SON DIES! THERE'S NO TIME FOR US TO LOSE!!
YOU MAY RETURN WITHOUT ME...
YOUR SON WILL LIVE!!!
....
I REQUEST HIM TO COME...AND HE COMMANDS ME TO GO... IS... IS HE TESTING ME?
YES, HE WANTS ME TO PROVE I BELIEVE HE CAN DO THIS ... WITHOUT EVEN SEEING IT! B-BUT AT THIS DISTANCE ... ? ... I ... I MUST TRUST HIM!
THANK YOU VERY MUCH FOR YOUR WORD!
I'M GOING BACK HOME!
THE NEXT DAY...

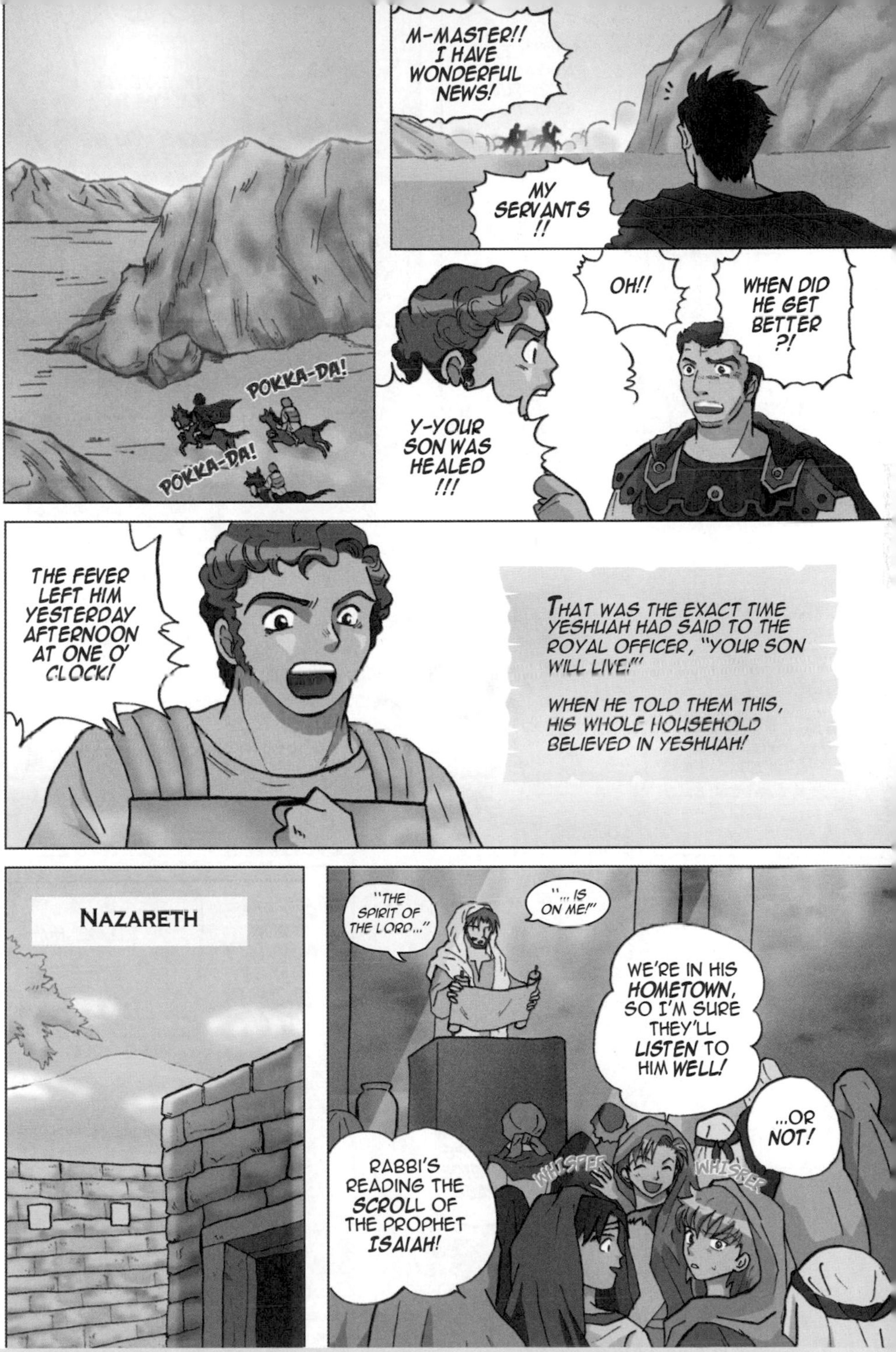
POKKA-DA!
POKKA-DA!
M-MASTER!! I HAVE WONDERFUL NEWS!
MY SERVANTS !!
OH!!
WHEN DID HE GET BETTER ?!
Y-YOUR SON WAS HEALED !!!
THE FEVER LEFT HIM YESTERDAY AFTERNOON AT ONE O' CLOCK!
THAT WAS THE EXACT TIME YESHUAH HAD SAID TO THE ROYAL OFFICER, "YOUR SON WILL LIVE!"
WHEN HE TOLD THEM THIS, HIS WHOLE HOUSEHOLD BELIEVED IN YESHUAH!
NAZARETH
"THE SPIRIT OF THE LORD..."
"... IS ON ME!"
WE'RE IN HIS HOMETOWN, SO I'M SURE THEY'LL LISTEN TO HIM WELL!
...OR NOT!
RABBI'S READING THE SCROLL OF THE PROPHET ISAIAH!
WHISPER
WHISPER

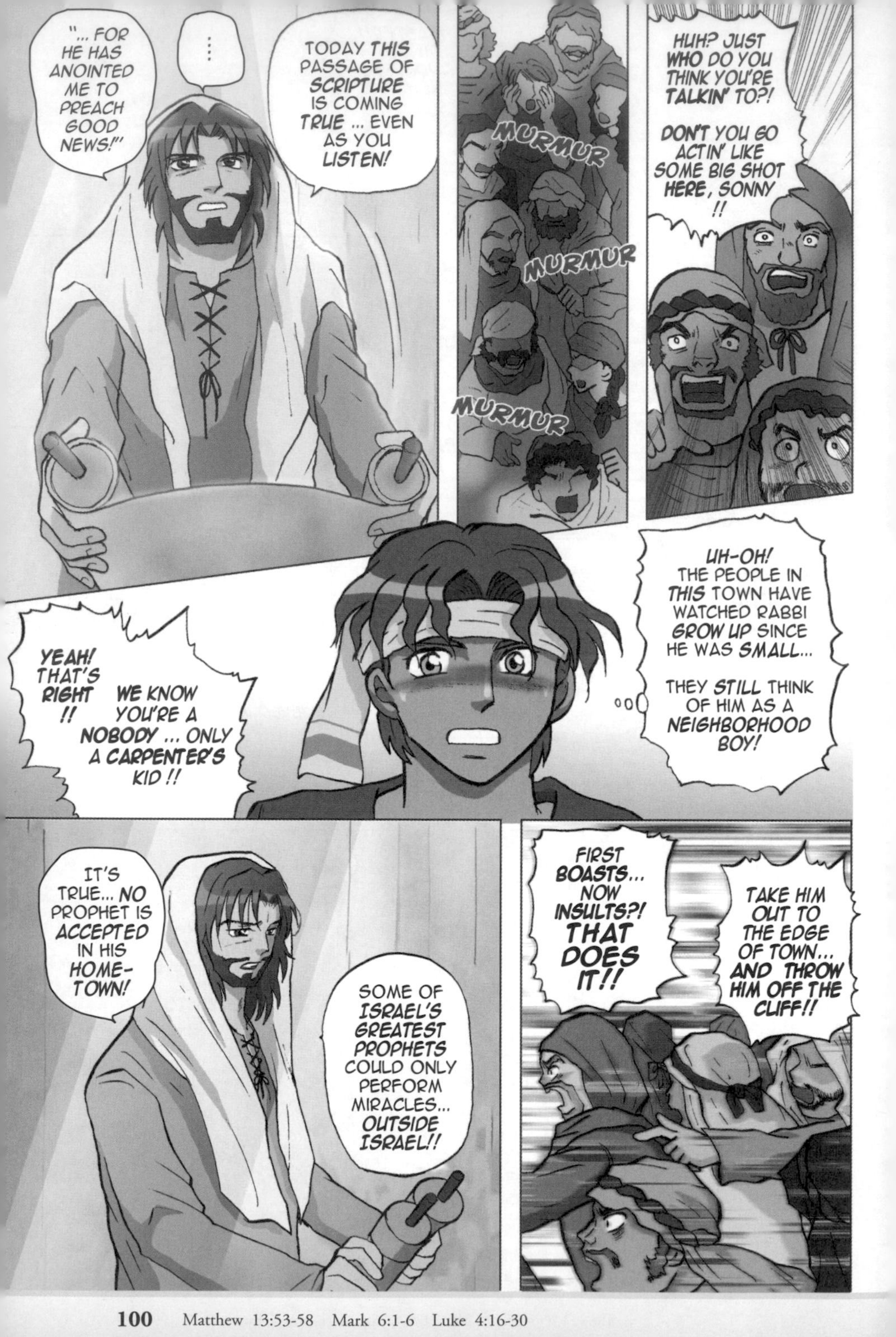
"... FOR HE HAS ANOINTED ME TO PREACH GOOD NEWS!"
...
TODAY THIS PASSAGE OF SCRIPTURE IS COMING TRUE ... EVEN AS YOU LISTEN!
MURMUR
MURMUR
MURMUR
HUH? JUST WHO DO YOU THINK YOU'RE TALKIN' TO?!
DON'T YOU GO ACTIN' LIKE SOME BIG SHOT HERE, SONNY !!
YEAH! THAT'S RIGHT !!
WE KNOW YOU'RE A NOBODY ... ONLY A CARPENTER'S KID !!
UH-OH! THE PEOPLE IN THIS TOWN HAVE WATCHED RABBI GROW UP SINCE HE WAS SMALL...
THEY STILL THINK OF HIM AS A NEIGHBORHOOD BOY!
IT'S TRUE... NO PROPHET IS ACCEPTED IN HIS HOME-TOWN!
SOME OF ISRAEL'S GREATEST PROPHETS COULD ONLY PERFORM MIRACLES... OUTSIDE ISRAEL!!
FIRST BOASTS... NOW INSULTS?! THAT DOES IT!!
TAKE HIM OUT TO THE EDGE OF TOWN... AND THROW HIM OFF THE CLIFF!!

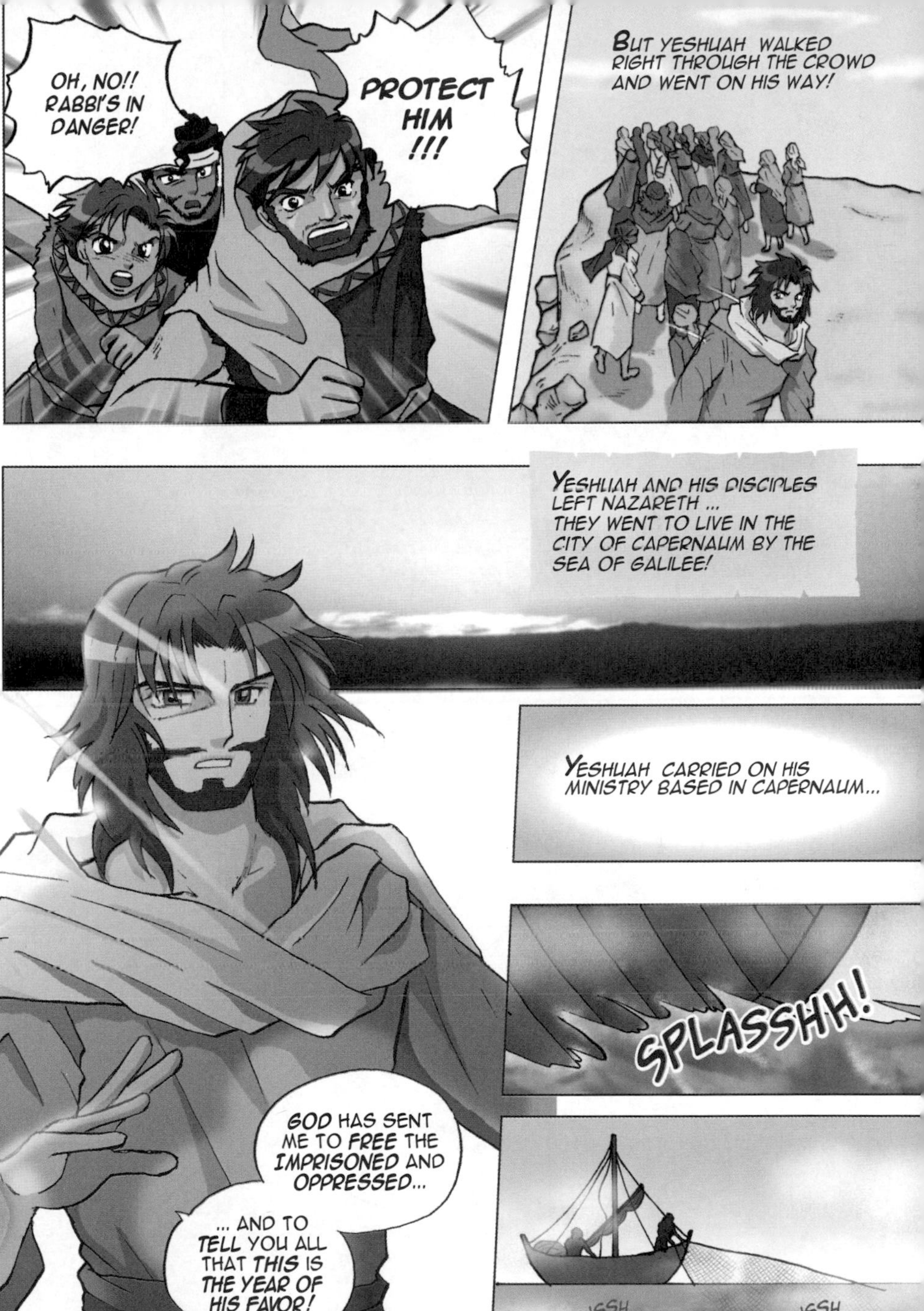
OH, NO!! RABBI'S IN DANGER!
PROTECT HIM !!!
BUT YESHUAH WALKED RIGHT THROUGH THE CROWD AND WENT ON HIS WAY!
YESHUAH AND HIS DISCIPLES LEFT NAZARETH ... THEY WENT TO LIVE IN THE CITY OF CAPERNAUM BY THE SEA OF GALILEE!
YESHUAH CARRIED ON HIS MINISTRY BASED IN CAPERNAUM...
SPLASSHH!
GOD HAS SENT ME TO FREE THE IMPRISONED AND OPPRESSED...
... AND TO TELL YOU ALL THAT THIS IS THE YEAR OF HIS FAVOR!
SWSSH
SWSSH

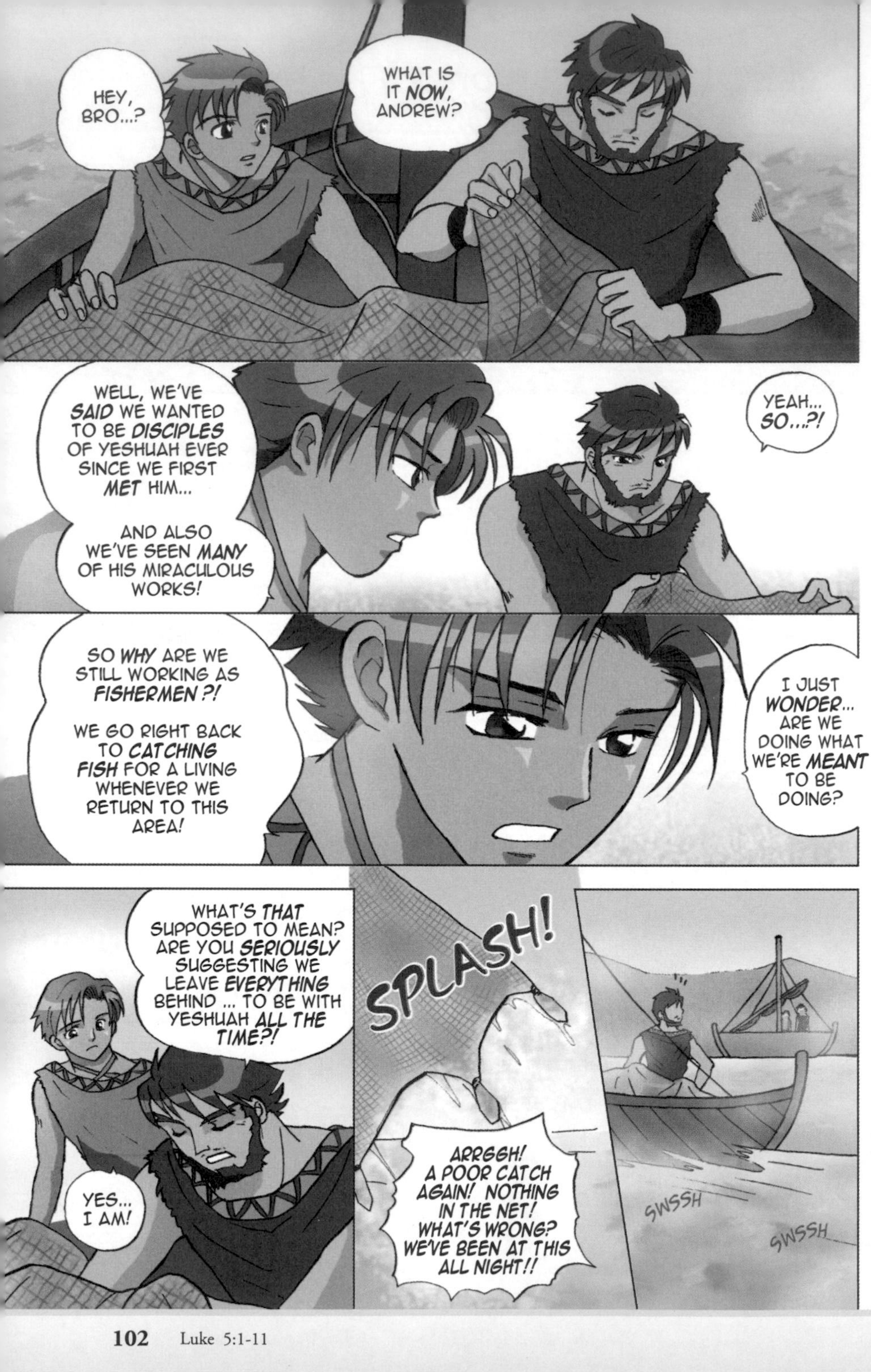
HEY, BRO...?
WHAT IS IT NOW, ANDREW?
WELL, WE'VE SAID WE WANTED TO BE DISCIPLES OF YESHUAH EVER SINCE WE FIRST MET HIM...
AND ALSO WE'VE SEEN MANY OF HIS MIRACULOUS WORKS!
YEAH... SO...?!
SO WHY ARE WE STILL WORKING AS FISHERMEN ?!
WE GO RIGHT BACK TO CATCHING FISH FOR A LIVING WHENEVER WE RETURN TO THIS AREA!
I JUST WONDER... ARE WE DOING WHAT WE'RE MEANT TO BE DOING?
WHAT'S THAT SUPPOSED TO MEAN? ARE YOU SERIOUSLY SUGGESTING WE LEAVE EVERYTHING BEHIND ... TO BE WITH YESHUAH ALL THE TIME?!
YES... I AM!
SPLASH!
ARRGGH! A POOR CATCH AGAIN! NOTHING IN THE NET! WHAT'S WRONG? WE'VE BEEN AT THIS ALL NIGHT!!
SWSSH
SWSSH

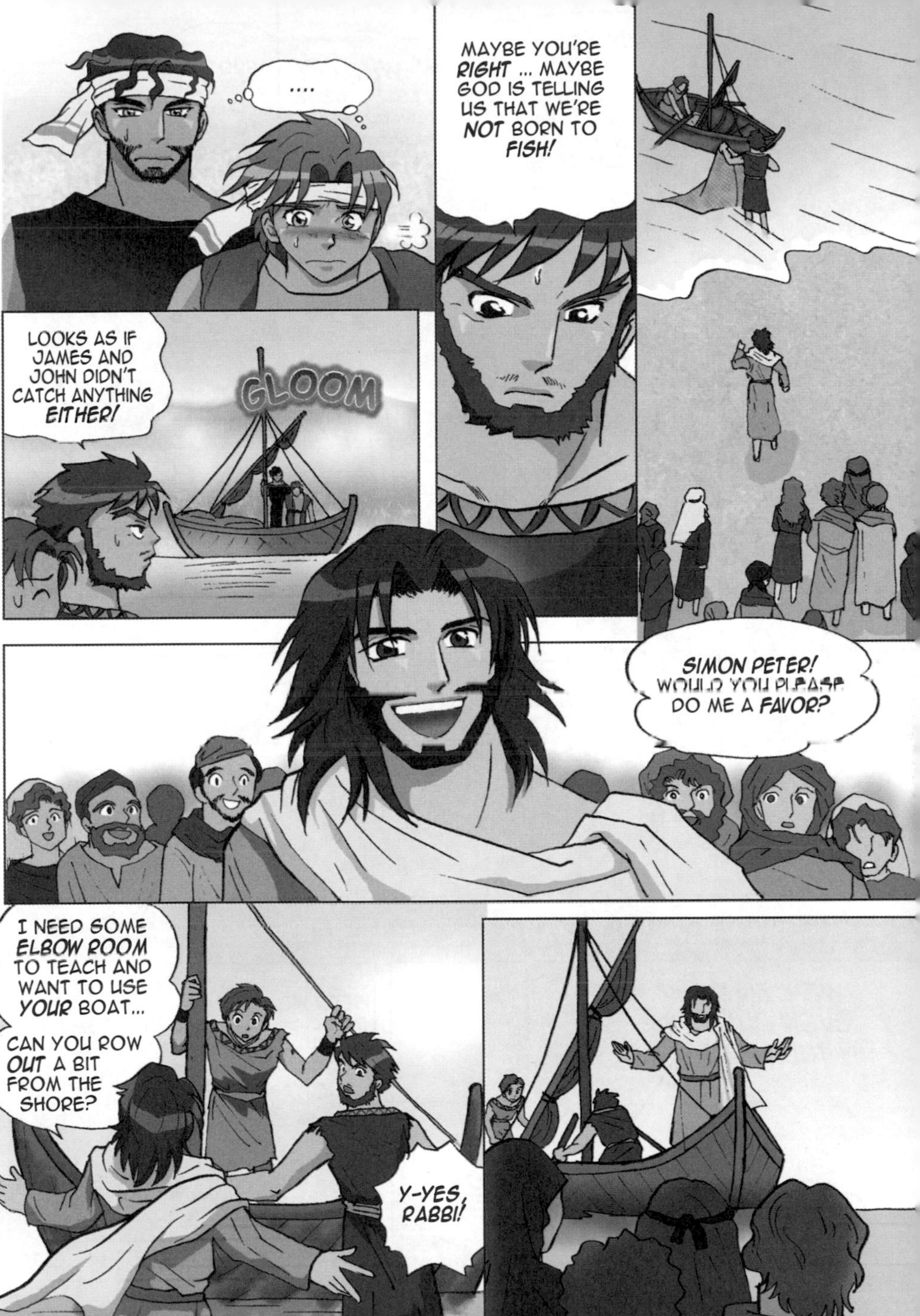
....
MAYBE YOU'RE RIGHT ... MAYBE GOD IS TELLING US THAT WE'RE NOT BORN TO FISH!
LOOKS AS IF JAMES AND JOHN DIDN'T CATCH ANYTHING EITHER!
GLOOM
SIMON PETER! WOULD YOU PLEASE DO ME A FAVOR?
I NEED SOME ELBOW ROOM TO TEACH AND WANT TO USE YOUR BOAT...
CAN YOU ROW OUT A BIT FROM THE SHORE?
Y-YES, RABBI!

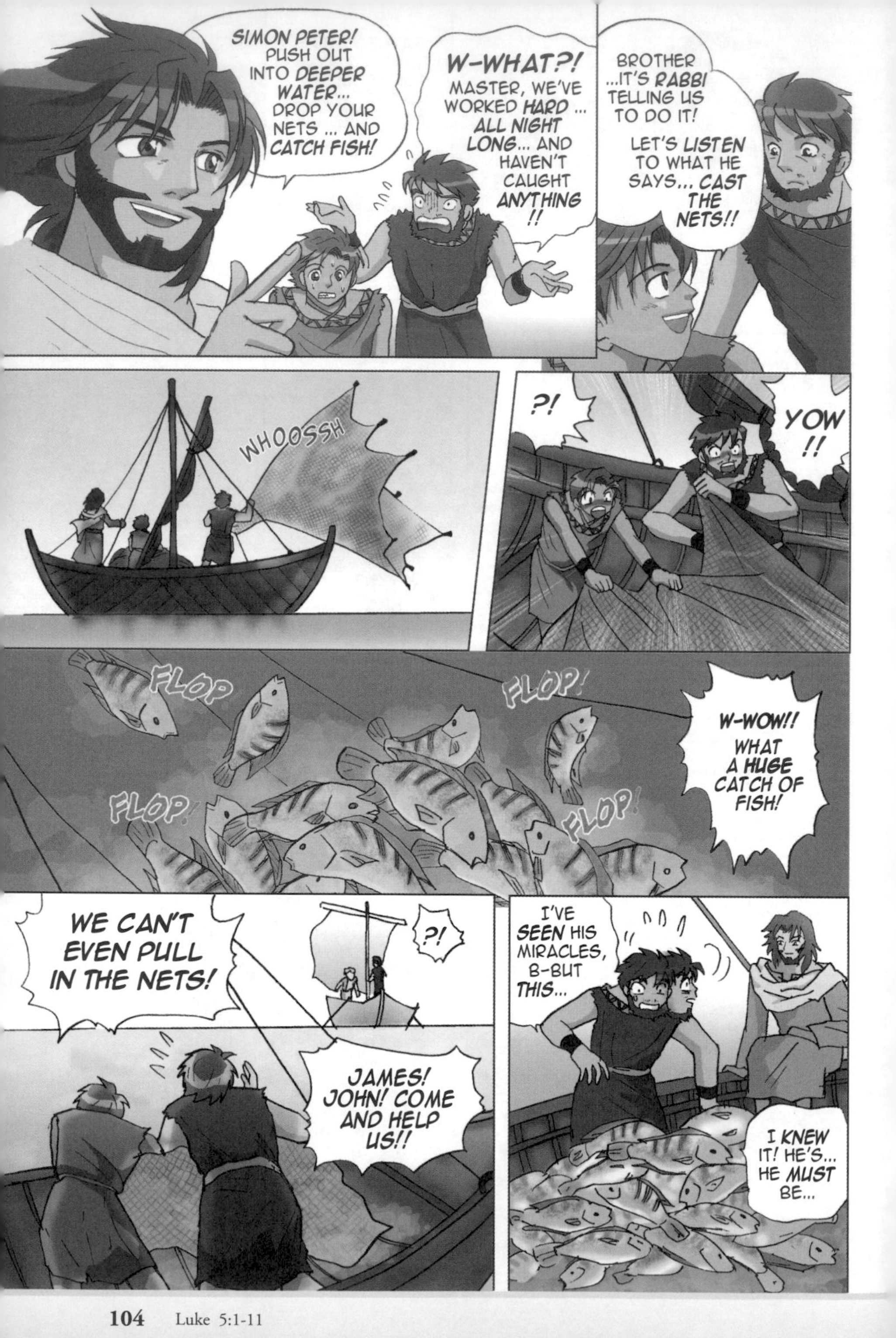
SIMON PETER! PUSH OUT INTO DEEPER WATER... DROP YOUR NETS ... AND CATCH FISH!
W-WHAT?! MASTER, WE'VE WORKED HARD ... ALL NIGHT LONG... AND HAVEN'T CAUGHT ANYTHING !!
BROTHER ...IT'S RABBI TELLING US TO DO IT!
LET'S LISTEN TO WHAT HE SAYS... CAST THE NETS!!
WHOOSSH
?!
YOW !!
FLOP
FLOP!
FLOP!
FLOP!
W-WOW!! WHAT A HUGE CATCH OF FISH!
WE CAN'T EVEN PULL IN THE NETS!
?!
JAMES! JOHN! COME AND HELP US!!
I'VE SEEN HIS MIRACLES, B-BUT THIS...
I KNEW IT! HE'S... HE MUST BE...

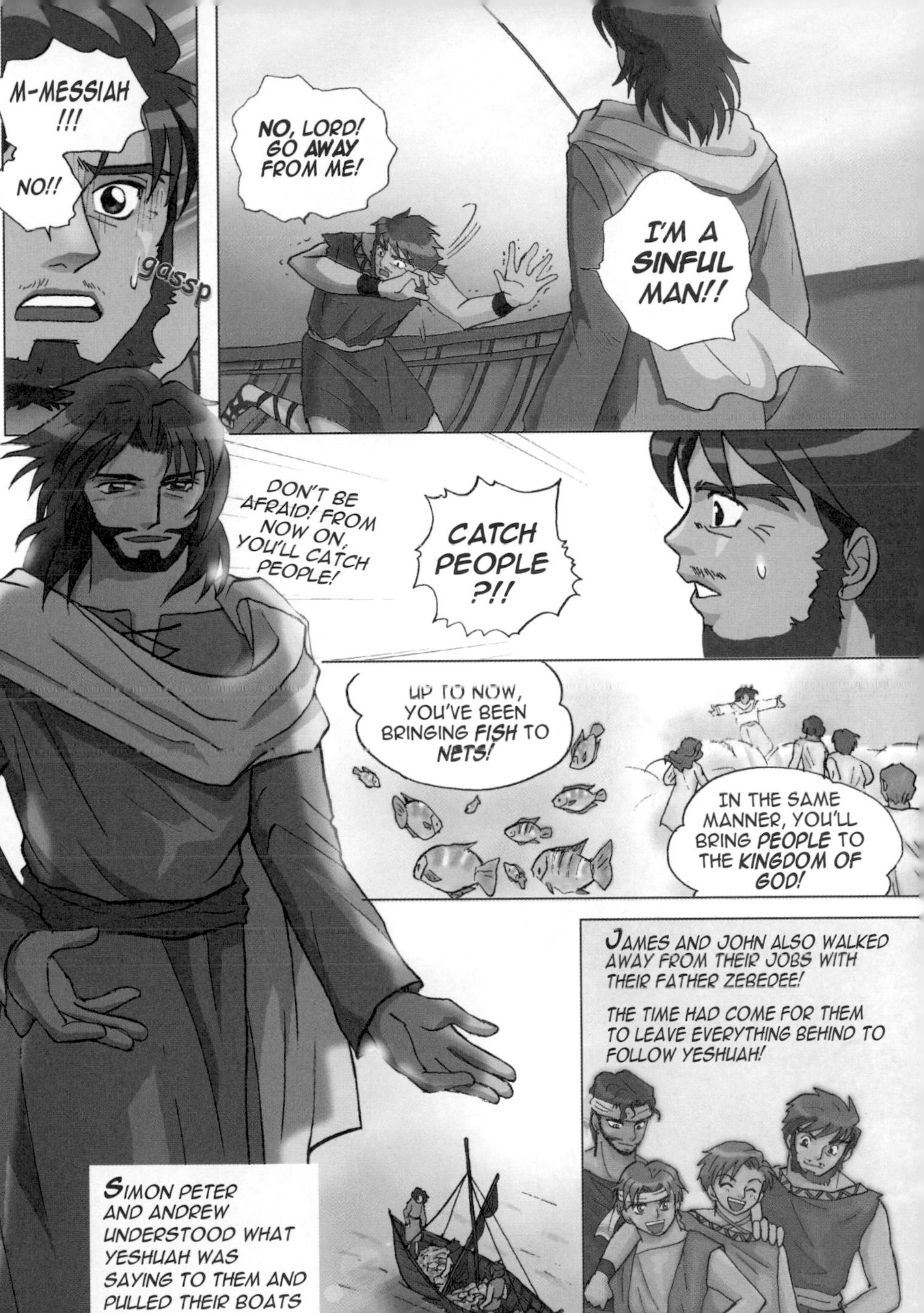
M-MESSIAH !!!
NO!!
gassp
NO, LORD! GO AWAY FROM ME!
I'M A SINFUL MAN!!
DON'T BE AFRAID! FROM NOW ON, YOU'LL CATCH PEOPLE!
CATCH PEOPLE ?!!
UP TO NOW, YOU'VE BEEN BRINGING FISH TO NETS!
IN THE SAME MANNER, YOU'LL BRING PEOPLE TO THE KINGDOM OF GOD!
JAMES AND JOHN ALSO WALKED AWAY FROM THEIR JOBS WITH THEIR FATHER ZEBEDEE!
THE TIME HAD COME FOR THEM TO LEAVE EVERYTHING BEHIND TO FOLLOW YESHUAH!
SIMON PETER AND ANDREW UNDERSTOOD WHAT YESHUAH WAS SAYING TO THEM AND PULLED THEIR BOATS UP ON SHORE...

Chapter II

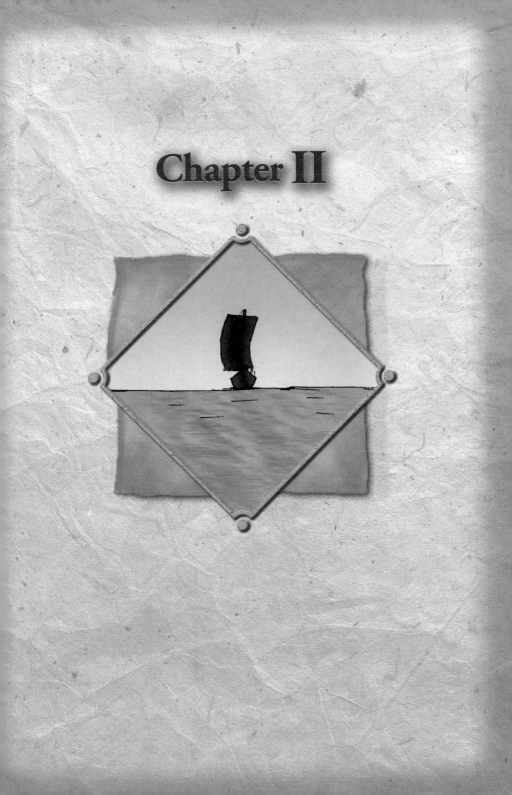

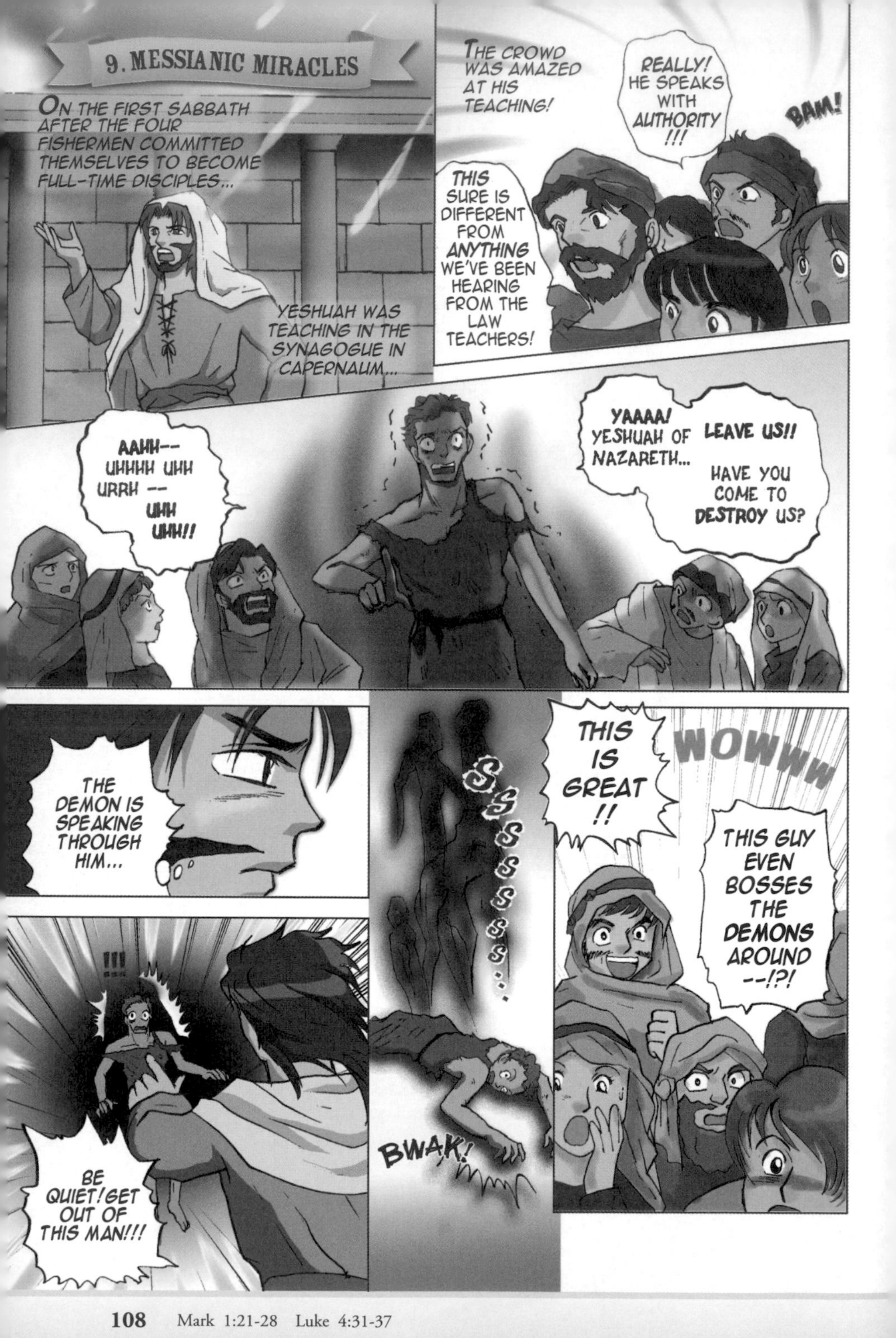
9. MESSIANIC MIRACLES
ON THE FIRST SABBATH AFTER THE FOUR FISHERMEN COMMITTED THEMSELVES TO BECOME FULL-TIME DISCIPLES...
YESHUAH WAS TEACHING IN THE SYNAGOGUE IN CAPERNAUM...
THE CROWD WAS AMAZED AT HIS TEACHING!
REALLY! HE SPEAKS WITH AUTHORITY !!!
BAM!
THIS SURE IS DIFFERENT FROM ANYTHING WE'VE BEEN HEARING FROM THE LAW TEACHERS!
YAAAA! YESHUAH OF NAZARETH... LEAVE US!! HAVE YOU COME TO DESTROY US?
AAHH-- UHHHH UHH URRH -- UHH UHH!!
THE DEMON IS SPEAKING THROUGH HIM...
BE QUIET! GET OUT OF THIS MAN!!!
SSSSSSS..
BWAK!
THIS IS GREAT !!
WOWWW
THIS GUY EVEN BOSSES THE DEMONS AROUND --!?!

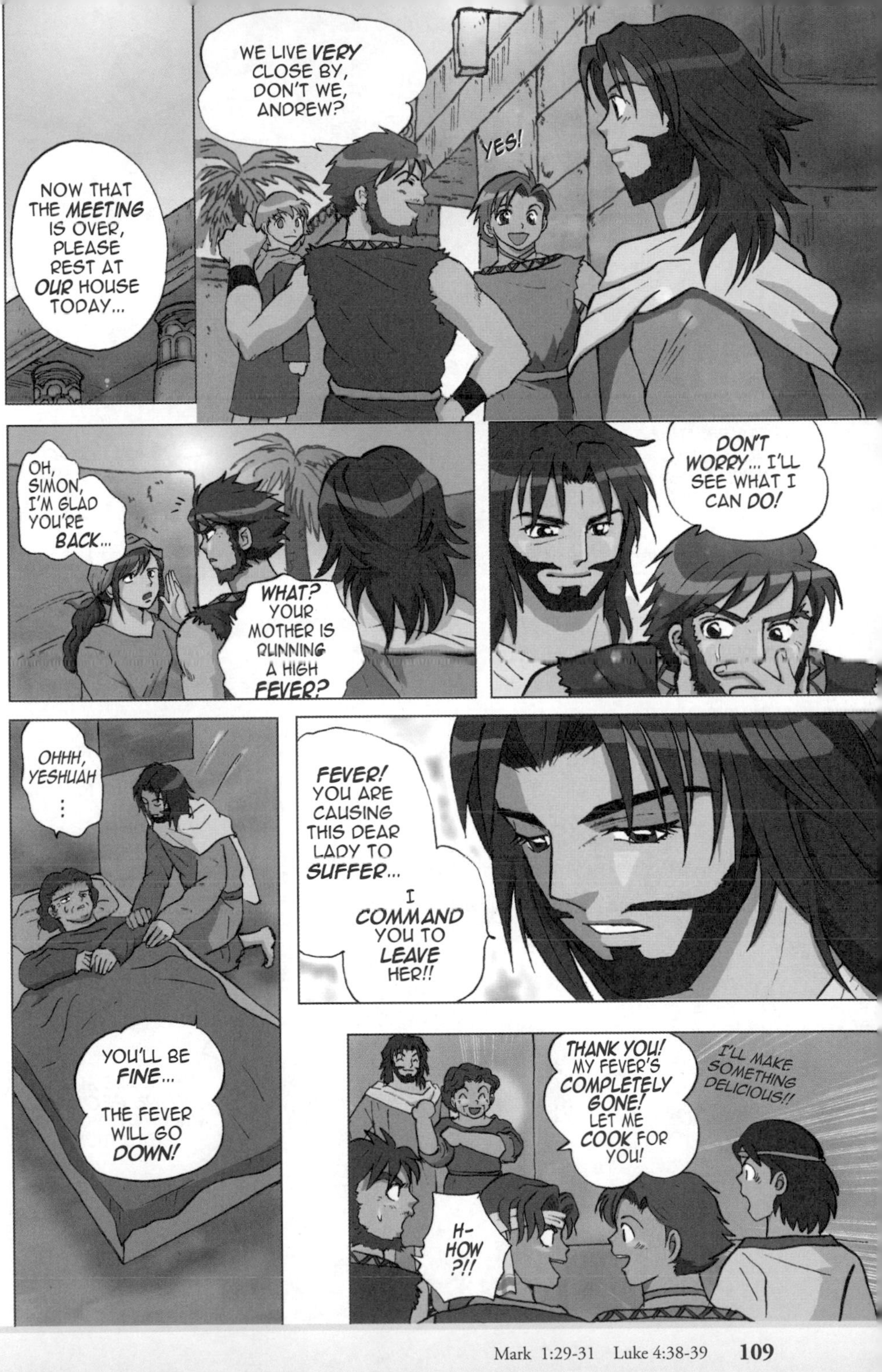
NOW THAT THE MEETING IS OVER, PLEASE REST AT OUR HOUSE TODAY...
WE LIVE VERY CLOSE BY, DON'T WE, ANDREW?
YES!
OH, SIMON, I'M GLAD YOU'RE BACK...
WHAT? YOUR MOTHER IS RUNNING A HIGH FEVER?
DON'T WORRY... I'LL SEE WHAT I CAN DO!
OHHH, YESHUAH ...
FEVER! YOU ARE CAUSING THIS DEAR LADY TO SUFFER...
I COMMAND YOU TO LEAVE HER!!
YOU'LL BE FINE...
THE FEVER WILL GO DOWN!
THANK YOU! MY FEVER'S COMPLETELY GONE! LET ME COOK FOR YOU!
I'LL MAKE SOMETHING DELICIOUS!!
H-HOW?!!

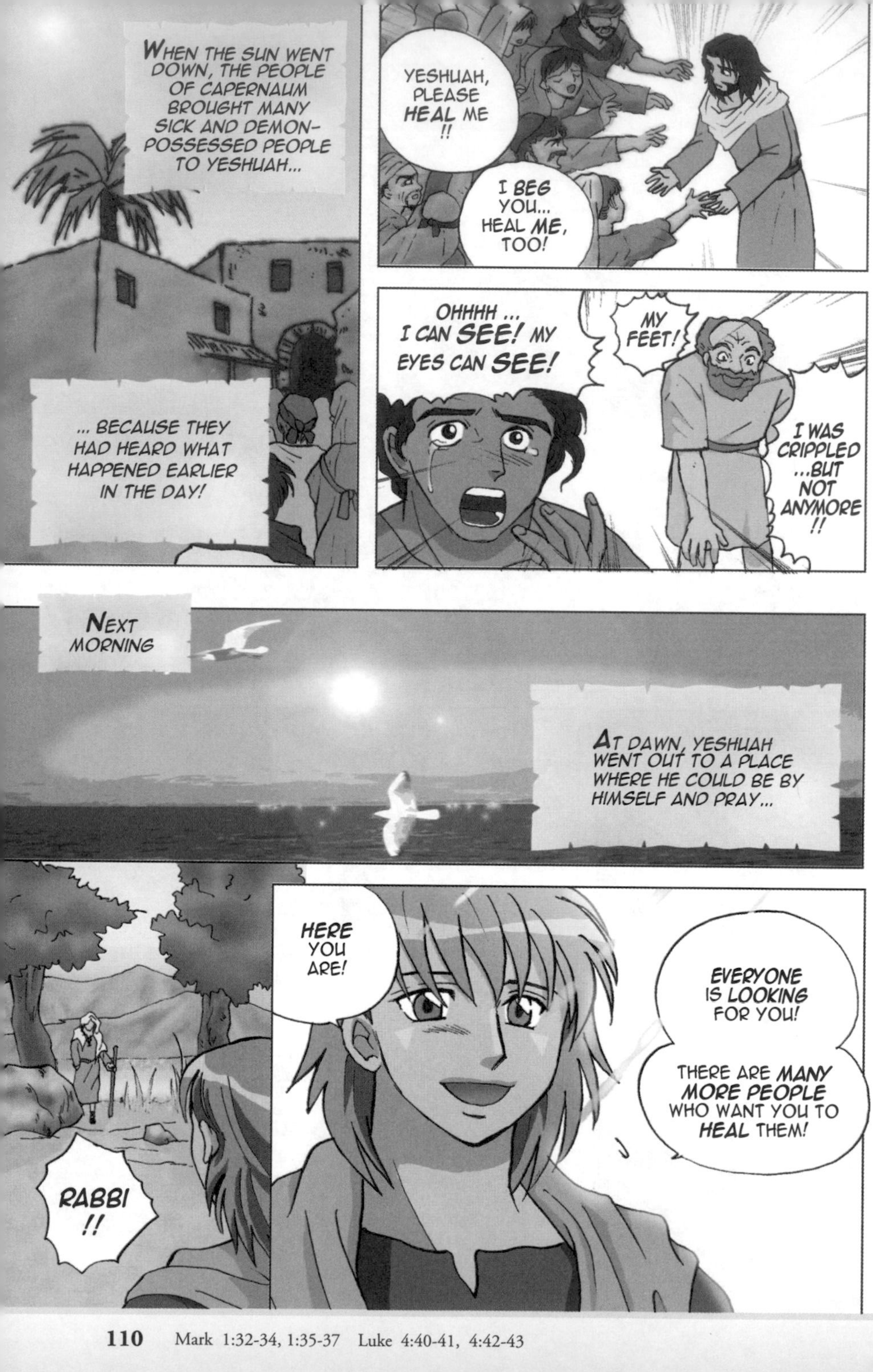
WHEN THE SUN WENT DOWN, THE PEOPLE OF CAPERNAUM BROUGHT MANY SICK AND DEMON-POSSESSED PEOPLE TO YESHUAH...
YESHUAH, PLEASE HEAL ME !!
I BEG YOU... HEAL ME, TOO!
... BECAUSE THEY HAD HEARD WHAT HAPPENED EARLIER IN THE DAY!
OHHHH ... I CAN SEE! MY EYES CAN SEE!
MY FEET!
I WAS CRIPPLED ...BUT NOT ANYMORE !!
NEXT MORNING
AT DAWN, YESHUAH WENT OUT TO A PLACE WHERE HE COULD BE BY HIMSELF AND PRAY...
RABBI !!
HERE YOU ARE!
EVERYONE IS LOOKING FOR YOU!
THERE ARE MANY MORE PEOPLE WHO WANT YOU TO HEAL THEM!

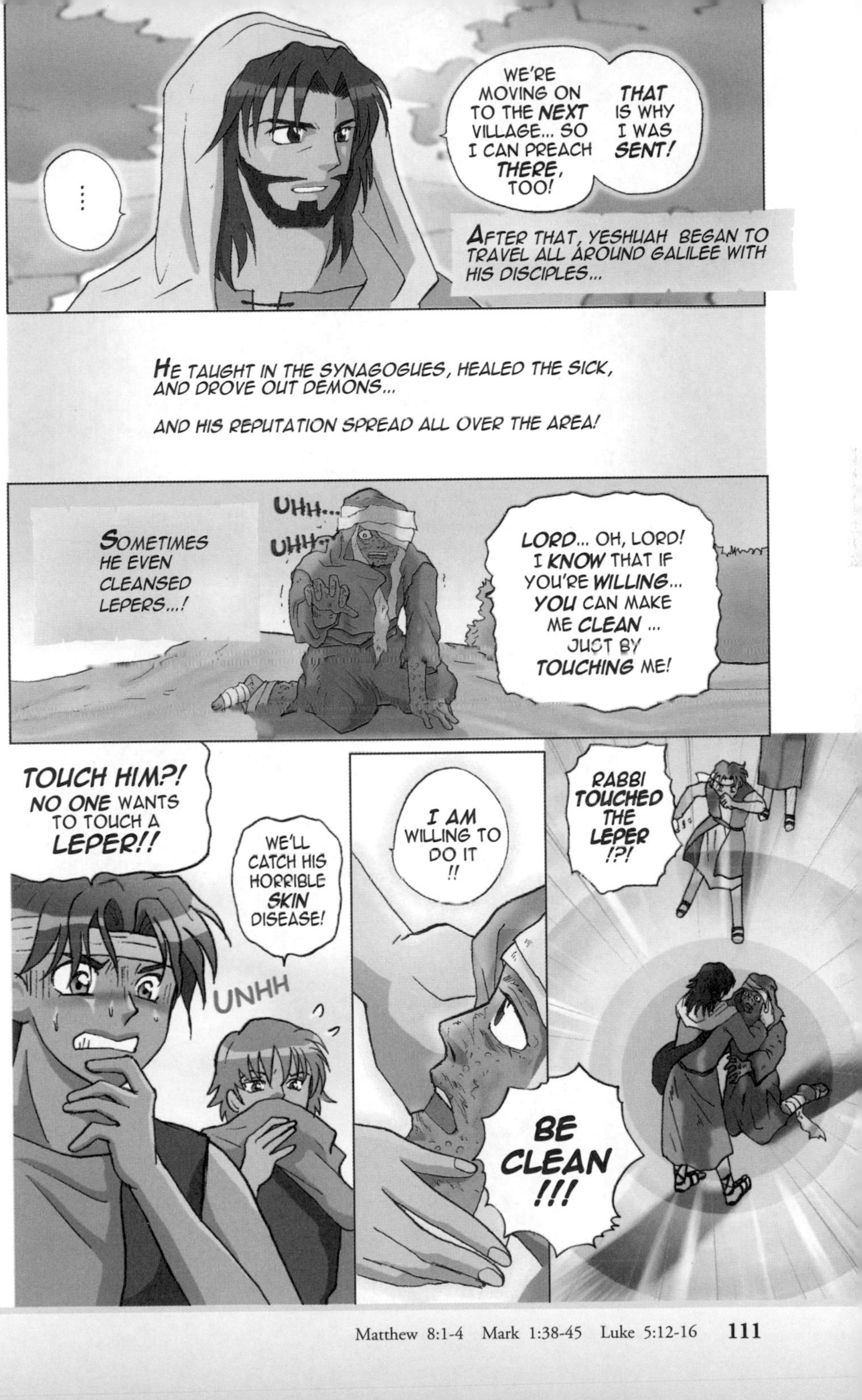

...
WE'RE MOVING ON TO THE NEXT VILLAGE... SO I CAN PREACH THERE, TOO!
THAT IS WHY I WAS SENT!
AFTER THAT, YESHUAH BEGAN TO TRAVEL ALL AROUND GALILEE WITH HIS DISCIPLES...
HE TAUGHT IN THE SYNAGOGUES, HEALED THE SICK, AND DROVE OUT DEMONS...
AND HIS REPUTATION SPREAD ALL OVER THE AREA!
SOMETIMES HE EVEN CLEANSED LEPERS...!
UHH...
UHH...
LORD... OH, LORD! I KNOW THAT IF YOU'RE WILLING... YOU CAN MAKE ME CLEAN ... JUST BY TOUCHING ME!
TOUCH HIM?! NO ONE WANTS TO TOUCH A LEPER!!
WE'LL CATCH HIS HORRIBLE SKIN DISEASE!
UNHH
I AM WILLING TO DO IT !!
BE CLEAN !!!
RABBI TOUCHED THE LEPER !?!

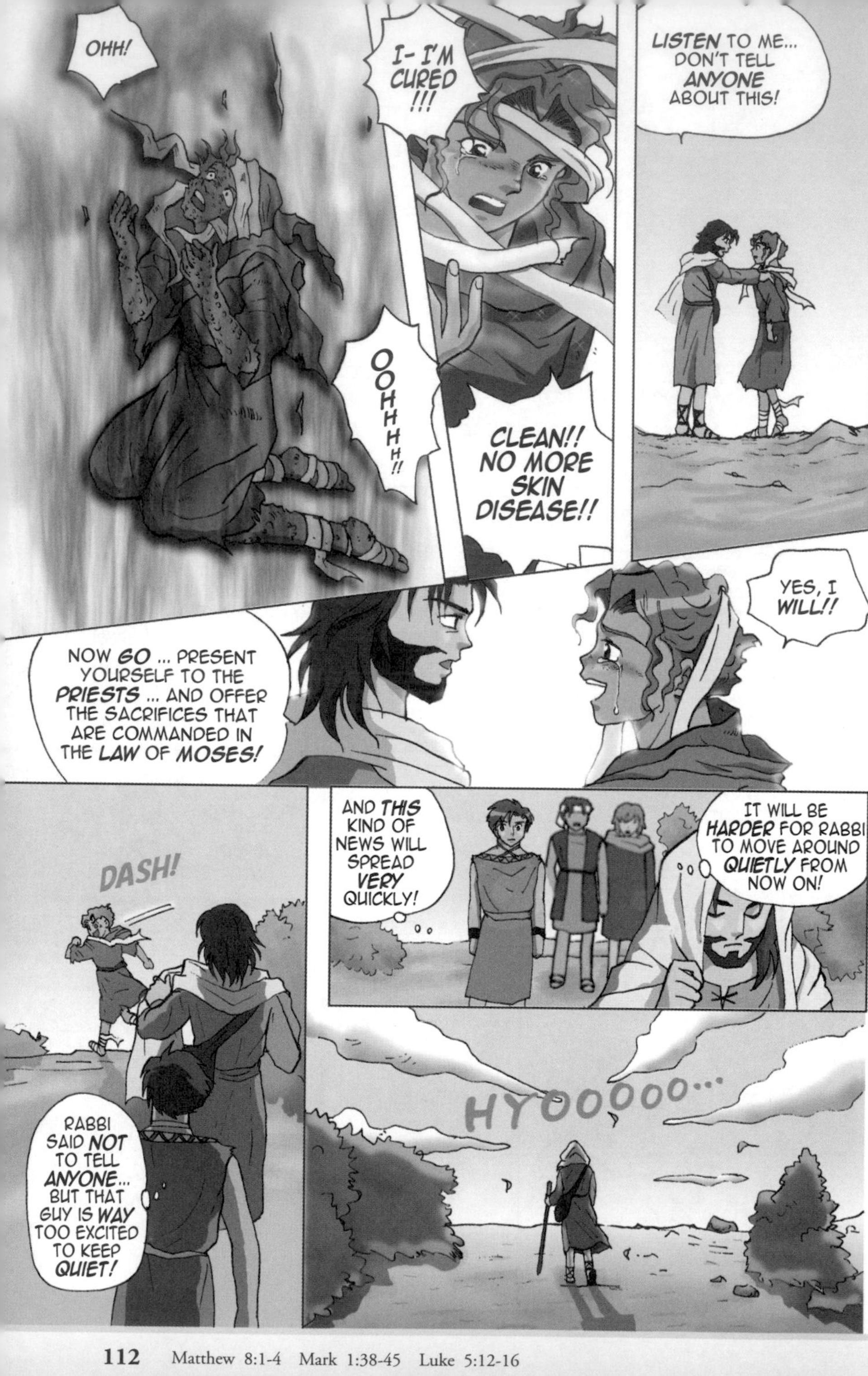
OHH!
I- I'M CURED !!!
OOHHHHH!!
CLEAN!! NO MORE SKIN DISEASE!!
LISTEN TO ME... DON'T TELL ANYONE ABOUT THIS!
NOW GO ... PRESENT YOURSELF TO THE PRIESTS ... AND OFFER THE SACRIFICES THAT ARE COMMANDED IN THE LAW OF MOSES!
YES, I WILL!!
DASH!
RABBI SAID NOT TO TELL ANYONE... BUT THAT GUY IS WAY TOO EXCITED TO KEEP QUIET!
AND THIS KIND OF NEWS WILL SPREAD VERY QUICKLY!
IT WILL BE HARDER FOR RABBI TO MOVE AROUND QUIETLY FROM NOW ON!
HYOOOOO...

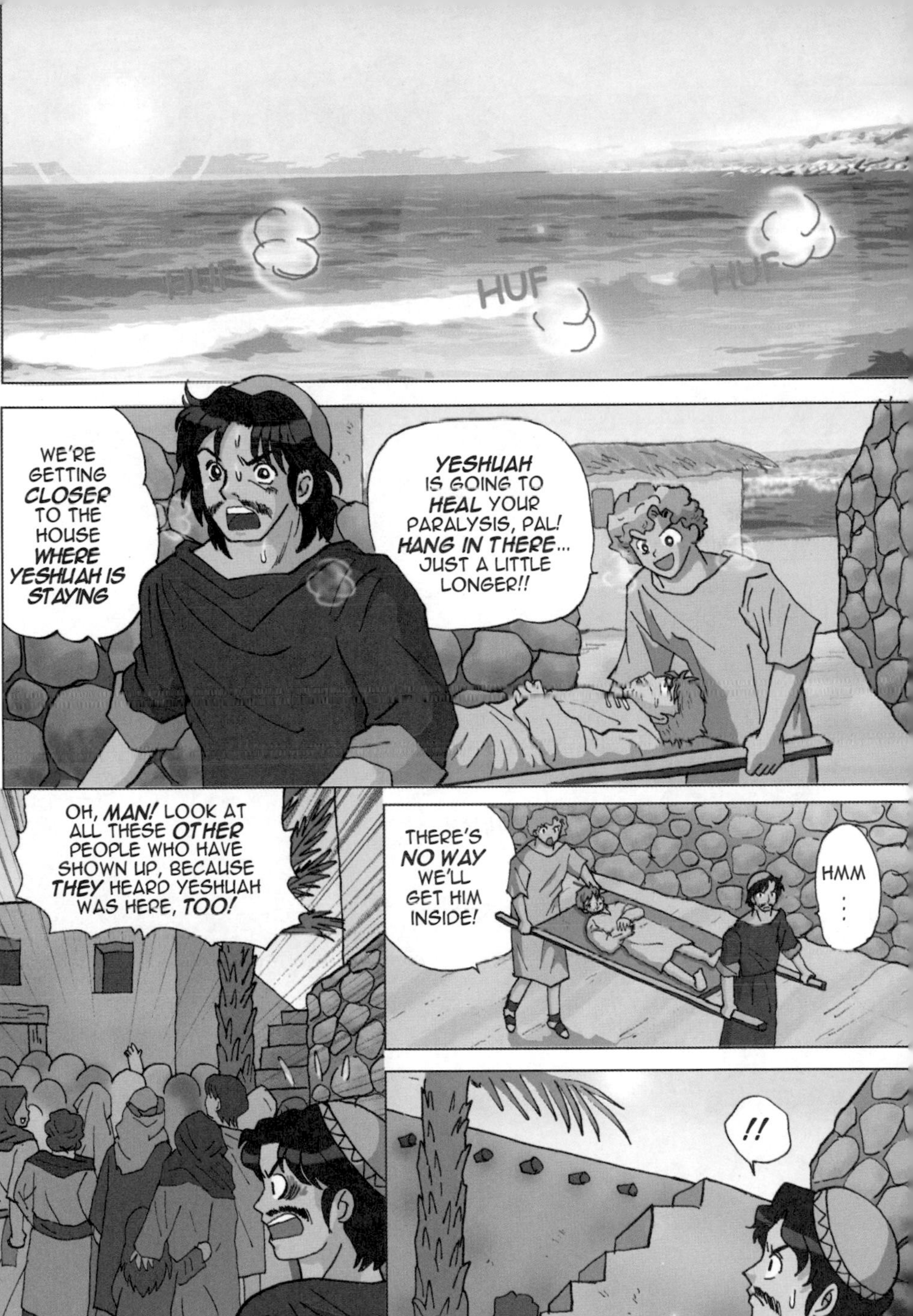
HUF
HUF
HUF
WE'RE GETTING CLOSER TO THE HOUSE WHERE YESHUAH IS STAYING
YESHUAH IS GOING TO HEAL YOUR PARALYSIS, PAL! HANG IN THERE... JUST A LITTLE LONGER!!
OH, MAN! LOOK AT ALL THESE OTHER PEOPLE WHO HAVE SHOWN UP, BECAUSE THEY HEARD YESHUAH WAS HERE, TOO!
THERE'S NO WAY WE'LL GET HIM INSIDE!
HMM ...
!!

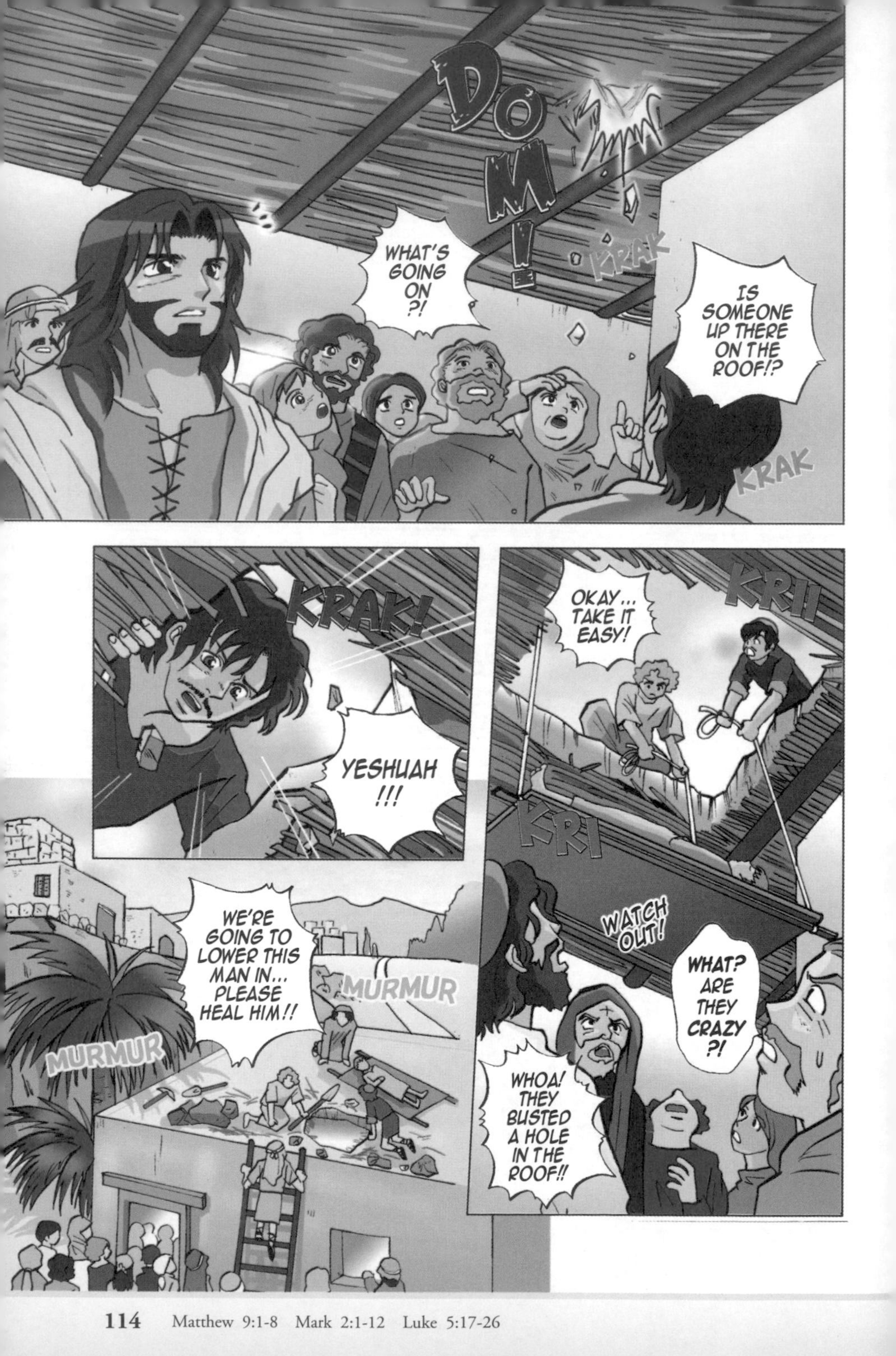
DOM!
WHAT'S GOING ON ?!
KRAK
IS SOMEONE UP THERE ON THE ROOF!?
KRAK
KRAK!
YESHUAH !!!
OKAY... TAKE IT EASY!
KRII
KRI
WATCH OUT!
WHAT? ARE THEY CRAZY ?!
WHOA! THEY BUSTED A HOLE IN THE ROOF!!
WE'RE GOING TO LOWER THIS MAN IN... PLEASE HEAL HIM!!
MURMUR
MURMUR

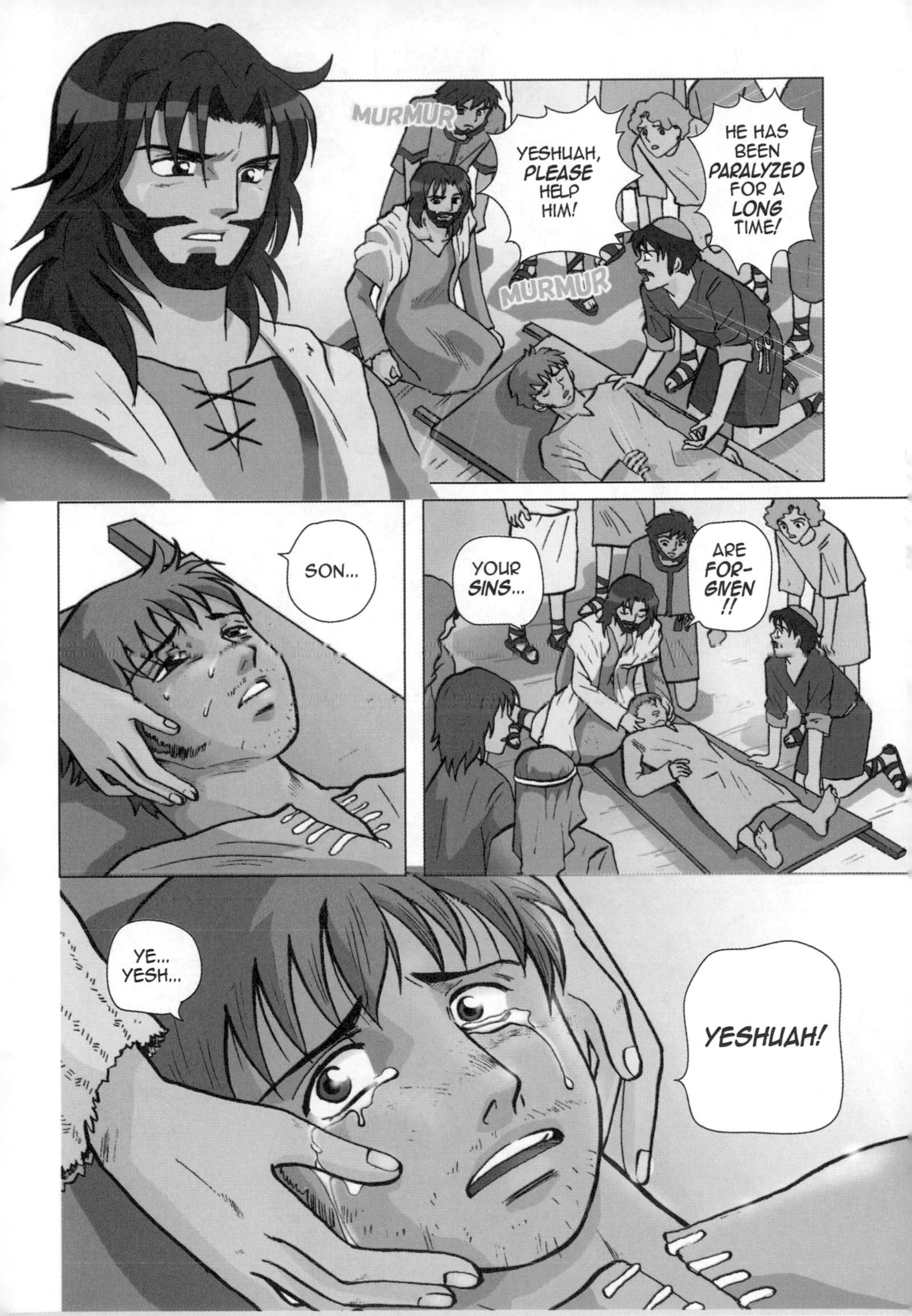
MURMUR
YESHUAH, PLEASE HELP HIM!
HE HAS BEEN PARALYZED FOR A LONG TIME!
MURMUR
SON...
YOUR SINS...
ARE FOR-GIVEN!!
YE... YESH...
YESHUAH!

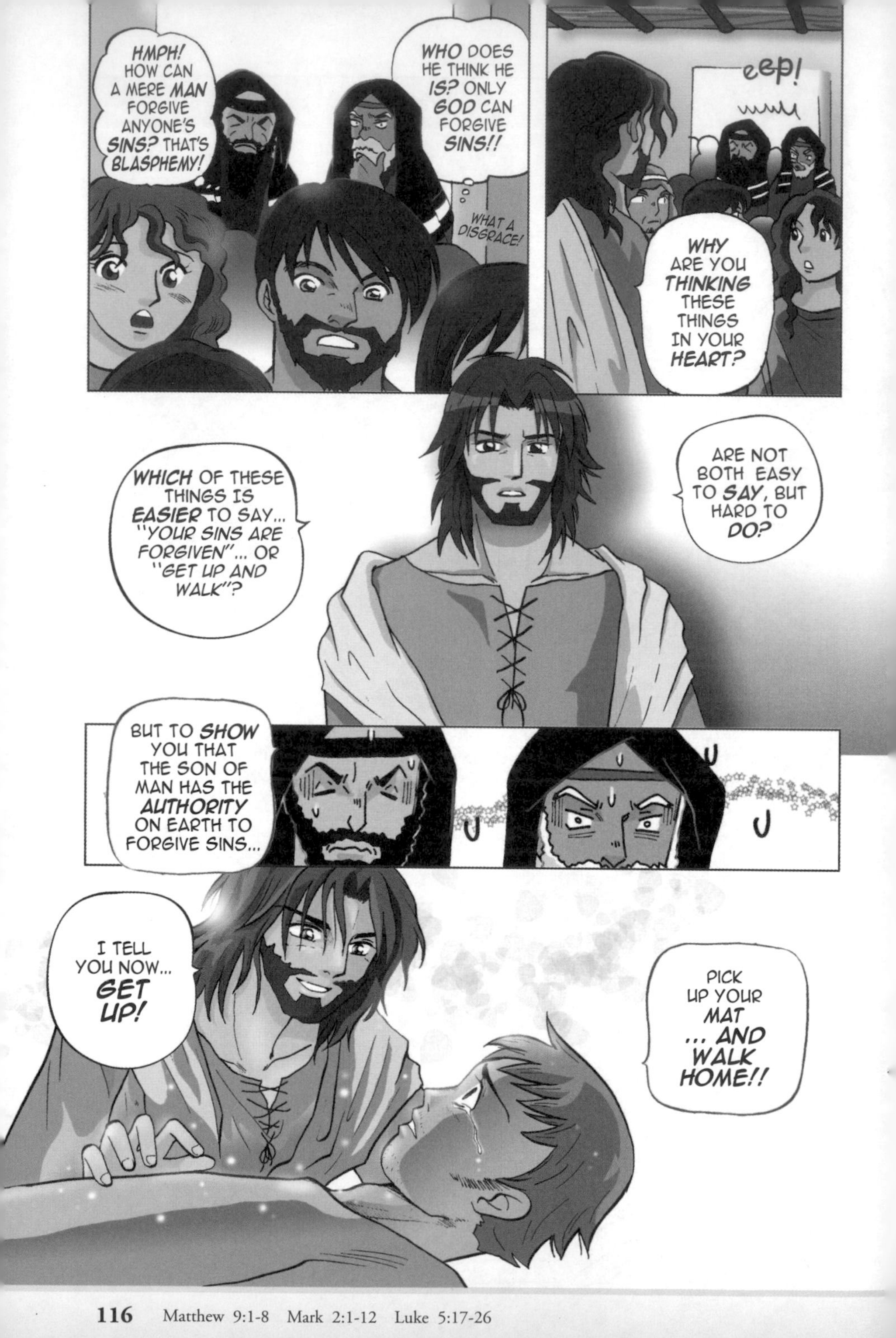
HMPH! HOW CAN A MERE MAN FORGIVE ANYONE'S SINS? THAT'S BLASPHEMY!
WHO DOES HE THINK HE IS? ONLY GOD CAN FORGIVE SINS!!
WHAT A DISGRACE!
eep!
WHY ARE YOU THINKING THESE THINGS IN YOUR HEART?
WHICH OF THESE THINGS IS EASIER TO SAY... "YOUR SINS ARE FORGIVEN"... OR "GET UP AND WALK"?
ARE NOT BOTH EASY TO SAY, BUT HARD TO DO?
BUT TO SHOW YOU THAT THE SON OF MAN HAS THE AUTHORITY ON EARTH TO FORGIVE SINS...
I TELL YOU NOW... GET UP!
PICK UP YOUR MAT ... AND WALK HOME!!

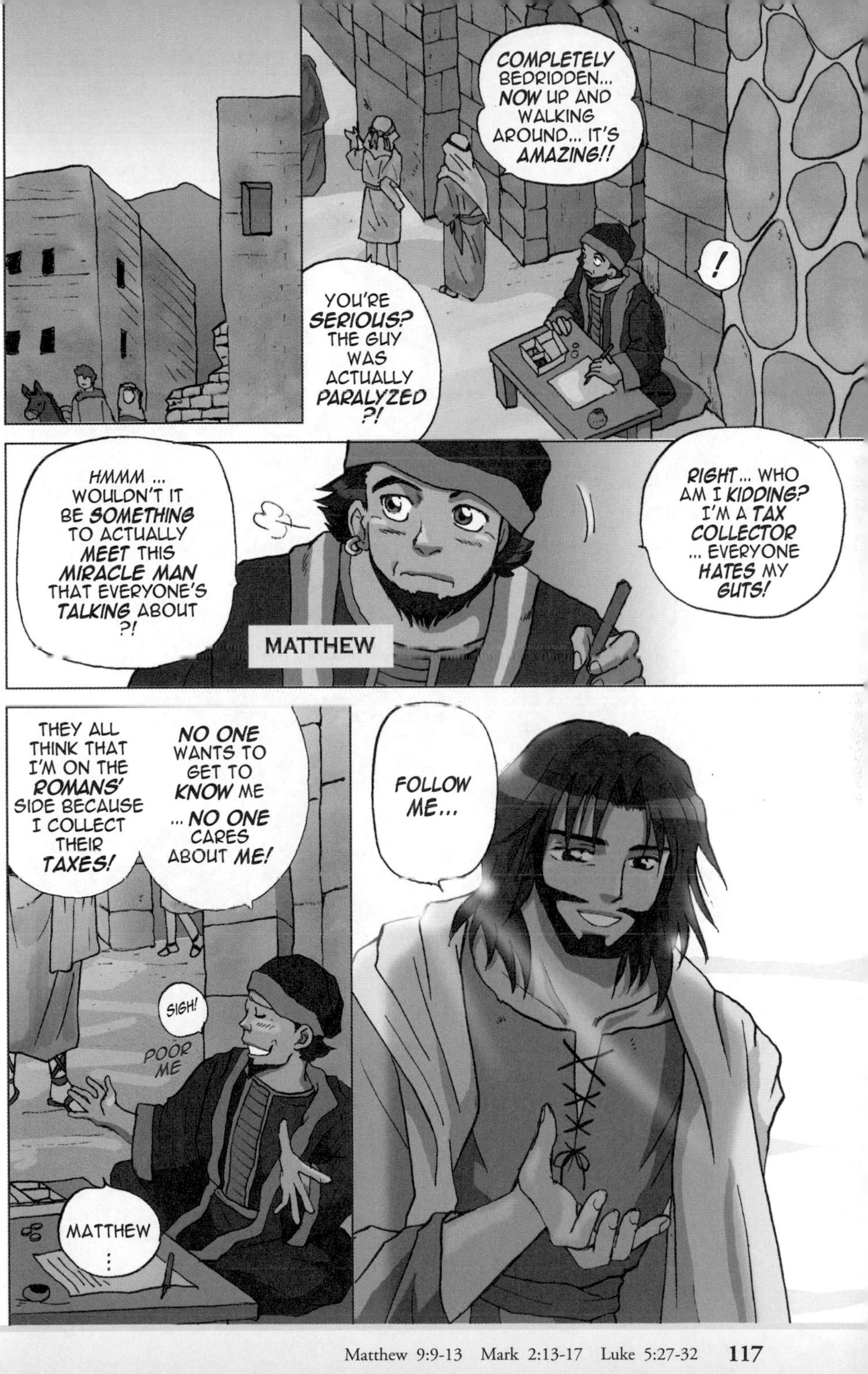
COMPLETELY BEDRIDDEN... NOW UP AND WALKING AROUND... IT'S AMAZING!!
YOU'RE SERIOUS? THE GUY WAS ACTUALLY PARALYZED ?!
!
HMMM ... WOULDN'T IT BE SOMETHING TO ACTUALLY MEET THIS MIRACLE MAN THAT EVERYONE'S TALKING ABOUT ?!
MATTHEW
RIGHT... WHO AM I KIDDING? I'M A TAX COLLECTOR ... EVERYONE HATES MY GUTS!
THEY ALL THINK THAT I'M ON THE ROMANS' SIDE BECAUSE I COLLECT THEIR TAXES!
NO ONE WANTS TO GET TO KNOW ME ... NO ONE CARES ABOUT ME!
SIGH!
POOR ME
MATTHEW ...
FOLLOW ME...

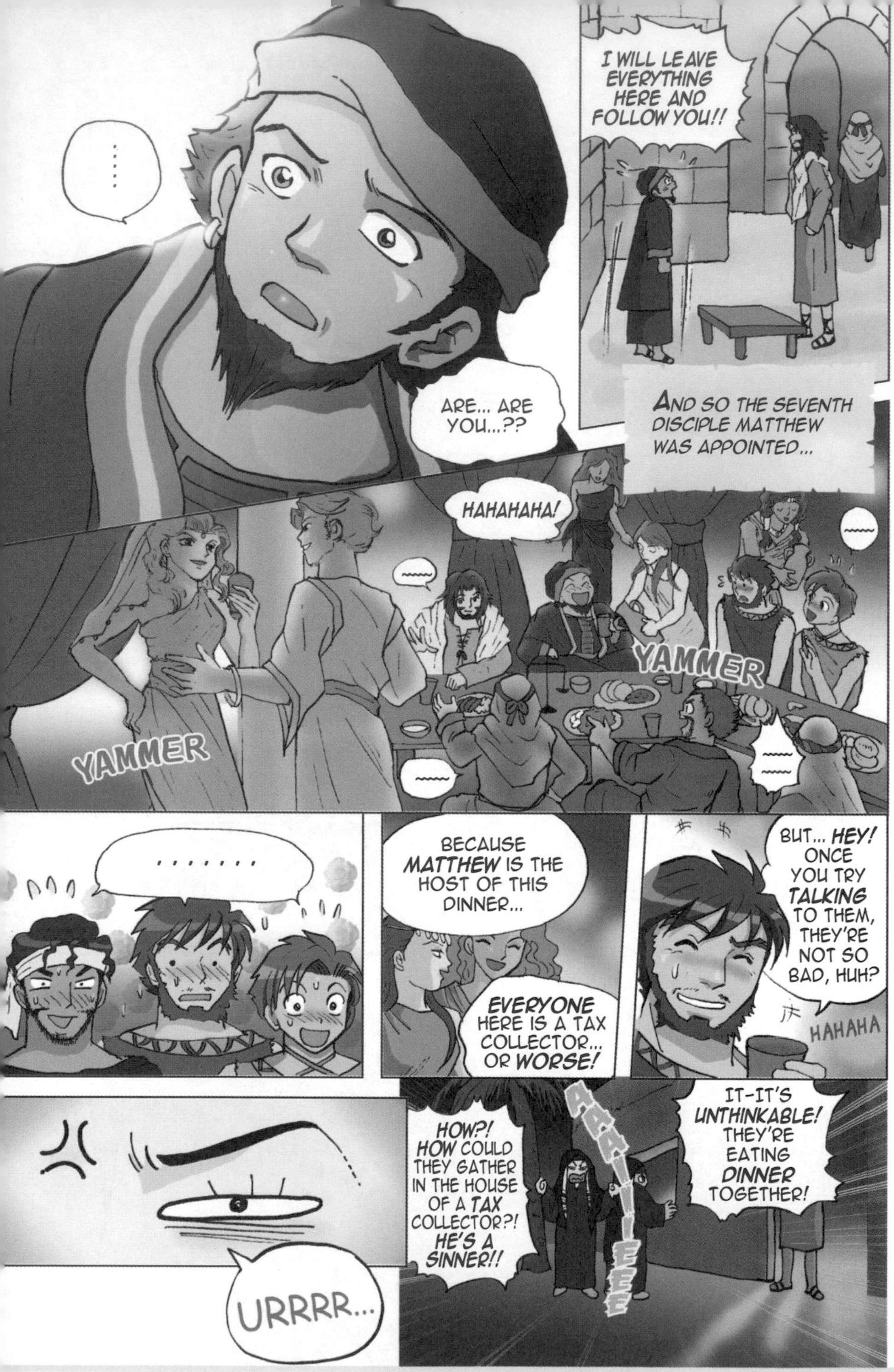
......
ARE... ARE YOU...??
I WILL LEAVE EVERYTHING HERE AND FOLLOW YOU!!
AND SO THE SEVENTH DISCIPLE MATTHEW WAS APPOINTED...
HAHAHAHA!
YAMMER
YAMMER
....
BECAUSE MATTHEW IS THE HOST OF THIS DINNER...
EVERYONE HERE IS A TAX COLLECTOR... OR WORSE!
BUT... HEY! ONCE YOU TRY TALKING TO THEM, THEY'RE NOT SO BAD, HUH?
HAHAHA
URRRR...
HOW?! HOW COULD THEY GATHER IN THE HOUSE OF A TAX COLLECTOR?! HE'S A SINNER!!
AAAIIIIEEE
IT-IT'S UNTHINKABLE! THEY'RE EATING DINNER TOGETHER!

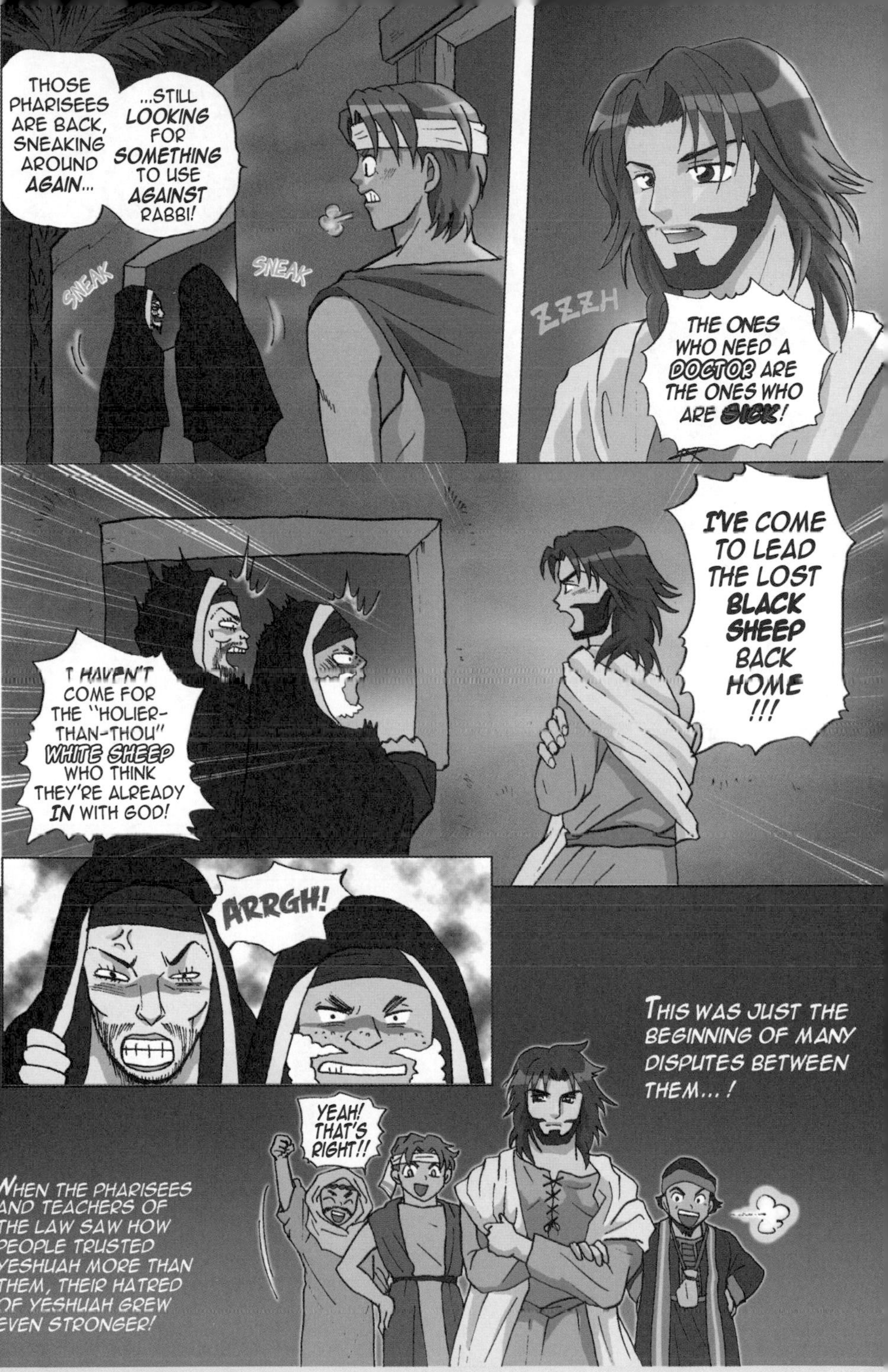
THOSE PHARISEES ARE BACK, SNEAKING AROUND AGAIN...
...STILL LOOKING FOR SOMETHING TO USE AGAINST RABBI!
SNEAK
SNEAK
ZZZH
THE ONES WHO NEED A DOCTOR ARE THE ONES WHO ARE SICK!
I'VE COME TO LEAD THE LOST BLACK SHEEP BACK HOME!!!
I HAVEN'T COME FOR THE "HOLIER-THAN-THOU" WHITE SHEEP WHO THINK THEY'RE ALREADY IN WITH GOD!
ARRGH!
THIS WAS JUST THE BEGINNING OF MANY DISPUTES BETWEEN THEM...!
YEAH! THAT'S RIGHT!!
WHEN THE PHARISEES AND TEACHERS OF THE LAW SAW HOW PEOPLE TRUSTED YESHUAH MORE THAN THEM, THEIR HATRED OF YESHUAH GREW EVEN STRONGER!

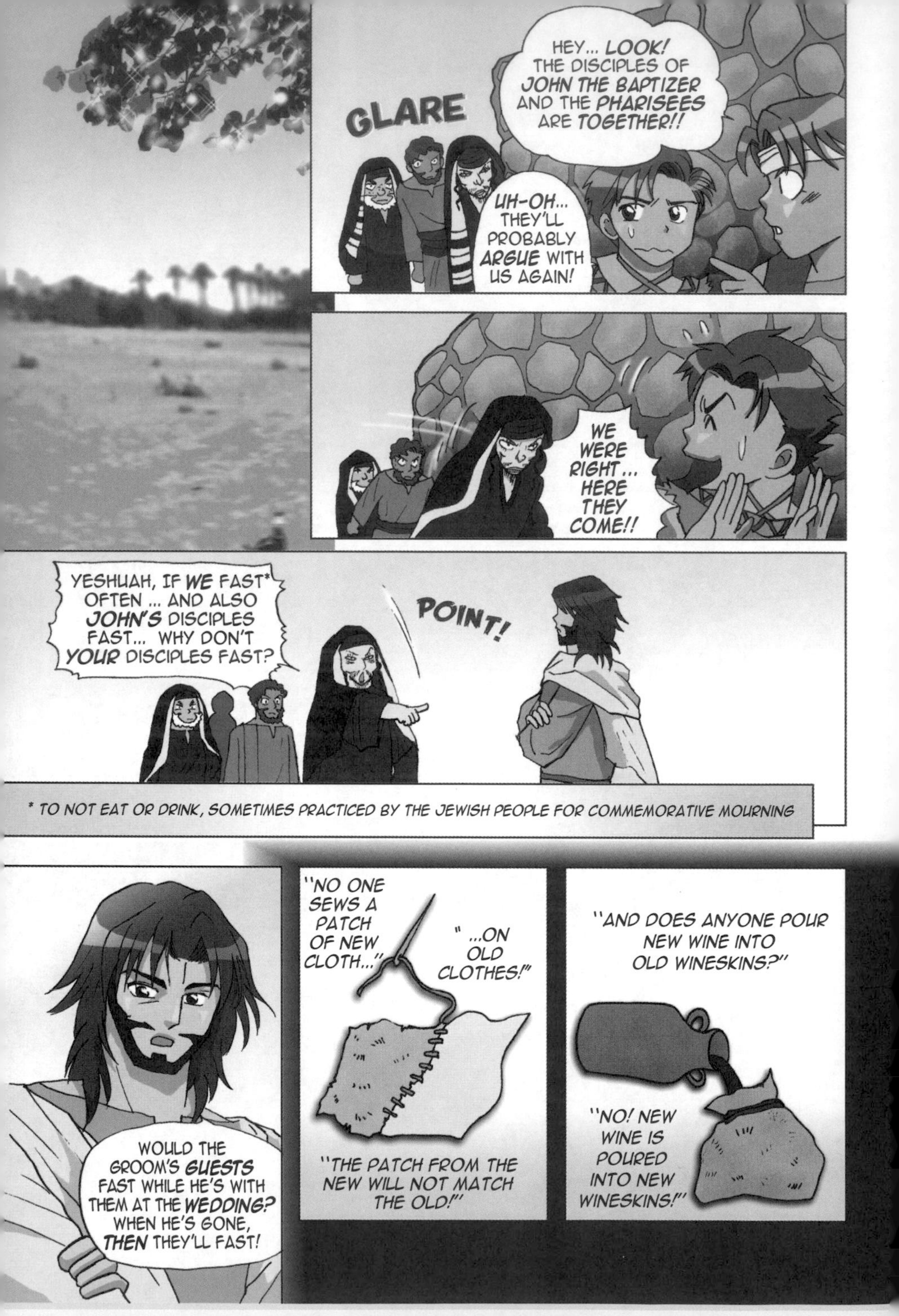
HEY... LOOK! THE DISCIPLES OF JOHN THE BAPTIZER AND THE PHARISEES ARE TOGETHER!!
GLARE
UH-OH... THEY'LL PROBABLY ARGUE WITH US AGAIN!
WE WERE RIGHT... HERE THEY COME!!
YESHUAH, IF WE FAST* OFTEN ... AND ALSO JOHN'S DISCIPLES FAST... WHY DON'T YOUR DISCIPLES FAST?
POINT!
* TO NOT EAT OR DRINK, SOMETIMES PRACTICED BY THE JEWISH PEOPLE FOR COMMEMORATIVE MOURNING
WOULD THE GROOM'S GUESTS FAST WHILE HE'S WITH THEM AT THE WEDDING? WHEN HE'S GONE, THEN THEY'LL FAST!
"NO ONE SEWS A PATCH OF NEW CLOTH..."
" ...ON OLD CLOTHES!"
"THE PATCH FROM THE NEW WILL NOT MATCH THE OLD!"
"AND DOES ANYONE POUR NEW WINE INTO OLD WINESKINS?"
"NO! NEW WINE IS POURED INTO NEW WINESKINS!"

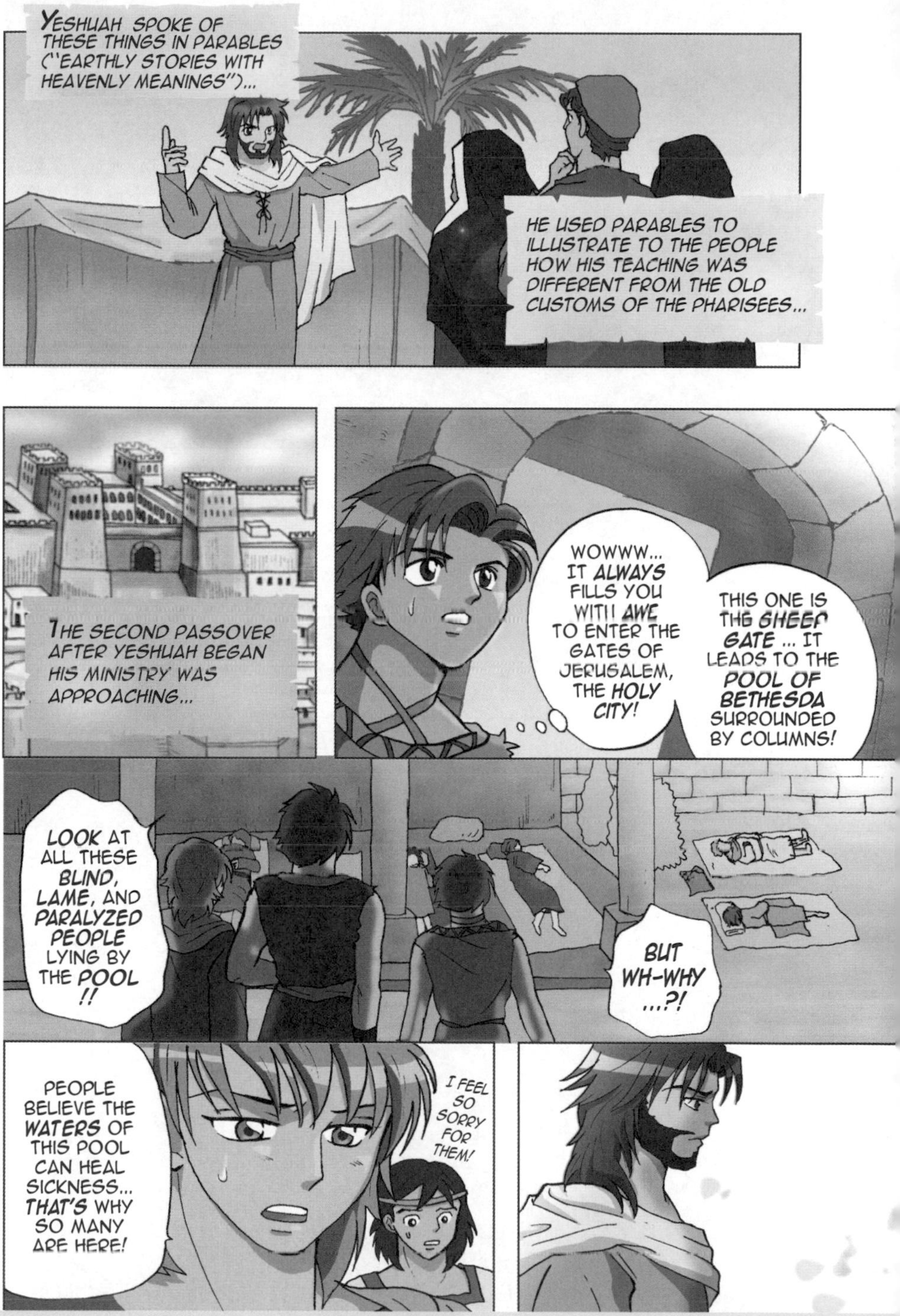

YESHUAH SPOKE OF THESE THINGS IN PARABLES ("EARTHLY STORIES WITH HEAVENLY MEANINGS")...
HE USED PARABLES TO ILLUSTRATE TO THE PEOPLE HOW HIS TEACHING WAS DIFFERENT FROM THE OLD CUSTOMS OF THE PHARISEES...
THE SECOND PASSOVER AFTER YESHUAH BEGAN HIS MINISTRY WAS APPROACHING...
WOWWW... IT ALWAYS FILLS YOU WITH AWE TO ENTER THE GATES OF JERUSALEM, THE HOLY CITY!
THIS ONE IS THE SHEEP GATE ... IT LEADS TO THE POOL OF BETHESDA SURROUNDED BY COLUMNS!
LOOK AT ALL THESE BLIND, LAME, AND PARALYZED PEOPLE LYING BY THE POOL !!
BUT WH-WHY ...?!
PEOPLE BELIEVE THE WATERS OF THIS POOL CAN HEAL SICKNESS... THAT'S WHY SO MANY ARE HERE!
I FEEL SO SORRY FOR THEM!

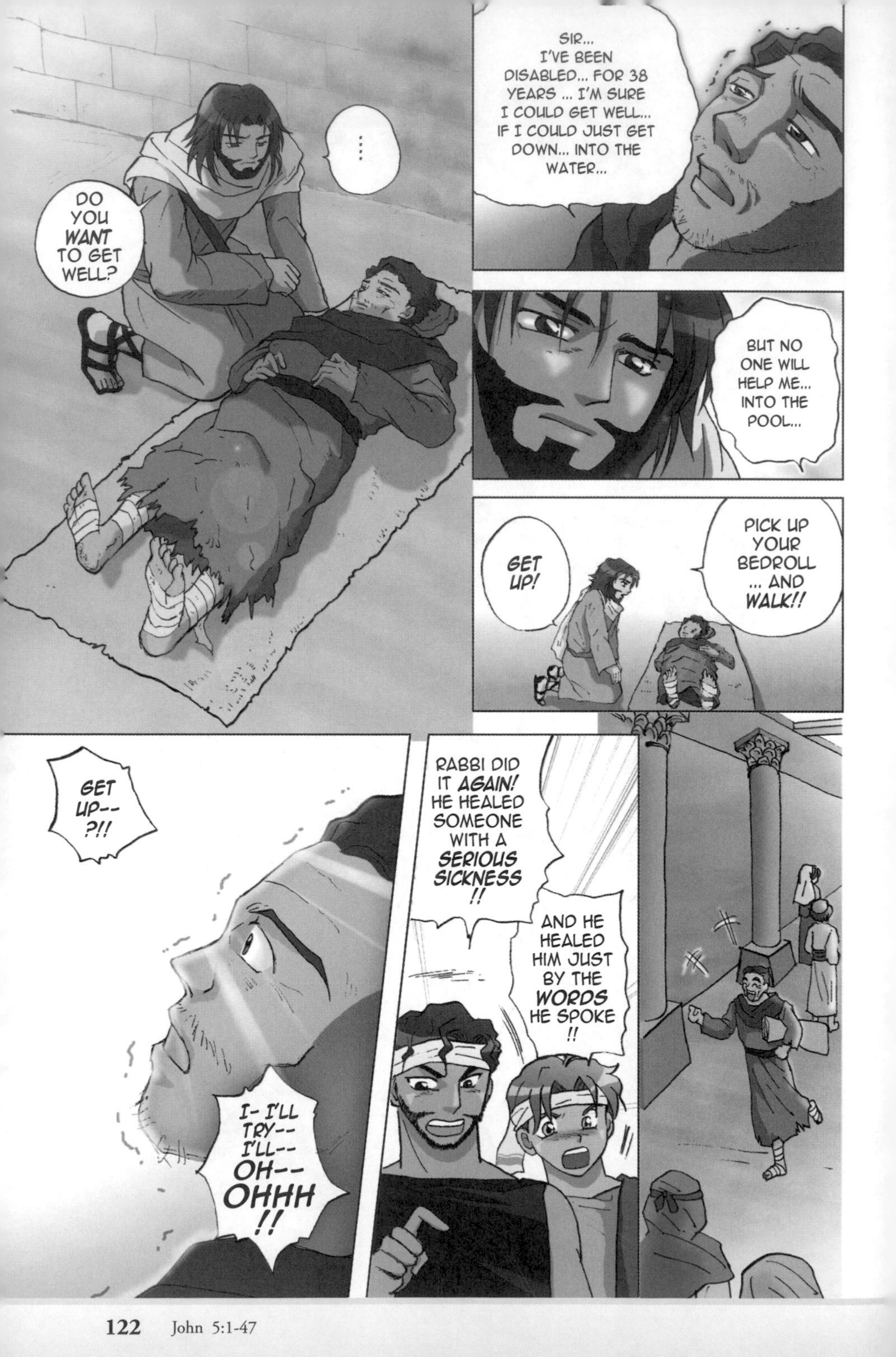
DO YOU WANT TO GET WELL?
...
SIR... I'VE BEEN DISABLED... FOR 38 YEARS ... I'M SURE I COULD GET WELL... IF I COULD JUST GET DOWN... INTO THE WATER...
BUT NO ONE WILL HELP ME... INTO THE POOL...
PICK UP YOUR BEDROLL ... AND WALK!!
GET UP!
GET UP--?!!
I- I'LL TRY-- I'LL-- OH-- OHHH !!
RABBI DID IT AGAIN! HE HEALED SOMEONE WITH A SERIOUS SICKNESS !!
AND HE HEALED HIM JUST BY THE WORDS HE SPOKE !!

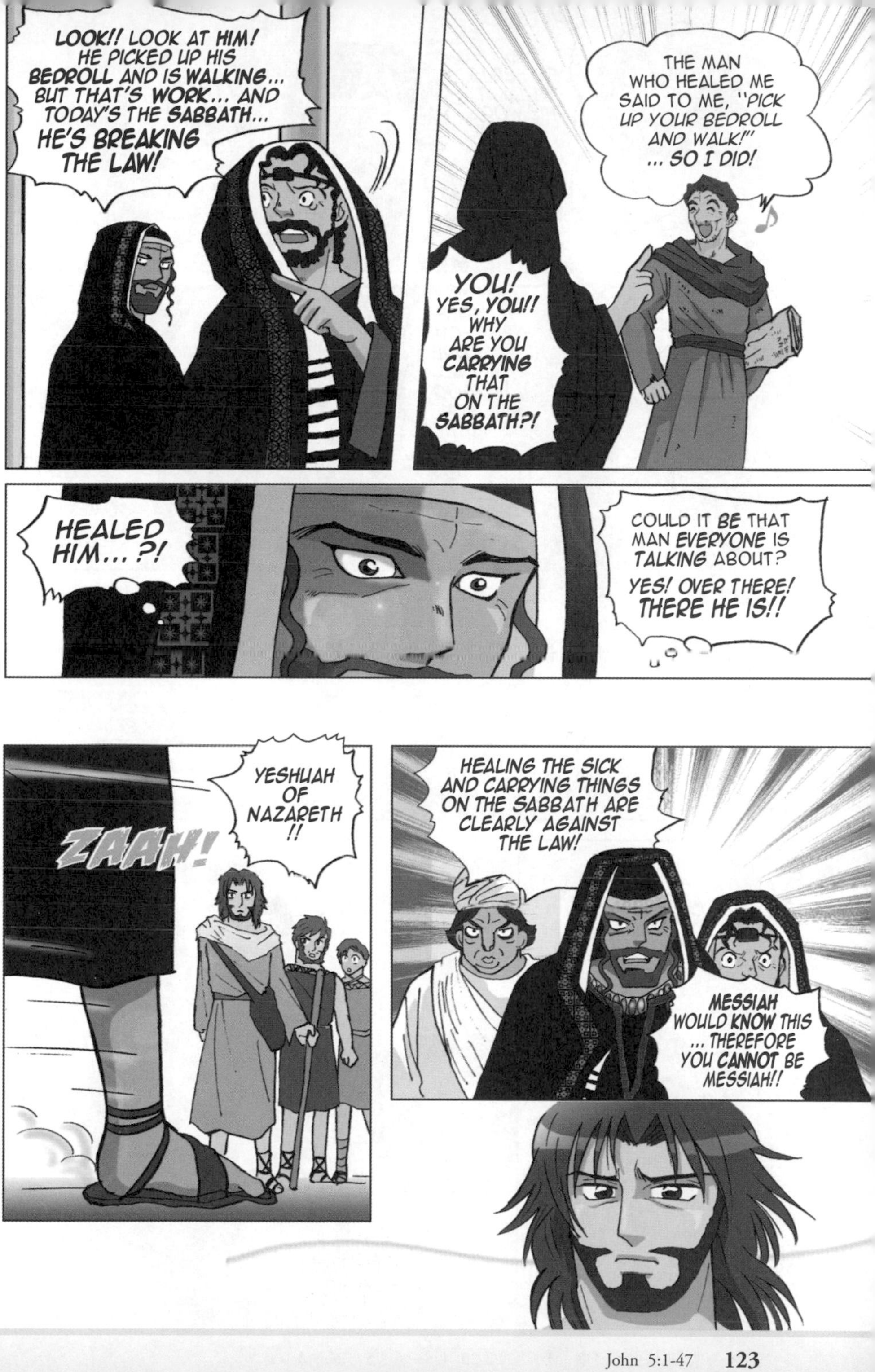
LOOK!! LOOK AT HIM! HE PICKED UP HIS BEDROLL AND IS WALKING... BUT THAT'S WORK... AND TODAY'S THE SABBATH... HE'S BREAKING THE LAW!
YOU! YES, YOU!! WHY ARE YOU CARRYING THAT ON THE SABBATH?!
THE MAN WHO HEALED ME SAID TO ME, "PICK UP YOUR BEDROLL AND WALK!" ... SO I DID!
HEALED HIM... ?!
COULD IT BE THAT MAN EVERYONE IS TALKING ABOUT? YES! OVER THERE! THERE HE IS!!
YESHUAH OF NAZARETH !!
ZAAH!
HEALING THE SICK AND CARRYING THINGS ON THE SABBATH ARE CLEARLY AGAINST THE LAW!
MESSIAH WOULD KNOW THIS ... THEREFORE YOU CANNOT BE MESSIAH!!

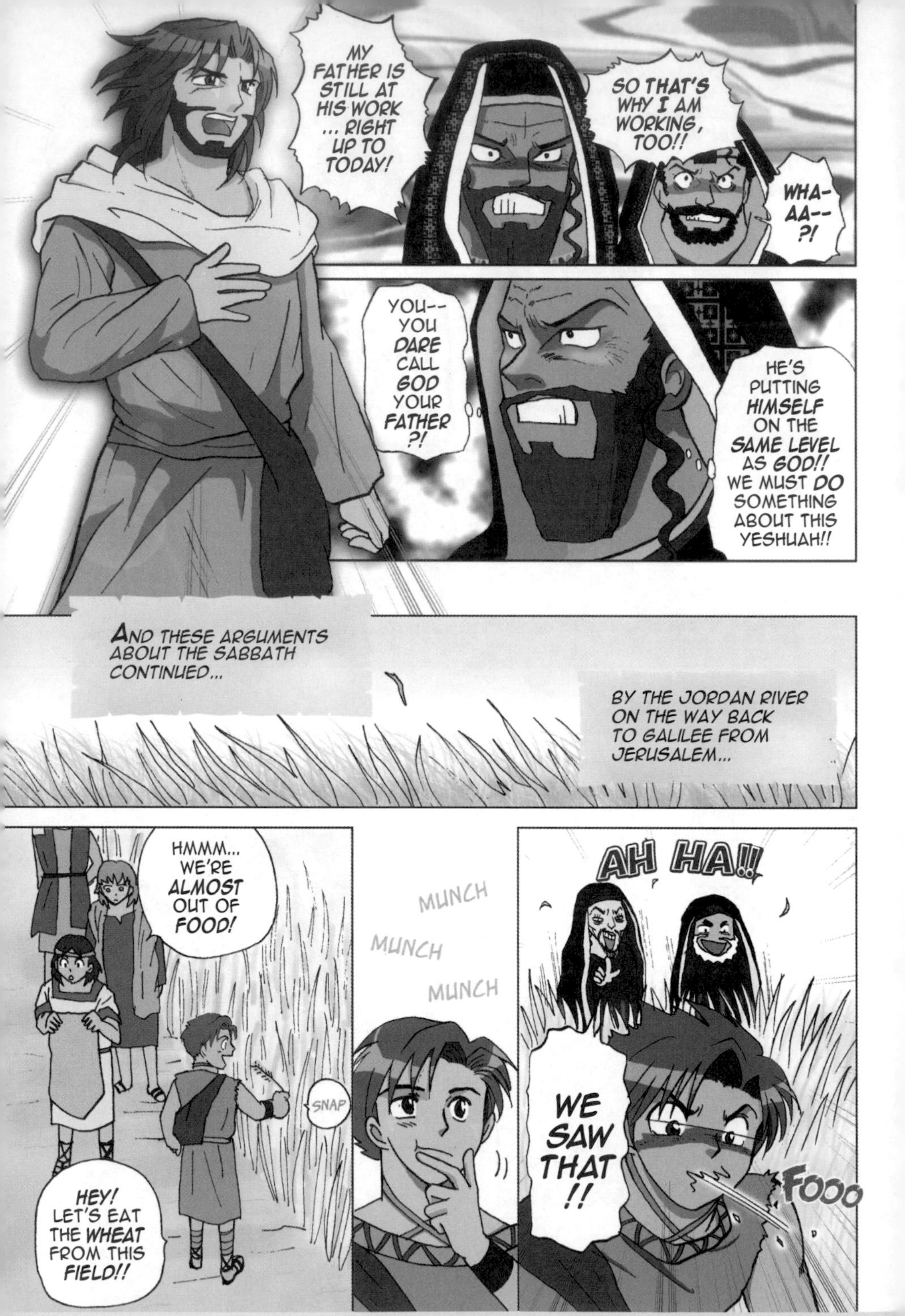
MY FATHER IS STILL AT HIS WORK ... RIGHT UP TO TODAY!
SO THAT'S WHY I AM WORKING, TOO!!
WHA-AA--?!
YOU-- YOU DARE CALL GOD YOUR FATHER?!
HE'S PUTTING HIMSELF ON THE SAME LEVEL AS GOD!! WE MUST DO SOMETHING ABOUT THIS YESHUAH!!
AND THESE ARGUMENTS ABOUT THE SABBATH CONTINUED...
BY THE JORDAN RIVER ON THE WAY BACK TO GALILEE FROM JERUSALEM...
HMMM... WE'RE ALMOST OUT OF FOOD!
SNAP
HEY! LET'S EAT THE WHEAT FROM THIS FIELD!!
MUNCH
MUNCH
MUNCH
AH HA!!
WE SAW THAT!!
FOOO

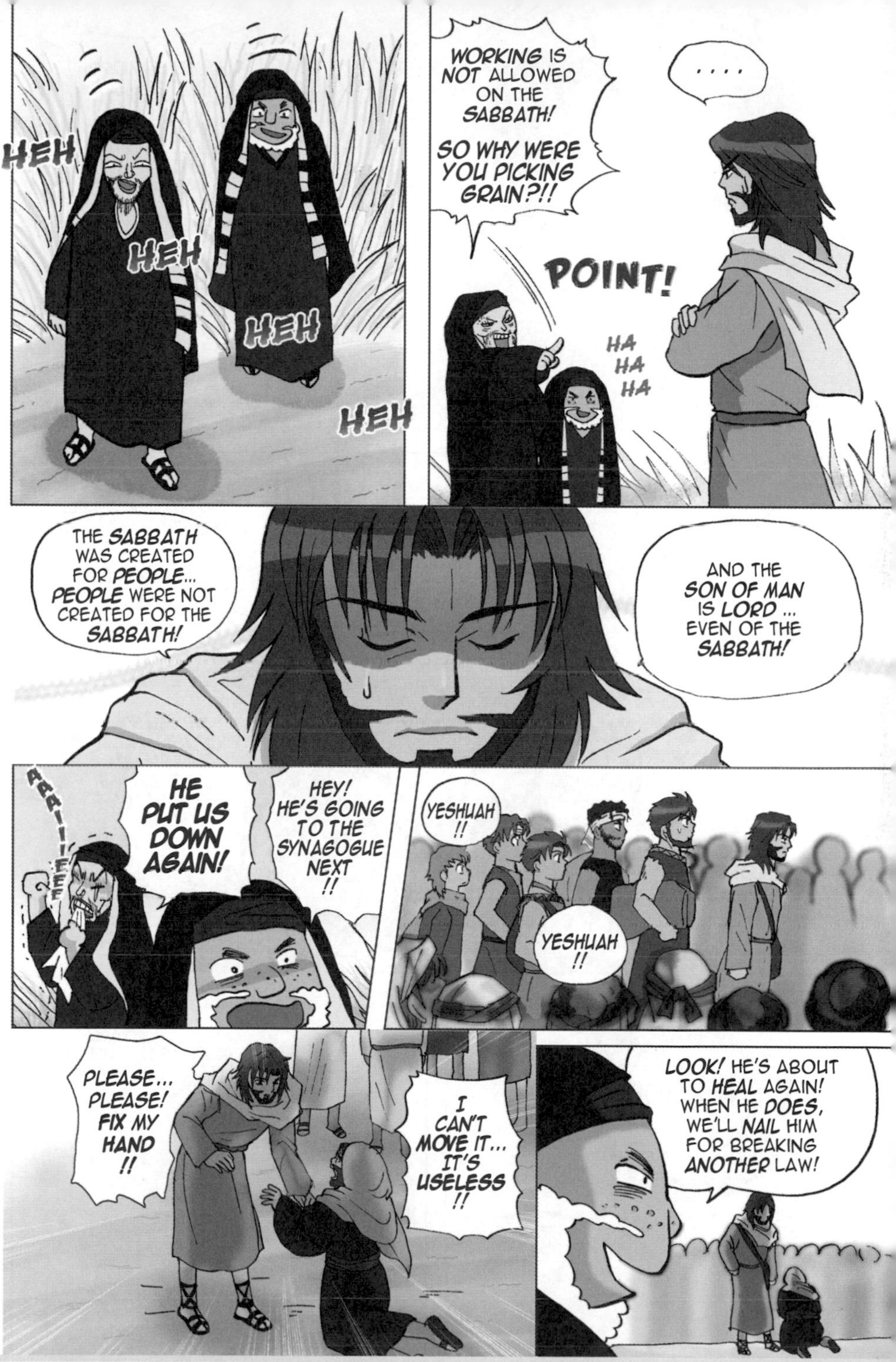
HEH
HEH
HEH
HEH
WORKING IS NOT ALLOWED ON THE SABBATH!
SO WHY WERE YOU PICKING GRAIN?!!
. . . .
POINT!
HA HA HA
THE SABBATH WAS CREATED FOR PEOPLE... PEOPLE WERE NOT CREATED FOR THE SABBATH!
AND THE SON OF MAN IS LORD ... EVEN OF THE SABBATH!
HE PUT US DOWN AGAIN!
HEY! HE'S GOING TO THE SYNAGOGUE NEXT !!
YESHUAH !!
YESHUAH !!
PLEASE... PLEASE! FIX MY HAND !!
I CAN'T MOVE IT... IT'S USELESS !!
LOOK! HE'S ABOUT TO HEAL AGAIN! WHEN HE DOES, WE'LL NAIL HIM FOR BREAKING ANOTHER LAW!

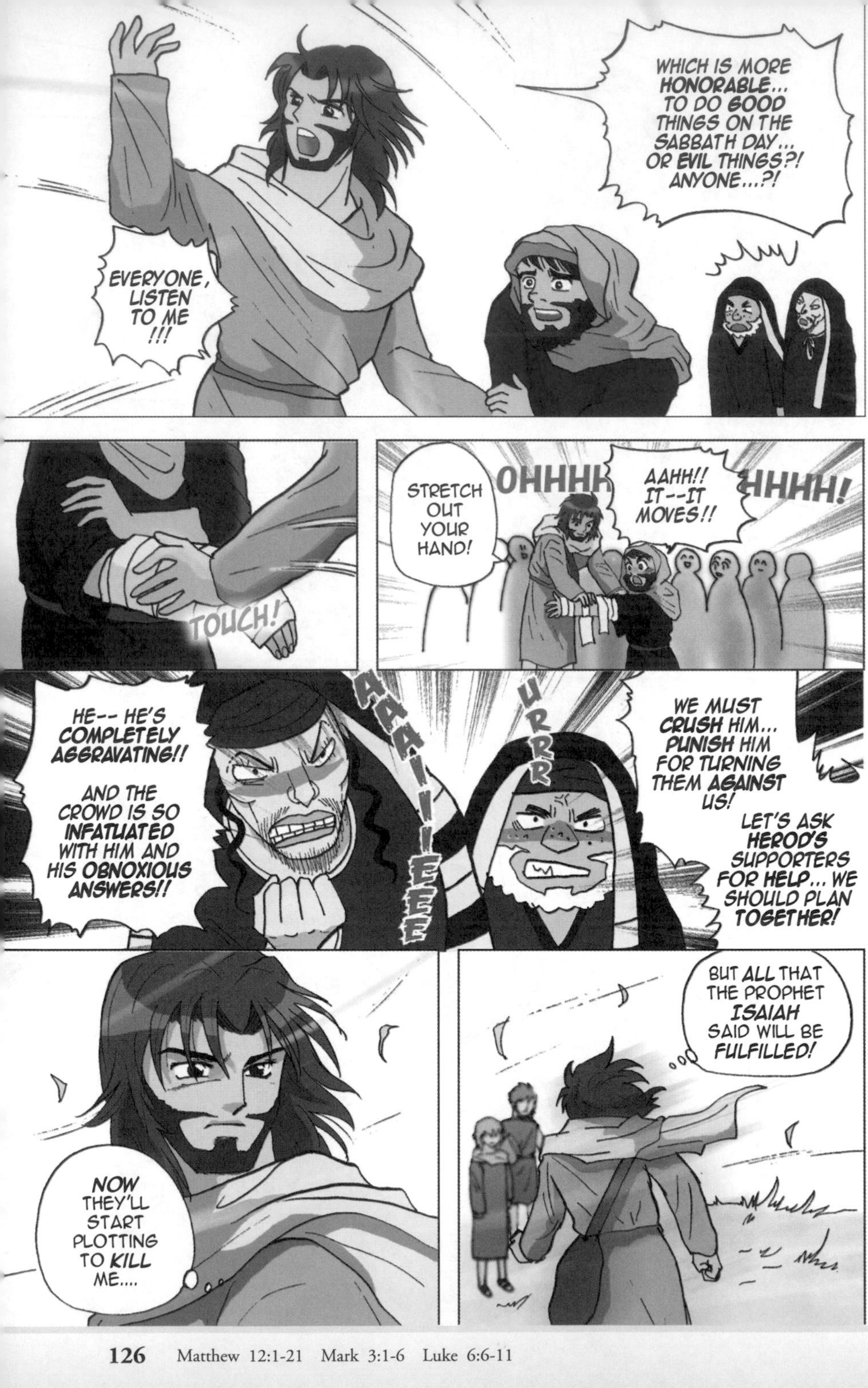

EVERYONE, LISTEN TO ME !!!
WHICH IS MORE HONORABLE... TO DO GOOD THINGS ON THE SABBATH DAY... OR EVIL THINGS?! ANYONE...?!
TOUCH!
STRETCH OUT YOUR HAND!
OHHHH HHHH!
AAHH!! IT--IT MOVES!!
HE-- HE'S COMPLETELY AGGRAVATING!!
AND THE CROWD IS SO INFATUATED WITH HIM AND HIS OBNOXIOUS ANSWERS!!
AAAIIIIEEE
URRR
WE MUST CRUSH HIM... PUNISH HIM FOR TURNING THEM AGAINST US!
LET'S ASK HEROD'S SUPPORTERS FOR HELP... WE SHOULD PLAN TOGETHER!
NOW THEY'LL START PLOTTING TO KILL ME....
BUT ALL THAT THE PROPHET ISAIAH SAID WILL BE FULFILLED!

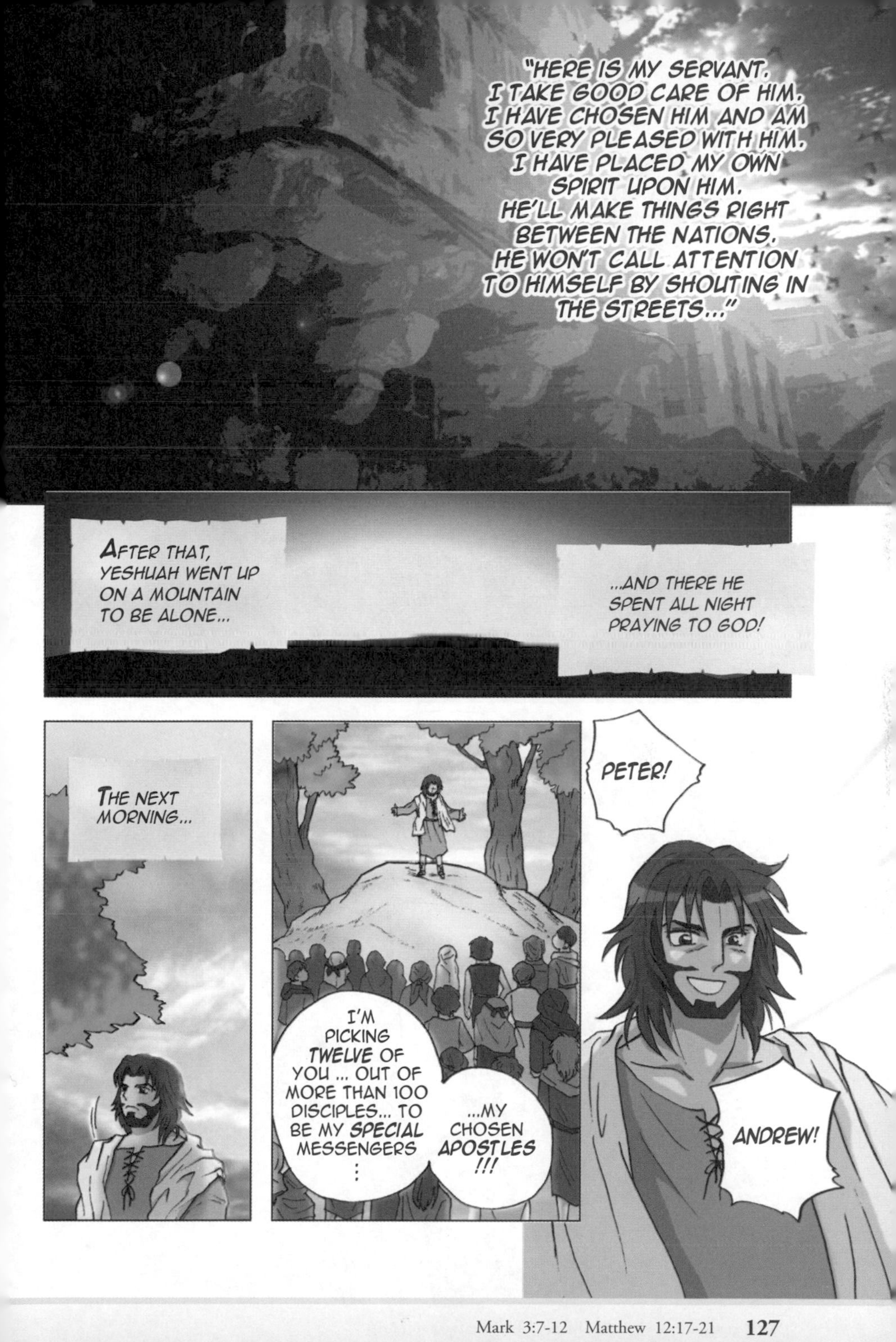
"HERE IS MY SERVANT. I TAKE GOOD CARE OF HIM. I HAVE CHOSEN HIM AND AM SO VERY PLEASED WITH HIM. I HAVE PLACED MY OWN SPIRIT UPON HIM. HE'LL MAKE THINGS RIGHT BETWEEN THE NATIONS. HE WON'T CALL ATTENTION TO HIMSELF BY SHOUTING IN THE STREETS..."
AFTER THAT, YESHUAH WENT UP ON A MOUNTAIN TO BE ALONE...
...AND THERE HE SPENT ALL NIGHT PRAYING TO GOD!
THE NEXT MORNING...
I'M PICKING TWELVE OF YOU ... OUT OF MORE THAN 100 DISCIPLES... TO BE MY SPECIAL MESSENGERS ...
...MY CHOSEN APOSTLES !!!
PETER!
ANDREW!

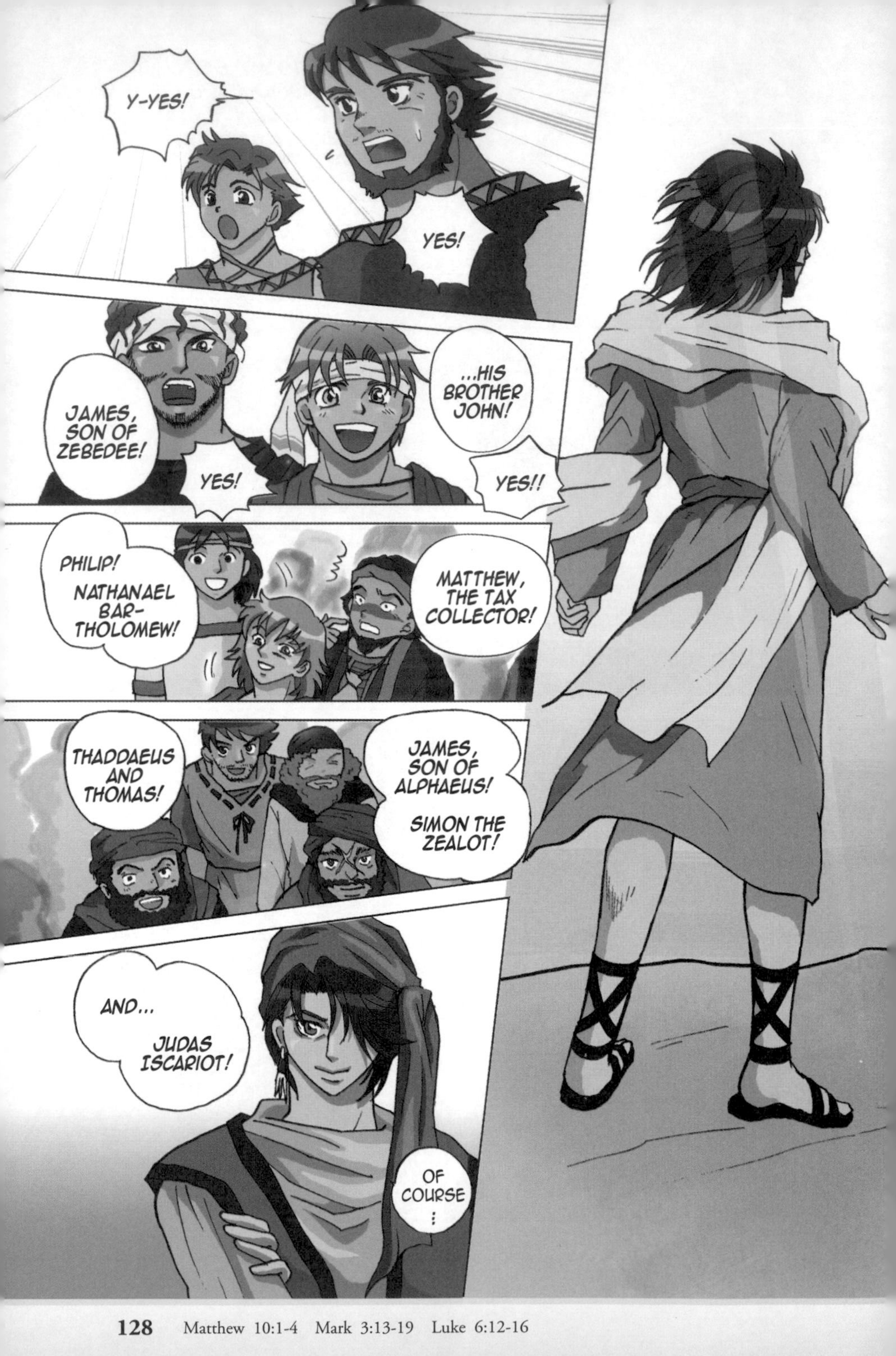
Y-YES!
YES!
JAMES, SON OF ZEBEDEE!
YES!
...HIS BROTHER JOHN!
YES!!
PHILIP!
NATHANAEL BAR-THOLOMEW!
MATTHEW, THE TAX COLLECTOR!
THADDAEUS AND THOMAS!
JAMES, SON OF ALPHAEUS!
SIMON THE ZEALOT!
AND...
JUDAS ISCARIOT!
OF COURSE
:

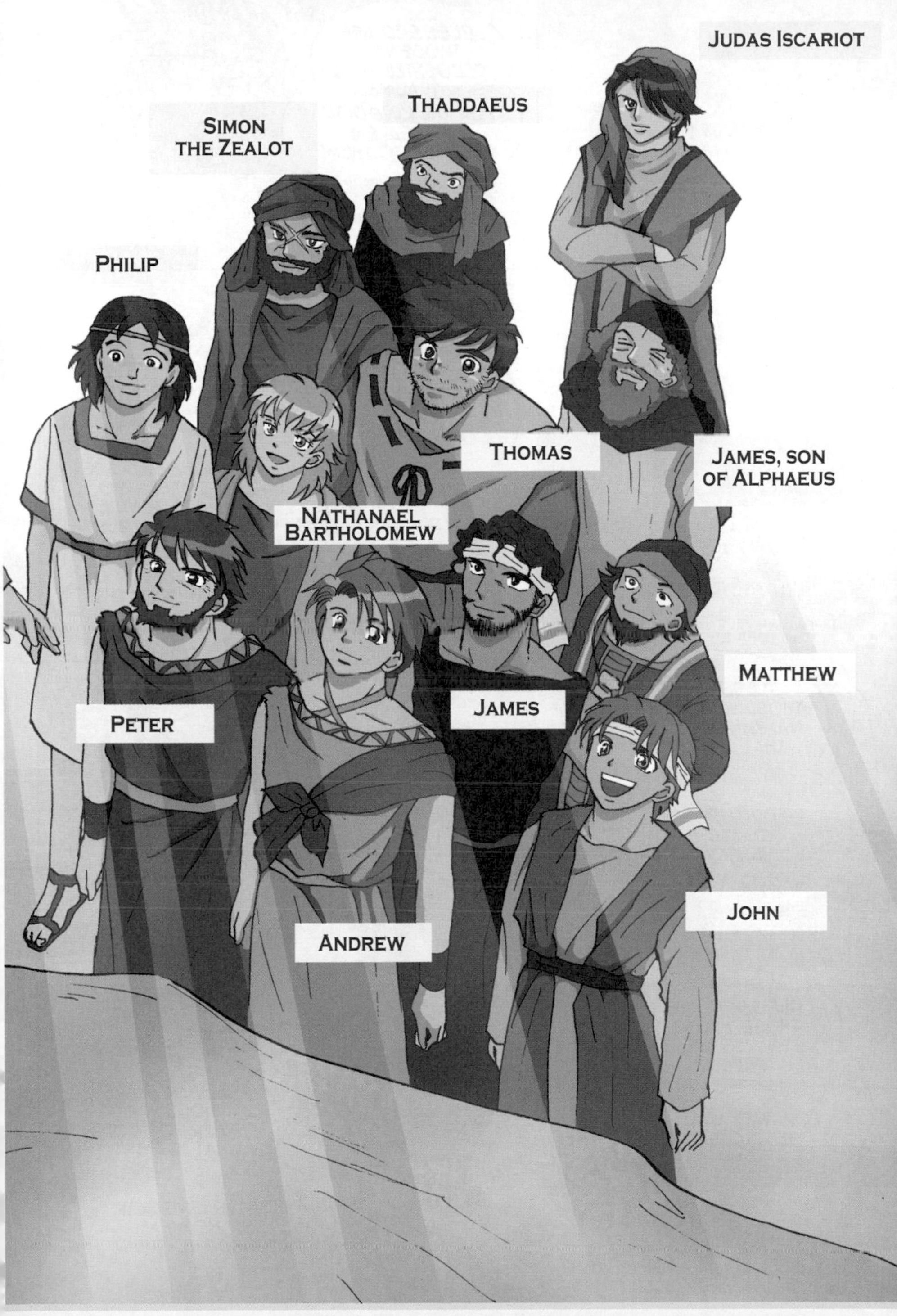
JUDAS ISCARIOT
THADDAEUS
SIMON
THE ZEALOT
PHILIP
THOMAS
JAMES, SON
OF ALPHAEUS
NATHANAEL
BARTHOLOMEW
MATTHEW
JAMES
PETER
JOHN
ANDREW

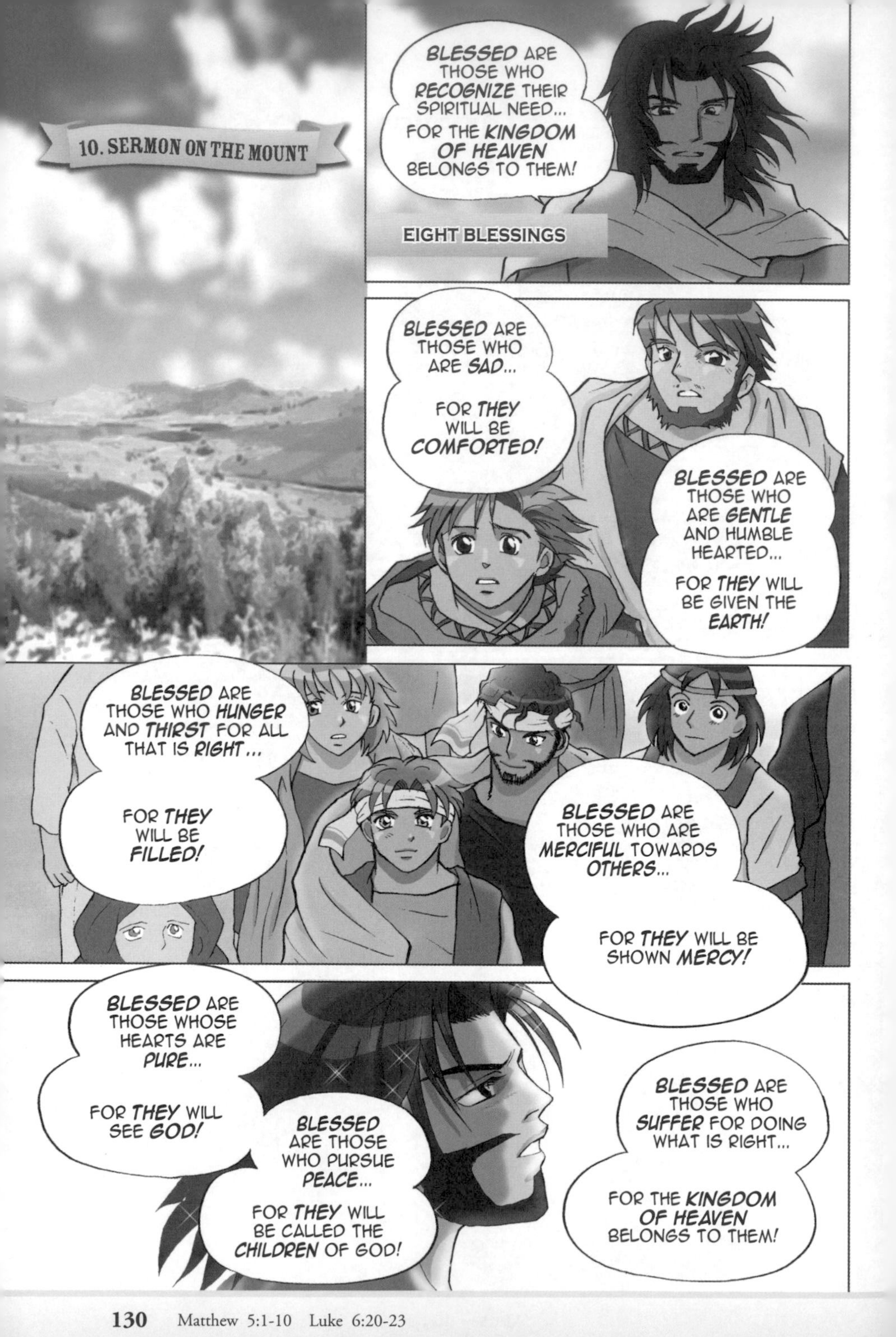

10. SERMON ON THE MOUNT
BLESSED ARE THOSE WHO RECOGNIZE THEIR SPIRITUAL NEED... FOR THE KINGDOM OF HEAVEN BELONGS TO THEM!
EIGHT BLESSINGS
BLESSED ARE THOSE WHO ARE SAD... FOR THEY WILL BE COMFORTED!
BLESSED ARE THOSE WHO ARE GENTLE AND HUMBLE HEARTED... FOR THEY WILL BE GIVEN THE EARTH!
BLESSED ARE THOSE WHO HUNGER AND THIRST FOR ALL THAT IS RIGHT... FOR THEY WILL BE FILLED!
BLESSED ARE THOSE WHO ARE MERCIFUL TOWARDS OTHERS... FOR THEY WILL BE SHOWN MERCY!
BLESSED ARE THOSE WHOSE HEARTS ARE PURE... FOR THEY WILL SEE GOD!
BLESSED ARE THOSE WHO PURSUE PEACE... FOR THEY WILL BE CALLED THE CHILDREN OF GOD!
BLESSED ARE THOSE WHO SUFFER FOR DOING WHAT IS RIGHT... FOR THE KINGDOM OF HEAVEN BELONGS TO THEM!

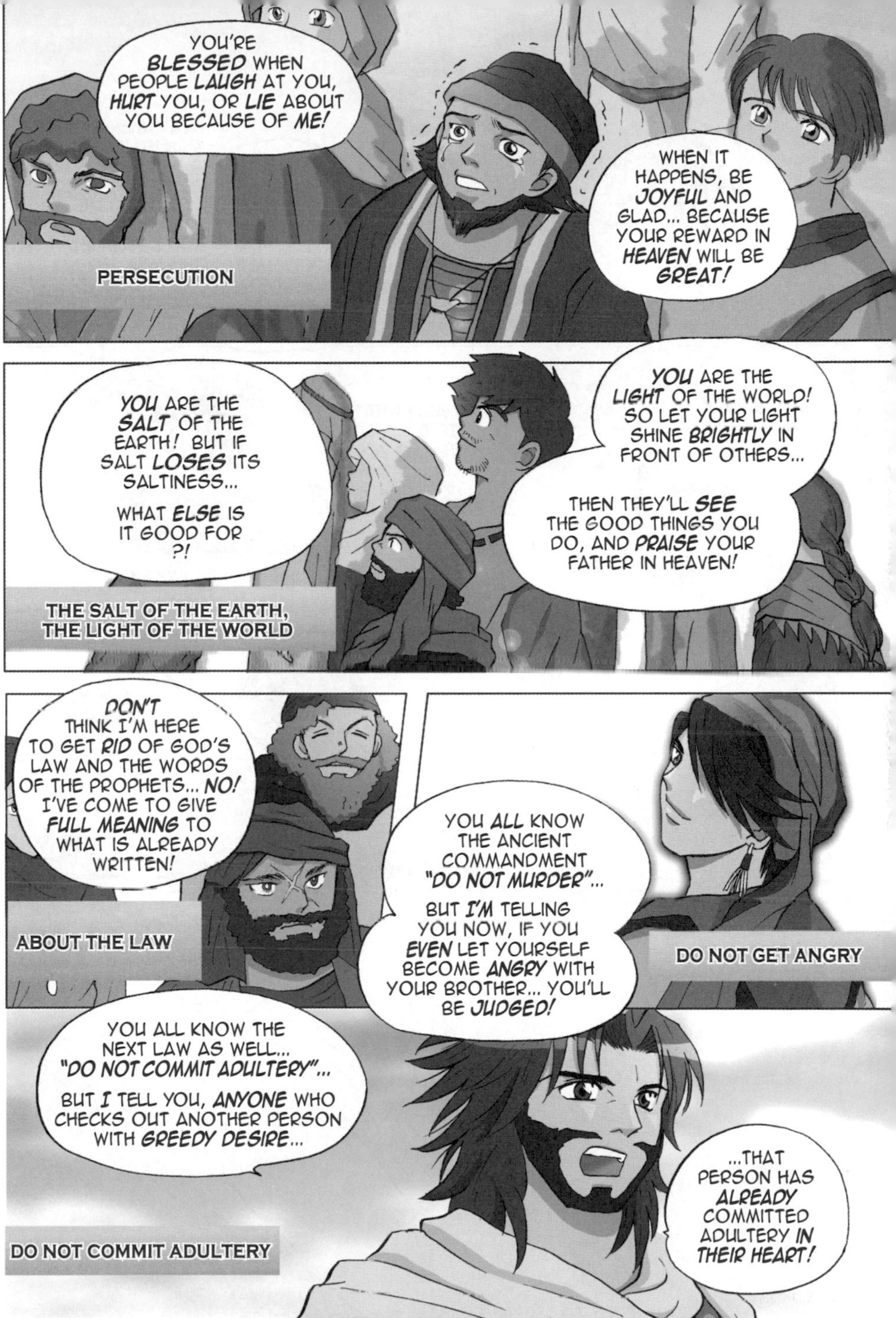
YOU'RE BLESSED WHEN PEOPLE LAUGH AT YOU, HURT YOU, OR LIE ABOUT YOU BECAUSE OF ME!
WHEN IT HAPPENS, BE JOYFUL AND GLAD... BECAUSE YOUR REWARD IN HEAVEN WILL BE GREAT!
PERSECUTION
YOU ARE THE SALT OF THE EARTH! BUT IF SALT LOSES ITS SALTINESS...
WHAT ELSE IS IT GOOD FOR ?!
YOU ARE THE LIGHT OF THE WORLD! SO LET YOUR LIGHT SHINE BRIGHTLY IN FRONT OF OTHERS...
THEN THEY'LL SEE THE GOOD THINGS YOU DO, AND PRAISE YOUR FATHER IN HEAVEN!
THE SALT OF THE EARTH, THE LIGHT OF THE WORLD
DON'T THINK I'M HERE TO GET RID OF GOD'S LAW AND THE WORDS OF THE PROPHETS... NO! I'VE COME TO GIVE FULL MEANING TO WHAT IS ALREADY WRITTEN!
ABOUT THE LAW
YOU ALL KNOW THE ANCIENT COMMANDMENT "DO NOT MURDER"...
BUT I'M TELLING YOU NOW, IF YOU EVEN LET YOURSELF BECOME ANGRY WITH YOUR BROTHER... YOU'LL BE JUDGED!
DO NOT GET ANGRY
YOU ALL KNOW THE NEXT LAW AS WELL... "DO NOT COMMIT ADULTERY"...
BUT I TELL YOU, ANYONE WHO CHECKS OUT ANOTHER PERSON WITH GREEDY DESIRE...
...THAT PERSON HAS ALREADY COMMITTED ADULTERY IN THEIR HEART!
DO NOT COMMIT ADULTERY

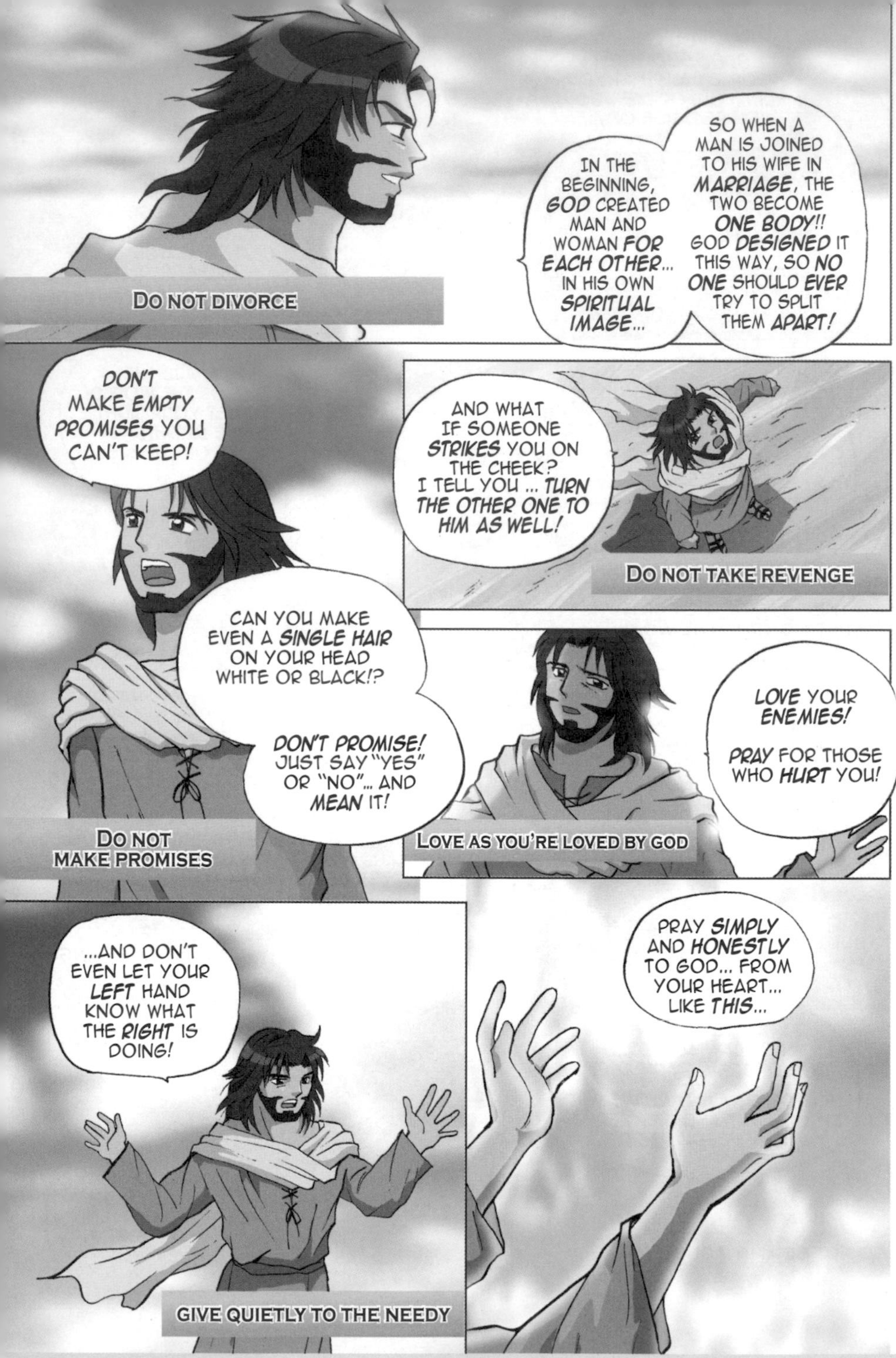
IN THE BEGINNING, GOD CREATED MAN AND WOMAN FOR EACH OTHER... IN HIS OWN SPIRITUAL IMAGE...
SO WHEN A MAN IS JOINED TO HIS WIFE IN MARRIAGE, THE TWO BECOME ONE BODY!! GOD DESIGNED IT THIS WAY, SO NO ONE SHOULD EVER TRY TO SPLIT THEM APART!
DO NOT DIVORCE
DON'T MAKE EMPTY PROMISES YOU CAN'T KEEP!
AND WHAT IF SOMEONE STRIKES YOU ON THE CHEEK? I TELL YOU ... TURN THE OTHER ONE TO HIM AS WELL!
DO NOT TAKE REVENGE
CAN YOU MAKE EVEN A SINGLE HAIR ON YOUR HEAD WHITE OR BLACK!?
DON'T PROMISE! JUST SAY "YES" OR "NO"... AND MEAN IT!
DO NOT MAKE PROMISES
LOVE YOUR ENEMIES!
PRAY FOR THOSE WHO HURT YOU!
LOVE AS YOU'RE LOVED BY GOD
...AND DON'T EVEN LET YOUR LEFT HAND KNOW WHAT THE RIGHT IS DOING!
GIVE QUIETLY TO THE NEEDY
PRAY SIMPLY AND HONESTLY TO GOD... FROM YOUR HEART... LIKE THIS...

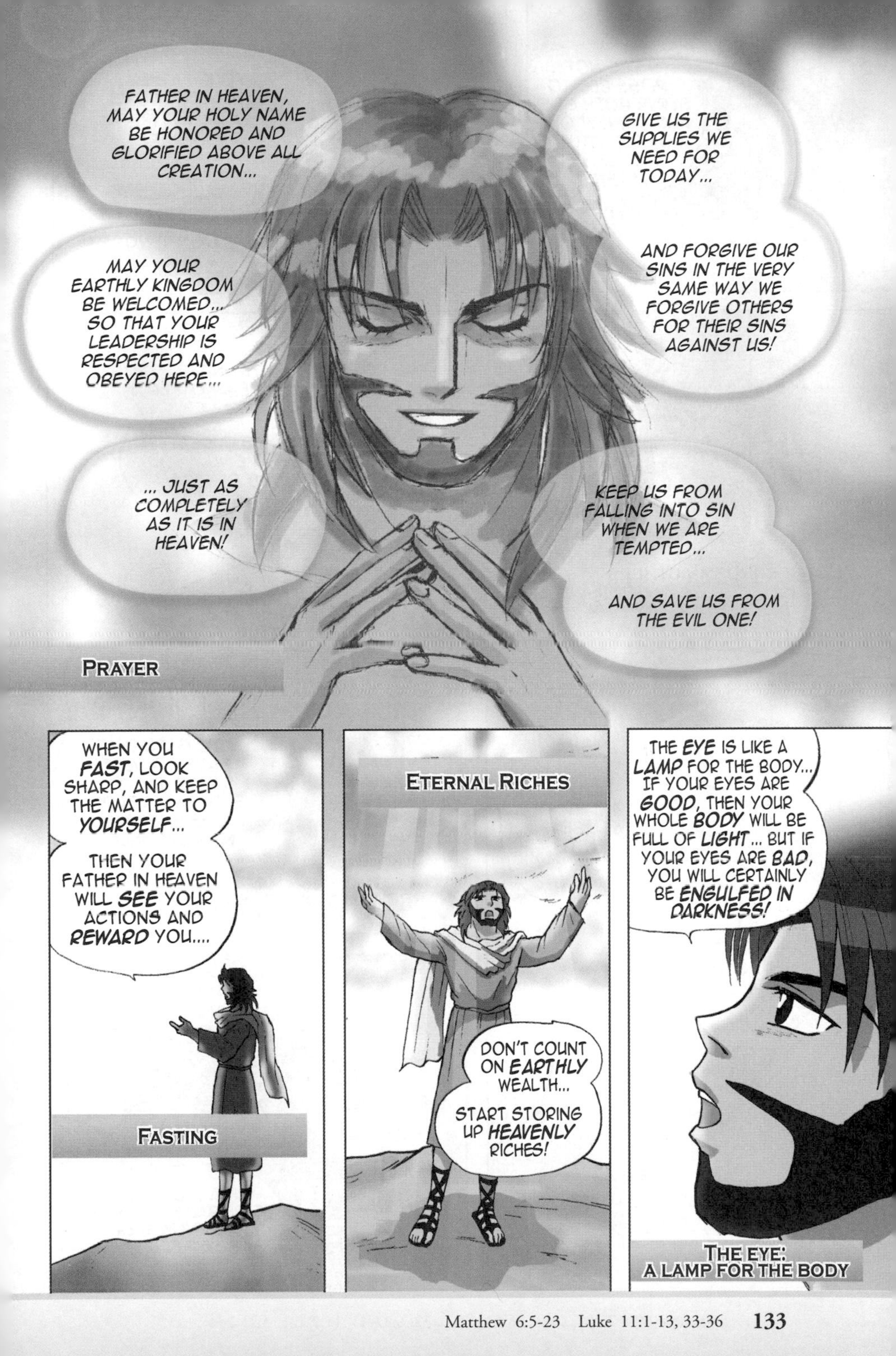
FATHER IN HEAVEN, MAY YOUR HOLY NAME BE HONORED AND GLORIFIED ABOVE ALL CREATION...
GIVE US THE SUPPLIES WE NEED FOR TODAY...
MAY YOUR EARTHLY KINGDOM BE WELCOMED... SO THAT YOUR LEADERSHIP IS RESPECTED AND OBEYED HERE...
AND FORGIVE OUR SINS IN THE VERY SAME WAY WE FORGIVE OTHERS FOR THEIR SINS AGAINST US!
... JUST AS COMPLETELY AS IT IS IN HEAVEN!
KEEP US FROM FALLING INTO SIN WHEN WE ARE TEMPTED...
AND SAVE US FROM THE EVIL ONE!
PRAYER
WHEN YOU FAST, LOOK SHARP, AND KEEP THE MATTER TO YOURSELF...
THEN YOUR FATHER IN HEAVEN WILL SEE YOUR ACTIONS AND REWARD YOU....
FASTING
ETERNAL RICHES
DON'T COUNT ON EARTHLY WEALTH...
START STORING UP HEAVENLY RICHES!
THE EYE IS LIKE A LAMP FOR THE BODY... IF YOUR EYES ARE GOOD, THEN YOUR WHOLE BODY WILL BE FULL OF LIGHT... BUT IF YOUR EYES ARE BAD, YOU WILL CERTAINLY BE ENGULFED IN DARKNESS!
THE EYE: A LAMP FOR THE BODY

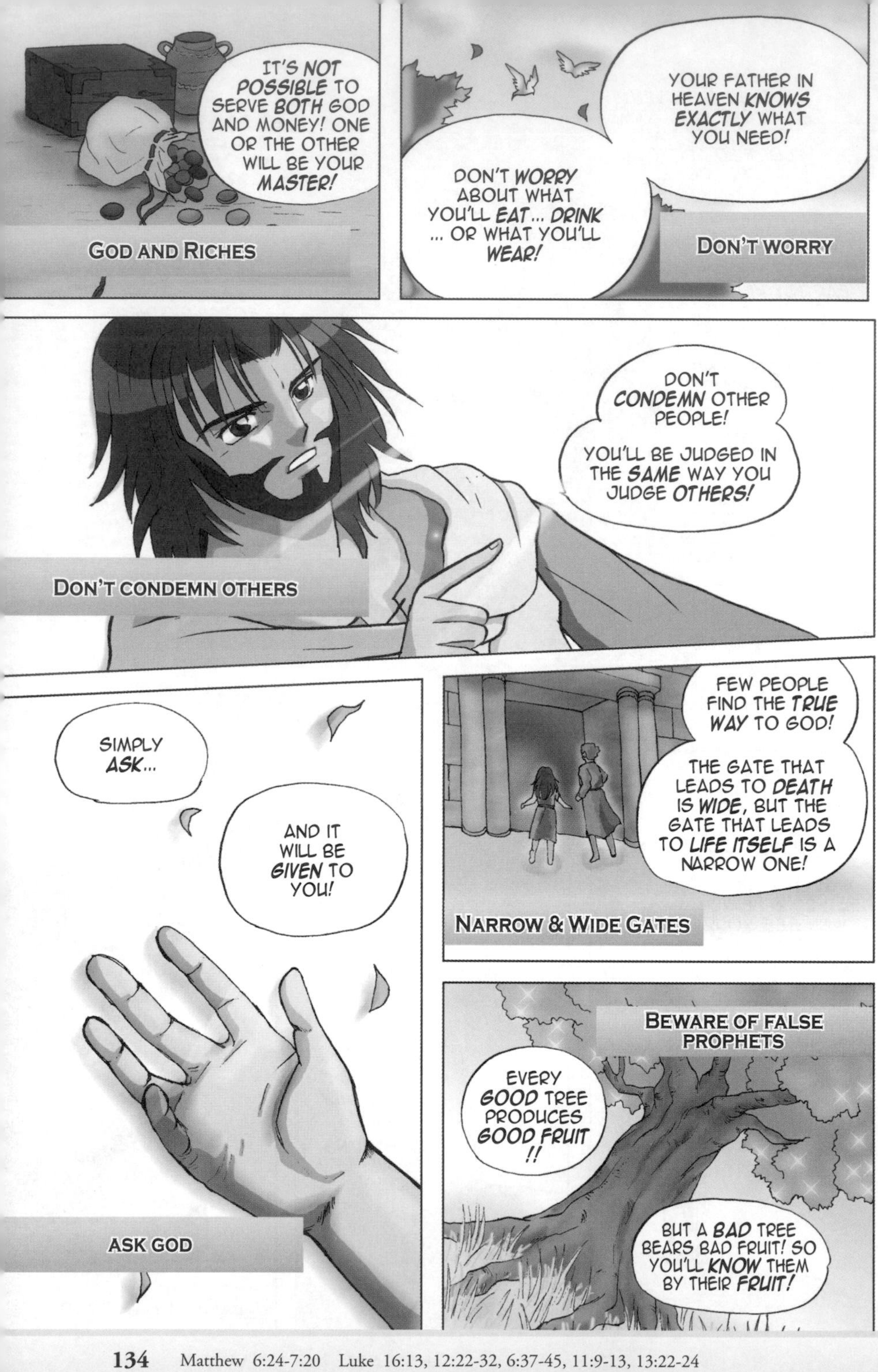
IT'S NOT POSSIBLE TO SERVE BOTH GOD AND MONEY! ONE OR THE OTHER WILL BE YOUR MASTER!
GOD AND RICHES
DON'T WORRY ABOUT WHAT YOU'LL EAT... DRINK ... OR WHAT YOU'LL WEAR!
YOUR FATHER IN HEAVEN KNOWS EXACTLY WHAT YOU NEED!
DON'T WORRY
DON'T CONDEMN OTHER PEOPLE!
YOU'LL BE JUDGED IN THE SAME WAY YOU JUDGE OTHERS!
DON'T CONDEMN OTHERS
SIMPLY ASK...
AND IT WILL BE GIVEN TO YOU!
ASK GOD
FEW PEOPLE FIND THE TRUE WAY TO GOD!
THE GATE THAT LEADS TO DEATH IS WIDE, BUT THE GATE THAT LEADS TO LIFE ITSELF IS A NARROW ONE!
NARROW & WIDE GATES
BEWARE OF FALSE PROPHETS
EVERY GOOD TREE PRODUCES GOOD FRUIT !!
BUT A BAD TREE BEARS BAD FRUIT! SO YOU'LL KNOW THEM BY THEIR FRUIT!

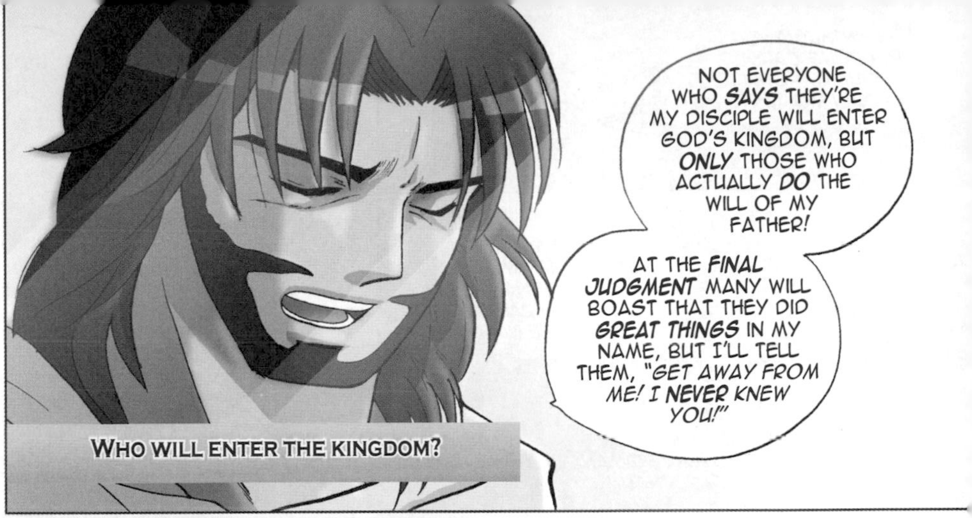

NOT EVERYONE WHO SAYS THEY'RE MY DISCIPLE WILL ENTER GOD'S KINGDOM, BUT ONLY THOSE WHO ACTUALLY DO THE WILL OF MY FATHER!
AT THE FINAL JUDGMENT MANY WILL BOAST THAT THEY DID GREAT THINGS IN MY NAME, BUT I'LL TELL THEM, "GET AWAY FROM ME! I NEVER KNEW YOU!"
WHO WILL ENTER THE KINGDOM?

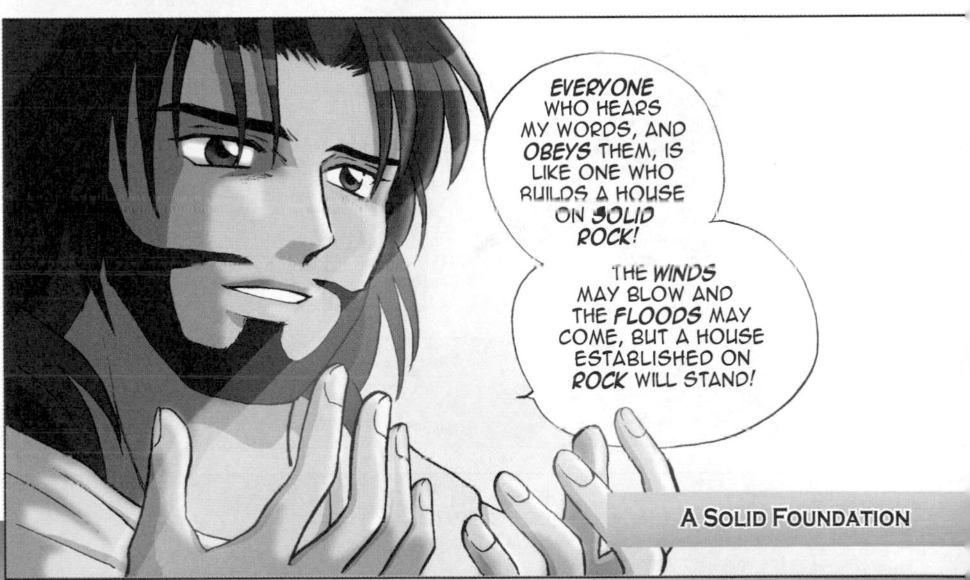

EVERYONE WHO HEARS MY WORDS, AND OBEYS THEM, IS LIKE ONE WHO BUILDS A HOUSE ON SOLID ROCK!
THE WINDS MAY BLOW AND THE FLOODS MAY COME, BUT A HOUSE ESTABLISHED ON ROCK WILL STAND!
A SOLID FOUNDATION

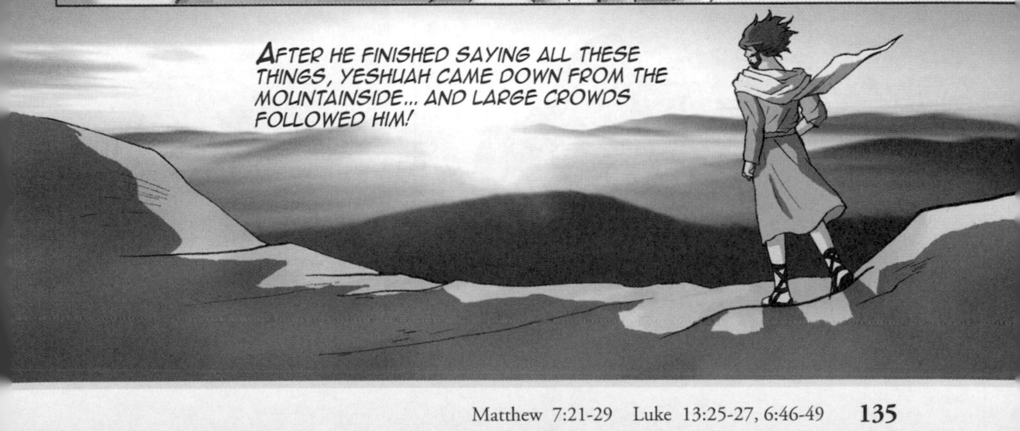

AFTER HE FINISHED SAYING ALL THESE THINGS, YESHUAH CAME DOWN FROM THE MOUNTAINSIDE... AND LARGE CROWDS FOLLOWED HIM!

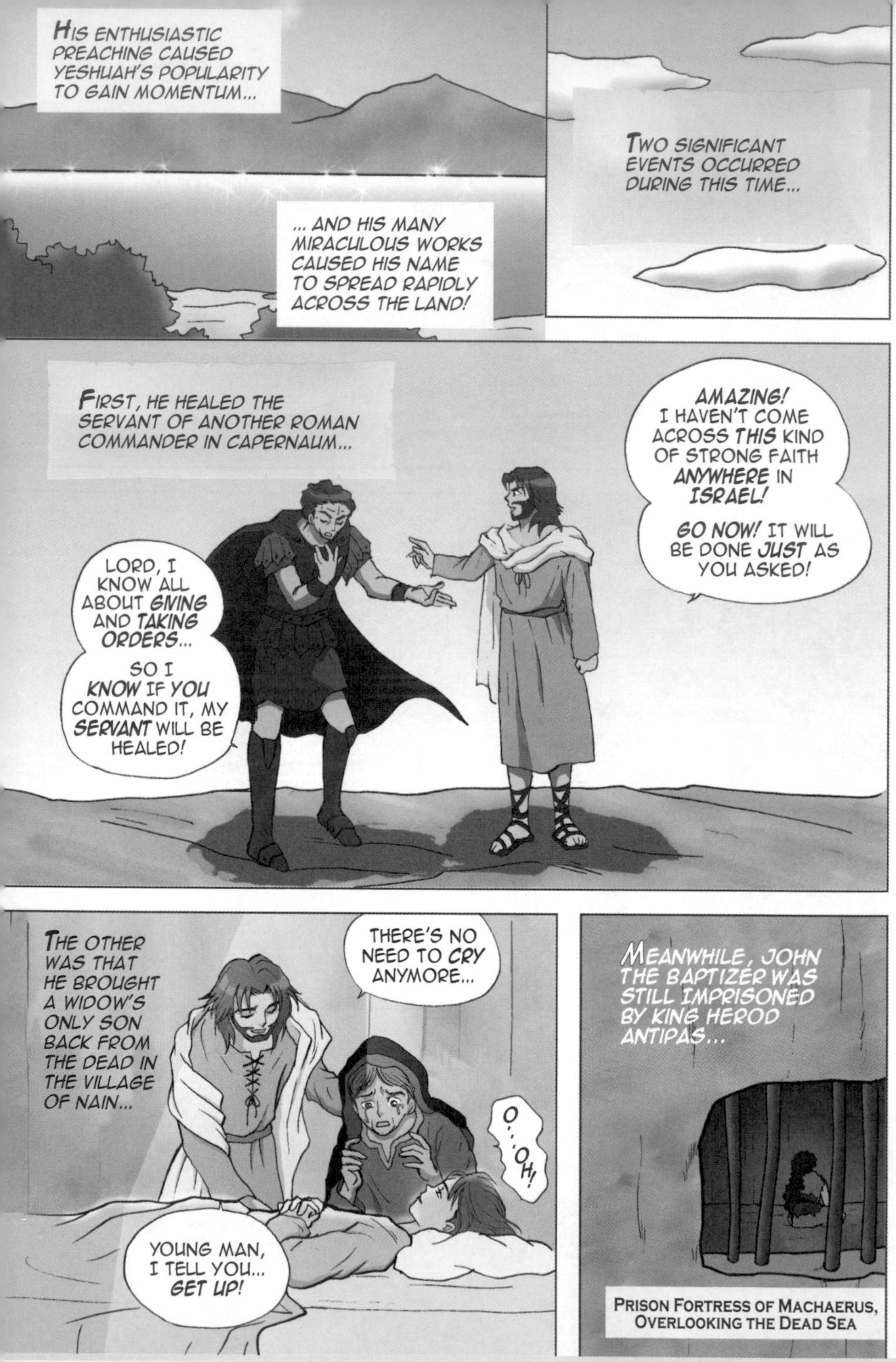
HIS ENTHUSIASTIC PREACHING CAUSED YESHUAH'S POPULARITY TO GAIN MOMENTUM...
... AND HIS MANY MIRACULOUS WORKS CAUSED HIS NAME TO SPREAD RAPIDLY ACROSS THE LAND!
TWO SIGNIFICANT EVENTS OCCURRED DURING THIS TIME...
FIRST, HE HEALED THE SERVANT OF ANOTHER ROMAN COMMANDER IN CAPERNAUM...
LORD, I KNOW ALL ABOUT GIVING AND TAKING ORDERS...
SO I KNOW IF YOU COMMAND IT, MY SERVANT WILL BE HEALED!
AMAZING! I HAVEN'T COME ACROSS THIS KIND OF STRONG FAITH ANYWHERE IN ISRAEL!
GO NOW! IT WILL BE DONE JUST AS YOU ASKED!
THE OTHER WAS THAT HE BROUGHT A WIDOW'S ONLY SON BACK FROM THE DEAD IN THE VILLAGE OF NAIN...
THERE'S NO NEED TO CRY ANYMORE...
O...OH!
YOUNG MAN, I TELL YOU... GET UP!
MEANWHILE, JOHN THE BAPTIZER WAS STILL IMPRISONED BY KING HEROD ANTIPAS...
PRISON FORTRESS OF MACHAERUS, OVERLOOKING THE DEAD SEA

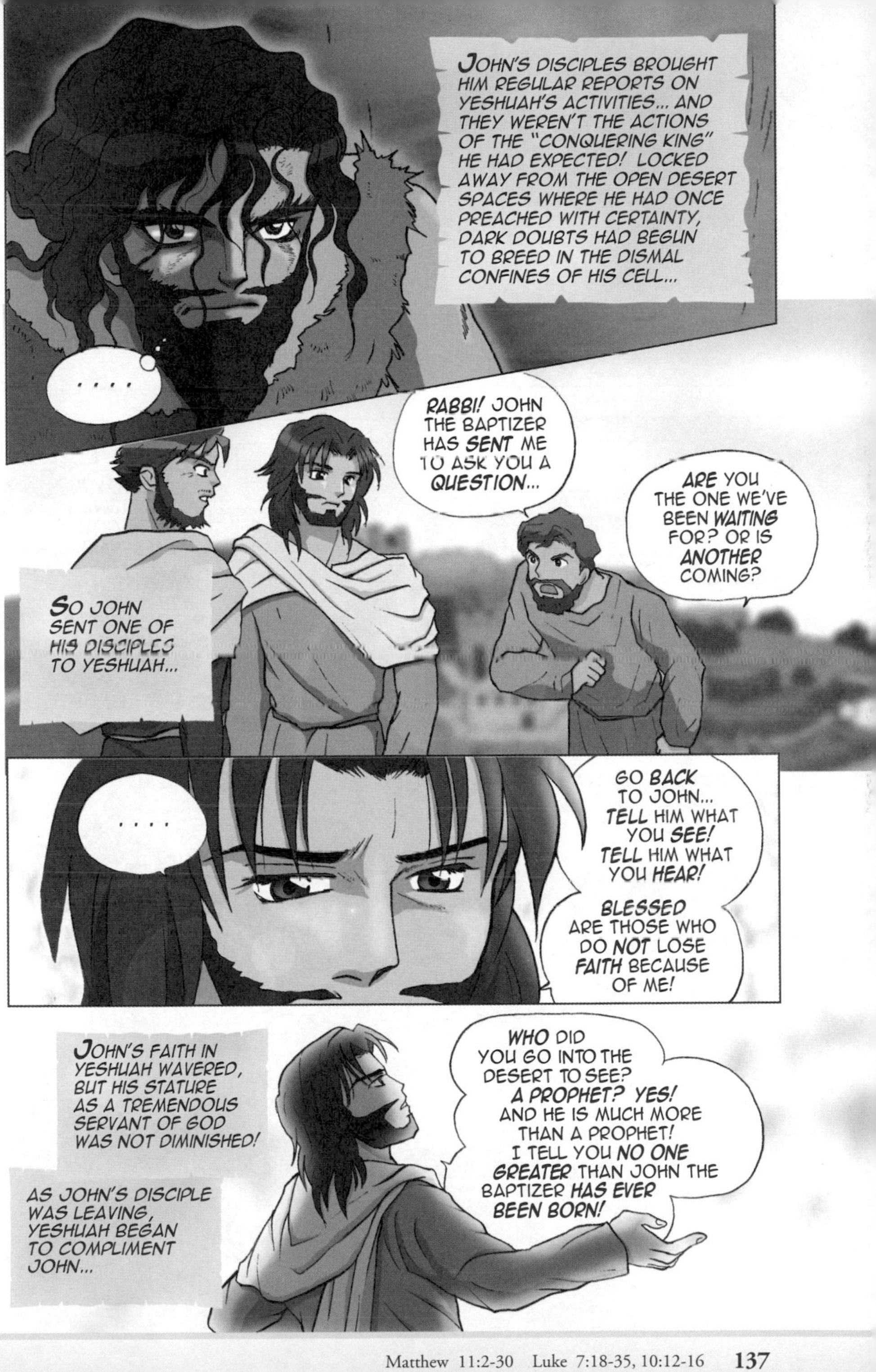
JOHN'S DISCIPLES BROUGHT HIM REGULAR REPORTS ON YESHUAH'S ACTIVITIES... AND THEY WEREN'T THE ACTIONS OF THE "CONQUERING KING" HE HAD EXPECTED! LOCKED AWAY FROM THE OPEN DESERT SPACES WHERE HE HAD ONCE PREACHED WITH CERTAINTY, DARK DOUBTS HAD BEGUN TO BREED IN THE DISMAL CONFINES OF HIS CELL...
.....
SO JOHN SENT ONE OF HIS DISCIPLES TO YESHUAH...
RABBI! JOHN THE BAPTIZER HAS SENT ME TO ASK YOU A QUESTION...
ARE YOU THE ONE WE'VE BEEN WAITING FOR? OR IS ANOTHER COMING?
.....
GO BACK TO JOHN... TELL HIM WHAT YOU SEE! TELL HIM WHAT YOU HEAR!
BLESSED ARE THOSE WHO DO NOT LOSE FAITH BECAUSE OF ME!
JOHN'S FAITH IN YESHUAH WAVERED, BUT HIS STATURE AS A TREMENDOUS SERVANT OF GOD WAS NOT DIMINISHED!
AS JOHN'S DISCIPLE WAS LEAVING, YESHUAH BEGAN TO COMPLIMENT JOHN...
WHO DID YOU GO INTO THE DESERT TO SEE? A PROPHET? YES! AND HE IS MUCH MORE THAN A PROPHET! I TELL YOU NO ONE GREATER THAN JOHN THE BAPTIZER HAS EVER BEEN BORN!

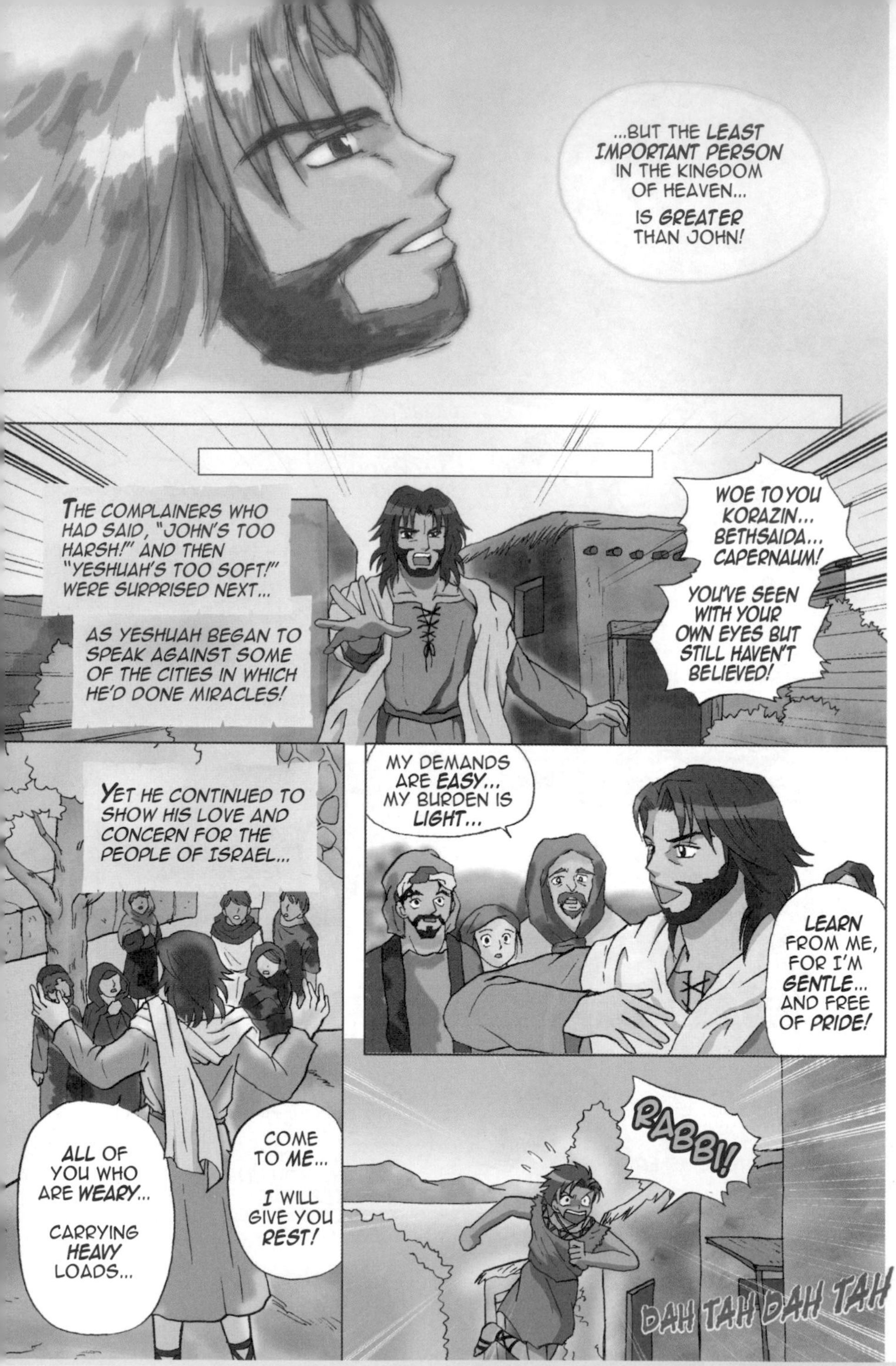

...BUT THE LEAST IMPORTANT PERSON IN THE KINGDOM OF HEAVEN...
IS GREATER THAN JOHN!
THE COMPLAINERS WHO HAD SAID, "JOHN'S TOO HARSH!" AND THEN "YESHUAH'S TOO SOFT!" WERE SURPRISED NEXT...
AS YESHUAH BEGAN TO SPEAK AGAINST SOME OF THE CITIES IN WHICH HE'D DONE MIRACLES!
WOE TO YOU KORAZIN... BETHSAIDA... CAPERNAUM!
YOU'VE SEEN WITH YOUR OWN EYES BUT STILL HAVEN'T BELIEVED!
YET HE CONTINUED TO SHOW HIS LOVE AND CONCERN FOR THE PEOPLE OF ISRAEL...
ALL OF YOU WHO ARE WEARY...
CARRYING HEAVY LOADS...
COME TO ME...
I WILL GIVE YOU REST!
MY DEMANDS ARE EASY... MY BURDEN IS LIGHT...
LEARN FROM ME, FOR I'M GENTLE... AND FREE OF PRIDE!
RABBI!
DAH TAH DAH TAH

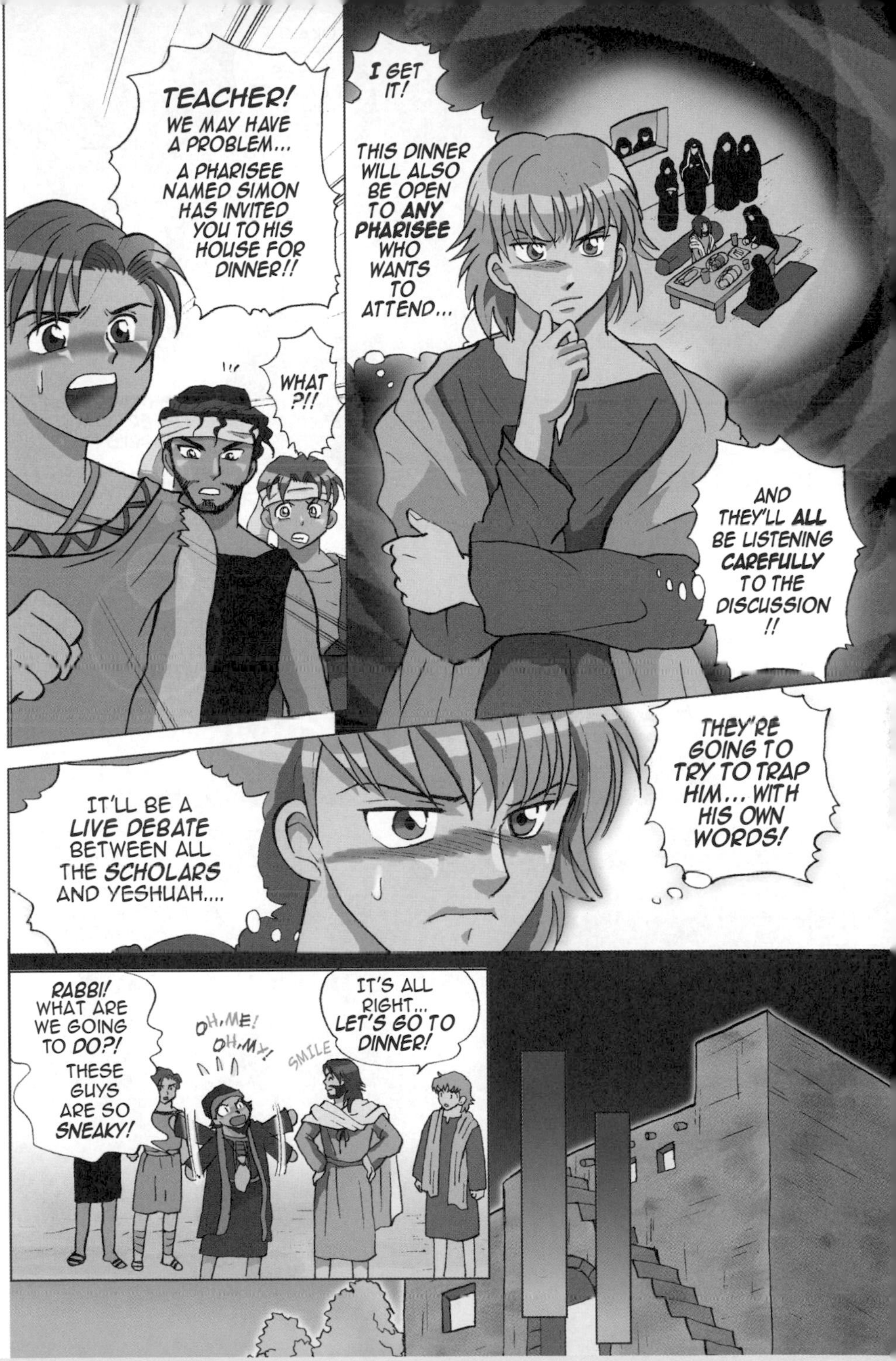
TEACHER! WE MAY HAVE A PROBLEM... A PHARISEE NAMED SIMON HAS INVITED YOU TO HIS HOUSE FOR DINNER!!
WHAT ?!!
I GET IT!
THIS DINNER WILL ALSO BE OPEN TO ANY PHARISEE WHO WANTS TO ATTEND...
AND THEY'LL ALL BE LISTENING CAREFULLY TO THE DISCUSSION !!
THEY'RE GOING TO TRY TO TRAP HIM... WITH HIS OWN WORDS!
IT'LL BE A LIVE DEBATE BETWEEN ALL THE SCHOLARS AND YESHUAH....
IT'S ALL RIGHT... LET'S GO TO DINNER!
SMILE
OH, ME! OH, MY!
RABBI! WHAT ARE WE GOING TO DO?! THESE GUYS ARE SO SNEAKY!

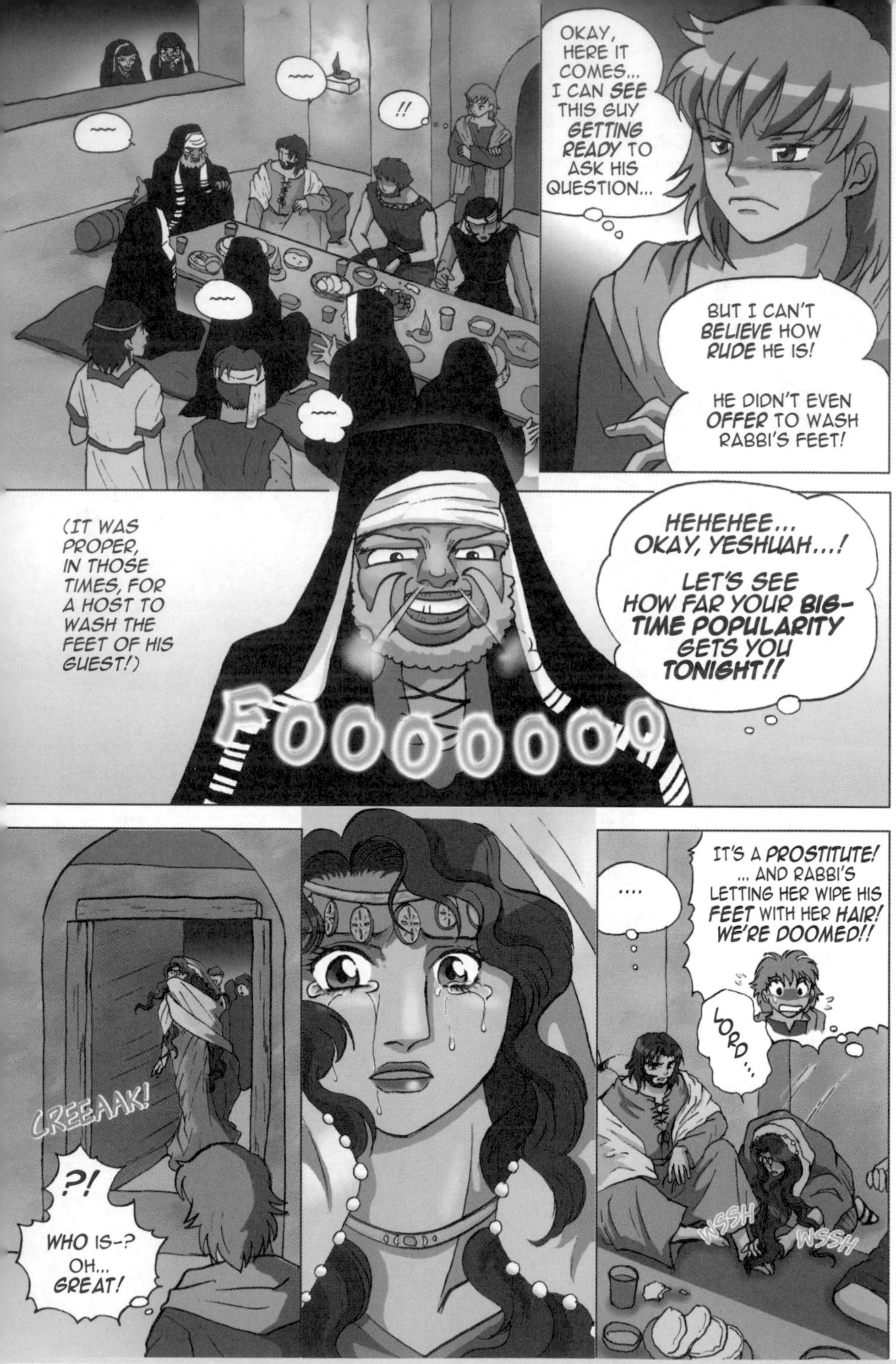
~~~
~~~
!!
~~~
~~~
OKAY, HERE IT COMES... I CAN SEE THIS GUY GETTING READY TO ASK HIS QUESTION...
BUT I CAN'T BELIEVE HOW RUDE HE IS!
HE DIDN'T EVEN OFFER TO WASH RABBI'S FEET!
(IT WAS PROPER, IN THOSE TIMES, FOR A HOST TO WASH THE FEET OF HIS GUEST!)
HEHEHEE... OKAY, YESHUAH...!
LET'S SEE HOW FAR YOUR BIG-TIME POPULARITY GETS YOU TONIGHT!!
FOOOOOOO
CREEAAK!
?!
WHO IS-? OH... GREAT!
....
IT'S A PROSTITUTE! ... AND RABBI'S LETTING HER WIPE HIS FEET WITH HER HAIR! WE'RE DOOMED!!
LORD...
WSSH
WSSH

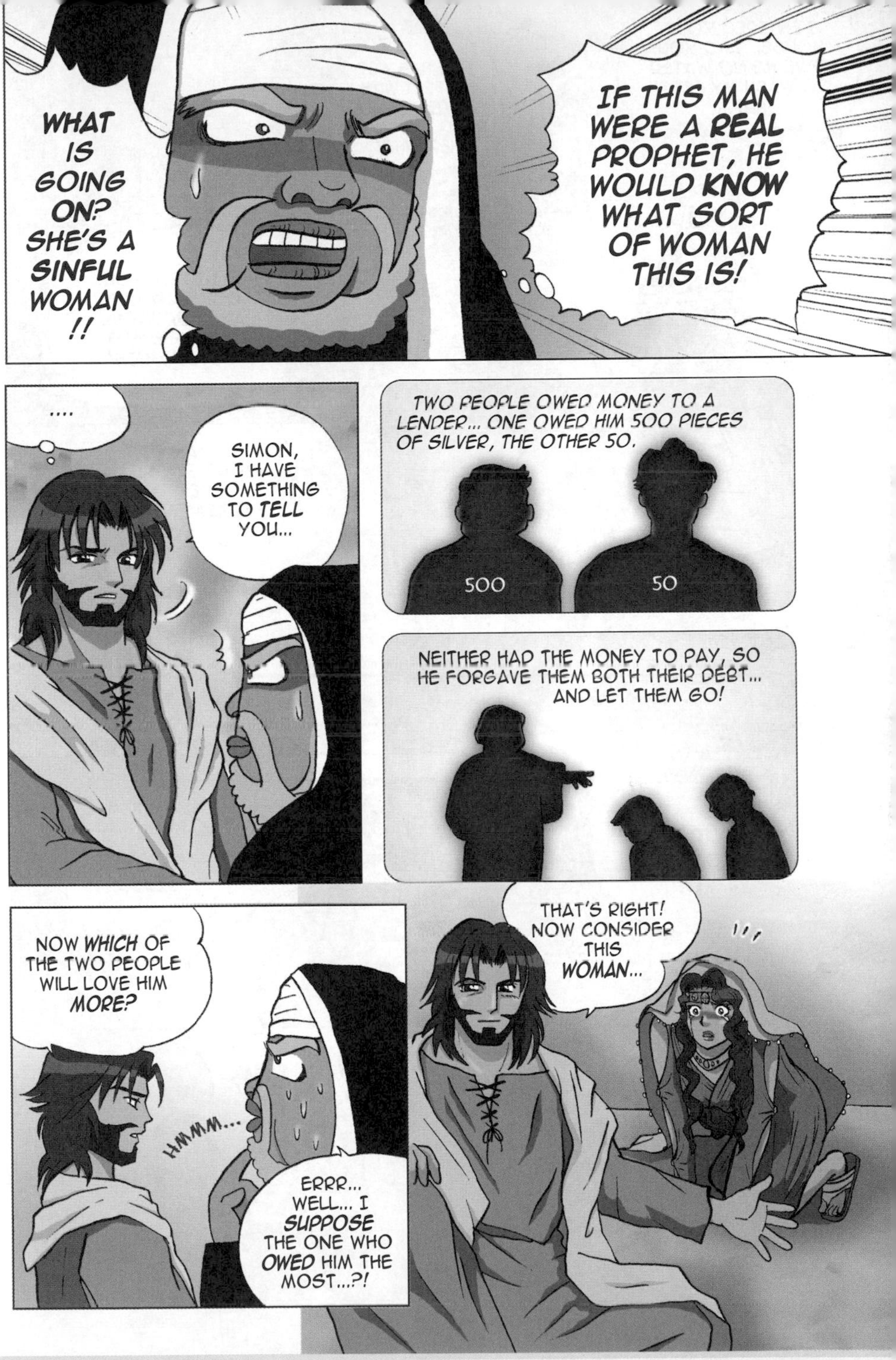
WHAT IS GOING ON? SHE'S A SINFUL WOMAN !!
IF THIS MAN WERE A REAL PROPHET, HE WOULD KNOW WHAT SORT OF WOMAN THIS IS!
....
SIMON, I HAVE SOMETHING TO TELL YOU...
TWO PEOPLE OWED MONEY TO A LENDER... ONE OWED HIM 500 PIECES OF SILVER, THE OTHER 50.
500
50
NEITHER HAD THE MONEY TO PAY, SO HE FORGAVE THEM BOTH THEIR DEBT... AND LET THEM GO!
NOW WHICH OF THE TWO PEOPLE WILL LOVE HIM MORE?
HMMM...
ERRR... WELL... I SUPPOSE THE ONE WHO OWED HIM THE MOST...?!
THAT'S RIGHT! NOW CONSIDER THIS WOMAN...

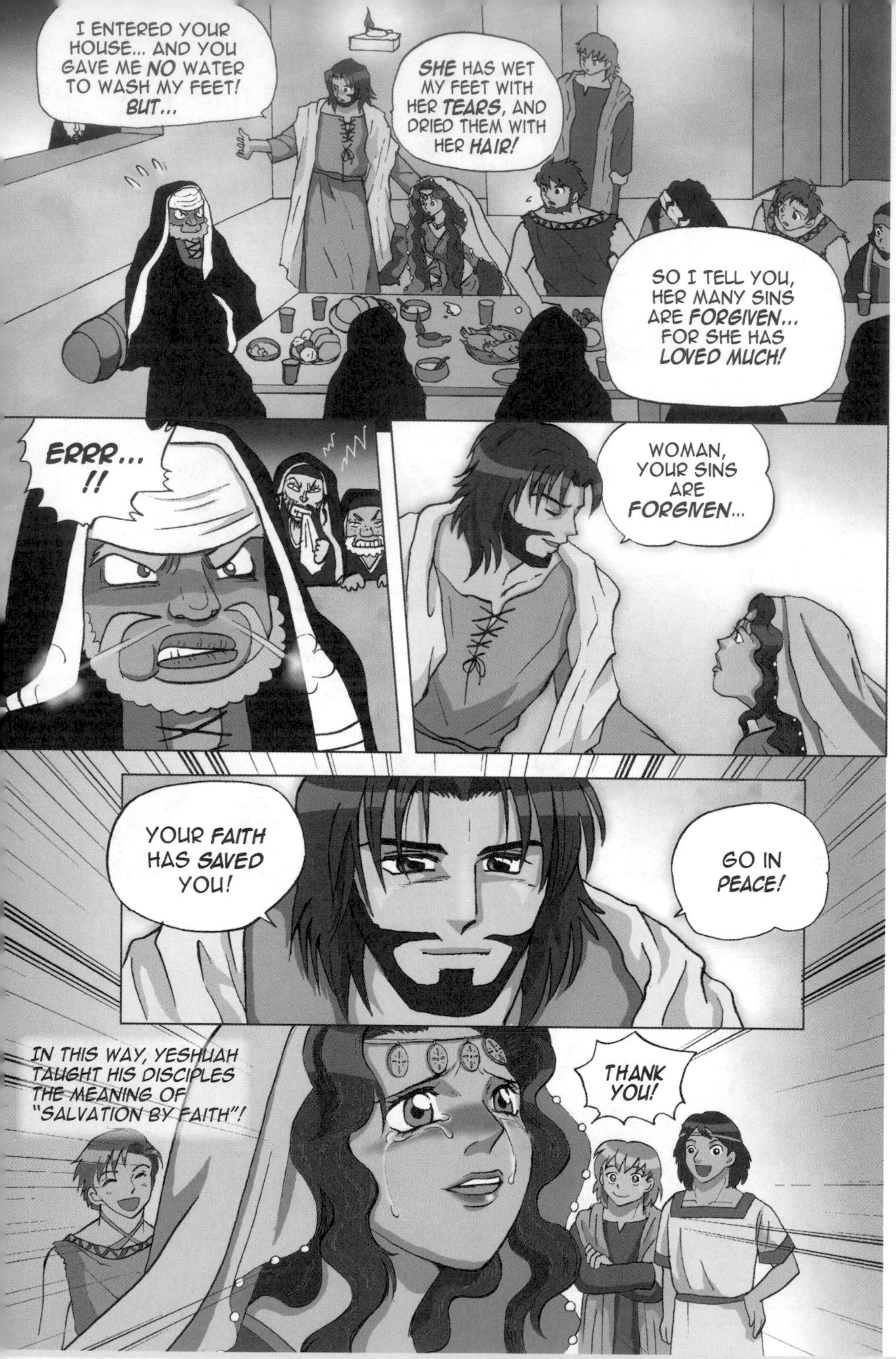
I ENTERED YOUR HOUSE... AND YOU GAVE ME NO WATER TO WASH MY FEET! BUT...
SHE HAS WET MY FEET WITH HER TEARS, AND DRIED THEM WITH HER HAIR!
SO I TELL YOU, HER MANY SINS ARE FORGIVEN... FOR SHE HAS LOVED MUCH!
ERRR... !!
WOMAN, YOUR SINS ARE FORGIVEN...
YOUR FAITH HAS SAVED YOU!
GO IN PEACE!
IN THIS WAY, YESHUAH TAUGHT HIS DISCIPLES THE MEANING OF "SALVATION BY FAITH"!
THANK YOU!

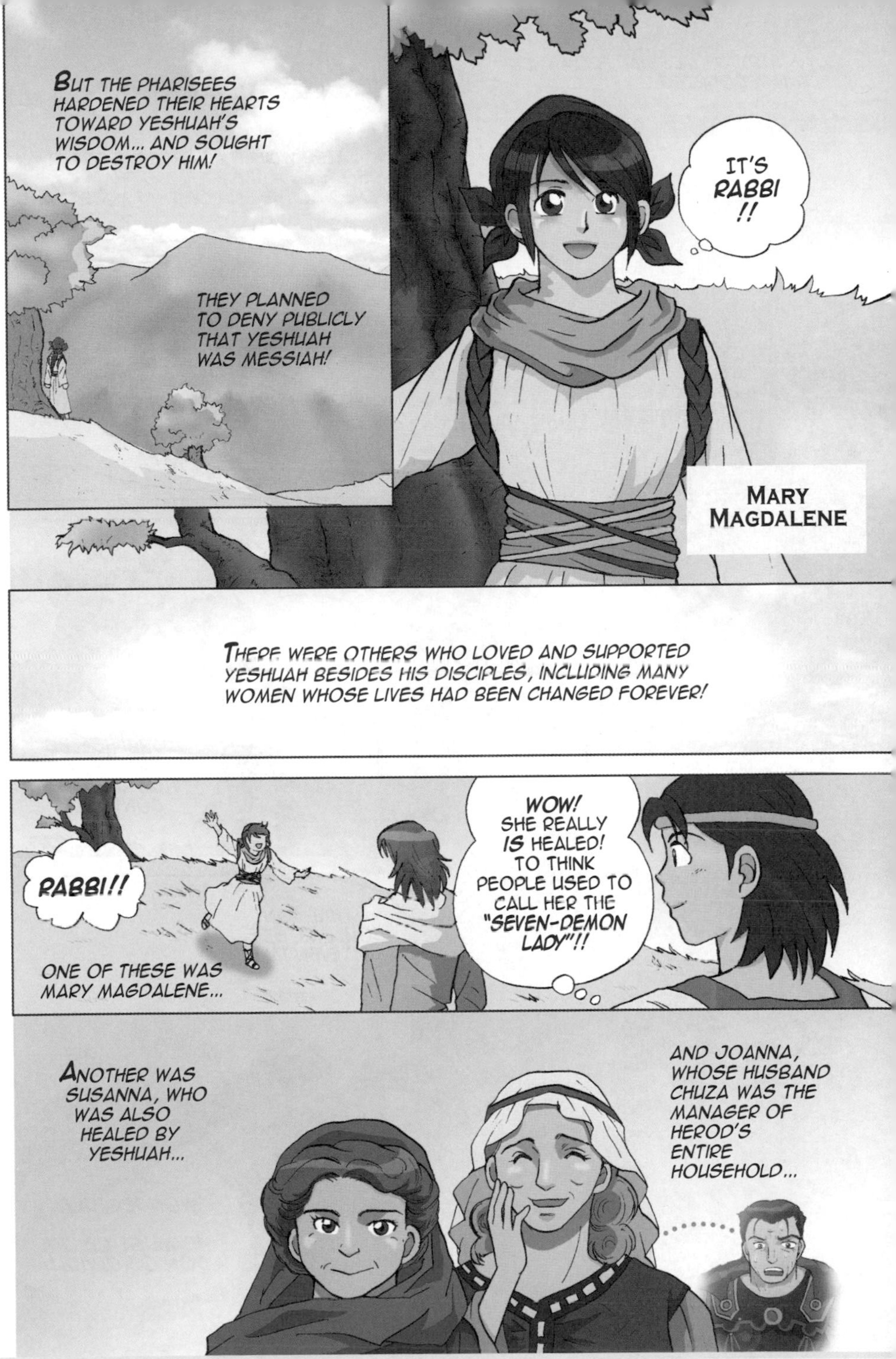
BUT THE PHARISEES HARDENED THEIR HEARTS TOWARD YESHUAH'S WISDOM... AND SOUGHT TO DESTROY HIM!
THEY PLANNED TO DENY PUBLICLY THAT YESHUAH WAS MESSIAH!
IT'S RABBI !!
MARY MAGDALENE
THERE WERE OTHERS WHO LOVED AND SUPPORTED YESHUAH BESIDES HIS DISCIPLES, INCLUDING MANY WOMEN WHOSE LIVES HAD BEEN CHANGED FOREVER!
RABBI!!
ONE OF THESE WAS MARY MAGDALENE...
WOW! SHE REALLY IS HEALED! TO THINK PEOPLE USED TO CALL HER THE "SEVEN-DEMON LADY"!!
ANOTHER WAS SUSANNA, WHO WAS ALSO HEALED BY YESHUAH...
AND JOANNA, WHOSE HUSBAND CHUZA WAS THE MANAGER OF HEROD'S ENTIRE HOUSEHOLD...

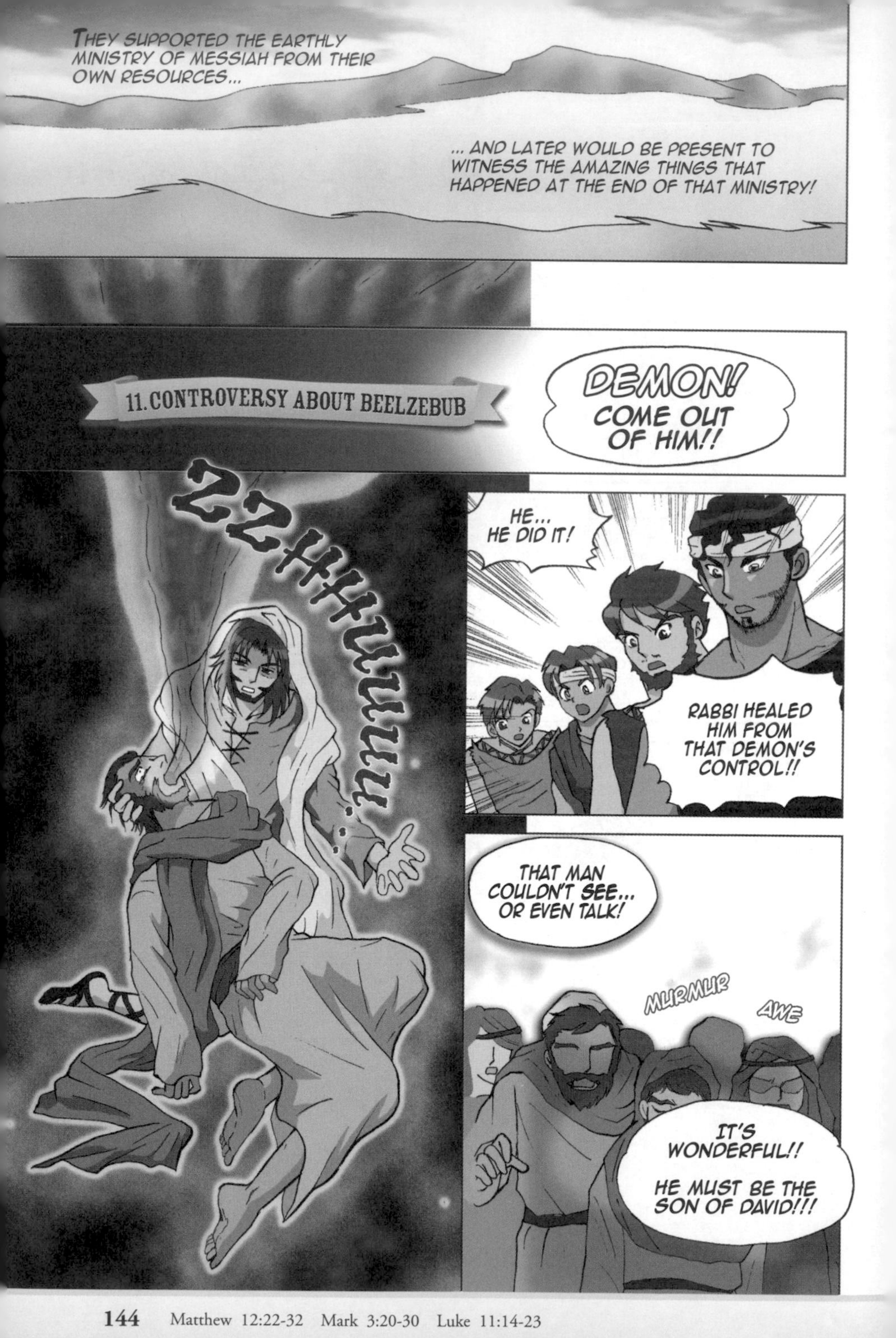
THEY SUPPORTED THE EARTHLY MINISTRY OF MESSIAH FROM THEIR OWN RESOURCES...
... AND LATER WOULD BE PRESENT TO WITNESS THE AMAZING THINGS THAT HAPPENED AT THE END OF THAT MINISTRY!
11. CONTROVERSY ABOUT BEELZEBUB
DEMON! COME OUT OF HIM!!
ZZHHHUUUUU...
HE... HE DID IT!
RABBI HEALED HIM FROM THAT DEMON'S CONTROL!!
THAT MAN COULDN'T SEE... OR EVEN TALK!
MURMUR
AWE
IT'S WONDERFUL!! HE MUST BE THE SON OF DAVID!!!

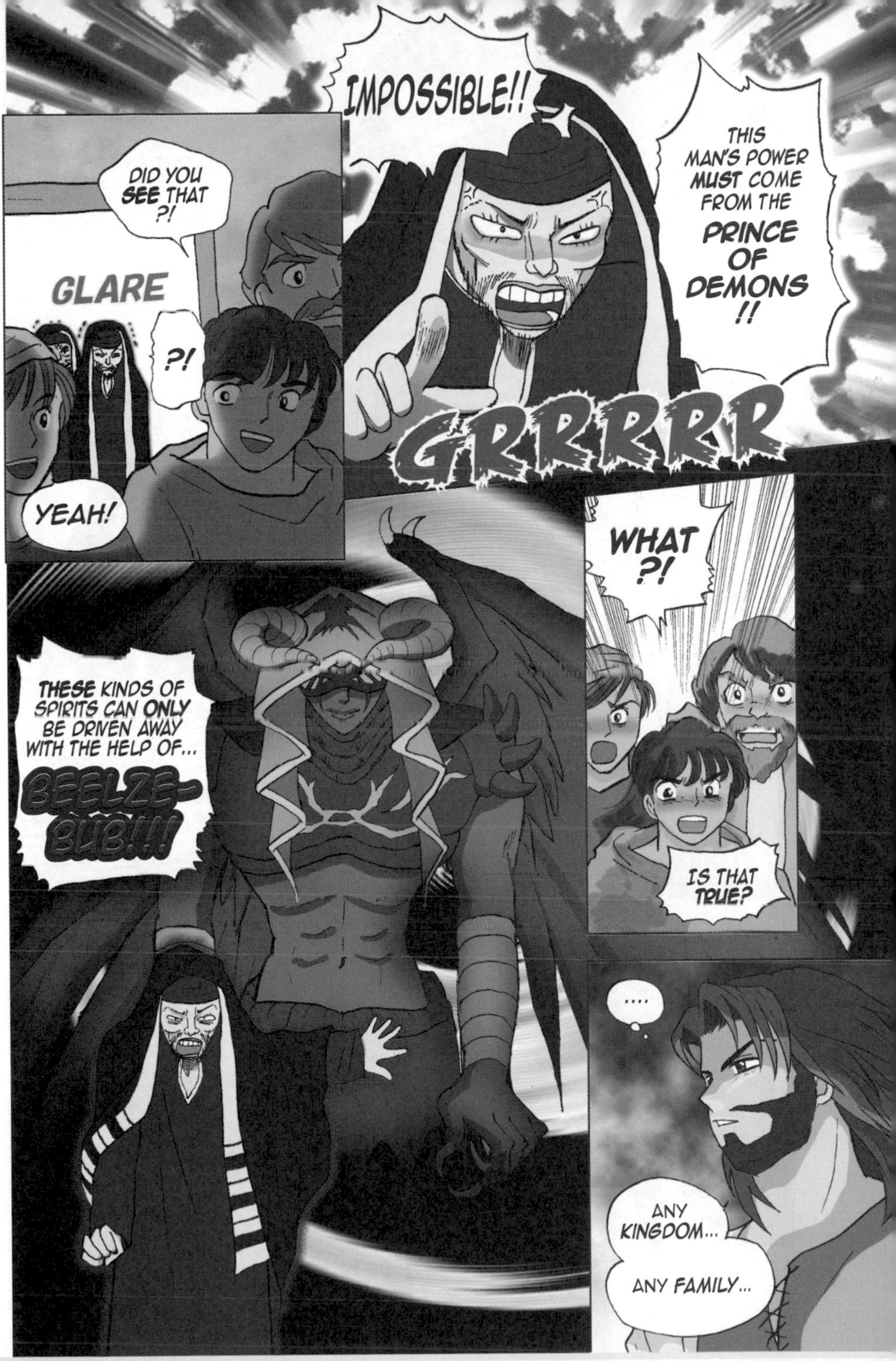
IMPOSSIBLE!!
THIS MAN'S POWER MUST COME FROM THE PRINCE OF DEMONS !!
GRRRRRR
DID YOU SEE THAT ?!
GLARE
?!
YEAH!
WHAT ?!
IS THAT TRUE?
THESE KINDS OF SPIRITS CAN ONLY BE DRIVEN AWAY WITH THE HELP OF...
BEELZE-BUB!!!
....
ANY KINGDOM...
ANY FAMILY...

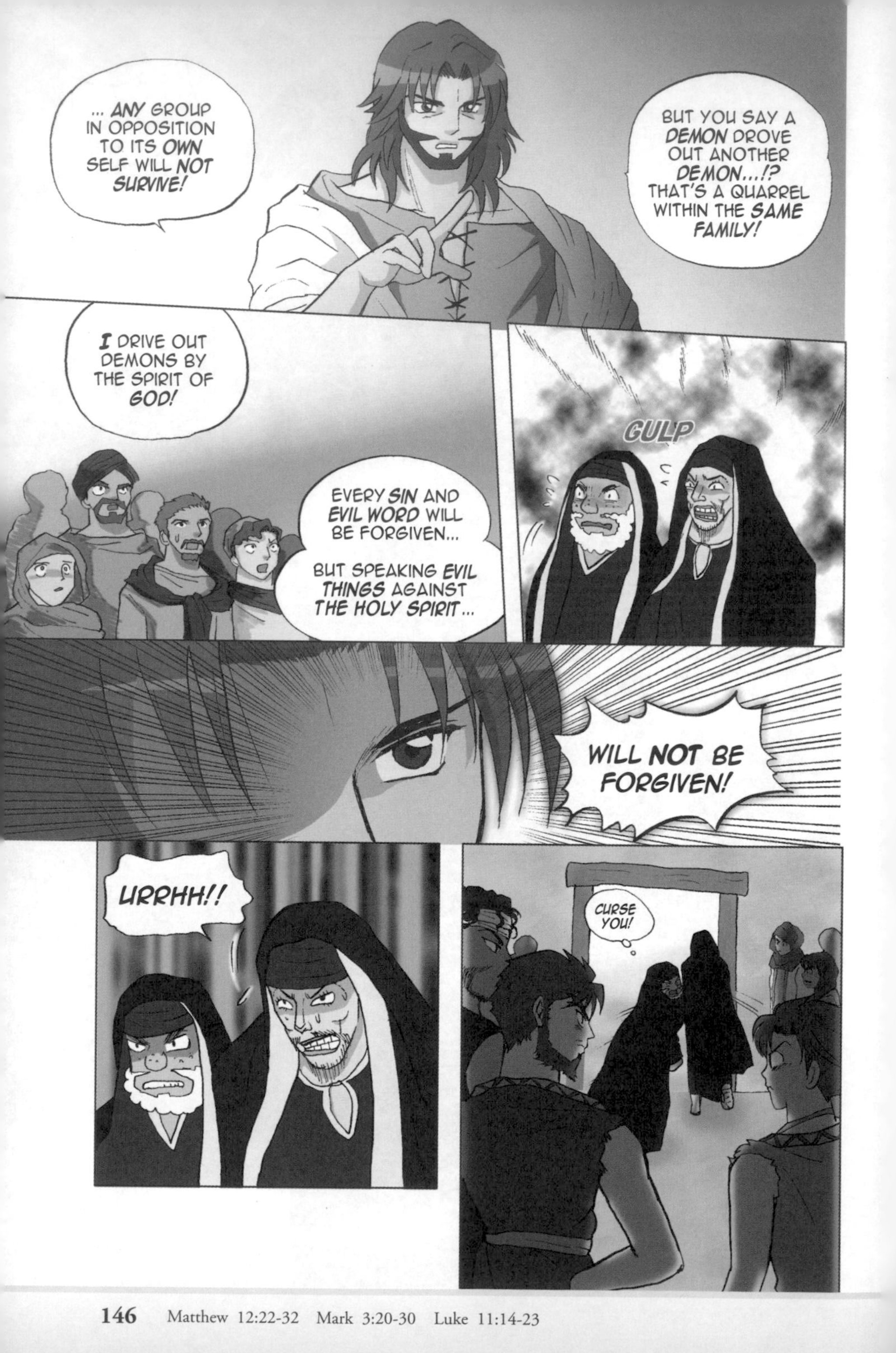
... ANY GROUP IN OPPOSITION TO ITS OWN SELF WILL NOT SURVIVE!
BUT YOU SAY A DEMON DROVE OUT ANOTHER DEMON...!? THAT'S A QUARREL WITHIN THE SAME FAMILY!
I DRIVE OUT DEMONS BY THE SPIRIT OF GOD!
EVERY SIN AND EVIL WORD WILL BE FORGIVEN...
BUT SPEAKING EVIL THINGS AGAINST THE HOLY SPIRIT...
GULP
WILL NOT BE FORGIVEN!
URRHH!!
CURSE YOU!

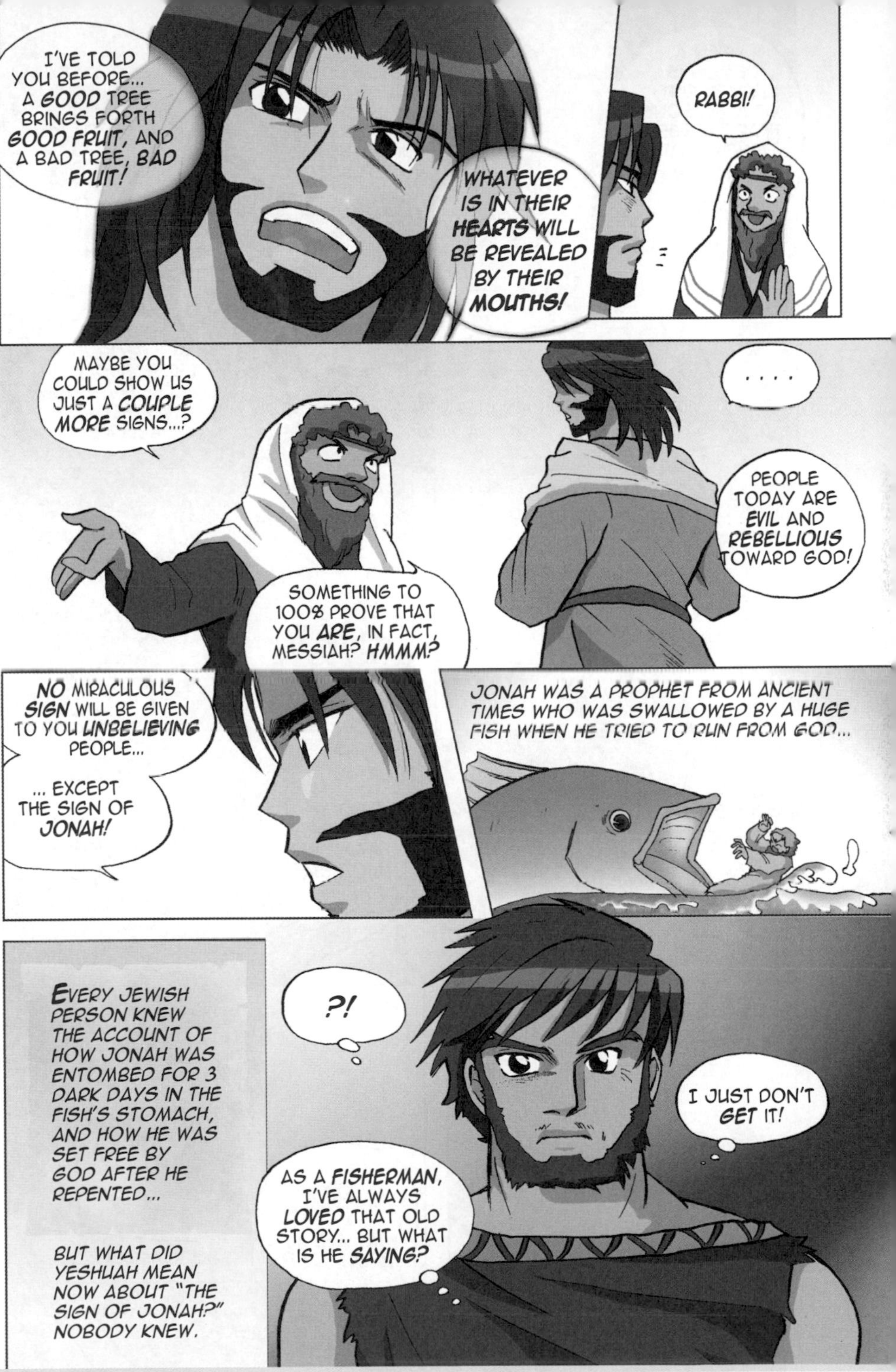
I'VE TOLD YOU BEFORE... A GOOD TREE BRINGS FORTH GOOD FRUIT, AND A BAD TREE, BAD FRUIT!
WHATEVER IS IN THEIR HEARTS WILL BE REVEALED BY THEIR MOUTHS!
RABBI!
MAYBE YOU COULD SHOW US JUST A COUPLE MORE SIGNS...?
SOMETHING TO 100% PROVE THAT YOU ARE, IN FACT, MESSIAH? HMMM?
....
PEOPLE TODAY ARE EVIL AND REBELLIOUS TOWARD GOD!
NO MIRACULOUS SIGN WILL BE GIVEN TO YOU UNBELIEVING PEOPLE...
... EXCEPT THE SIGN OF JONAH!
JONAH WAS A PROPHET FROM ANCIENT TIMES WHO WAS SWALLOWED BY A HUGE FISH WHEN HE TRIED TO RUN FROM GOD...
EVERY JEWISH PERSON KNEW THE ACCOUNT OF HOW JONAH WAS ENTOMBED FOR 3 DARK DAYS IN THE FISH'S STOMACH, AND HOW HE WAS SET FREE BY GOD AFTER HE REPENTED...
BUT WHAT DID YESHUAH MEAN NOW ABOUT "THE SIGN OF JONAH?" NOBODY KNEW.
?!
I JUST DON'T GET IT!
AS A FISHERMAN, I'VE ALWAYS LOVED THAT OLD STORY... BUT WHAT IS HE SAYING?

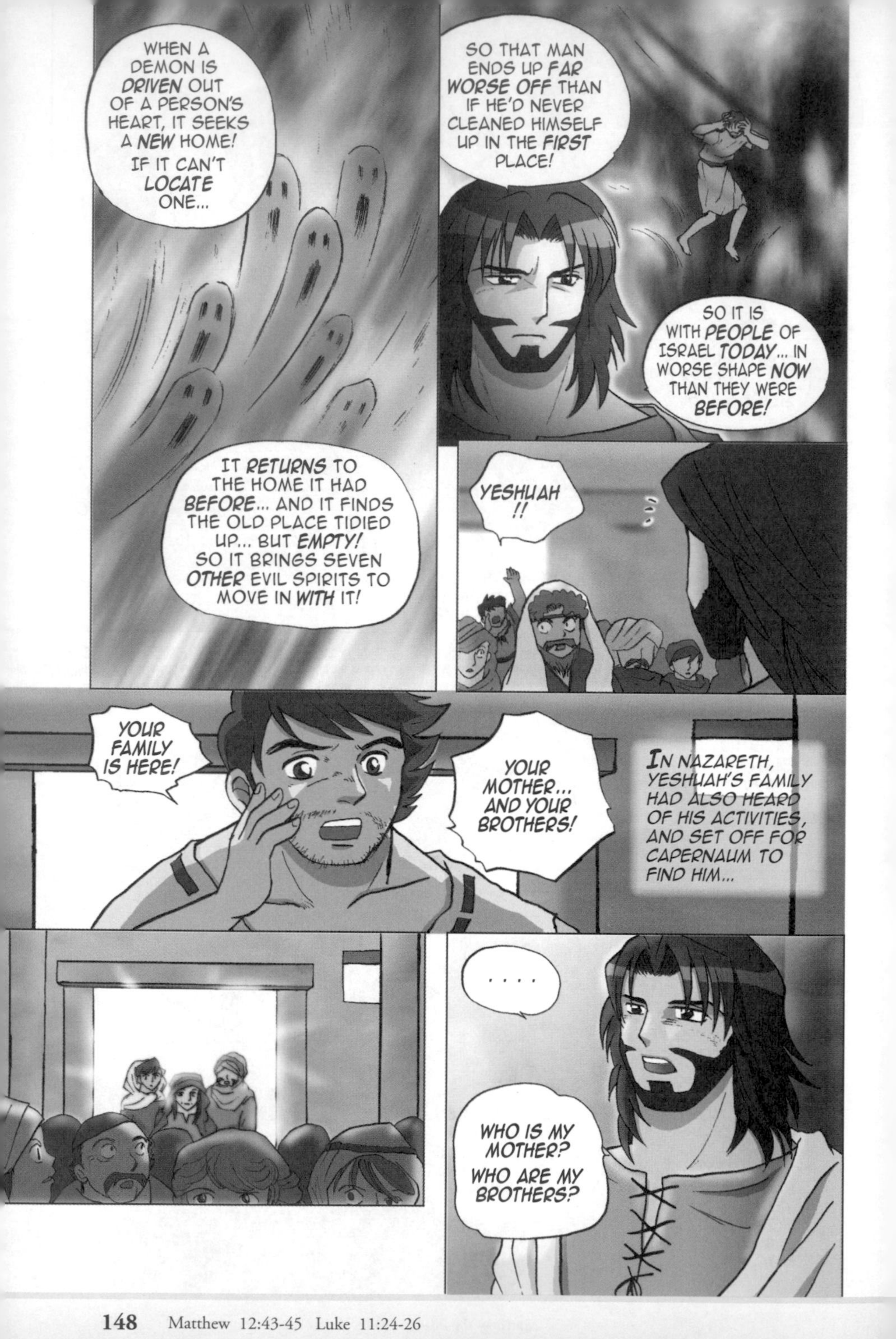
WHEN A DEMON IS DRIVEN OUT OF A PERSON'S HEART, IT SEEKS A NEW HOME! IF IT CAN'T LOCATE ONE...
IT RETURNS TO THE HOME IT HAD BEFORE... AND IT FINDS THE OLD PLACE TIDIED UP... BUT EMPTY! SO IT BRINGS SEVEN OTHER EVIL SPIRITS TO MOVE IN WITH IT!
SO THAT MAN ENDS UP FAR WORSE OFF THAN IF HE'D NEVER CLEANED HIMSELF UP IN THE FIRST PLACE!
SO IT IS WITH PEOPLE OF ISRAEL TODAY... IN WORSE SHAPE NOW THAN THEY WERE BEFORE!
YESHUAH !!
IN NAZARETH, YESHUAH'S FAMILY HAD ALSO HEARD OF HIS ACTIVITIES, AND SET OFF FOR CAPERNAUM TO FIND HIM...
YOUR FAMILY IS HERE!
YOUR MOTHER... AND YOUR BROTHERS!
. . . .
WHO IS MY MOTHER? WHO ARE MY BROTHERS?

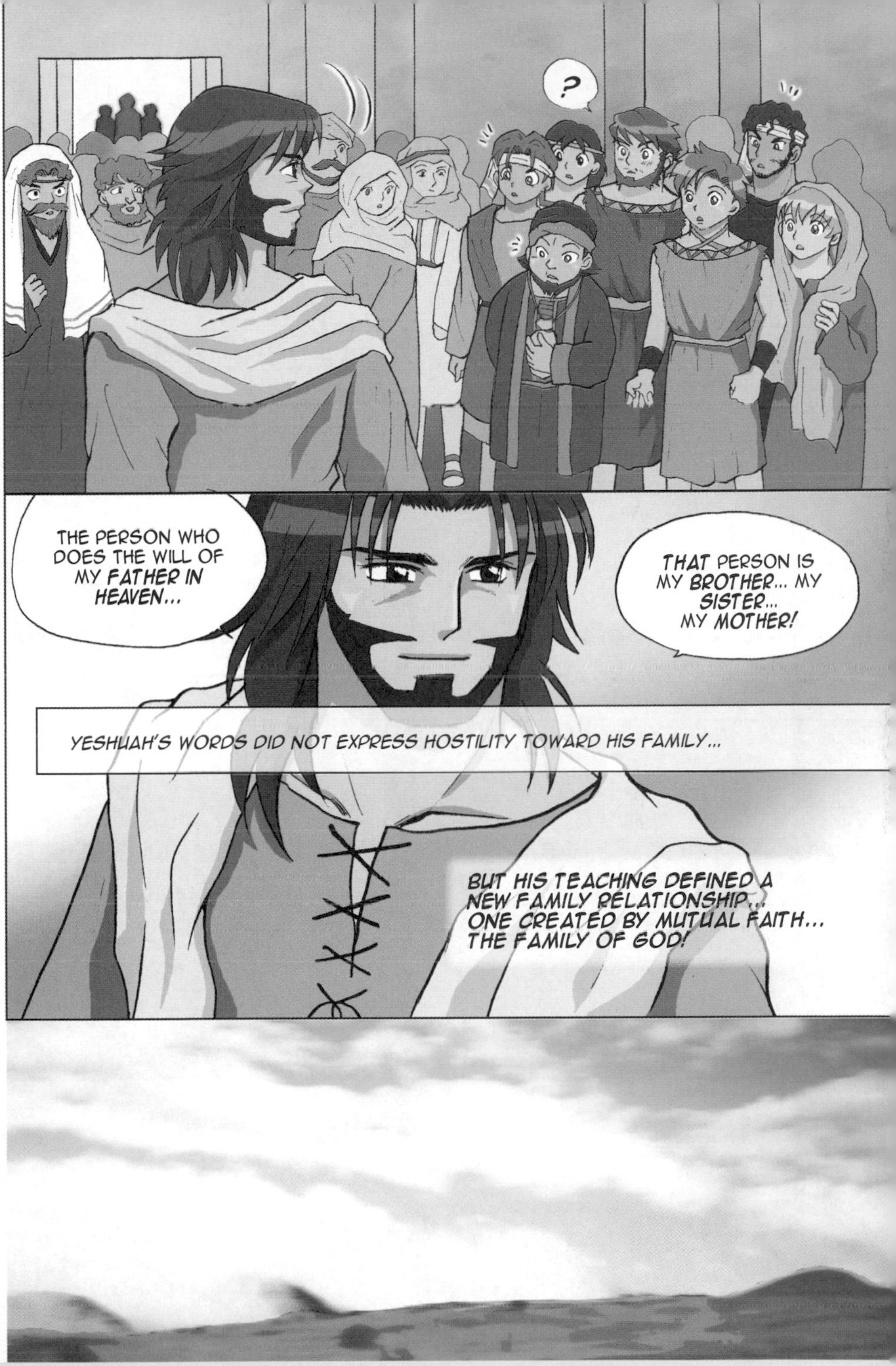
?
THE PERSON WHO DOES THE WILL OF MY FATHER IN HEAVEN...
THAT PERSON IS MY BROTHER... MY SISTER... MY MOTHER!
YESHUAH'S WORDS DID NOT EXPRESS HOSTILITY TOWARD HIS FAMILY...
BUT HIS TEACHING DEFINED A NEW FAMILY RELATIONSHIP... ONE CREATED BY MUTUAL FAITH... THE FAMILY OF GOD!

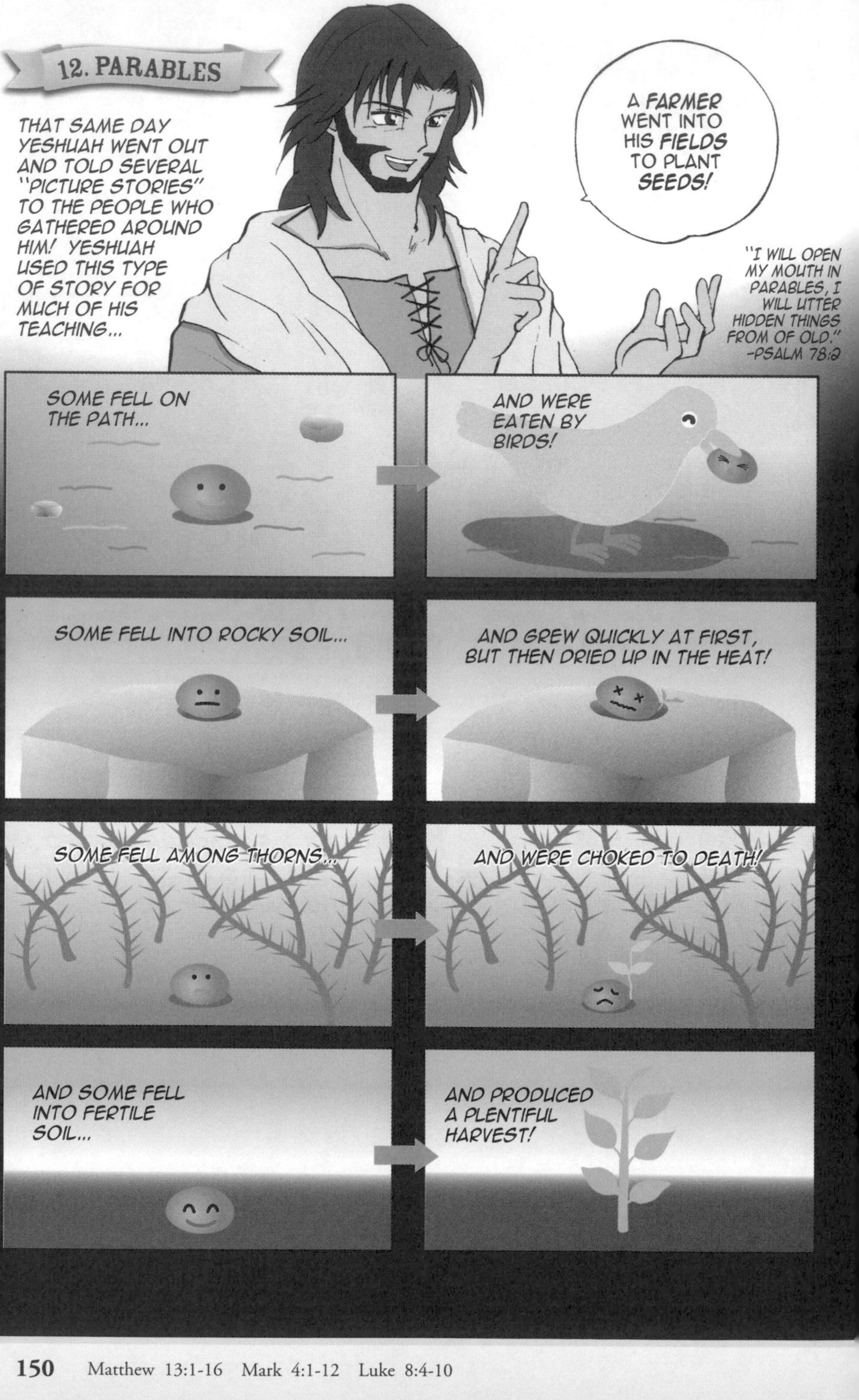
12. PARABLES
THAT SAME DAY YESHUAH WENT OUT AND TOLD SEVERAL "PICTURE STORIES" TO THE PEOPLE WHO GATHERED AROUND HIM! YESHUAH USED THIS TYPE OF STORY FOR MUCH OF HIS TEACHING...
A FARMER WENT INTO HIS FIELDS TO PLANT SEEDS!
"I WILL OPEN MY MOUTH IN PARABLES, I WILL UTTER HIDDEN THINGS FROM OF OLD." -PSALM 78:2
SOME FELL ON THE PATH...
AND WERE EATEN BY BIRDS!
SOME FELL INTO ROCKY SOIL...
AND GREW QUICKLY AT FIRST, BUT THEN DRIED UP IN THE HEAT!
SOME FELL AMONG THORNS...
AND WERE CHOKED TO DEATH!
AND SOME FELL INTO FERTILE SOIL...
AND PRODUCED A PLENTIFUL HARVEST!

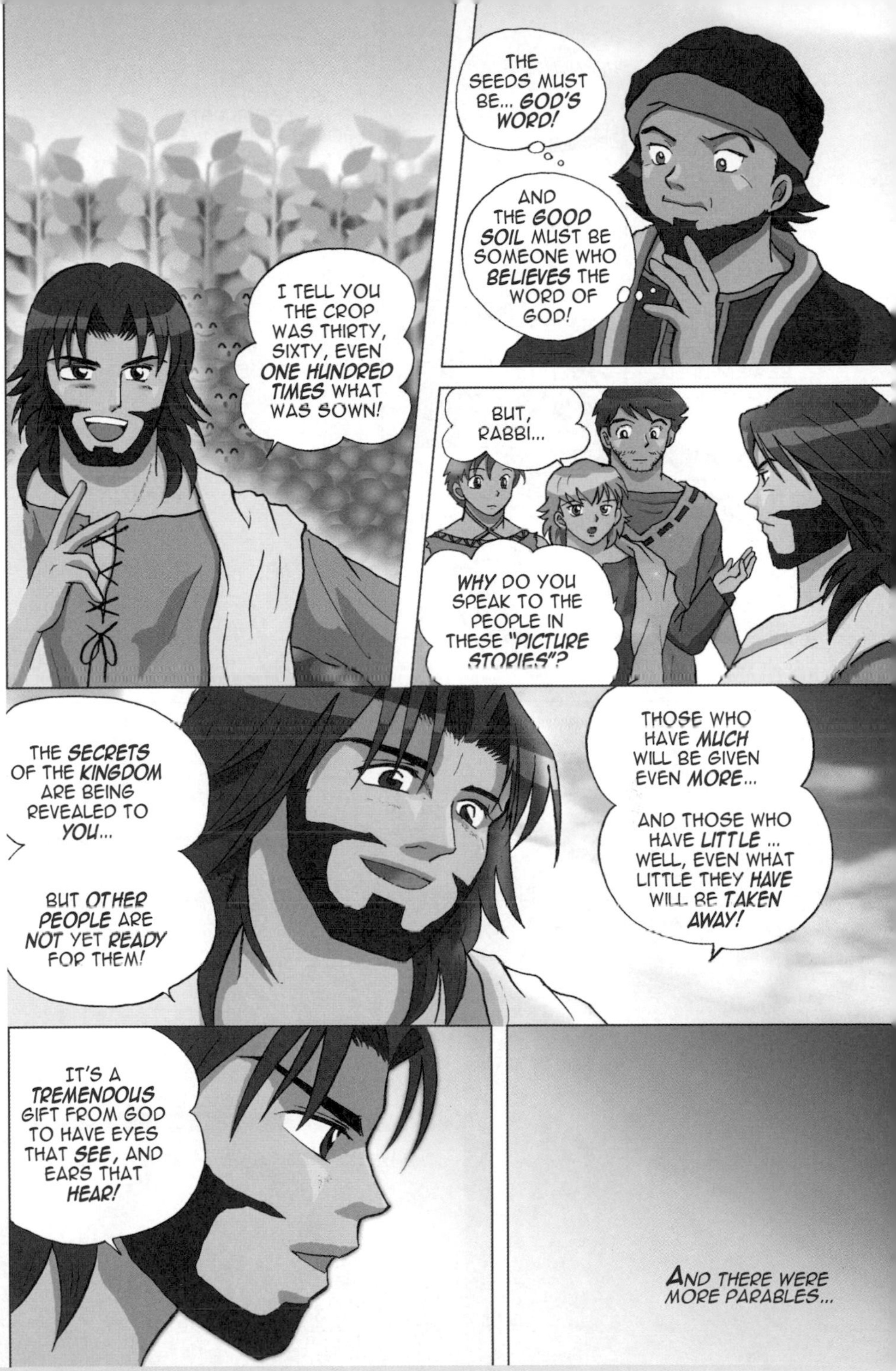
I TELL YOU THE CROP WAS THIRTY, SIXTY, EVEN ONE HUNDRED TIMES WHAT WAS SOWN!
THE SEEDS MUST BE... GOD'S WORD!
AND THE GOOD SOIL MUST BE SOMEONE WHO BELIEVES THE WORD OF GOD!
BUT, RABBI...
WHY DO YOU SPEAK TO THE PEOPLE IN THESE "PICTURE STORIES"?
THE SECRETS OF THE KINGDOM ARE BEING REVEALED TO YOU...
BUT OTHER PEOPLE ARE NOT YET READY FOR THEM!
THOSE WHO HAVE MUCH WILL BE GIVEN EVEN MORE...
AND THOSE WHO HAVE LITTLE ... WELL, EVEN WHAT LITTLE THEY HAVE WILL BE TAKEN AWAY!
IT'S A TREMENDOUS GIFT FROM GOD TO HAVE EYES THAT SEE, AND EARS THAT HEAR!
AND THERE WERE MORE PARABLES...

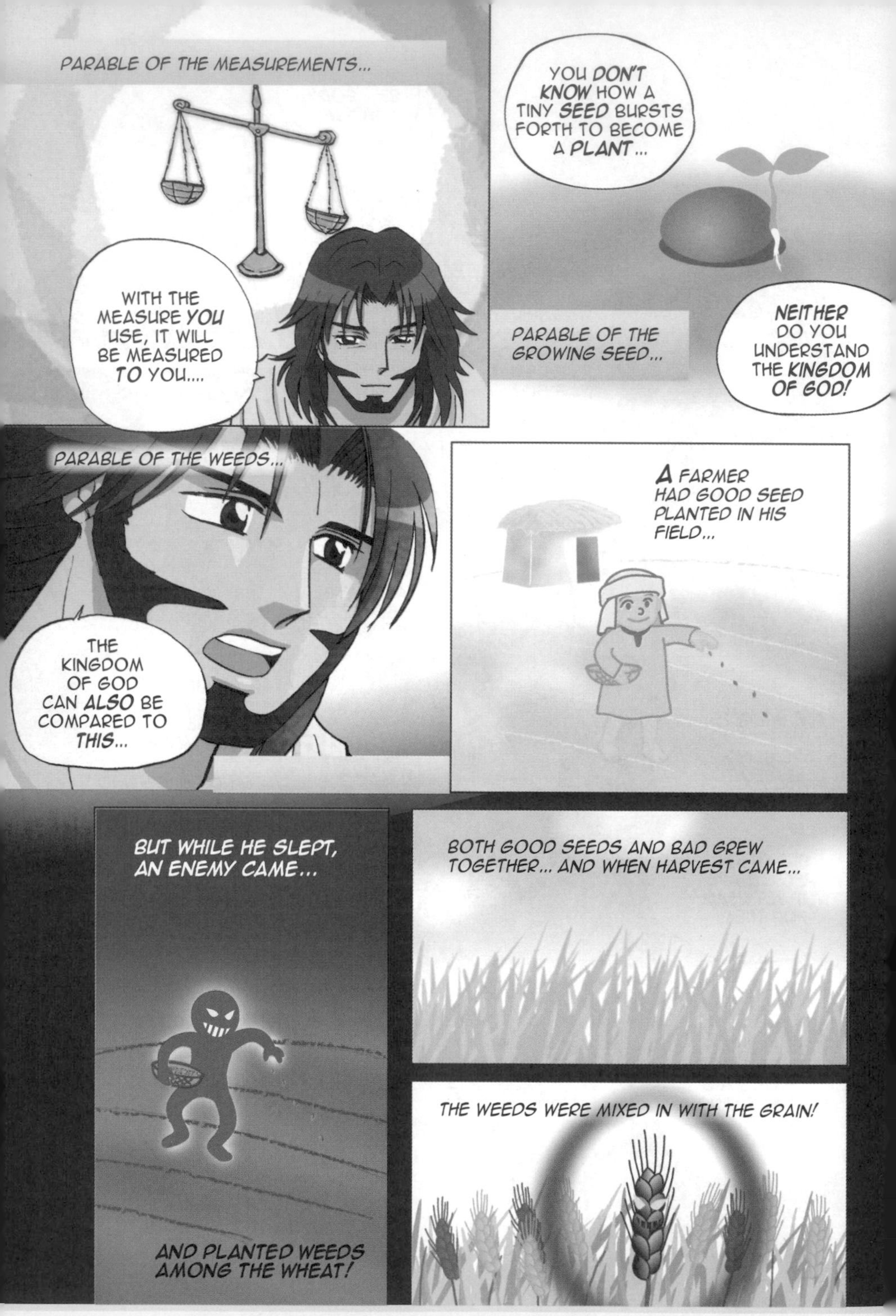

PARABLE OF THE MEASUREMENTS...
WITH THE MEASURE YOU USE, IT WILL BE MEASURED TO YOU....
YOU DON'T KNOW HOW A TINY SEED BURSTS FORTH TO BECOME A PLANT...
PARABLE OF THE GROWING SEED...
NEITHER DO YOU UNDERSTAND THE KINGDOM OF GOD!
PARABLE OF THE WEEDS...
THE KINGDOM OF GOD CAN ALSO BE COMPARED TO THIS...
A FARMER HAD GOOD SEED PLANTED IN HIS FIELD...
BUT WHILE HE SLEPT, AN ENEMY CAME...
AND PLANTED WEEDS AMONG THE WHEAT!
BOTH GOOD SEEDS AND BAD GREW TOGETHER... AND WHEN HARVEST CAME...
THE WEEDS WERE MIXED IN WITH THE GRAIN!

 Matthew 13:24-42 Mark 4:24-27

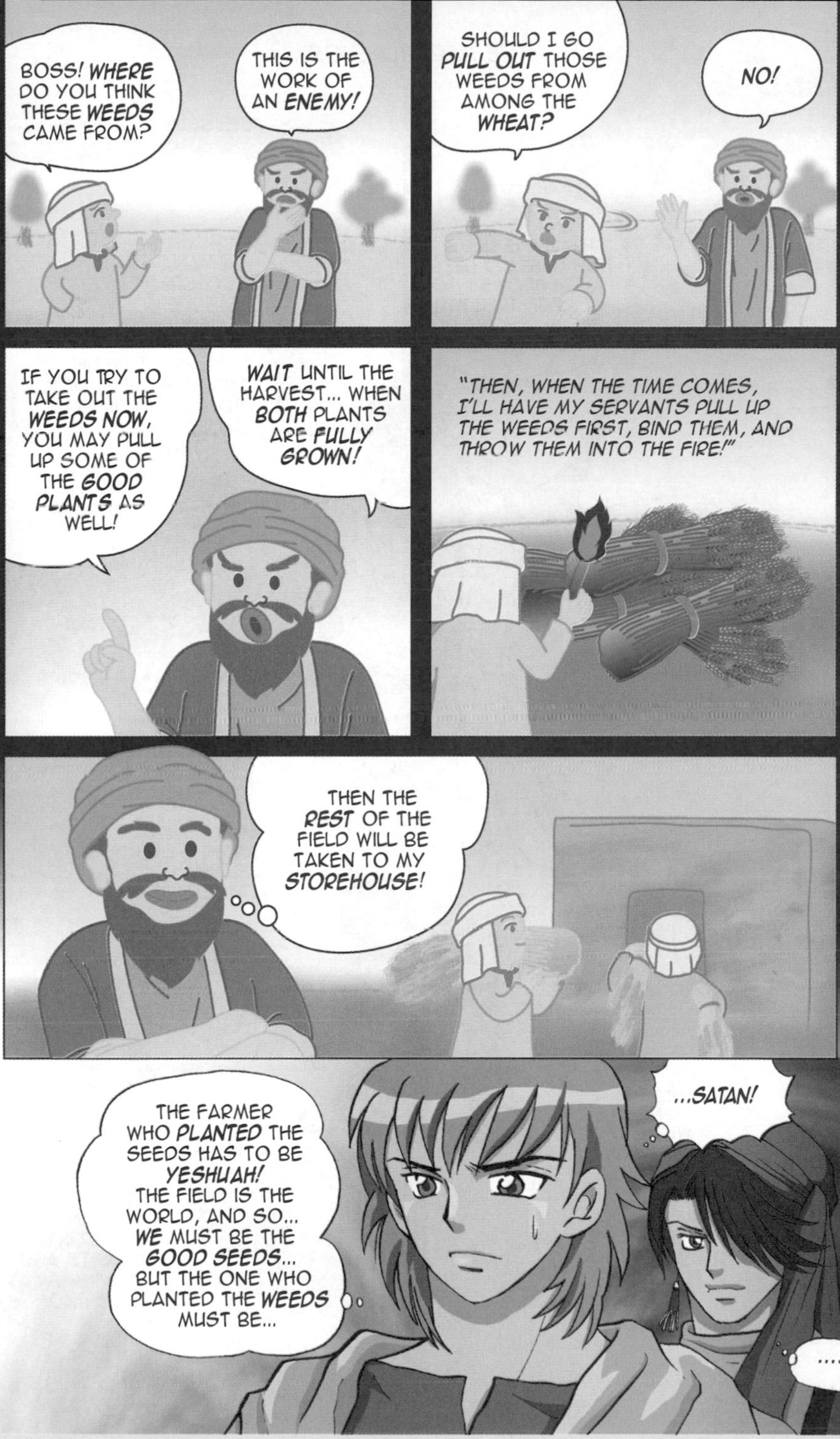
BOSS! WHERE DO YOU THINK THESE WEEDS CAME FROM?
THIS IS THE WORK OF AN ENEMY!
SHOULD I GO PULL OUT THOSE WEEDS FROM AMONG THE WHEAT?
NO!
IF YOU TRY TO TAKE OUT THE WEEDS NOW, YOU MAY PULL UP SOME OF THE GOOD PLANTS AS WELL!
WAIT UNTIL THE HARVEST... WHEN BOTH PLANTS ARE FULLY GROWN!
"THEN, WHEN THE TIME COMES, I'LL HAVE MY SERVANTS PULL UP THE WEEDS FIRST, BIND THEM, AND THROW THEM INTO THE FIRE!"
THEN THE REST OF THE FIELD WILL BE TAKEN TO MY STOREHOUSE!
THE FARMER WHO PLANTED THE SEEDS HAS TO BE YESHUAH! THE FIELD IS THE WORLD, AND SO... WE MUST BE THE GOOD SEEDS... BUT THE ONE WHO PLANTED THE WEEDS MUST BE...
...SATAN!
....

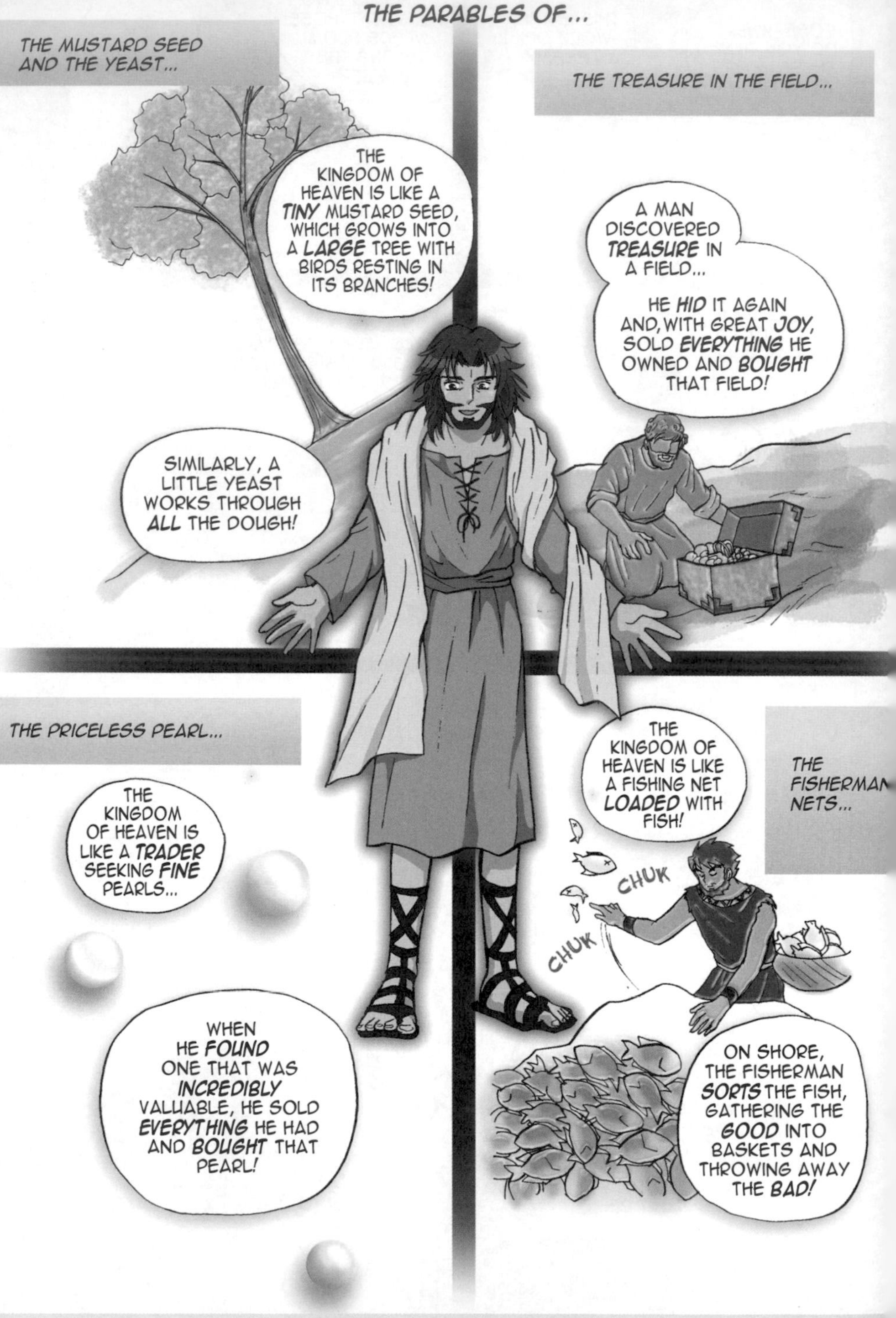
THE PARABLES OF...
THE MUSTARD SEED AND THE YEAST...
THE KINGDOM OF HEAVEN IS LIKE A TINY MUSTARD SEED, WHICH GROWS INTO A LARGE TREE WITH BIRDS RESTING IN ITS BRANCHES!
SIMILARLY, A LITTLE YEAST WORKS THROUGH ALL THE DOUGH!
THE TREASURE IN THE FIELD...
A MAN DISCOVERED TREASURE IN A FIELD...
HE HID IT AGAIN AND, WITH GREAT JOY, SOLD EVERYTHING HE OWNED AND BOUGHT THAT FIELD!
THE PRICELESS PEARL...
THE KINGDOM OF HEAVEN IS LIKE A TRADER SEEKING FINE PEARLS...
WHEN HE FOUND ONE THAT WAS INCREDIBLY VALUABLE, HE SOLD EVERYTHING HE HAD AND BOUGHT THAT PEARL!
THE FISHERMAN NETS...
THE KINGDOM OF HEAVEN IS LIKE A FISHING NET LOADED WITH FISH!
CHUK
CHUK
ON SHORE, THE FISHERMAN SORTS THE FISH, GATHERING THE GOOD INTO BASKETS AND THROWING AWAY THE BAD!

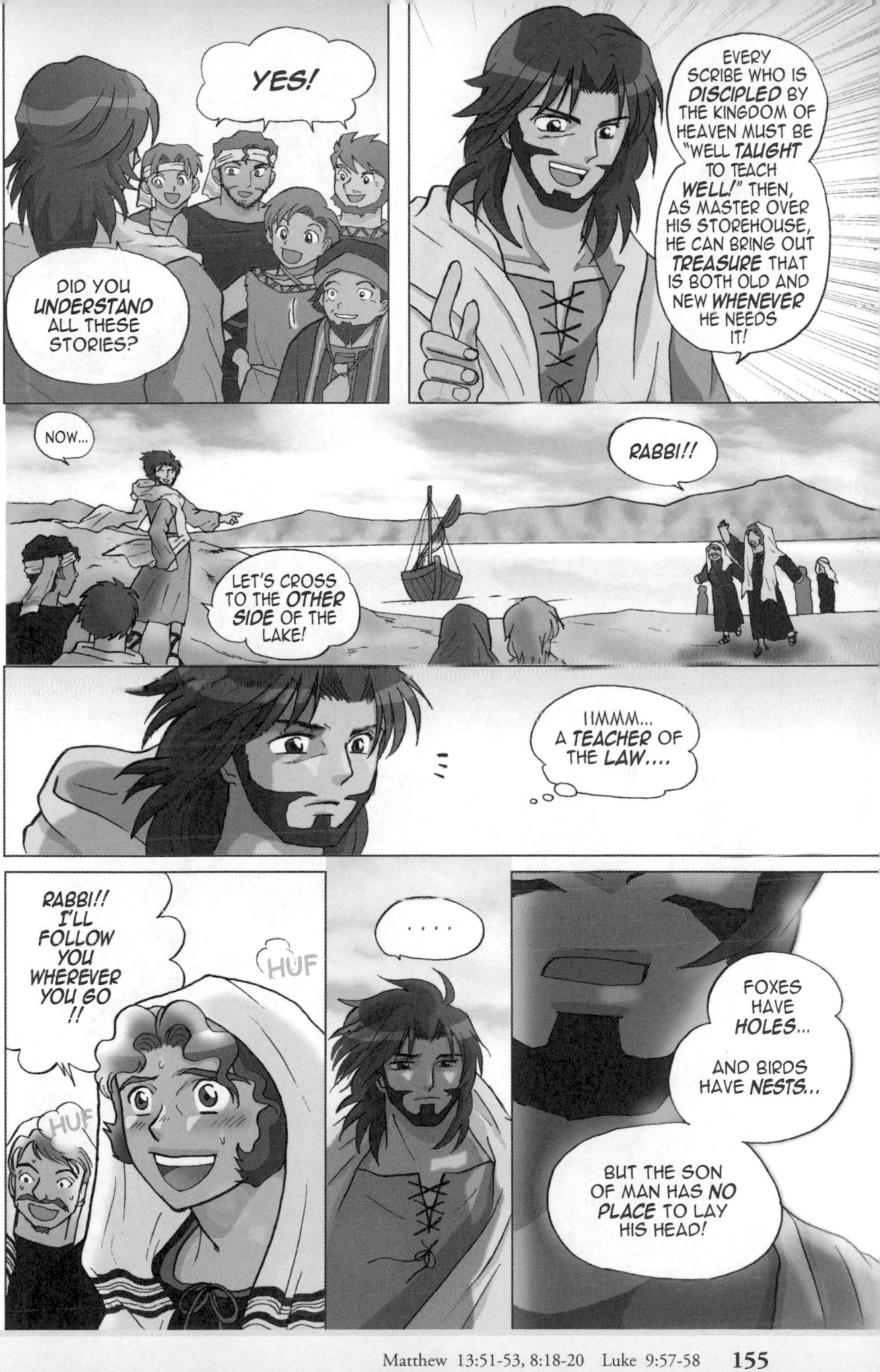
DID YOU UNDERSTAND ALL THESE STORIES?
YES!
EVERY SCRIBE WHO IS DISCIPLED BY THE KINGDOM OF HEAVEN MUST BE "WELL TAUGHT TO TEACH WELL!" THEN, AS MASTER OVER HIS STOREHOUSE, HE CAN BRING OUT TREASURE THAT IS BOTH OLD AND NEW WHENEVER HE NEEDS IT!
NOW...
LET'S CROSS TO THE OTHER SIDE OF THE LAKE!
RABBI!!
HMMM... A TEACHER OF THE LAW....
RABBI!! I'LL FOLLOW YOU WHEREVER YOU GO !!
HUF
HUF
....
FOXES HAVE HOLES...
AND BIRDS HAVE NESTS...
BUT THE SON OF MAN HAS NO PLACE TO LAY HIS HEAD!

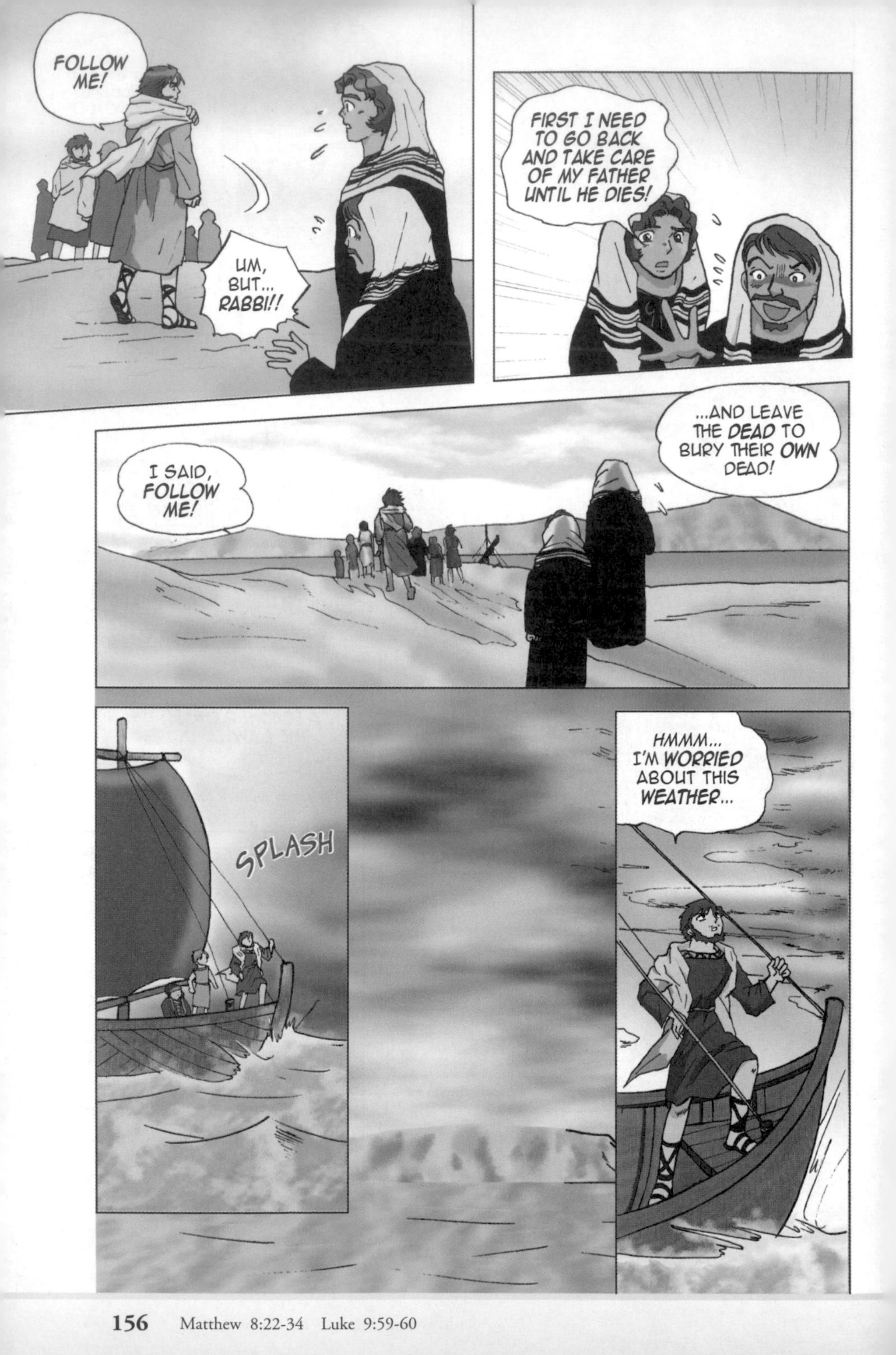
FOLLOW ME!
UM, BUT... RABBI!!
FIRST I NEED TO GO BACK AND TAKE CARE OF MY FATHER UNTIL HE DIES!
I SAID, FOLLOW ME!
...AND LEAVE THE DEAD TO BURY THEIR OWN DEAD!
SPLASH
HMMM... I'M WORRIED ABOUT THIS WEATHER...

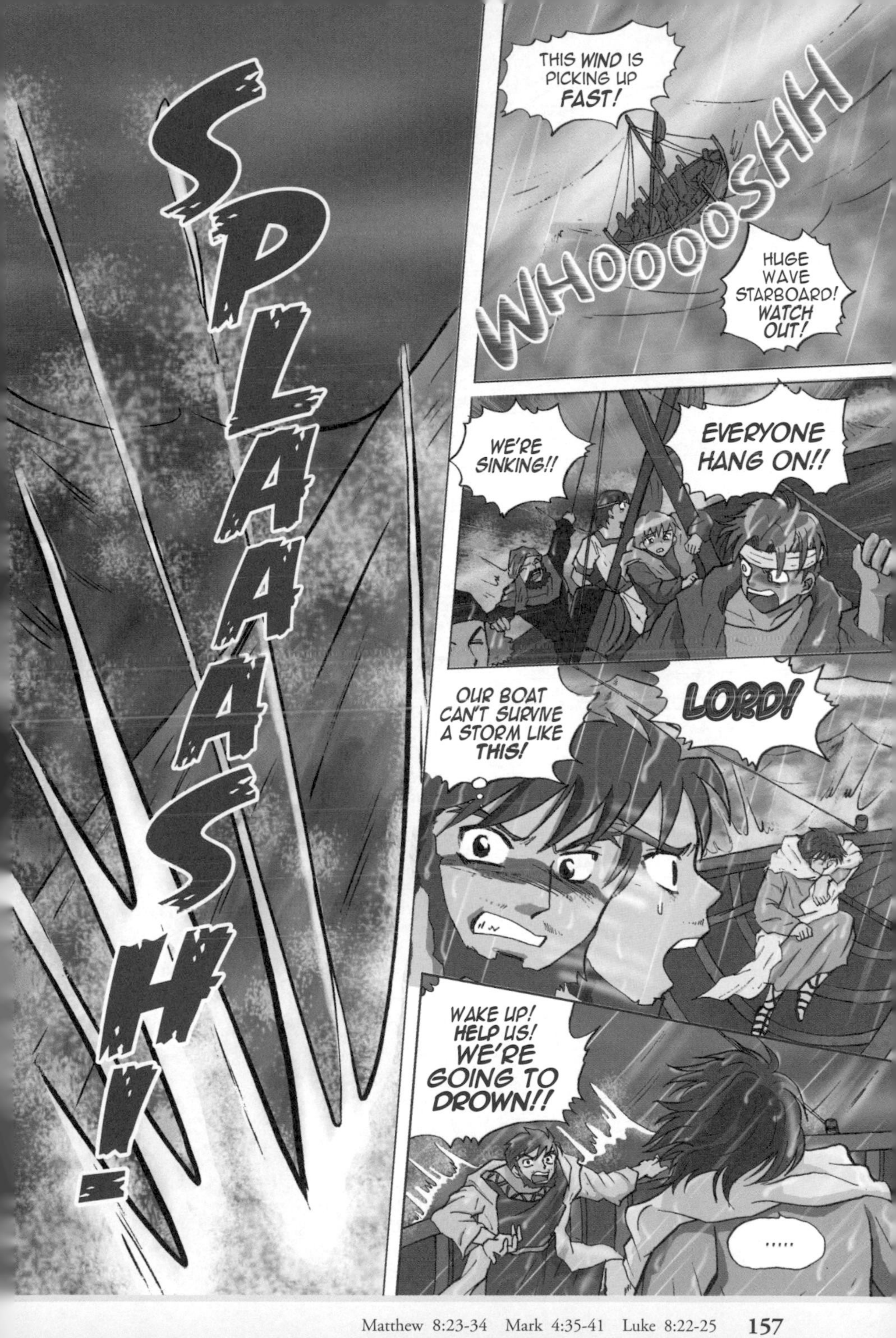
THIS WIND IS PICKING UP FAST!
WHOOOOSHH
HUGE WAVE STARBOARD! WATCH OUT!
WE'RE SINKING!!
EVERYONE HANG ON!!
SPLAASH!
OUR BOAT CAN'T SURVIVE A STORM LIKE THIS!
LORD!
WAKE UP! HELP US! WE'RE GOING TO DROWN!!
.....

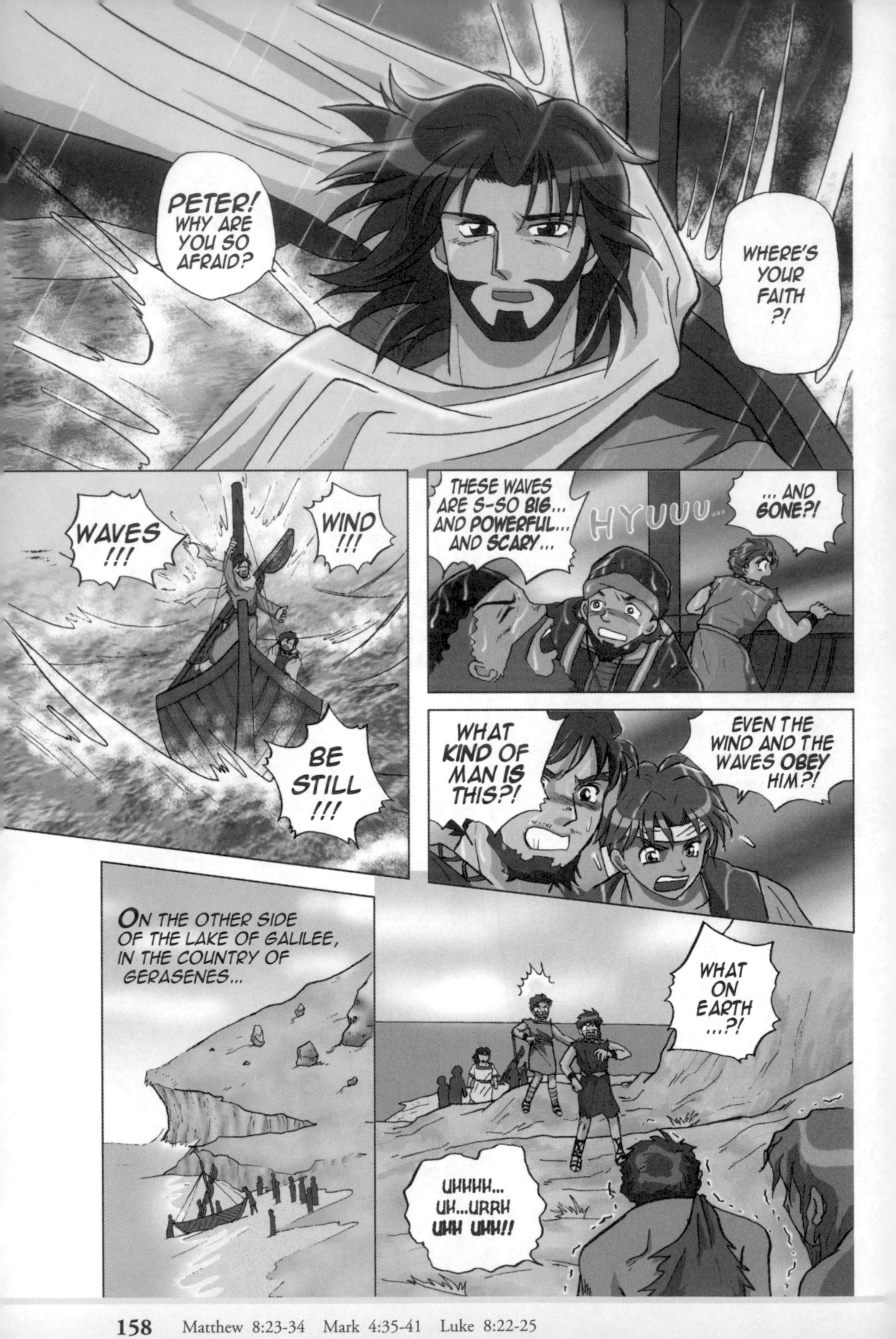
PETER! WHY ARE YOU SO AFRAID?
WHERE'S YOUR FAITH ?!
WAVES !!!
WIND !!!
BE STILL !!!
THESE WAVES ARE S-SO BIG... AND POWERFUL... AND SCARY...
HYUUU...
... AND GONE?!
WHAT KIND OF MAN IS THIS?!
EVEN THE WIND AND THE WAVES OBEY HIM?!
ON THE OTHER SIDE OF THE LAKE OF GALILEE, IN THE COUNTRY OF GERASENES...
WHAT ON EARTH ...?!
UHHHH... UH...URRH UHH UHH!!

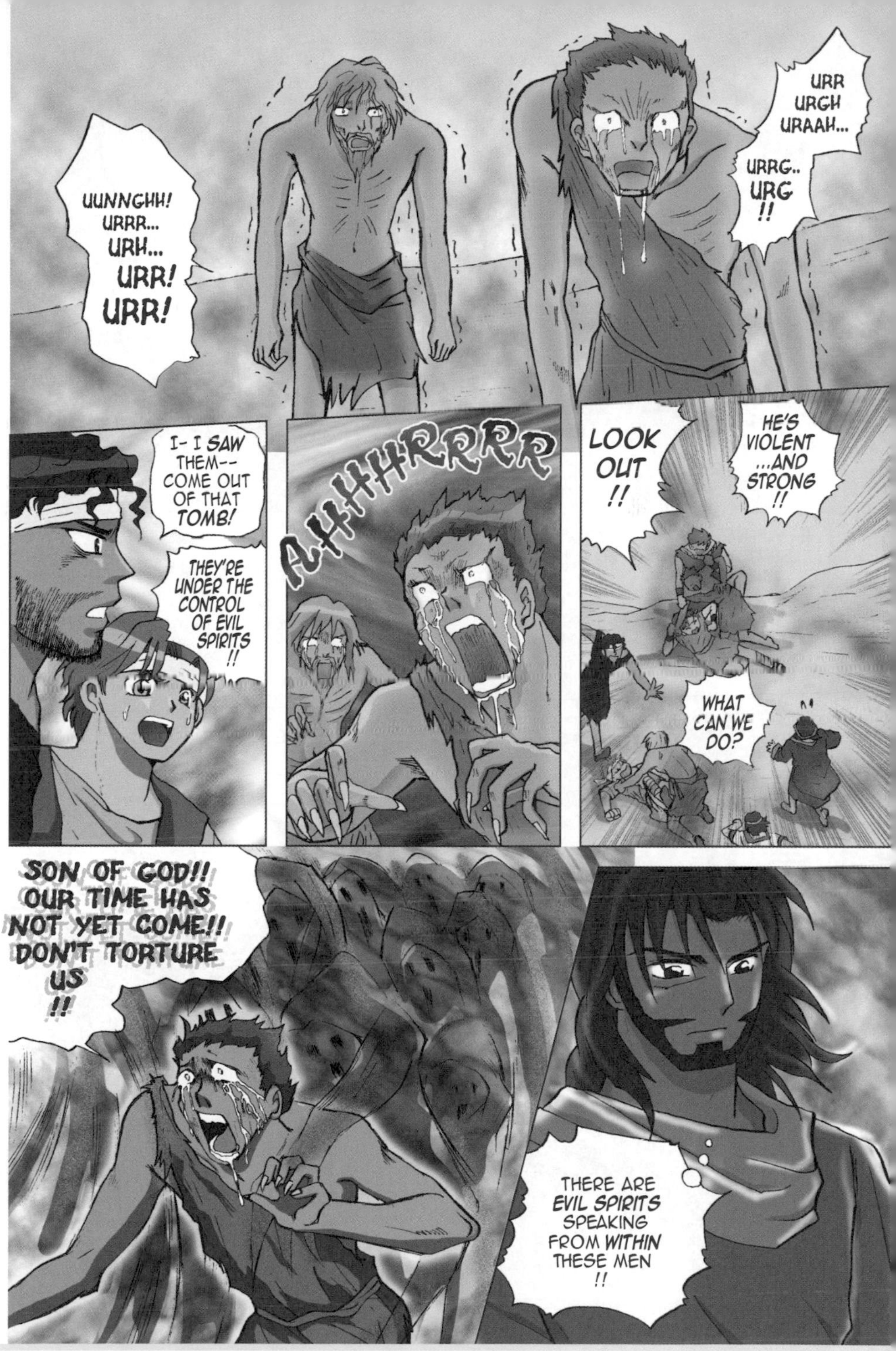
UUNNGHH! URRR... URH... URR! URR!
URR URGH URAAH...
URRG.. URG !!
I- I SAW THEM-- COME OUT OF THAT TOMB!
THEY'RE UNDER THE CONTROL OF EVIL SPIRITS !!
AHHHRRRRR
LOOK OUT !!
HE'S VIOLENT ...AND STRONG !!
WHAT CAN WE DO?
SON OF GOD!! OUR TIME HAS NOT YET COME!!! DON'T TORTURE US !!
THERE ARE EVIL SPIRITS SPEAKING FROM WITHIN THESE MEN !!

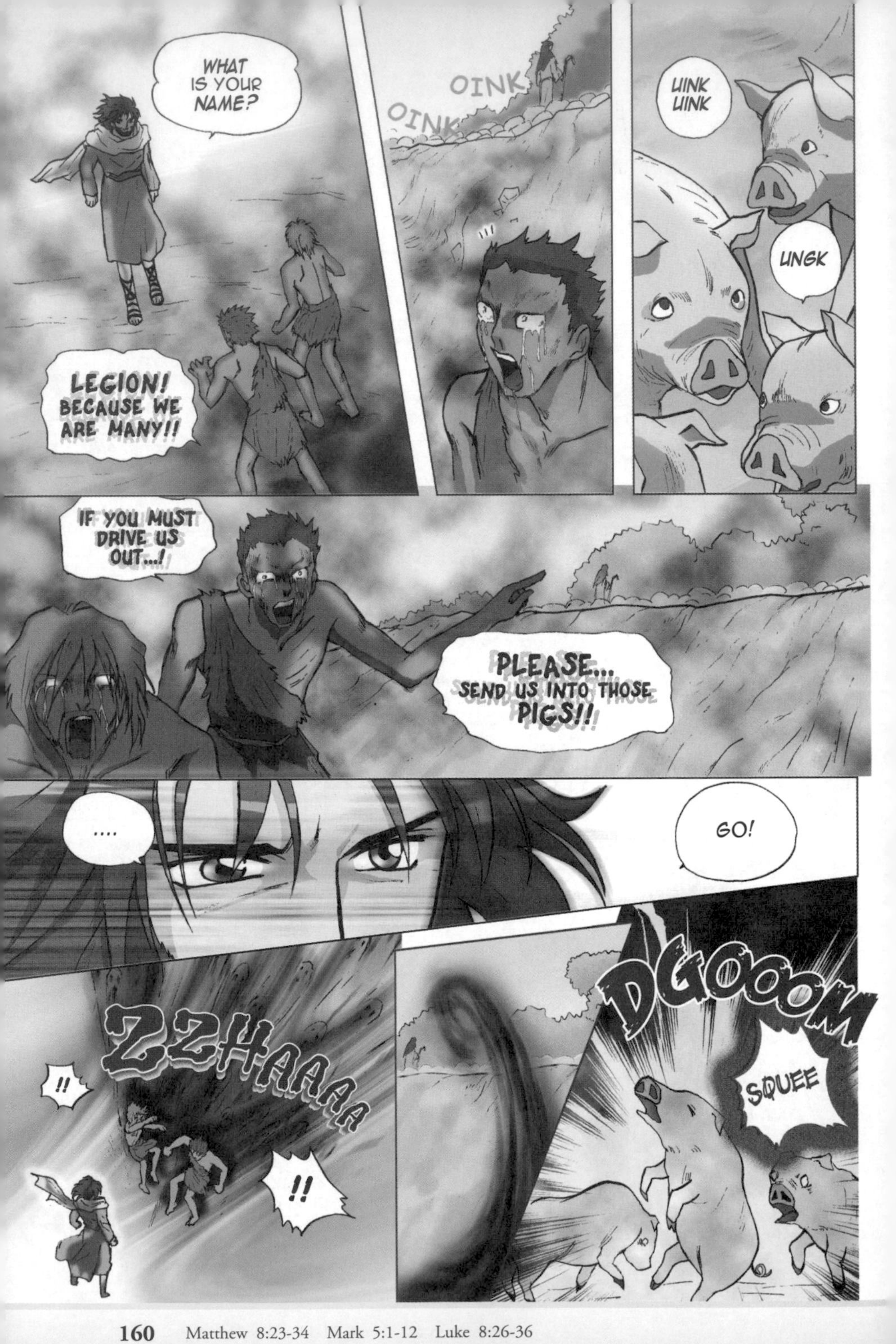
WHAT IS YOUR NAME?
LEGION! BECAUSE WE ARE MANY!!
OINK
OINK
!!!
UINK UINK
UNGK
IF YOU MUST DRIVE US OUT...!
PLEASE... SEND US INTO THOSE PIGS!!
....
GO!
ZZHAAAAA
!!
!!
DGOOOM
SQUEE

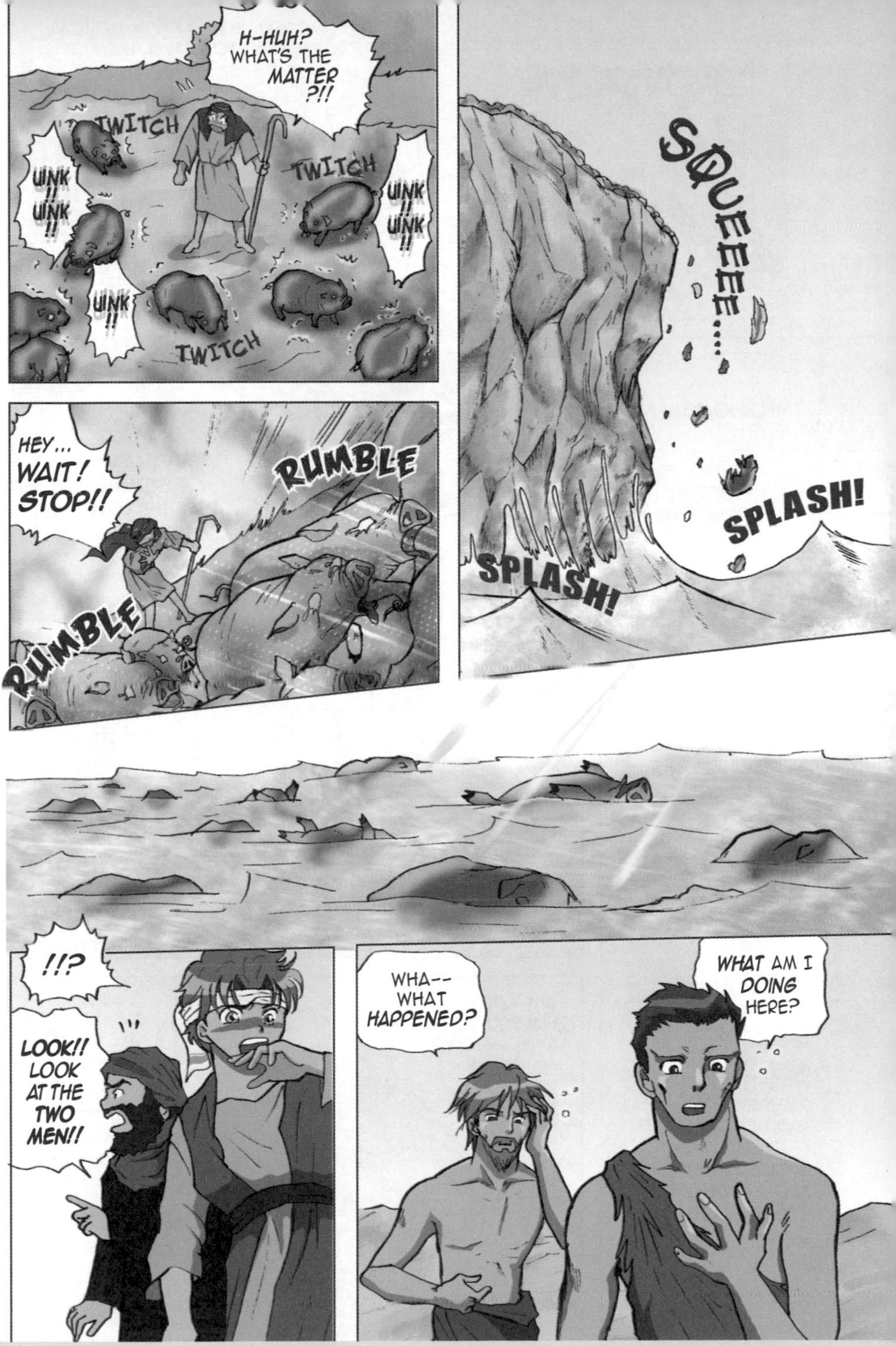
H-HUH? WHAT'S THE MATTER ?!!
TWITCH
UINK!! UINK!!
TWITCH
UINK!! UINK!!
UINK!!
TWITCH
SQUEEEE....
HEY... WAIT! STOP!!
RUMBLE
RUMBLE
SPLASH!
SPLASH!
!!?
LOOK!! LOOK AT THE TWO MEN!!
WHA-- WHAT HAPPENED?
WHAT AM I DOING HERE?

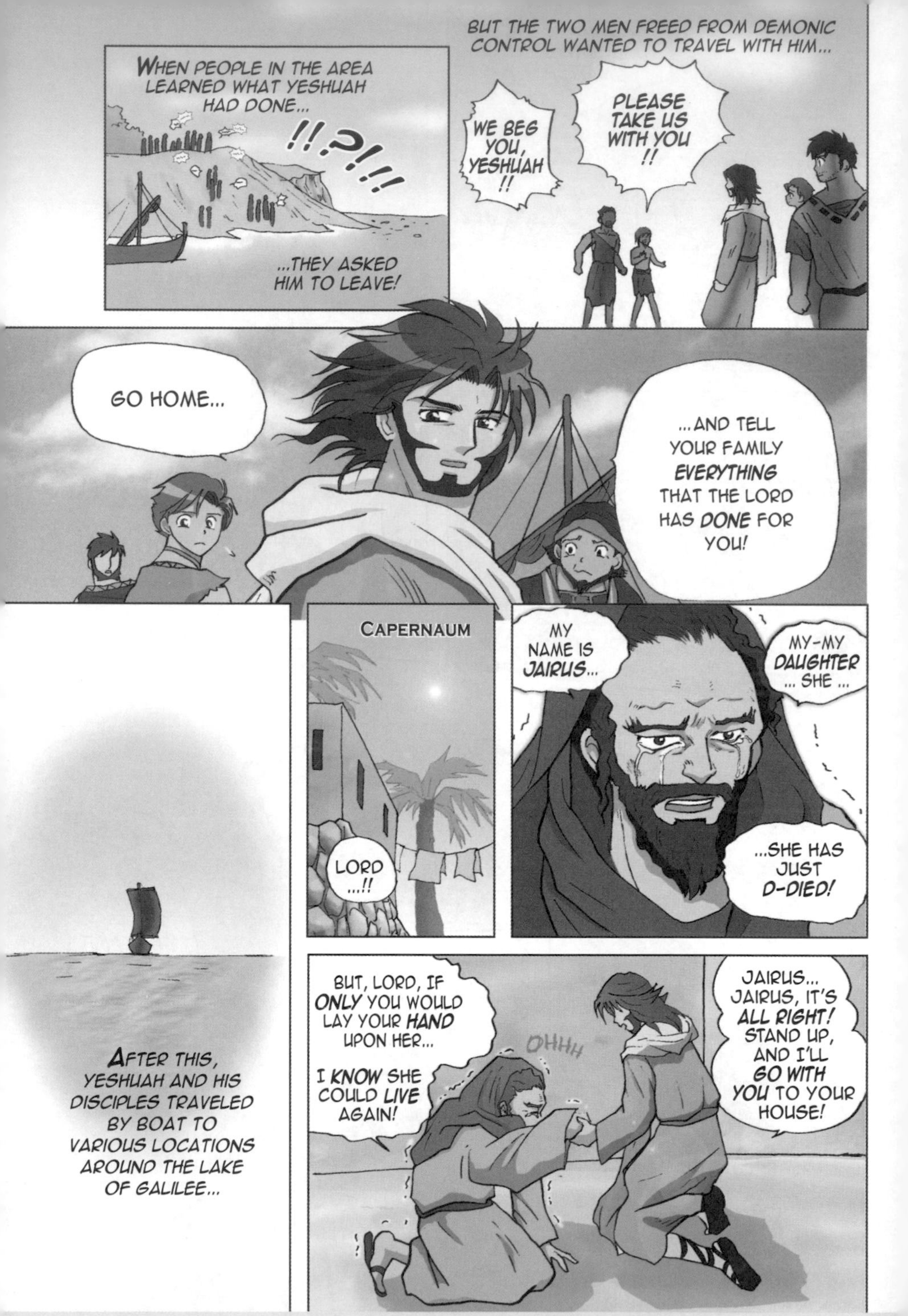
WHEN PEOPLE IN THE AREA LEARNED WHAT YESHUAH HAD DONE...
!!?!!!
...THEY ASKED HIM TO LEAVE!
BUT THE TWO MEN FREED FROM DEMONIC CONTROL WANTED TO TRAVEL WITH HIM...
WE BEG YOU, YESHUAH !!
PLEASE TAKE US WITH YOU !!
GO HOME...
...AND TELL YOUR FAMILY EVERYTHING THAT THE LORD HAS DONE FOR YOU!
AFTER THIS, YESHUAH AND HIS DISCIPLES TRAVELED BY BOAT TO VARIOUS LOCATIONS AROUND THE LAKE OF GALILEE...
CAPERNAUM
LORD ...!!
MY NAME IS JAIRUS...
MY-MY DAUGHTER ... SHE ...
...SHE HAS JUST D-DIED!
BUT, LORD, IF ONLY YOU WOULD LAY YOUR HAND UPON HER...
I KNOW SHE COULD LIVE AGAIN!
OHHH
JAIRUS... JAIRUS, IT'S ALL RIGHT! STAND UP, AND I'LL GO WITH YOU TO YOUR HOUSE!

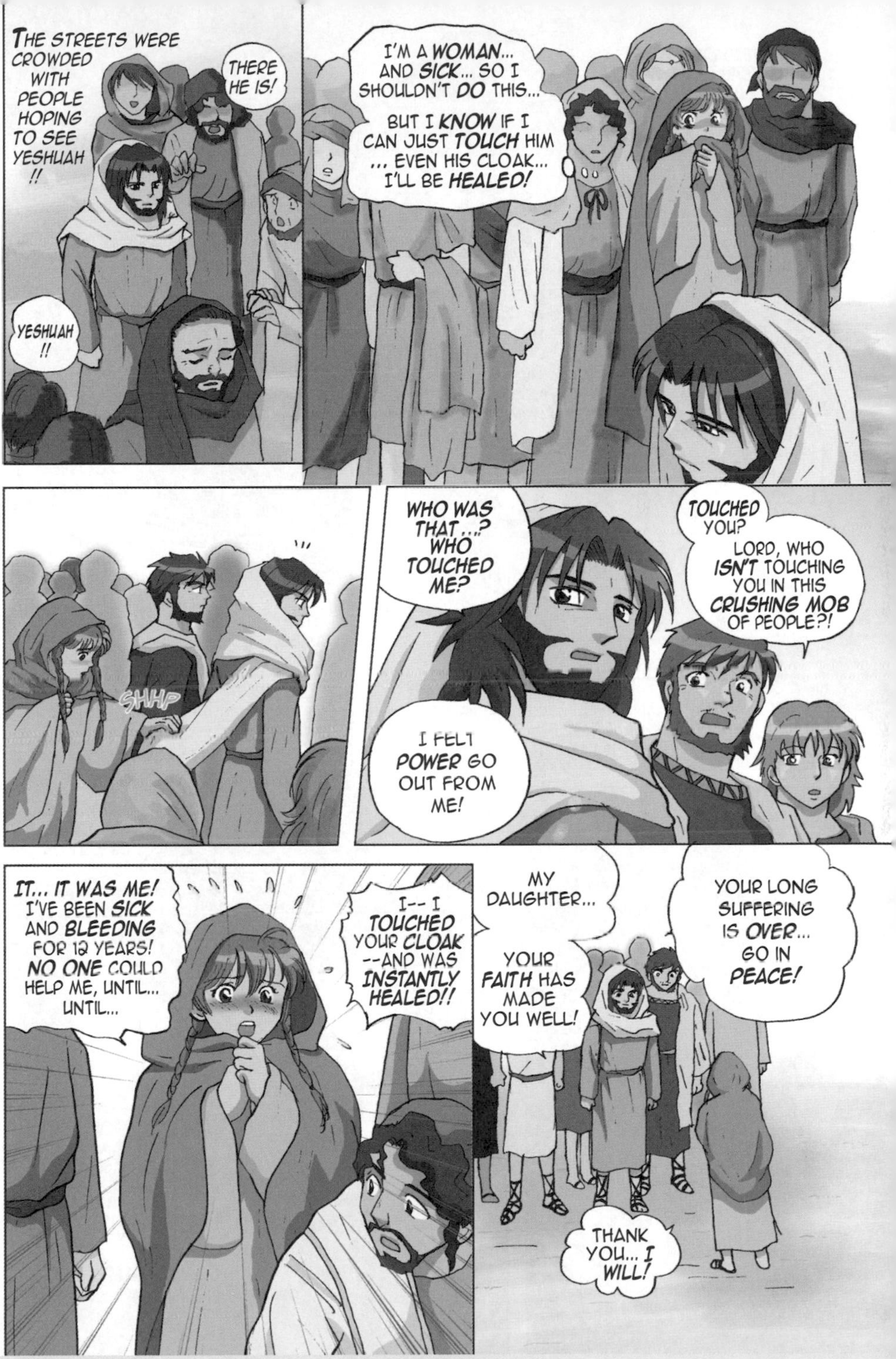
THE STREETS WERE CROWDED WITH PEOPLE HOPING TO SEE YESHUAH !!
THERE HE IS!
YESHUAH !!
I'M A WOMAN... AND SICK... SO I SHOULDN'T DO THIS...
BUT I KNOW IF I CAN JUST TOUCH HIM ... EVEN HIS CLOAK... I'LL BE HEALED!
SHHP
WHO WAS THAT...? WHO TOUCHED ME?
I FELT POWER GO OUT FROM ME!
TOUCHED YOU?
LORD, WHO ISN'T TOUCHING YOU IN THIS CRUSHING MOB OF PEOPLE?!
IT... IT WAS ME! I'VE BEEN SICK AND BLEEDING FOR 12 YEARS! NO ONE COULD HELP ME, UNTIL... UNTIL...
I-- I TOUCHED YOUR CLOAK --AND WAS INSTANTLY HEALED!!
MY DAUGHTER...
YOUR FAITH HAS MADE YOU WELL!
YOUR LONG SUFFERING IS OVER... GO IN PEACE!
THANK YOU... I WILL!

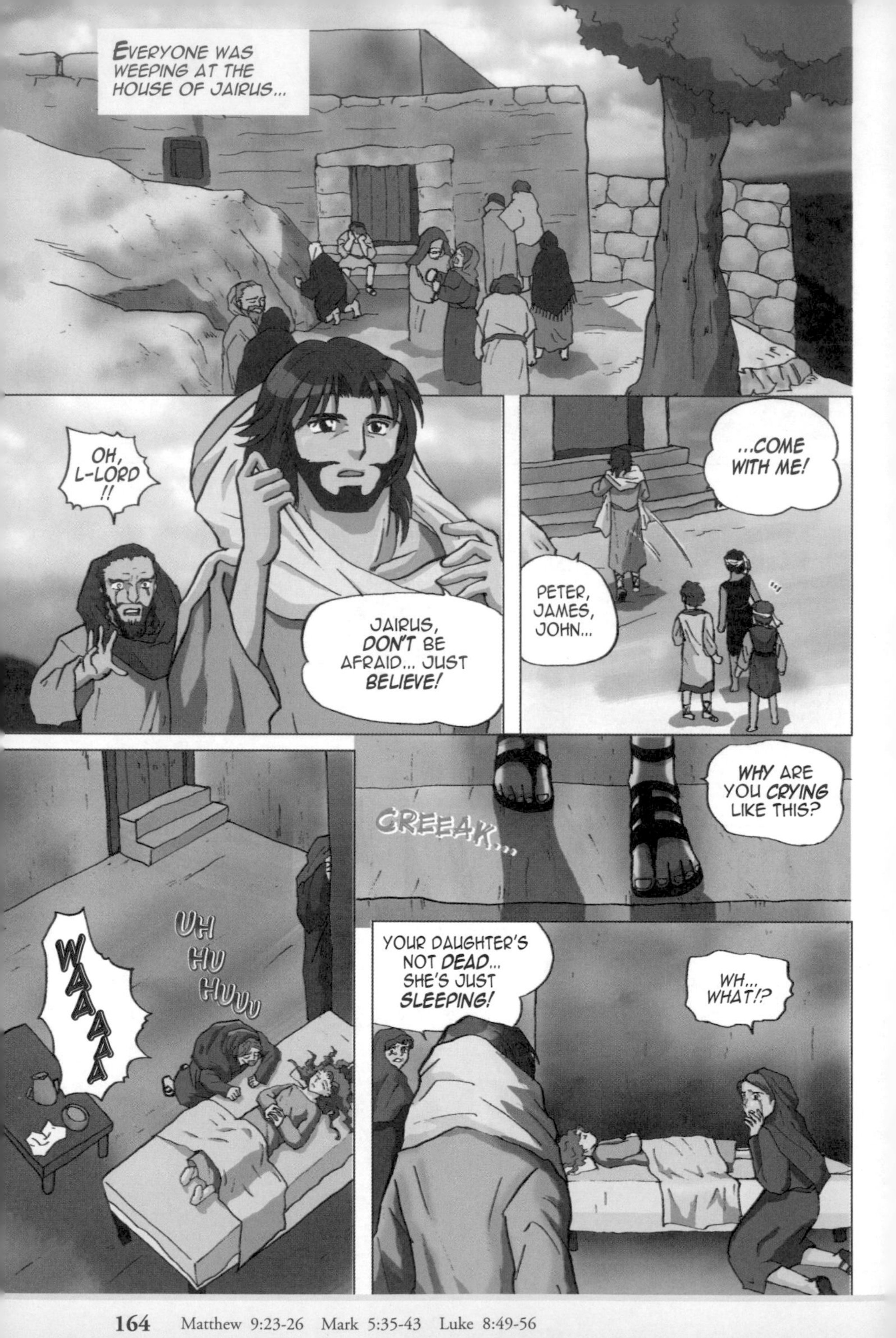
EVERYONE WAS WEEPING AT THE HOUSE OF JAIRUS...
OH, L-LORD !!
JAIRUS, DON'T BE AFRAID... JUST BELIEVE!
...COME WITH ME!
PETER, JAMES, JOHN...
CREEAK...
WHY ARE YOU CRYING LIKE THIS?
WAAAAA
UH HU HUUU
YOUR DAUGHTER'S NOT DEAD... SHE'S JUST SLEEPING!
WH... WHAT!?

 Matthew 9:23-26 Mark 5:35-43 Luke 8:49-56

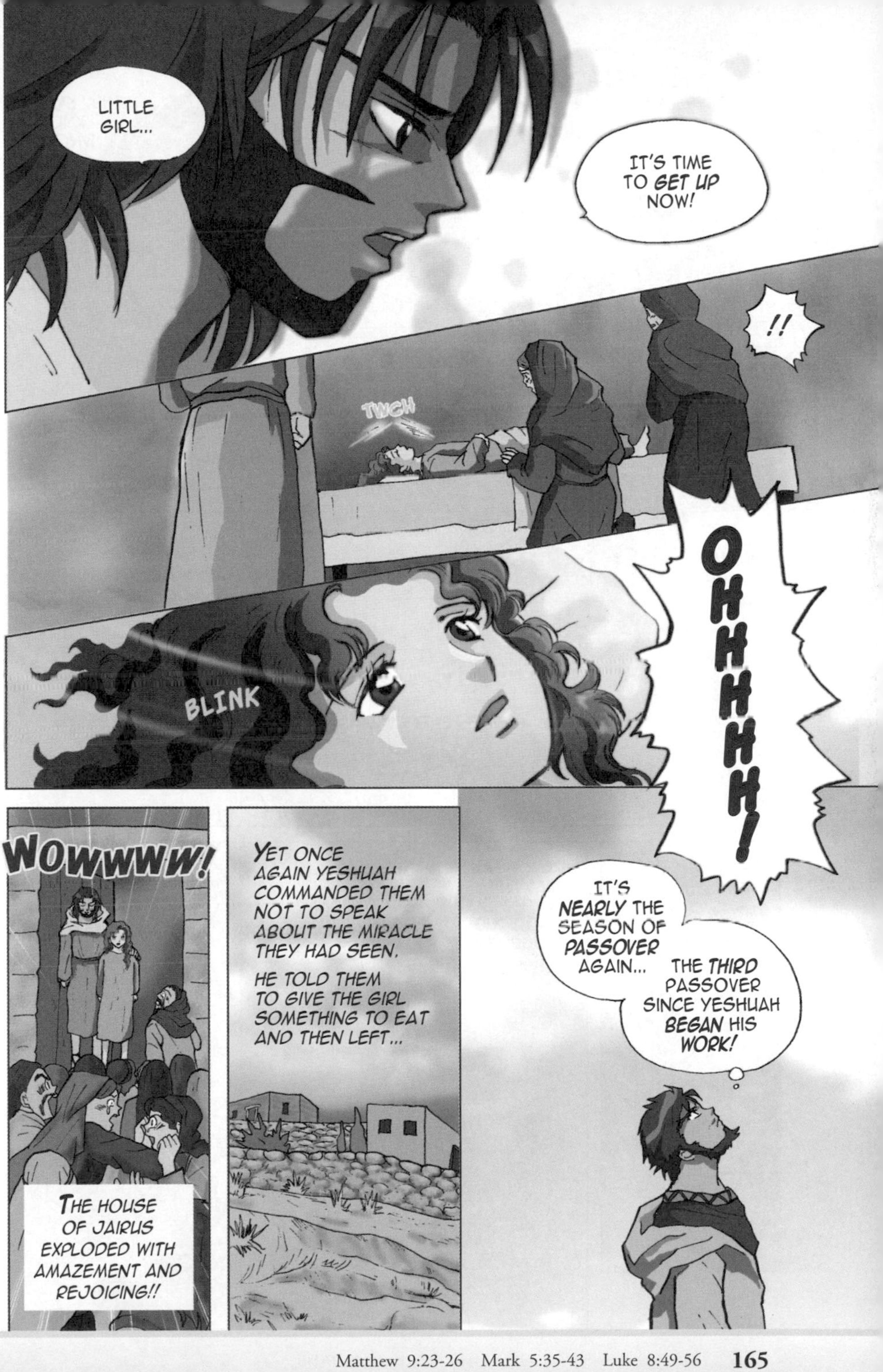

LITTLE GIRL...
IT'S TIME TO GET UP NOW!
!!
TWCH
BLINK
OHHHHHH!
WOWWWW!
THE HOUSE OF JAIRUS EXPLODED WITH AMAZEMENT AND REJOICING!!
YET ONCE AGAIN YESHUAH COMMANDED THEM NOT TO SPEAK ABOUT THE MIRACLE THEY HAD SEEN.
HE TOLD THEM TO GIVE THE GIRL SOMETHING TO EAT AND THEN LEFT...
IT'S NEARLY THE SEASON OF PASSOVER AGAIN...
THE THIRD PASSOVER SINCE YESHUAH BEGAN HIS WORK!

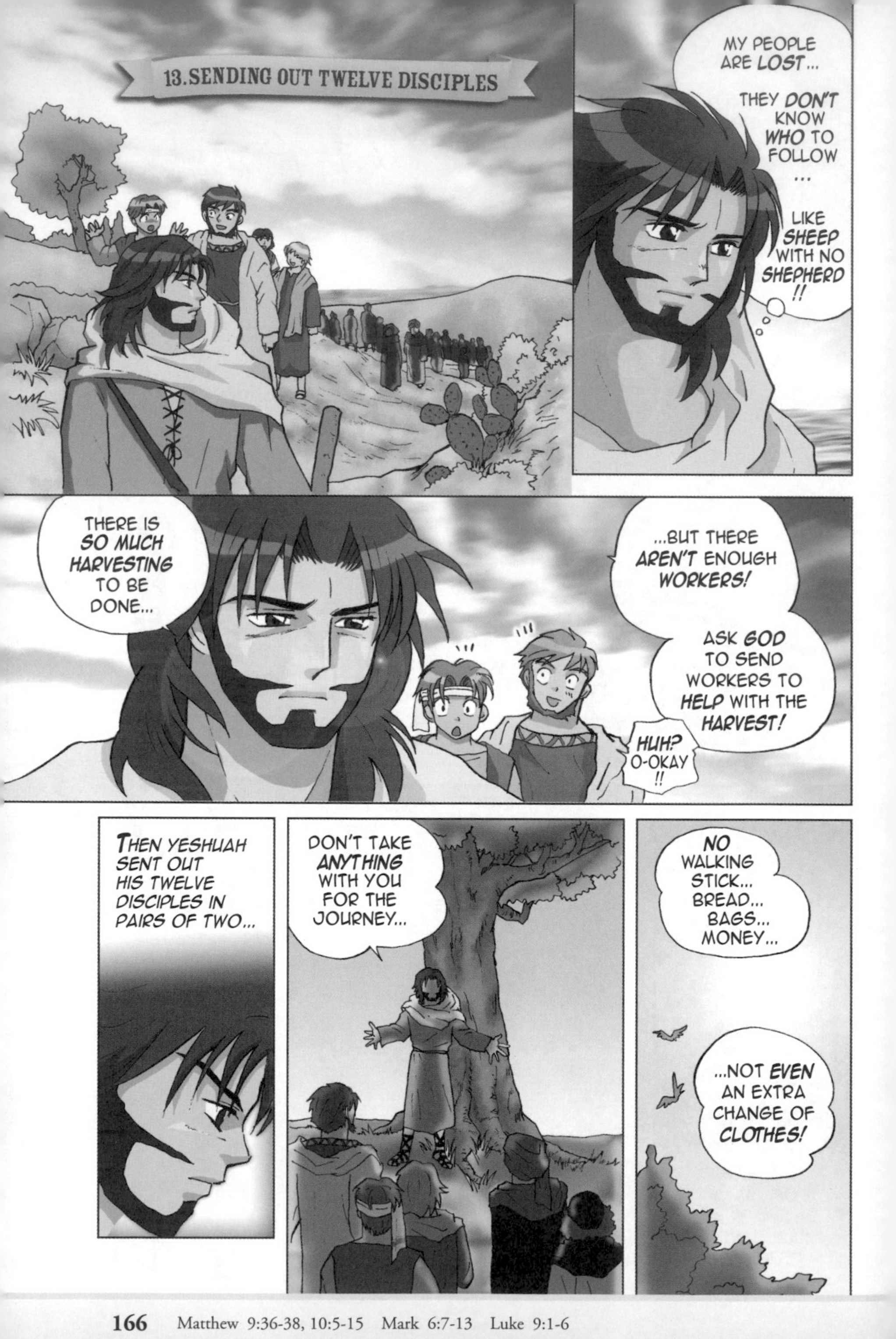
13. SENDING OUT TWELVE DISCIPLES
MY PEOPLE ARE LOST...
THEY DON'T KNOW WHO TO FOLLOW ...
LIKE SHEEP WITH NO SHEPHERD !!
THERE IS SO MUCH HARVESTING TO BE DONE...
...BUT THERE AREN'T ENOUGH WORKERS!
ASK GOD TO SEND WORKERS TO HELP WITH THE HARVEST!
HUH? O-OKAY !!
THEN YESHUAH SENT OUT HIS TWELVE DISCIPLES IN PAIRS OF TWO...
DON'T TAKE ANYTHING WITH YOU FOR THE JOURNEY...
NO WALKING STICK... BREAD... BAGS... MONEY...
...NOT EVEN AN EXTRA CHANGE OF CLOTHES!

 Matthew 9:36-38, 10:5-15 Mark 6:7-13 Luke 9:1-6

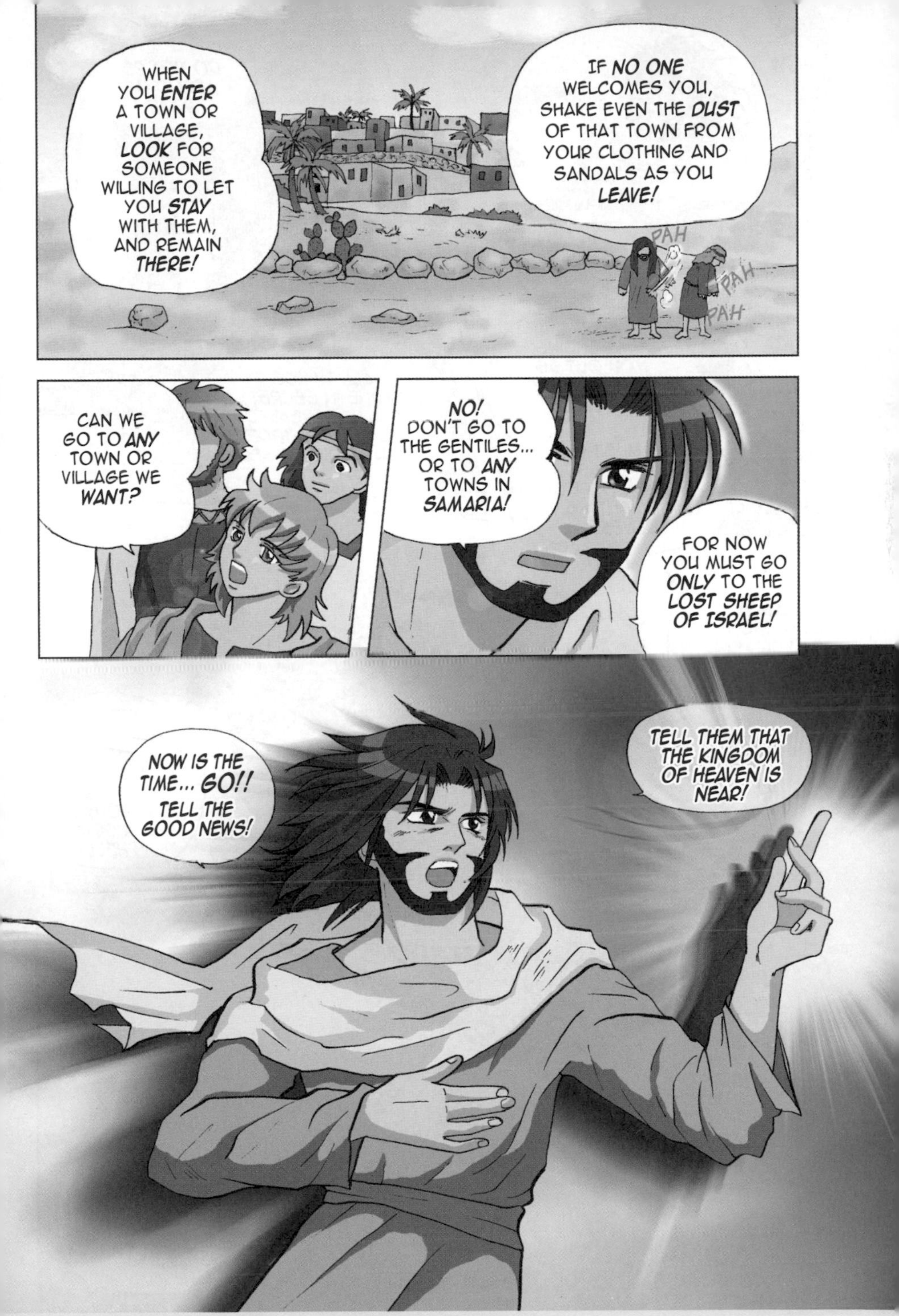
WHEN YOU ENTER A TOWN OR VILLAGE, LOOK FOR SOMEONE WILLING TO LET YOU STAY WITH THEM, AND REMAIN THERE!
IF NO ONE WELCOMES YOU, SHAKE EVEN THE DUST OF THAT TOWN FROM YOUR CLOTHING AND SANDALS AS YOU LEAVE!
PAH
PAH
PAH
CAN WE GO TO ANY TOWN OR VILLAGE WE WANT?
NO! DON'T GO TO THE GENTILES... OR TO ANY TOWNS IN SAMARIA!
FOR NOW YOU MUST GO ONLY TO THE LOST SHEEP OF ISRAEL!
NOW IS THE TIME... GO!! TELL THE GOOD NEWS!
TELL THEM THAT THE KINGDOM OF HEAVEN IS NEAR!

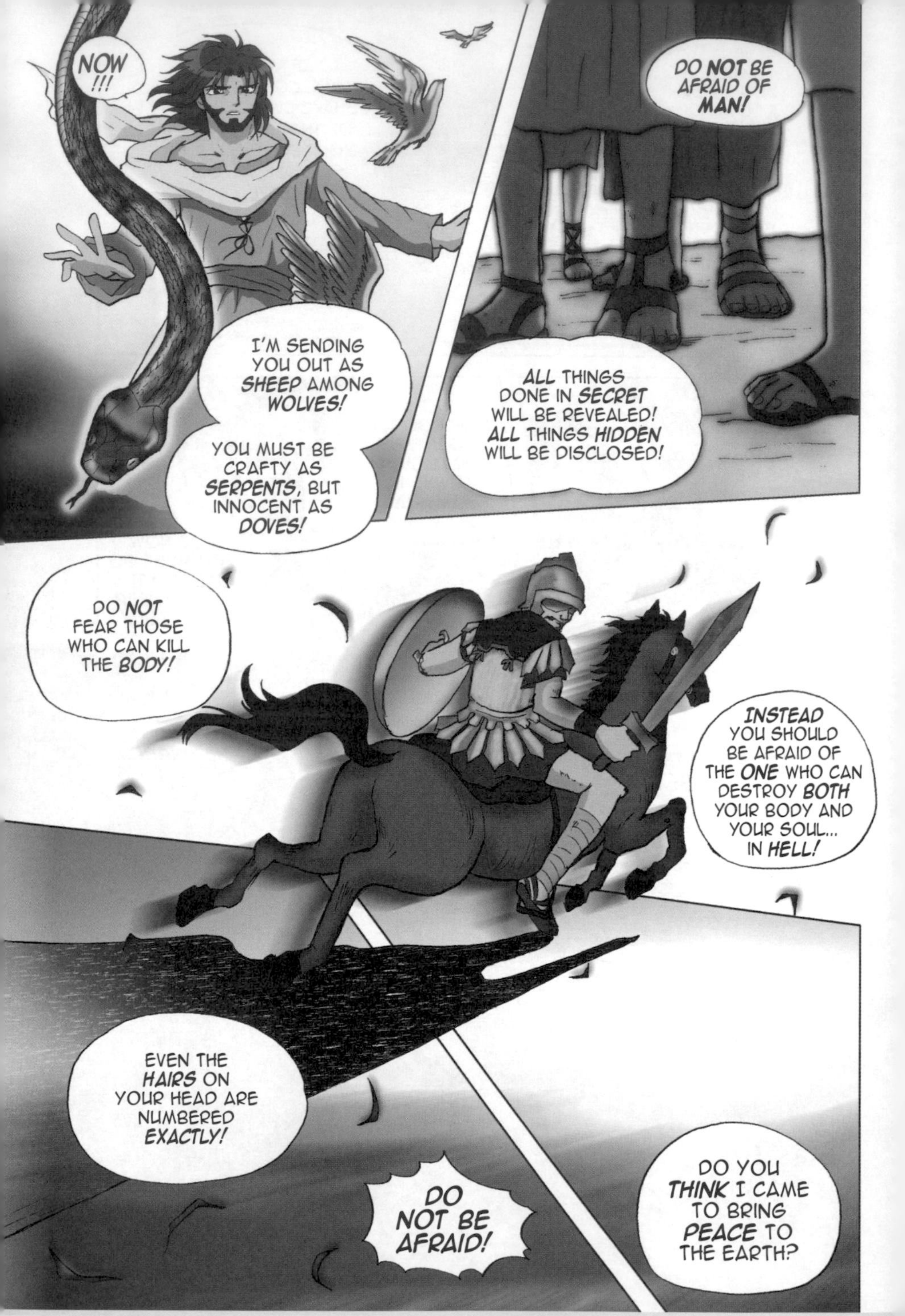
NOW !!!
I'M SENDING YOU OUT AS SHEEP AMONG WOLVES!
YOU MUST BE CRAFTY AS SERPENTS, BUT INNOCENT AS DOVES!
DO NOT BE AFRAID OF MAN!
ALL THINGS DONE IN SECRET WILL BE REVEALED! ALL THINGS HIDDEN WILL BE DISCLOSED!
DO NOT FEAR THOSE WHO CAN KILL THE BODY!
INSTEAD YOU SHOULD BE AFRAID OF THE ONE WHO CAN DESTROY BOTH YOUR BODY AND YOUR SOUL... IN HELL!
EVEN THE HAIRS ON YOUR HEAD ARE NUMBERED EXACTLY!
DO NOT BE AFRAID!
DO YOU THINK I CAME TO BRING PEACE TO THE EARTH?

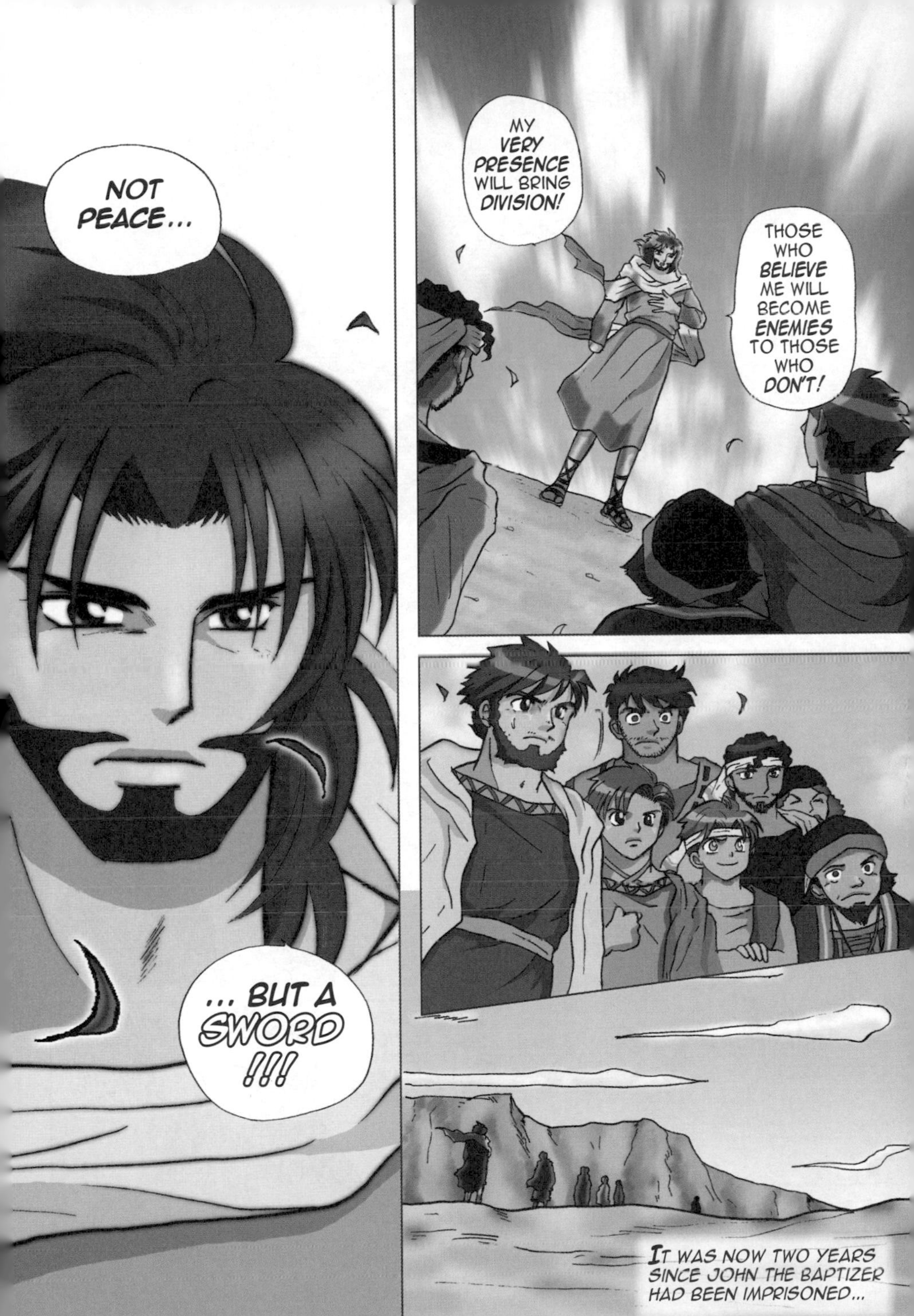
NOT PEACE...
... BUT A SWORD !!!
MY VERY PRESENCE WILL BRING DIVISION!
THOSE WHO BELIEVE ME WILL BECOME ENEMIES TO THOSE WHO DON'T!
IT WAS NOW TWO YEARS SINCE JOHN THE BAPTIZER HAD BEEN IMPRISONED...

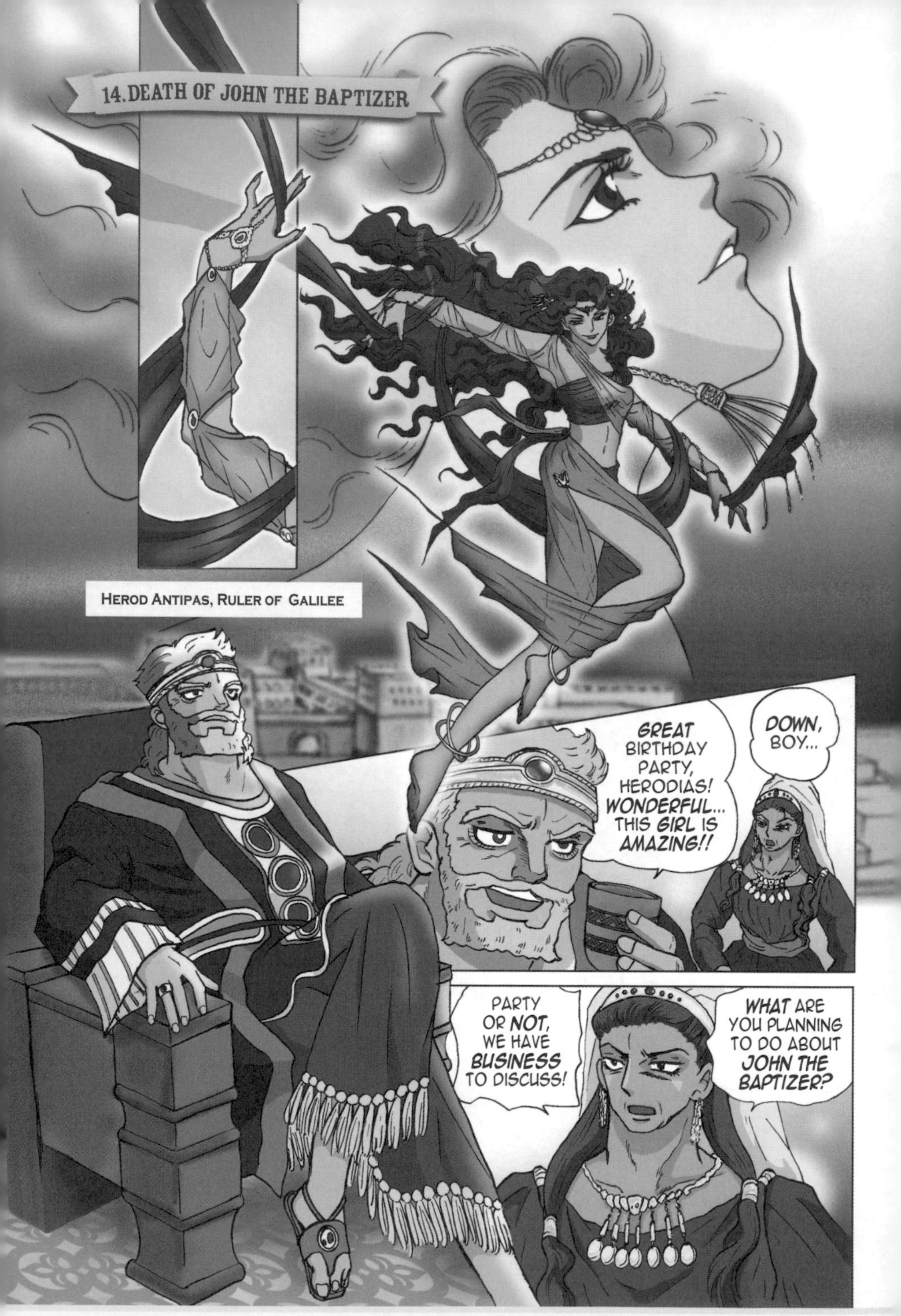

14. DEATH OF JOHN THE BAPTIZER
HEROD ANTIPAS, RULER OF GALILEE
GREAT BIRTHDAY PARTY, HERODIAS! WONDERFUL... THIS GIRL IS AMAZING!!
DOWN, BOY...
PARTY OR NOT, WE HAVE BUSINESS TO DISCUSS!
WHAT ARE YOU PLANNING TO DO ABOUT JOHN THE BAPTIZER?

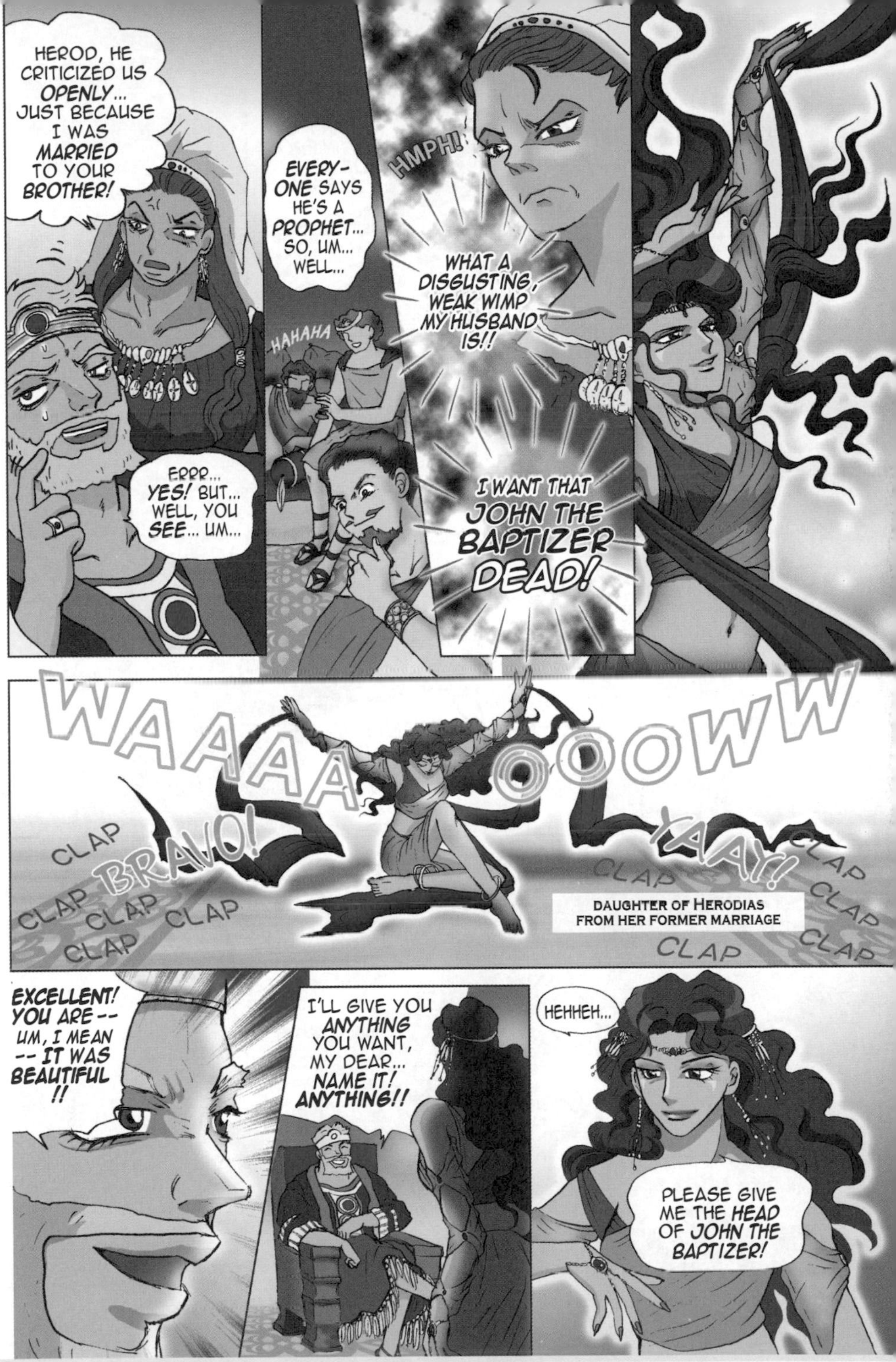
HEROD, HE CRITICIZED US OPENLY... JUST BECAUSE I WAS MARRIED TO YOUR BROTHER!
ERRR... YES! BUT... WELL, YOU SEE... UM...
EVERY-ONE SAYS HE'S A PROPHET... SO, UM... WELL...
HAHAHA
HMPH!
WHAT A DISGUSTING, WEAK WIMP MY HUSBAND IS!!
I WANT THAT JOHN THE BAPTIZER DEAD!
WAAAAAOOOOWW
CLAP
BRAVO!
CLAP CLAP CLAP CLAP
YAAAY!
CLAP CLAP CLAP CLAP CLAP
DAUGHTER OF HERODIAS FROM HER FORMER MARRIAGE
EXCELLENT! YOU ARE -- UM, I MEAN -- IT WAS BEAUTIFUL!!
I'LL GIVE YOU ANYTHING YOU WANT, MY DEAR... NAME IT! ANYTHING!!
HEHHEH...
PLEASE GIVE ME THE HEAD OF JOHN THE BAPTIZER!

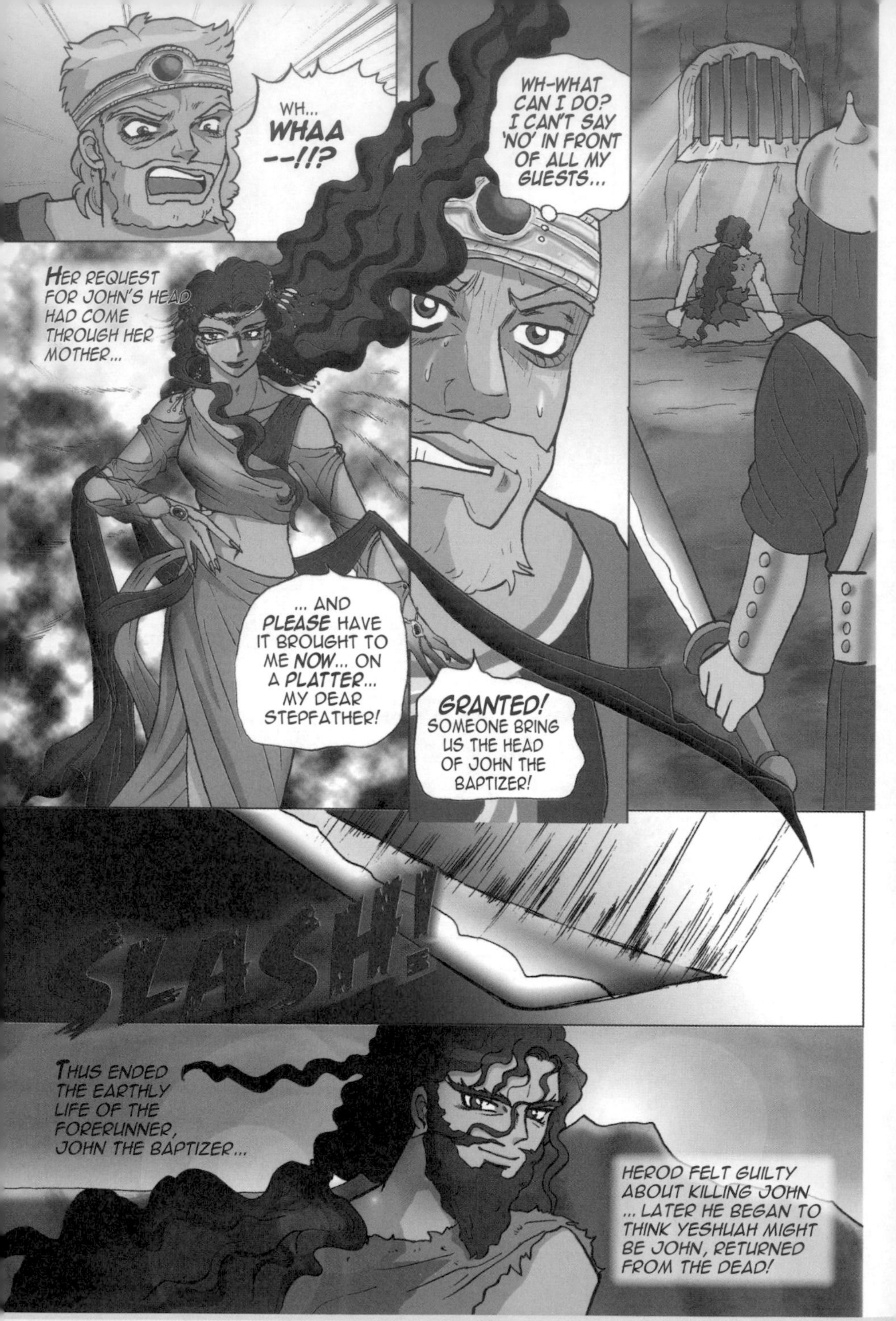
WH... WHAA --!!?
WH-WHAT CAN I DO? I CAN'T SAY 'NO' IN FRONT OF ALL MY GUESTS...
HER REQUEST FOR JOHN'S HEAD HAD COME THROUGH HER MOTHER...
... AND PLEASE HAVE IT BROUGHT TO ME NOW... ON A PLATTER... MY DEAR STEPFATHER!
GRANTED! SOMEONE BRING US THE HEAD OF JOHN THE BAPTIZER!
SLASH!
THUS ENDED THE EARTHLY LIFE OF THE FORERUNNER, JOHN THE BAPTIZER...
HEROD FELT GUILTY ABOUT KILLING JOHN ... LATER HE BEGAN TO THINK YESHUAH MIGHT BE JOHN, RETURNED FROM THE DEAD!

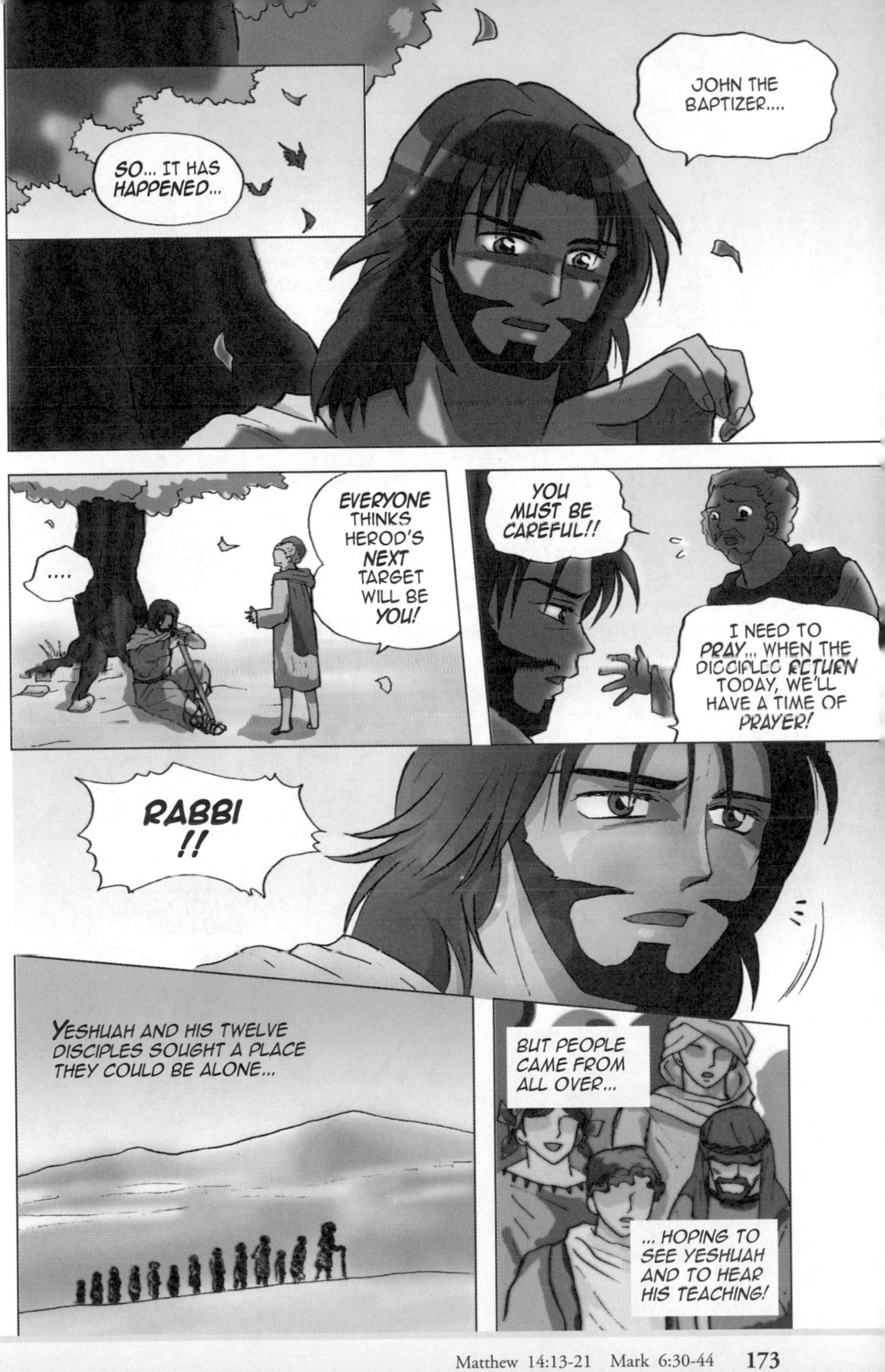
SO... IT HAS HAPPENED...
JOHN THE BAPTIZER....
....
EVERYONE THINKS HEROD'S NEXT TARGET WILL BE YOU!
YOU MUST BE CAREFUL!!
I NEED TO PRAY... WHEN THE DISCIPLES RETURN TODAY, WE'LL HAVE A TIME OF PRAYER!
RABBI !!
YESHUAH AND HIS TWELVE DISCIPLES SOUGHT A PLACE THEY COULD BE ALONE...
BUT PEOPLE CAME FROM ALL OVER...
... HOPING TO SEE YESHUAH AND TO HEAR HIS TEACHING!

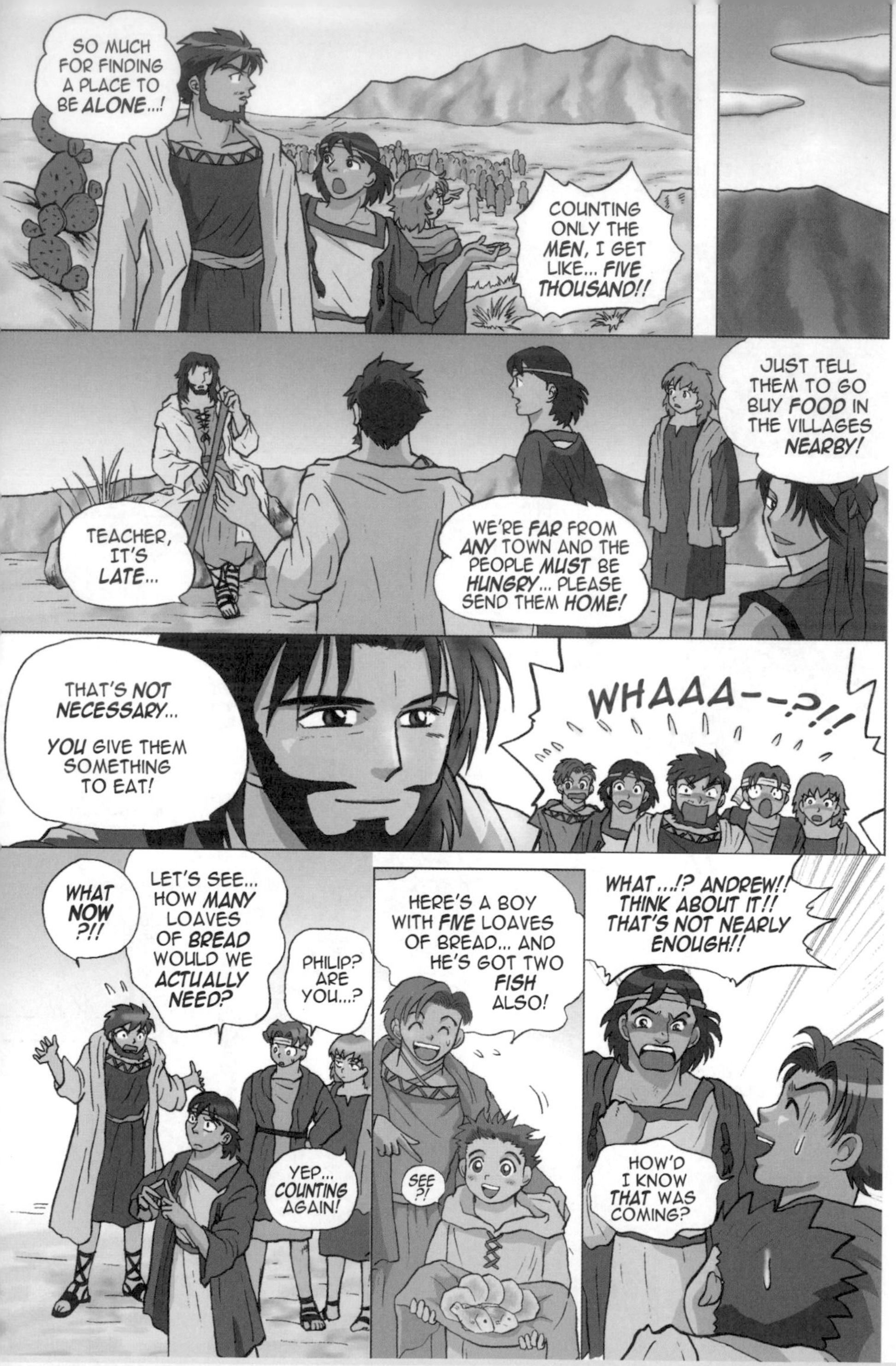

SO MUCH FOR FINDING A PLACE TO BE ALONE...!
COUNTING ONLY THE MEN, I GET LIKE... FIVE THOUSAND!!
JUST TELL THEM TO GO BUY FOOD IN THE VILLAGES NEARBY!
TEACHER, IT'S LATE...
WE'RE FAR FROM ANY TOWN AND THE PEOPLE MUST BE HUNGRY... PLEASE SEND THEM HOME!
THAT'S NOT NECESSARY...
YOU GIVE THEM SOMETHING TO EAT!
WHAAA--?!!
WHAT NOW?!!
LET'S SEE... HOW MANY LOAVES OF BREAD WOULD WE ACTUALLY NEED?
PHILIP? ARE YOU...?
YEP... COUNTING AGAIN!
HERE'S A BOY WITH FIVE LOAVES OF BREAD... AND HE'S GOT TWO FISH ALSO!
SEE?!
WHAT...!? ANDREW!! THINK ABOUT IT!! THAT'S NOT NEARLY ENOUGH!!
HOW'D I KNOW THAT WAS COMING?

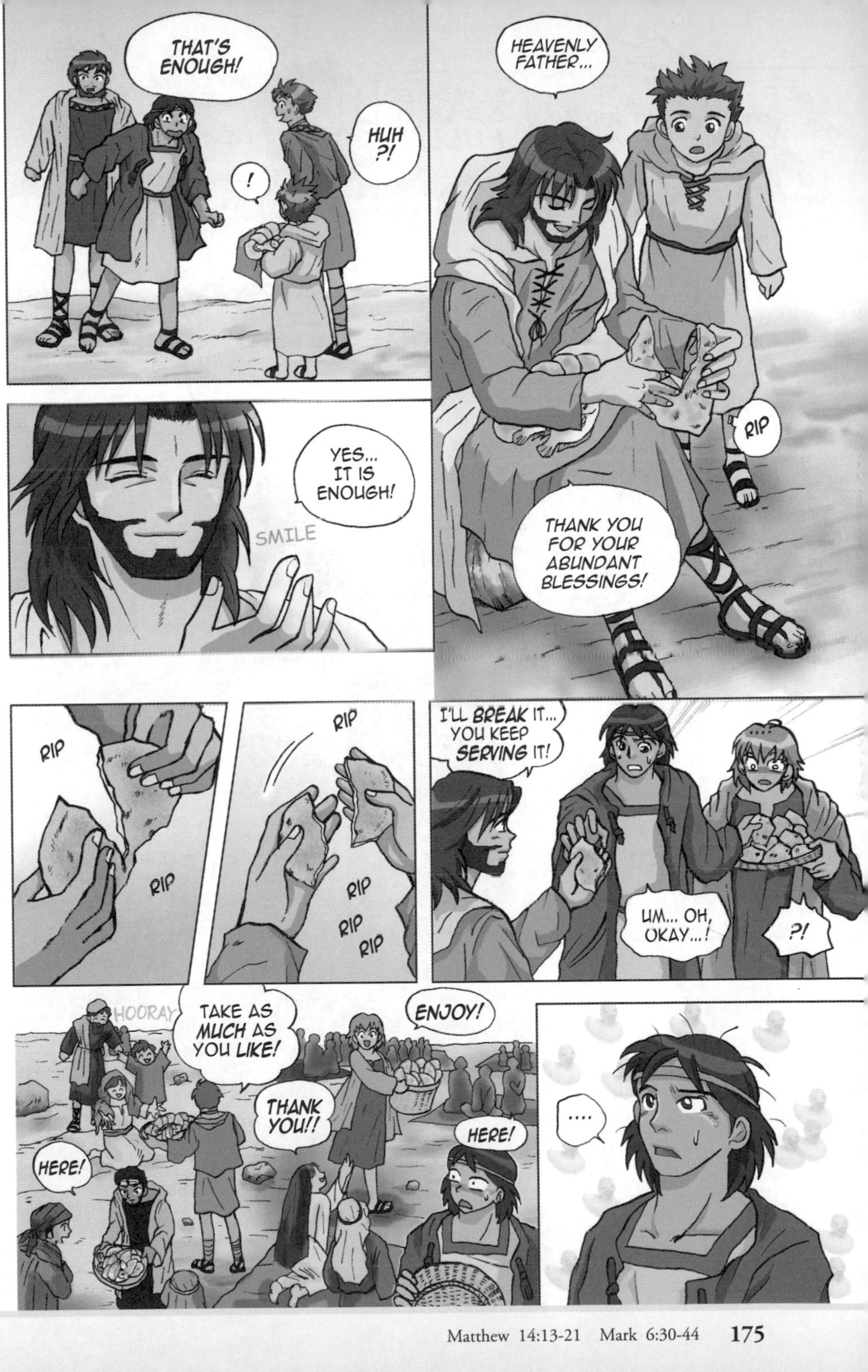
THAT'S ENOUGH!
HUH ?!
!
HEAVENLY FATHER...
RIP
YES... IT IS ENOUGH!
SMILE
THANK YOU FOR YOUR ABUNDANT BLESSINGS!
RIP
RIP
RIP
RIP
RIP
RIP
I'LL BREAK IT... YOU KEEP SERVING IT!
UM... OH, OKAY...!
?!
HOORAY
TAKE AS MUCH AS YOU LIKE!
ENJOY!
THANK YOU!!
HERE!
HERE!
....

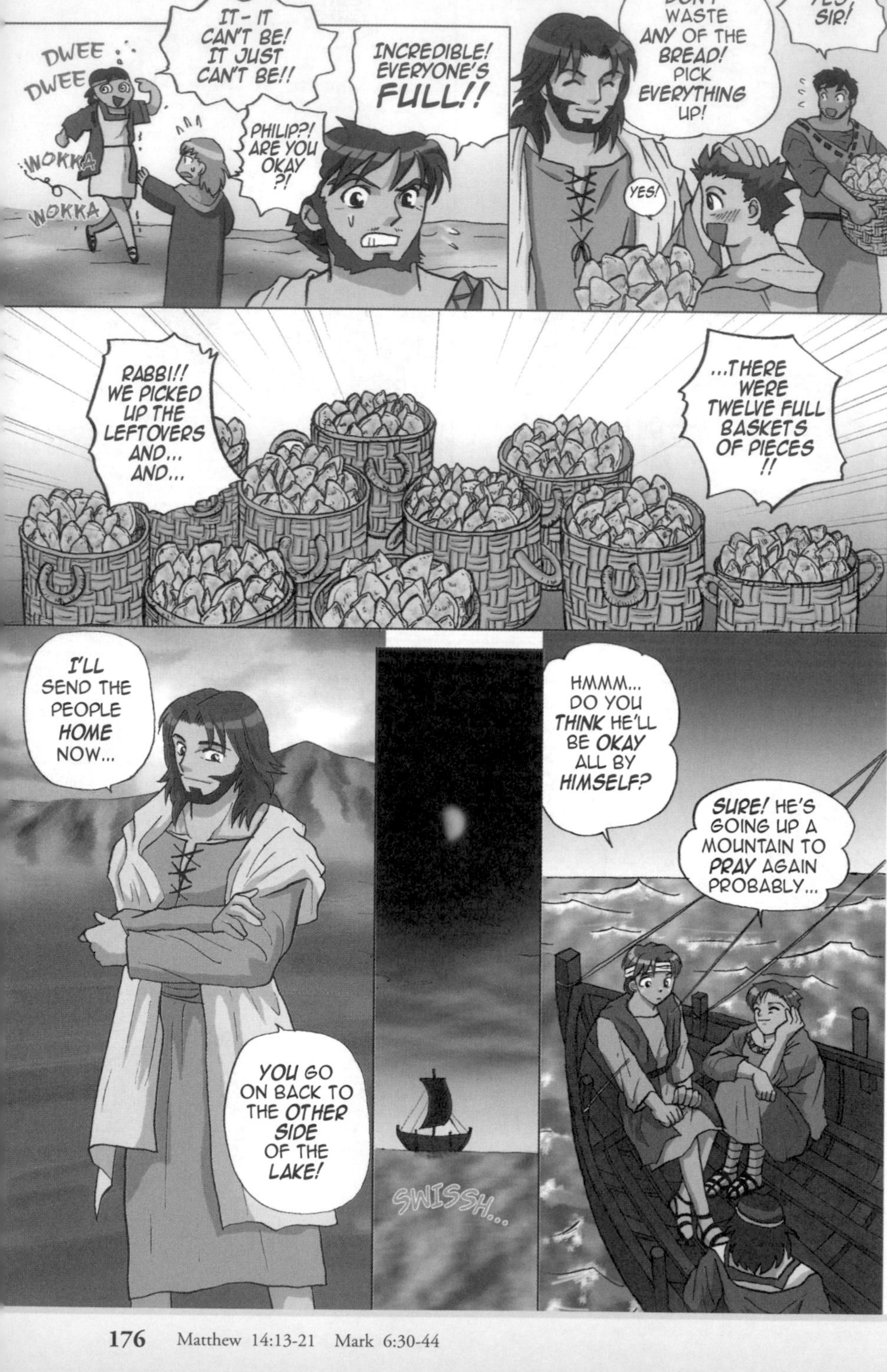
DWEE DWEE
WOKKA WOKKA
IT - IT CAN'T BE! IT JUST CAN'T BE!!
PHILIP?! ARE YOU OKAY ?!
INCREDIBLE! EVERYONE'S FULL!!
DON'T WASTE ANY OF THE BREAD! PICK EVERYTHING UP!
YES!
YES, SIR!
RABBI!! WE PICKED UP THE LEFTOVERS AND... AND...
...THERE WERE TWELVE FULL BASKETS OF PIECES !!
I'LL SEND THE PEOPLE HOME NOW...
YOU GO ON BACK TO THE OTHER SIDE OF THE LAKE!
SWISSH...
HMMM... DO YOU THINK HE'LL BE OKAY ALL BY HIMSELF?
SURE! HE'S GOING UP A MOUNTAIN TO PRAY AGAIN PROBABLY...

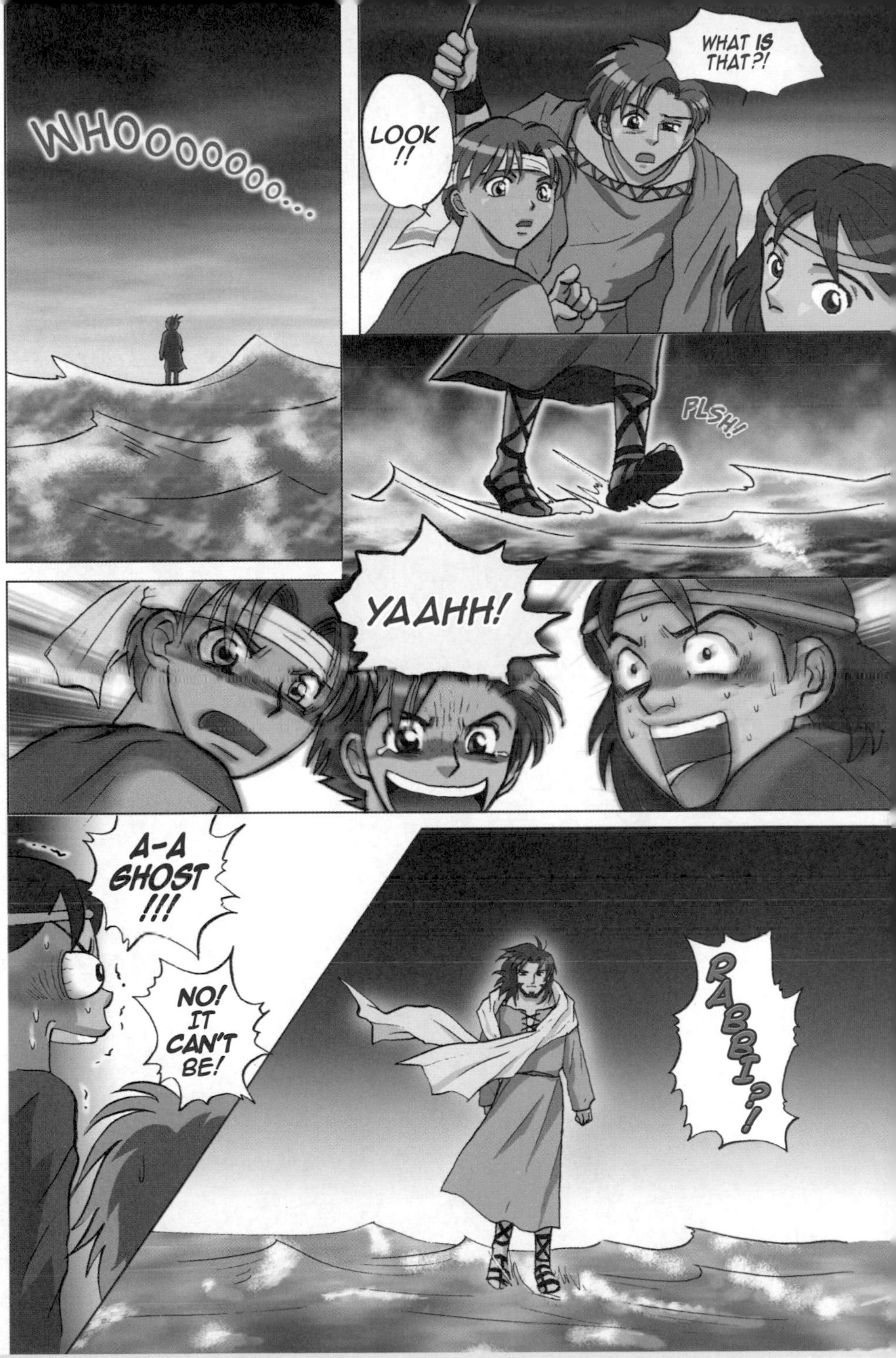
WHOOOOOOOO...
WHAT IS THAT?!
LOOK !!
PLSH!
YAAHH!
A-A GHOST !!!
NO! IT CAN'T BE!
RABBI?!

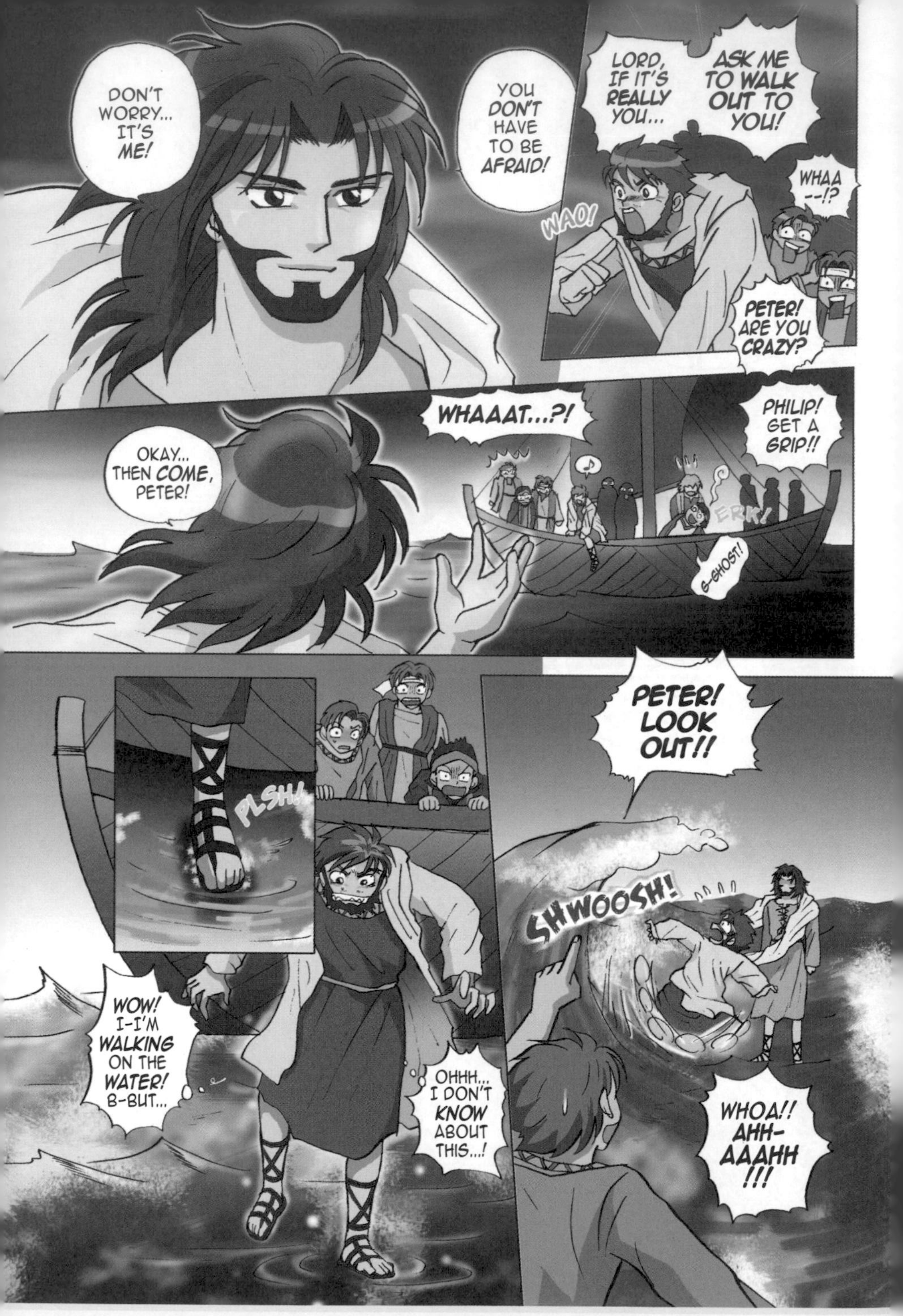
DON'T WORRY... IT'S ME!
YOU DON'T HAVE TO BE AFRAID!
LORD, IF IT'S REALLY YOU...
ASK ME TO WALK OUT TO YOU!
WAO!
WHAA--!?
PETER! ARE YOU CRAZY?
OKAY... THEN COME, PETER!
WHAAAT...?!
PHILIP! GET A GRIP!!
ERK!
G-GHOST!
PLSH!
WOW! I-I'M WALKING ON THE WATER! B-BUT...
OHHH... I DON'T KNOW ABOUT THIS...!
PETER! LOOK OUT!!
SHWOOSH!
WHOA!! AHH-AAAHH!!!

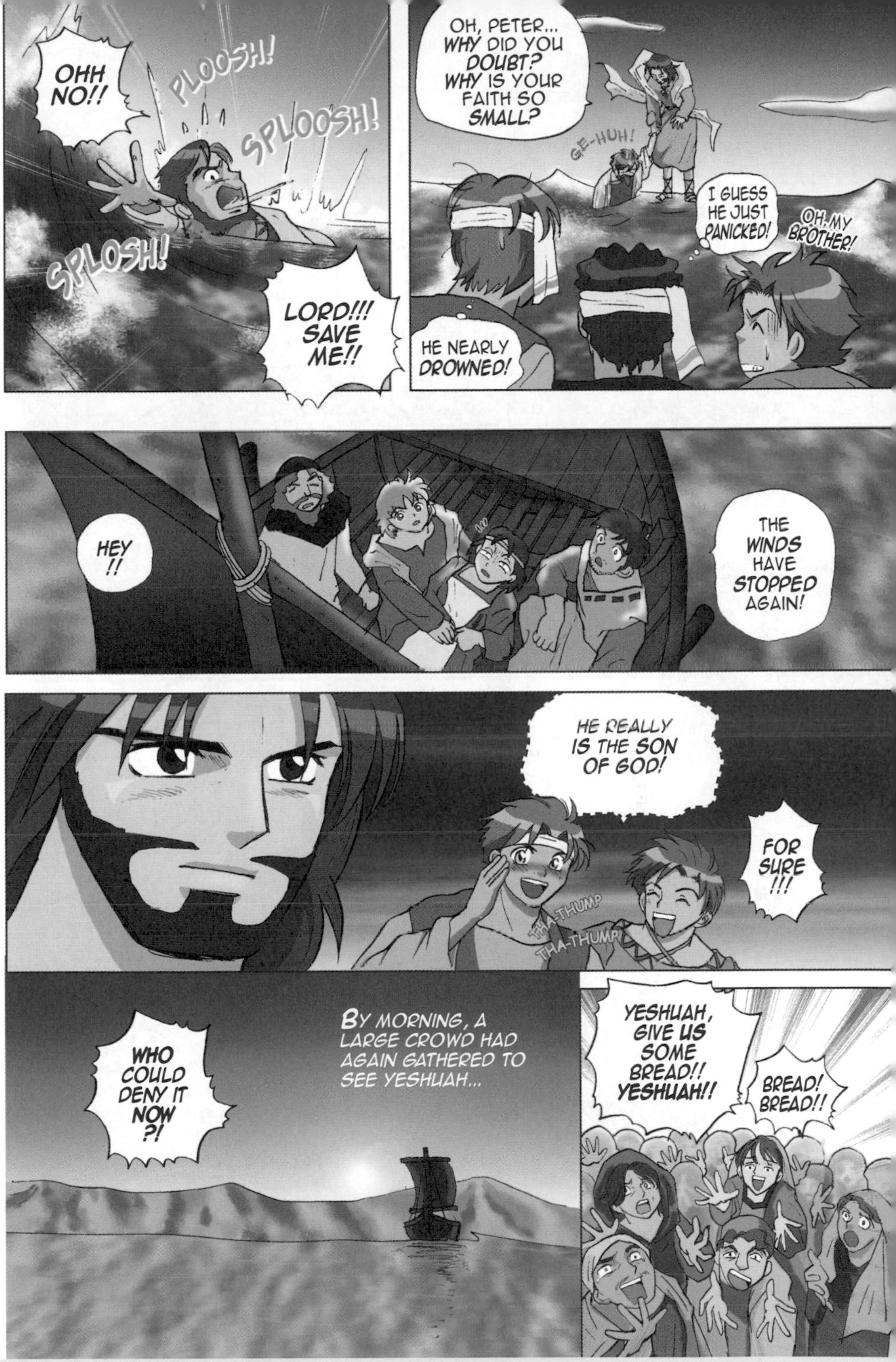
OHH NO!!
PLOOSH!
SPLOOSH!
SPLOSH!
LORD!!! SAVE ME!!
OH, PETER... WHY DID YOU DOUBT? WHY IS YOUR FAITH SO SMALL?
GE-HUH!
I GUESS HE JUST PANICKED!
OH, MY BROTHER!
HE NEARLY DROWNED!
HEY !!
THE WINDS HAVE STOPPED AGAIN!
HE REALLY IS THE SON OF GOD!
FOR SURE !!!
THA-THUMP
THA-THUMP
WHO COULD DENY IT NOW ?!
BY MORNING, A LARGE CROWD HAD AGAIN GATHERED TO SEE YESHUAH...
YESHUAH, GIVE US SOME BREAD!! YESHUAH!!
BREAD! BREAD!!

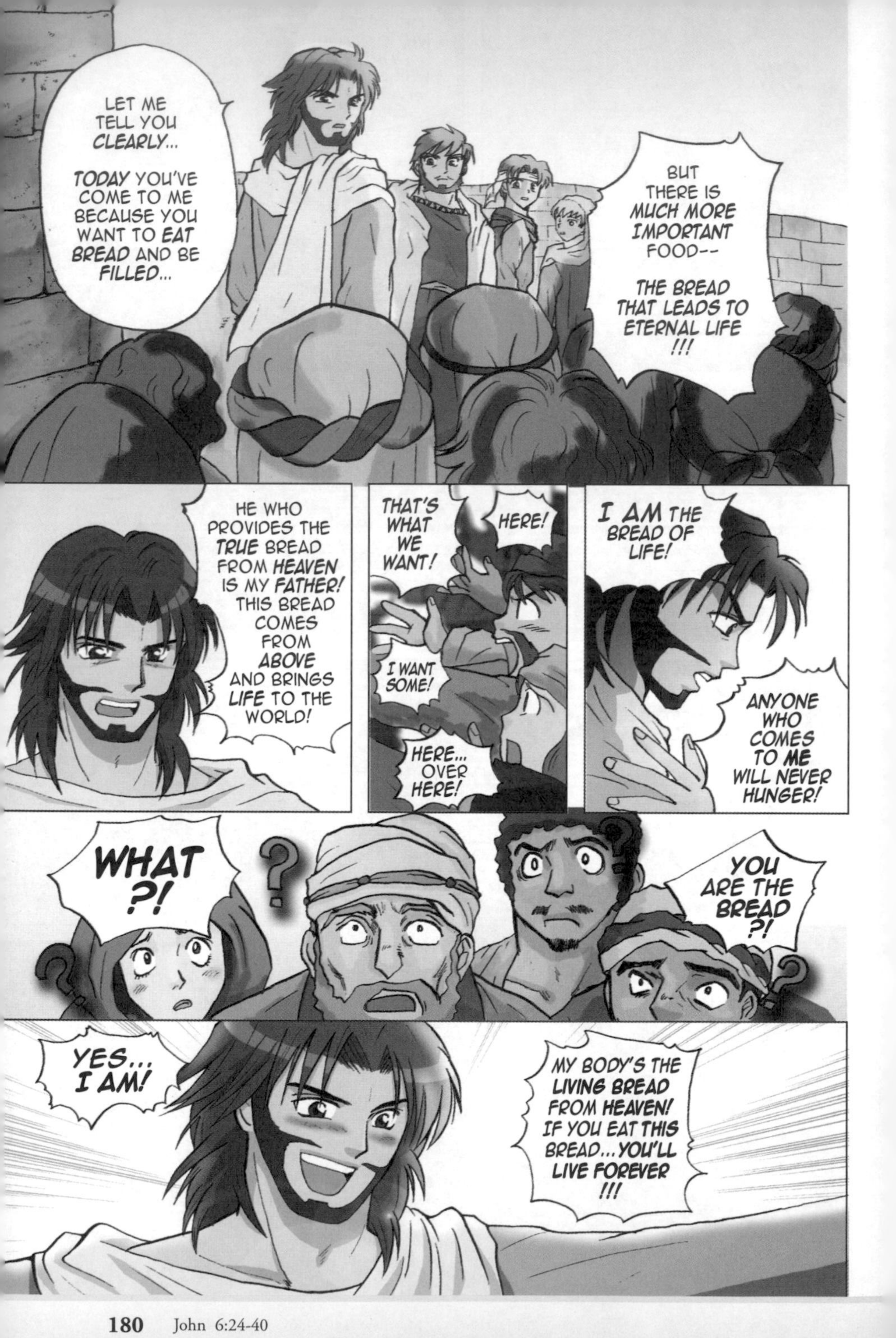
LET ME TELL YOU CLEARLY...
TODAY YOU'VE COME TO ME BECAUSE YOU WANT TO EAT BREAD AND BE FILLED...
BUT THERE IS MUCH MORE IMPORTANT FOOD--
THE BREAD THAT LEADS TO ETERNAL LIFE !!!
HE WHO PROVIDES THE TRUE BREAD FROM HEAVEN IS MY FATHER! THIS BREAD COMES FROM ABOVE AND BRINGS LIFE TO THE WORLD!
THAT'S WHAT WE WANT!
HERE!
I WANT SOME!
HERE... OVER HERE!
I AM THE BREAD OF LIFE!
ANYONE WHO COMES TO ME WILL NEVER HUNGER!
WHAT ?!
YOU ARE THE BREAD ?!
YES... I AM!
MY BODY'S THE LIVING BREAD FROM HEAVEN! IF YOU EAT THIS BREAD... YOU'LL LIVE FOREVER !!!

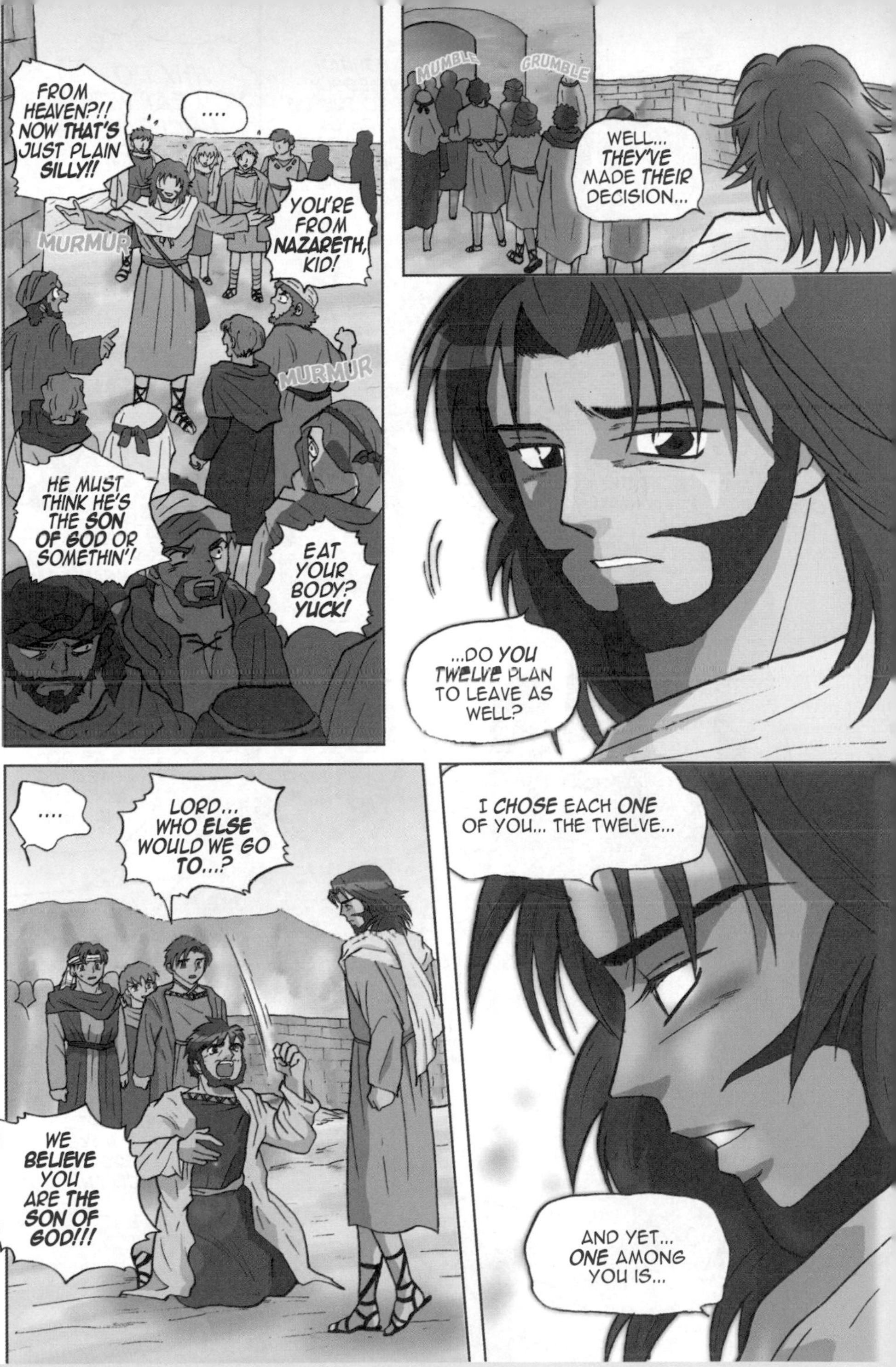
FROM HEAVEN?!! NOW THAT'S JUST PLAIN SILLY!!
....
MURMUR
YOU'RE FROM NAZARETH, KID!
MURMUR
HE MUST THINK HE'S THE SON OF GOD OR SOMETHIN'!
EAT YOUR BODY? YUCK!
MUMBLE
GRUMBLE
WELL... THEY'VE MADE THEIR DECISION...
...DO YOU TWELVE PLAN TO LEAVE AS WELL?
....
LORD... WHO ELSE WOULD WE GO TO...?
WE BELIEVE YOU ARE THE SON OF GOD!!!
I CHOSE EACH ONE OF YOU... THE TWELVE...
AND YET... ONE AMONG YOU IS...

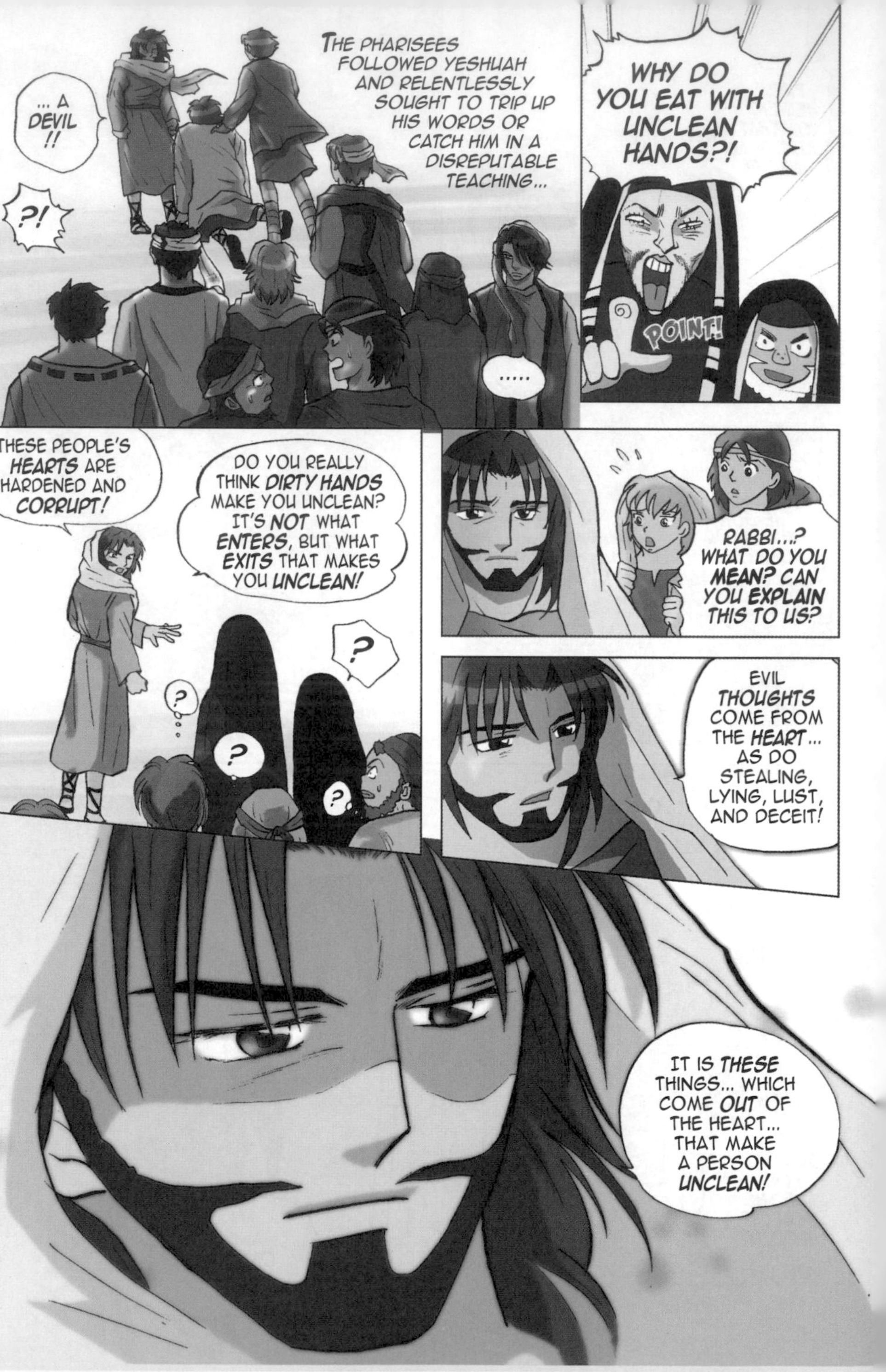
THE PHARISEES FOLLOWED YESHUAH AND RELENTLESSLY SOUGHT TO TRIP UP HIS WORDS OR CATCH HIM IN A DISREPUTABLE TEACHING...
... A DEVIL !!
?!
......
WHY DO YOU EAT WITH UNCLEAN HANDS?!
POINT!
THESE PEOPLE'S HEARTS ARE HARDENED AND CORRUPT!
DO YOU REALLY THINK DIRTY HANDS MAKE YOU UNCLEAN? IT'S NOT WHAT ENTERS, BUT WHAT EXITS THAT MAKES YOU UNCLEAN!
?
?
?
?
RABBI...? WHAT DO YOU MEAN? CAN YOU EXPLAIN THIS TO US?
EVIL THOUGHTS COME FROM THE HEART... AS DO STEALING, LYING, LUST, AND DECEIT!
IT IS THESE THINGS... WHICH COME OUT OF THE HEART... THAT MAKE A PERSON UNCLEAN!

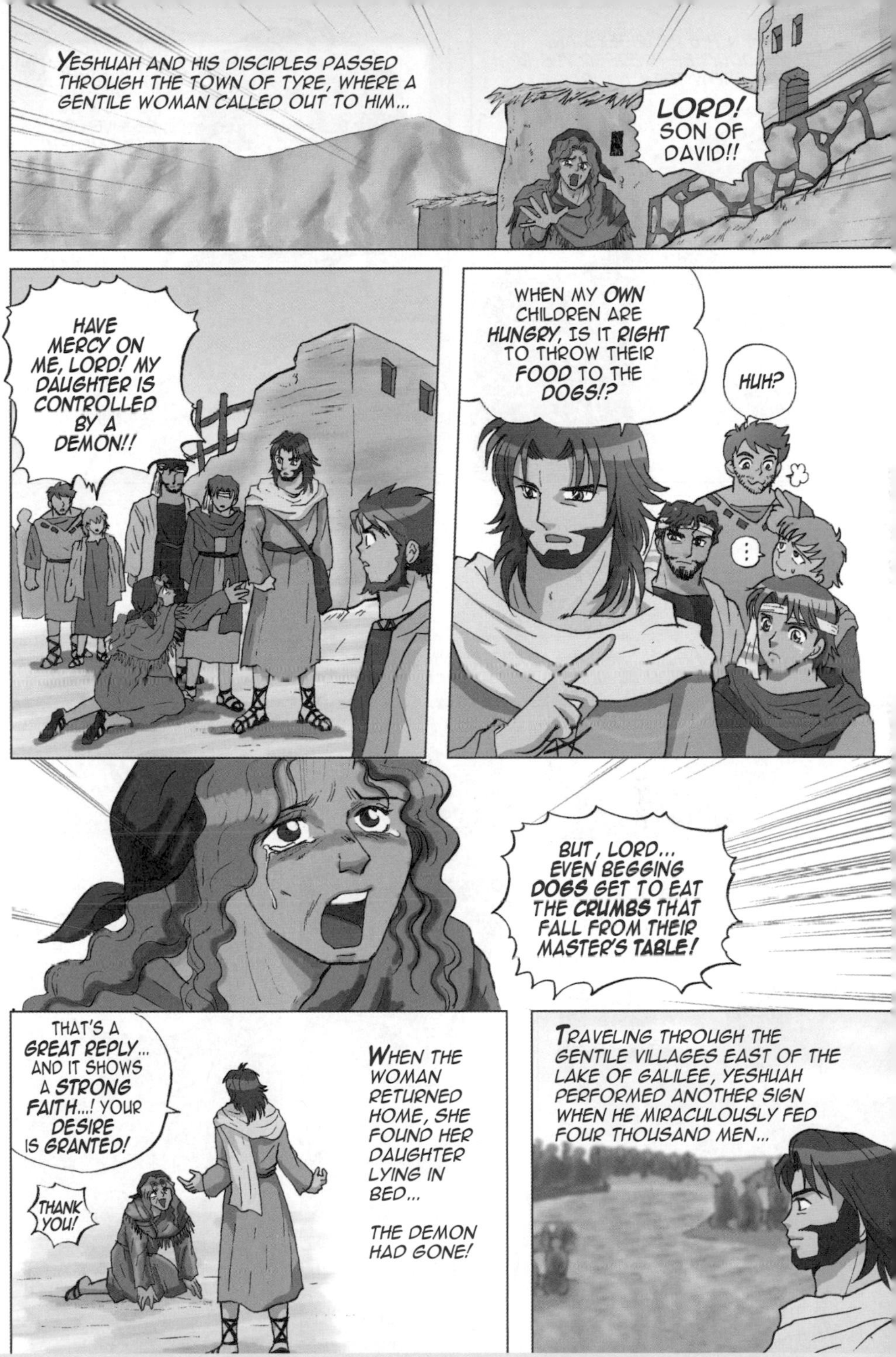
YESHUAH AND HIS DISCIPLES PASSED THROUGH THE TOWN OF TYRE, WHERE A GENTILE WOMAN CALLED OUT TO HIM...
LORD! SON OF DAVID!!
HAVE MERCY ON ME, LORD! MY DAUGHTER IS CONTROLLED BY A DEMON!!
WHEN MY OWN CHILDREN ARE HUNGRY, IS IT RIGHT TO THROW THEIR FOOD TO THE DOGS!?
HUH?
BUT, LORD... EVEN BEGGING DOGS GET TO EAT THE CRUMBS THAT FALL FROM THEIR MASTER'S TABLE!
THAT'S A GREAT REPLY... AND IT SHOWS A STRONG FAITH...! YOUR DESIRE IS GRANTED!
THANK YOU!
WHEN THE WOMAN RETURNED HOME, SHE FOUND HER DAUGHTER LYING IN BED...
THE DEMON HAD GONE!
TRAVELING THROUGH THE GENTILE VILLAGES EAST OF THE LAKE OF GALILEE, YESHUAH PERFORMED ANOTHER SIGN WHEN HE MIRACULOUSLY FED FOUR THOUSAND MEN...

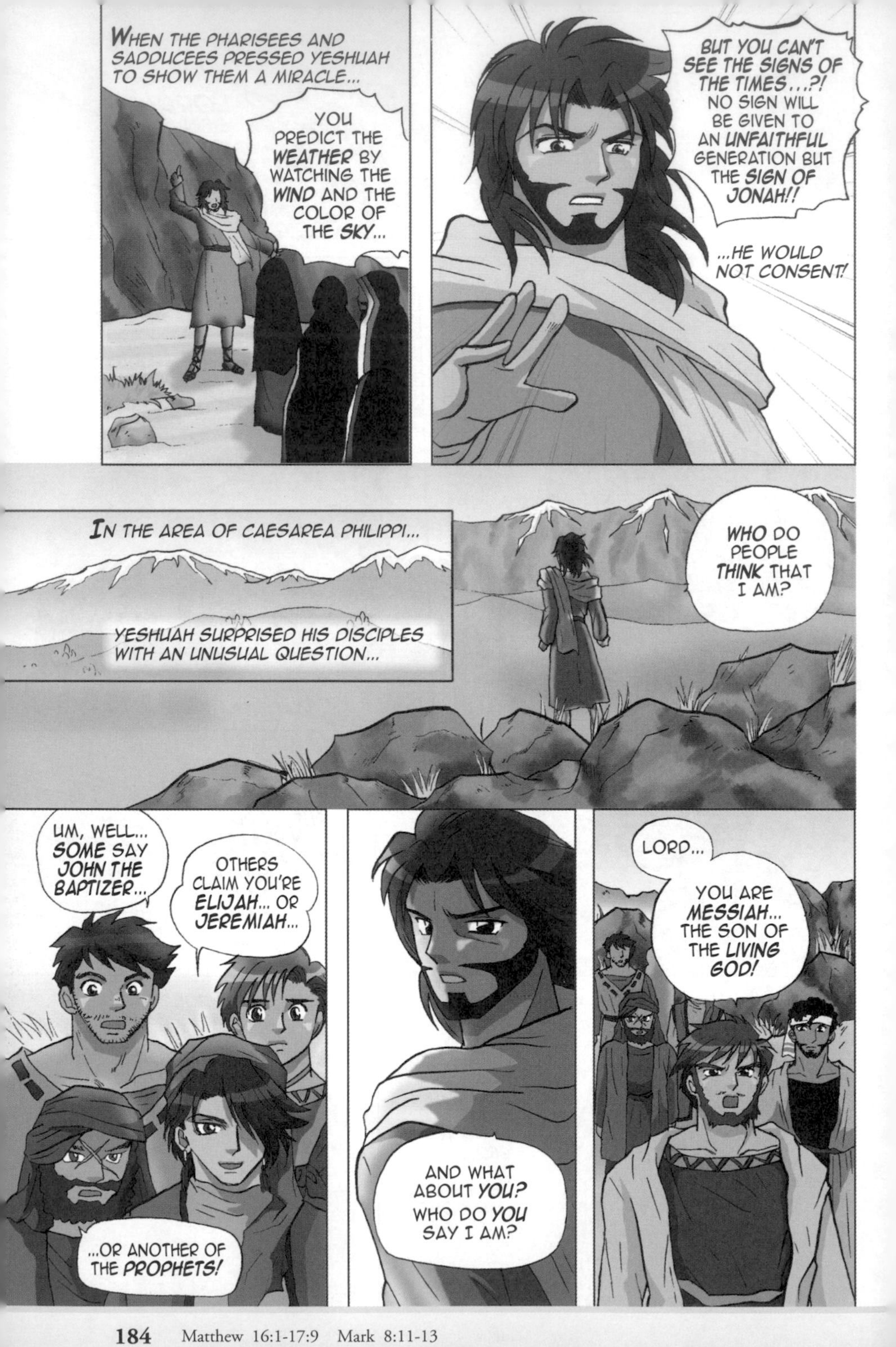

WHEN THE PHARISEES AND SADDUCEES PRESSED YESHUAH TO SHOW THEM A MIRACLE...
YOU PREDICT THE WEATHER BY WATCHING THE WIND AND THE COLOR OF THE SKY...
BUT YOU CAN'T SEE THE SIGNS OF THE TIMES...?! NO SIGN WILL BE GIVEN TO AN UNFAITHFUL GENERATION BUT THE SIGN OF JONAH!!
...HE WOULD NOT CONSENT!
IN THE AREA OF CAESAREA PHILIPPI...
YESHUAH SURPRISED HIS DISCIPLES WITH AN UNUSUAL QUESTION...
WHO DO PEOPLE THINK THAT I AM?
UM, WELL... SOME SAY JOHN THE BAPTIZER...
OTHERS CLAIM YOU'RE ELIJAH... OR JEREMIAH...
...OR ANOTHER OF THE PROPHETS!
AND WHAT ABOUT YOU? WHO DO YOU SAY I AM?
LORD...
YOU ARE MESSIAH... THE SON OF THE LIVING GOD!

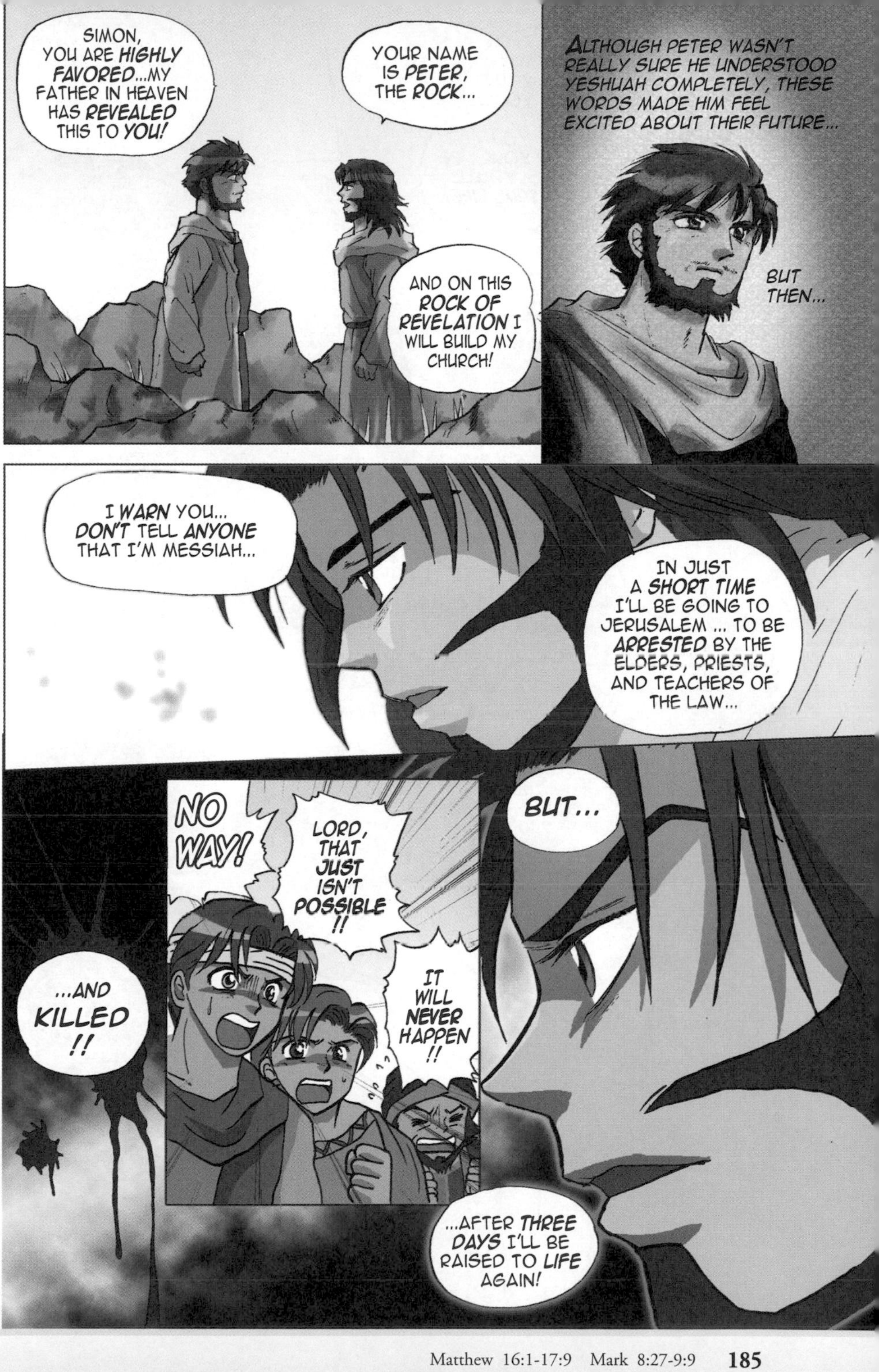
SIMON, YOU ARE HIGHLY FAVORED...MY FATHER IN HEAVEN HAS REVEALED THIS TO YOU!
YOUR NAME IS PETER, THE ROCK...
AND ON THIS ROCK OF REVELATION I WILL BUILD MY CHURCH!
ALTHOUGH PETER WASN'T REALLY SURE HE UNDERSTOOD YESHUAH COMPLETELY, THESE WORDS MADE HIM FEEL EXCITED ABOUT THEIR FUTURE...
BUT THEN...
I WARN YOU... DON'T TELL ANYONE THAT I'M MESSIAH...
IN JUST A SHORT TIME I'LL BE GOING TO JERUSALEM ... TO BE ARRESTED BY THE ELDERS, PRIESTS, AND TEACHERS OF THE LAW...
...AND KILLED !!
BUT...
...AFTER THREE DAYS I'LL BE RAISED TO LIFE AGAIN!
NO WAY!
LORD, THAT JUST ISN'T POSSIBLE !!
IT WILL NEVER HAPPEN !!

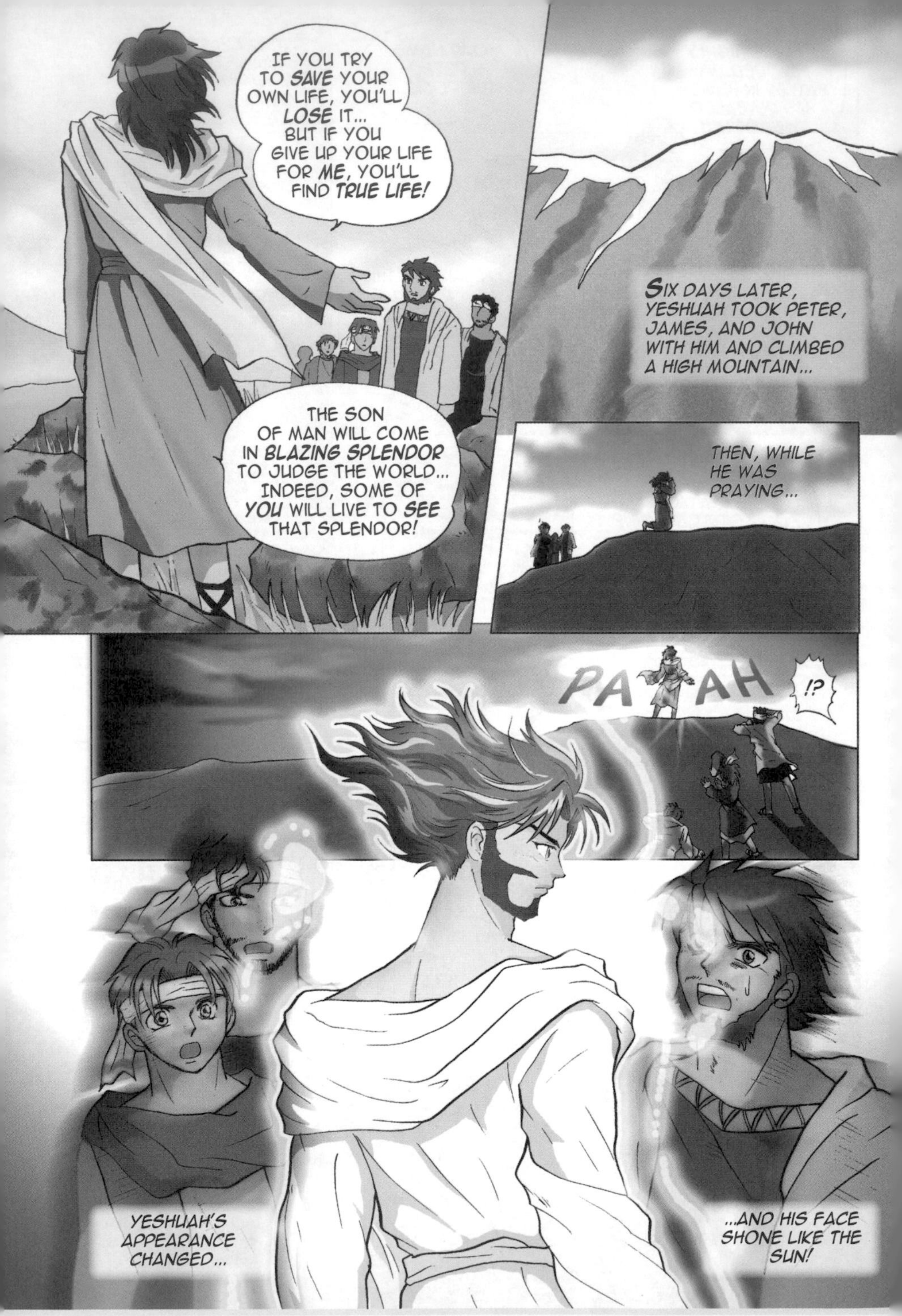
IF YOU TRY TO SAVE YOUR OWN LIFE, YOU'LL LOSE IT... BUT IF YOU GIVE UP YOUR LIFE FOR ME, YOU'LL FIND TRUE LIFE!
THE SON OF MAN WILL COME IN BLAZING SPLENDOR TO JUDGE THE WORLD... INDEED, SOME OF YOU WILL LIVE TO SEE THAT SPLENDOR!
SIX DAYS LATER, YESHUAH TOOK PETER, JAMES, AND JOHN WITH HIM AND CLIMBED A HIGH MOUNTAIN...
THEN, WHILE HE WAS PRAYING...
PA AH
!?
YESHUAH'S APPEARANCE CHANGED...
...AND HIS FACE SHONE LIKE THE SUN!

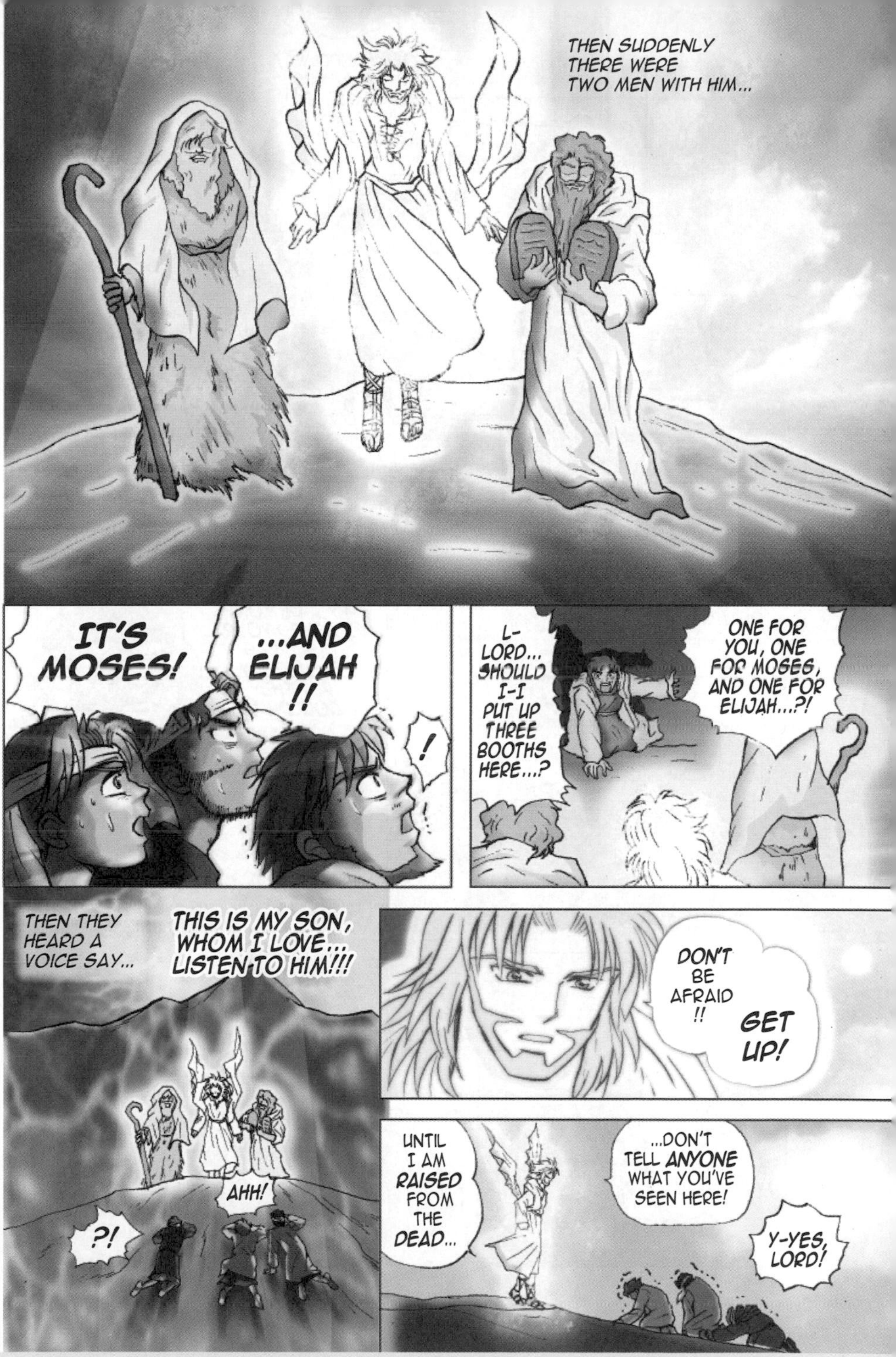

THEN SUDDENLY THERE WERE TWO MEN WITH HIM...
IT'S MOSES!
...AND ELIJAH !!
!
L- LORD... SHOULD I-I PUT UP THREE BOOTHS HERE...?
ONE FOR YOU, ONE FOR MOSES, AND ONE FOR ELIJAH...?!
THEN THEY HEARD A VOICE SAY...
THIS IS MY SON, WHOM I LOVE... LISTEN TO HIM!!!
AHH!
?!
DON'T BE AFRAID !!
GET UP!
UNTIL I AM RAISED FROM THE DEAD...
...DON'T TELL ANYONE WHAT YOU'VE SEEN HERE!
Y-YES, LORD!

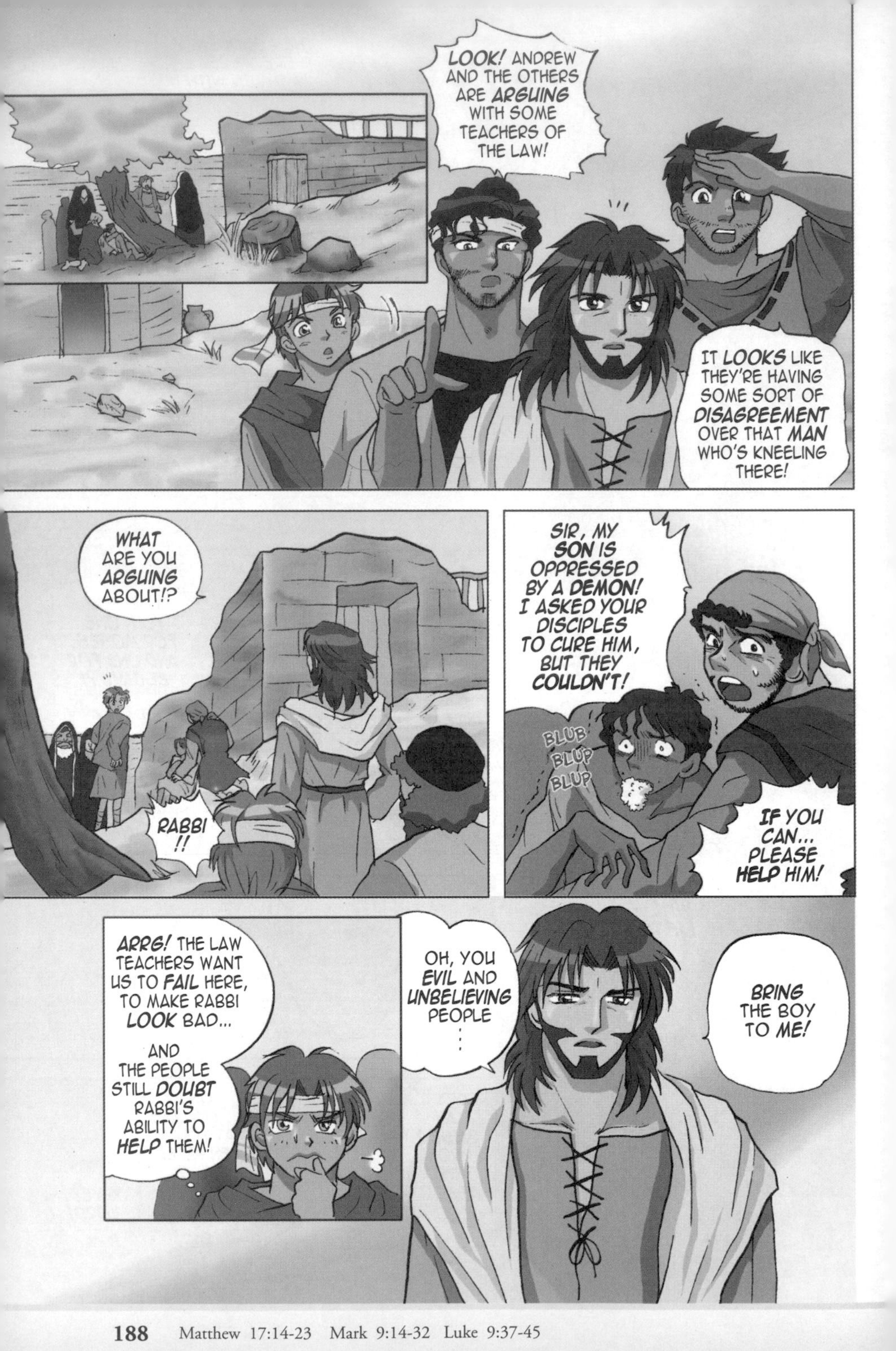
LOOK! ANDREW AND THE OTHERS ARE ARGUING WITH SOME TEACHERS OF THE LAW!
IT LOOKS LIKE THEY'RE HAVING SOME SORT OF DISAGREEMENT OVER THAT MAN WHO'S KNEELING THERE!
WHAT ARE YOU ARGUING ABOUT!?
RABBI !!
SIR, MY SON IS OPPRESSED BY A DEMON! I ASKED YOUR DISCIPLES TO CURE HIM, BUT THEY COULDN'T!
BLUB BLUP BLUP
IF YOU CAN... PLEASE HELP HIM!
ARRG! THE LAW TEACHERS WANT US TO FAIL HERE, TO MAKE RABBI LOOK BAD...
AND THE PEOPLE STILL DOUBT RABBI'S ABILITY TO HELP THEM!
OH, YOU EVIL AND UNBELIEVING PEOPLE ...
BRING THE BOY TO ME!

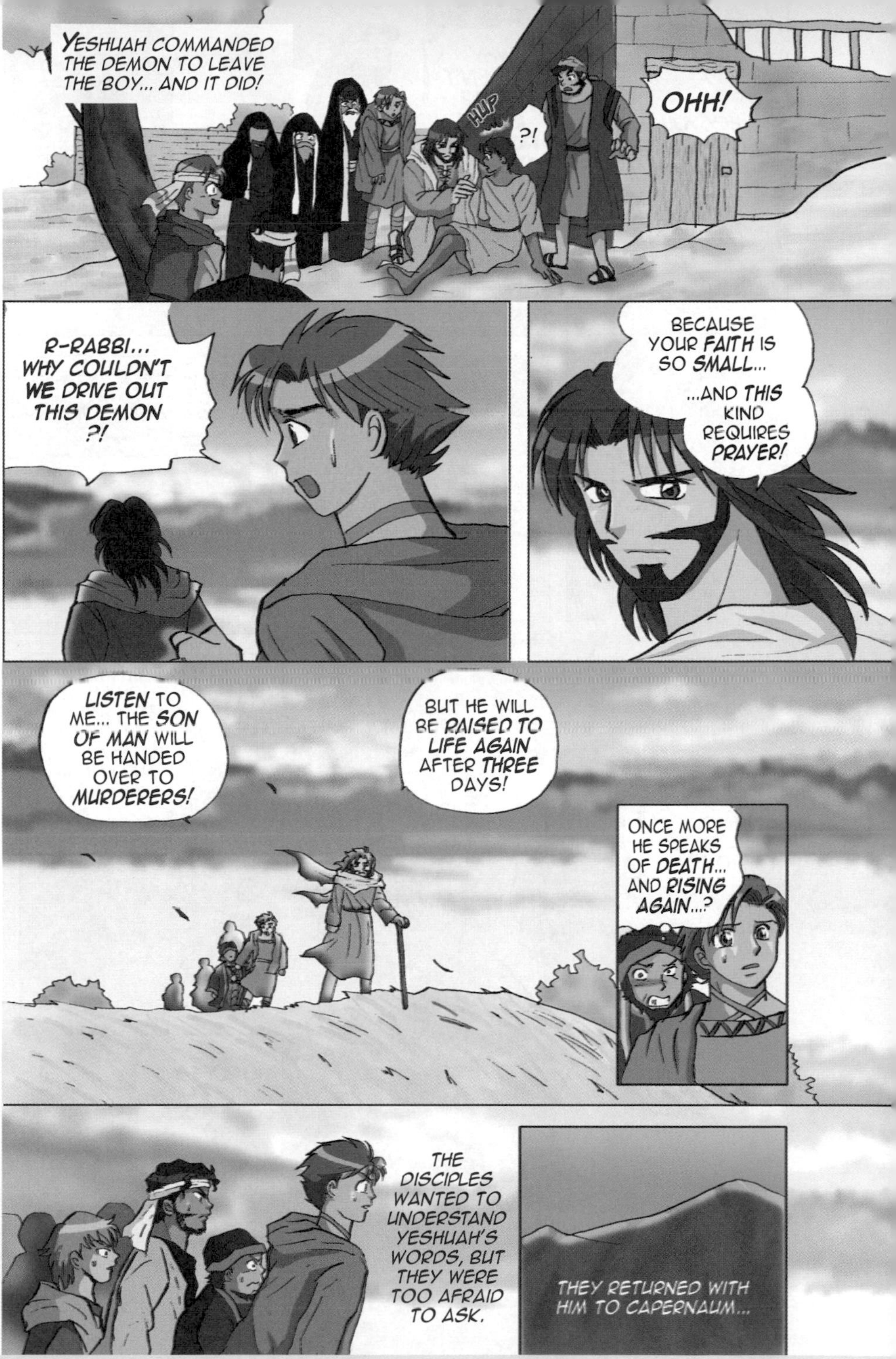
YESHUAH COMMANDED THE DEMON TO LEAVE THE BOY... AND IT DID!
HUP
?!
OHH!
R-RABBI... WHY COULDN'T WE DRIVE OUT THIS DEMON ?!
BECAUSE YOUR FAITH IS SO SMALL...
...AND THIS KIND REQUIRES PRAYER!
LISTEN TO ME... THE SON OF MAN WILL BE HANDED OVER TO MURDERERS!
BUT HE WILL BE RAISED TO LIFE AGAIN AFTER THREE DAYS!
ONCE MORE HE SPEAKS OF DEATH... AND RISING AGAIN...?
THE DISCIPLES WANTED TO UNDERSTAND YESHUAH'S WORDS, BUT THEY WERE TOO AFRAID TO ASK.
THEY RETURNED WITH HIM TO CAPERNAUM...

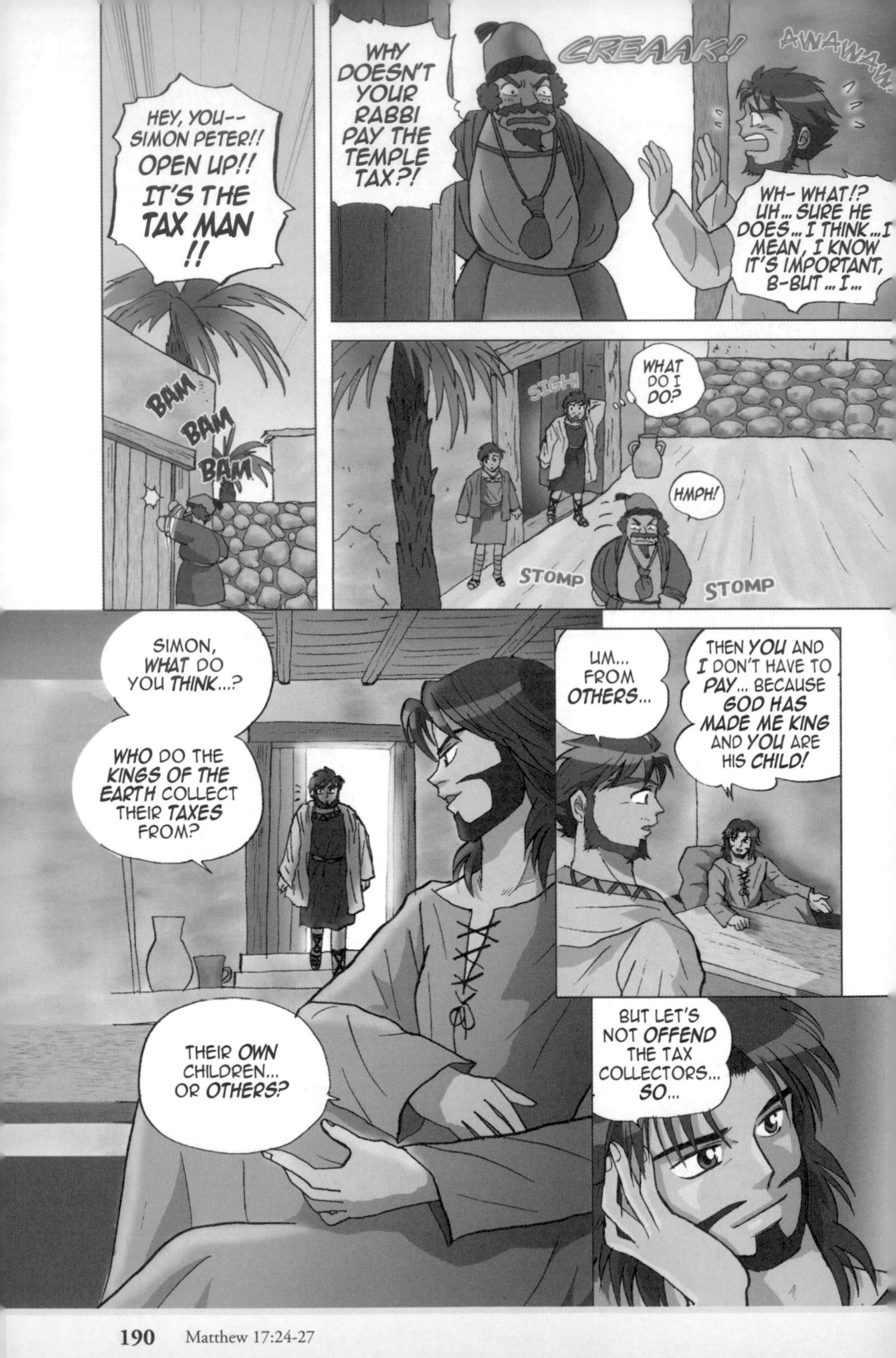

HEY, YOU-- SIMON PETER!! OPEN UP!! IT'S THE TAX MAN !!
BAM BAM BAM
WHY DOESN'T YOUR RABBI PAY THE TEMPLE TAX?!
CREAAK!
AWAWAW
WH- WHAT!? UH... SURE HE DOES... I THINK... I MEAN, I KNOW IT'S IMPORTANT, B-BUT ... I...
SIGH!
WHAT DO I DO?
HMPH!
STOMP
STOMP
SIMON, WHAT DO YOU THINK...?
WHO DO THE KINGS OF THE EARTH COLLECT THEIR TAXES FROM?
THEIR OWN CHILDREN... OR OTHERS?
UM... FROM OTHERS...
THEN YOU AND I DON'T HAVE TO PAY... BECAUSE GOD HAS MADE ME KING AND YOU ARE HIS CHILD!
BUT LET'S NOT OFFEND THE TAX COLLECTORS... SO...

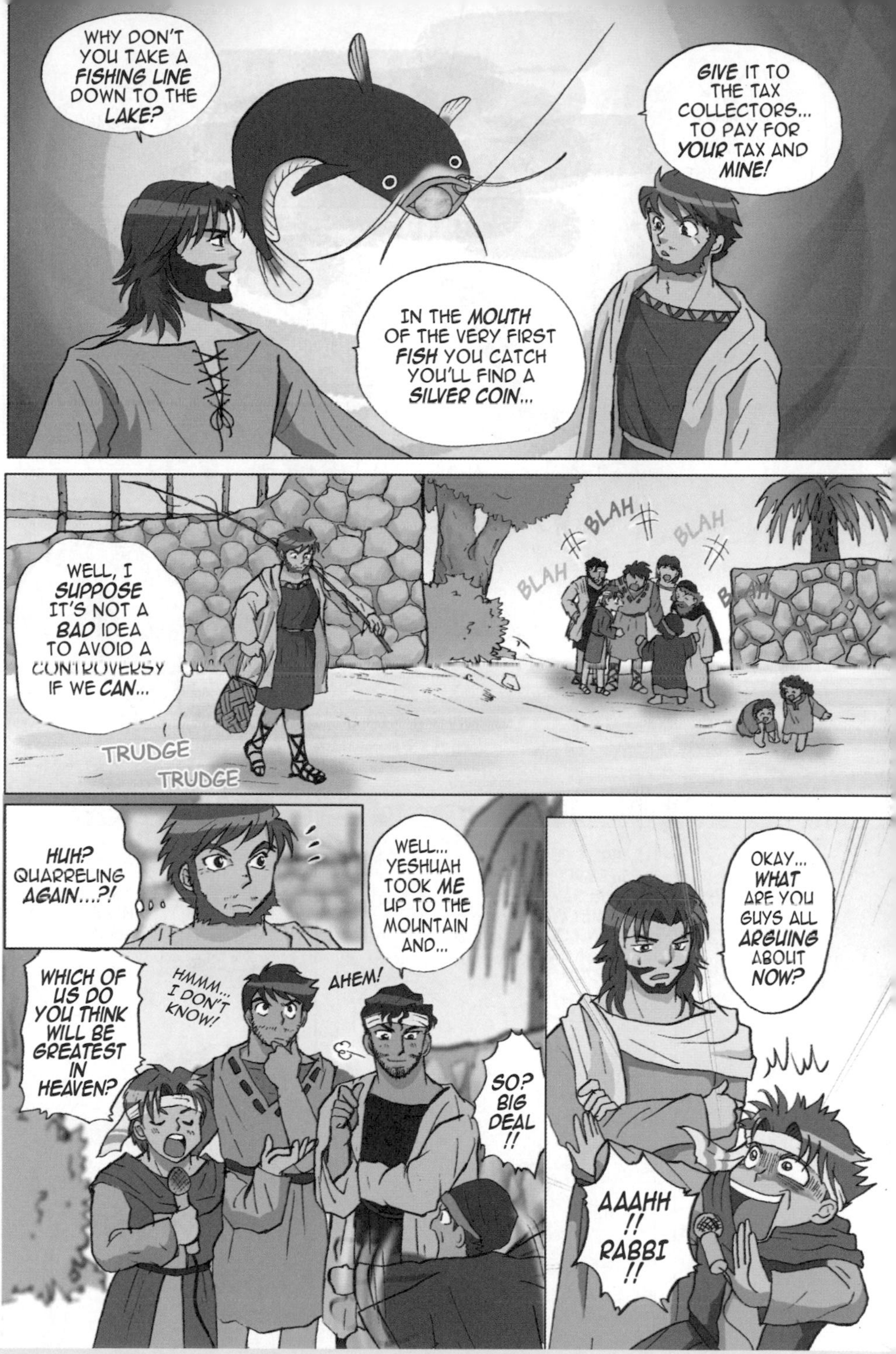
WHY DON'T YOU TAKE A FISHING LINE DOWN TO THE LAKE?
IN THE MOUTH OF THE VERY FIRST FISH YOU CATCH YOU'LL FIND A SILVER COIN...
GIVE IT TO THE TAX COLLECTORS... TO PAY FOR YOUR TAX AND MINE!
WELL, I SUPPOSE IT'S NOT A BAD IDEA TO AVOID A CONTROVERSY IF WE CAN...
TRUDGE
TRUDGE
BLAH
BLAH
BLAH
BLAH
HUH? QUARRELING AGAIN...?!
WELL... YESHUAH TOOK ME UP TO THE MOUNTAIN AND...
AHEM!
HMMM... I DON'T KNOW!
WHICH OF US DO YOU THINK WILL BE GREATEST IN HEAVEN?
SO? BIG DEAL !!
OKAY... WHAT ARE YOU GUYS ALL ARGUING ABOUT NOW?
AAAHH !! RABBI !!

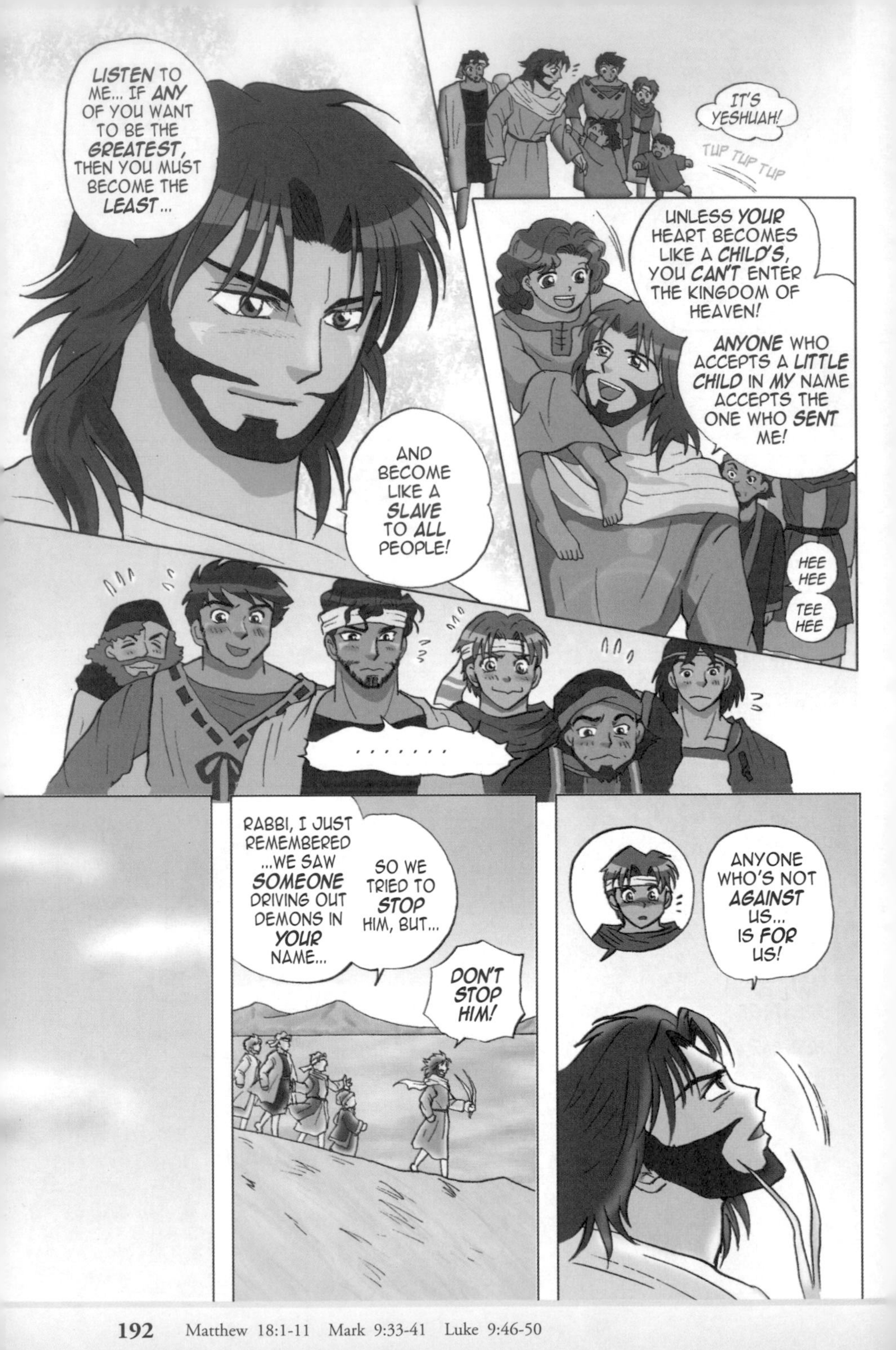
LISTEN TO ME... IF ANY OF YOU WANT TO BE THE GREATEST, THEN YOU MUST BECOME THE LEAST...
AND BECOME LIKE A SLAVE TO ALL PEOPLE!
IT'S YESHUAH!
TUP TUP TUP
UNLESS YOUR HEART BECOMES LIKE A CHILD'S, YOU CAN'T ENTER THE KINGDOM OF HEAVEN!
ANYONE WHO ACCEPTS A LITTLE CHILD IN MY NAME ACCEPTS THE ONE WHO SENT ME!
HEE HEE
TEE HEE
. . . .
RABBI, I JUST REMEMBERED ...WE SAW SOMEONE DRIVING OUT DEMONS IN YOUR NAME...
SO WE TRIED TO STOP HIM, BUT...
DON'T STOP HIM!
ANYONE WHO'S NOT AGAINST US... IS FOR US!

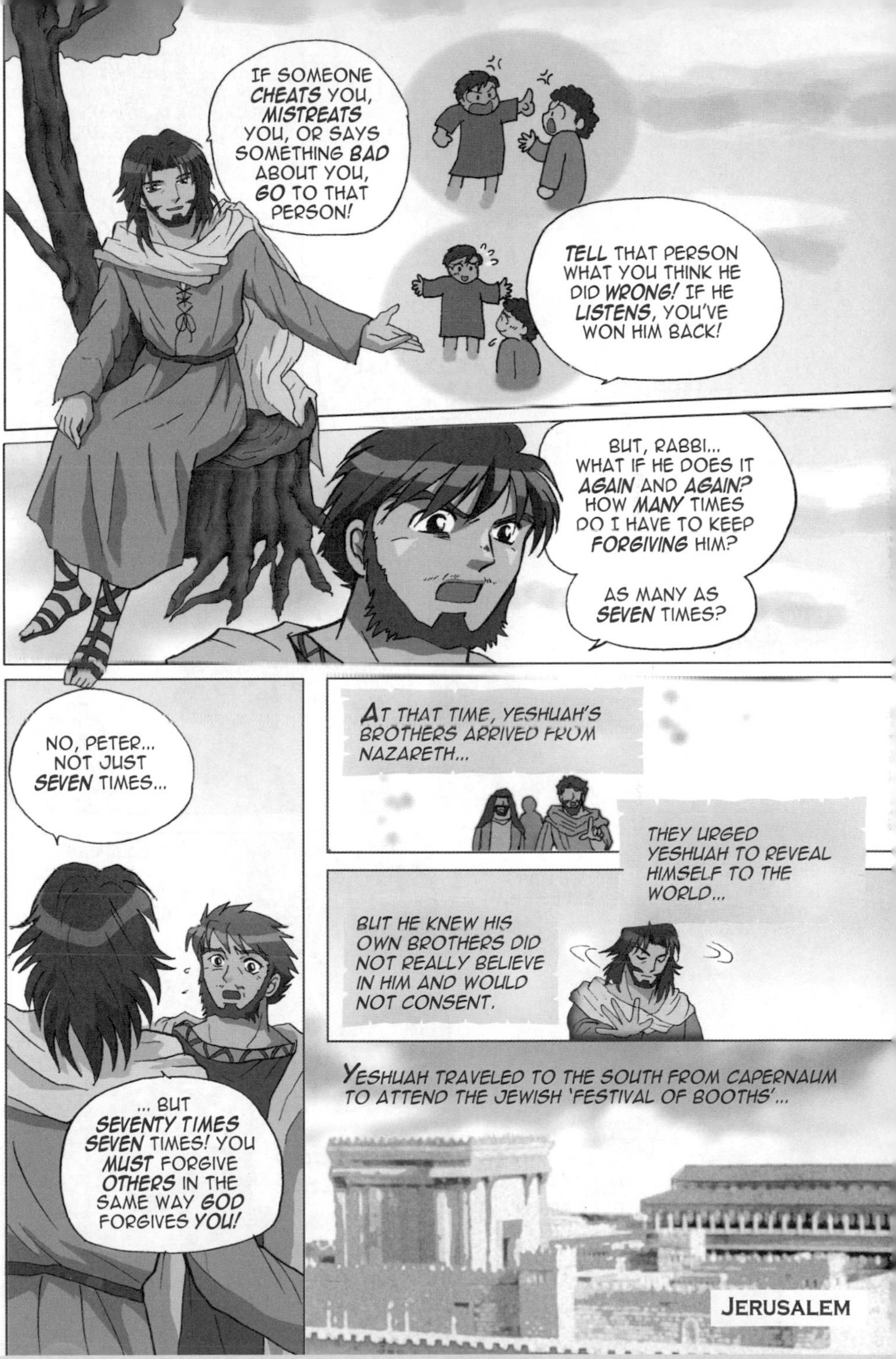

IF SOMEONE CHEATS YOU, MISTREATS YOU, OR SAYS SOMETHING BAD ABOUT YOU, GO TO THAT PERSON!
TELL THAT PERSON WHAT YOU THINK HE DID WRONG! IF HE LISTENS, YOU'VE WON HIM BACK!
BUT, RABBI... WHAT IF HE DOES IT AGAIN AND AGAIN? HOW MANY TIMES DO I HAVE TO KEEP FORGIVING HIM?
AS MANY AS SEVEN TIMES?
NO, PETER... NOT JUST SEVEN TIMES...
... BUT SEVENTY TIMES SEVEN TIMES! YOU MUST FORGIVE OTHERS IN THE SAME WAY GOD FORGIVES YOU!
AT THAT TIME, YESHUAH'S BROTHERS ARRIVED FROM NAZARETH...
THEY URGED YESHUAH TO REVEAL HIMSELF TO THE WORLD...
BUT HE KNEW HIS OWN BROTHERS DID NOT REALLY BELIEVE IN HIM AND WOULD NOT CONSENT.
YESHUAH TRAVELED TO THE SOUTH FROM CAPERNAUM TO ATTEND THE JEWISH 'FESTIVAL OF BOOTHS'...
JERUSALEM

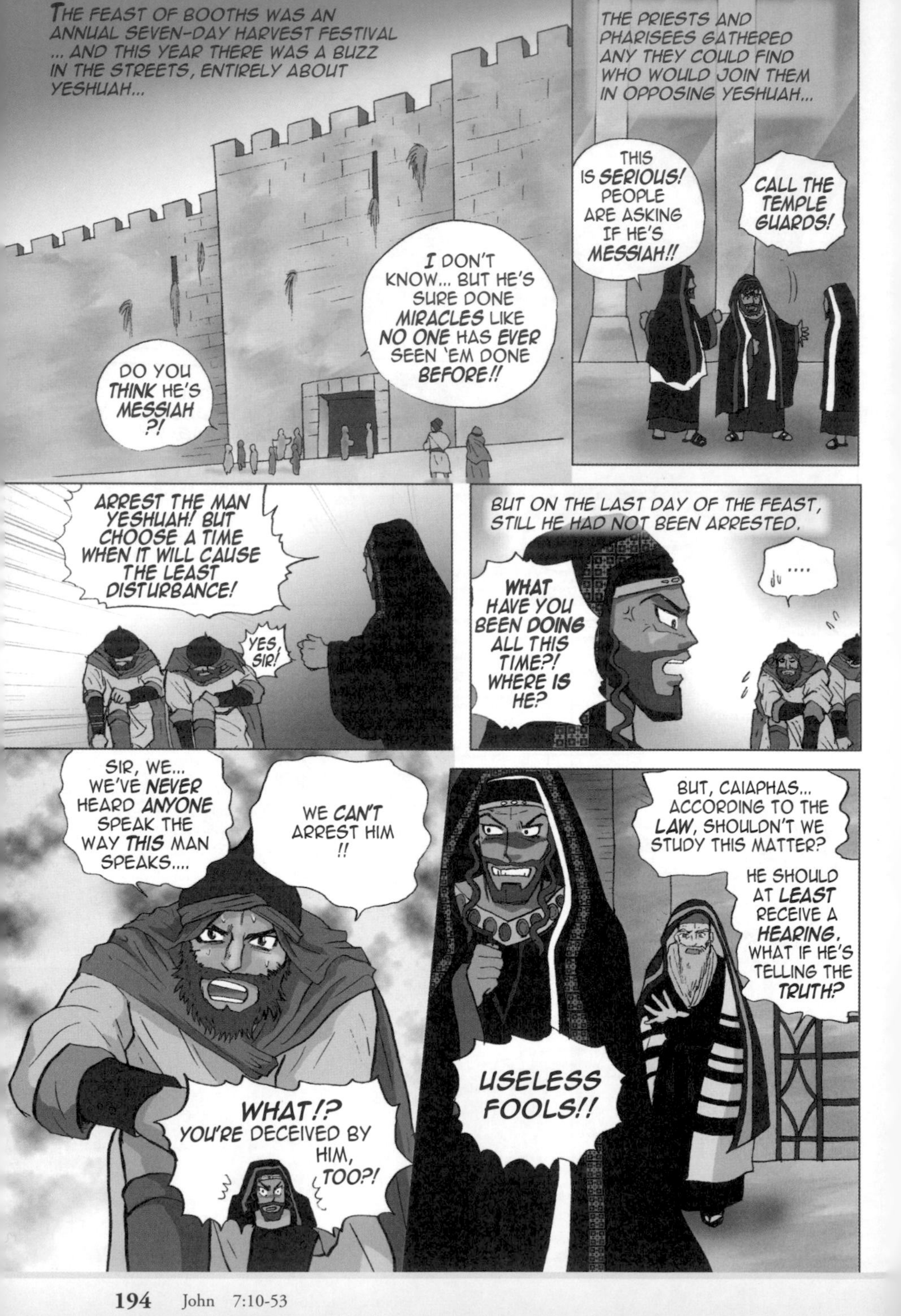
THE FEAST OF BOOTHS WAS AN ANNUAL SEVEN-DAY HARVEST FESTIVAL ... AND THIS YEAR THERE WAS A BUZZ IN THE STREETS, ENTIRELY ABOUT YESHUAH...
DO YOU THINK HE'S MESSIAH ?!
I DON'T KNOW... BUT HE'S SURE DONE MIRACLES LIKE NO ONE HAS EVER SEEN 'EM DONE BEFORE!!
THE PRIESTS AND PHARISEES GATHERED ANY THEY COULD FIND WHO WOULD JOIN THEM IN OPPOSING YESHUAH...
THIS IS SERIOUS! PEOPLE ARE ASKING IF HE'S MESSIAH!!
CALL THE TEMPLE GUARDS!
ARREST THE MAN YESHUAH! BUT CHOOSE A TIME WHEN IT WILL CAUSE THE LEAST DISTURBANCE!
YES, SIR!
BUT ON THE LAST DAY OF THE FEAST, STILL HE HAD NOT BEEN ARRESTED.
WHAT HAVE YOU BEEN DOING ALL THIS TIME?! WHERE IS HE?
....
SIR, WE... WE'VE NEVER HEARD ANYONE SPEAK THE WAY THIS MAN SPEAKS....
WE CAN'T ARREST HIM !!
WHAT!? YOU'RE DECEIVED BY HIM, TOO?!
USELESS FOOLS!!
BUT, CAIAPHAS... ACCORDING TO THE LAW, SHOULDN'T WE STUDY THIS MATTER?
HE SHOULD AT LEAST RECEIVE A HEARING. WHAT IF HE'S TELLING THE TRUTH?

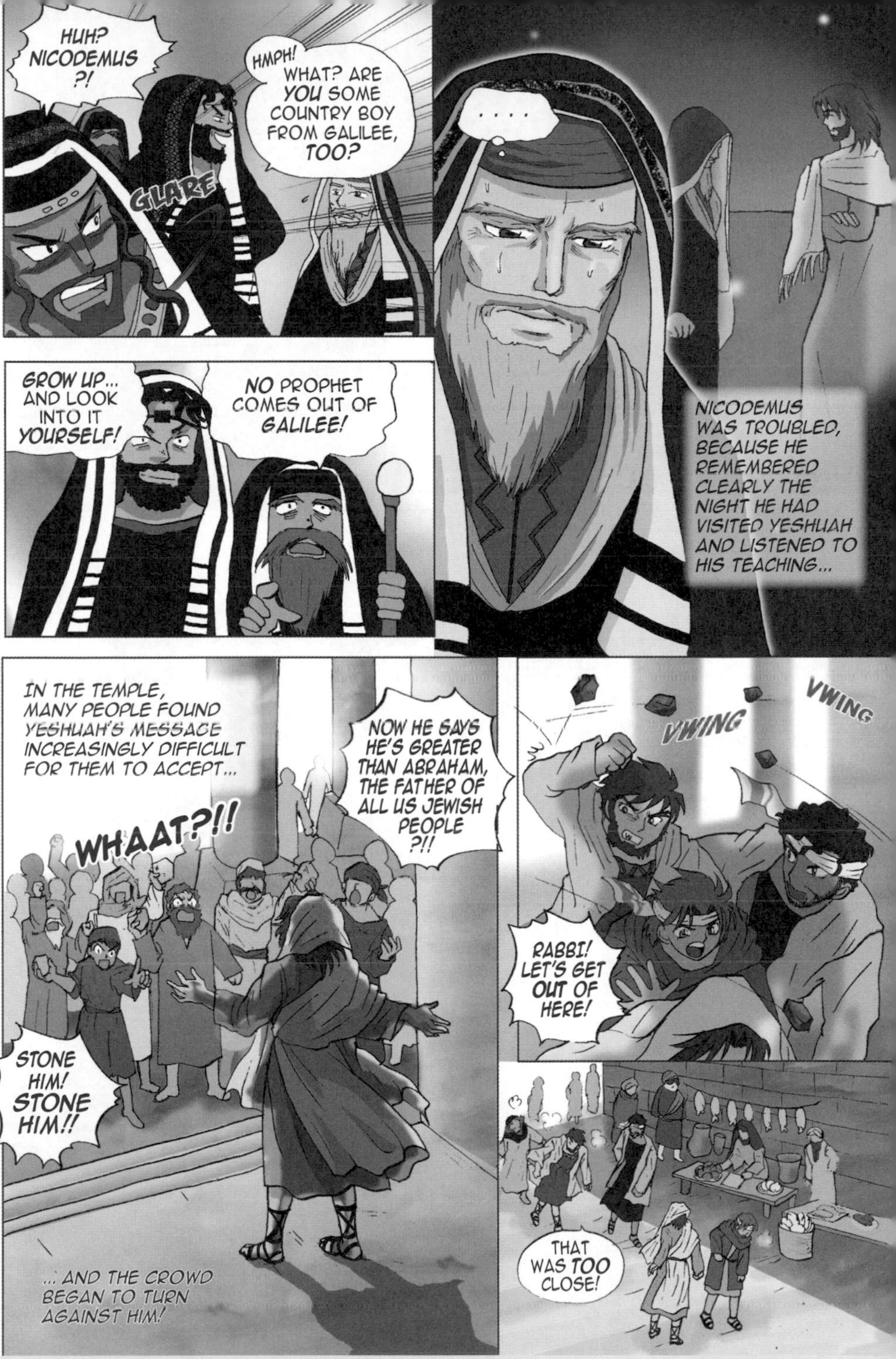
HUH? NICODEMUS ?!
HMPH! WHAT? ARE YOU SOME COUNTRY BOY FROM GALILEE, TOO?
GLARE
....
GROW UP... AND LOOK INTO IT YOURSELF!
NO PROPHET COMES OUT OF GALILEE!
NICODEMUS WAS TROUBLED, BECAUSE HE REMEMBERED CLEARLY THE NIGHT HE HAD VISITED YESHUAH AND LISTENED TO HIS TEACHING...
IN THE TEMPLE, MANY PEOPLE FOUND YESHUAH'S MESSAGE INCREASINGLY DIFFICULT FOR THEM TO ACCEPT...
NOW HE SAYS HE'S GREATER THAN ABRAHAM, THE FATHER OF ALL US JEWISH PEOPLE ?!!
WHAAT?!!
STONE HIM! STONE HIM!!
... AND THE CROWD BEGAN TO TURN AGAINST HIM!
VWING
VWING
RABBI! LET'S GET OUT OF HERE!
THAT WAS TOO CLOSE!

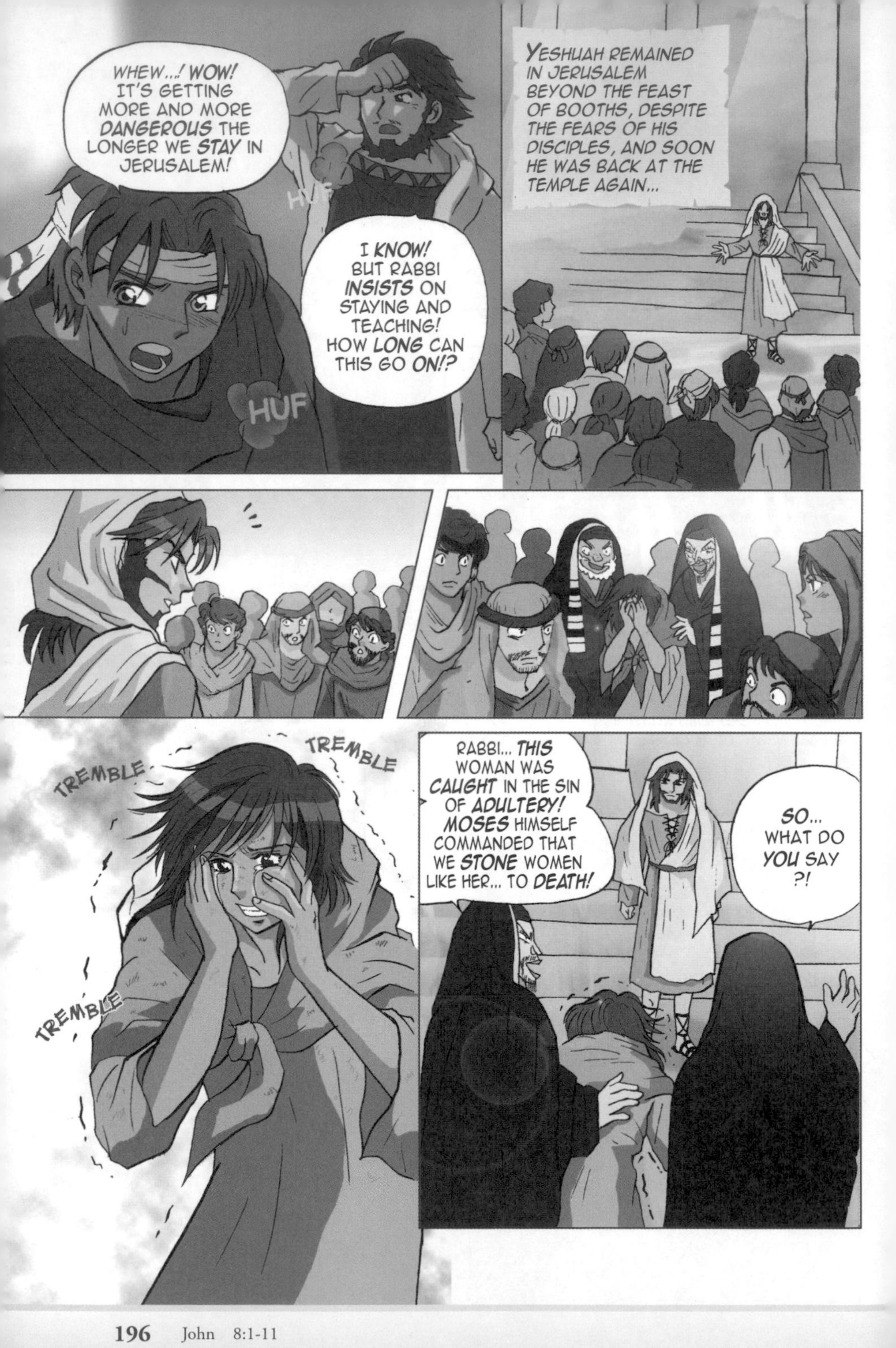
WHEW...! WOW! IT'S GETTING MORE AND MORE DANGEROUS THE LONGER WE STAY IN JERUSALEM!
HUF
HUF
I KNOW! BUT RABBI INSISTS ON STAYING AND TEACHING! HOW LONG CAN THIS GO ON!?
YESHUAH REMAINED IN JERUSALEM BEYOND THE FEAST OF BOOTHS, DESPITE THE FEARS OF HIS DISCIPLES, AND SOON HE WAS BACK AT THE TEMPLE AGAIN...
TREMBLE
TREMBLE
TREMBLE
RABBI... THIS WOMAN WAS CAUGHT IN THE SIN OF ADULTERY! MOSES HIMSELF COMMANDED THAT WE STONE WOMEN LIKE HER... TO DEATH!
SO... WHAT DO YOU SAY ?!

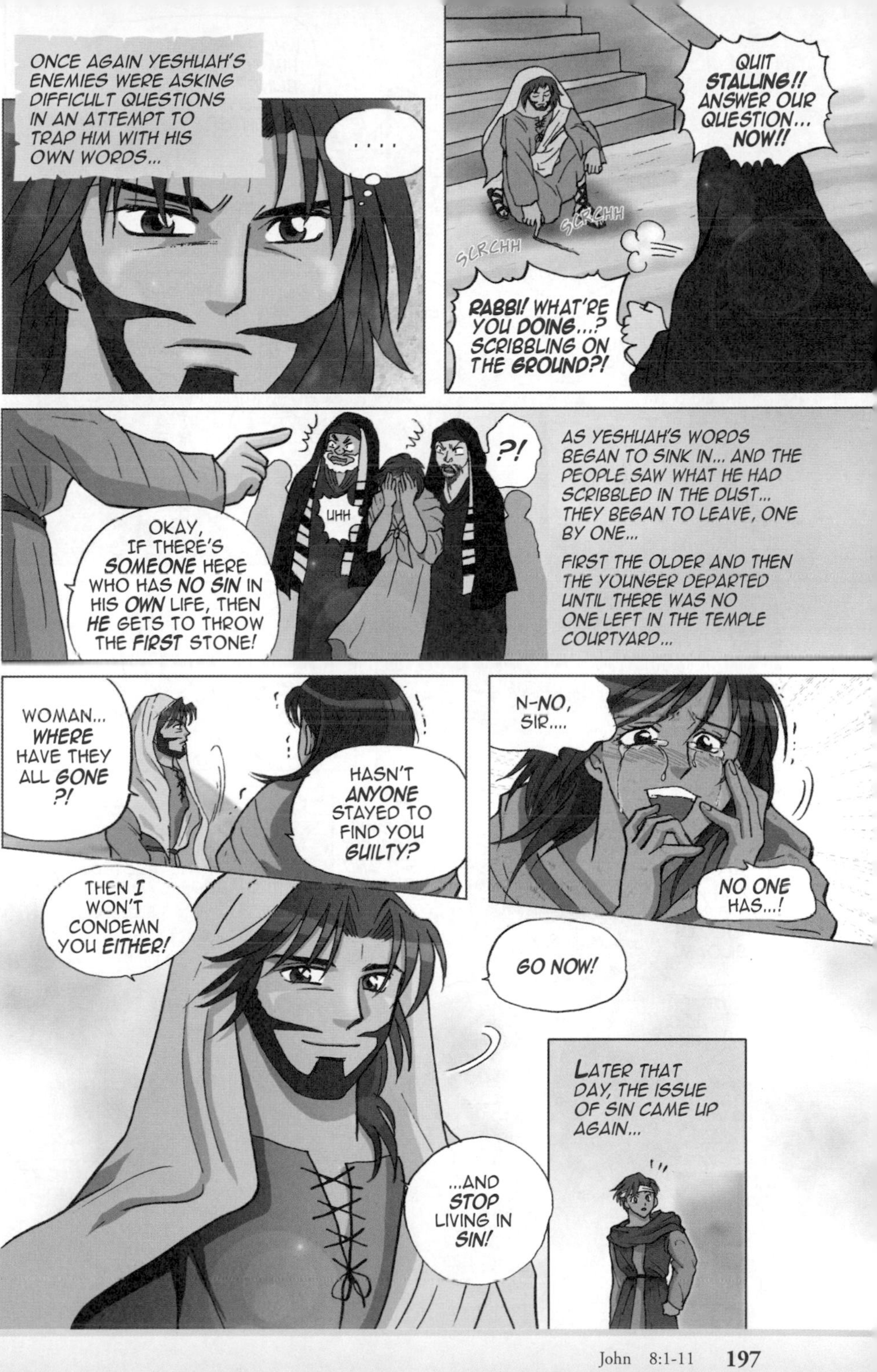
ONCE AGAIN YESHUAH'S ENEMIES WERE ASKING DIFFICULT QUESTIONS IN AN ATTEMPT TO TRAP HIM WITH HIS OWN WORDS...
....
QUIT STALLING!! ANSWER OUR QUESTION... NOW!!
SCRCHH
SCRCHH
RABBI! WHAT'RE YOU DOING...? SCRIBBLING ON THE GROUND?!
?!
UHH
OKAY, IF THERE'S SOMEONE HERE WHO HAS NO SIN IN HIS OWN LIFE, THEN HE GETS TO THROW THE FIRST STONE!
AS YESHUAH'S WORDS BEGAN TO SINK IN... AND THE PEOPLE SAW WHAT HE HAD SCRIBBLED IN THE DUST... THEY BEGAN TO LEAVE, ONE BY ONE...
FIRST THE OLDER AND THEN THE YOUNGER DEPARTED UNTIL THERE WAS NO ONE LEFT IN THE TEMPLE COURTYARD...
WOMAN... WHERE HAVE THEY ALL GONE ?!
HASN'T ANYONE STAYED TO FIND YOU GUILTY?
N-NO, SIR....
NO ONE HAS...!
THEN I WON'T CONDEMN YOU EITHER!
GO NOW!
...AND STOP LIVING IN SIN!
LATER THAT DAY, THE ISSUE OF SIN CAME UP AGAIN...

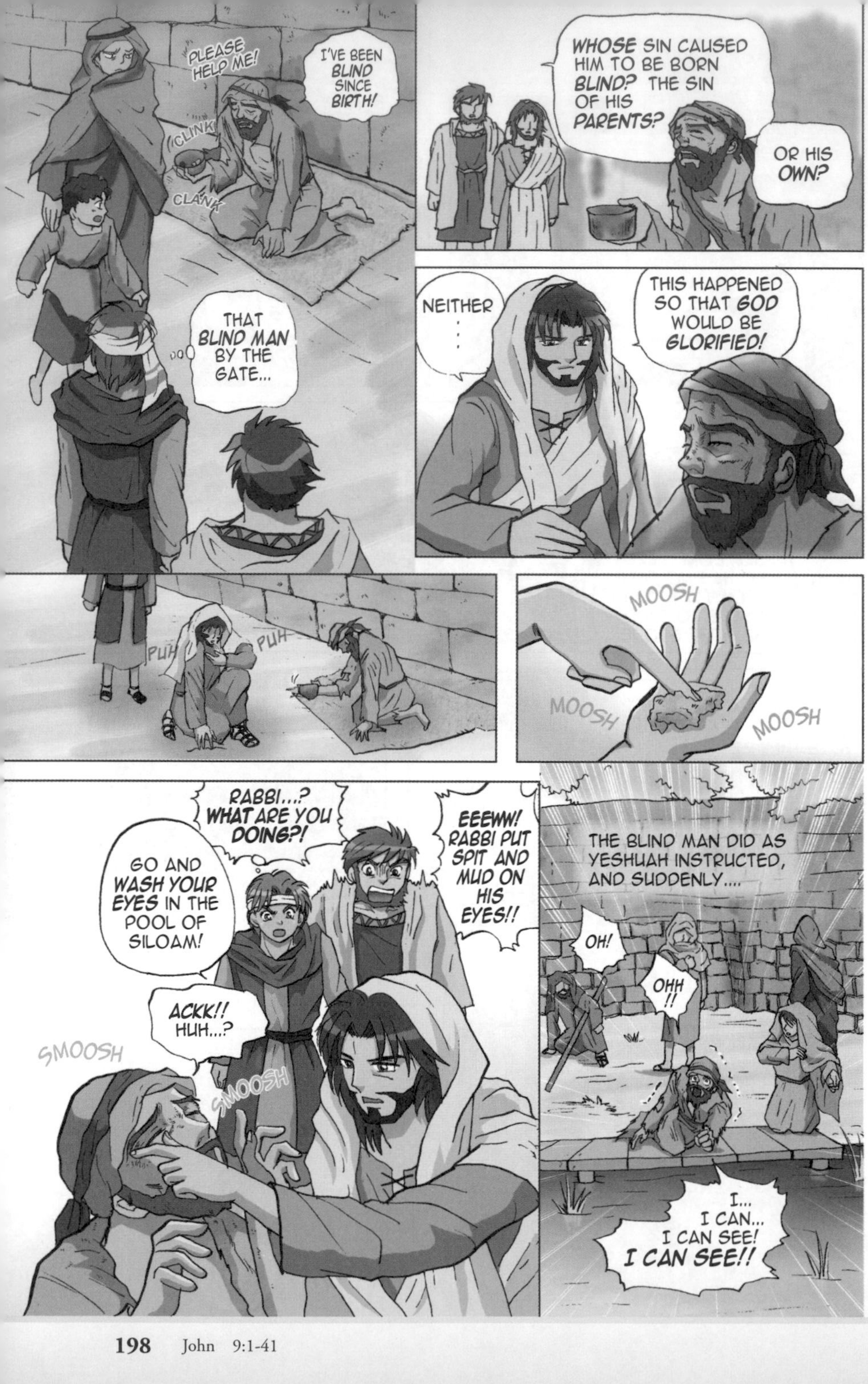
PLEASE HELP ME!
I'VE BEEN BLIND SINCE BIRTH!
CLINK
CLANK
THAT BLIND MAN BY THE GATE...
WHOSE SIN CAUSED HIM TO BE BORN BLIND? THE SIN OF HIS PARENTS?
OR HIS OWN?
NEITHER . . .
THIS HAPPENED SO THAT GOD WOULD BE GLORIFIED!
PUH
PUH
MOOSH
MOOSH
MOOSH
RABBI...? WHAT ARE YOU DOING?!
EEEWW! RABBI PUT SPIT AND MUD ON HIS EYES!!
GO AND WASH YOUR EYES IN THE POOL OF SILOAM!
ACKK!! HUH...?
SMOOSH
SMOOSH
THE BLIND MAN DID AS YESHUAH INSTRUCTED, AND SUDDENLY....
OH!
OHH !!
I... I CAN... I CAN SEE! I CAN SEE!!

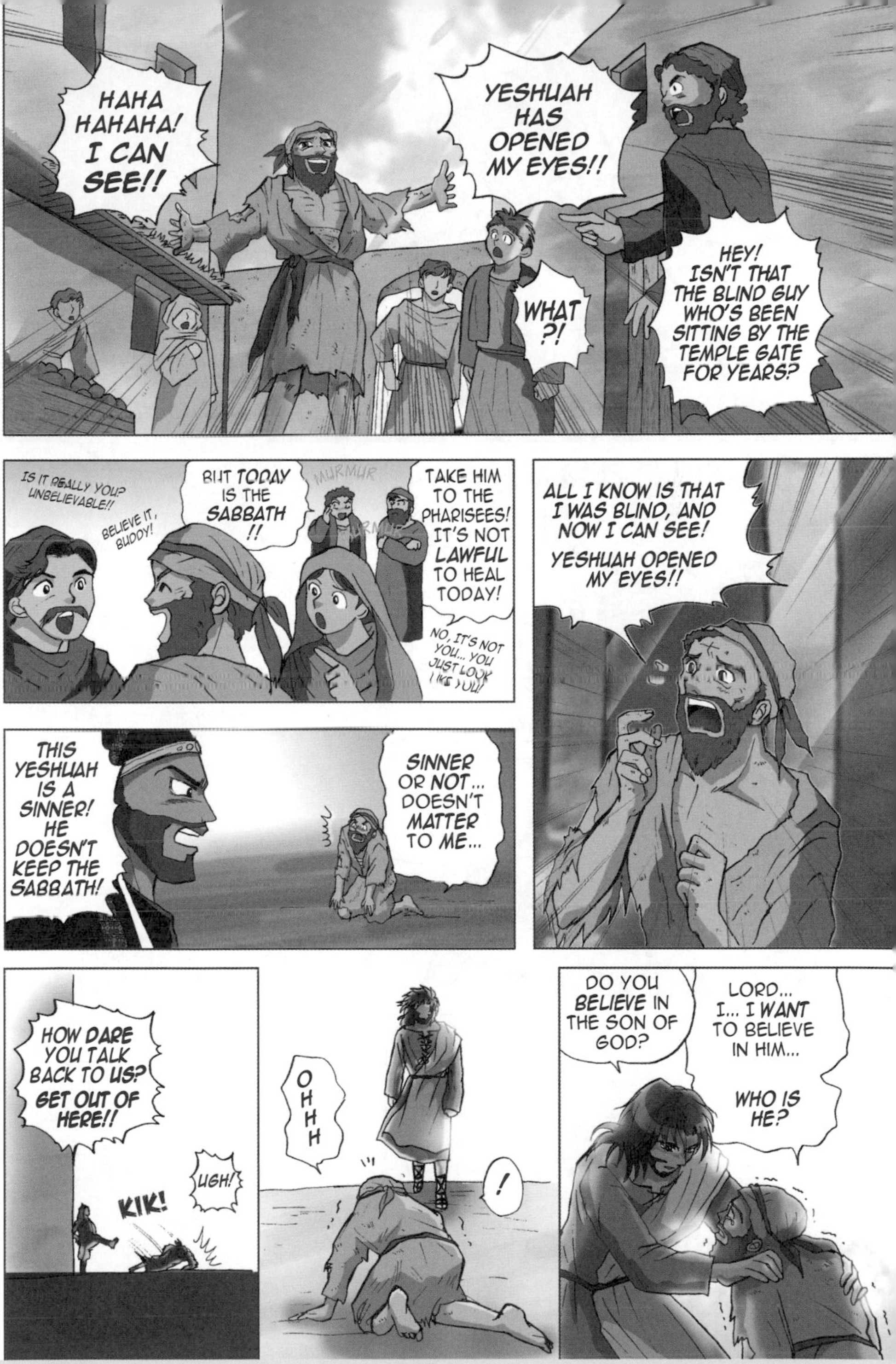
HAHA HAHAHA! I CAN SEE!!
YESHUAH HAS OPENED MY EYES!!
HEY! ISN'T THAT THE BLIND GUY WHO'S BEEN SITTING BY THE TEMPLE GATE FOR YEARS?
WHAT?!
IS IT REALLY YOU? UNBELIEVABLE!!
BELIEVE IT, BUDDY!
BUT TODAY IS THE SABBATH!!
MURMUR
TAKE HIM TO THE PHARISEES! IT'S NOT LAWFUL TO HEAL TODAY!
NO, IT'S NOT YOU... YOU JUST LOOK LIKE YOU!
ALL I KNOW IS THAT I WAS BLIND, AND NOW I CAN SEE!
YESHUAH OPENED MY EYES!!
THIS YESHUAH IS A SINNER! HE DOESN'T KEEP THE SABBATH!
SINNER OR NOT... DOESN'T MATTER TO ME...
HOW DARE YOU TALK BACK TO US? GET OUT OF HERE!!
UGH!
KIK!
OHHH
!
DO YOU BELIEVE IN THE SON OF GOD?
LORD... I... I WANT TO BELIEVE IN HIM...
WHO IS HE?

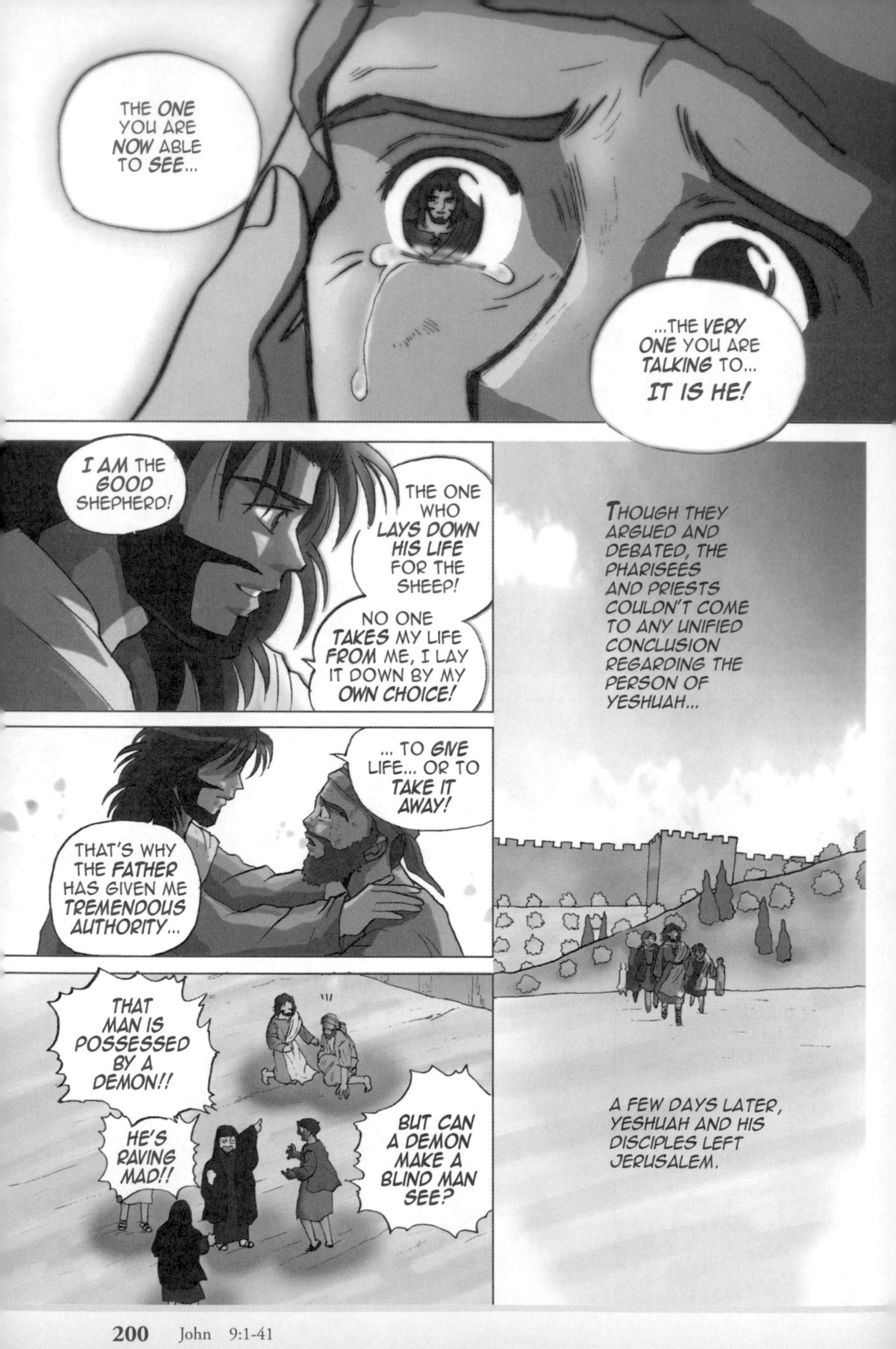
THE ONE YOU ARE NOW ABLE TO SEE...
...THE VERY ONE YOU ARE TALKING TO... IT IS HE!
I AM THE GOOD SHEPHERD!
THE ONE WHO LAYS DOWN HIS LIFE FOR THE SHEEP!
NO ONE TAKES MY LIFE FROM ME, I LAY IT DOWN BY MY OWN CHOICE!
THAT'S WHY THE FATHER HAS GIVEN ME TREMENDOUS AUTHORITY...
... TO GIVE LIFE... OR TO TAKE IT AWAY!
THAT MAN IS POSSESSED BY A DEMON!!
HE'S RAVING MAD!!
BUT CAN A DEMON MAKE A BLIND MAN SEE?
THOUGH THEY ARGUED AND DEBATED, THE PHARISEES AND PRIESTS COULDN'T COME TO ANY UNIFIED CONCLUSION REGARDING THE PERSON OF YESHUAH...
A FEW DAYS LATER, YESHUAH AND HIS DISCIPLES LEFT JERUSALEM.

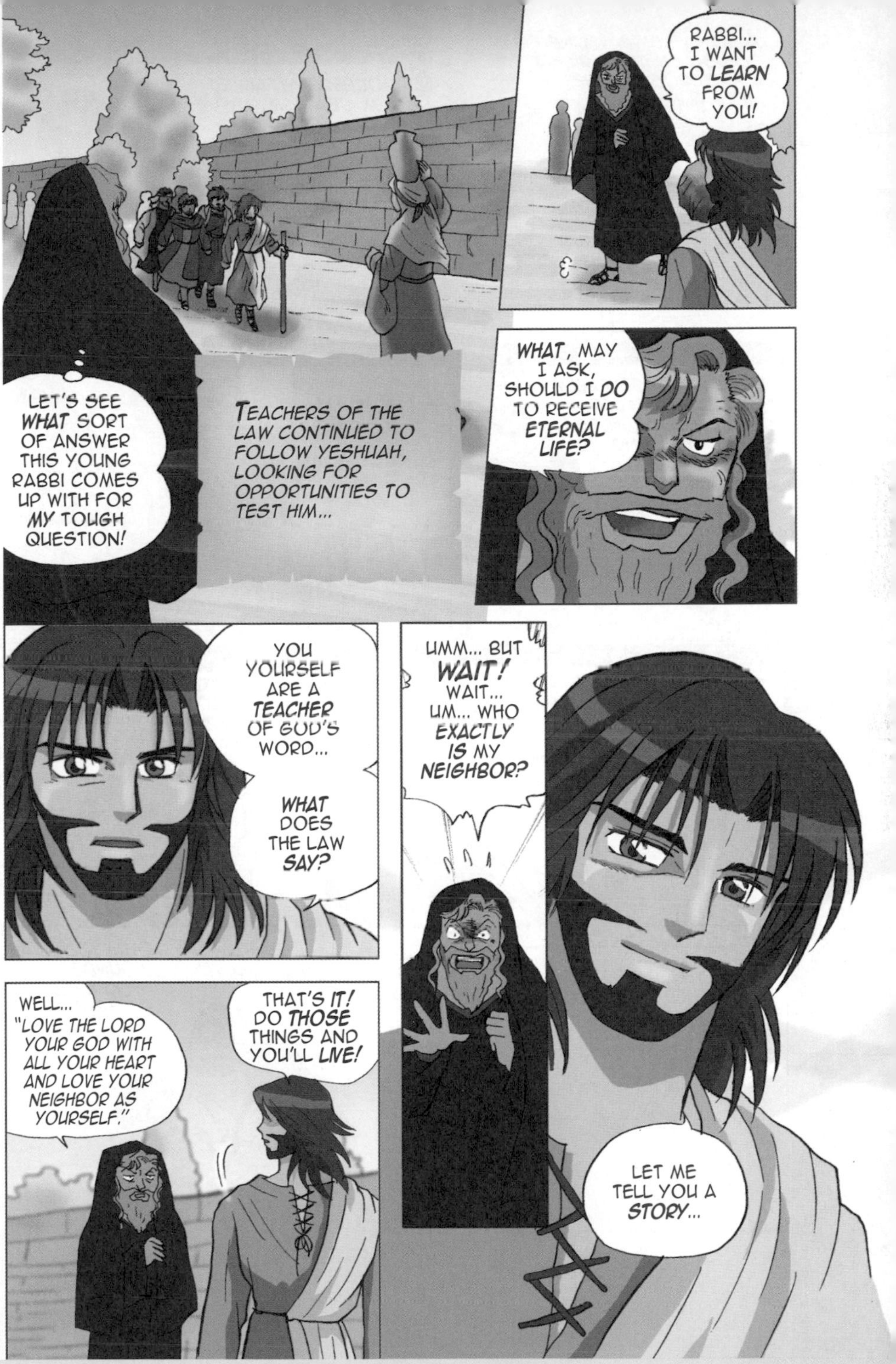
RABBI... I WANT TO LEARN FROM YOU!
LET'S SEE WHAT SORT OF ANSWER THIS YOUNG RABBI COMES UP WITH FOR MY TOUGH QUESTION!
TEACHERS OF THE LAW CONTINUED TO FOLLOW YESHUAH, LOOKING FOR OPPORTUNITIES TO TEST HIM...
WHAT, MAY I ASK, SHOULD I DO TO RECEIVE ETERNAL LIFE?
YOU YOURSELF ARE A TEACHER OF GOD'S WORD...
WHAT DOES THE LAW SAY?
WELL... "LOVE THE LORD YOUR GOD WITH ALL YOUR HEART AND LOVE YOUR NEIGHBOR AS YOURSELF."
THAT'S IT! DO THOSE THINGS AND YOU'LL LIVE!
UMM... BUT WAIT! WAIT... UM... WHO EXACTLY IS MY NEIGHBOR?
LET ME TELL YOU A STORY...

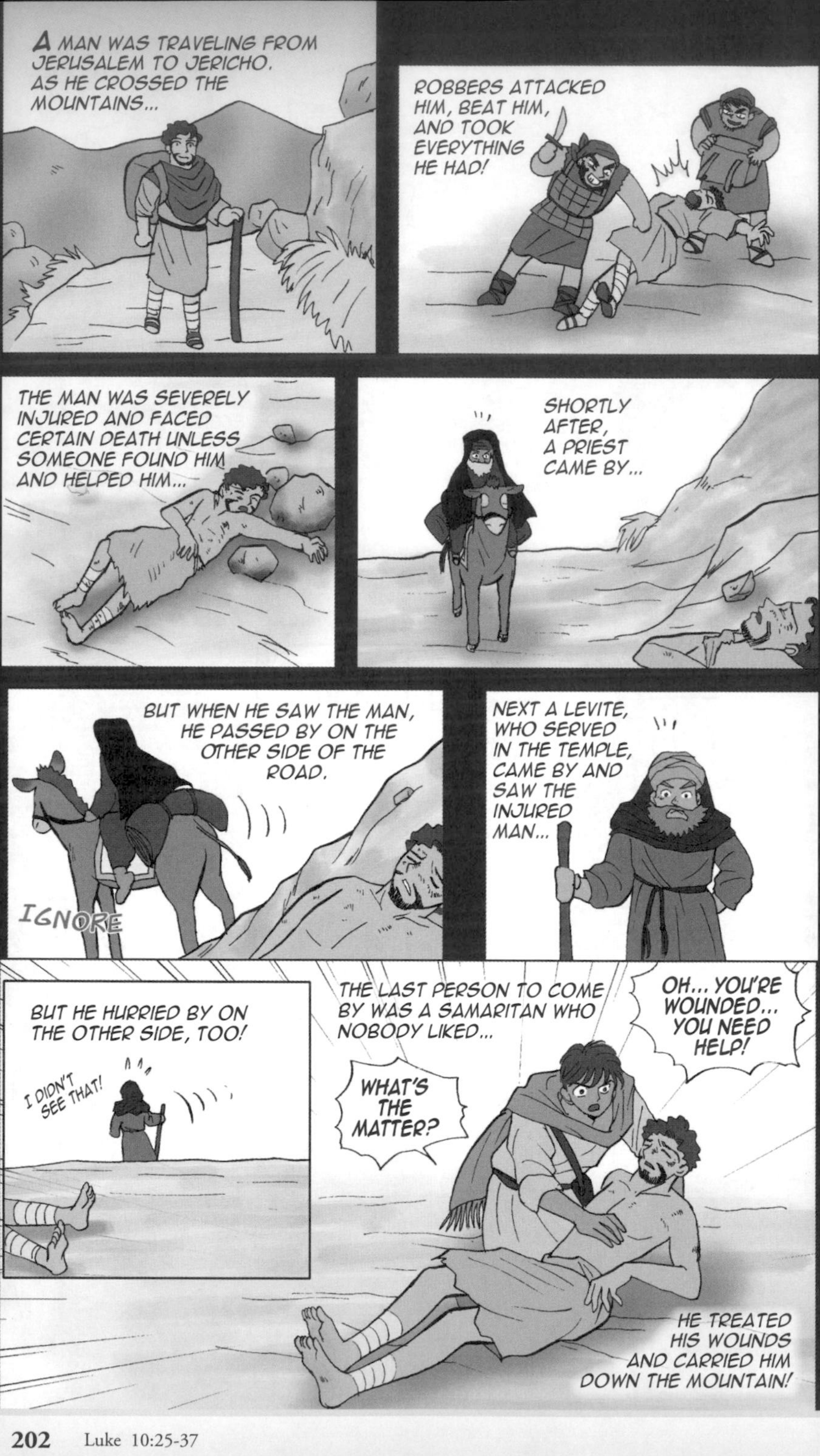
A MAN WAS TRAVELING FROM JERUSALEM TO JERICHO. AS HE CROSSED THE MOUNTAINS...
ROBBERS ATTACKED HIM, BEAT HIM, AND TOOK EVERYTHING HE HAD!
THE MAN WAS SEVERELY INJURED AND FACED CERTAIN DEATH UNLESS SOMEONE FOUND HIM AND HELPED HIM...
SHORTLY AFTER, A PRIEST CAME BY...
BUT WHEN HE SAW THE MAN, HE PASSED BY ON THE OTHER SIDE OF THE ROAD.
IGNORE
NEXT A LEVITE, WHO SERVED IN THE TEMPLE, CAME BY AND SAW THE INJURED MAN...
BUT HE HURRIED BY ON THE OTHER SIDE, TOO!
I DIDN'T SEE THAT!
THE LAST PERSON TO COME BY WAS A SAMARITAN WHO NOBODY LIKED...
OH... YOU'RE WOUNDED... YOU NEED HELP!
WHAT'S THE MATTER?
HE TREATED HIS WOUNDS AND CARRIED HIM DOWN THE MOUNTAIN!

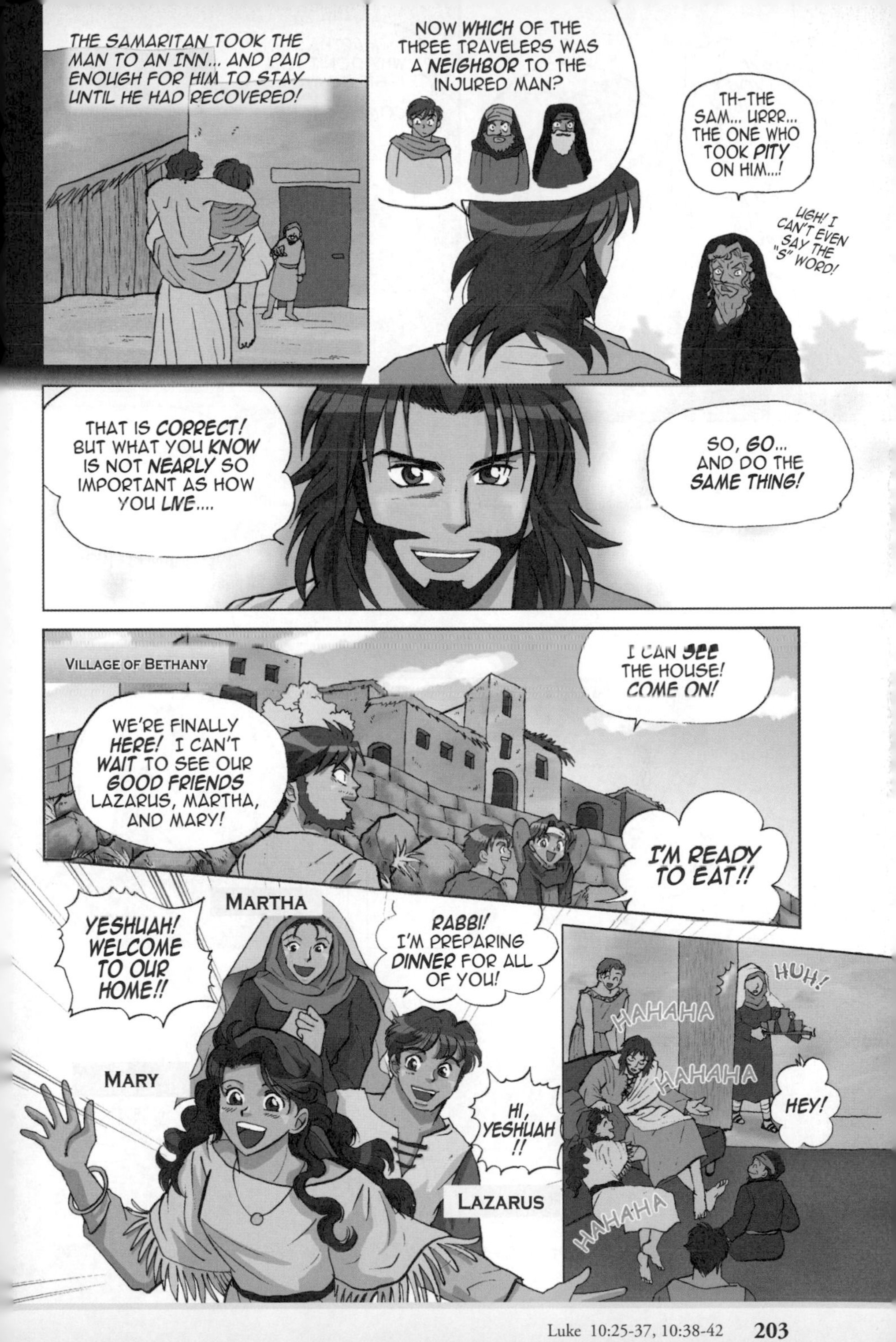
THE SAMARITAN TOOK THE MAN TO AN INN... AND PAID ENOUGH FOR HIM TO STAY UNTIL HE HAD RECOVERED!
NOW WHICH OF THE THREE TRAVELERS WAS A NEIGHBOR TO THE INJURED MAN?
TH-THE SAM... URRR... THE ONE WHO TOOK PITY ON HIM...!
UGH! I CAN'T EVEN SAY THE "S" WORD!
THAT IS CORRECT! BUT WHAT YOU KNOW IS NOT NEARLY SO IMPORTANT AS HOW YOU LIVE....
SO, GO... AND DO THE SAME THING!
VILLAGE OF BETHANY
I CAN SEE THE HOUSE! COME ON!
WE'RE FINALLY HERE! I CAN'T WAIT TO SEE OUR GOOD FRIENDS LAZARUS, MARTHA, AND MARY!
I'M READY TO EAT!!
YESHUAH! WELCOME TO OUR HOME!!
MARTHA
RABBI! I'M PREPARING DINNER FOR ALL OF YOU!
MARY
HI, YESHUAH!!
LAZARUS
HUH!
HAHAHA
HAHAHA
HEY!
HAHAHA

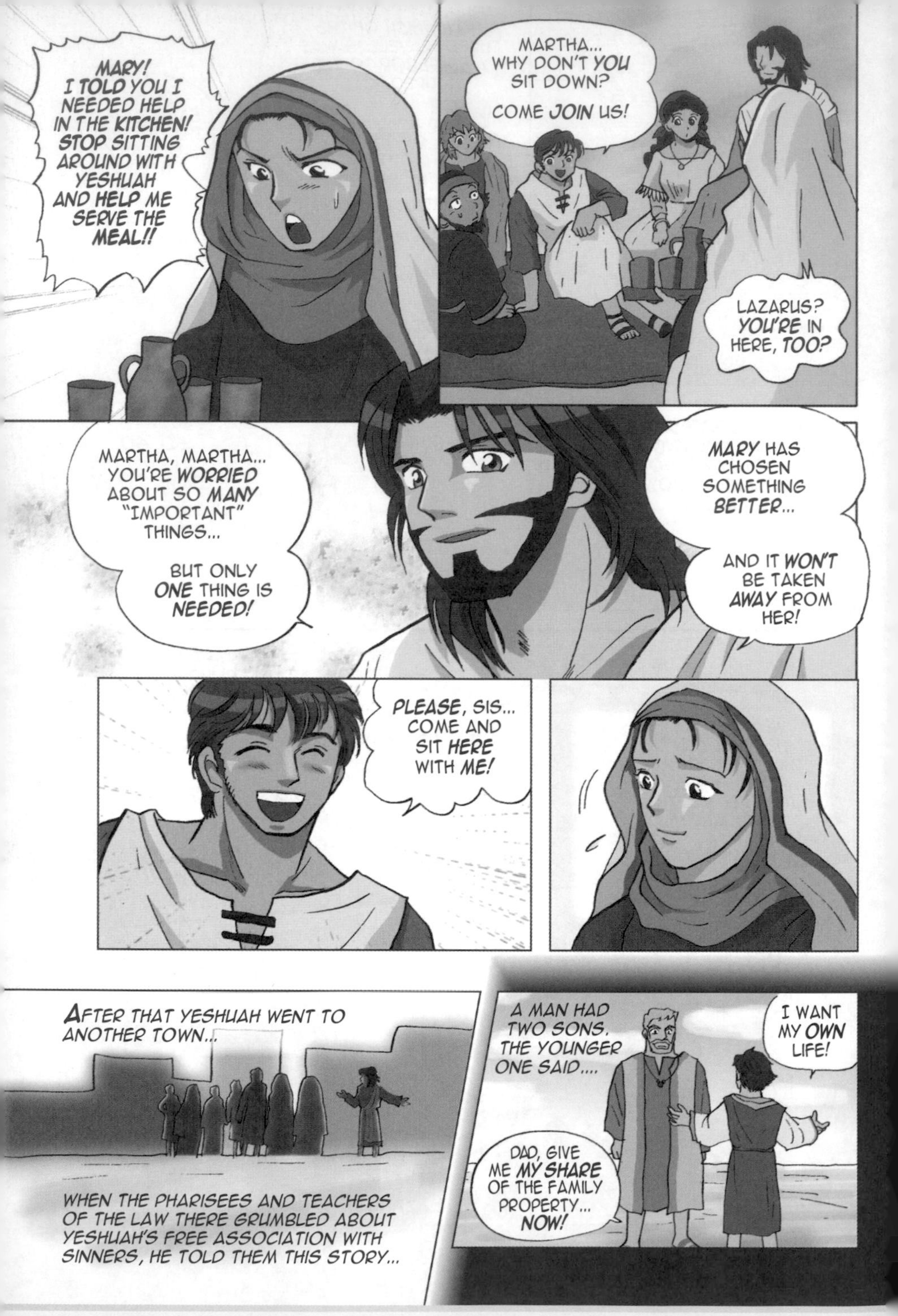
MARY! I TOLD YOU I NEEDED HELP IN THE KITCHEN! STOP SITTING AROUND WITH YESHUAH AND HELP ME SERVE THE MEAL!!
MARTHA... WHY DON'T YOU SIT DOWN?
COME JOIN US!
LAZARUS? YOU'RE IN HERE, TOO?
MARTHA, MARTHA... YOU'RE WORRIED ABOUT SO MANY "IMPORTANT" THINGS...
BUT ONLY ONE THING IS NEEDED!
MARY HAS CHOSEN SOMETHING BETTER...
AND IT WON'T BE TAKEN AWAY FROM HER!
PLEASE, SIS... COME AND SIT HERE WITH ME!
AFTER THAT YESHUAH WENT TO ANOTHER TOWN...
WHEN THE PHARISEES AND TEACHERS OF THE LAW THERE GRUMBLED ABOUT YESHUAH'S FREE ASSOCIATION WITH SINNERS, HE TOLD THEM THIS STORY...
A MAN HAD TWO SONS. THE YOUNGER ONE SAID....
I WANT MY OWN LIFE!
DAD, GIVE ME MY SHARE OF THE FAMILY PROPERTY... NOW!

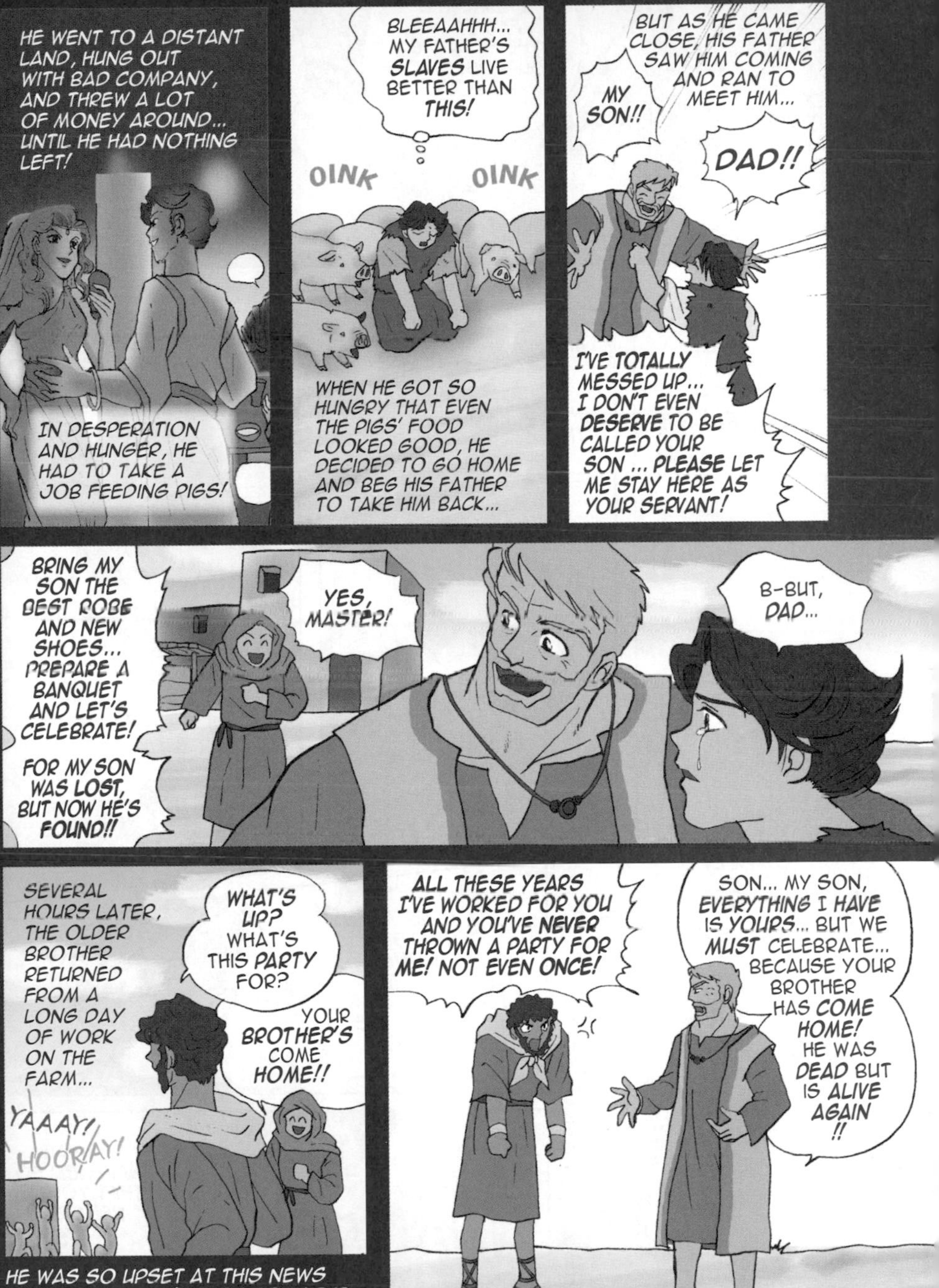
HE WENT TO A DISTANT LAND, HUNG OUT WITH BAD COMPANY, AND THREW A LOT OF MONEY AROUND... UNTIL HE HAD NOTHING LEFT!
IN DESPERATION AND HUNGER, HE HAD TO TAKE A JOB FEEDING PIGS!
BLEEAAHHH... MY FATHER'S SLAVES LIVE BETTER THAN THIS!
OINK
OINK
WHEN HE GOT SO HUNGRY THAT EVEN THE PIGS' FOOD LOOKED GOOD, HE DECIDED TO GO HOME AND BEG HIS FATHER TO TAKE HIM BACK...
BUT AS HE CAME CLOSE, HIS FATHER SAW HIM COMING AND RAN TO MEET HIM...
MY SON!!
DAD!!
I'VE TOTALLY MESSED UP... I DON'T EVEN DESERVE TO BE CALLED YOUR SON ... PLEASE LET ME STAY HERE AS YOUR SERVANT!
BRING MY SON THE BEST ROBE AND NEW SHOES... PREPARE A BANQUET AND LET'S CELEBRATE!
FOR MY SON WAS LOST, BUT NOW HE'S FOUND!!
YES, MASTER!
B-BUT, DAD...
SEVERAL HOURS LATER, THE OLDER BROTHER RETURNED FROM A LONG DAY OF WORK ON THE FARM...
WHAT'S UP? WHAT'S THIS PARTY FOR?
YOUR BROTHER'S COME HOME!!
YAAAY!
HOORAY!
HE WAS SO UPSET AT THIS NEWS THAT HE WOULDN'T EVEN GO IN THE HOUSE ... SO HIS FATHER CAME OUT.
ALL THESE YEARS I'VE WORKED FOR YOU AND YOU'VE NEVER THROWN A PARTY FOR ME! NOT EVEN ONCE!
SON... MY SON, EVERYTHING I HAVE IS YOURS... BUT WE MUST CELEBRATE... BECAUSE YOUR BROTHER HAS COME HOME! HE WAS DEAD BUT IS ALIVE AGAIN !!

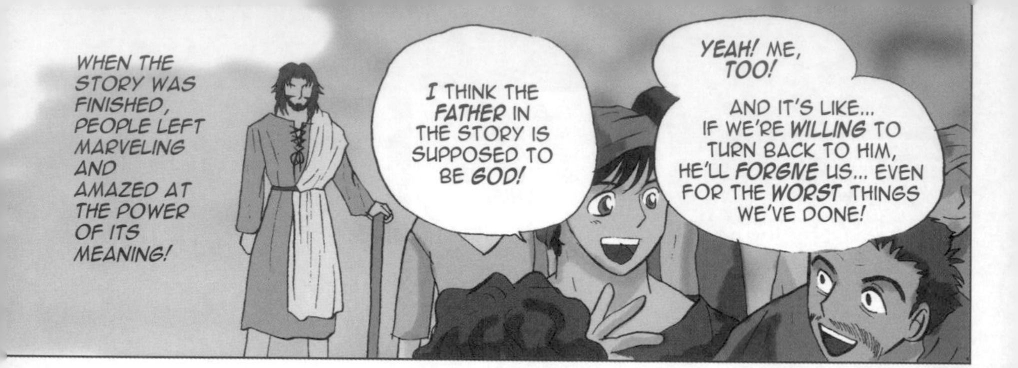
WHEN THE STORY WAS FINISHED, PEOPLE LEFT MARVELING AND AMAZED AT THE POWER OF ITS MEANING!
I THINK THE FATHER IN THE STORY IS SUPPOSED TO BE GOD!
YEAH! ME, TOO!
AND IT'S LIKE... IF WE'RE WILLING TO TURN BACK TO HIM, HE'LL FORGIVE US... EVEN FOR THE WORST THINGS WE'VE DONE!

15. LAZARUS DIES

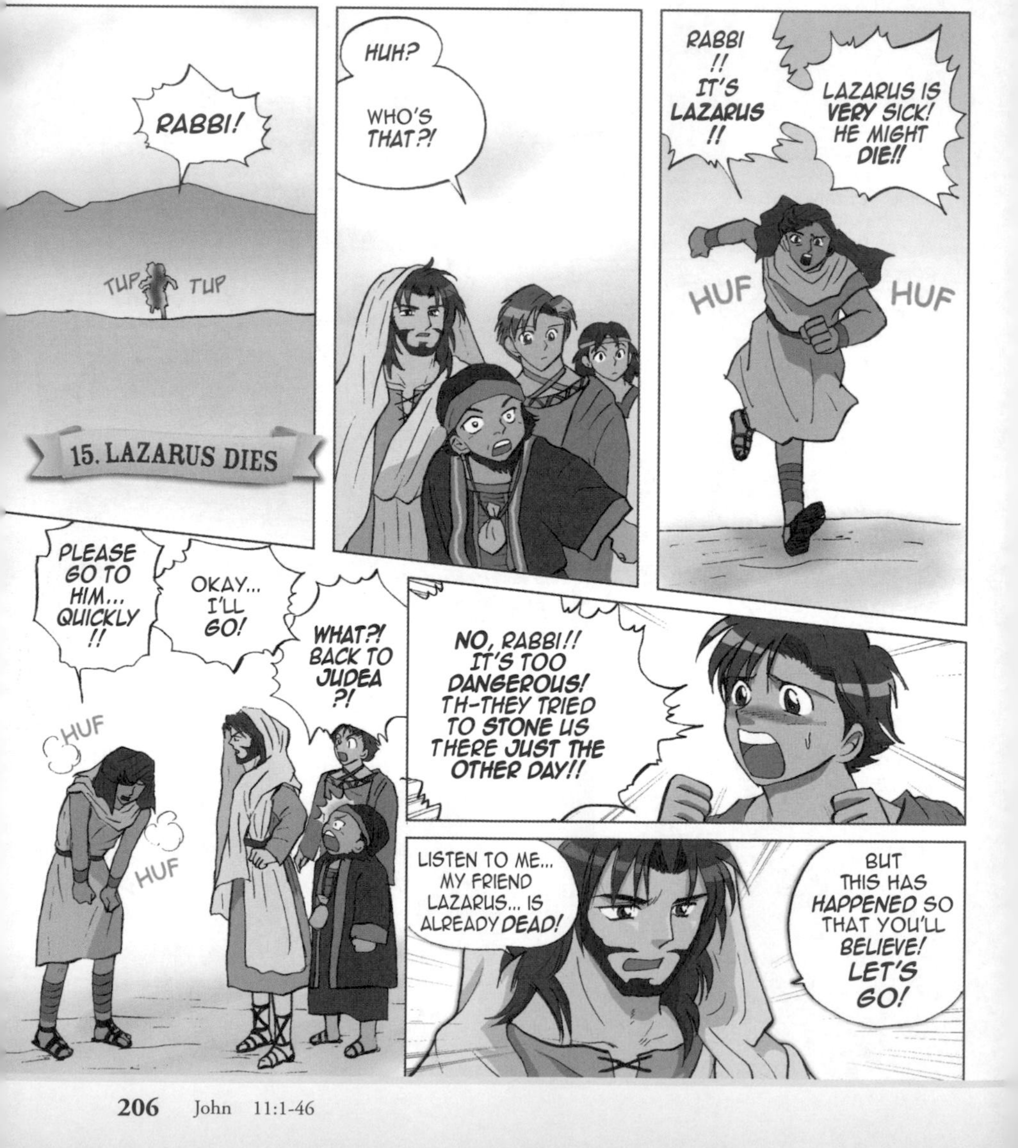
RABBI!
TUP TUP
HUH?
WHO'S THAT?!
RABBI !! IT'S LAZARUS !!
LAZARUS IS VERY SICK! HE MIGHT DIE!!
HUF HUF
PLEASE GO TO HIM... QUICKLY !!
OKAY... I'LL GO!
WHAT?! BACK TO JUDEA ?!
HUF
HUF
NO, RABBI!! IT'S TOO DANGEROUS! TH-THEY TRIED TO STONE US THERE JUST THE OTHER DAY!!
LISTEN TO ME... MY FRIEND LAZARUS... IS ALREADY DEAD!
BUT THIS HAS HAPPENED SO THAT YOU'LL BELIEVE! LET'S GO!

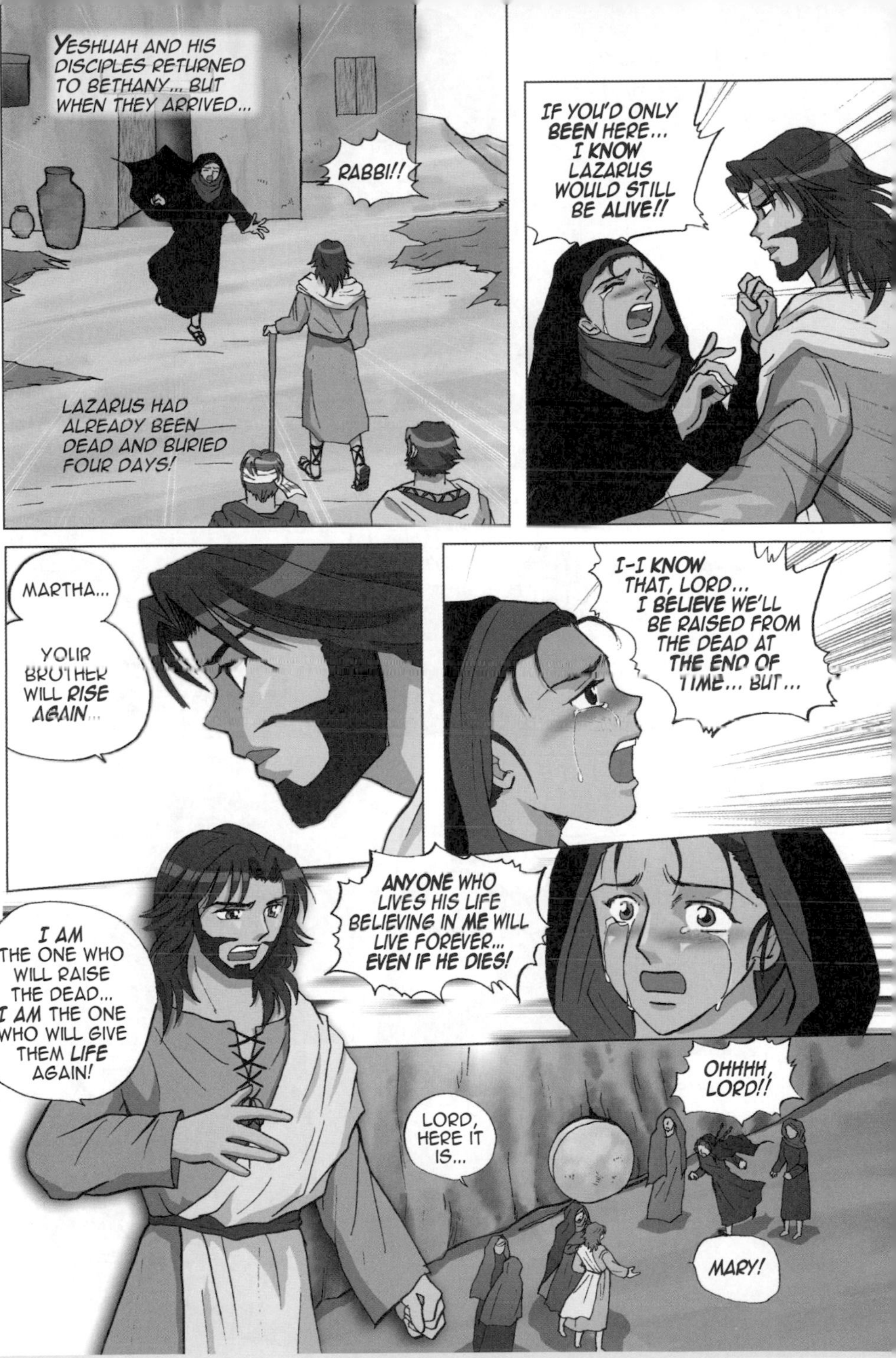
YESHUAH AND HIS DISCIPLES RETURNED TO BETHANY... BUT WHEN THEY ARRIVED...
RABBI!!
LAZARUS HAD ALREADY BEEN DEAD AND BURIED FOUR DAYS!
IF YOU'D ONLY BEEN HERE... I KNOW LAZARUS WOULD STILL BE ALIVE!!
MARTHA...
YOUR BROTHER WILL RISE AGAIN...
I-I KNOW THAT, LORD... I BELIEVE WE'LL BE RAISED FROM THE DEAD AT THE END OF TIME... BUT...
I AM THE ONE WHO WILL RAISE THE DEAD... I AM THE ONE WHO WILL GIVE THEM LIFE AGAIN!
ANYONE WHO LIVES HIS LIFE BELIEVING IN ME WILL LIVE FOREVER... EVEN IF HE DIES!
OHHHH, LORD!!
LORD, HERE IT IS...
MARY!

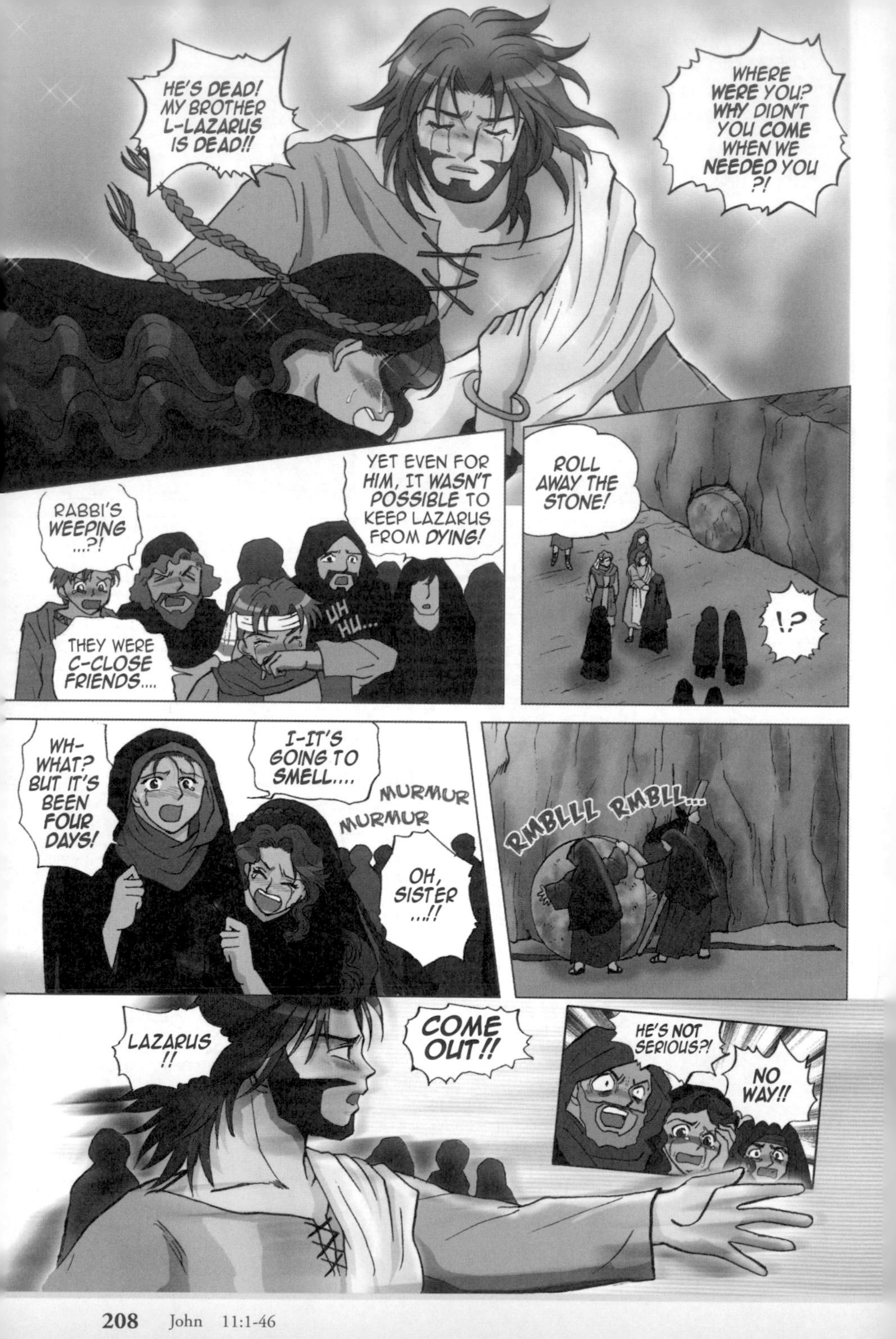
HE'S DEAD! MY BROTHER L-LAZARUS IS DEAD!!
WHERE WERE YOU? WHY DIDN'T YOU COME WHEN WE NEEDED YOU ?!
YET EVEN FOR HIM, IT WASN'T POSSIBLE TO KEEP LAZARUS FROM DYING!
RABBI'S WEEPING ...?!
UH HU...
THEY WERE C-CLOSE FRIENDS....
ROLL AWAY THE STONE!
!?
WH- WHAT? BUT IT'S BEEN FOUR DAYS!
I-IT'S GOING TO SMELL....
MURMUR
MURMUR
OH, SISTER ...!!
RMBLLL RMBLL...
LAZARUS !!
COME OUT!!
HE'S NOT SERIOUS?!
NO WAY!!

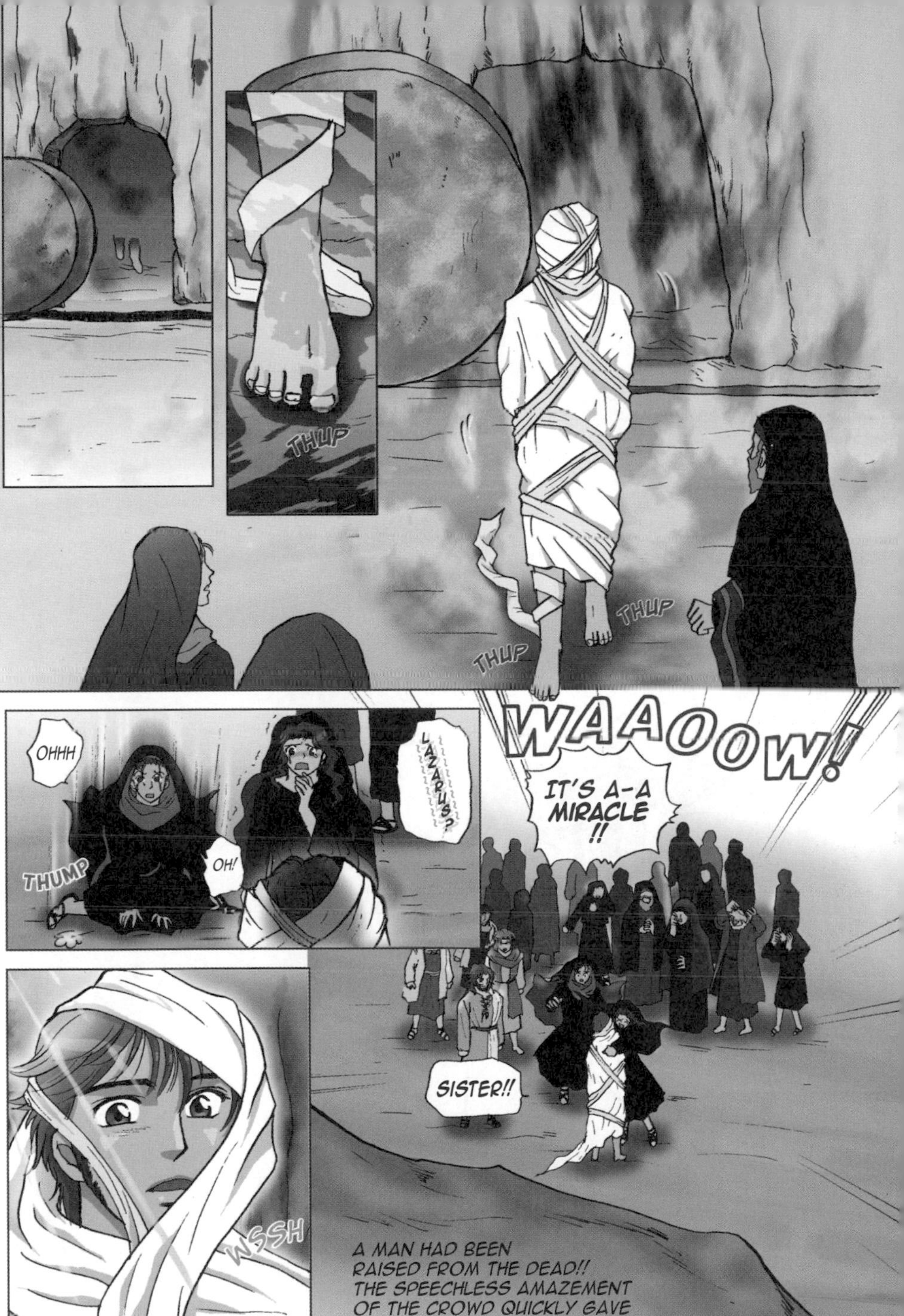
THUP
THUP
THUP
OHHH
THUMP
LAZARUS?
OH!
WAAOOOW!
IT'S A-A MIRACLE !!
SISTER!!
WSSH
A MAN HAD BEEN RAISED FROM THE DEAD!! THE SPEECHLESS AMAZEMENT OF THE CROWD QUICKLY GAVE WAY TO CRIES OF "HE'S MESSIAH!" AND "THE SON OF GOD!"

Chapter III

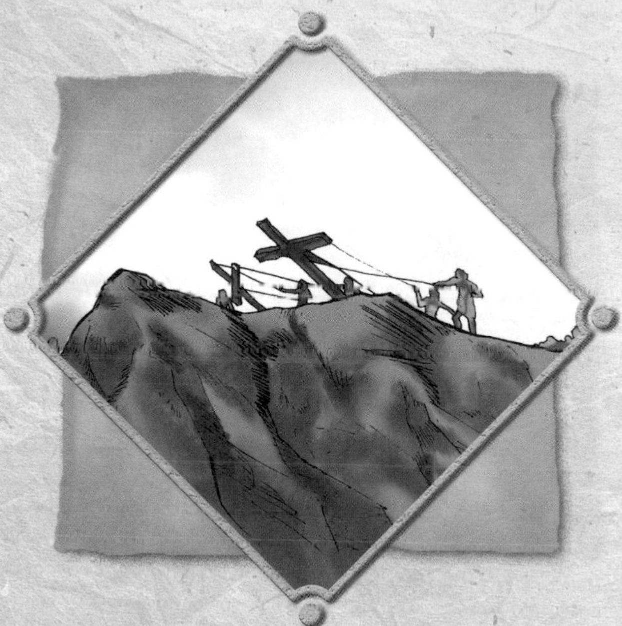

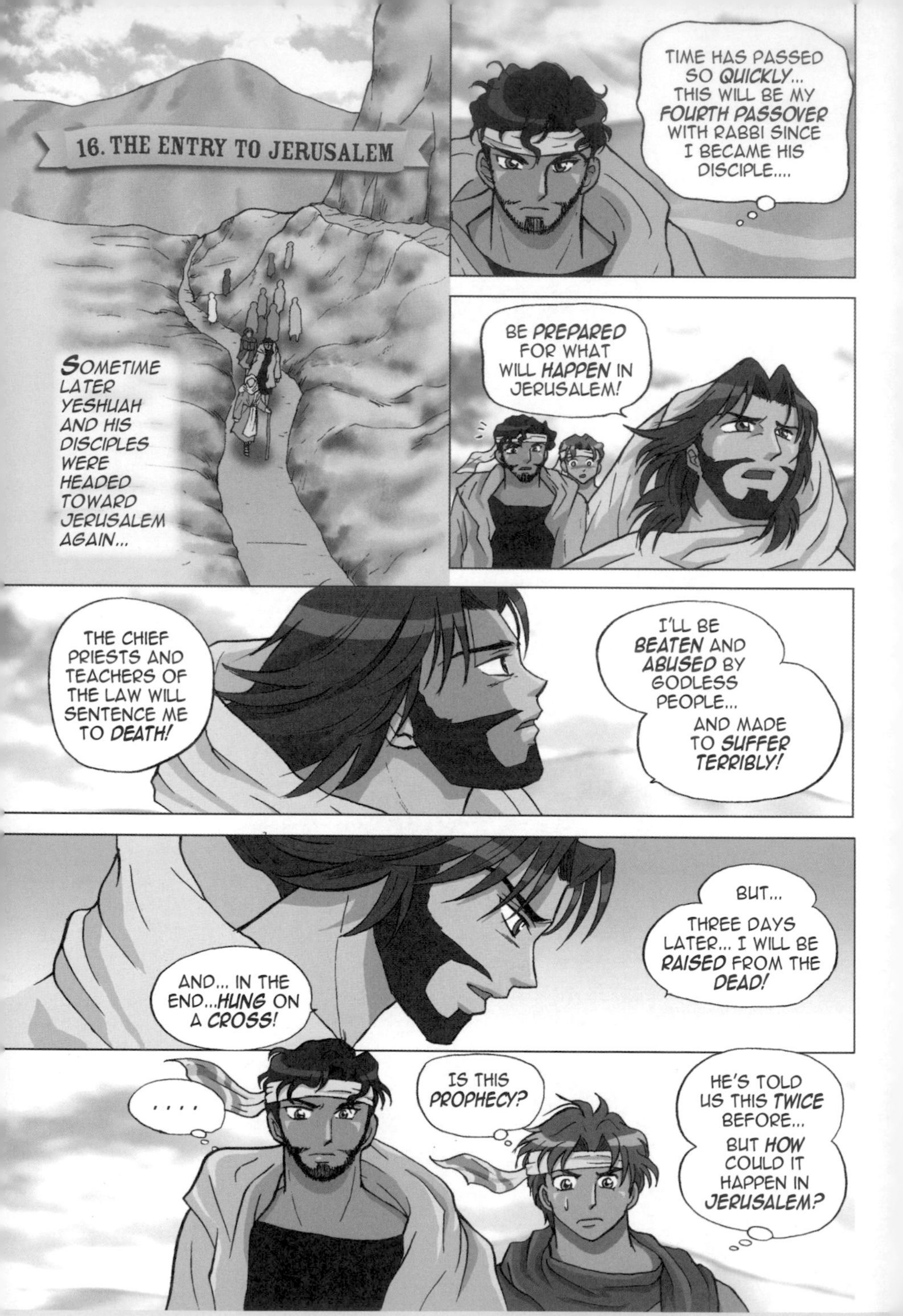
16. THE ENTRY TO JERUSALEM
SOMETIME LATER YESHUAH AND HIS DISCIPLES WERE HEADED TOWARD JERUSALEM AGAIN...
TIME HAS PASSED SO QUICKLY... THIS WILL BE MY FOURTH PASSOVER WITH RABBI SINCE I BECAME HIS DISCIPLE....
BE PREPARED FOR WHAT WILL HAPPEN IN JERUSALEM!
THE CHIEF PRIESTS AND TEACHERS OF THE LAW WILL SENTENCE ME TO DEATH!
I'LL BE BEATEN AND ABUSED BY GODLESS PEOPLE...
AND MADE TO SUFFER TERRIBLY!
AND... IN THE END...HUNG ON A CROSS!
BUT...
THREE DAYS LATER... I WILL BE RAISED FROM THE DEAD!
....
IS THIS PROPHECY?
HE'S TOLD US THIS TWICE BEFORE...
BUT HOW COULD IT HAPPEN IN JERUSALEM?

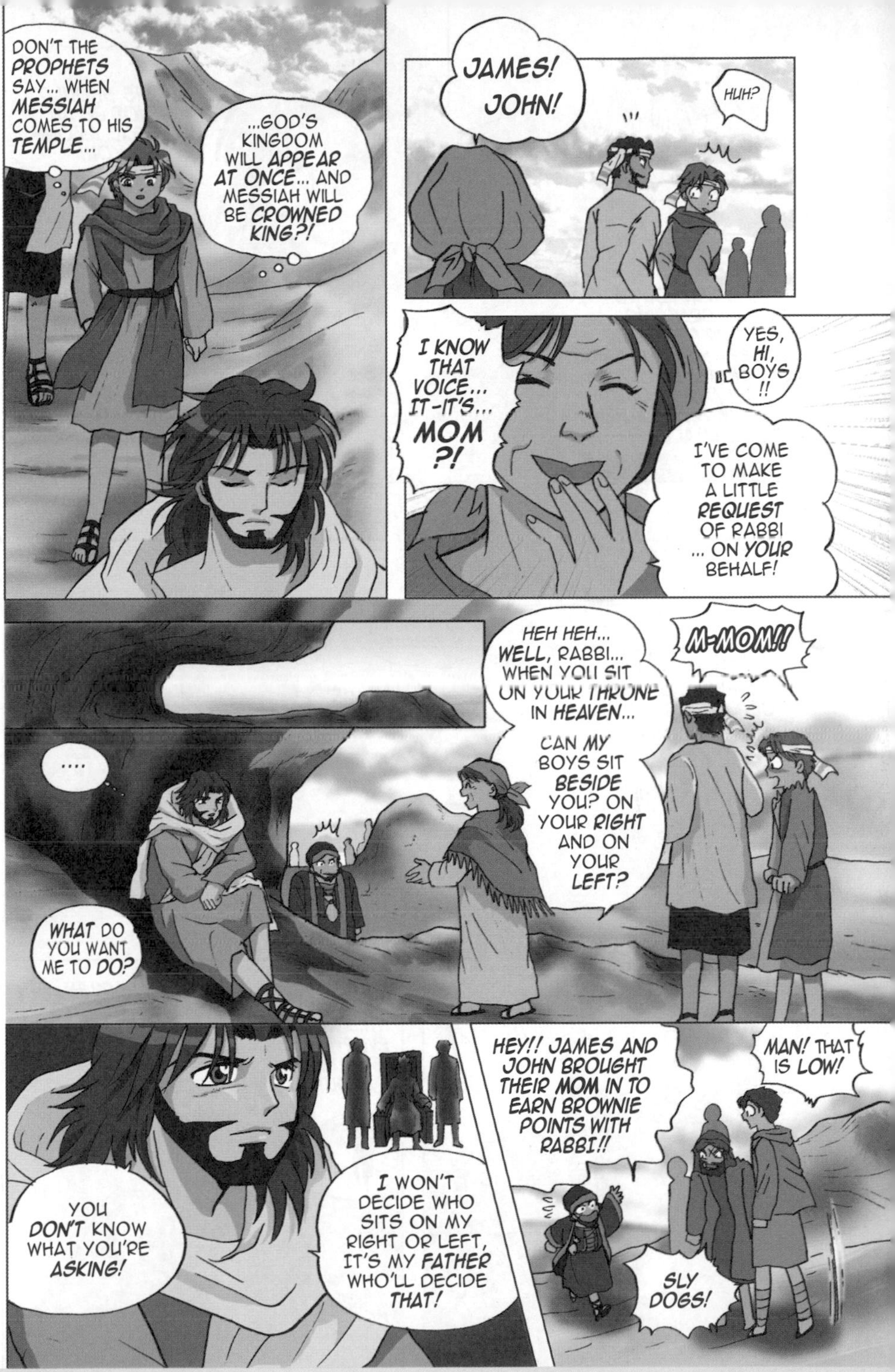

DON'T THE PROPHETS SAY... WHEN MESSIAH COMES TO HIS TEMPLE...
...GOD'S KINGDOM WILL APPEAR AT ONCE... AND MESSIAH WILL BE CROWNED KING?!
JAMES! JOHN!
HUH?
I KNOW THAT VOICE... IT-IT'S... MOM?!
YES, HI, BOYS!!
I'VE COME TO MAKE A LITTLE REQUEST OF RABBI ... ON YOUR BEHALF!
HEH HEH... WELL, RABBI... WHEN YOU SIT ON YOUR THRONE IN HEAVEN...
M-MOM!!
CAN MY BOYS SIT BESIDE YOU? ON YOUR RIGHT AND ON YOUR LEFT?
....
WHAT DO YOU WANT ME TO DO?
YOU DON'T KNOW WHAT YOU'RE ASKING!
I WON'T DECIDE WHO SITS ON MY RIGHT OR LEFT, IT'S MY FATHER WHO'LL DECIDE THAT!
HEY!! JAMES AND JOHN BROUGHT THEIR MOM IN TO EARN BROWNIE POINTS WITH RABBI!!
MAN! THAT IS LOW!
SLY DOGS!

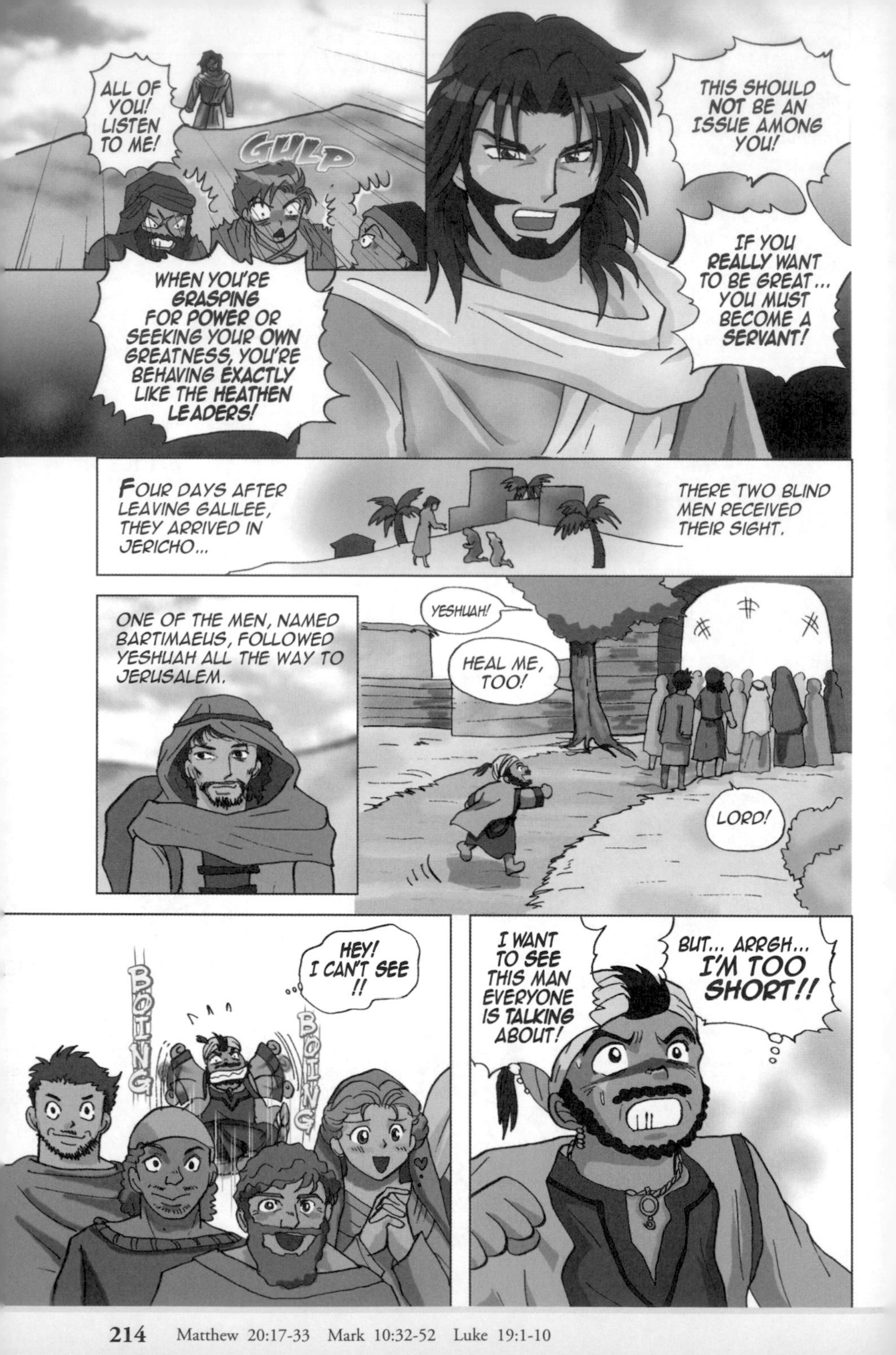
ALL OF YOU! LISTEN TO ME!
GULP
THIS SHOULD NOT BE AN ISSUE AMONG YOU!
WHEN YOU'RE GRASPING FOR POWER OR SEEKING YOUR OWN GREATNESS, YOU'RE BEHAVING EXACTLY LIKE THE HEATHEN LEADERS!
IF YOU REALLY WANT TO BE GREAT... YOU MUST BECOME A SERVANT!
FOUR DAYS AFTER LEAVING GALILEE, THEY ARRIVED IN JERICHO...
THERE TWO BLIND MEN RECEIVED THEIR SIGHT.
ONE OF THE MEN, NAMED BARTIMAEUS, FOLLOWED YESHUAH ALL THE WAY TO JERUSALEM.
YESHUAH!
HEAL ME, TOO!
LORD!
BOING
BOING
HEY! I CAN'T SEE !!
I WANT TO SEE THIS MAN EVERYONE IS TALKING ABOUT!
BUT... ARRGH... I'M TOO SHORT!!

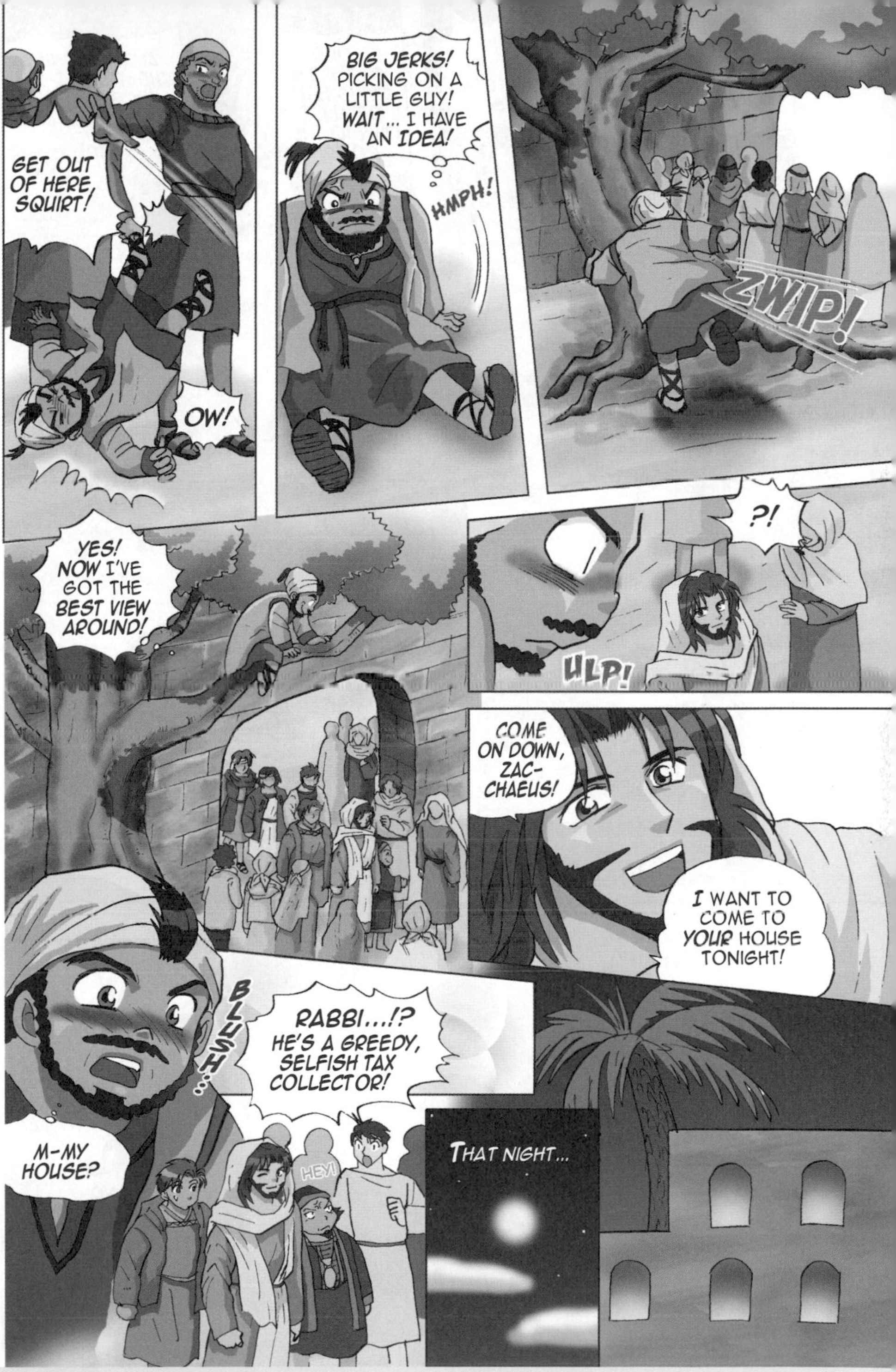
GET OUT OF HERE, SQUIRT!
OW!
BIG JERKS! PICKING ON A LITTLE GUY! WAIT... I HAVE AN IDEA!
HMPH!
ZWIP!
YES! NOW I'VE GOT THE BEST VIEW AROUND!
?!
ULP!
COME ON DOWN, ZAC-CHAEUS!
I WANT TO COME TO YOUR HOUSE TONIGHT!
BLUSH...
M-MY HOUSE?
RABBI...!? HE'S A GREEDY, SELFISH TAX COLLECTOR!
HEY!
THAT NIGHT...

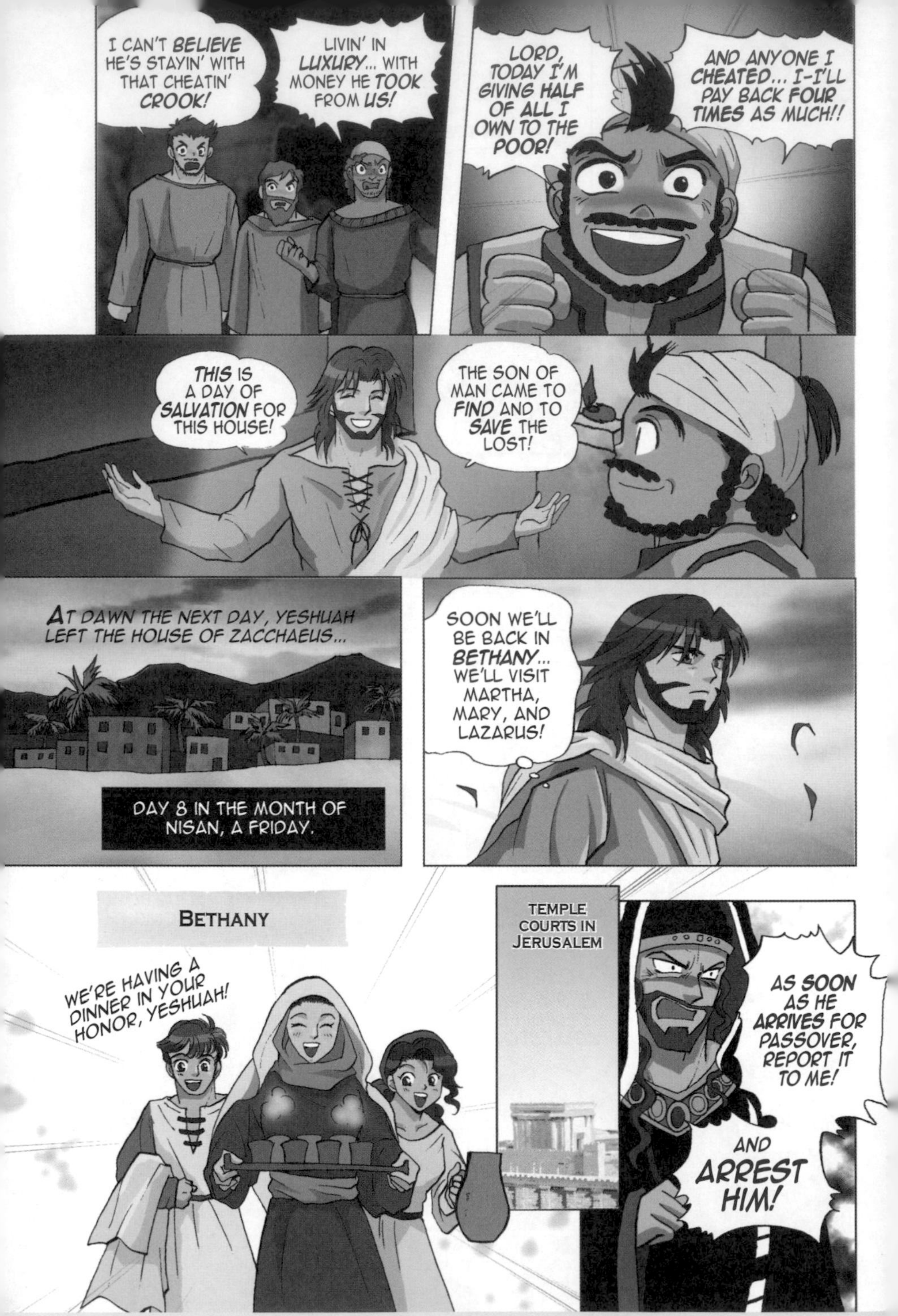

I CAN'T BELIEVE HE'S STAYIN' WITH THAT CHEATIN' CROOK!
LIVIN' IN LUXURY... WITH MONEY HE TOOK FROM US!
LORD, TODAY I'M GIVING HALF OF ALL I OWN TO THE POOR!
AND ANYONE I CHEATED... I-I'LL PAY BACK FOUR TIMES AS MUCH!!
THIS IS A DAY OF SALVATION FOR THIS HOUSE!
THE SON OF MAN CAME TO FIND AND TO SAVE THE LOST!
AT DAWN THE NEXT DAY, YESHUAH LEFT THE HOUSE OF ZACCHAEUS...
DAY 8 IN THE MONTH OF NISAN, A FRIDAY.
SOON WE'LL BE BACK IN BETHANY... WE'LL VISIT MARTHA, MARY, AND LAZARUS!
BETHANY
WE'RE HAVING A DINNER IN YOUR HONOR, YESHUAH!
TEMPLE COURTS IN JERUSALEM
AS SOON AS HE ARRIVES FOR PASSOVER, REPORT IT TO ME!
AND ARREST HIM!

 Matthew 26:3-4 Mark 14:1-2 Luke 19:1-10 John 12:1-2

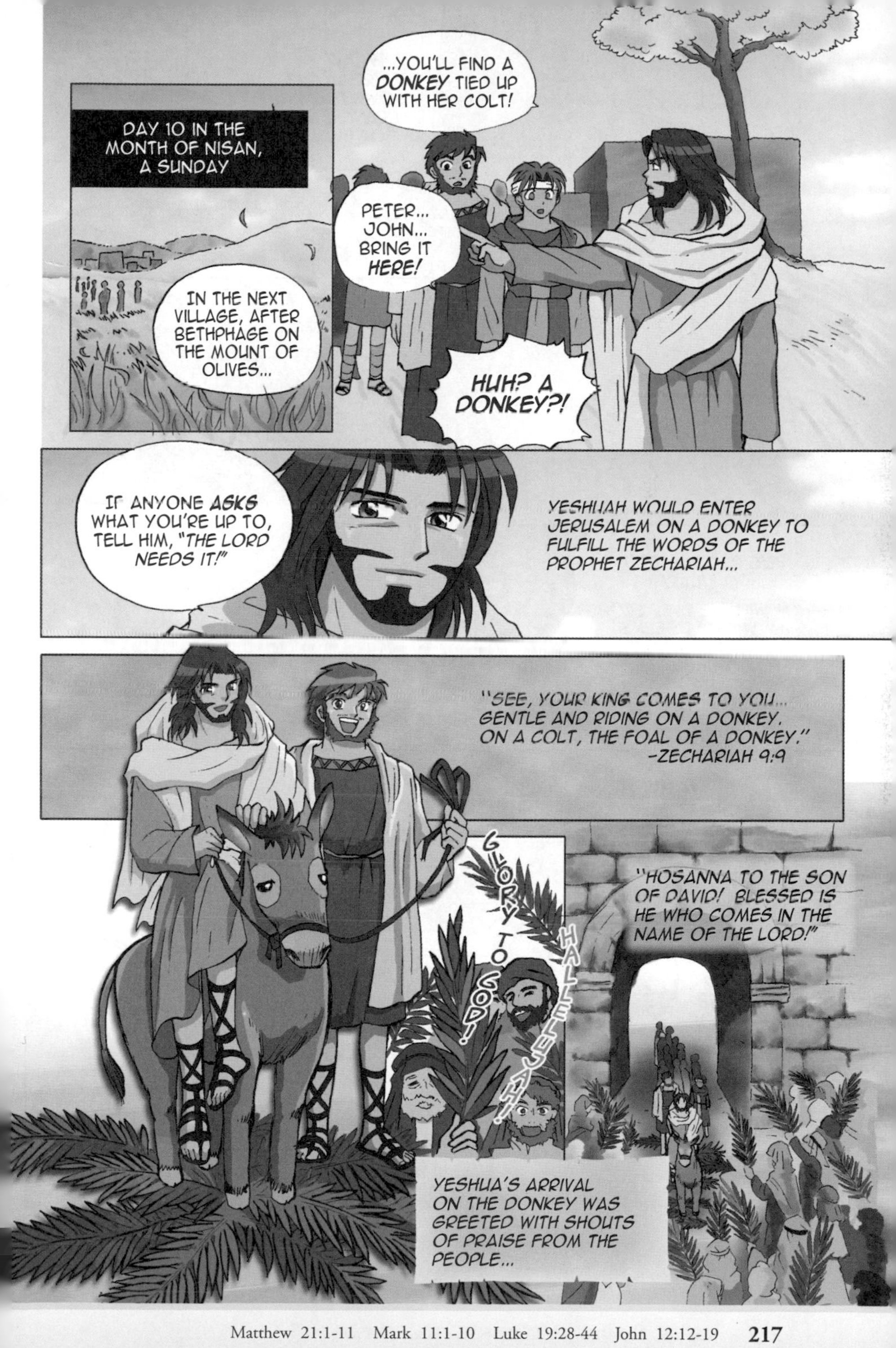
DAY 10 IN THE MONTH OF NISAN, A SUNDAY
IN THE NEXT VILLAGE, AFTER BETHPHAGE ON THE MOUNT OF OLIVES...
PETER... JOHN... BRING IT HERE!
...YOU'LL FIND A DONKEY TIED UP WITH HER COLT!
HUH? A DONKEY?!
IF ANYONE ASKS WHAT YOU'RE UP TO, TELL HIM, "THE LORD NEEDS IT!"
YESHUAH WOULD ENTER JERUSALEM ON A DONKEY TO FULFILL THE WORDS OF THE PROPHET ZECHARIAH...
"SEE, YOUR KING COMES TO YOU... GENTLE AND RIDING ON A DONKEY. ON A COLT, THE FOAL OF A DONKEY." -ZECHARIAH 9:9
GLORY TO GOD!
HALLELUJAH!
"HOSANNA TO THE SON OF DAVID! BLESSED IS HE WHO COMES IN THE NAME OF THE LORD!"
YESHUA'S ARRIVAL ON THE DONKEY WAS GREETED WITH SHOUTS OF PRAISE FROM THE PEOPLE...

Matthew 21:1-11 Mark 11:1-10 Luke 19:28-44 John 12:12-19

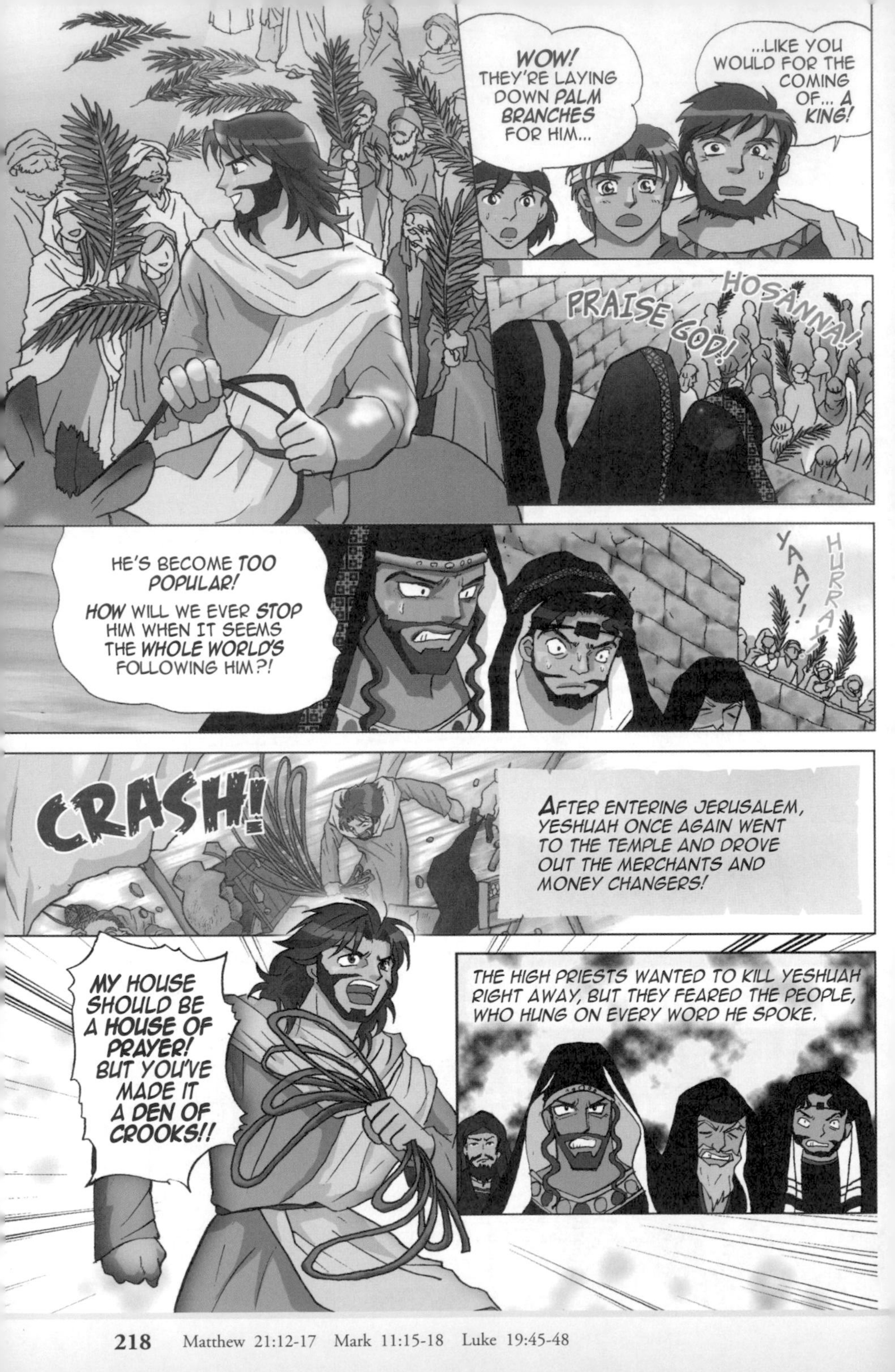
WOW! THEY'RE LAYING DOWN PALM BRANCHES FOR HIM...
...LIKE YOU WOULD FOR THE COMING OF... A KING!
PRAISE GOD!
HOSANNA!
HE'S BECOME TOO POPULAR! HOW WILL WE EVER STOP HIM WHEN IT SEEMS THE WHOLE WORLD'S FOLLOWING HIM?!
YAAY!
HURRAY!
CRASH!
AFTER ENTERING JERUSALEM, YESHUAH ONCE AGAIN WENT TO THE TEMPLE AND DROVE OUT THE MERCHANTS AND MONEY CHANGERS!
MY HOUSE SHOULD BE A HOUSE OF PRAYER! BUT YOU'VE MADE IT A DEN OF CROOKS!!
THE HIGH PRIESTS WANTED TO KILL YESHUAH RIGHT AWAY, BUT THEY FEARED THE PEOPLE, WHO HUNG ON EVERY WORD HE SPOKE.

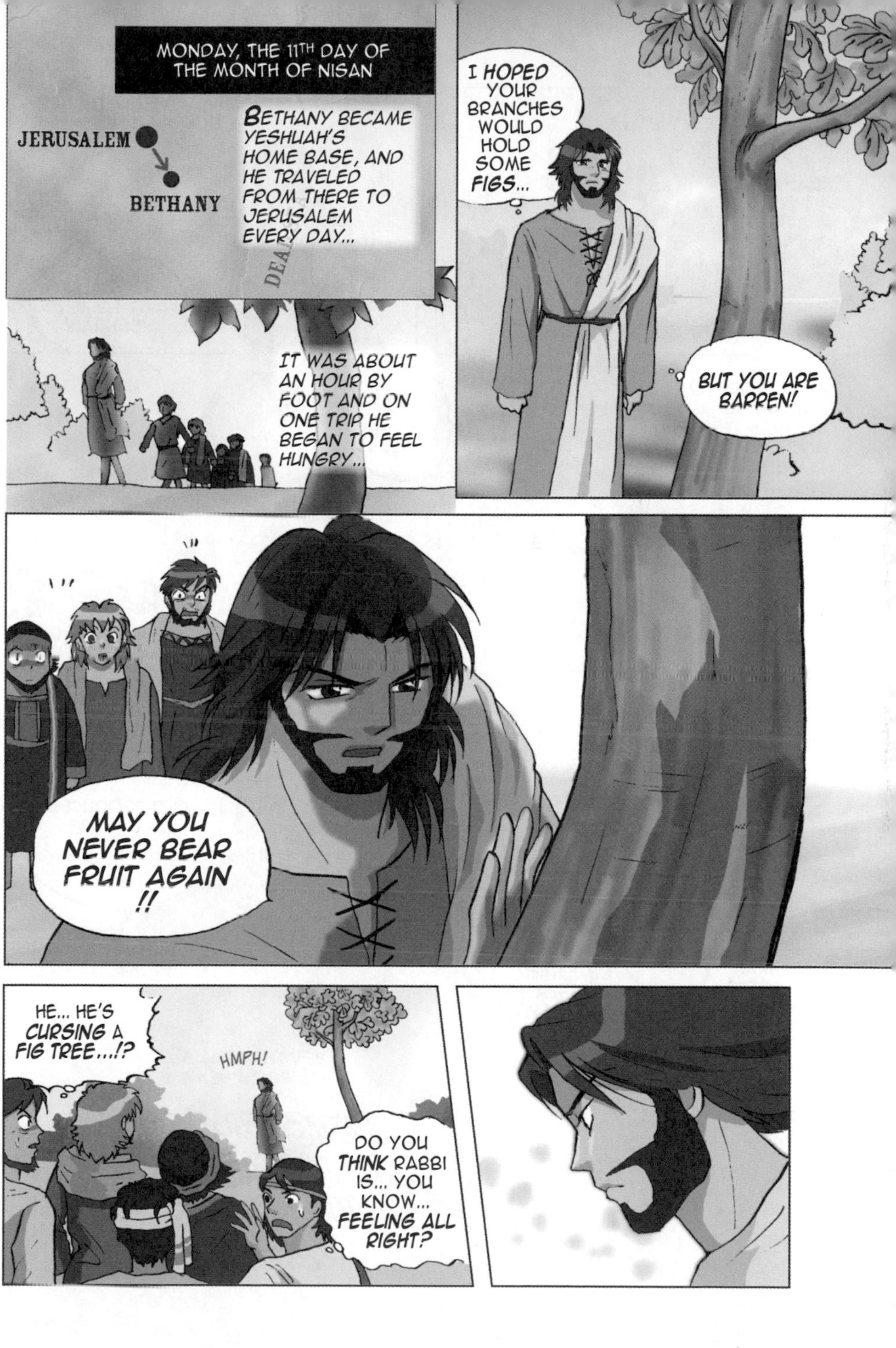
MONDAY, THE 11TH DAY OF THE MONTH OF NISAN
JERUSALEM
BETHANY
BETHANY BECAME YESHUAH'S HOME BASE, AND HE TRAVELED FROM THERE TO JERUSALEM EVERY DAY...
IT WAS ABOUT AN HOUR BY FOOT AND ON ONE TRIP HE BEGAN TO FEEL HUNGRY...
I HOPED YOUR BRANCHES WOULD HOLD SOME FIGS...
BUT YOU ARE BARREN!
MAY YOU NEVER BEAR FRUIT AGAIN !!
HE... HE'S CURSING A FIG TREE...!?
HMPH!
DO YOU THINK RABBI IS... YOU KNOW... FEELING ALL RIGHT?

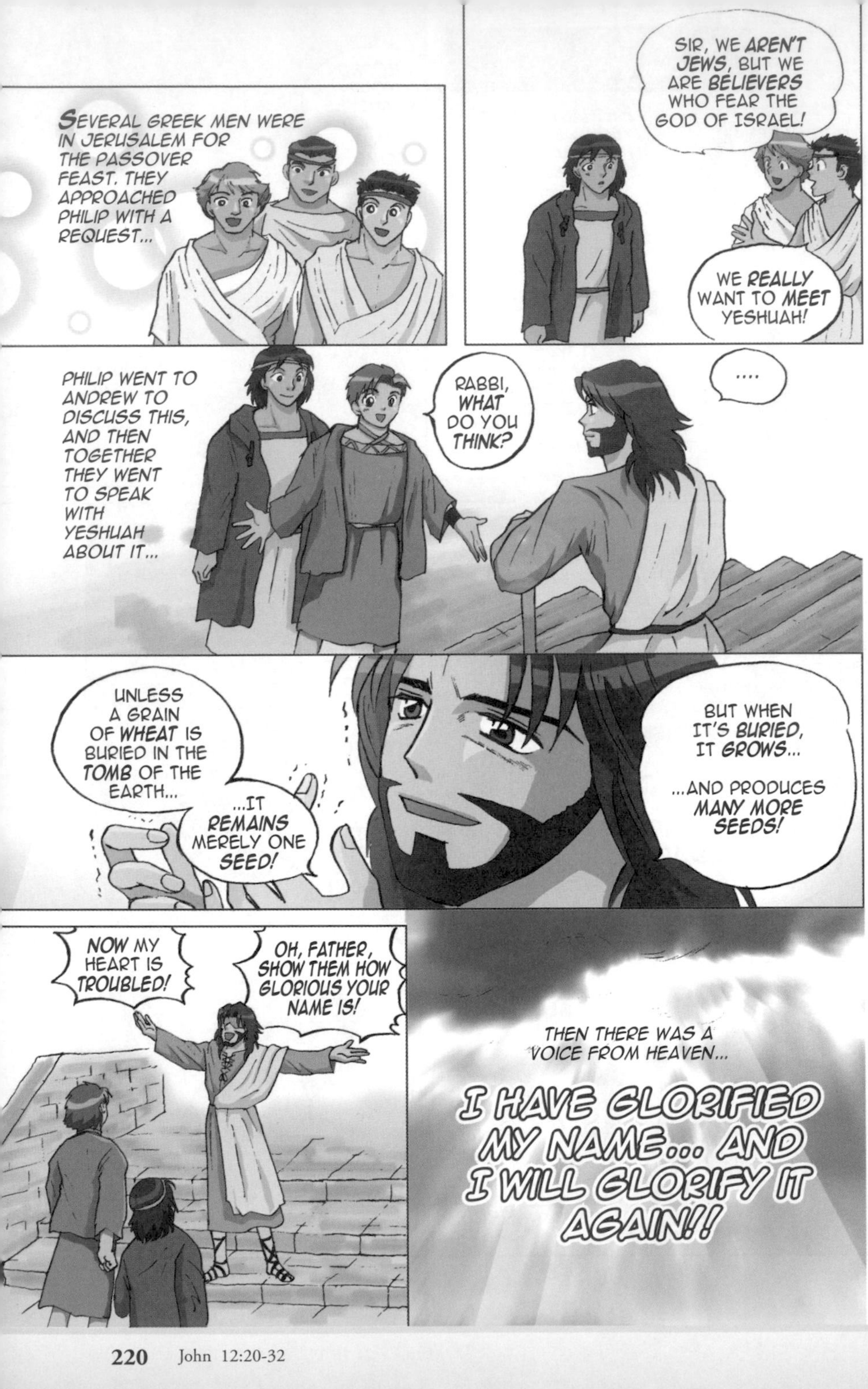
SEVERAL GREEK MEN WERE IN JERUSALEM FOR THE PASSOVER FEAST. THEY APPROACHED PHILIP WITH A REQUEST...
SIR, WE AREN'T JEWS, BUT WE ARE BELIEVERS WHO FEAR THE GOD OF ISRAEL!
WE REALLY WANT TO MEET YESHUAH!
PHILIP WENT TO ANDREW TO DISCUSS THIS, AND THEN TOGETHER THEY WENT TO SPEAK WITH YESHUAH ABOUT IT...
RABBI, WHAT DO YOU THINK?
....
UNLESS A GRAIN OF WHEAT IS BURIED IN THE TOMB OF THE EARTH...
...IT REMAINS MERELY ONE SEED!
BUT WHEN IT'S BURIED, IT GROWS...
...AND PRODUCES MANY MORE SEEDS!
NOW MY HEART IS TROUBLED!
OH, FATHER, SHOW THEM HOW GLORIOUS YOUR NAME IS!
THEN THERE WAS A VOICE FROM HEAVEN...
I HAVE GLORIFIED MY NAME... AND I WILL GLORIFY IT AGAIN!!

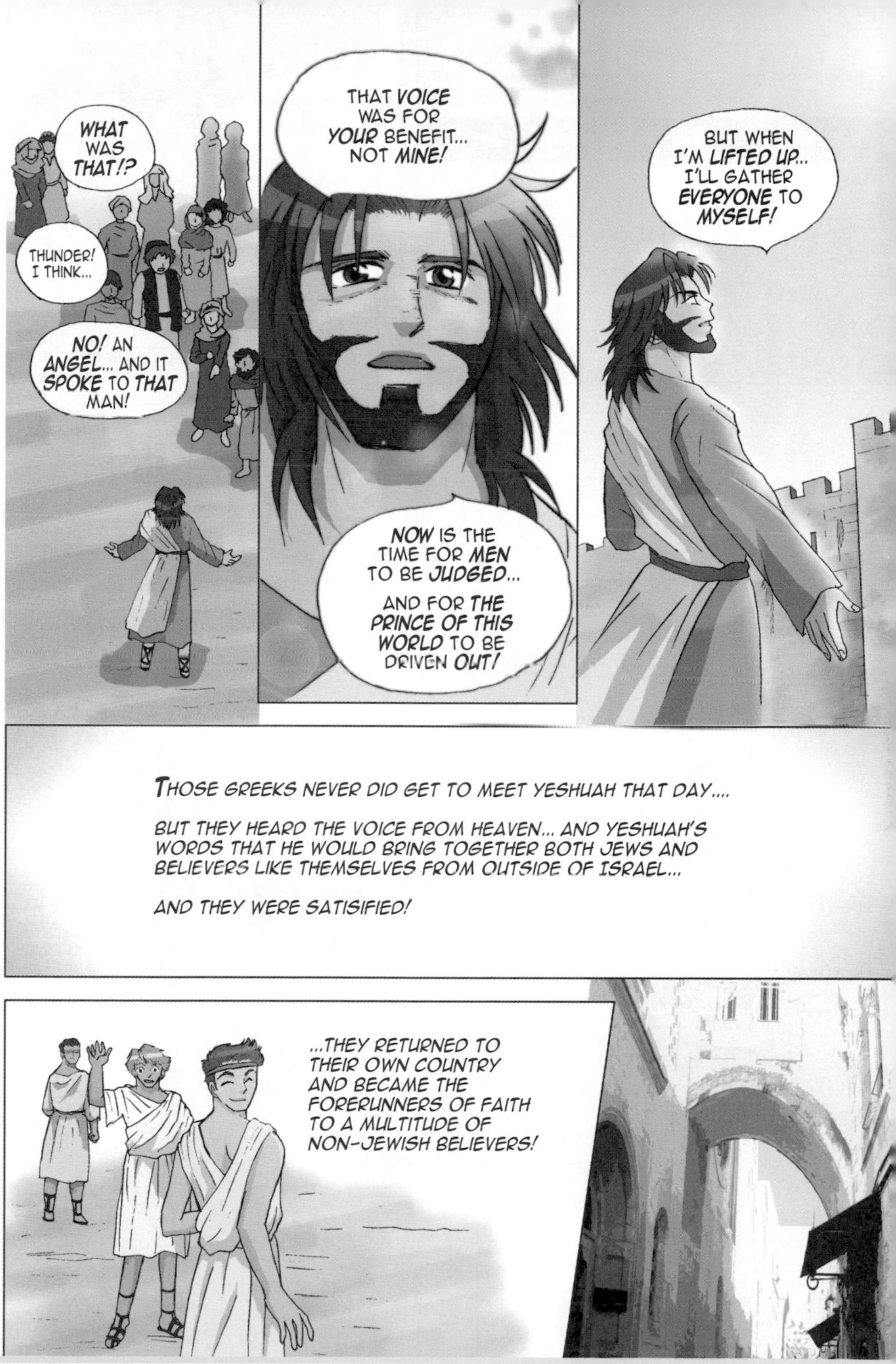
WHAT WAS THAT!?
THUNDER! I THINK...
NO! AN ANGEL... AND IT SPOKE TO THAT MAN!
THAT VOICE WAS FOR YOUR BENEFIT... NOT MINE!
NOW IS THE TIME FOR MEN TO BE JUDGED...
AND FOR THE PRINCE OF THIS WORLD TO BE DRIVEN OUT!
BUT WHEN I'M LIFTED UP... I'LL GATHER EVERYONE TO MYSELF!
THOSE GREEKS NEVER DID GET TO MEET YESHUAH THAT DAY....
BUT THEY HEARD THE VOICE FROM HEAVEN... AND YESHUAH'S WORDS THAT HE WOULD BRING TOGETHER BOTH JEWS AND BELIEVERS LIKE THEMSELVES FROM OUTSIDE OF ISRAEL...
AND THEY WERE SATISIFIED!
...THEY RETURNED TO THEIR OWN COUNTRY AND BECAME THE FORERUNNERS OF FAITH TO A MULTITUDE OF NON-JEWISH BELIEVERS!

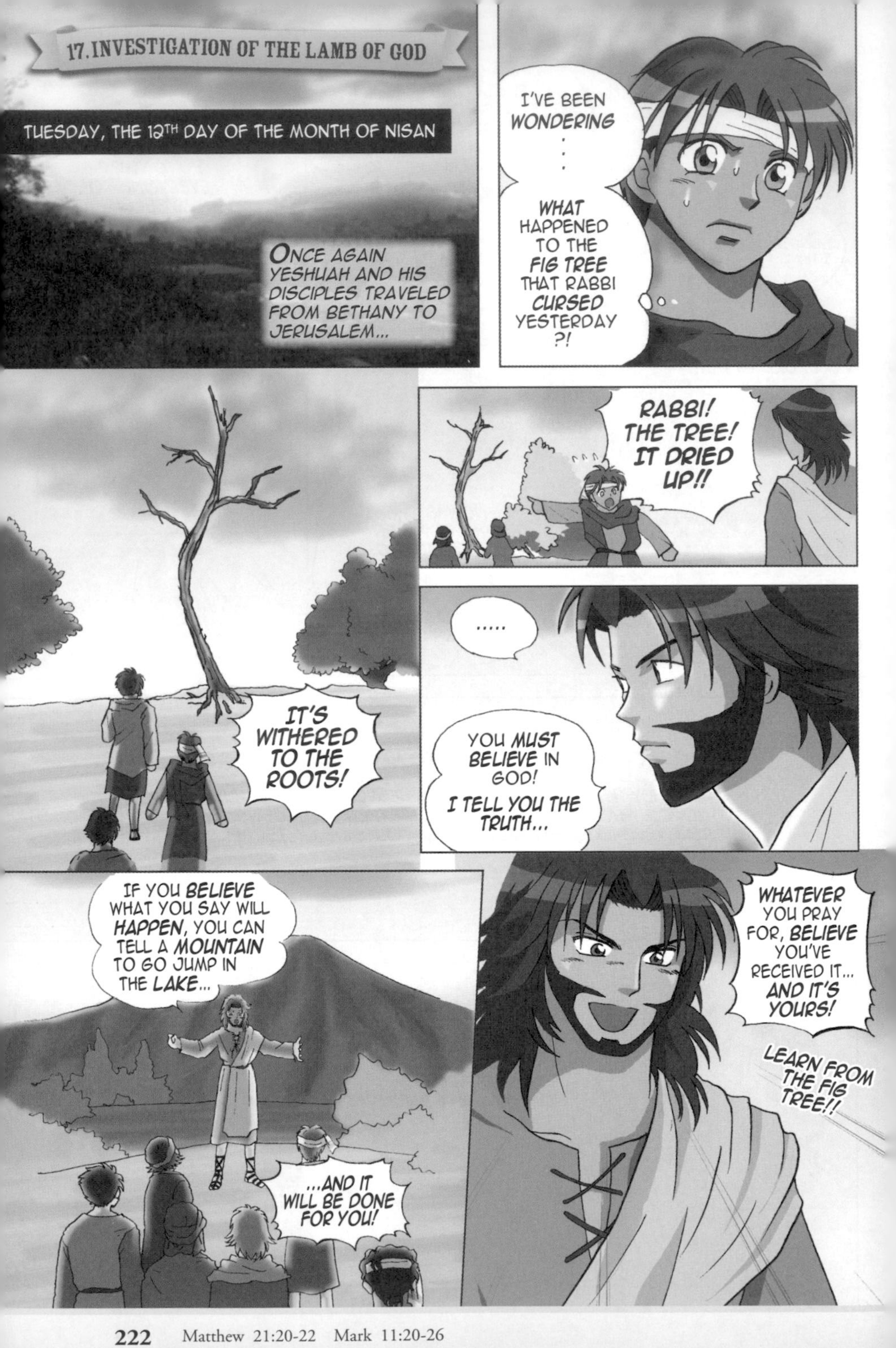
17. INVESTIGATION OF THE LAMB OF GOD
TUESDAY, THE 12TH DAY OF THE MONTH OF NISAN
ONCE AGAIN YESHUAH AND HIS DISCIPLES TRAVELED FROM BETHANY TO JERUSALEM...
I'VE BEEN WONDERING . . .
WHAT HAPPENED TO THE FIG TREE THAT RABBI CURSED YESTERDAY ?!
IT'S WITHERED TO THE ROOTS!
RABBI! THE TREE! IT DRIED UP!!
.....
YOU MUST BELIEVE IN GOD!
I TELL YOU THE TRUTH...
IF YOU BELIEVE WHAT YOU SAY WILL HAPPEN, YOU CAN TELL A MOUNTAIN TO GO JUMP IN THE LAKE...
...AND IT WILL BE DONE FOR YOU!
WHATEVER YOU PRAY FOR, BELIEVE YOU'VE RECEIVED IT... AND IT'S YOURS!
LEARN FROM THE FIG TREE!!

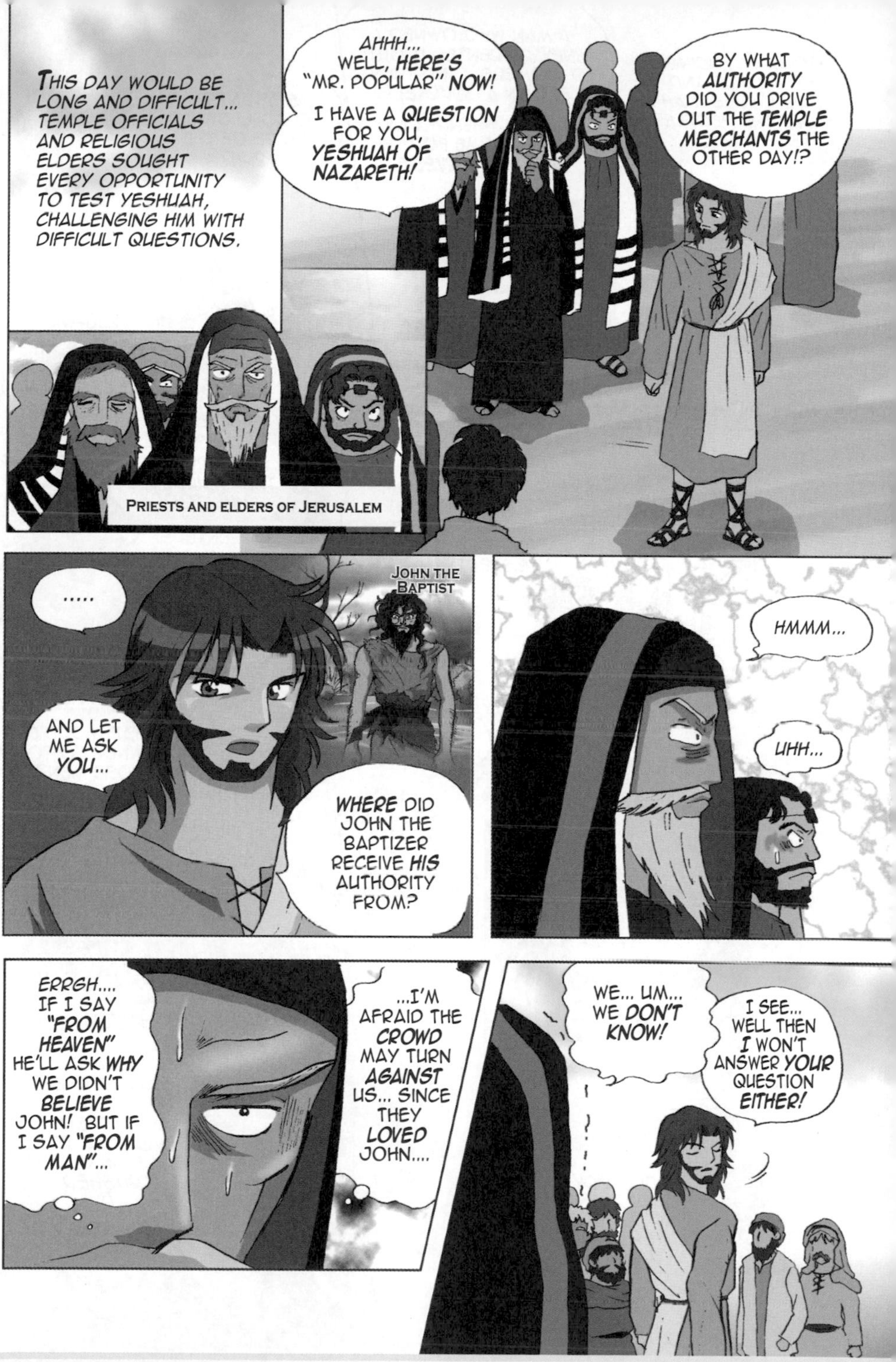

THIS DAY WOULD BE LONG AND DIFFICULT... TEMPLE OFFICIALS AND RELIGIOUS ELDERS SOUGHT EVERY OPPORTUNITY TO TEST YESHUAH, CHALLENGING HIM WITH DIFFICULT QUESTIONS.
AHHH... WELL, HERE'S "MR. POPULAR" NOW!
I HAVE A QUESTION FOR YOU, YESHUAH OF NAZARETH!
BY WHAT AUTHORITY DID YOU DRIVE OUT THE TEMPLE MERCHANTS THE OTHER DAY!?
PRIESTS AND ELDERS OF JERUSALEM
.....
JOHN THE BAPTIST
AND LET ME ASK YOU...
WHERE DID JOHN THE BAPTIZER RECEIVE HIS AUTHORITY FROM?
HMMM...
UHH...
ERRGH.... IF I SAY "FROM HEAVEN" HE'LL ASK WHY WE DIDN'T BELIEVE JOHN! BUT IF I SAY "FROM MAN"...
...I'M AFRAID THE CROWD MAY TURN AGAINST US... SINCE THEY LOVED JOHN....
WE... UM... WE DON'T KNOW!
I SEE... WELL THEN I WON'T ANSWER YOUR QUESTION EITHER!

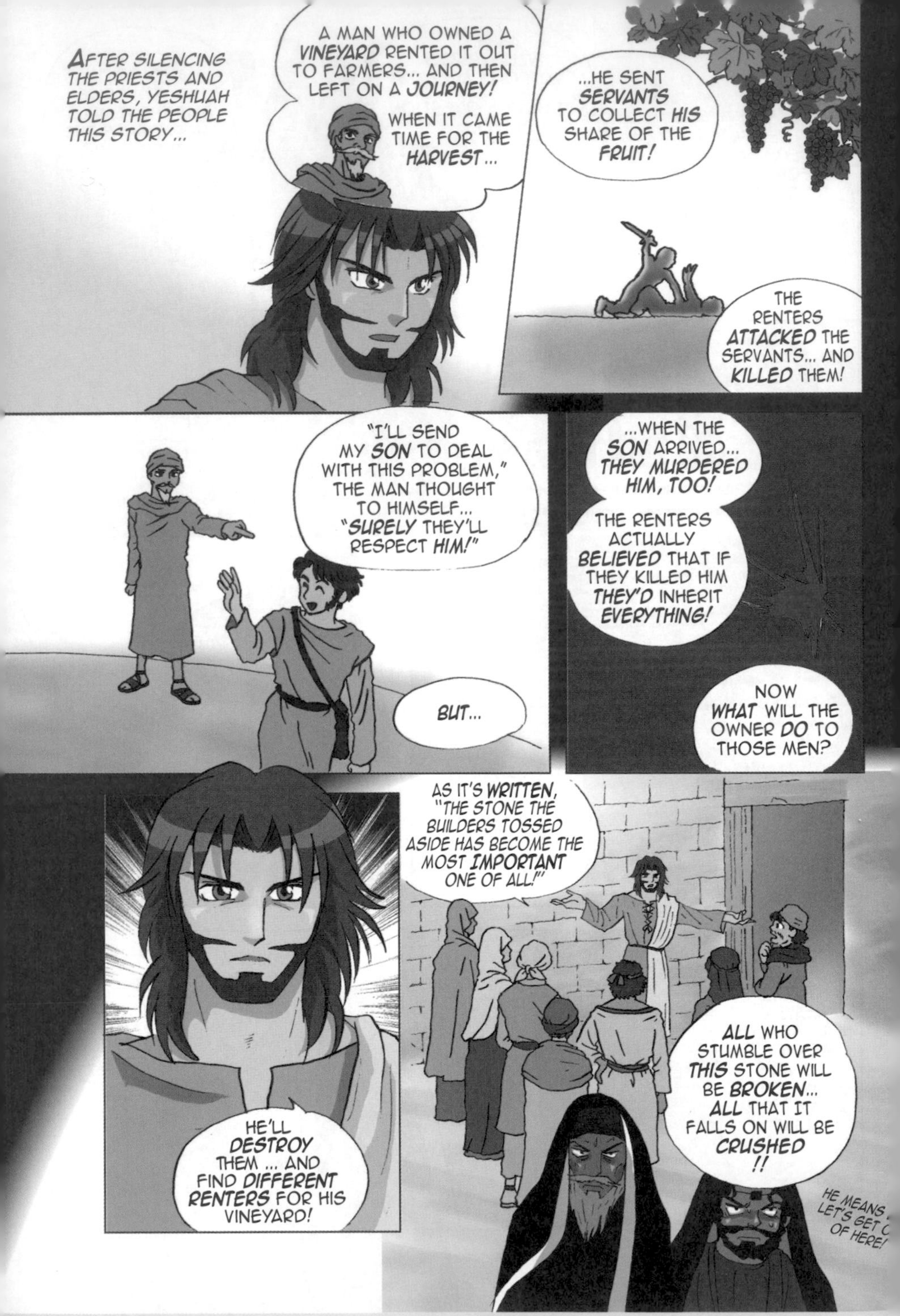
AFTER SILENCING THE PRIESTS AND ELDERS, YESHUAH TOLD THE PEOPLE THIS STORY...
A MAN WHO OWNED A VINEYARD RENTED IT OUT TO FARMERS... AND THEN LEFT ON A JOURNEY!
WHEN IT CAME TIME FOR THE HARVEST...
...HE SENT SERVANTS TO COLLECT HIS SHARE OF THE FRUIT!
THE RENTERS ATTACKED THE SERVANTS... AND KILLED THEM!
"I'LL SEND MY SON TO DEAL WITH THIS PROBLEM," THE MAN THOUGHT TO HIMSELF... "SURELY THEY'LL RESPECT HIM!"
BUT...
...WHEN THE SON ARRIVED... THEY MURDERED HIM, TOO!
THE RENTERS ACTUALLY BELIEVED THAT IF THEY KILLED HIM THEY'D INHERIT EVERYTHING!
NOW WHAT WILL THE OWNER DO TO THOSE MEN?
HE'LL DESTROY THEM ... AND FIND DIFFERENT RENTERS FOR HIS VINEYARD!
AS IT'S WRITTEN, "THE STONE THE BUILDERS TOSSED ASIDE HAS BECOME THE MOST IMPORTANT ONE OF ALL!"
ALL WHO STUMBLE OVER THIS STONE WILL BE BROKEN... ALL THAT IT FALLS ON WILL BE CRUSHED !!
HE MEANS... LET'S GET OF HERE!

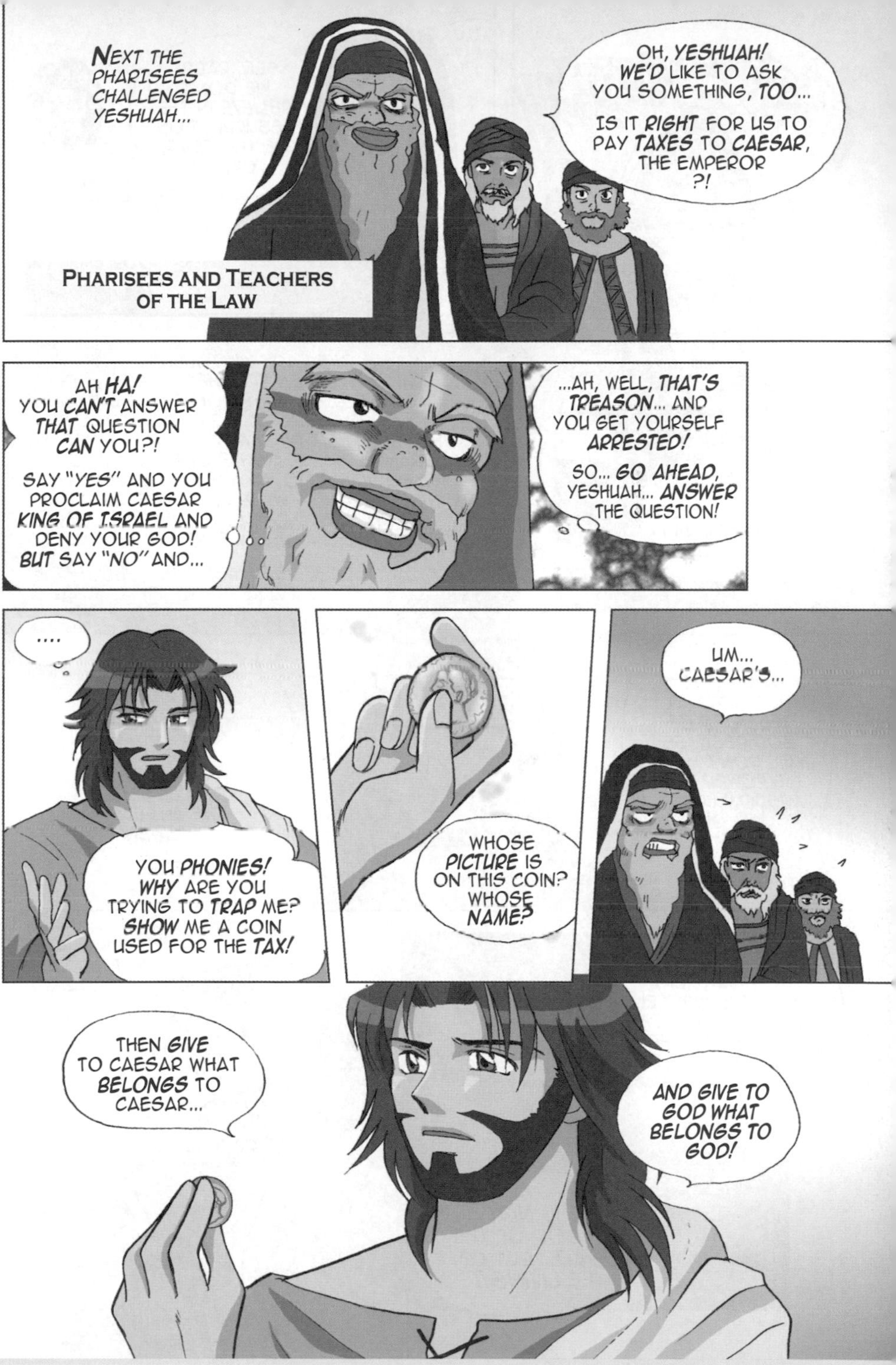
NEXT THE PHARISEES CHALLENGED YESHUAH...
OH, YESHUAH! WE'D LIKE TO ASK YOU SOMETHING, TOO...
IS IT RIGHT FOR US TO PAY TAXES TO CAESAR, THE EMPEROR ?!
PHARISEES AND TEACHERS OF THE LAW
AH HA! YOU CAN'T ANSWER THAT QUESTION CAN YOU?!
SAY "YES" AND YOU PROCLAIM CAESAR KING OF ISRAEL AND DENY YOUR GOD! BUT SAY "NO" AND...
...AH, WELL, THAT'S TREASON... AND YOU GET YOURSELF ARRESTED!
SO... GO AHEAD, YESHUAH... ANSWER THE QUESTION!
....
YOU PHONIES! WHY ARE YOU TRYING TO TRAP ME? SHOW ME A COIN USED FOR THE TAX!
WHOSE PICTURE IS ON THIS COIN? WHOSE NAME?
UM... CAESAR'S...
THEN GIVE TO CAESAR WHAT BELONGS TO CAESAR...
AND GIVE TO GOD WHAT BELONGS TO GOD!

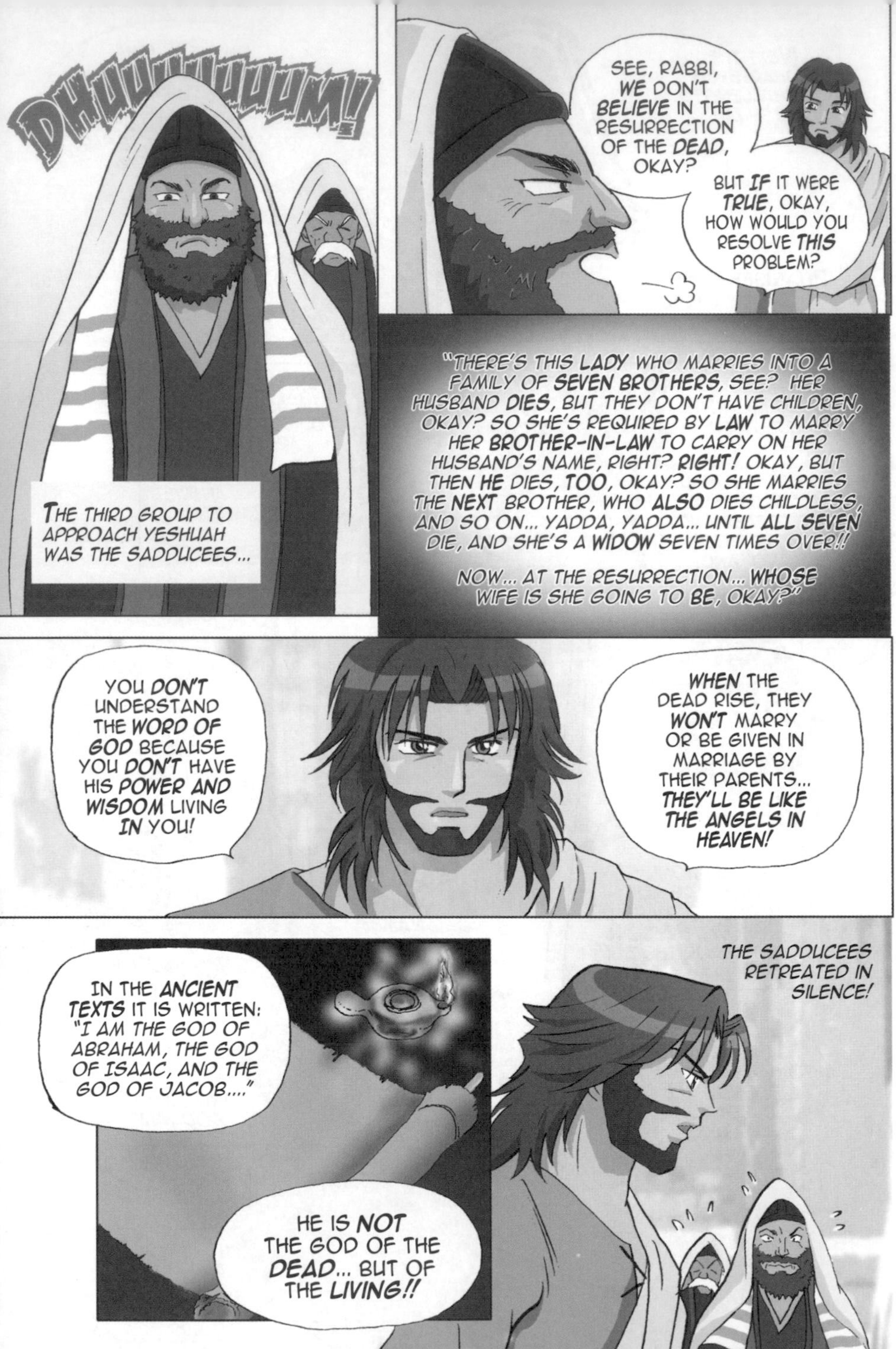
DHUUUUUUUM!!
THE THIRD GROUP TO APPROACH YESHUAH WAS THE SADDUCEES...
SEE, RABBI, WE DON'T BELIEVE IN THE RESURRECTION OF THE DEAD, OKAY?
BUT IF IT WERE TRUE, OKAY, HOW WOULD YOU RESOLVE THIS PROBLEM?
"THERE'S THIS LADY WHO MARRIES INTO A FAMILY OF SEVEN BROTHERS, SEE? HER HUSBAND DIES, BUT THEY DON'T HAVE CHILDREN, OKAY? SO SHE'S REQUIRED BY LAW TO MARRY HER BROTHER-IN-LAW TO CARRY ON HER HUSBAND'S NAME, RIGHT? RIGHT! OKAY, BUT THEN HE DIES, TOO, OKAY? SO SHE MARRIES THE NEXT BROTHER, WHO ALSO DIES CHILDLESS, AND SO ON... YADDA, YADDA... UNTIL ALL SEVEN DIE, AND SHE'S A WIDOW SEVEN TIMES OVER!!
NOW... AT THE RESURRECTION... WHOSE WIFE IS SHE GOING TO BE, OKAY?"
YOU DON'T UNDERSTAND THE WORD OF GOD BECAUSE YOU DON'T HAVE HIS POWER AND WISDOM LIVING IN YOU!
WHEN THE DEAD RISE, THEY WON'T MARRY OR BE GIVEN IN MARRIAGE BY THEIR PARENTS... THEY'LL BE LIKE THE ANGELS IN HEAVEN!
IN THE ANCIENT TEXTS IT IS WRITTEN: "I AM THE GOD OF ABRAHAM, THE GOD OF ISAAC, AND THE GOD OF JACOB...."
HE IS NOT THE GOD OF THE DEAD... BUT OF THE LIVING!!
THE SADDUCEES RETREATED IN SILENCE!

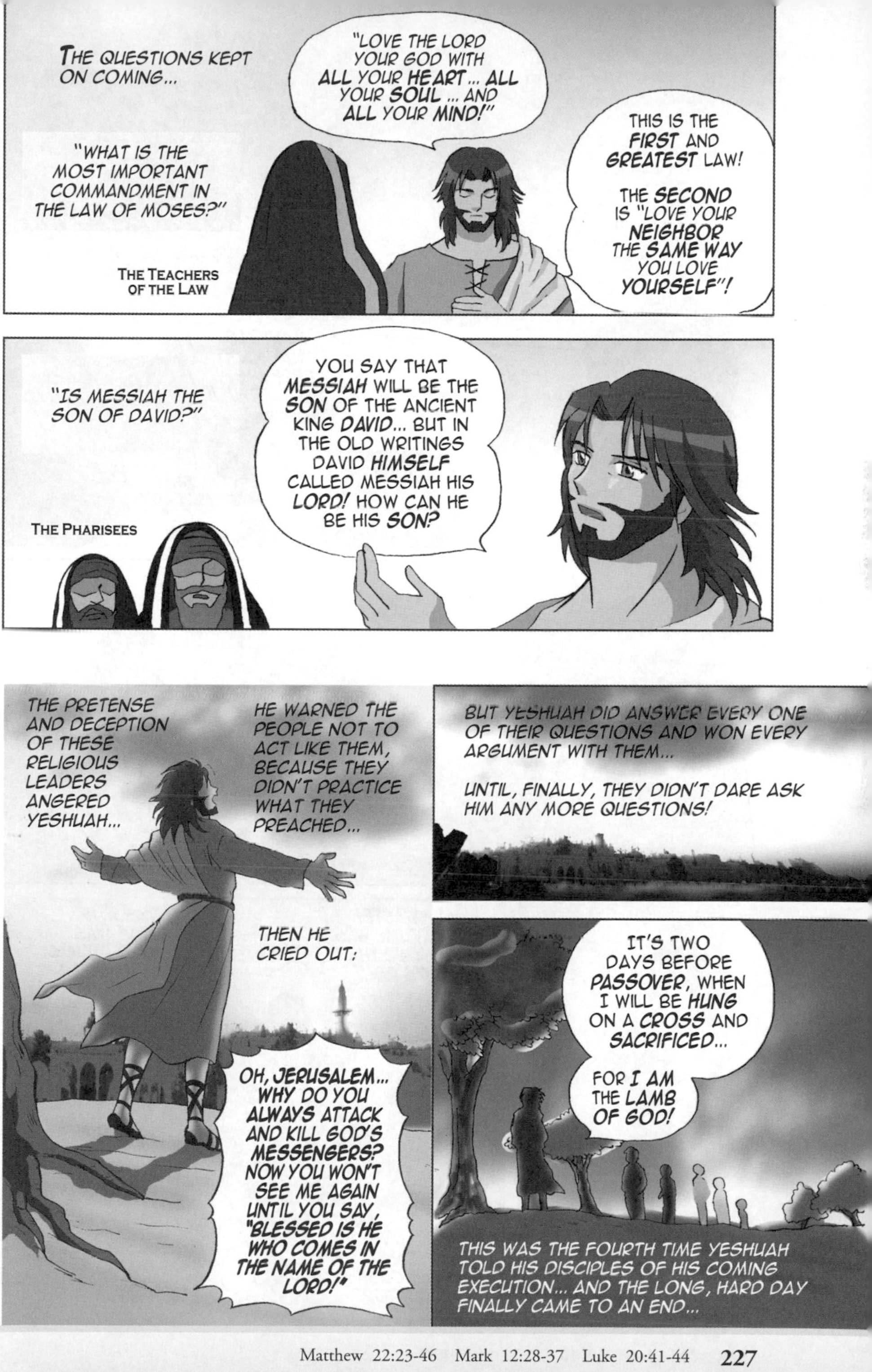
THE QUESTIONS KEPT ON COMING...
"WHAT IS THE MOST IMPORTANT COMMANDMENT IN THE LAW OF MOSES?"
THE TEACHERS OF THE LAW
"LOVE THE LORD YOUR GOD WITH ALL YOUR HEART... ALL YOUR SOUL ... AND ALL YOUR MIND!"
THIS IS THE FIRST AND GREATEST LAW!
THE SECOND IS "LOVE YOUR NEIGHBOR THE SAME WAY YOU LOVE YOURSELF"!
"IS MESSIAH THE SON OF DAVID?"
THE PHARISEES
YOU SAY THAT MESSIAH WILL BE THE SON OF THE ANCIENT KING DAVID... BUT IN THE OLD WRITINGS DAVID HIMSELF CALLED MESSIAH HIS LORD! HOW CAN HE BE HIS SON?
THE PRETENSE AND DECEPTION OF THESE RELIGIOUS LEADERS ANGERED YESHUAH...
HE WARNED THE PEOPLE NOT TO ACT LIKE THEM, BECAUSE THEY DIDN'T PRACTICE WHAT THEY PREACHED...
THEN HE CRIED OUT:
OH, JERUSALEM... WHY DO YOU ALWAYS ATTACK AND KILL GOD'S MESSENGERS? NOW YOU WON'T SEE ME AGAIN UNTIL YOU SAY, "BLESSED IS HE WHO COMES IN THE NAME OF THE LORD!"
BUT YESHUAH DID ANSWER EVERY ONE OF THEIR QUESTIONS AND WON EVERY ARGUMENT WITH THEM...
UNTIL, FINALLY, THEY DIDN'T DARE ASK HIM ANY MORE QUESTIONS!
IT'S TWO DAYS BEFORE PASSOVER, WHEN I WILL BE HUNG ON A CROSS AND SACRIFICED...
FOR I AM THE LAMB OF GOD!
THIS WAS THE FOURTH TIME YESHUAH TOLD HIS DISCIPLES OF HIS COMING EXECUTION... AND THE LONG, HARD DAY FINALLY CAME TO AN END...

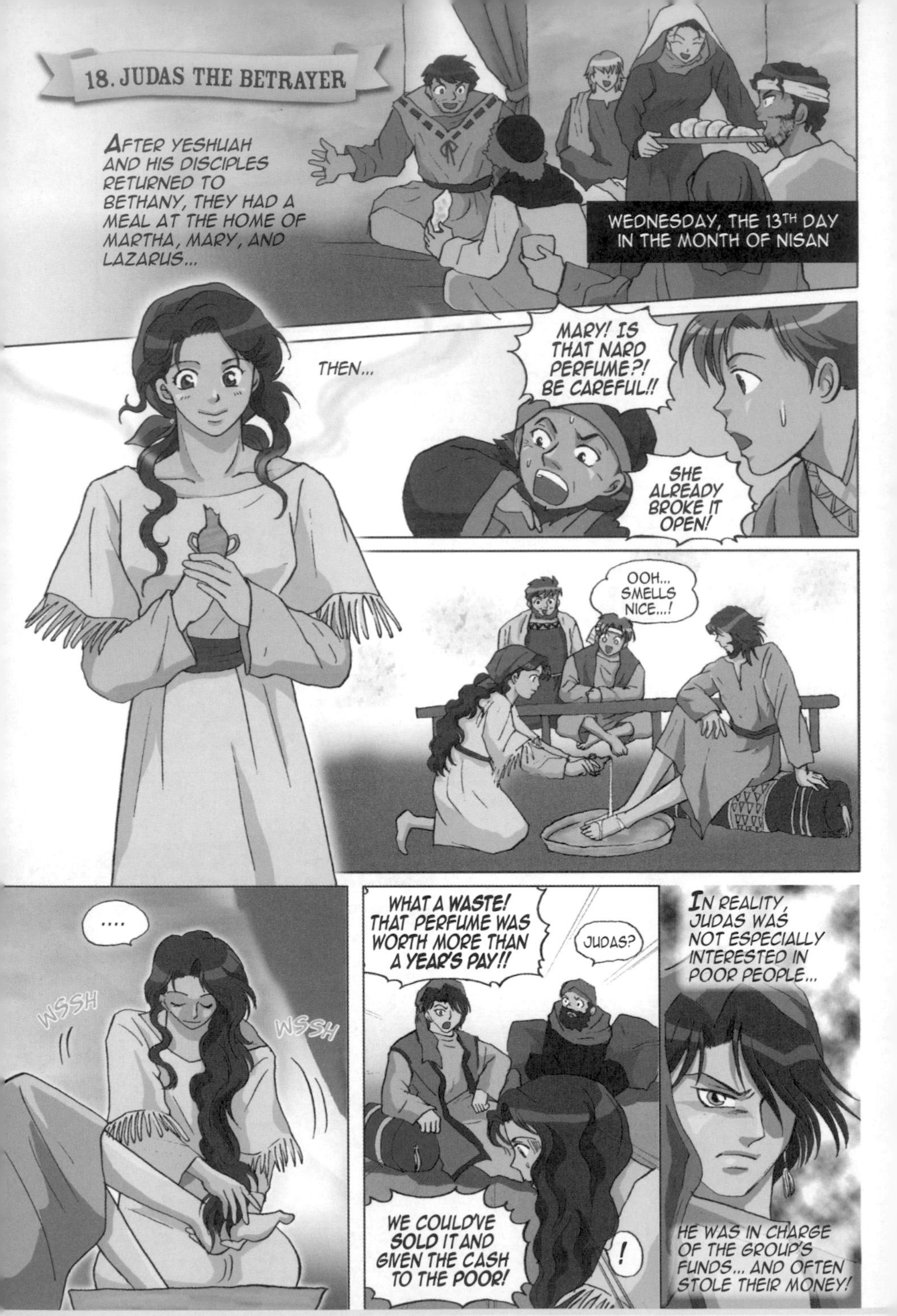
18. JUDAS THE BETRAYER
AFTER YESHUAH AND HIS DISCIPLES RETURNED TO BETHANY, THEY HAD A MEAL AT THE HOME OF MARTHA, MARY, AND LAZARUS...
WEDNESDAY, THE 13TH DAY IN THE MONTH OF NISAN
THEN...
MARY! IS THAT NARD PERFUME?! BE CAREFUL!!
SHE ALREADY BROKE IT OPEN!
OOH... SMELLS NICE...!
....
WSSH
WSSH
WHAT A WASTE! THAT PERFUME WAS WORTH MORE THAN A YEAR'S PAY!!
JUDAS?
WE COULD'VE SOLD IT AND GIVEN THE CASH TO THE POOR!
!
IN REALITY, JUDAS WAS NOT ESPECIALLY INTERESTED IN POOR PEOPLE...
HE WAS IN CHARGE OF THE GROUP'S FUNDS... AND OFTEN STOLE THEIR MONEY!

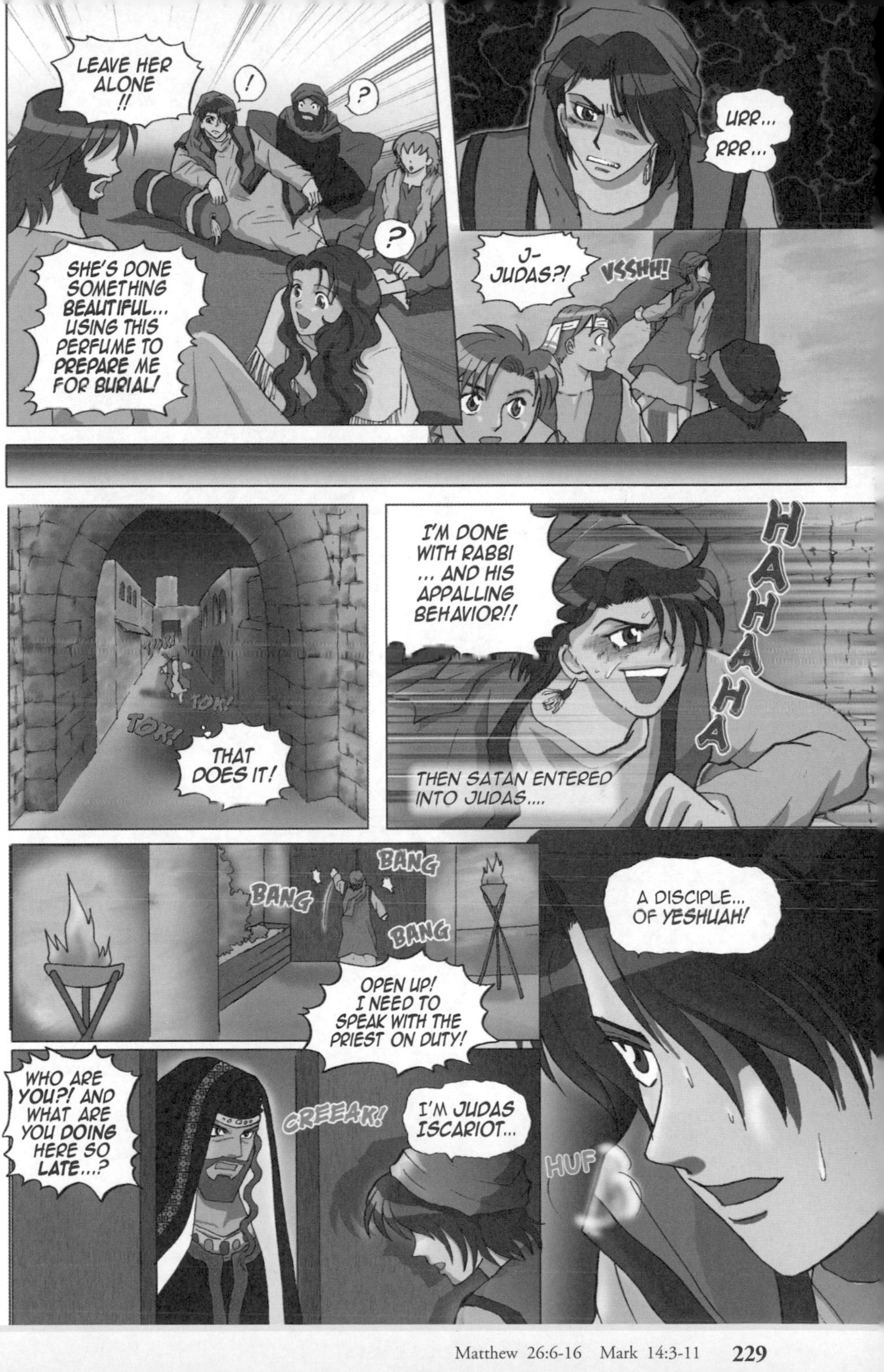
LEAVE HER ALONE !!
!
?
?
SHE'S DONE SOMETHING BEAUTIFUL... USING THIS PERFUME TO PREPARE ME FOR BURIAL!
URR... RRR...
J- JUDAS?!
VSSHH!
TOK!
TOK!
THAT DOES IT!
I'M DONE WITH RABBI ... AND HIS APPALLING BEHAVIOR!!
HAHAHAHA
THEN SATAN ENTERED INTO JUDAS....
BANG
BANG
BANG
OPEN UP! I NEED TO SPEAK WITH THE PRIEST ON DUTY!
A DISCIPLE... OF YESHUAH!
WHO ARE YOU?! AND WHAT ARE YOU DOING HERE SO LATE...?
CREEAK!
I'M JUDAS ISCARIOT...
HUF

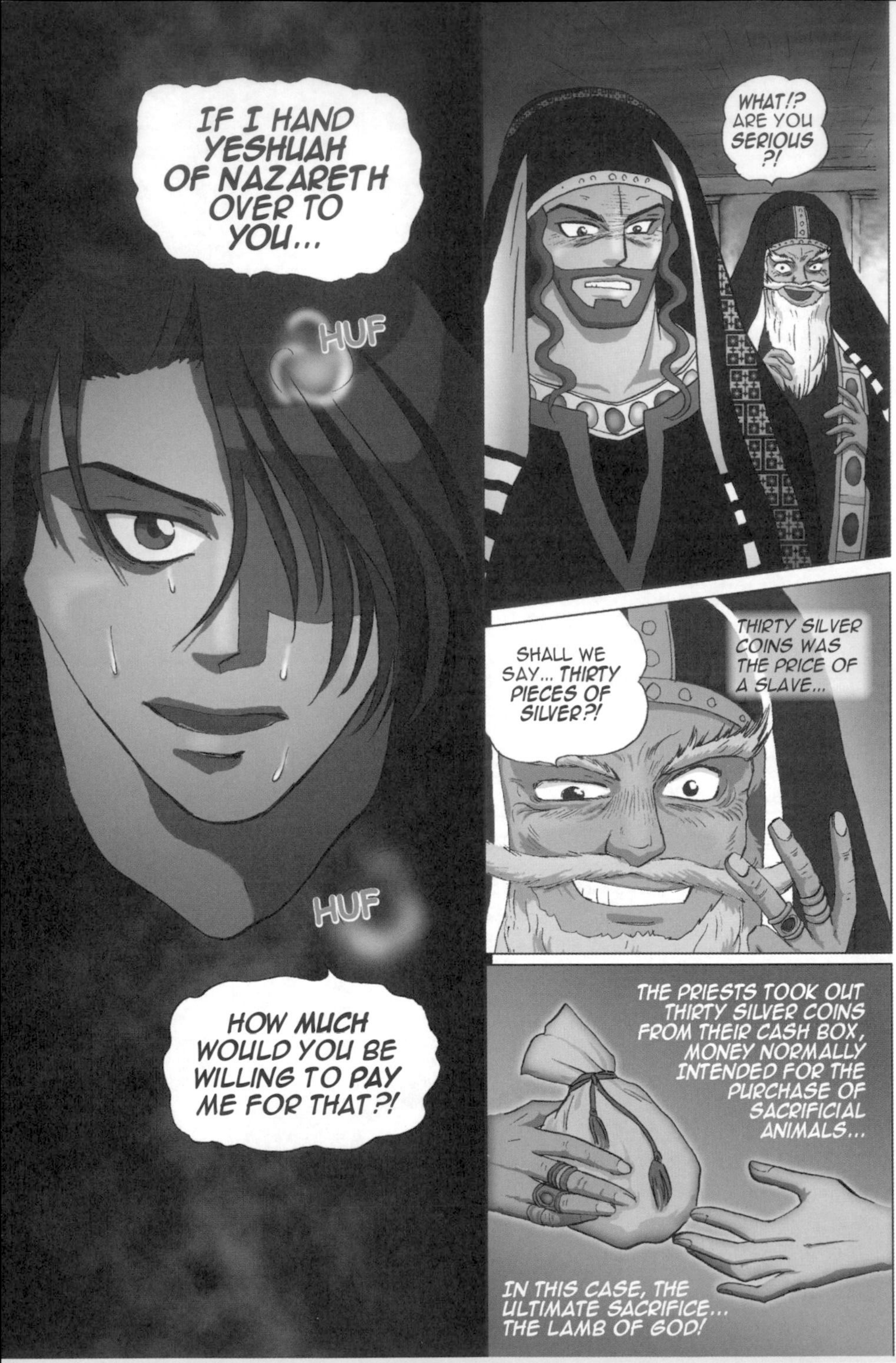
IF I HAND YESHUAH OF NAZARETH OVER TO YOU...
HUF
HUF
HOW MUCH WOULD YOU BE WILLING TO PAY ME FOR THAT?!
WHAT!? ARE YOU SERIOUS ?!
SHALL WE SAY... THIRTY PIECES OF SILVER?!
THIRTY SILVER COINS WAS THE PRICE OF A SLAVE...
THE PRIESTS TOOK OUT THIRTY SILVER COINS FROM THEIR CASH BOX, MONEY NORMALLY INTENDED FOR THE PURCHASE OF SACRIFICIAL ANIMALS...
IN THIS CASE, THE ULTIMATE SACRIFICE... THE LAMB OF GOD!

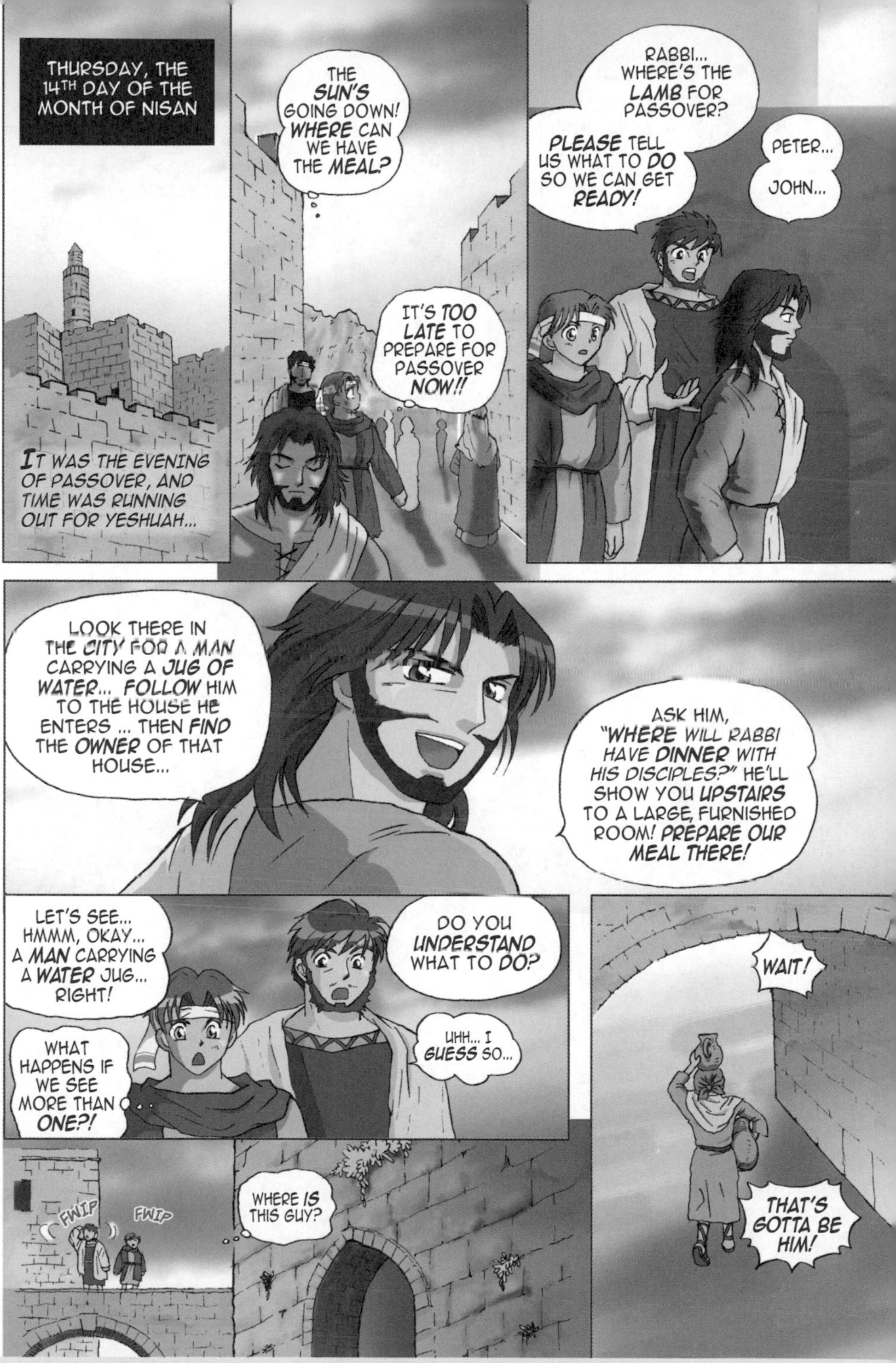
THURSDAY, THE 14TH DAY OF THE MONTH OF NISAN
IT WAS THE EVENING OF PASSOVER, AND TIME WAS RUNNING OUT FOR YESHUAH...
THE SUN'S GOING DOWN! WHERE CAN WE HAVE THE MEAL?
IT'S TOO LATE TO PREPARE FOR PASSOVER NOW!!
RABBI... WHERE'S THE LAMB FOR PASSOVER?
PLEASE TELL US WHAT TO DO SO WE CAN GET READY!
PETER... JOHN...
LOOK THERE IN THE CITY FOR A MAN CARRYING A JUG OF WATER... FOLLOW HIM TO THE HOUSE HE ENTERS ... THEN FIND THE OWNER OF THAT HOUSE...
ASK HIM, "WHERE WILL RABBI HAVE DINNER WITH HIS DISCIPLES?" HE'LL SHOW YOU UPSTAIRS TO A LARGE, FURNISHED ROOM! PREPARE OUR MEAL THERE!
DO YOU UNDERSTAND WHAT TO DO?
LET'S SEE... HMMM, OKAY... A MAN CARRYING A WATER JUG... RIGHT!
UHH... I GUESS SO...
WHAT HAPPENS IF WE SEE MORE THAN ONE?!
FWIP
FWIP
WHERE IS THIS GUY?
WAIT!
THAT'S GOTTA BE HIM!

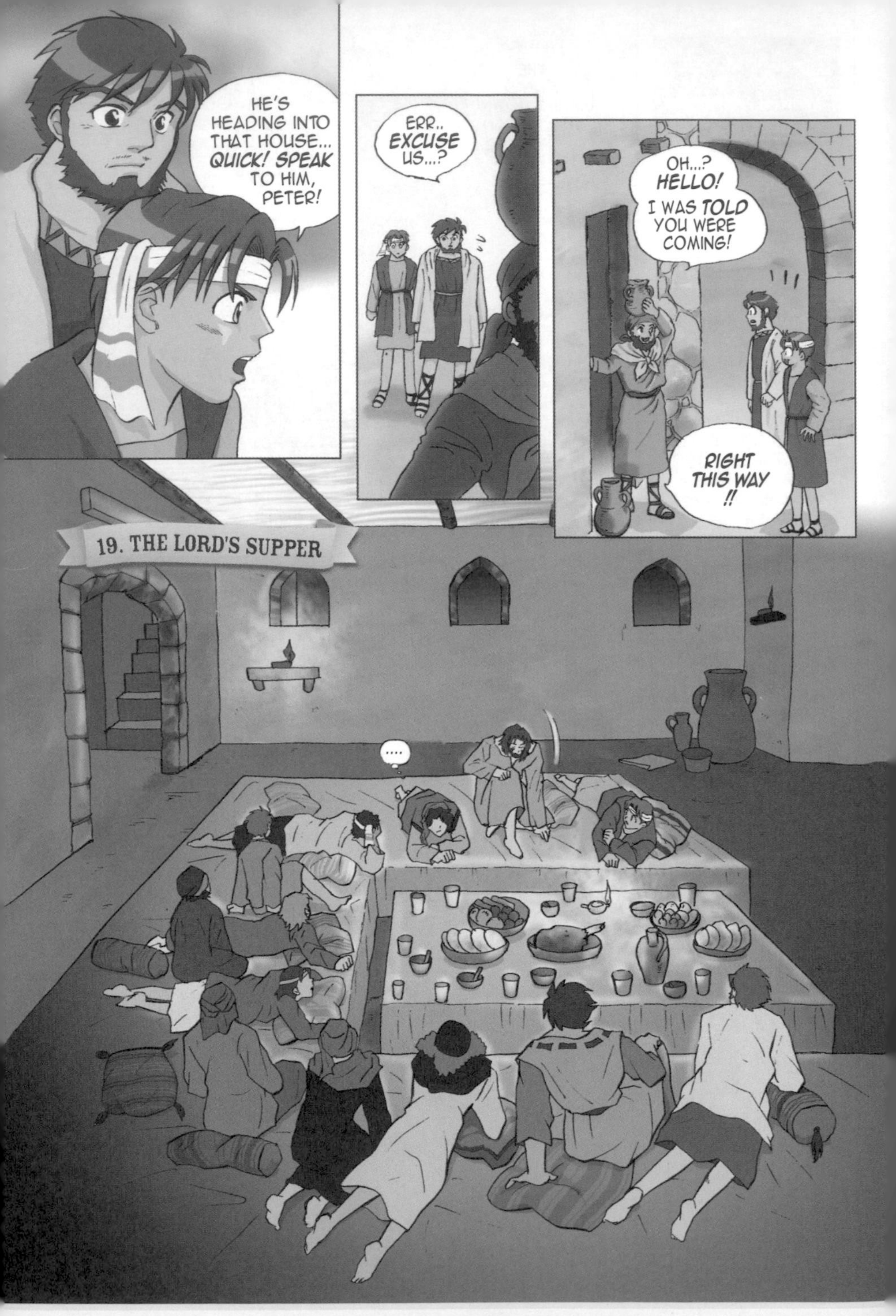
HE'S HEADING INTO THAT HOUSE... QUICK! SPEAK TO HIM, PETER!
ERR.. EXCUSE US...?
OH...? HELLO! I WAS TOLD YOU WERE COMING!
RIGHT THIS WAY !!
19. THE LORD'S SUPPER
....

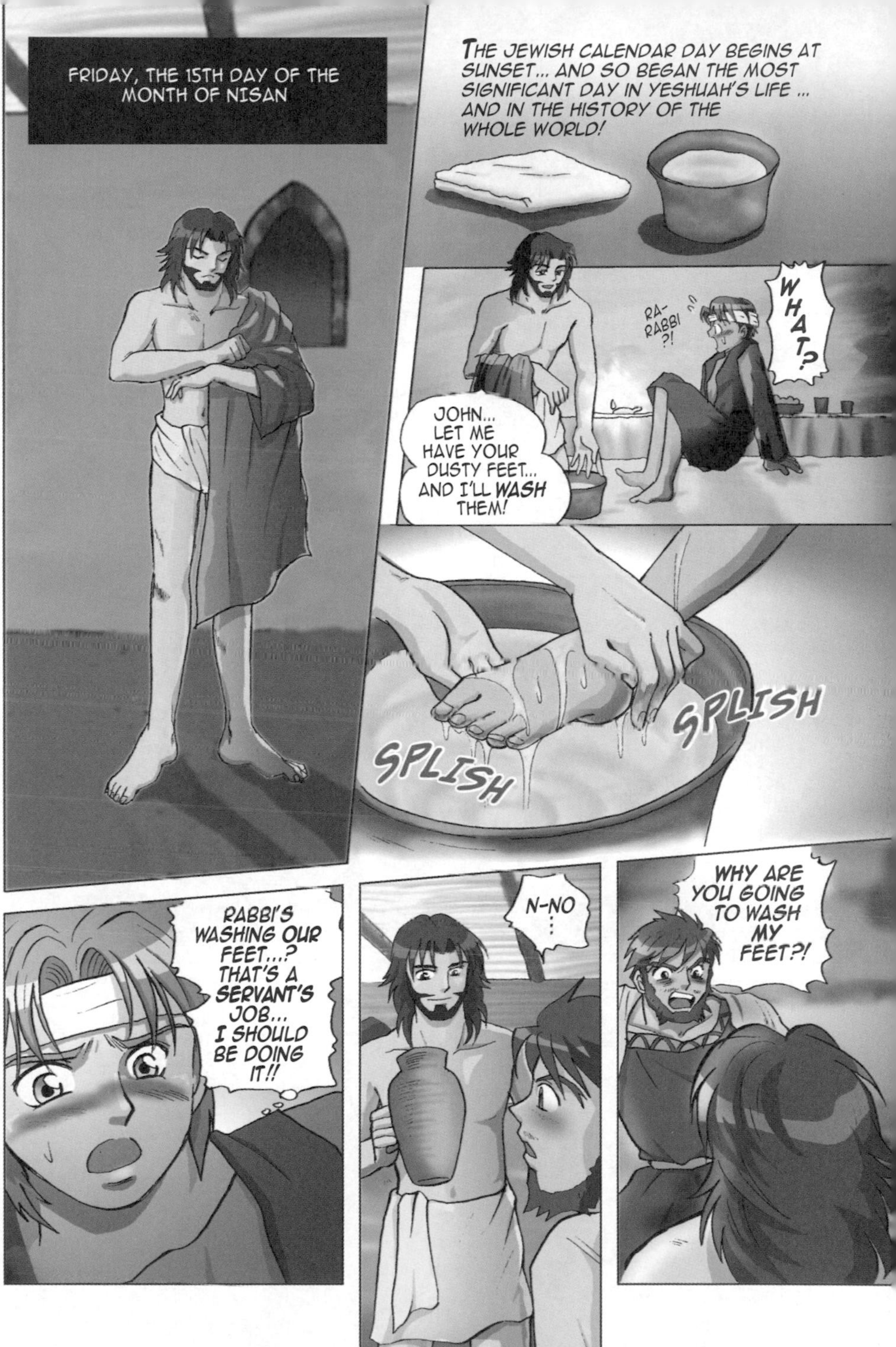
FRIDAY, THE 15TH DAY OF THE MONTH OF NISAN
THE JEWISH CALENDAR DAY BEGINS AT SUNSET... AND SO BEGAN THE MOST SIGNIFICANT DAY IN YESHUAH'S LIFE ... AND IN THE HISTORY OF THE WHOLE WORLD!
JOHN... LET ME HAVE YOUR DUSTY FEET... AND I'LL WASH THEM!
RA-RABBI ?!
WHAT?
SPLISH
SPLISH
RABBI'S WASHING OUR FEET...? THAT'S A SERVANT'S JOB... I SHOULD BE DOING IT!!
N-NO ...
WHY ARE YOU GOING TO WASH MY FEET?!

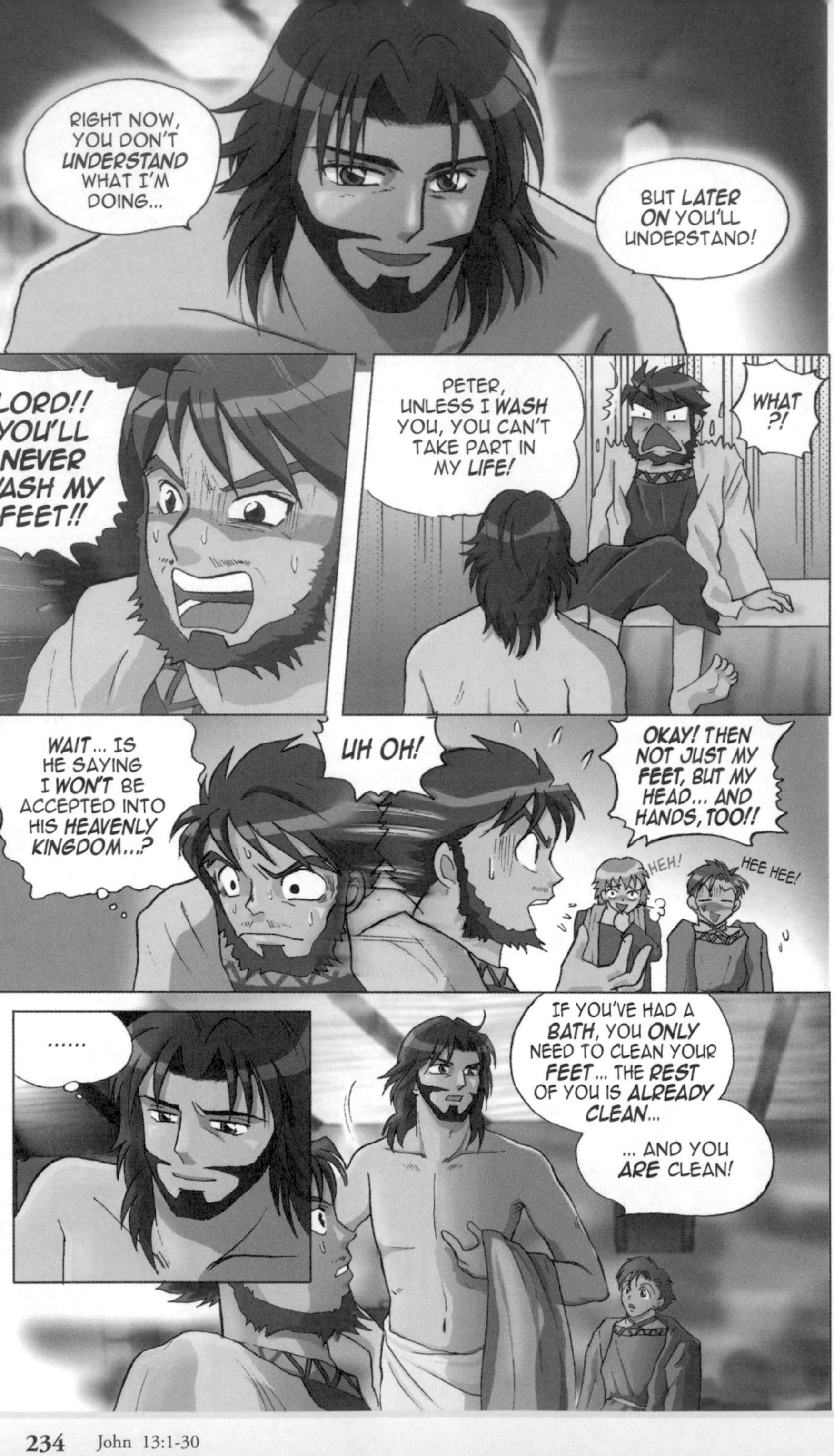
RIGHT NOW, YOU DON'T UNDERSTAND WHAT I'M DOING...
BUT LATER ON YOU'LL UNDERSTAND!
LORD!! YOU'LL NEVER WASH MY FEET!!
PETER, UNLESS I WASH YOU, YOU CAN'T TAKE PART IN MY LIFE!
WHAT ?!
WAIT... IS HE SAYING I WON'T BE ACCEPTED INTO HIS HEAVENLY KINGDOM...?
UH OH!
OKAY! THEN NOT JUST MY FEET, BUT MY HEAD... AND HANDS, TOO!!
HEH!
HEE HEE!
......
IF YOU'VE HAD A BATH, YOU ONLY NEED TO CLEAN YOUR FEET... THE REST OF YOU IS ALREADY CLEAN...
... AND YOU ARE CLEAN!

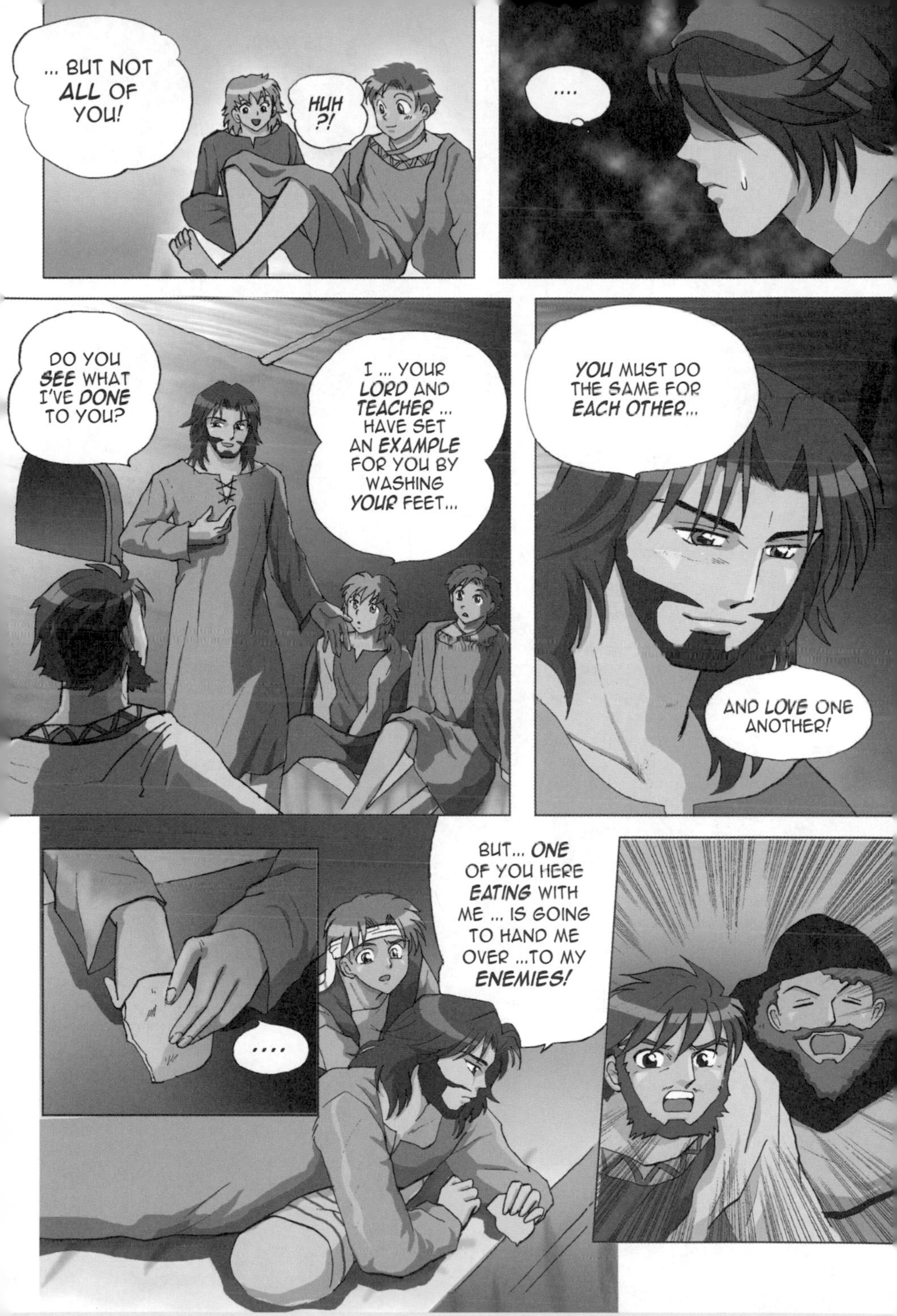
... BUT NOT ALL OF YOU!
HUH ?!
....
DO YOU SEE WHAT I'VE DONE TO YOU?
I ... YOUR LORD AND TEACHER ... HAVE SET AN EXAMPLE FOR YOU BY WASHING YOUR FEET...
YOU MUST DO THE SAME FOR EACH OTHER...
AND LOVE ONE ANOTHER!
....
BUT... ONE OF YOU HERE EATING WITH ME ... IS GOING TO HAND ME OVER ...TO MY ENEMIES!

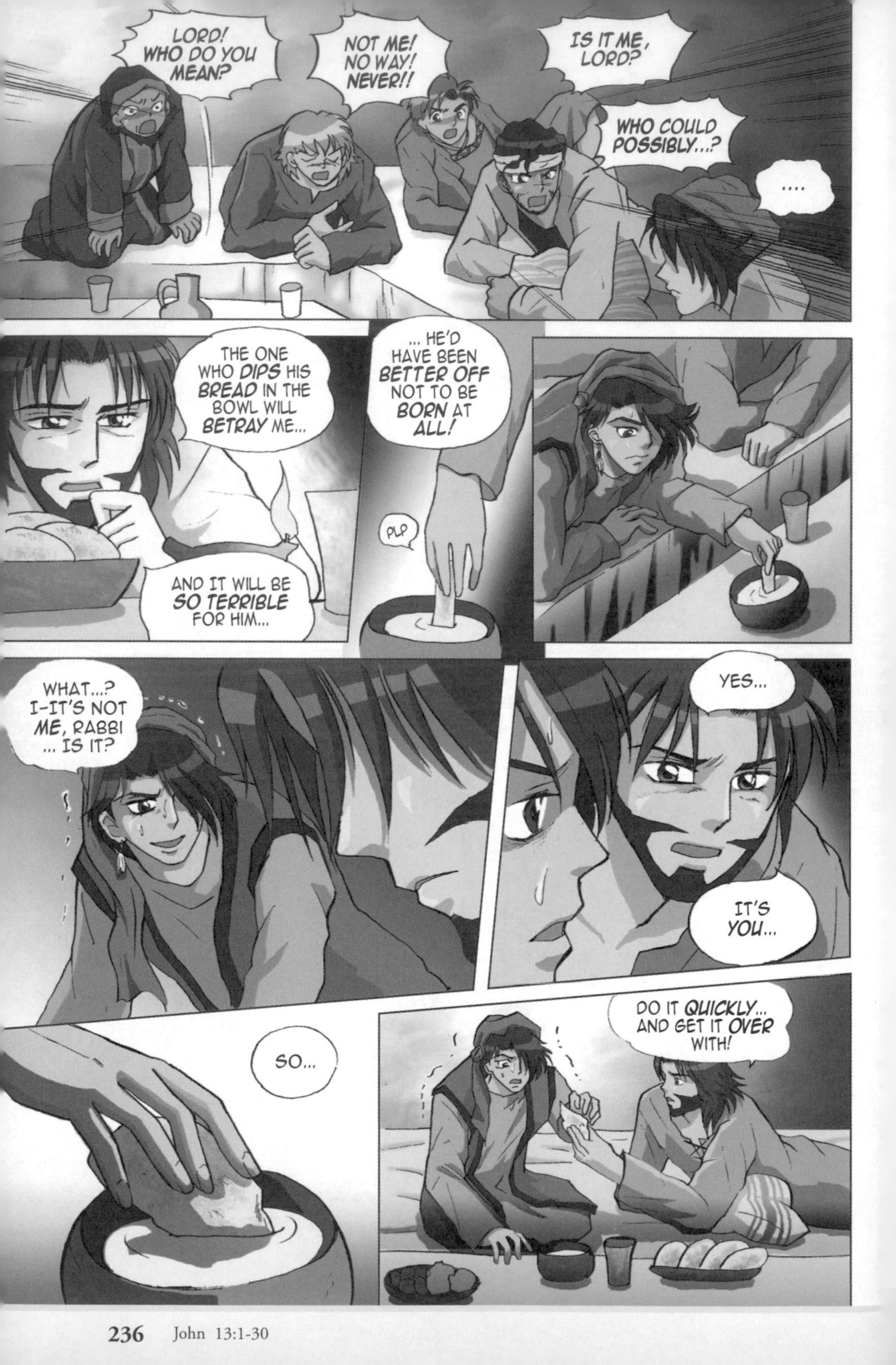

LORD! WHO DO YOU MEAN?
NOT ME! NO WAY! NEVER!!
IS IT ME, LORD?
WHO COULD POSSIBLY...?
....
THE ONE WHO DIPS HIS BREAD IN THE BOWL WILL BETRAY ME...
AND IT WILL BE SO TERRIBLE FOR HIM...
... HE'D HAVE BEEN BETTER OFF NOT TO BE BORN AT ALL!
PLP
WHAT...? I-IT'S NOT ME, RABBI ... IS IT?
YES...
IT'S YOU...
SO...
DO IT QUICKLY... AND GET IT OVER WITH!

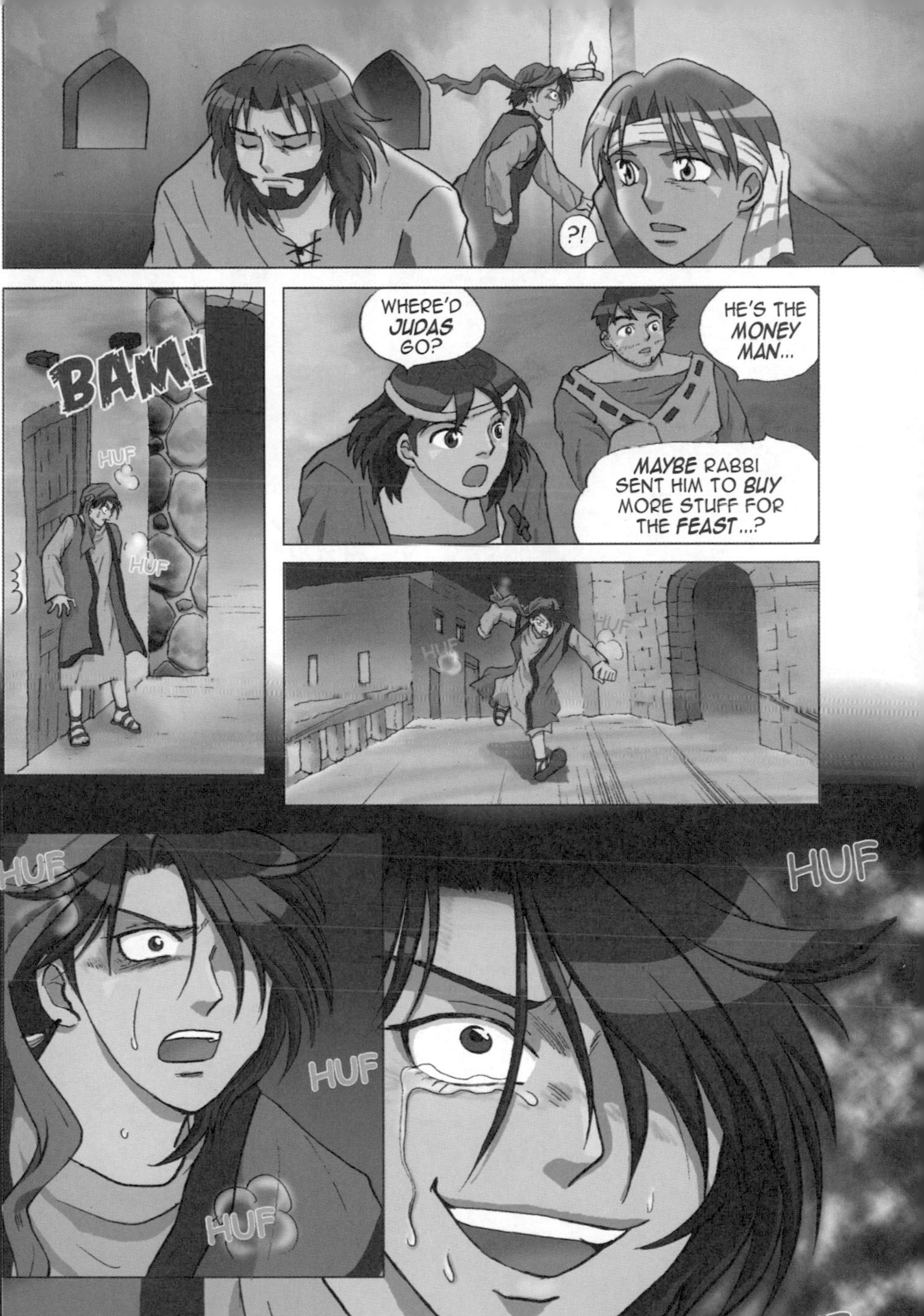
?!
BAM!
HUF
HUF
WHERE'D JUDAS GO?
HE'S THE MONEY MAN...
MAYBE RABBI SENT HIM TO BUY MORE STUFF FOR THE FEAST...?
HUF
HUF
HUF
HUF
HUF
HUF
HUF

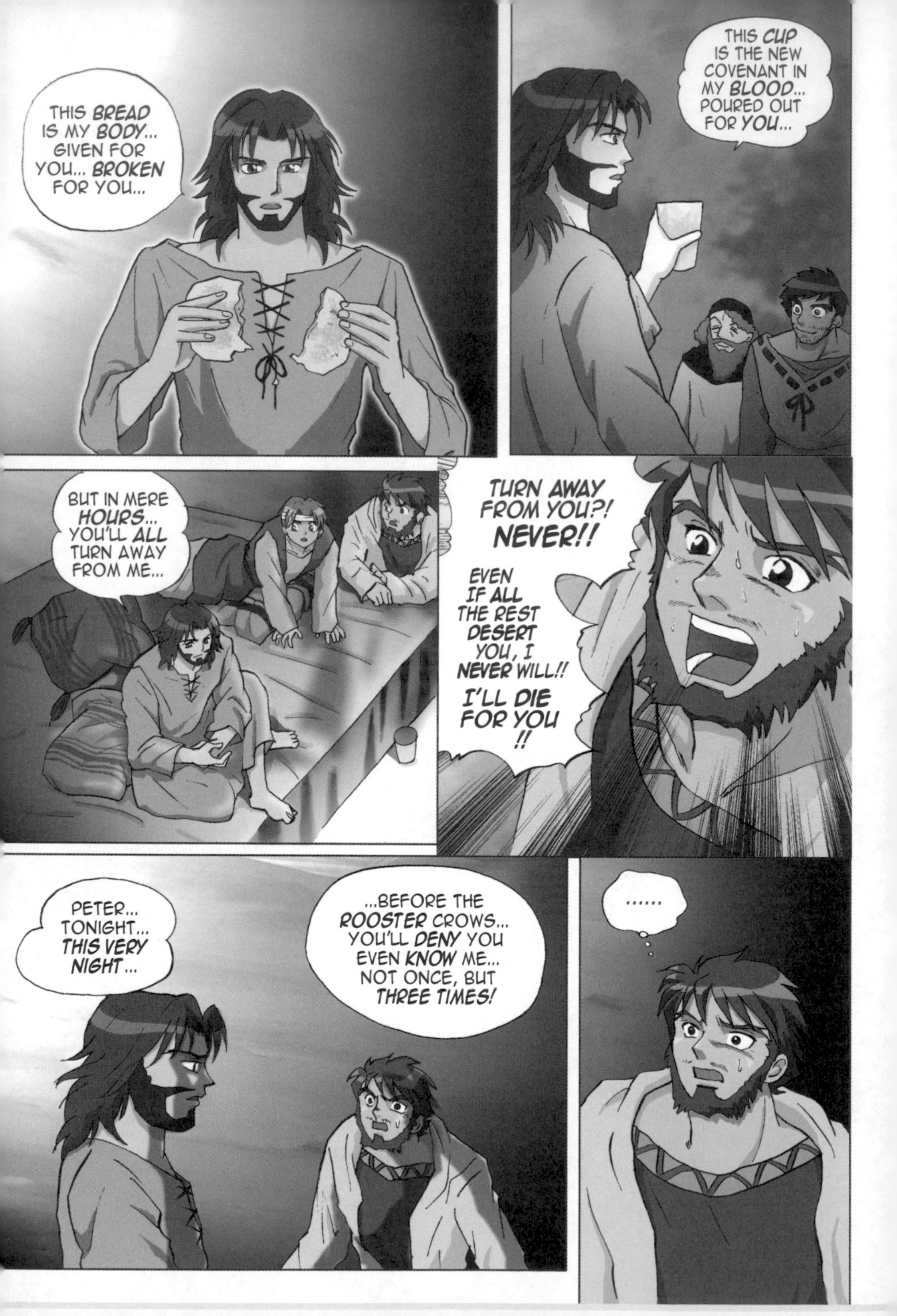
THIS BREAD IS MY BODY... GIVEN FOR YOU... BROKEN FOR YOU...
THIS CUP IS THE NEW COVENANT IN MY BLOOD... POURED OUT FOR YOU...
BUT IN MERE HOURS... YOU'LL ALL TURN AWAY FROM ME...
TURN AWAY FROM YOU?! NEVER!!
EVEN IF ALL THE REST DESERT YOU, I NEVER WILL!!
I'LL DIE FOR YOU!!
PETER... TONIGHT... THIS VERY NIGHT...
...BEFORE THE ROOSTER CROWS... YOU'LL DENY YOU EVEN KNOW ME... NOT ONCE, BUT THREE TIMES!
......

 Matthew 26:26-35 Mark 14:22-31 Luke 22:15-20, 22:31-34 John 13:36-38

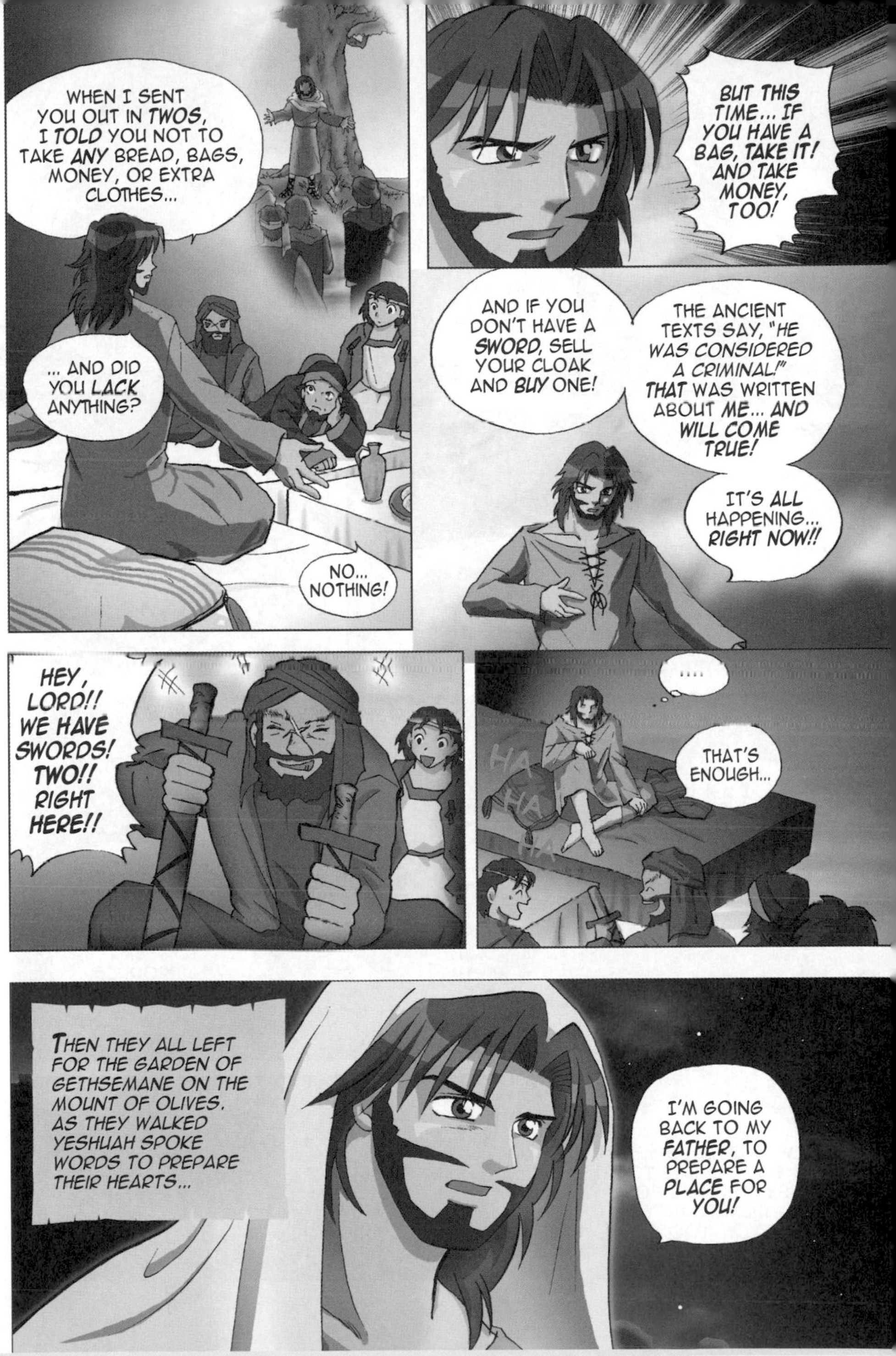
WHEN I SENT YOU OUT IN TWOS, I TOLD YOU NOT TO TAKE ANY BREAD, BAGS, MONEY, OR EXTRA CLOTHES...
... AND DID YOU LACK ANYTHING?
NO... NOTHING!
BUT THIS TIME... IF YOU HAVE A BAG, TAKE IT! AND TAKE MONEY, TOO!
AND IF YOU DON'T HAVE A SWORD, SELL YOUR CLOAK AND BUY ONE!
THE ANCIENT TEXTS SAY, "HE WAS CONSIDERED A CRIMINAL!" THAT WAS WRITTEN ABOUT ME... AND WILL COME TRUE!
IT'S ALL HAPPENING... RIGHT NOW!!
HEY, LORD!! WE HAVE SWORDS! TWO!! RIGHT HERE!!
....
HA HA HA
THAT'S ENOUGH...
THEN THEY ALL LEFT FOR THE GARDEN OF GETHSEMANE ON THE MOUNT OF OLIVES. AS THEY WALKED YESHUAH SPOKE WORDS TO PREPARE THEIR HEARTS...
I'M GOING BACK TO MY FATHER, TO PREPARE A PLACE FOR YOU!

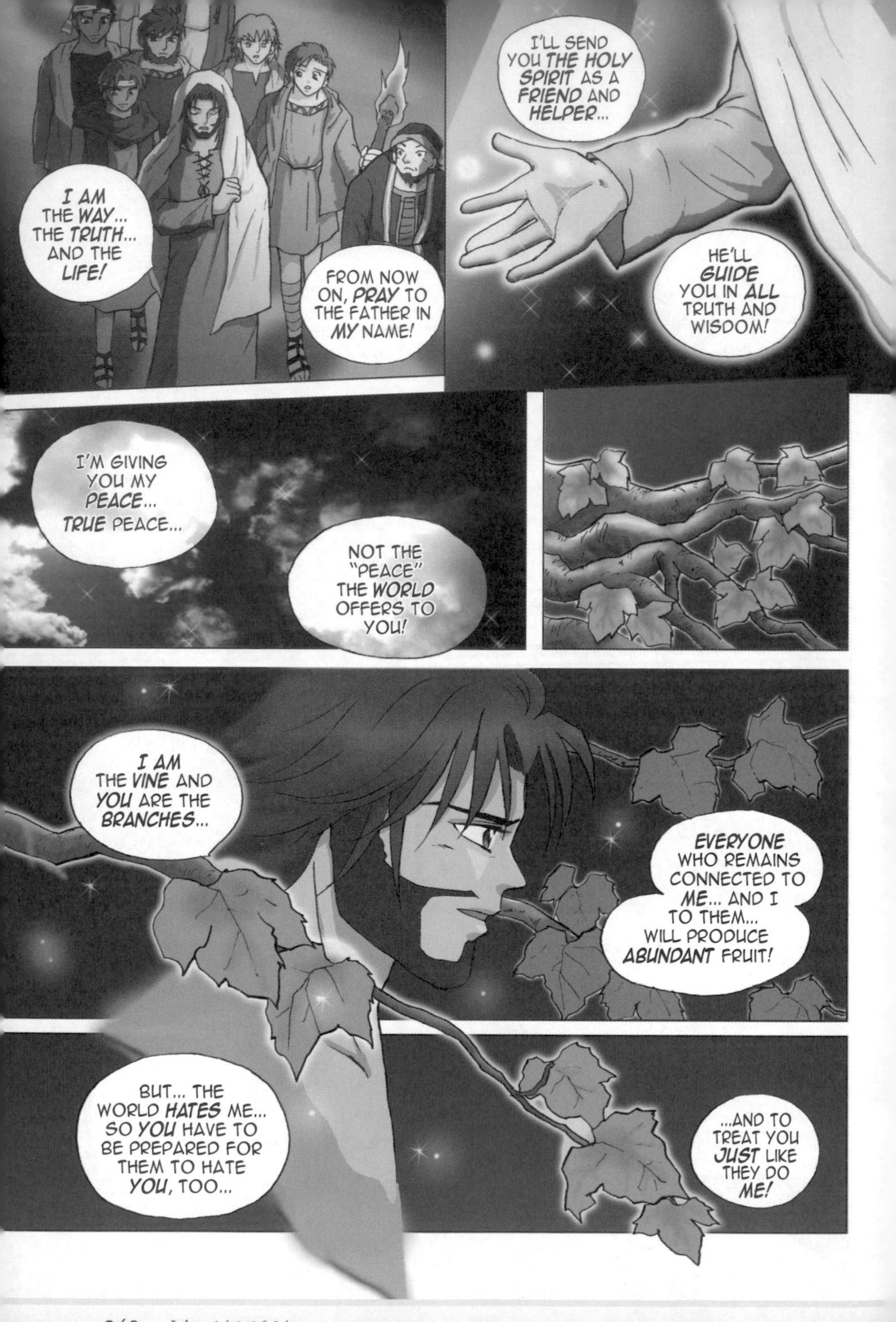
I AM THE WAY... THE TRUTH... AND THE LIFE!
FROM NOW ON, PRAY TO THE FATHER IN MY NAME!
I'LL SEND YOU THE HOLY SPIRIT AS A FRIEND AND HELPER...
HE'LL GUIDE YOU IN ALL TRUTH AND WISDOM!
I'M GIVING YOU MY PEACE... TRUE PEACE...
NOT THE "PEACE" THE WORLD OFFERS TO YOU!
I AM THE VINE AND YOU ARE THE BRANCHES...
EVERYONE WHO REMAINS CONNECTED TO ME... AND I TO THEM... WILL PRODUCE ABUNDANT FRUIT!
BUT... THE WORLD HATES ME... SO YOU HAVE TO BE PREPARED FOR THEM TO HATE YOU, TOO...
...AND TO TREAT YOU JUST LIKE THEY DO ME!

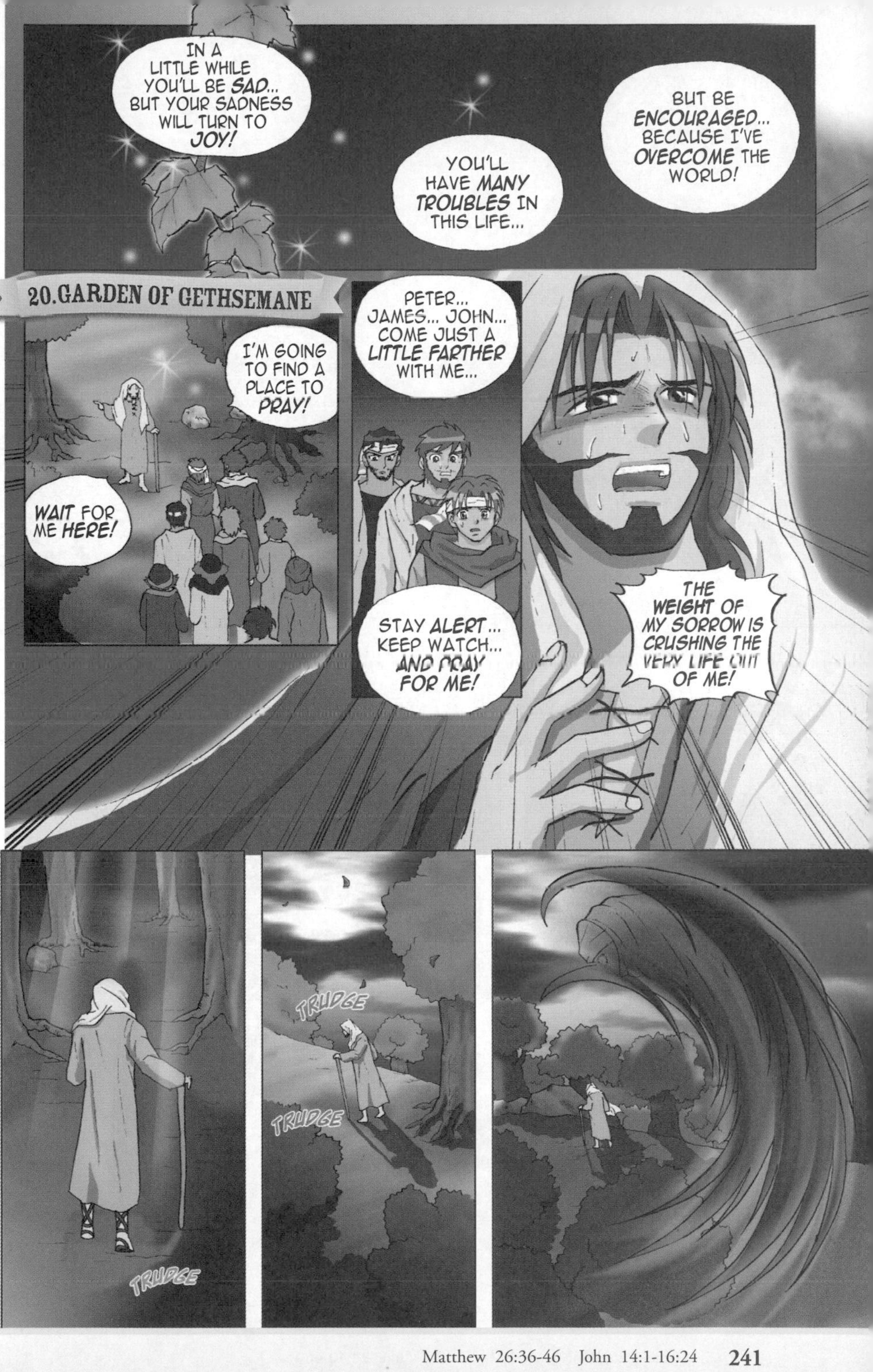
IN A LITTLE WHILE YOU'LL BE SAD... BUT YOUR SADNESS WILL TURN TO JOY!
YOU'LL HAVE MANY TROUBLES IN THIS LIFE...
BUT BE ENCOURAGED... BECAUSE I'VE OVERCOME THE WORLD!
20.GARDEN OF GETHSEMANE
I'M GOING TO FIND A PLACE TO PRAY!
WAIT FOR ME HERE!
PETER... JAMES... JOHN... COME JUST A LITTLE FARTHER WITH ME...
STAY ALERT... KEEP WATCH... AND PRAY FOR ME!
THE WEIGHT OF MY SORROW IS CRUSHING THE VERY LIFE OUT OF ME!
TRUDGE
TRUDGE
TRUDGE

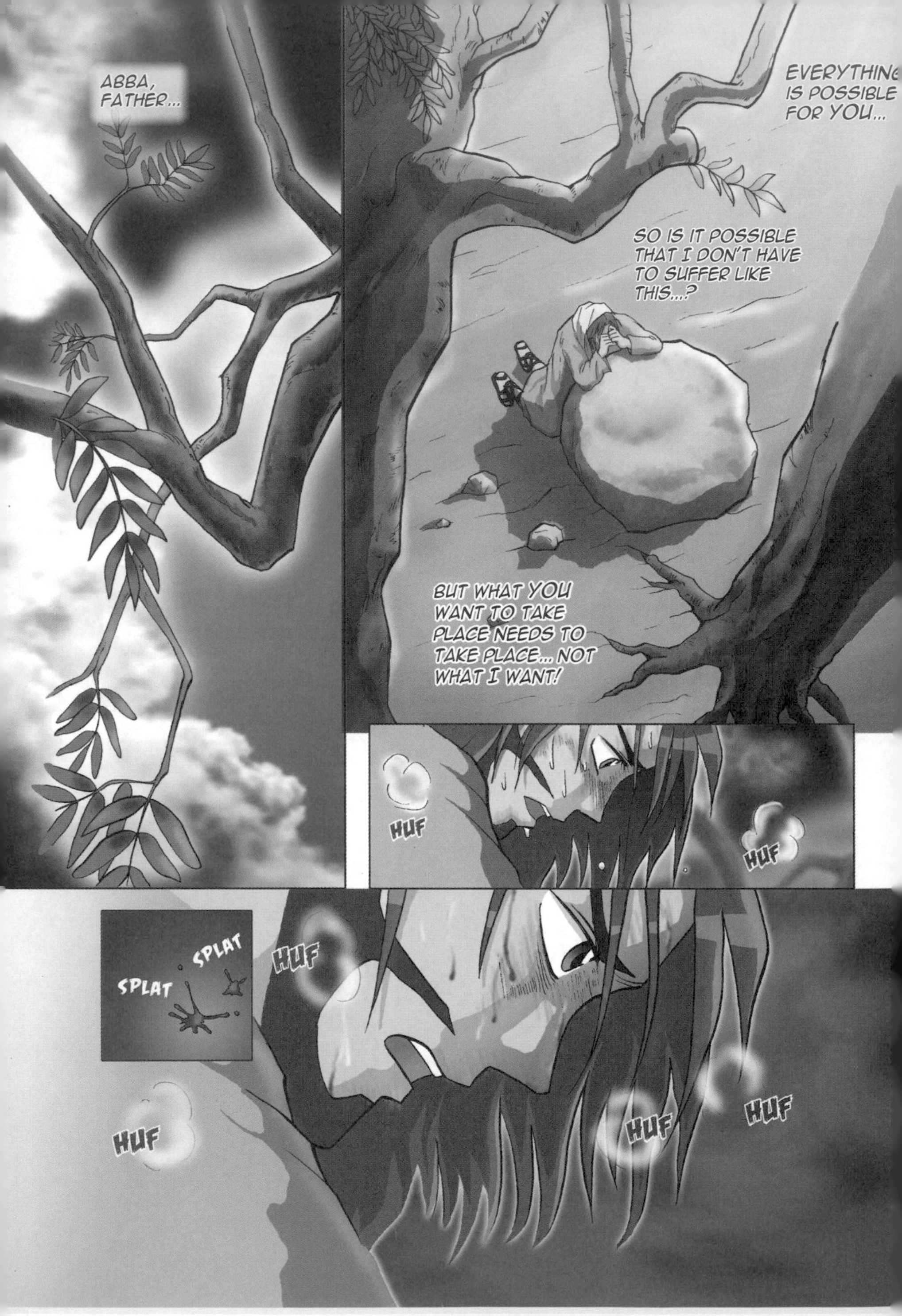

ABBA, FATHER...
EVERYTHING IS POSSIBLE FOR YOU...
SO IS IT POSSIBLE THAT I DON'T HAVE TO SUFFER LIKE THIS...?
BUT WHAT YOU WANT TO TAKE PLACE NEEDS TO TAKE PLACE... NOT WHAT I WANT!
HUF
HUF
SPLAT
SPLAT
HUF
HUF
HUF
HUF

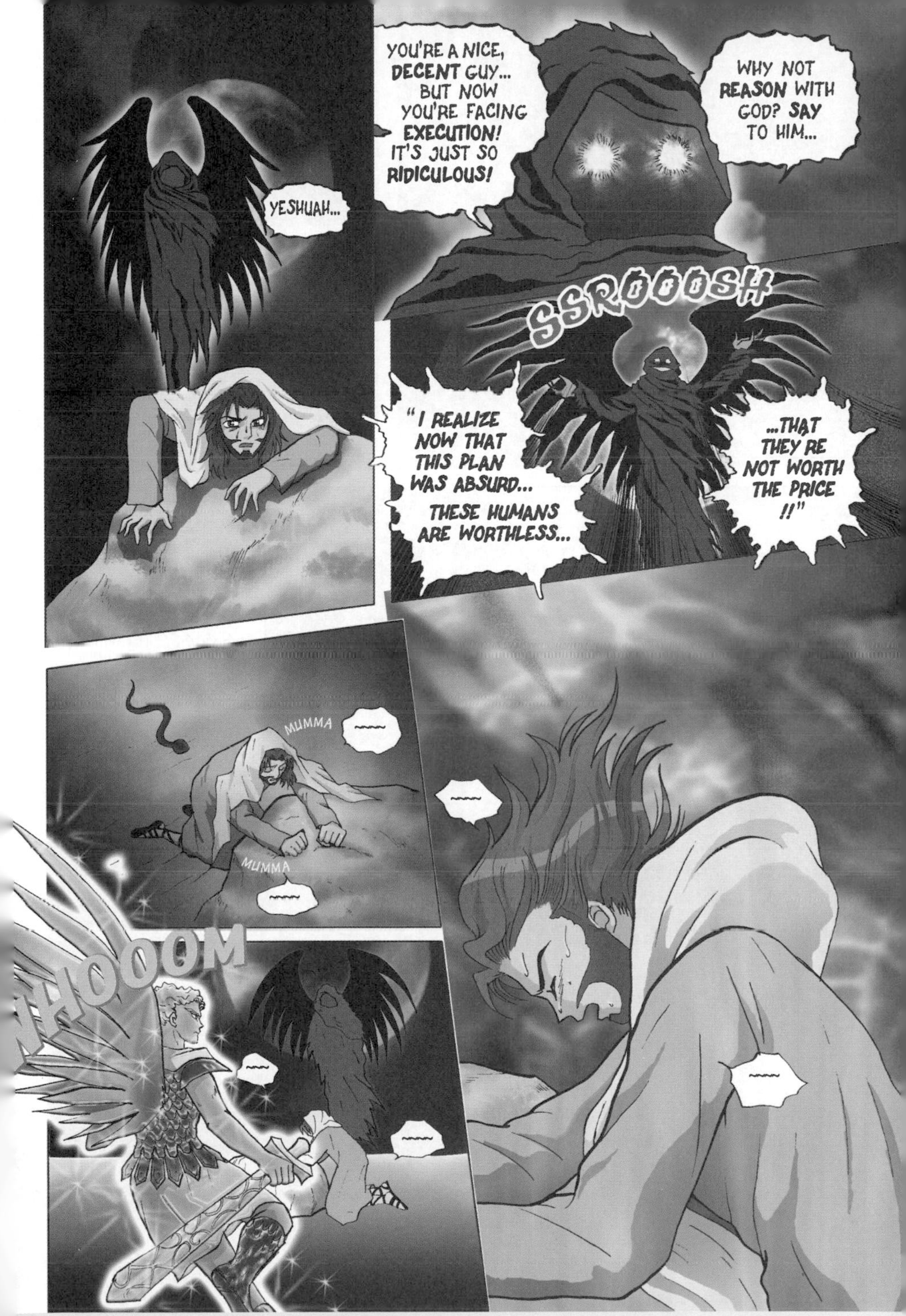
YESHUAH...
YOU'RE A NICE, DECENT GUY... BUT NOW YOU'RE FACING EXECUTION! IT'S JUST SO RIDICULOUS!
WHY NOT REASON WITH GOD? SAY TO HIM...
SSROOOOSH
"I REALIZE NOW THAT THIS PLAN WAS ABSURD... THESE HUMANS ARE WORTHLESS...
...THAT THEY RE NOT WORTH THE PRICE !!"
MUMMA
MUMMA
WHOOOM

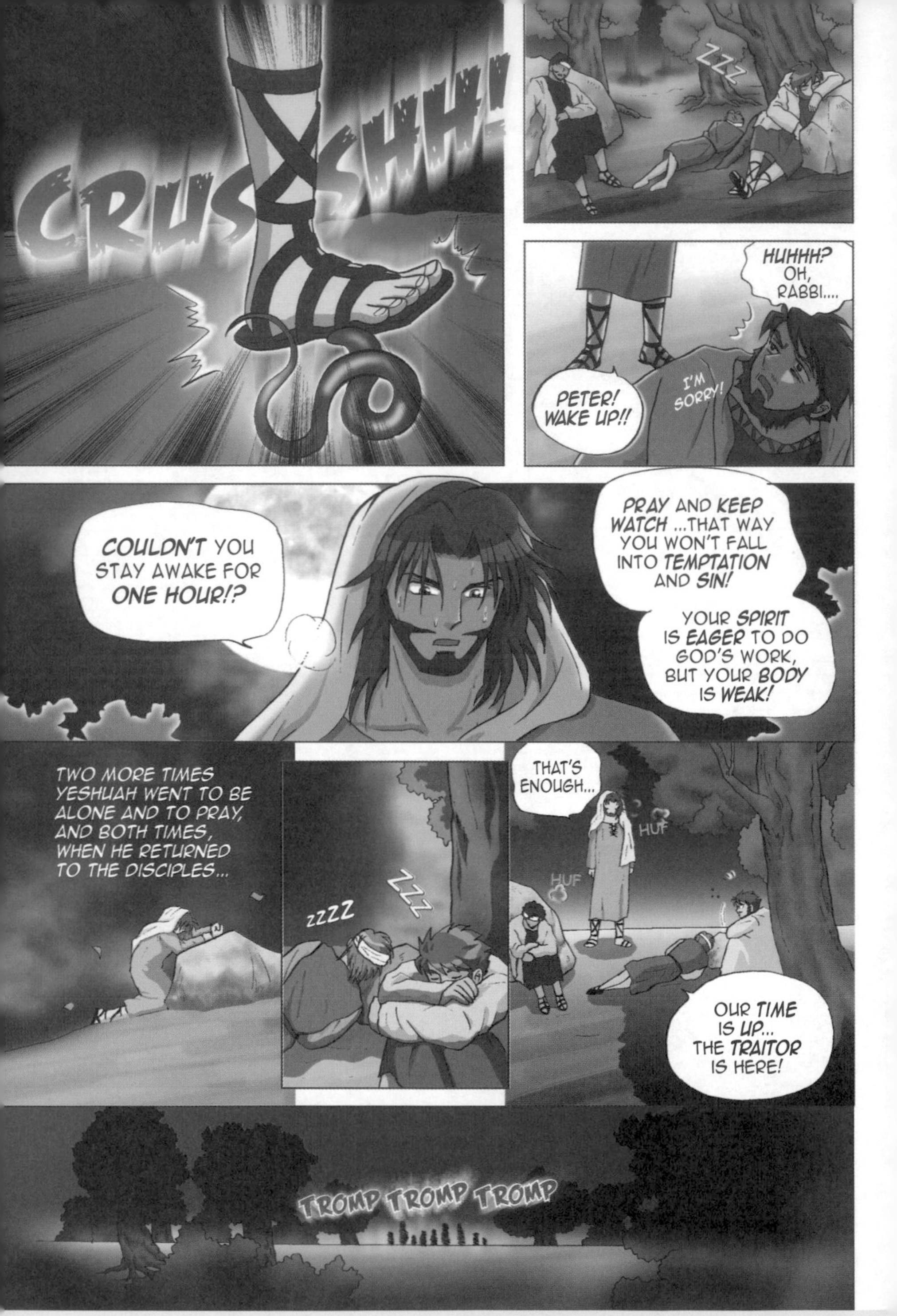
CRUSHHH!
ZZZ
HUHHH? OH, RABBI....
PETER! WAKE UP!!
I'M SORRY!
COULDN'T YOU STAY AWAKE FOR ONE HOUR!?
PRAY AND KEEP WATCH ...THAT WAY YOU WON'T FALL INTO TEMPTATION AND SIN!
YOUR SPIRIT IS EAGER TO DO GOD'S WORK, BUT YOUR BODY IS WEAK!
TWO MORE TIMES YESHUAH WENT TO BE ALONE AND TO PRAY, AND BOTH TIMES, WHEN HE RETURNED TO THE DISCIPLES...
zZZZ
ZZZ
THAT'S ENOUGH...
HUF
HUF
OUR TIME IS UP... THE TRAITOR IS HERE!
TROMP TROMP TROMP

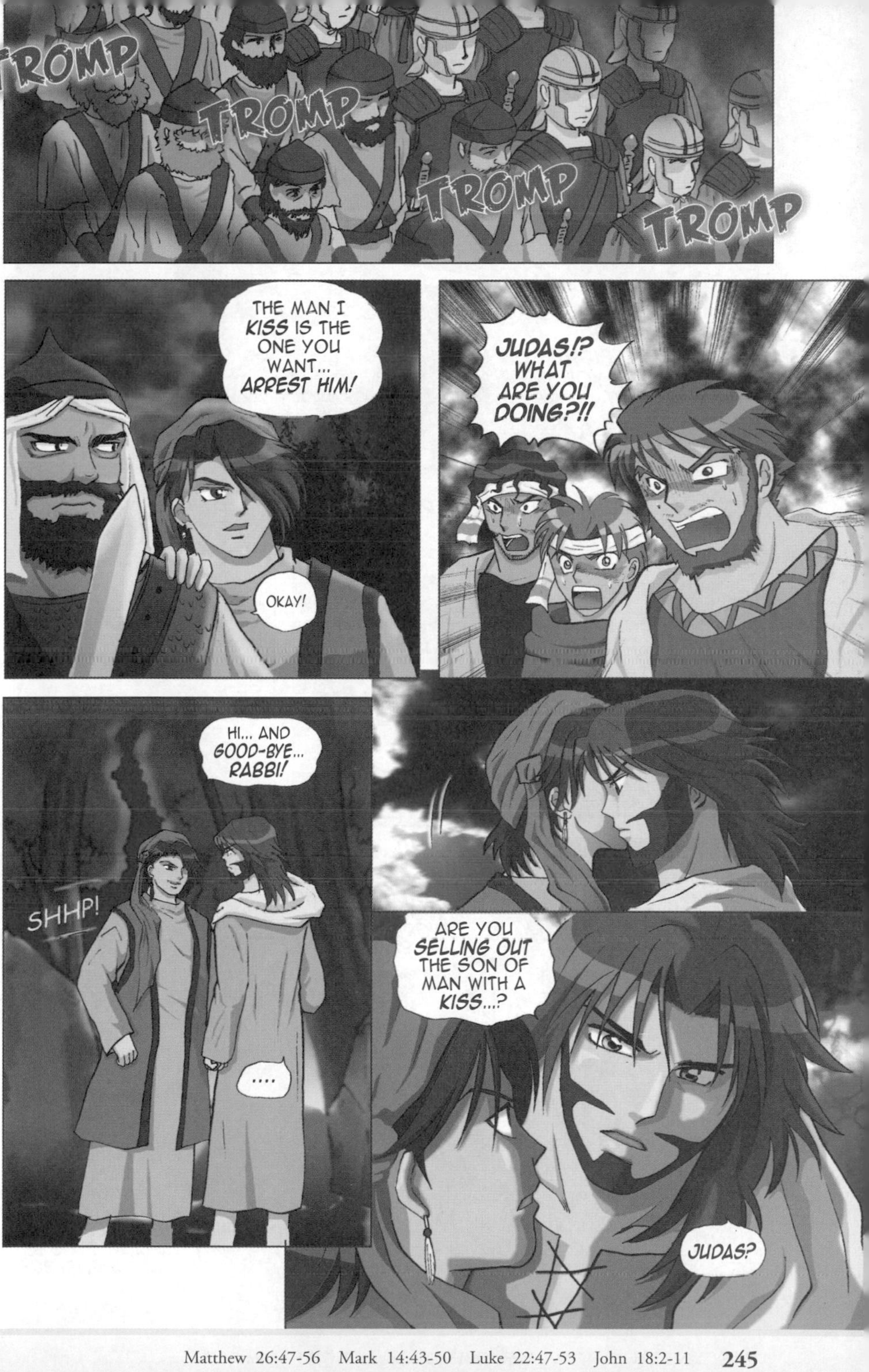
TROMP
TROMP
TROMP
TROMP
THE MAN I KISS IS THE ONE YOU WANT... ARREST HIM!
OKAY!
JUDAS!? WHAT ARE YOU DOING?!!
HI... AND GOOD-BYE... RABBI!
SHHP!
....
ARE YOU SELLING OUT THE SON OF MAN WITH A KISS...?
JUDAS?

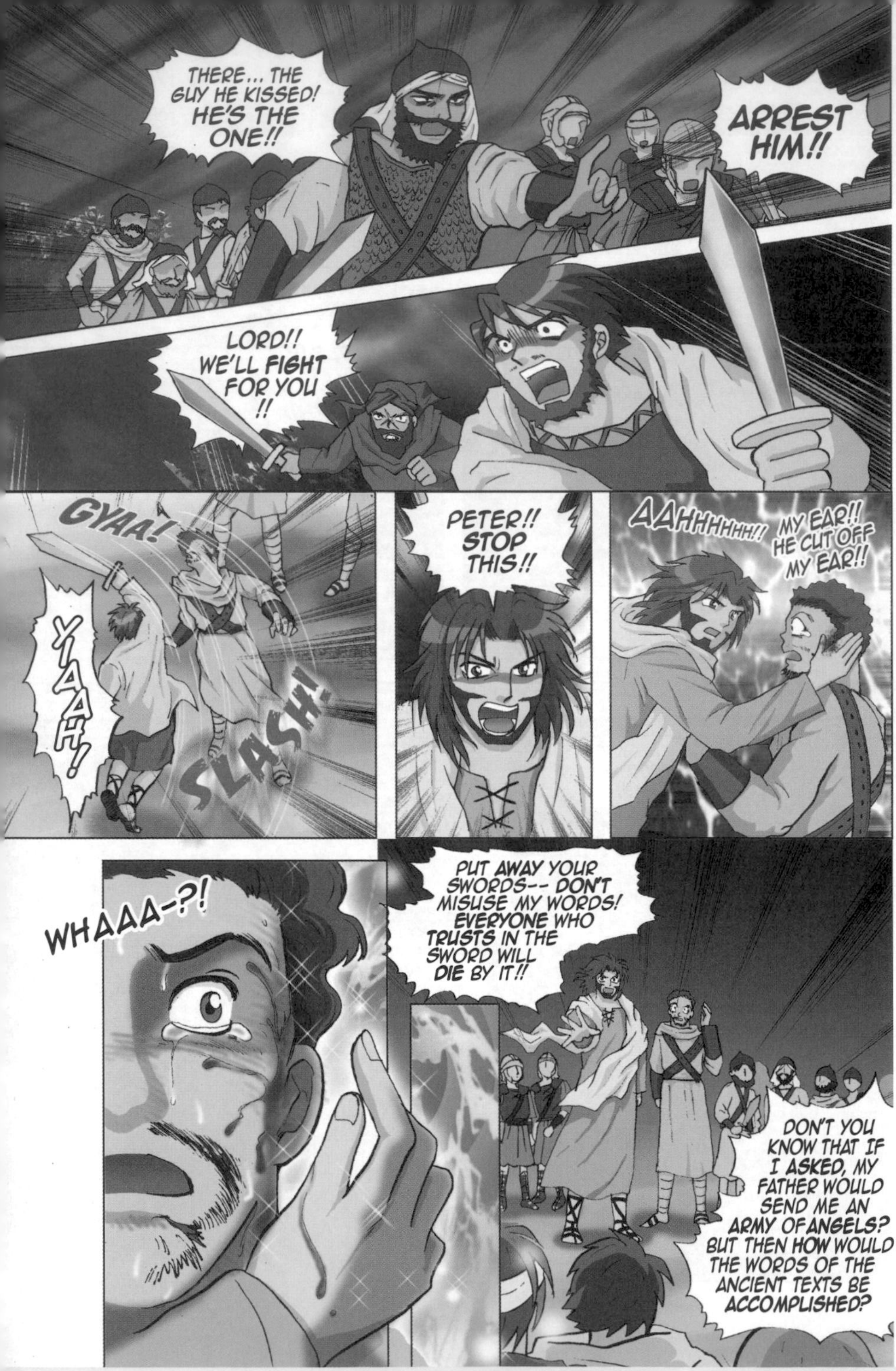
THERE... THE GUY HE KISSED! HE'S THE ONE!!
ARREST HIM!!
LORD!! WE'LL FIGHT FOR YOU !!
GYAA!
YIAAAH!
SLASH!
PETER!! STOP THIS!!
AAHHHHHHH!!
MY EAR!! HE CUT OFF MY EAR!!
WHAAA-?!
PUT AWAY YOUR SWORDS-- DON'T MISUSE MY WORDS! EVERYONE WHO TRUSTS IN THE SWORD WILL DIE BY IT!!
DON'T YOU KNOW THAT IF I ASKED, MY FATHER WOULD SEND ME AN ARMY OF ANGELS? BUT THEN HOW WOULD THE WORDS OF THE ANCIENT TEXTS BE ACCOMPLISHED?

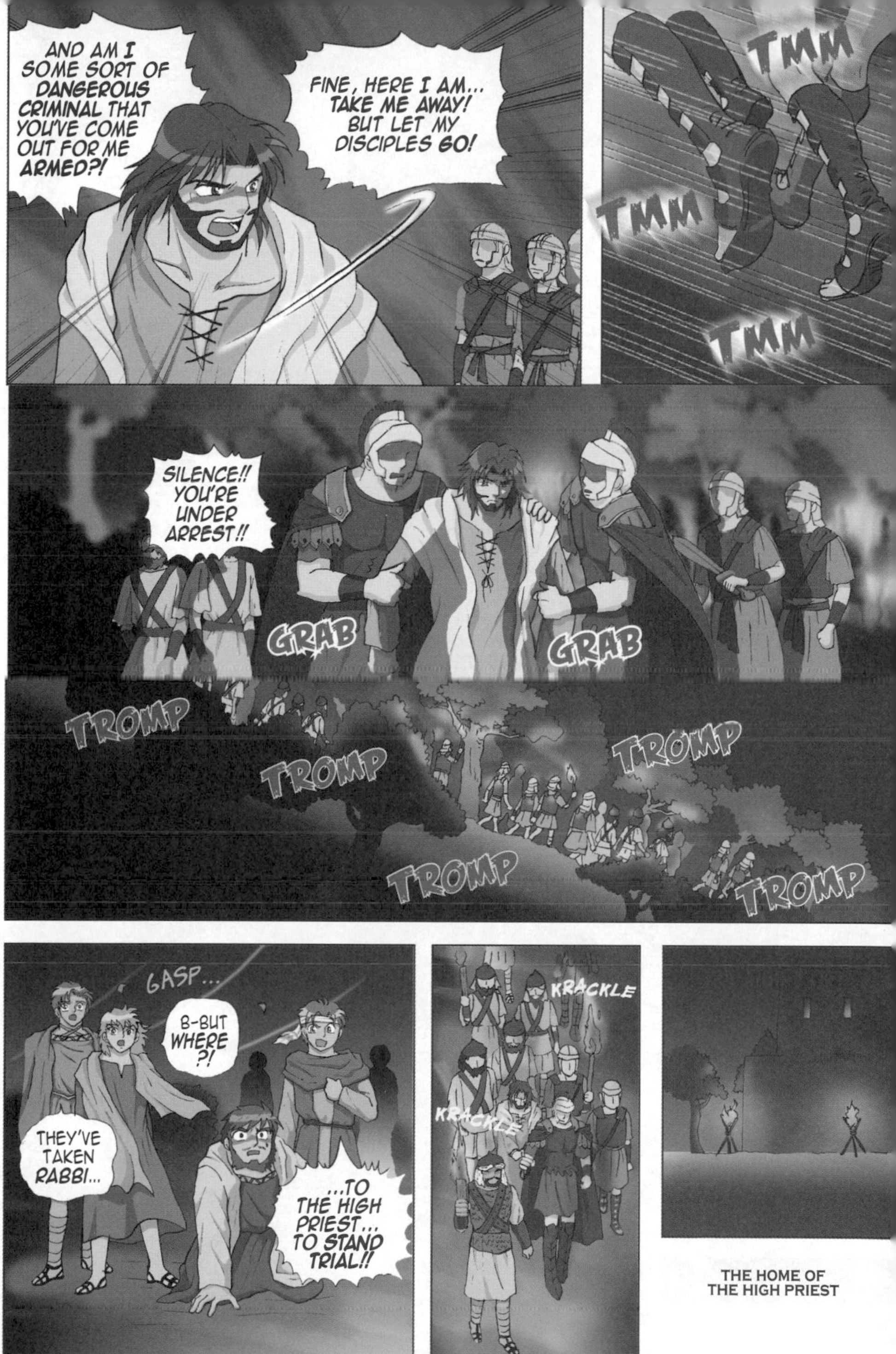
AND AM I SOME SORT OF DANGEROUS CRIMINAL THAT YOU'VE COME OUT FOR ME ARMED?!
FINE, HERE I AM... TAKE ME AWAY! BUT LET MY DISCIPLES GO!
TMM
TMM
TMM
SILENCE!! YOU'RE UNDER ARREST!!
GRAB
GRAB
TROMP
TROMP
TROMP
TROMP
TROMP
GASP...
B-BUT WHERE ?!
THEY'VE TAKEN RABBI...
...TO THE HIGH PRIEST... TO STAND TRIAL!!
KRACKLE
KRACKLE
THE HOME OF THE HIGH PRIEST

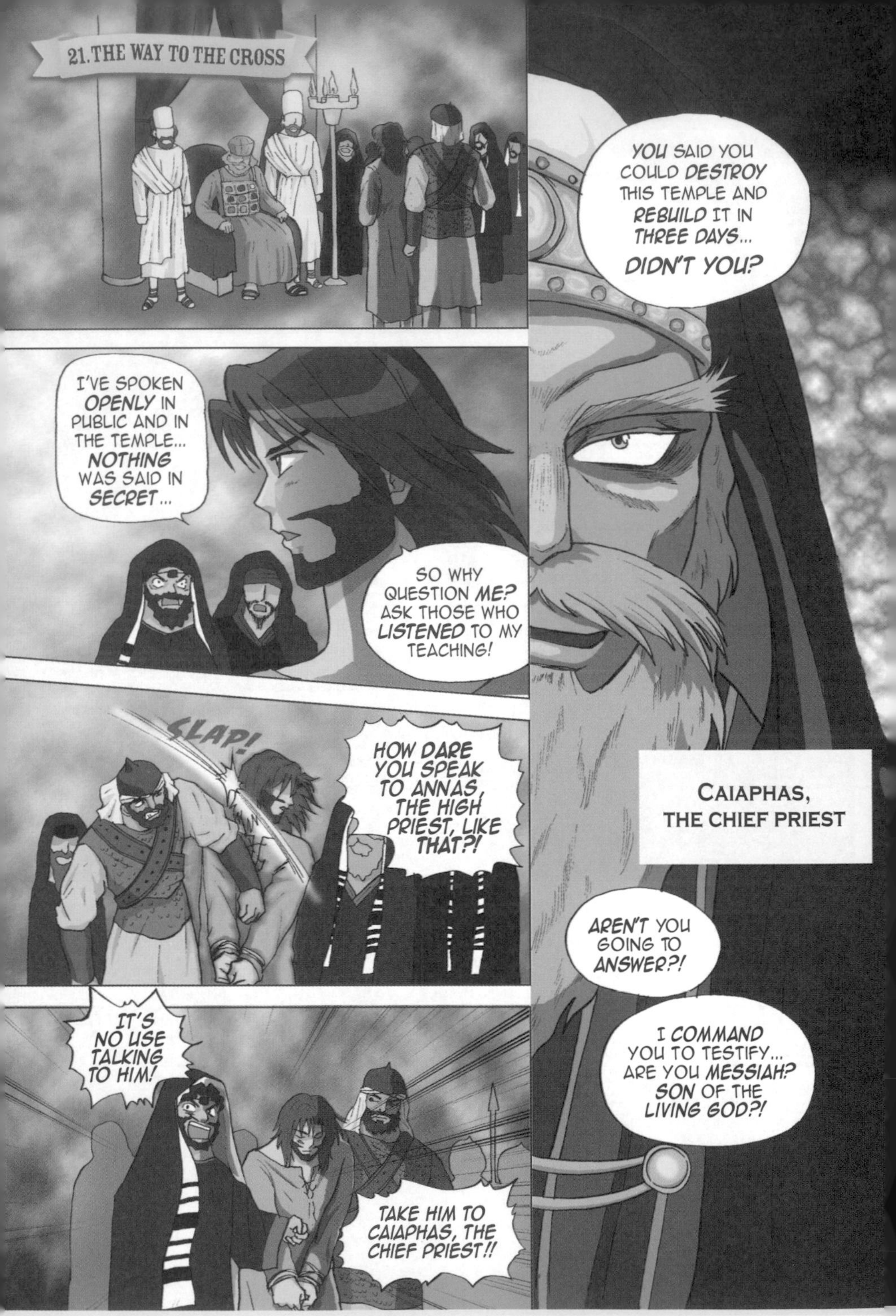
21. THE WAY TO THE CROSS
I'VE SPOKEN OPENLY IN PUBLIC AND IN THE TEMPLE... NOTHING WAS SAID IN SECRET...
SO WHY QUESTION ME? ASK THOSE WHO LISTENED TO MY TEACHING!
SLAP!
HOW DARE YOU SPEAK TO ANNAS, THE HIGH PRIEST, LIKE THAT?!
IT'S NO USE TALKING TO HIM!
TAKE HIM TO CAIAPHAS, THE CHIEF PRIEST!!
YOU SAID YOU COULD DESTROY THIS TEMPLE AND REBUILD IT IN THREE DAYS... DIDN'T YOU?
CAIAPHAS, THE CHIEF PRIEST
AREN'T YOU GOING TO ANSWER?!
I COMMAND YOU TO TESTIFY... ARE YOU MESSIAH? SON OF THE LIVING GOD?!

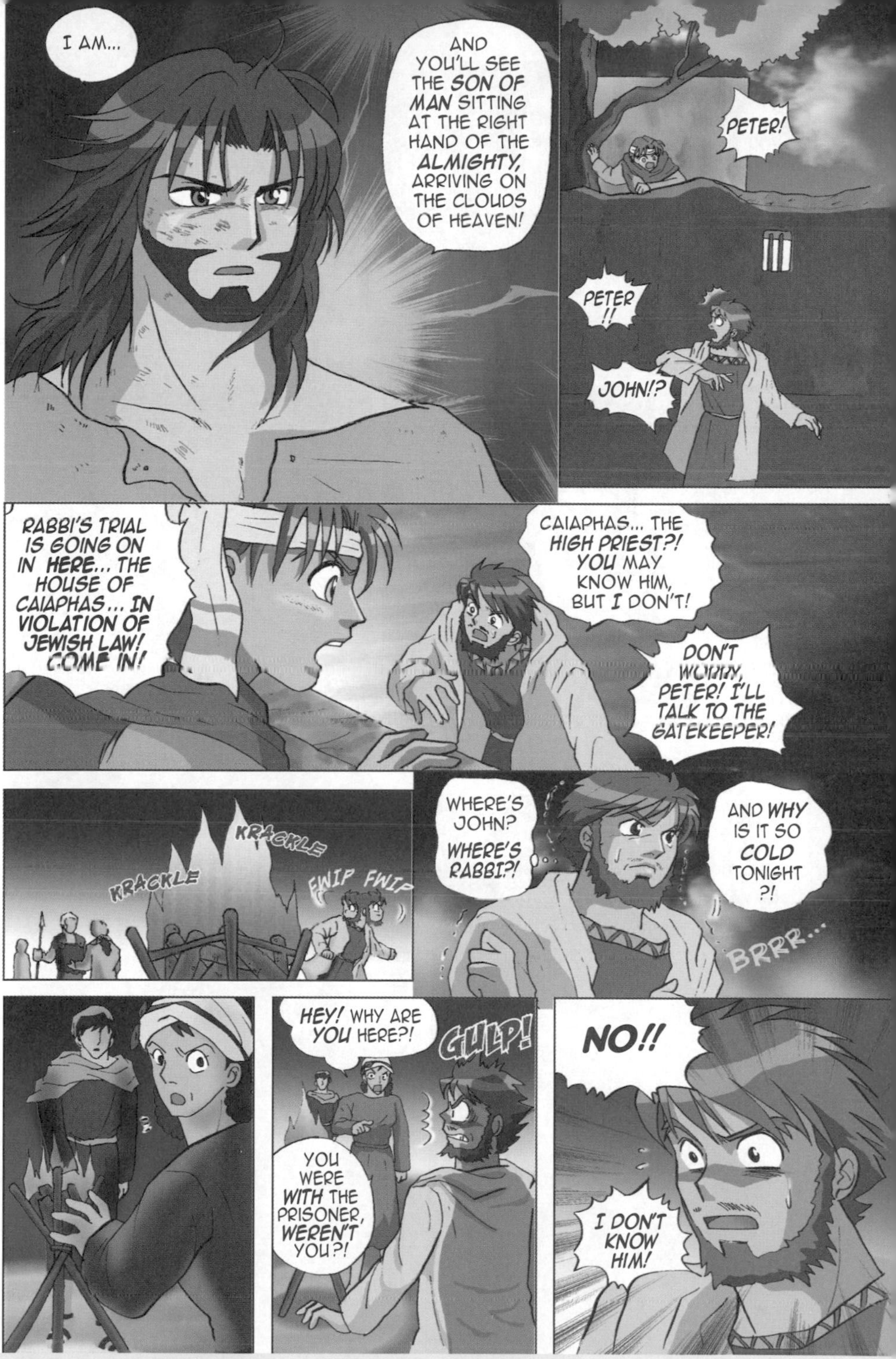
I AM...
AND YOU'LL SEE THE SON OF MAN SITTING AT THE RIGHT HAND OF THE ALMIGHTY, ARRIVING ON THE CLOUDS OF HEAVEN!
PETER!
PETER !!
JOHN!?
RABBI'S TRIAL IS GOING ON IN HERE... THE HOUSE OF CAIAPHAS... IN VIOLATION OF JEWISH LAW! COME IN!
CAIAPHAS... THE HIGH PRIEST?! YOU MAY KNOW HIM, BUT I DON'T!
DON'T WORRY, PETER! I'LL TALK TO THE GATEKEEPER!
KRACKLE
KRACKLE
FWIP FWIP
WHERE'S JOHN? WHERE'S RABBI?!
AND WHY IS IT SO COLD TONIGHT ?!
BRRR...
HEY! WHY ARE YOU HERE?!
GULP!
YOU WERE WITH THE PRISONER, WEREN'T YOU?!
NO!!
I DON'T KNOW HIM!

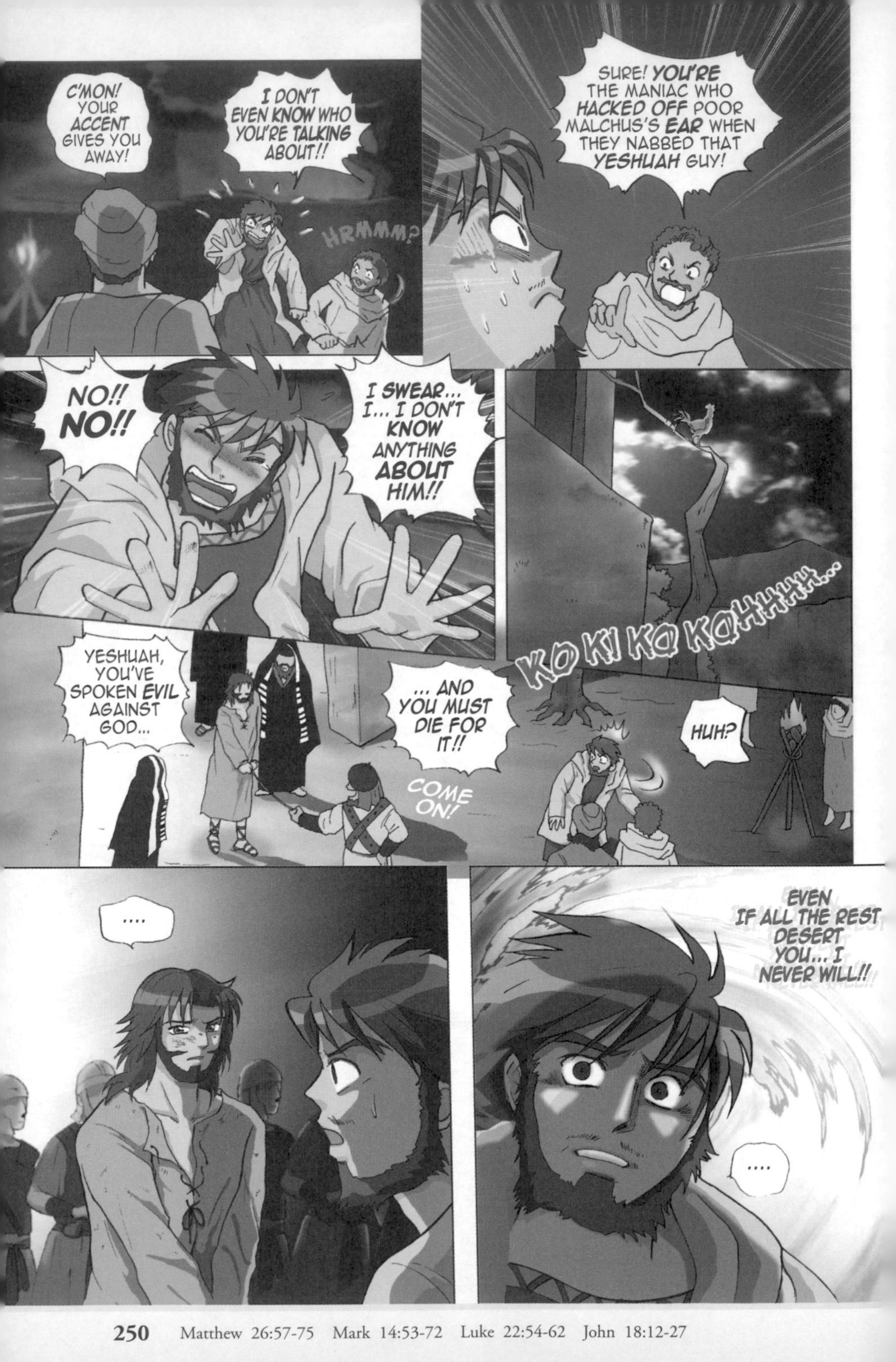
C'MON! YOUR ACCENT GIVES YOU AWAY!
I DON'T EVEN KNOW WHO YOU'RE TALKING ABOUT!!
HRMMM?
SURE! YOU'RE THE MANIAC WHO HACKED OFF POOR MALCHUS'S EAR WHEN THEY NABBED THAT YESHUAH GUY!
NO!! NO!!
I SWEAR... I... I DON'T KNOW ANYTHING ABOUT HIM!!
KO KI KO KOHHHH...
YESHUAH, YOU'VE SPOKEN EVIL AGAINST GOD...
... AND YOU MUST DIE FOR IT!!
COME ON!
HUH?
....
EVEN IF ALL THE REST DESERT YOU... I NEVER WILL!!
....

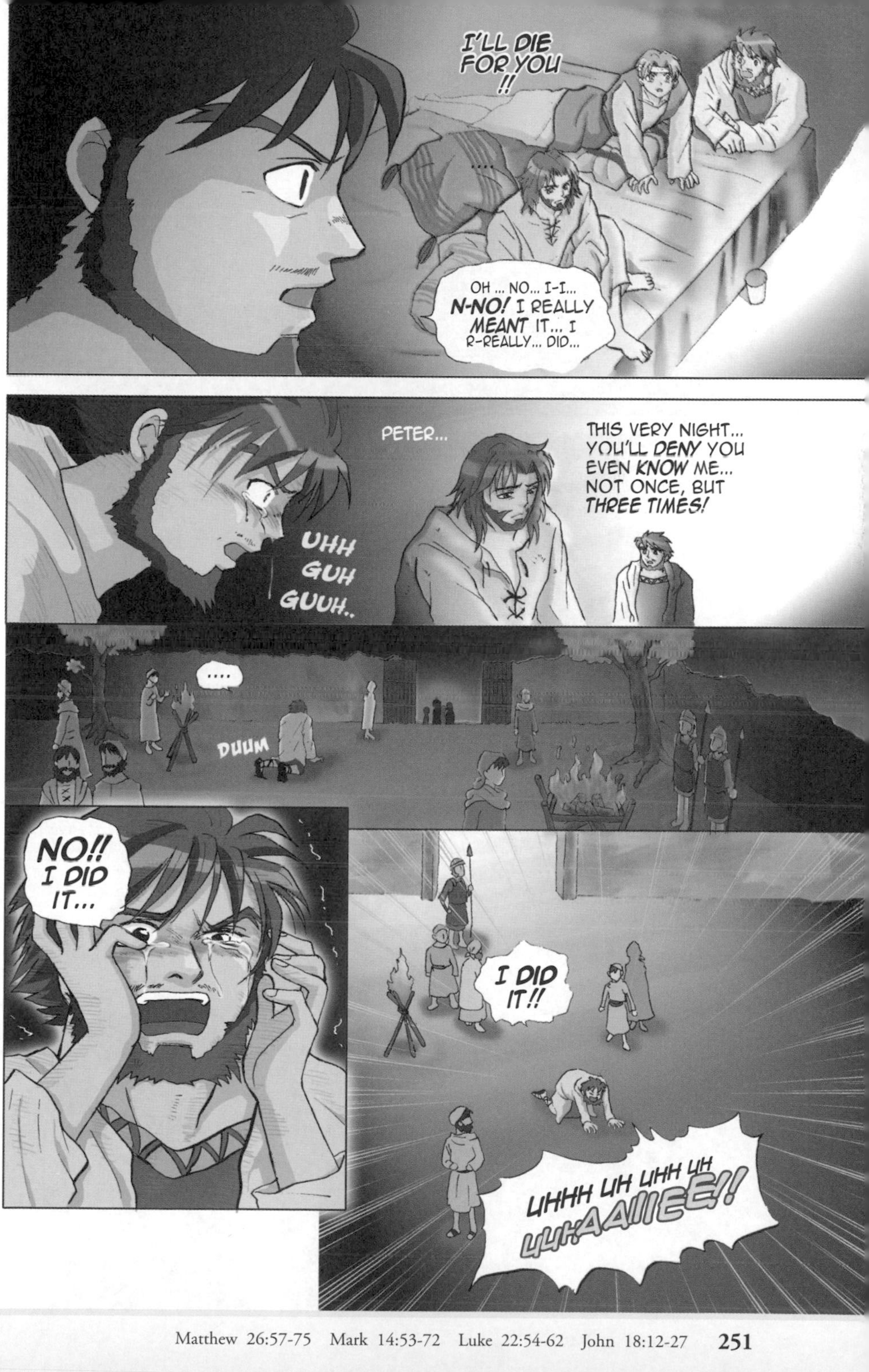
I'LL DIE FOR YOU !!
....
OH ... NO... I-I... N-NO! I REALLY MEANT IT... I R-REALLY... DID...
PETER...
THIS VERY NIGHT... YOU'LL DENY YOU EVEN KNOW ME... NOT ONCE, BUT THREE TIMES!
UHH GUH GUUH..
....
DUUM
NO!! I DID IT...
I DID IT!!
UHHH UH UHH UH UUHAAIIIEE!!

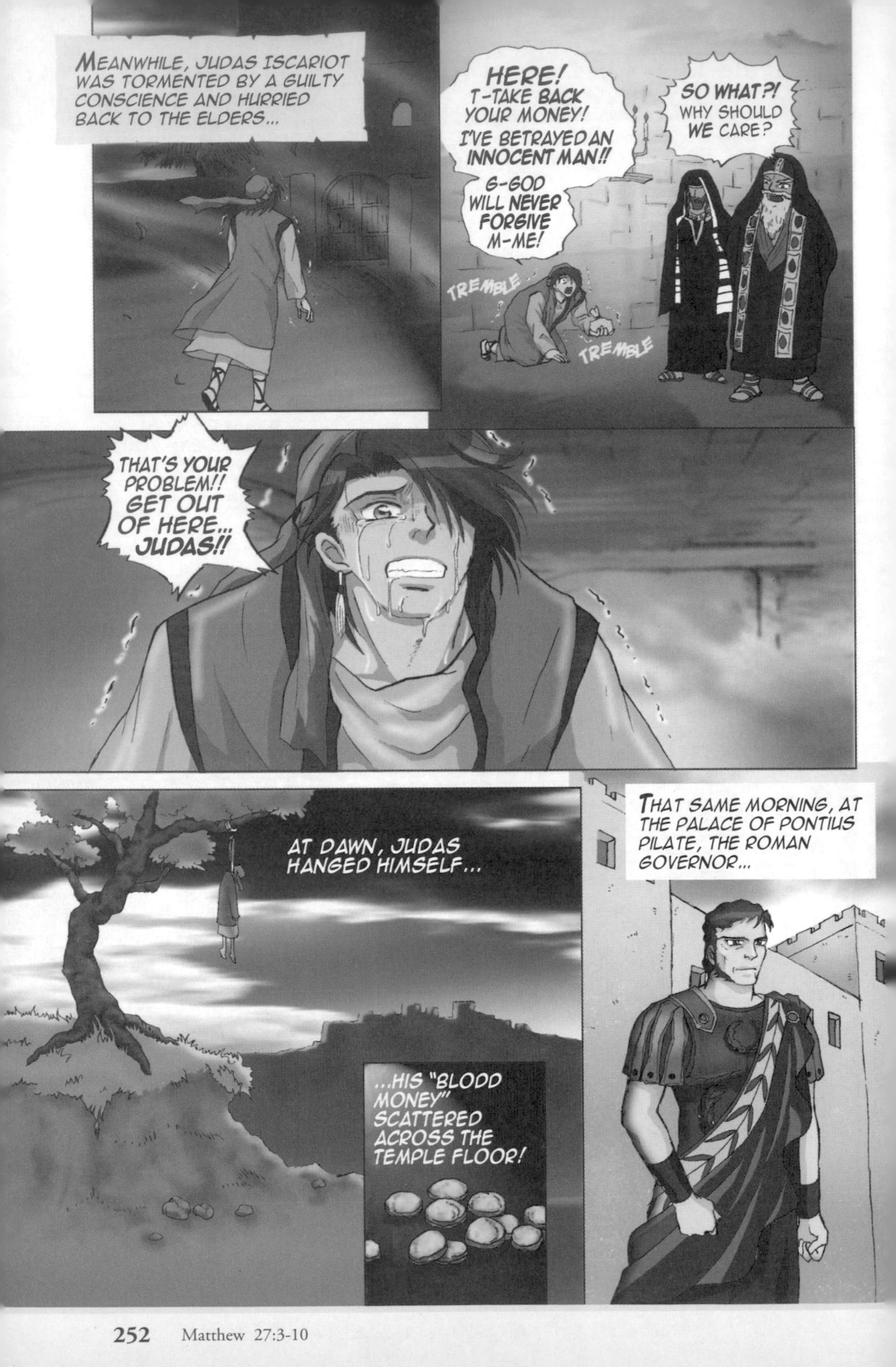
MEANWHILE, JUDAS ISCARIOT WAS TORMENTED BY A GUILTY CONSCIENCE AND HURRIED BACK TO THE ELDERS...
HERE! T-TAKE BACK YOUR MONEY! I'VE BETRAYED AN INNOCENT MAN!!
G-GOD WILL NEVER FORGIVE M-ME!
SO WHAT?! WHY SHOULD WE CARE?
TREMBLE
TREMBLE
THAT'S YOUR PROBLEM!! GET OUT OF HERE... JUDAS!!
AT DAWN, JUDAS HANGED HIMSELF...
...HIS "BLOOD MONEY" SCATTERED ACROSS THE TEMPLE FLOOR!
THAT SAME MORNING, AT THE PALACE OF PONTIUS PILATE, THE ROMAN GOVERNOR...

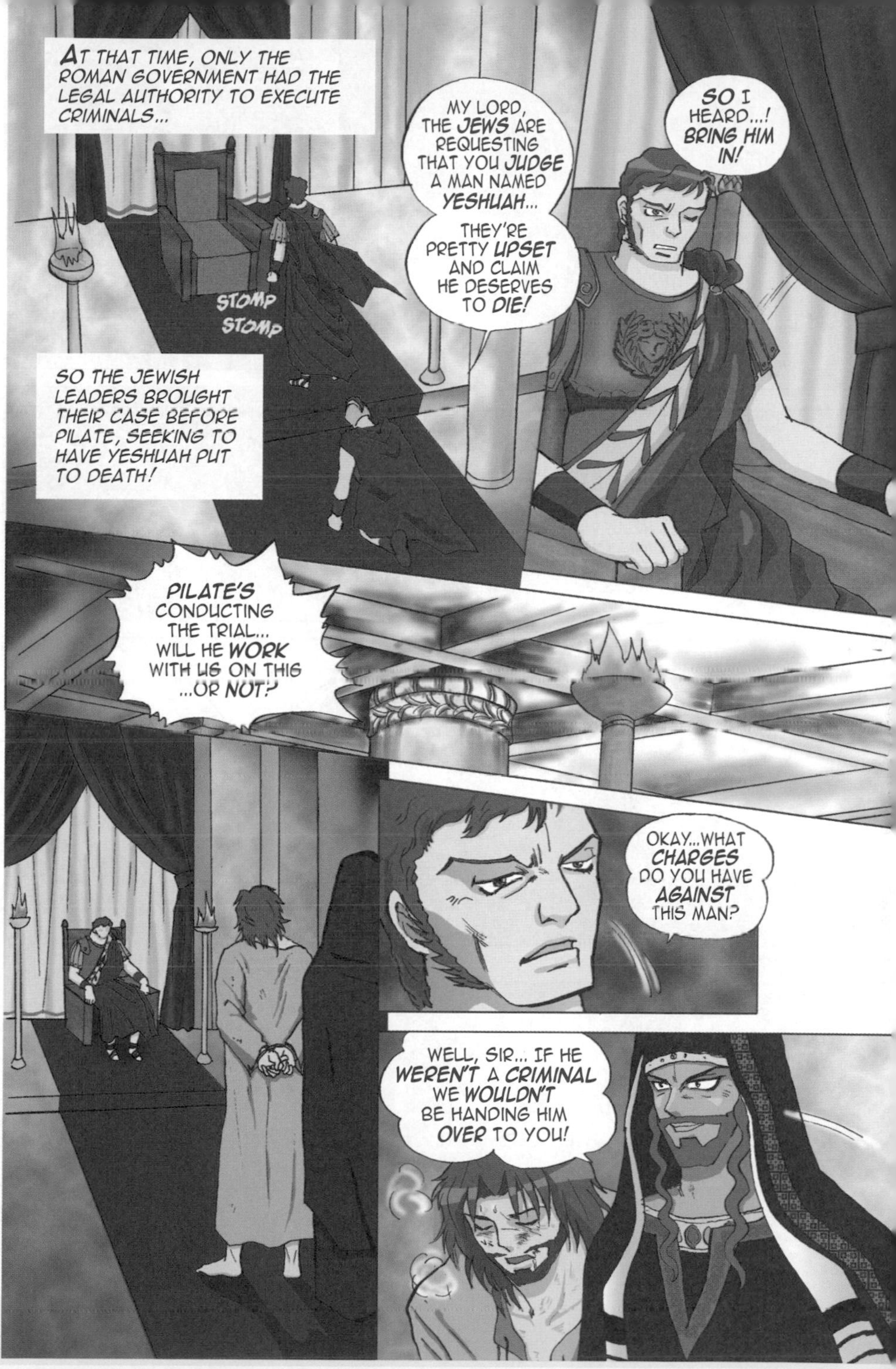
AT THAT TIME, ONLY THE ROMAN GOVERNMENT HAD THE LEGAL AUTHORITY TO EXECUTE CRIMINALS...
MY LORD, THE JEWS ARE REQUESTING THAT YOU JUDGE A MAN NAMED YESHUAH...
THEY'RE PRETTY UPSET AND CLAIM HE DESERVES TO DIE!
SO I HEARD...! BRING HIM IN!
STOMP
STOMP
SO THE JEWISH LEADERS BROUGHT THEIR CASE BEFORE PILATE, SEEKING TO HAVE YESHUAH PUT TO DEATH!
PILATE'S CONDUCTING THE TRIAL... WILL HE WORK WITH US ON THIS ...OR NOT?
OKAY...WHAT CHARGES DO YOU HAVE AGAINST THIS MAN?
WELL, SIR... IF HE WEREN'T A CRIMINAL WE WOULDN'T BE HANDING HIM OVER TO YOU!

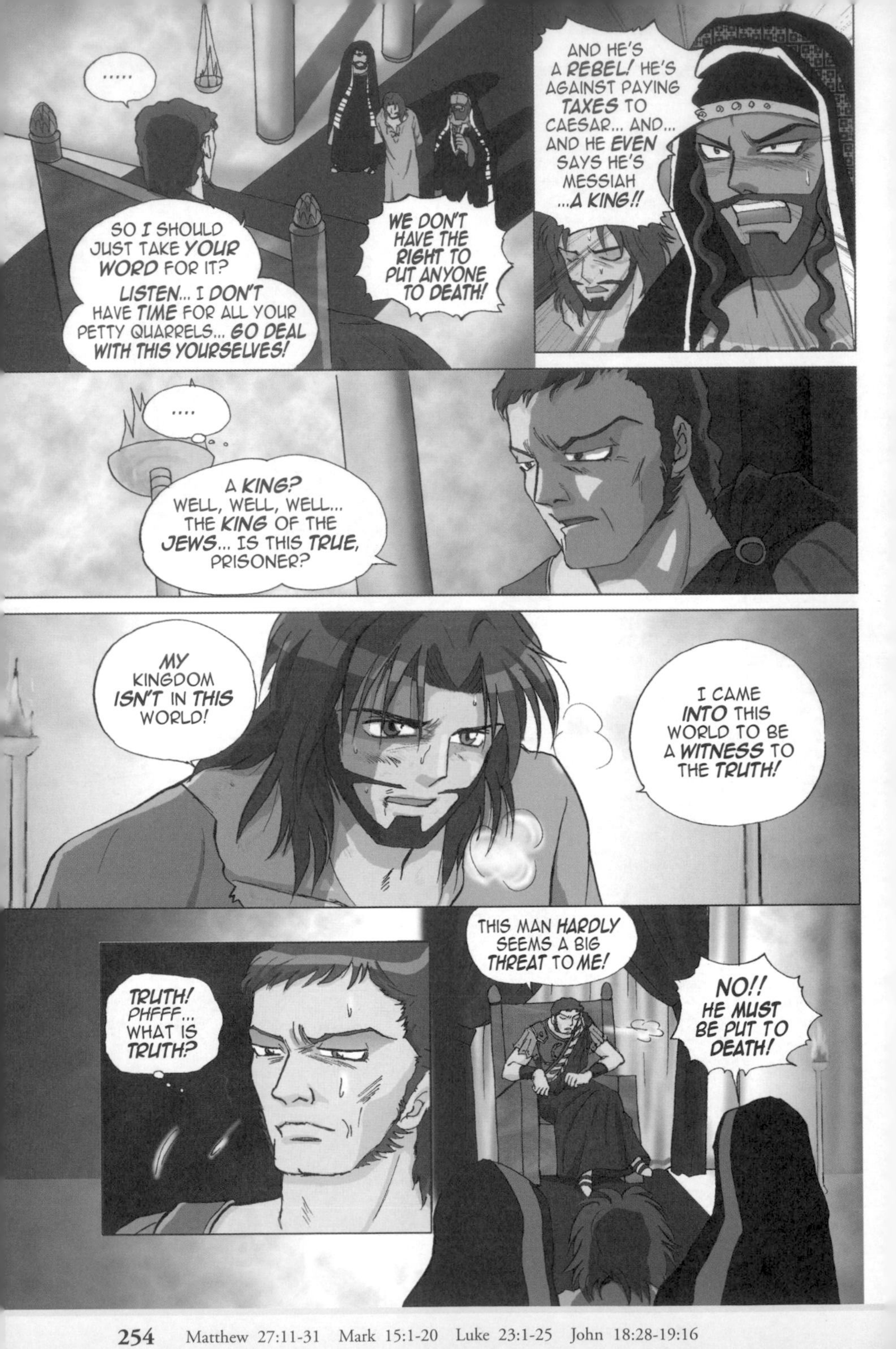
......
SO I SHOULD JUST TAKE YOUR WORD FOR IT? LISTEN... I DON'T HAVE TIME FOR ALL YOUR PETTY QUARRELS... GO DEAL WITH THIS YOURSELVES!
WE DON'T HAVE THE RIGHT TO PUT ANYONE TO DEATH!
AND HE'S A REBEL! HE'S AGAINST PAYING TAXES TO CAESAR... AND... AND HE EVEN SAYS HE'S MESSIAH ...A KING!!
....
A KING? WELL, WELL, WELL... THE KING OF THE JEWS... IS THIS TRUE, PRISONER?
MY KINGDOM ISN'T IN THIS WORLD!
I CAME INTO THIS WORLD TO BE A WITNESS TO THE TRUTH!
TRUTH! PHFFF... WHAT IS TRUTH?
THIS MAN HARDLY SEEMS A BIG THREAT TO ME!
NO!! HE MUST BE PUT TO DEATH!

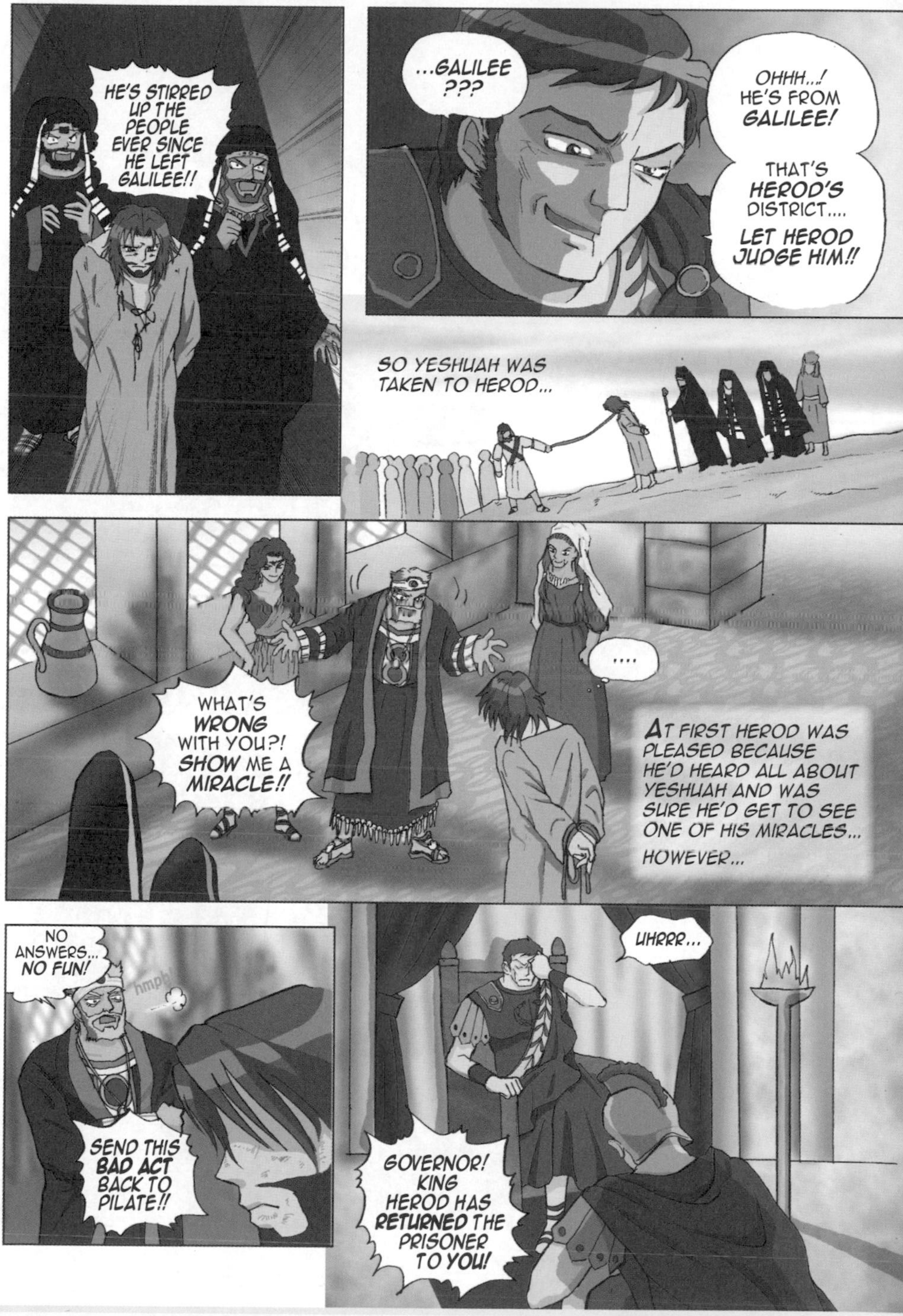
HE'S STIRRED UP THE PEOPLE EVER SINCE HE LEFT GALILEE!!
...GALILEE ???
OHHH...! HE'S FROM GALILEE!
THAT'S HEROD'S DISTRICT....
LET HEROD JUDGE HIM!!
SO YESHUAH WAS TAKEN TO HEROD...
WHAT'S WRONG WITH YOU?! SHOW ME A MIRACLE!!
....
AT FIRST HEROD WAS PLEASED BECAUSE HE'D HEARD ALL ABOUT YESHUAH AND WAS SURE HE'D GET TO SEE ONE OF HIS MIRACLES...
HOWEVER...
NO ANSWERS... NO FUN!
hmph!
SEND THIS BAD ACT BACK TO PILATE!!
UHRRR...
GOVERNOR! KING HEROD HAS RETURNED THE PRISONER TO YOU!

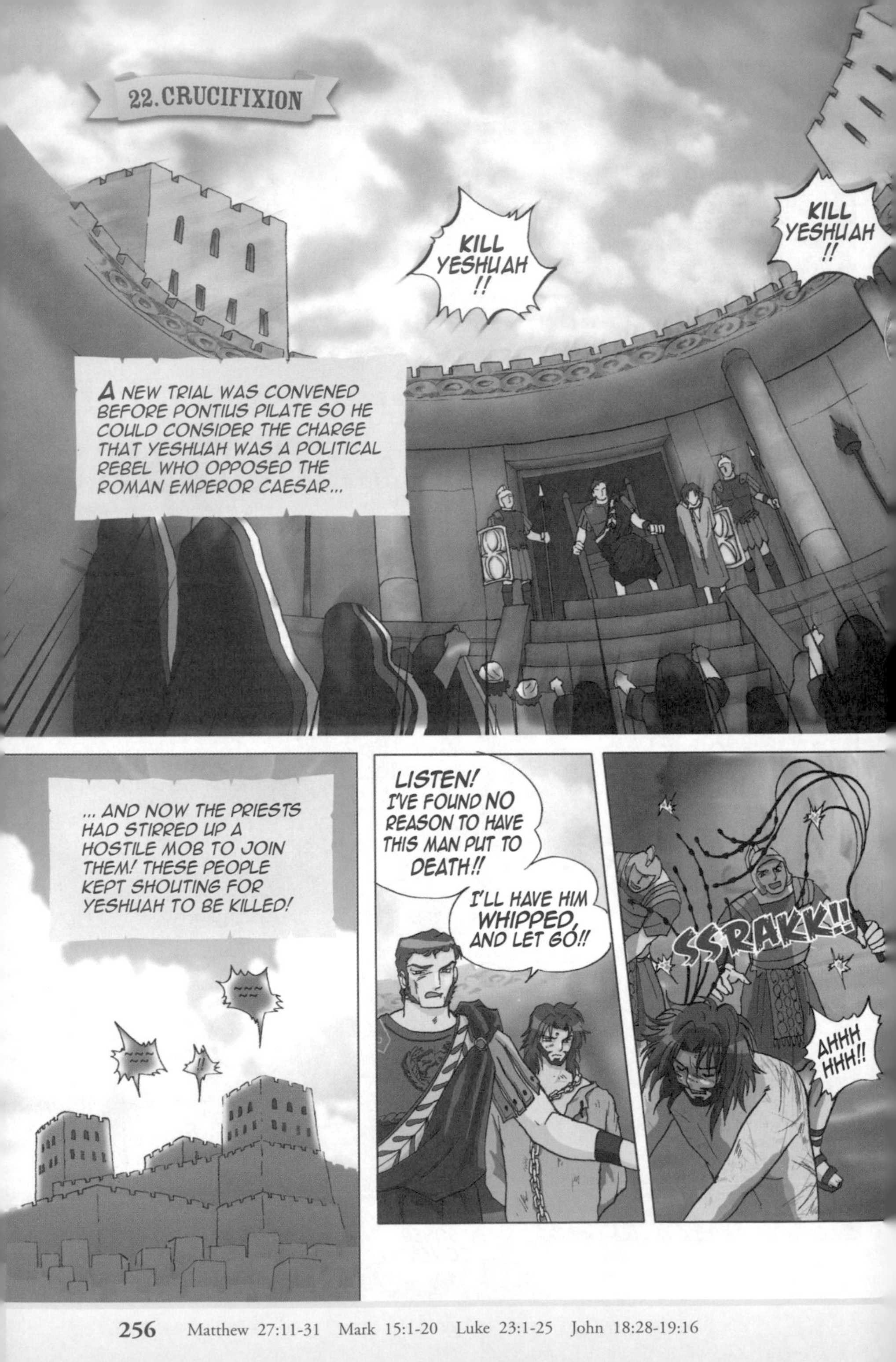
22. CRUCIFIXION
KILL YESHUAH !!
KILL YESHUAH !!
A NEW TRIAL WAS CONVENED BEFORE PONTIUS PILATE SO HE COULD CONSIDER THE CHARGE THAT YESHUAH WAS A POLITICAL REBEL WHO OPPOSED THE ROMAN EMPEROR CAESAR...
... AND NOW THE PRIESTS HAD STIRRED UP A HOSTILE MOB TO JOIN THEM! THESE PEOPLE KEPT SHOUTING FOR YESHUAH TO BE KILLED!
~~~ ~~
~~~ ~~
!!
LISTEN! I'VE FOUND NO REASON TO HAVE THIS MAN PUT TO DEATH!!
I'LL HAVE HIM WHIPPED, AND LET GO!!
SSRAKK!!
AHHH HHH!!

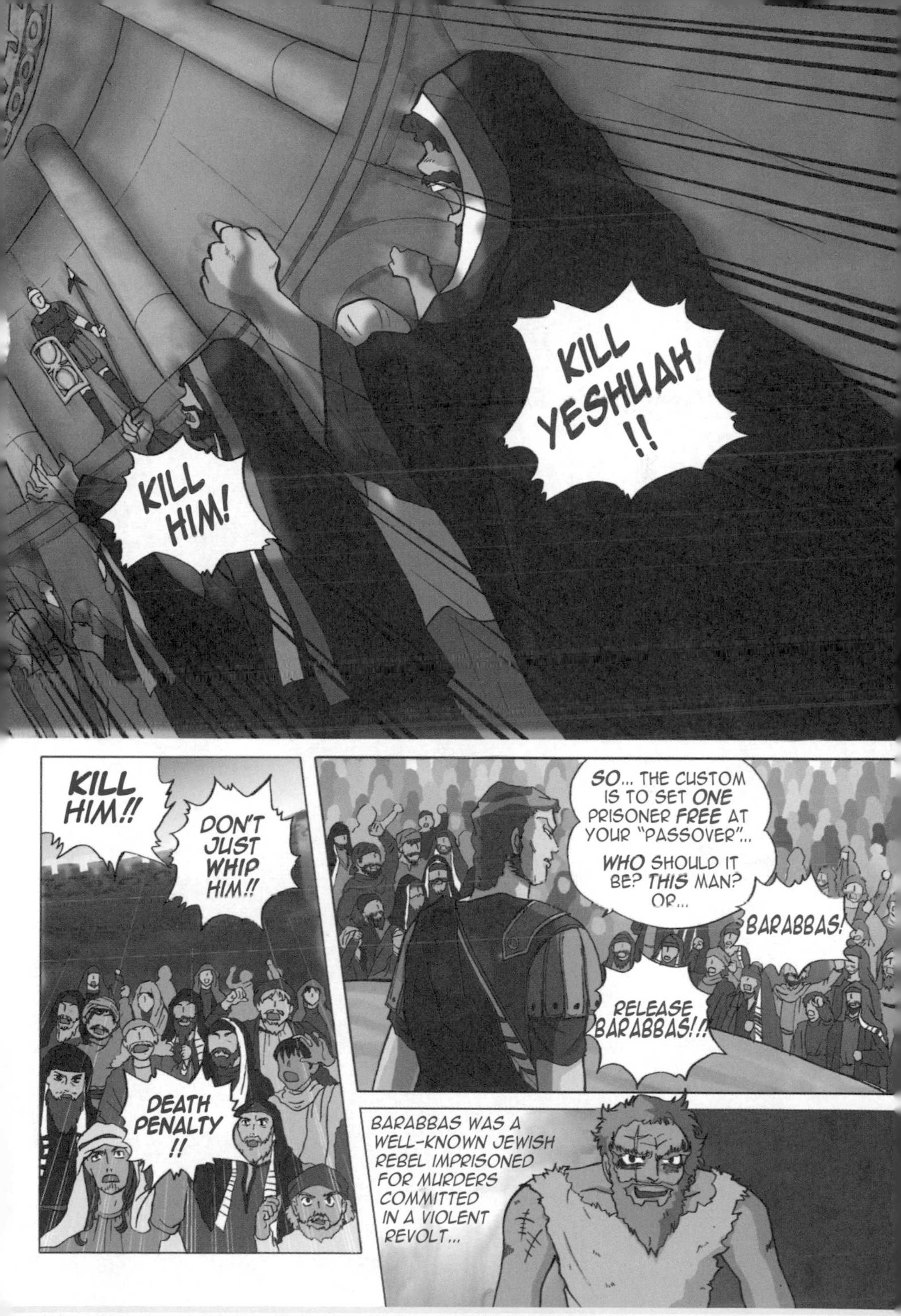
KILL YESHUAH !!
KILL HIM!
KILL HIM!!
DON'T JUST WHIP HIM!!
DEATH PENALTY !!
SO... THE CUSTOM IS TO SET ONE PRISONER FREE AT YOUR "PASSOVER"...
WHO SHOULD IT BE? THIS MAN? OR...
BARABBAS!
RELEASE BARABBAS!!
BARABBAS WAS A WELL-KNOWN JEWISH REBEL IMPRISONED FOR MURDERS COMMITTED IN A VIOLENT REVOLT...

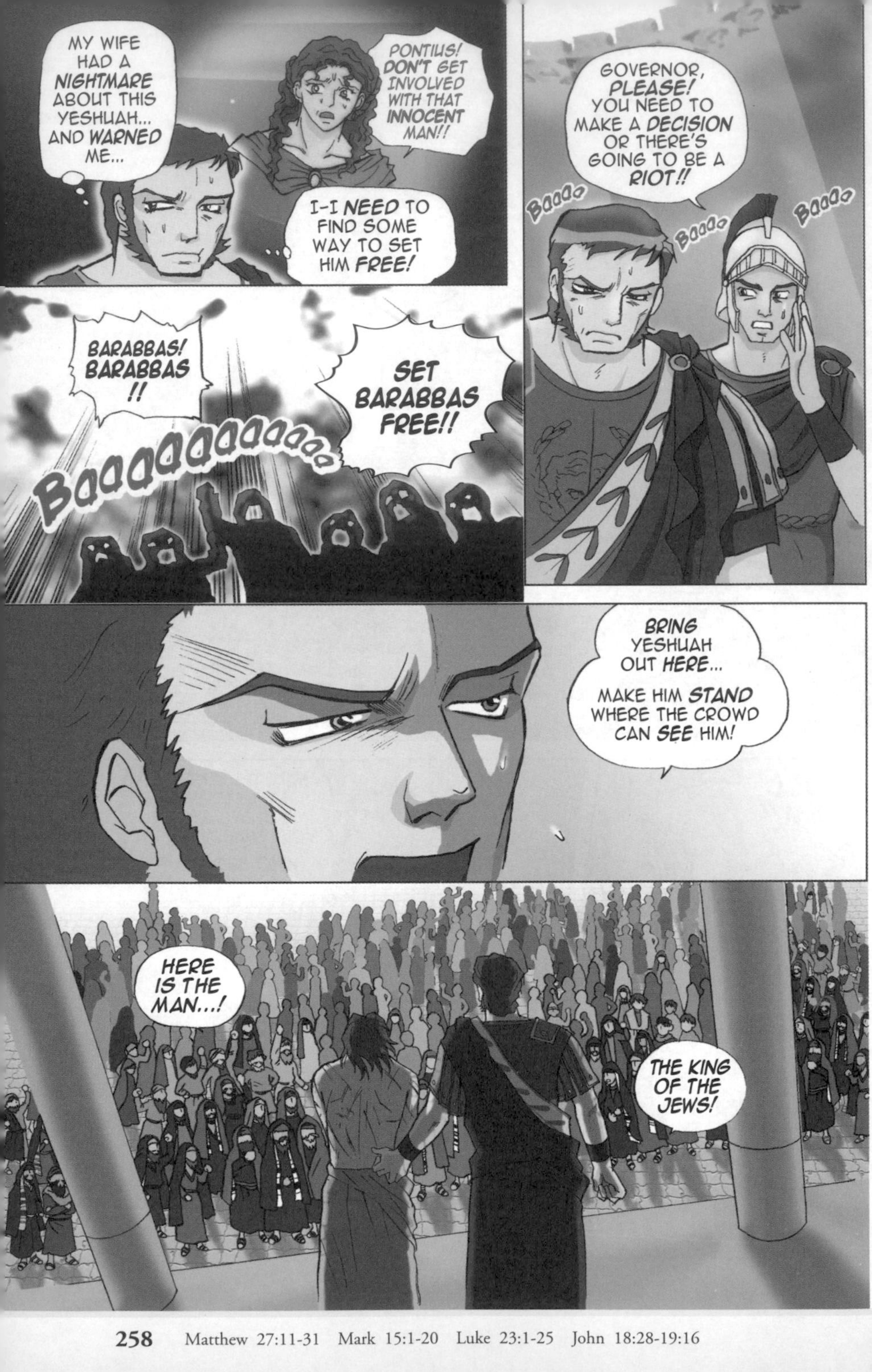
MY WIFE HAD A NIGHTMARE ABOUT THIS YESHUAH... AND WARNED ME...
PONTIUS! DON'T GET INVOLVED WITH THAT INNOCENT MAN!!
I-I NEED TO FIND SOME WAY TO SET HIM FREE!
GOVERNOR, PLEASE! YOU NEED TO MAKE A DECISION OR THERE'S GOING TO BE A RIOT!!
Baaaa
Baaaa
Baaaa
BARABBAS! BARABBAS!!
SET BARABBAS FREE!!
Baaaaaaaaaaa
BRING YESHUAH OUT HERE...
MAKE HIM STAND WHERE THE CROWD CAN SEE HIM!
HERE IS THE MAN...!
THE KING OF THE JEWS!

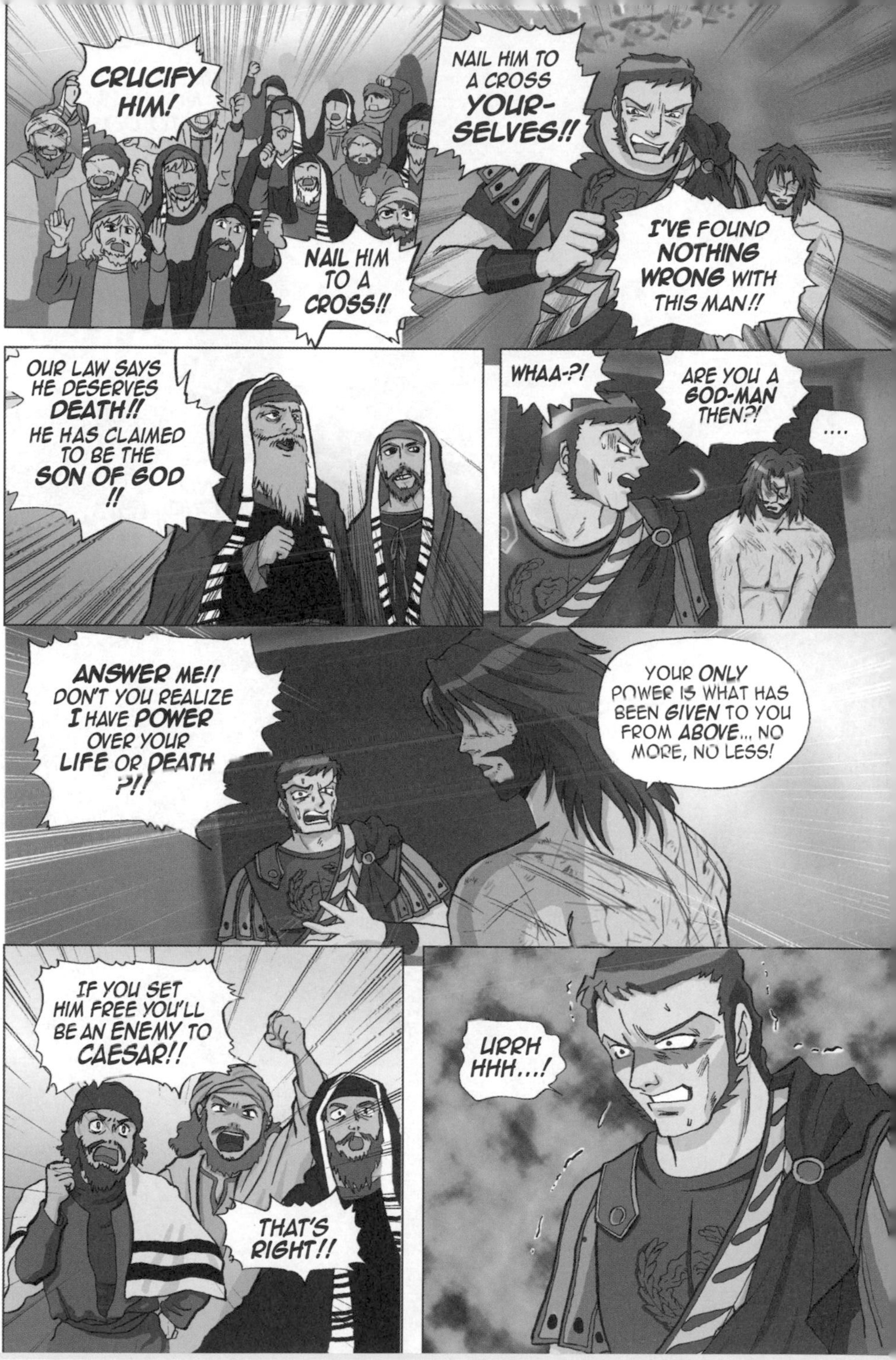
CRUCIFY HIM!
NAIL HIM TO A CROSS!!
NAIL HIM TO A CROSS YOURSELVES!!
I'VE FOUND NOTHING WRONG WITH THIS MAN!!
OUR LAW SAYS HE DESERVES DEATH!! HE HAS CLAIMED TO BE THE SON OF GOD!!
WHAA-?!
ARE YOU A GOD-MAN THEN?!
....
ANSWER ME!! DON'T YOU REALIZE I HAVE POWER OVER YOUR LIFE OR DEATH?!!
YOUR ONLY POWER IS WHAT HAS BEEN GIVEN TO YOU FROM ABOVE... NO MORE, NO LESS!
IF YOU SET HIM FREE YOU'LL BE AN ENEMY TO CAESAR!!
THAT'S RIGHT!!
URRH HHH...!

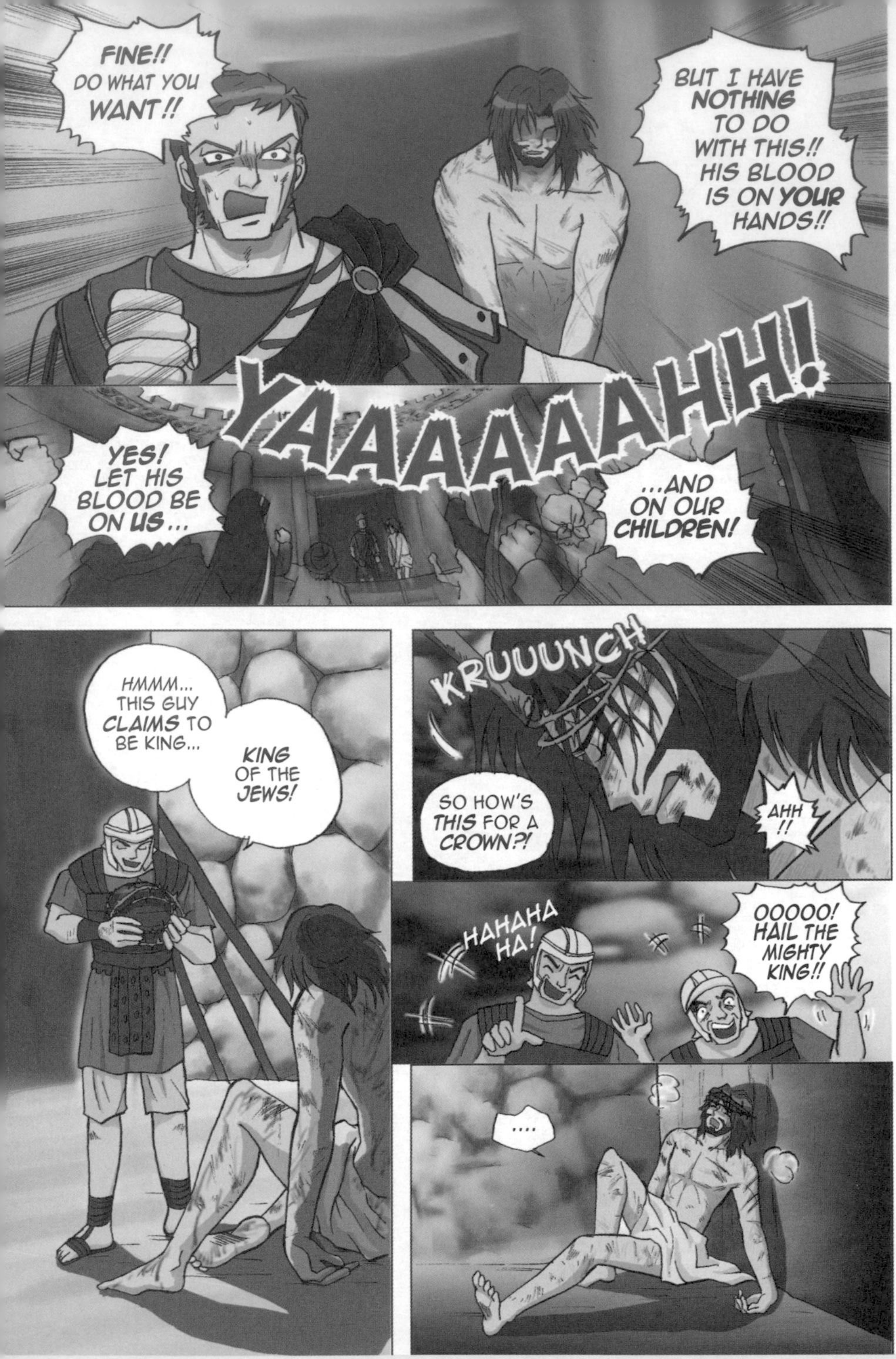
FINE!! DO WHAT YOU WANT!!
BUT I HAVE NOTHING TO DO WITH THIS!! HIS BLOOD IS ON YOUR HANDS!!
YAAAAAAHH!
YES! LET HIS BLOOD BE ON US...
...AND ON OUR CHILDREN!
HMMM... THIS GUY CLAIMS TO BE KING...
KING OF THE JEWS!
KRUUUNCH
SO HOW'S THIS FOR A CROWN?!
AHH !!
HAHAHA HA!
OOOOO! HAIL THE MIGHTY KING!!
....

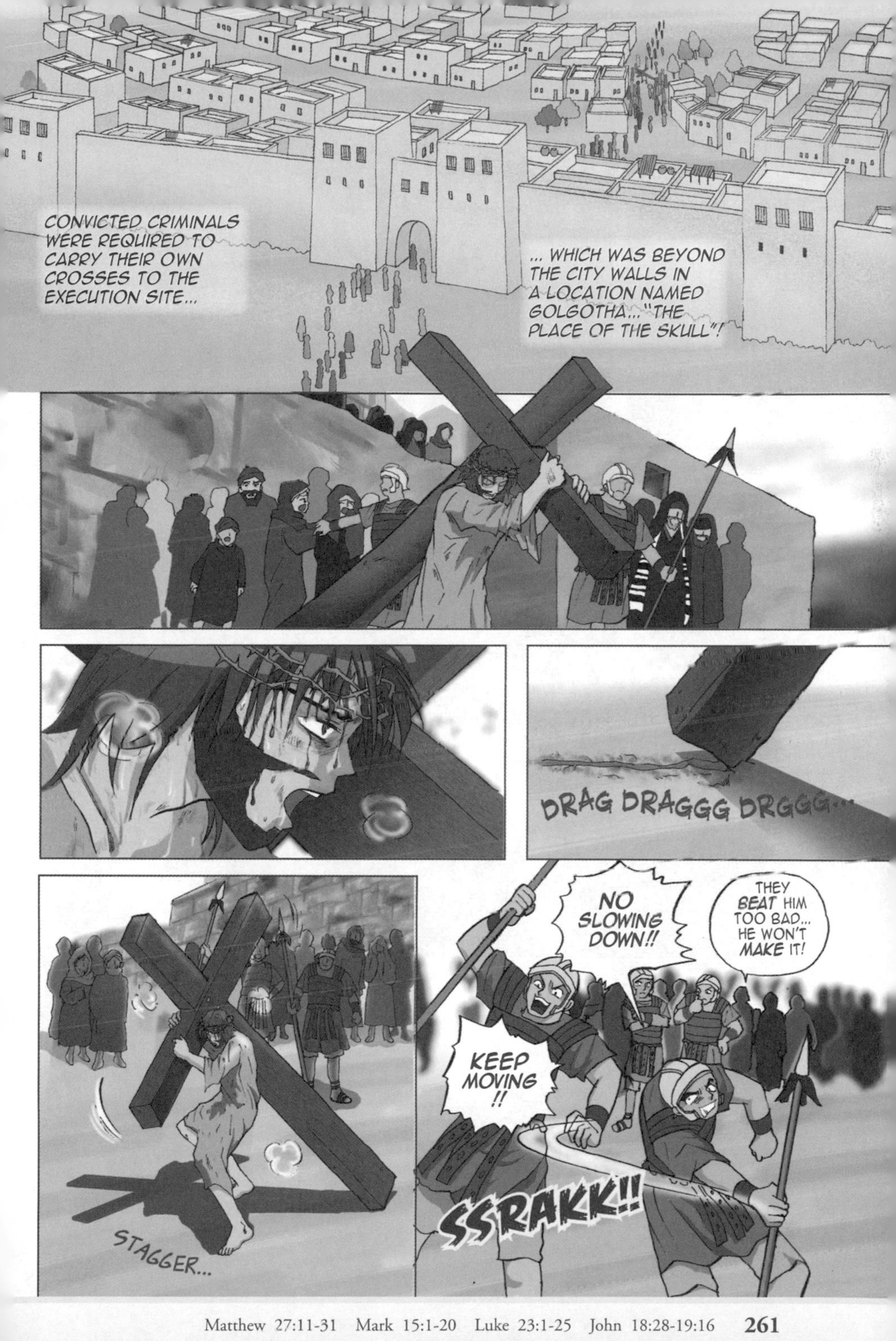
CONVICTED CRIMINALS WERE REQUIRED TO CARRY THEIR OWN CROSSES TO THE EXECUTION SITE...
... WHICH WAS BEYOND THE CITY WALLS IN A LOCATION NAMED GOLGOTHA... "THE PLACE OF THE SKULL"!
DRAG DRAGGG DRGGG...
STAGGER...
NO SLOWING DOWN!!
THEY BEAT HIM TOO BAD... HE WON'T MAKE IT!
KEEP MOVING !!
SSRAKK!!

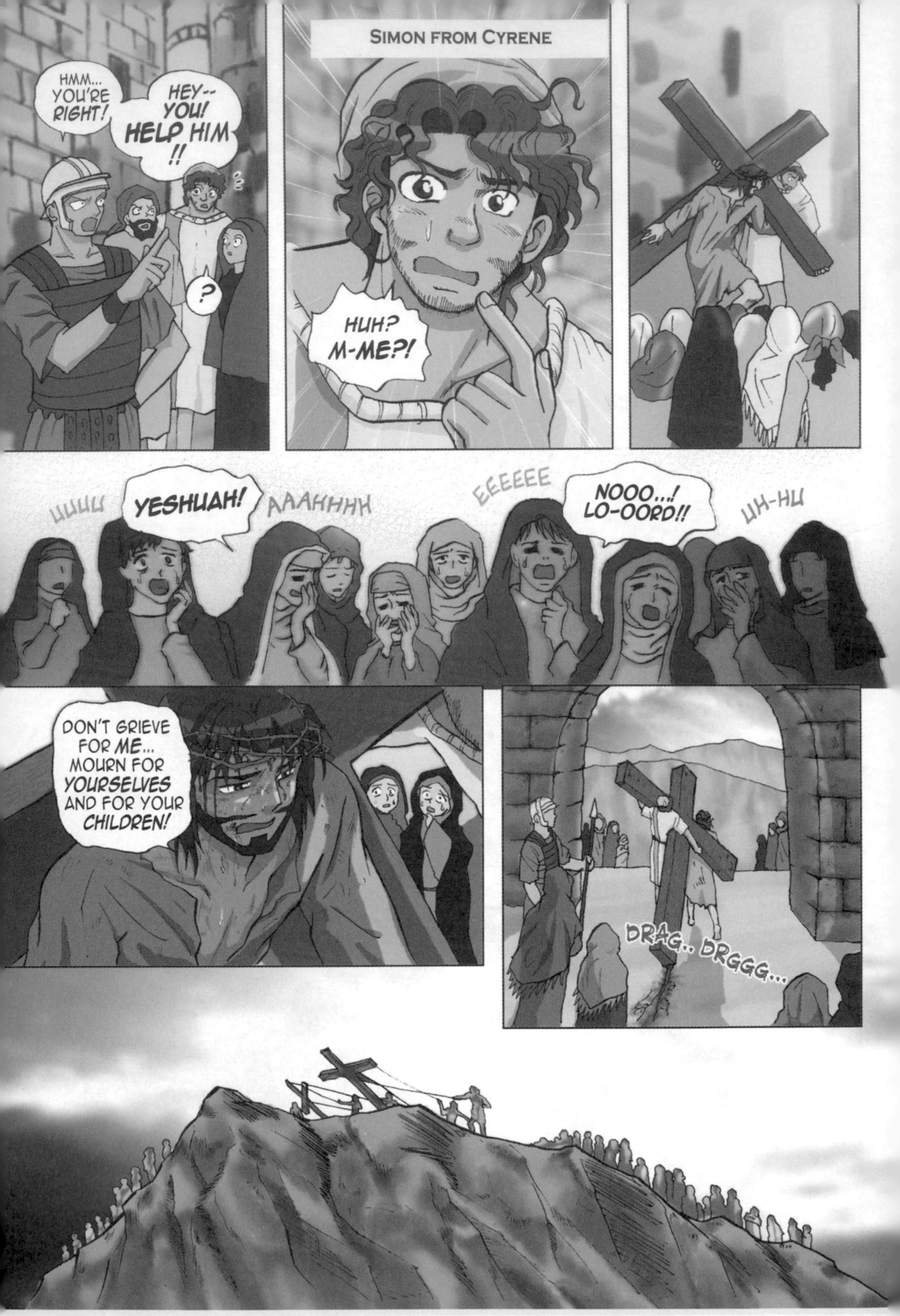
HMM... YOU'RE RIGHT!
HEY-- YOU! HELP HIM !!
?
SIMON FROM CYRENE
HUH? M-ME?!
UUUU
YESHUAH!
AAAHHHH
EEEEEE
NOOO...! LO-OORD!!
UH-HU
DON'T GRIEVE FOR ME... MOURN FOR YOURSELVES AND FOR YOUR CHILDREN!
DRAG.. DRGGG...

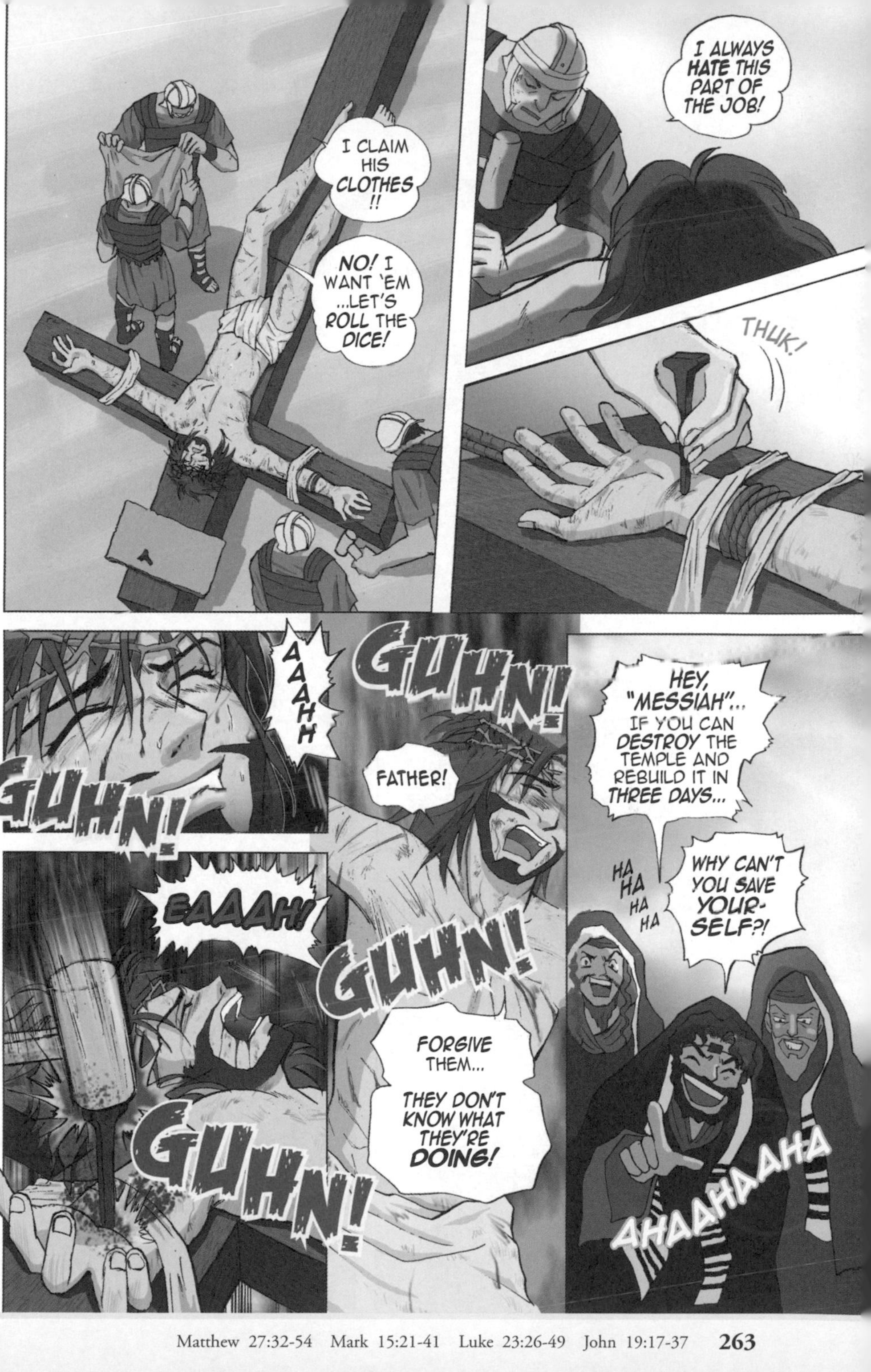
I CLAIM HIS CLOTHES !!
NO! I WANT 'EM ...LET'S ROLL THE DICE!
I ALWAYS HATE THIS PART OF THE JOB!
THUK!
AAAHH
GUHN!
GUHN!
FATHER!
EAAAH!
GUHN!
GUHN!
FORGIVE THEM...
THEY DON'T KNOW WHAT THEY'RE DOING!
HEY, "MESSIAH"... IF YOU CAN DESTROY THE TEMPLE AND REBUILD IT IN THREE DAYS...
HA HA HA HA
WHY CAN'T YOU SAVE YOUR-SELF?!
AHAAHAAHAAHA

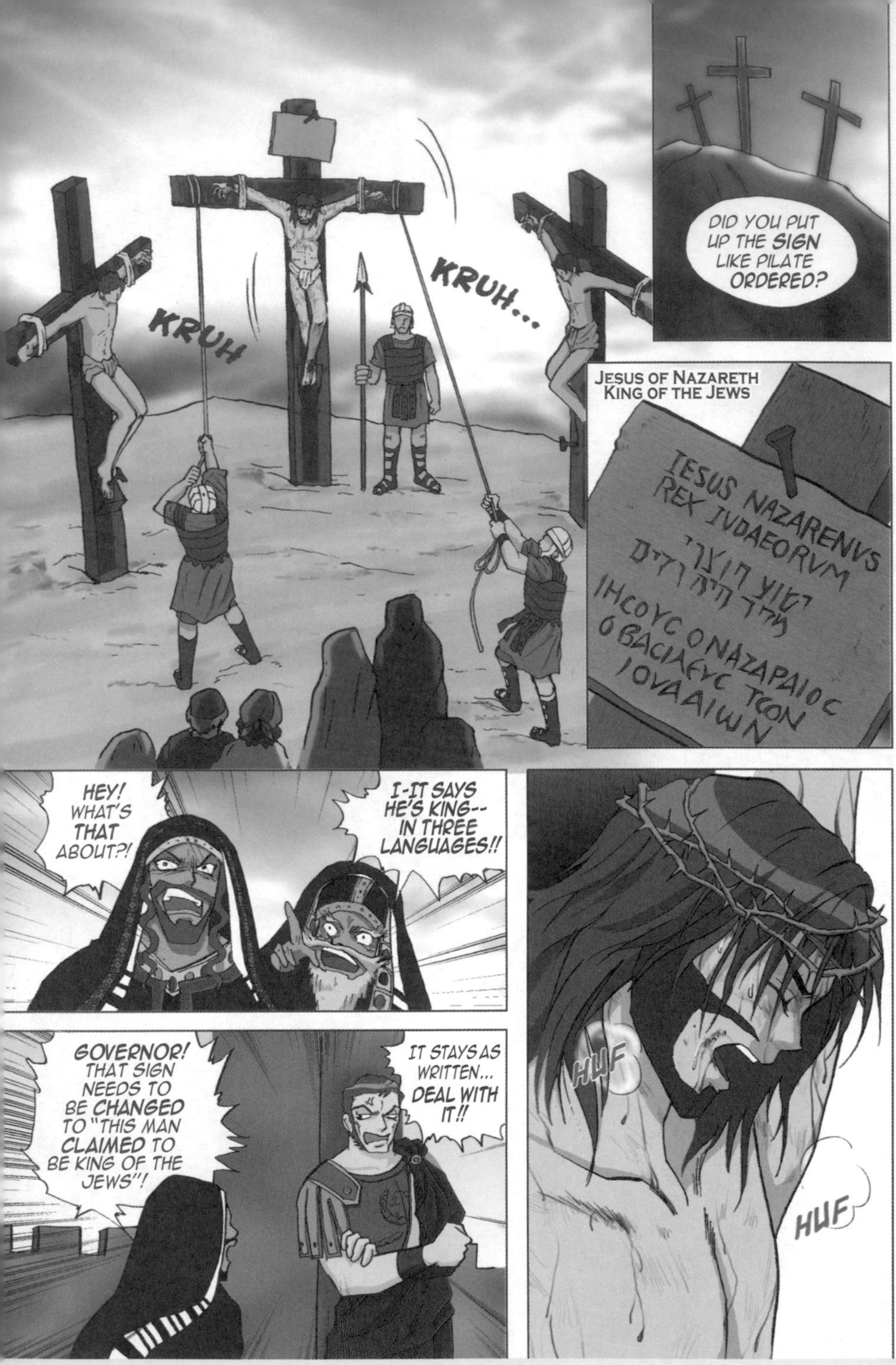
KRUH
KRUH...
DID YOU PUT UP THE SIGN LIKE PILATE ORDERED?
JESUS OF NAZARETH KING OF THE JEWS
IESUS NAZARENVS REX IVDAEORVM
HEY! WHAT'S THAT ABOUT?!
I-IT SAYS HE'S KING-- IN THREE LANGUAGES!!
GOVERNOR! THAT SIGN NEEDS TO BE CHANGED TO "THIS MAN CLAIMED TO BE KING OF THE JEWS"!
IT STAYS AS WRITTEN... DEAL WITH IT!!
HUF
HUF

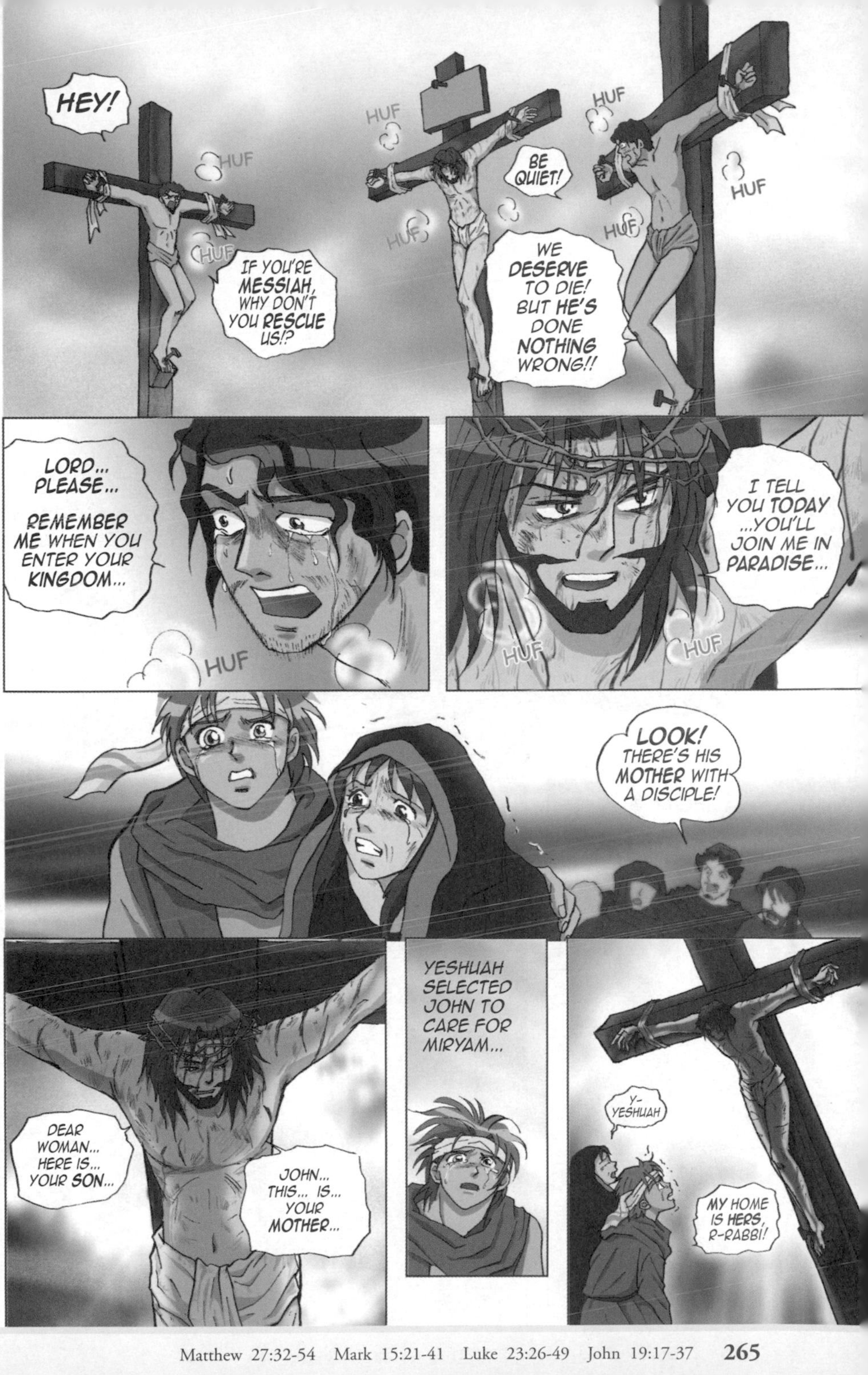
HEY!
HUF
HUF
IF YOU'RE MESSIAH, WHY DON'T YOU RESCUE US!?
HUF
HUF
BE QUIET!
HUF
HUF
HUF
WE DESERVE TO DIE! BUT HE'S DONE NOTHING WRONG!!
LORD... PLEASE... REMEMBER ME WHEN YOU ENTER YOUR KINGDOM...
HUF
I TELL YOU TODAY ...YOU'LL JOIN ME IN PARADISE...
HUF
HUF
LOOK! THERE'S HIS MOTHER WITH A DISCIPLE!
DEAR WOMAN... HERE IS... YOUR SON...
JOHN... THIS... IS... YOUR MOTHER...
YESHUAH SELECTED JOHN TO CARE FOR MIRYAM...
Y-YESHUAH
MY HOME IS HERS, R-RABBI!

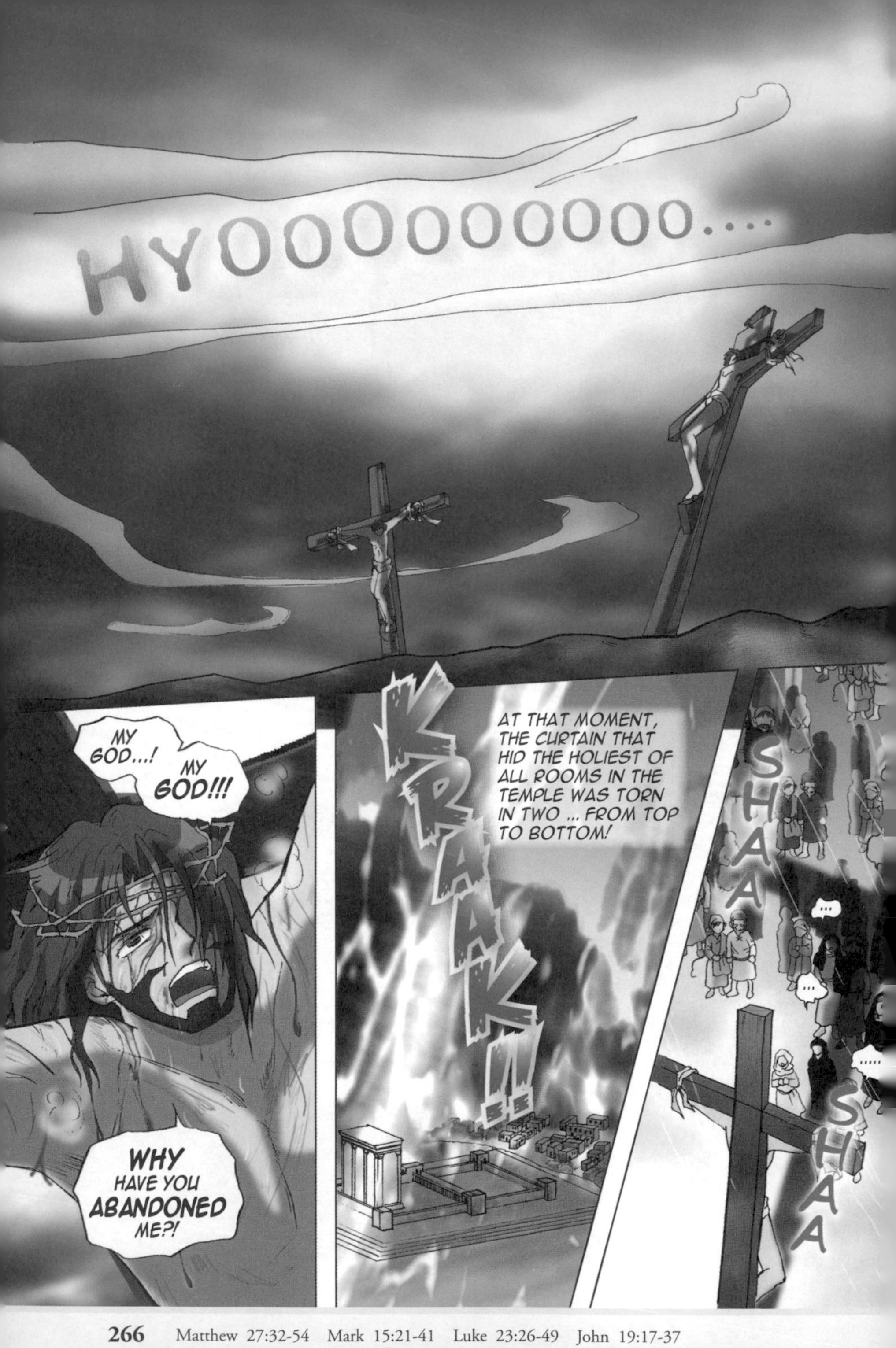
HYOOOOOOOO....
MY GOD...!
MY GOD!!!
WHY HAVE YOU ABANDONED ME?!
KRAAK!!
AT THAT MOMENT, THE CURTAIN THAT HID THE HOLIEST OF ALL ROOMS IN THE TEMPLE WAS TORN IN TWO ... FROM TOP TO BOTTOM!
SHAA
...
...
.....
SHAA

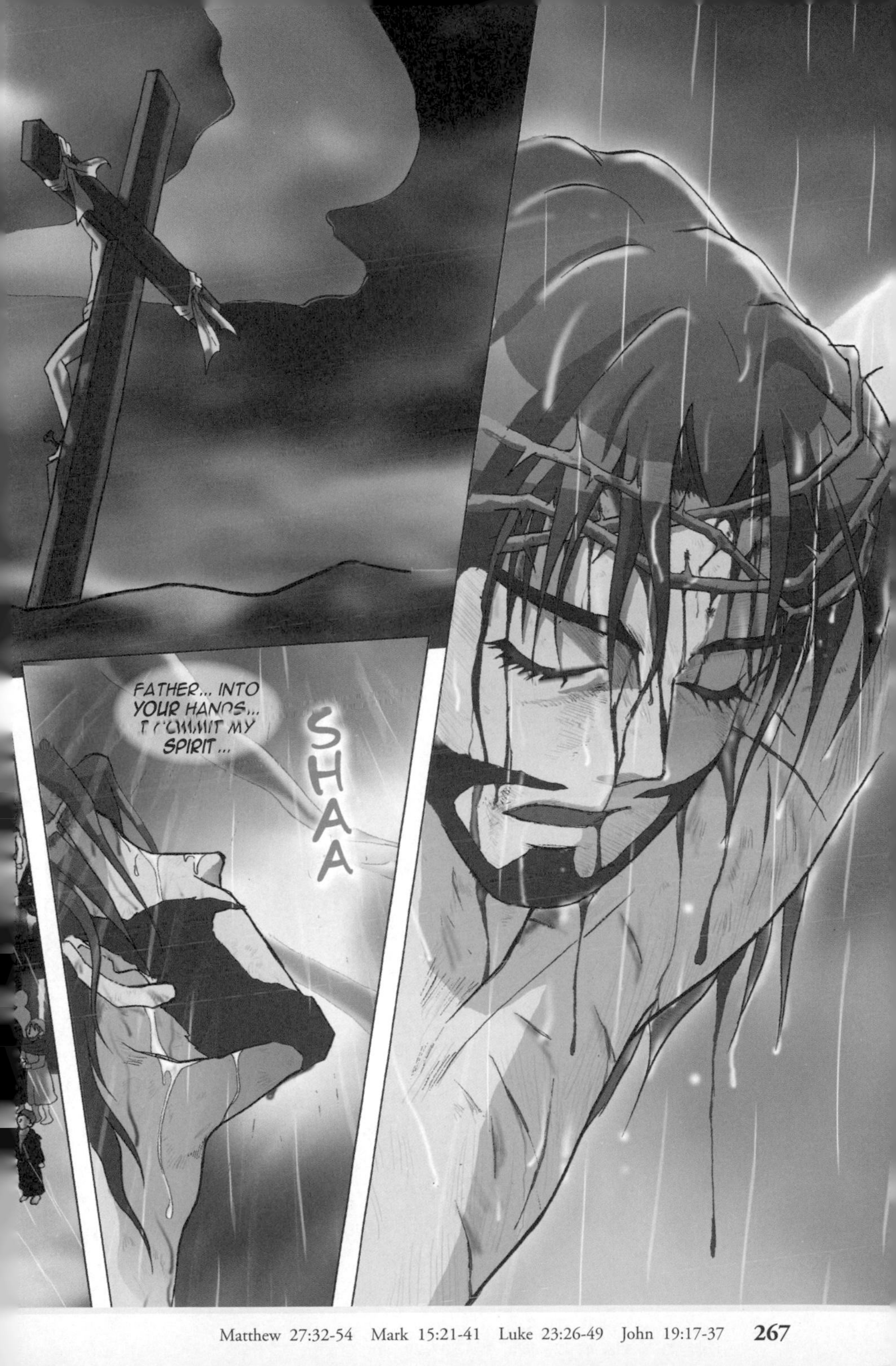
FATHER... INTO YOUR HANDS... I COMMIT MY SPIRIT...
SHAA

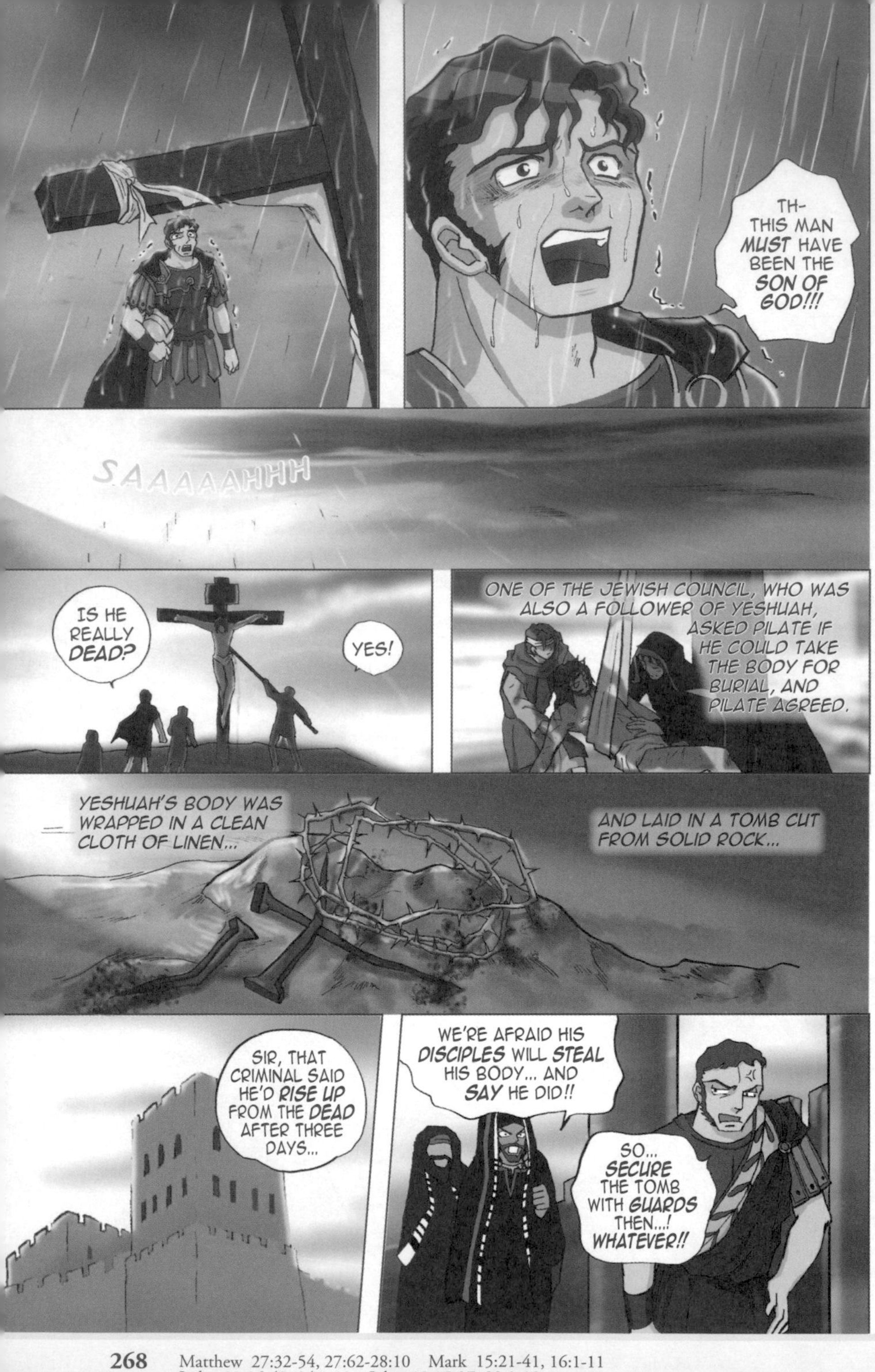
TH- THIS MAN MUST HAVE BEEN THE SON OF GOD!!!
SAAAAAHHH
IS HE REALLY DEAD?
YES!
ONE OF THE JEWISH COUNCIL, WHO WAS ALSO A FOLLOWER OF YESHUAH, ASKED PILATE IF HE COULD TAKE THE BODY FOR BURIAL, AND PILATE AGREED.
YESHUAH'S BODY WAS WRAPPED IN A CLEAN CLOTH OF LINEN...
AND LAID IN A TOMB CUT FROM SOLID ROCK...
SIR, THAT CRIMINAL SAID HE'D RISE UP FROM THE DEAD AFTER THREE DAYS...
WE'RE AFRAID HIS DISCIPLES WILL STEAL HIS BODY... AND SAY HE DID!!
SO... SECURE THE TOMB WITH GUARDS THEN...! WHATEVER!!

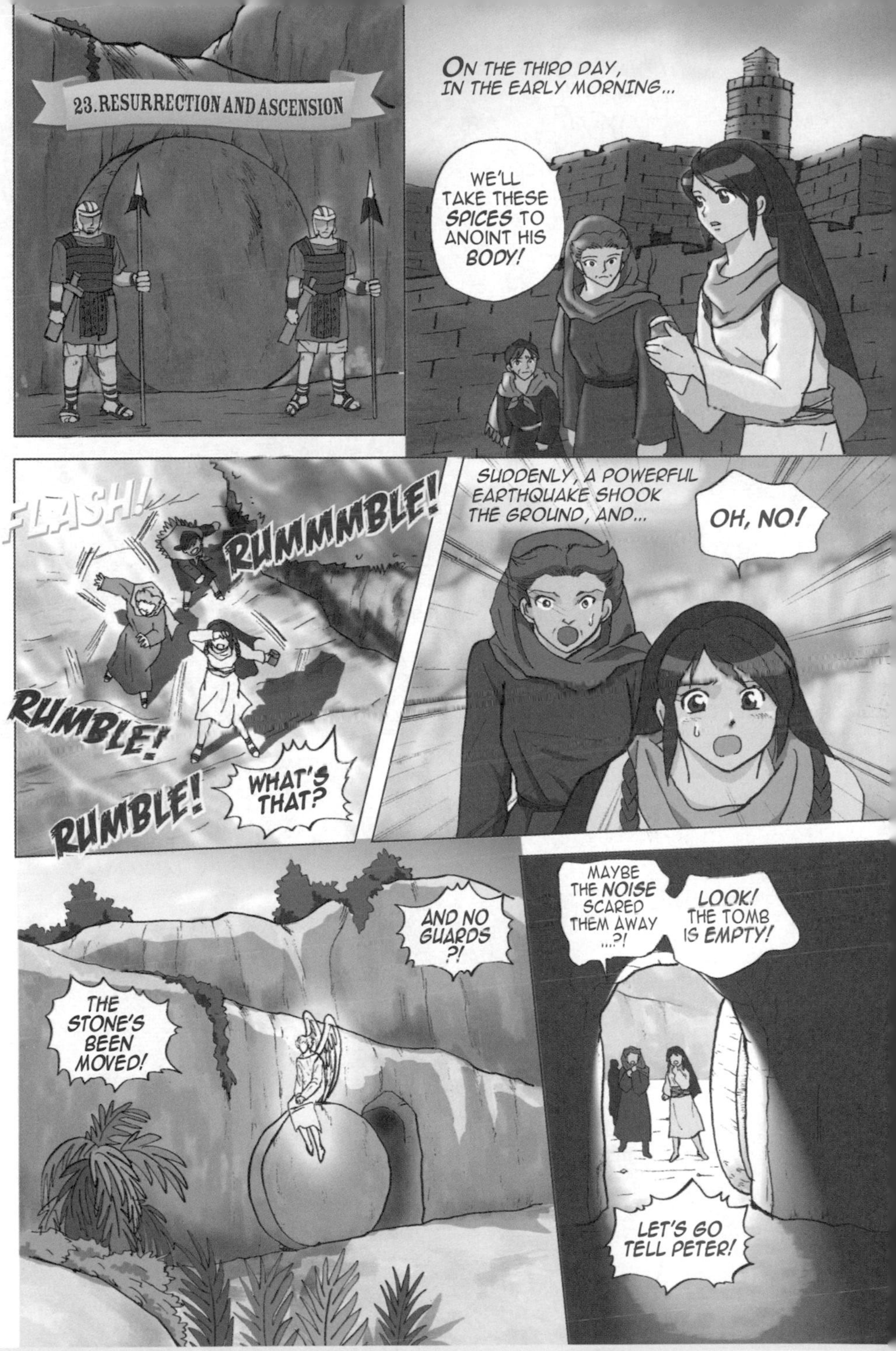
23. RESURRECTION AND ASCENSION
ON THE THIRD DAY, IN THE EARLY MORNING...
WE'LL TAKE THESE SPICES TO ANOINT HIS BODY!
FLASH!
RUMMMBLE!
RUMBLE!
RUMBLE!
WHAT'S THAT?
SUDDENLY, A POWERFUL EARTHQUAKE SHOOK THE GROUND, AND...
OH, NO!
AND NO GUARDS ?!
THE STONE'S BEEN MOVED!
MAYBE THE NOISE SCARED THEM AWAY ...?!
LOOK! THE TOMB IS EMPTY!
LET'S GO TELL PETER!

Matthew 27:62-28:10 Mark 16:1-11 Luke 24:1-12 John 20:1-18

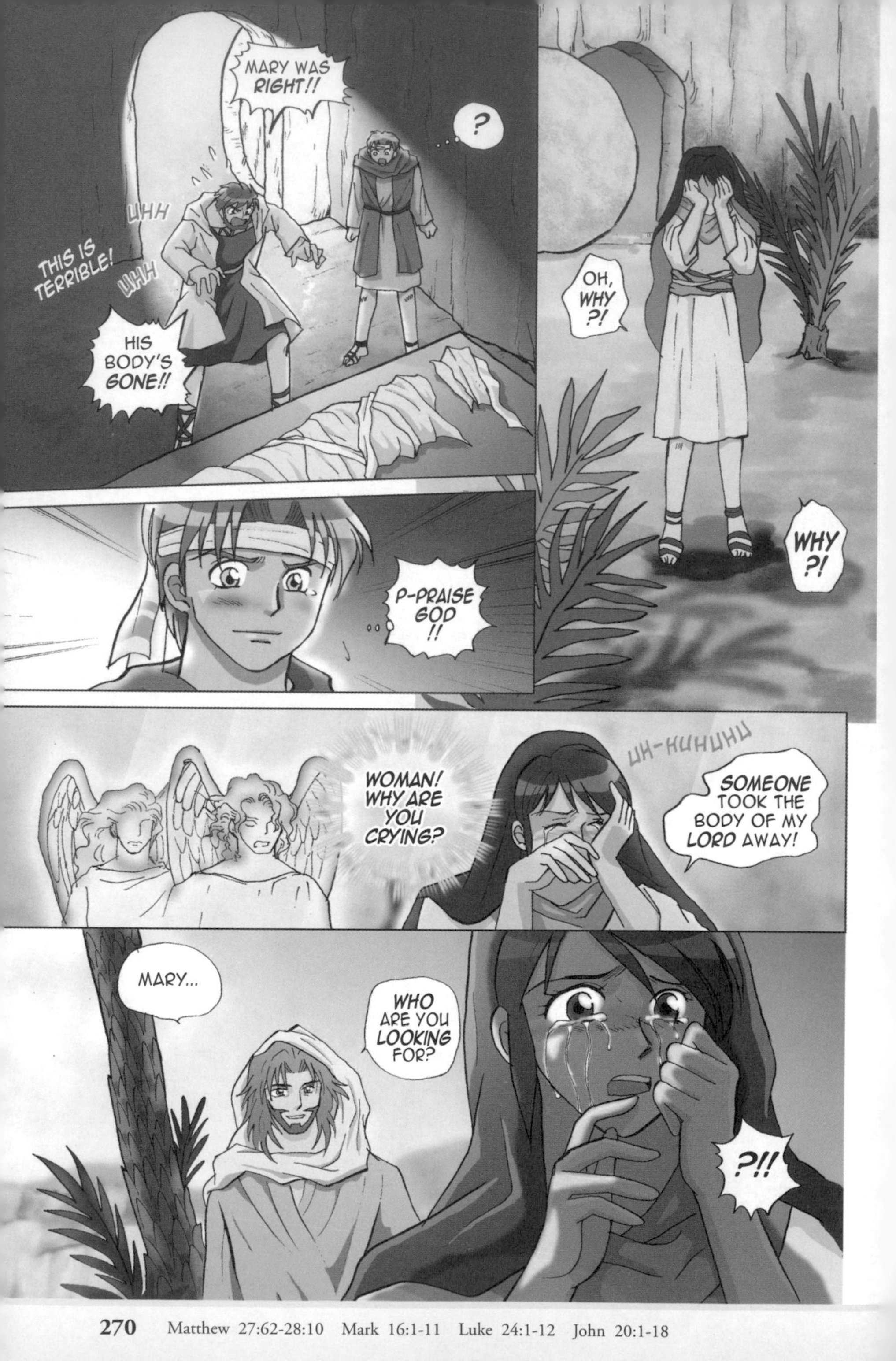
MARY WAS RIGHT!!
?
UHH
THIS IS TERRIBLE!
UHH
HIS BODY'S GONE!!
P-PRAISE GOD !!
OH, WHY ?!
WHY ?!
UH-HUHUHU
WOMAN! WHY ARE YOU CRYING?
SOMEONE TOOK THE BODY OF MY LORD AWAY!
MARY...
WHO ARE YOU LOOKING FOR?
?!!

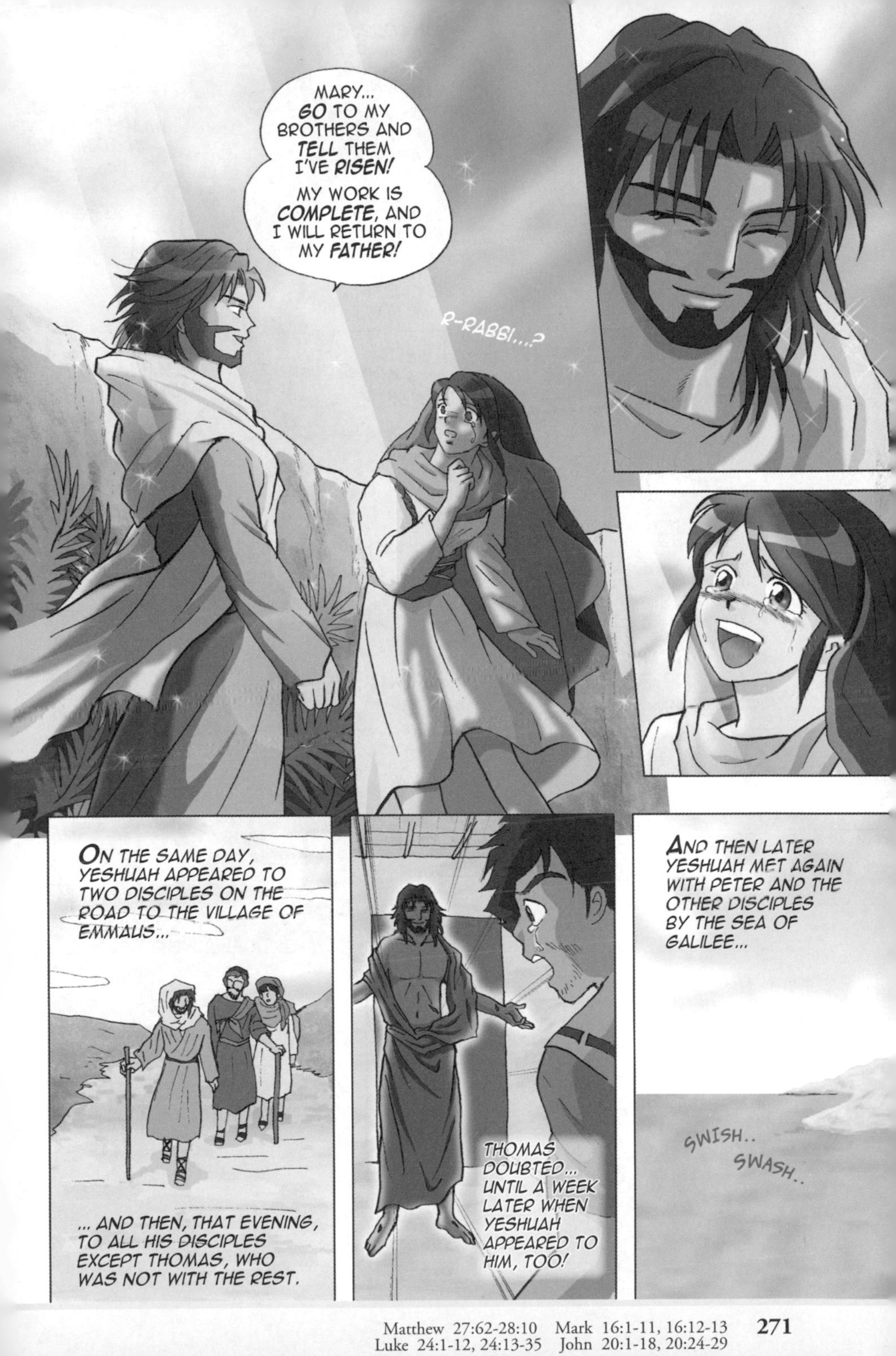
MARY... GO TO MY BROTHERS AND TELL THEM I'VE RISEN!
MY WORK IS COMPLETE, AND I WILL RETURN TO MY FATHER!
R-RABBI...?
ON THE SAME DAY, YESHUAH APPEARED TO TWO DISCIPLES ON THE ROAD TO THE VILLAGE OF EMMAUS...
... AND THEN, THAT EVENING, TO ALL HIS DISCIPLES EXCEPT THOMAS, WHO WAS NOT WITH THE REST.
THOMAS DOUBTED... UNTIL A WEEK LATER WHEN YESHUAH APPEARED TO HIM, TOO!
AND THEN LATER YESHUAH MET AGAIN WITH PETER AND THE OTHER DISCIPLES BY THE SEA OF GALILEE...
SWISH..
SWASH..

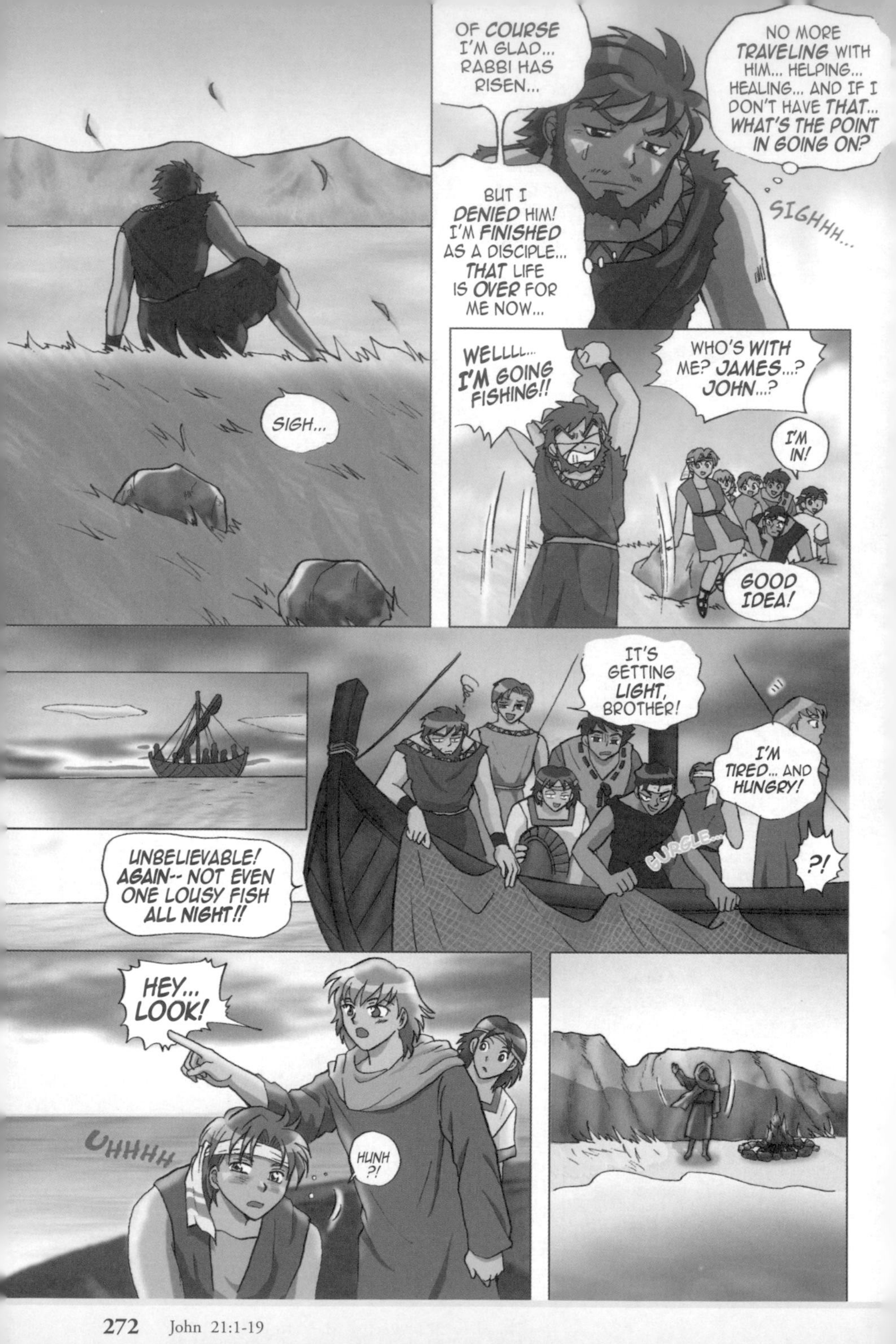
SIGH...
OF COURSE I'M GLAD... RABBI HAS RISEN...
BUT I DENIED HIM! I'M FINISHED AS A DISCIPLE... THAT LIFE IS OVER FOR ME NOW...
NO MORE TRAVELING WITH HIM... HELPING... HEALING... AND IF I DON'T HAVE THAT... WHAT'S THE POINT IN GOING ON?
SIGHHH...
WELLLL... I'M GOING FISHING!!
WHO'S WITH ME? JAMES...? JOHN...?
I'M IN!
GOOD IDEA!
UNBELIEVABLE! AGAIN-- NOT EVEN ONE LOUSY FISH ALL NIGHT!!
IT'S GETTING LIGHT, BROTHER!
I'M TIRED... AND HUNGRY!
GURGLE...
?!
HEY... LOOK!
UHHHH
HUNH ?!

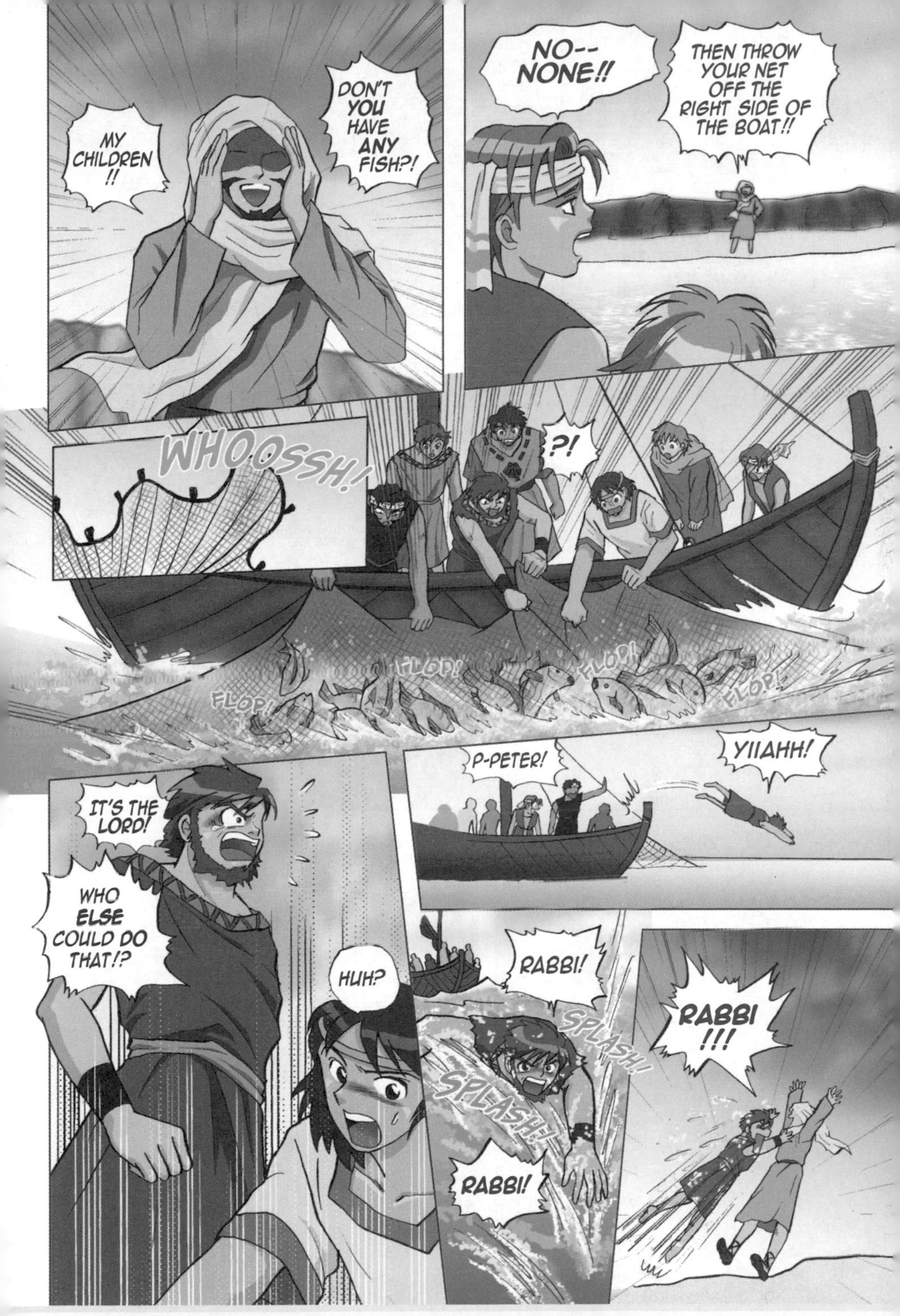
MY CHILDREN !!
DON'T YOU HAVE ANY FISH?!
NO-- NONE!!
THEN THROW YOUR NET OFF THE RIGHT SIDE OF THE BOAT!!
WHOOSSH!
?!
FLOP!
FLOP!
FLOP!
FLOP!
IT'S THE LORD!
WHO ELSE COULD DO THAT!?
HUH?
P-PETER!
YIIAHH!
RABBI!
SPLASH!
SPLASH!
RABBI!
RABBI !!!

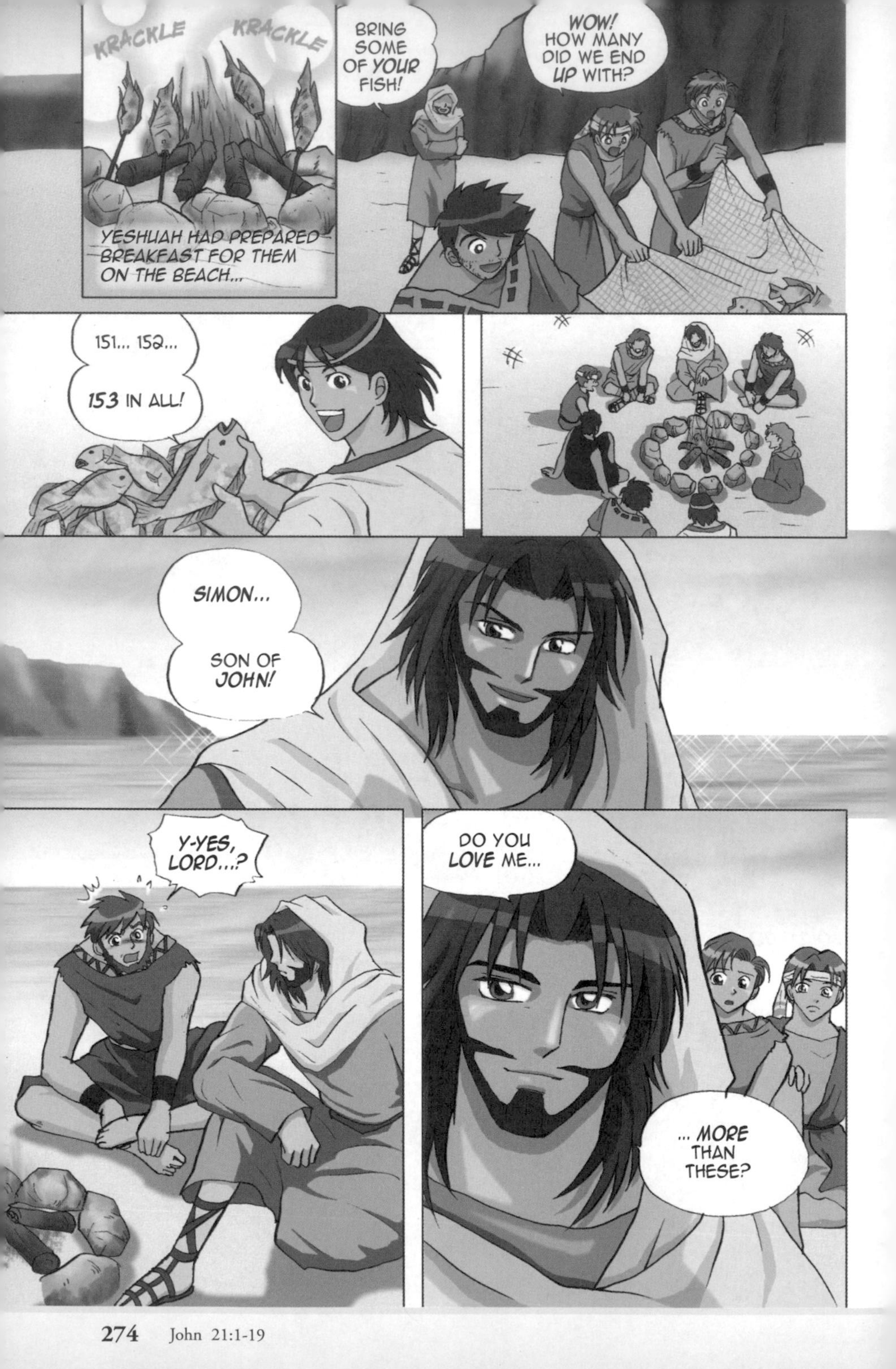
KRACKLE KRACKLE
YESHUAH HAD PREPARED BREAKFAST FOR THEM ON THE BEACH...
BRING SOME OF YOUR FISH!
WOW! HOW MANY DID WE END UP WITH?
151... 152...
153 IN ALL!
SIMON...
SON OF JOHN!
Y-YES, LORD...?
DO YOU LOVE ME...
... MORE THAN THESE?

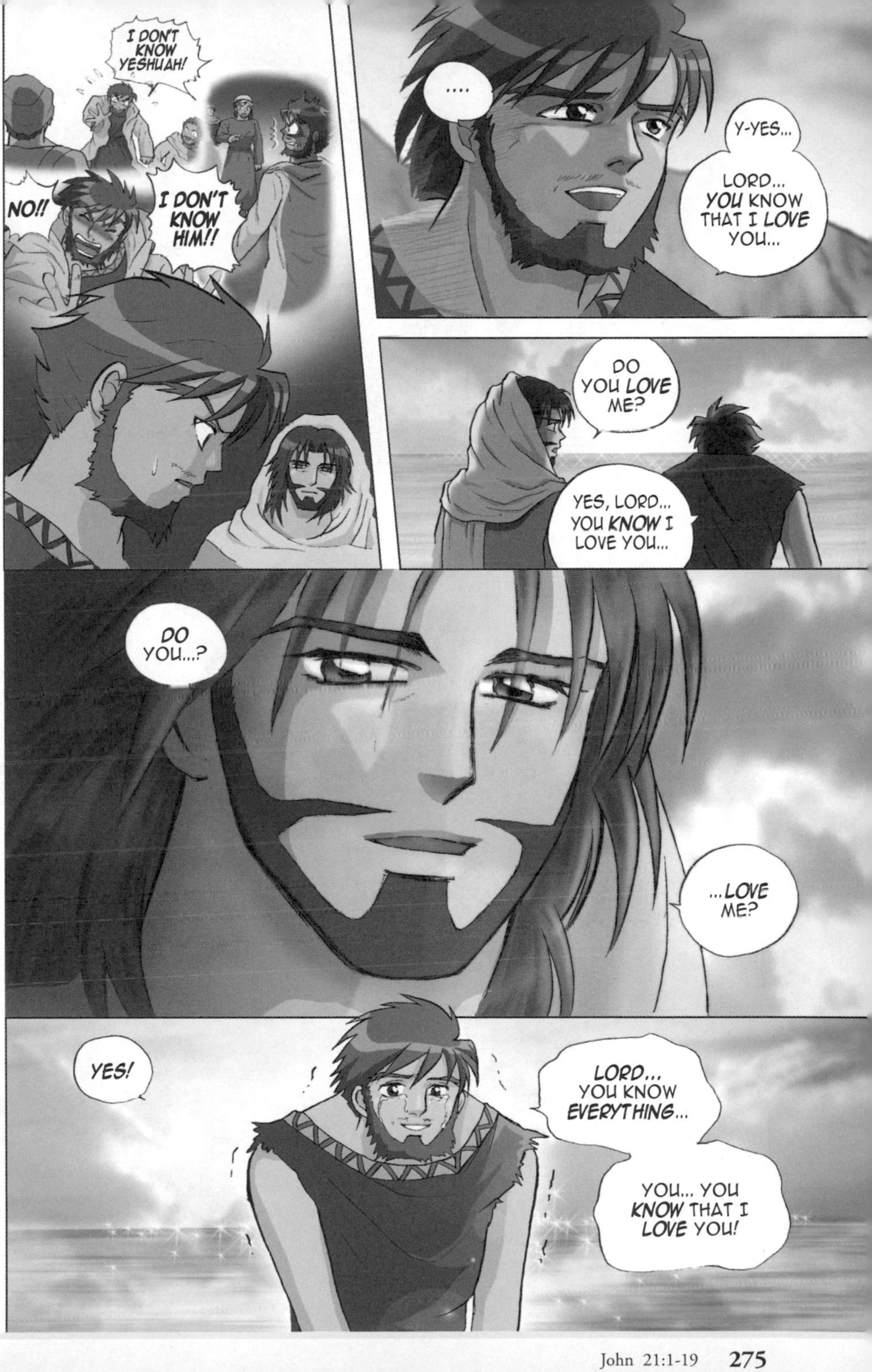
I DON'T KNOW YESHUAH!
NO!!
I DON'T KNOW HIM!!
....
Y-YES...
LORD... YOU KNOW THAT I LOVE YOU...
DO YOU LOVE ME?
YES, LORD... YOU KNOW I LOVE YOU...
DO YOU...?
...LOVE ME?
YES!
LORD... YOU KNOW EVERYTHING...
YOU... YOU KNOW THAT I LOVE YOU!

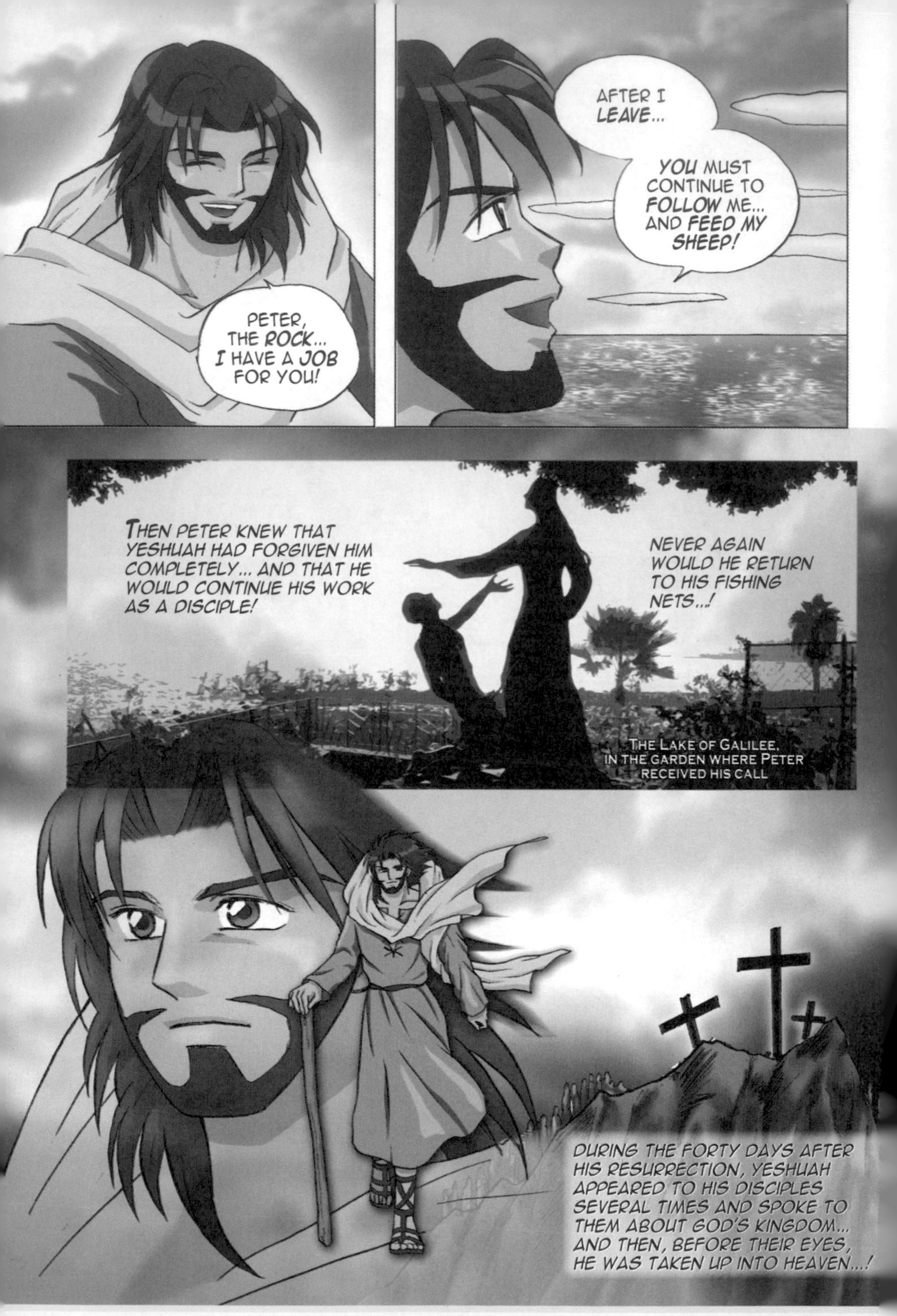
PETER, THE ROCK... I HAVE A JOB FOR YOU!
AFTER I LEAVE...
YOU MUST CONTINUE TO FOLLOW ME... AND FEED MY SHEEP!
THEN PETER KNEW THAT YESHUAH HAD FORGIVEN HIM COMPLETELY... AND THAT HE WOULD CONTINUE HIS WORK AS A DISCIPLE!
NEVER AGAIN WOULD HE RETURN TO HIS FISHING NETS...!
THE LAKE OF GALILEE, IN THE GARDEN WHERE PETER RECEIVED HIS CALL
DURING THE FORTY DAYS AFTER HIS RESURRECTION, YESHUAH APPEARED TO HIS DISCIPLES SEVERAL TIMES AND SPOKE TO THEM ABOUT GOD'S KINGDOM... AND THEN, BEFORE THEIR EYES, HE WAS TAKEN UP INTO HEAVEN...!

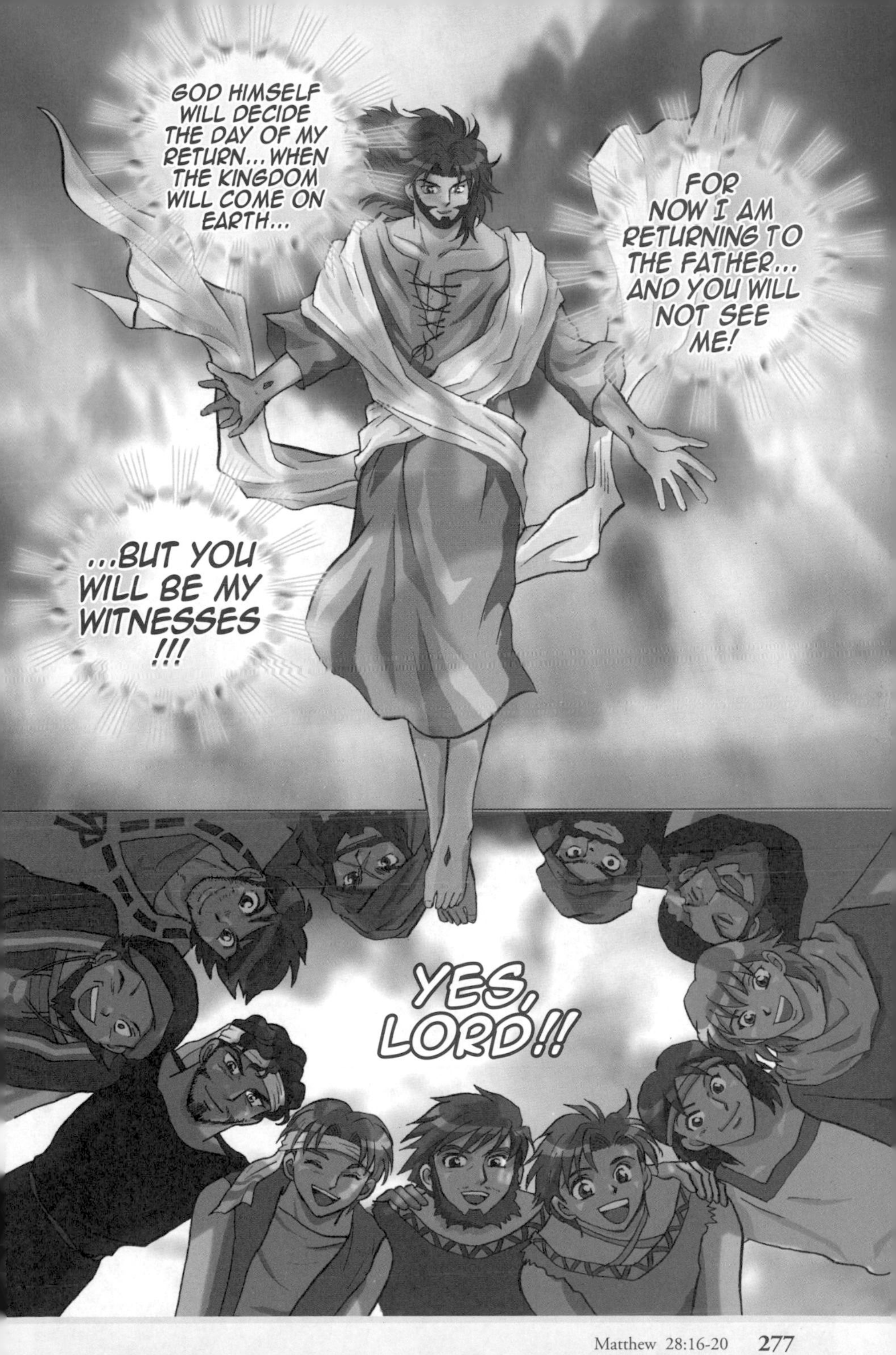
GOD HIMSELF WILL DECIDE THE DAY OF MY RETURN...WHEN THE KINGDOM WILL COME ON EARTH...
FOR NOW I AM RETURNING TO THE FATHER... AND YOU WILL NOT SEE ME!
...BUT YOU WILL BE MY WITNESSES !!!
YES, LORD!!

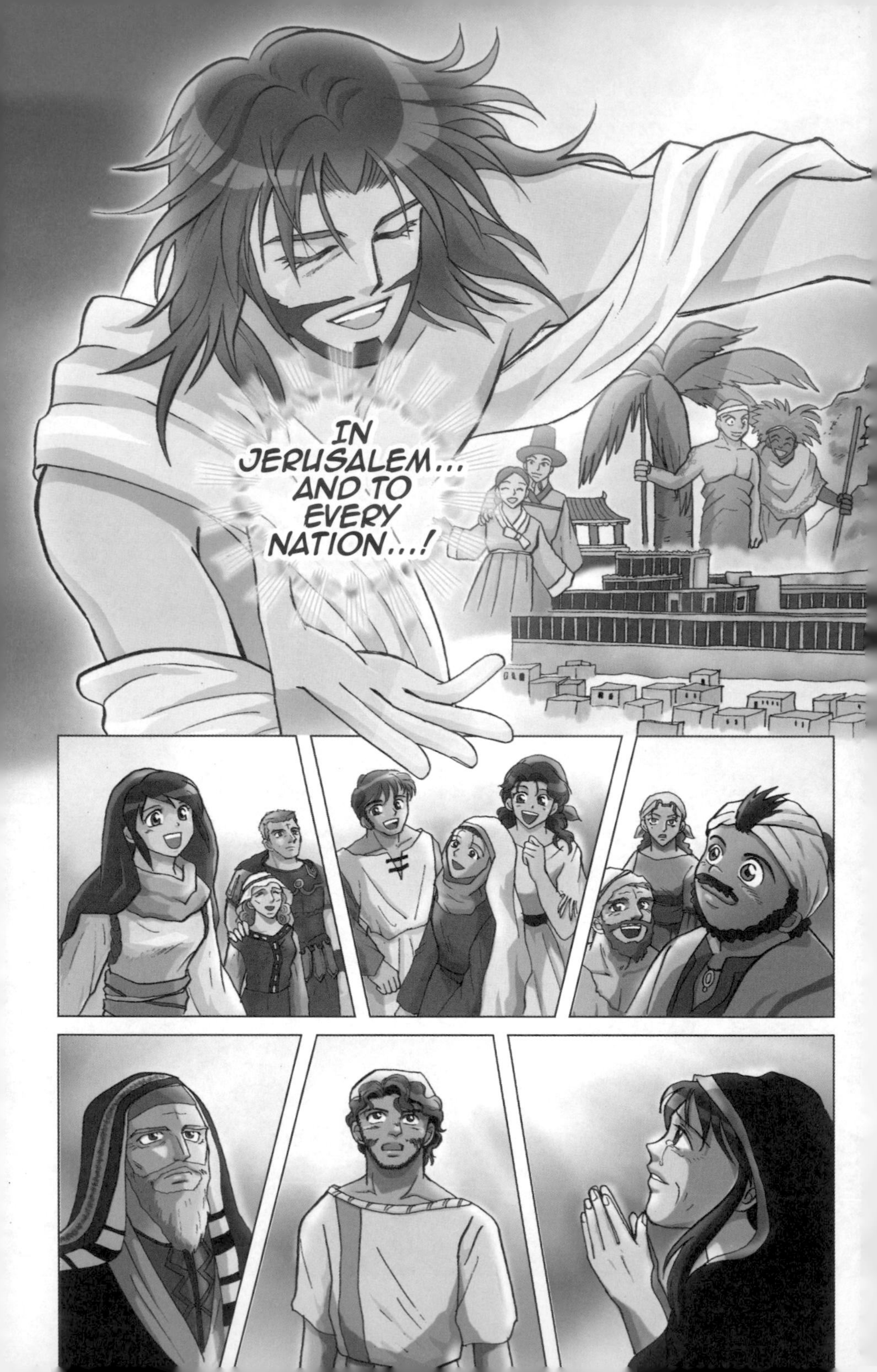
IN JERUSALEM... AND TO EVERY NATION...!

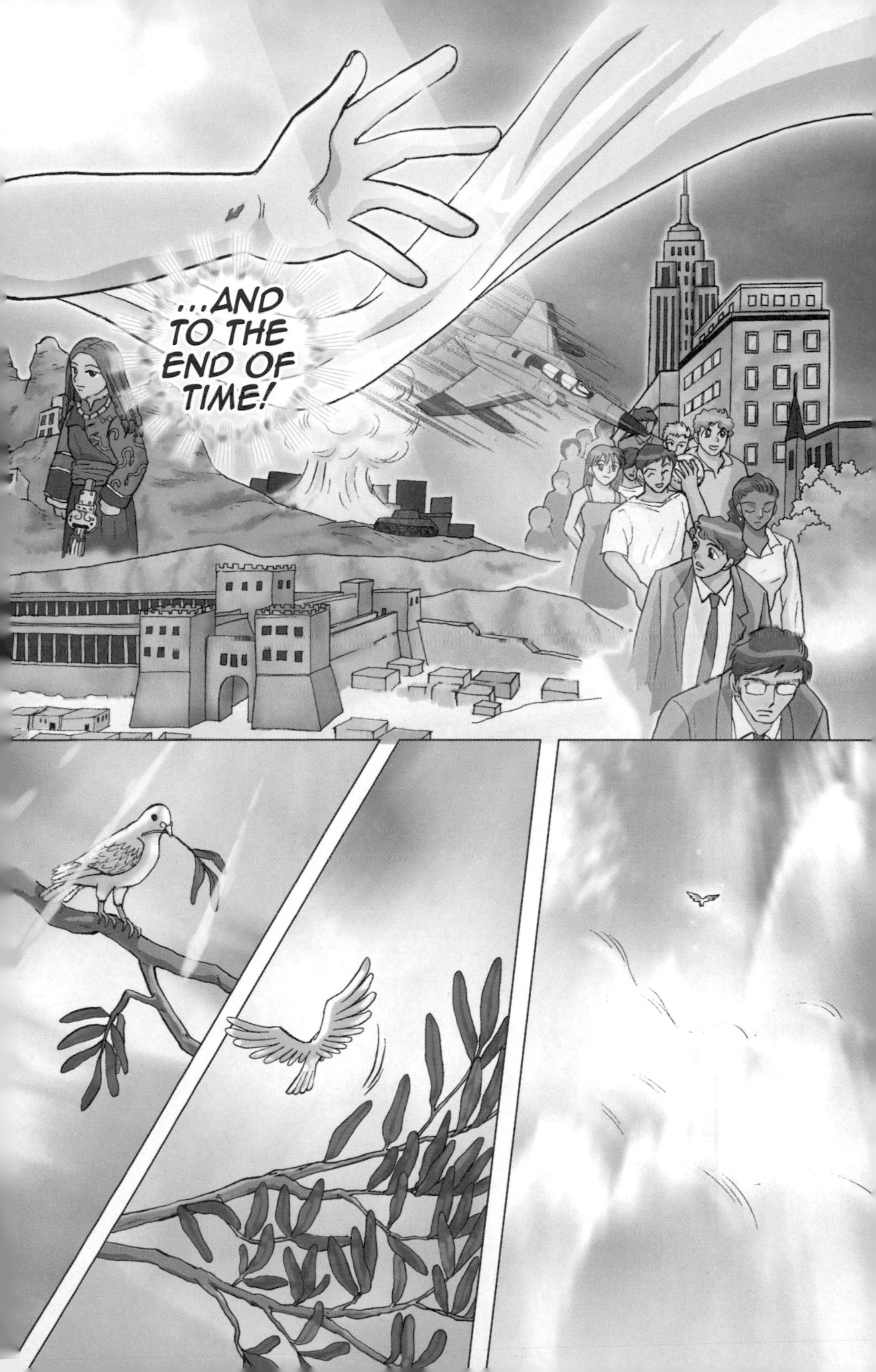
...AND TO THE END OF TIME!

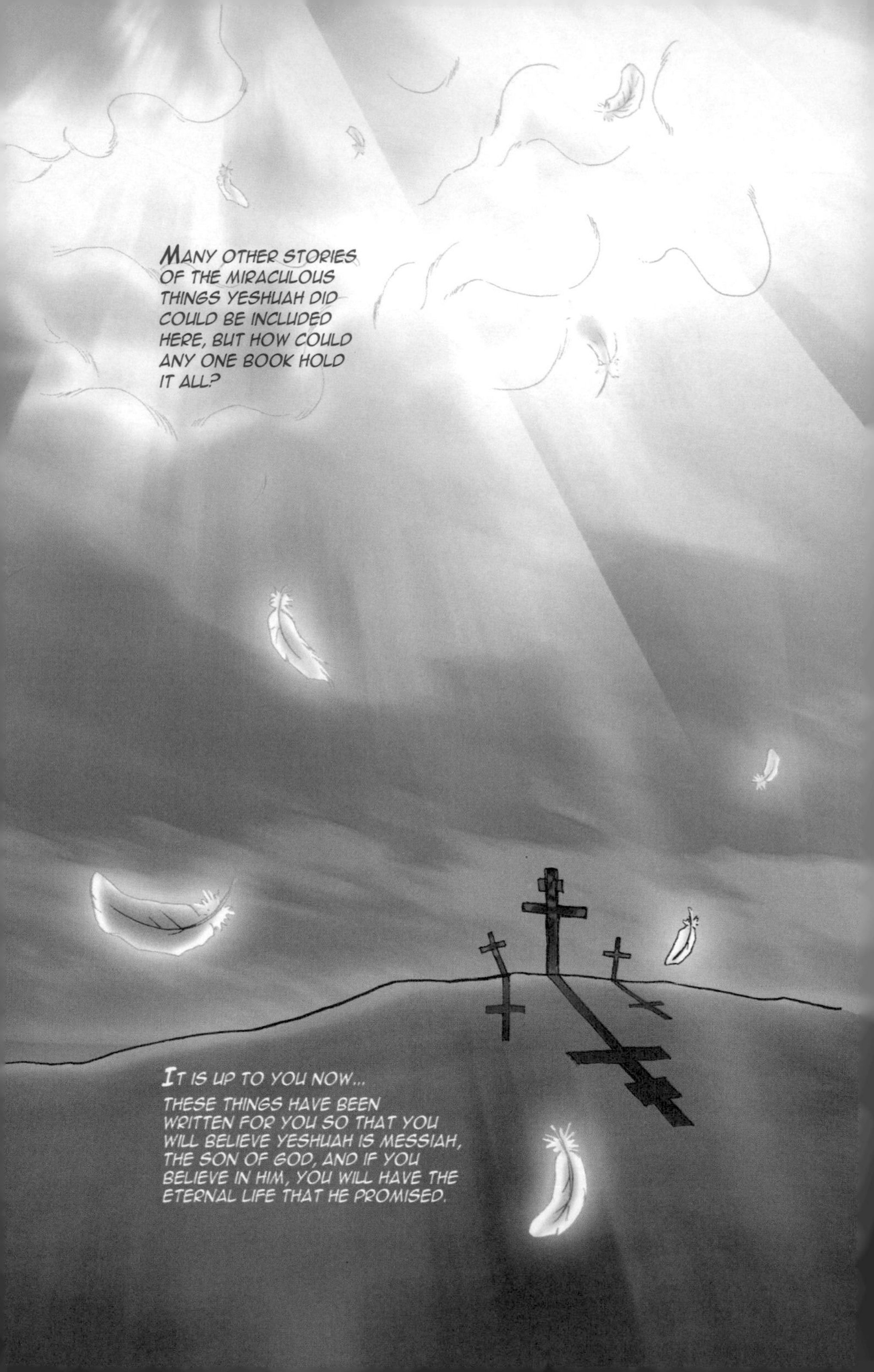
MANY OTHER STORIES OF THE MIRACULOUS THINGS YESHUAH DID COULD BE INCLUDED HERE, BUT HOW COULD ANY ONE BOOK HOLD IT ALL?
IT IS UP TO YOU NOW...
THESE THINGS HAVE BEEN WRITTEN FOR YOU SO THAT YOU WILL BELIEVE YESHUAH IS MESSIAH, THE SON OF GOD, AND IF YOU BELIEVE IN HIM, YOU WILL HAVE THE ETERNAL LIFE THAT HE PROMISED.

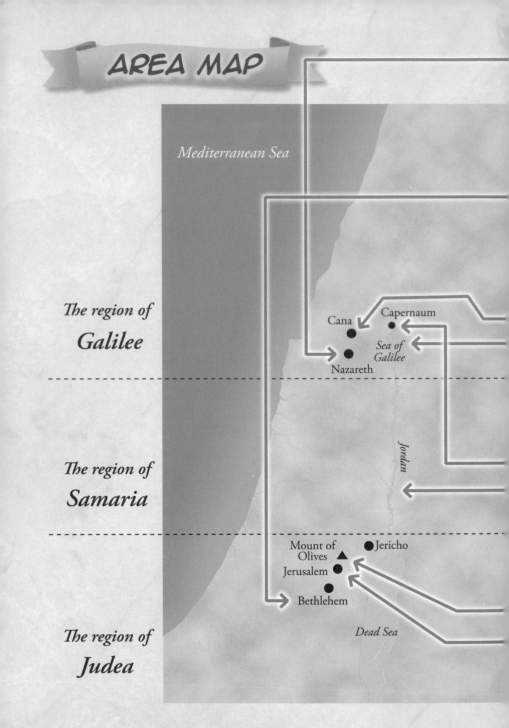

Mediterranean Sea

The region of
Galilee

Cana Capernaum

Sea of
Galilee

Nazareth

Jordan

The region of
Samaria

Mount of   Jericho
Olives ▲

Jerusalem

Bethlehem

Dead Sea

The region of
Judea

NAZARETH

A village in northern Galilee, where Miryam and Yosef live. This is where Miryam saw the angel who told her that she would become the mother of Yeshuah!

BETHLEHEM

A town in Judea, known as "the City of the Great King." Yeshuah is born there when Yosef and Miryam are visiting as part of a population study.

CANA

A town in Galilee to the north of Nazareth. Yeshuah presents a groom and bride with an amazing wedding gift in this place!

SEA OF GALILEE

A large freshwater lake through which the Jordan River flows from north to south ... and the site of miracles that defy any human logic!

The hometown of Peter and Andrew, which Yeshuah uses as a base of operations.

CAPERNAUM

JORDAN

The place where John the Baptizer immerses people in water as a "rite of passage." Even Yeshuah asks John to immerse him, too.

MOUNT OF OLIVES

Yeshuah spends a lot of time at the foot of this mountain ridge, in the Garden of Gethsemane.

JERUSALEM

"The City of Peace," a sacred town in Judea where the "Feast of Passover" is celebrated every spring. This is the place where Messiah will face terrible trials ... and experience the greatest triumph in the history of the world!

CHARACTER PROFILES

Messiah Yeshuah

Anyone who meets him can tell in seconds that Yeshuah's not like any man ever seen before in this world ... But is he really Messiah, the liberating God-King that everyone's been waiting for? How could Messiah possibly be a working man from a backward town like Nazareth?

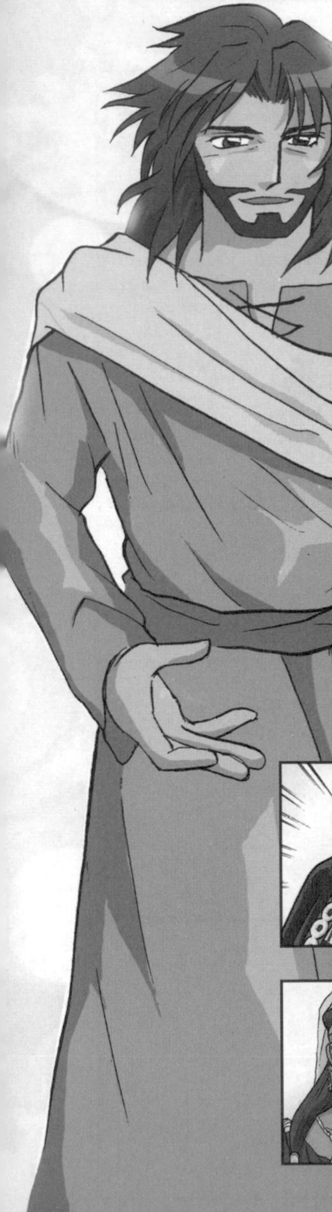

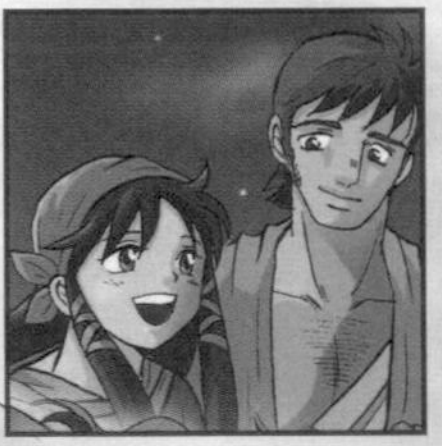

Yosef & Miryam

This decent, young couple descended from the greatest king in history and are Yeshuah's parents ... or at least Miryam is his mother. Questions have circulated for years about who his father really is!

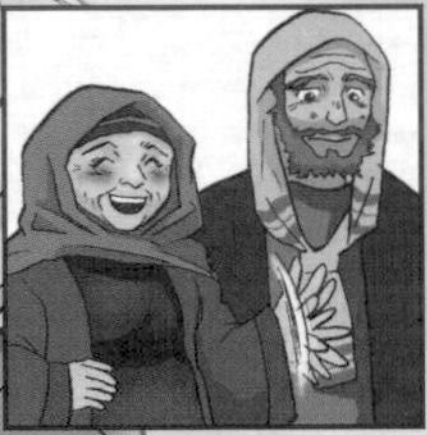

Zechariah & Elizabeth

Miryam's relative Elizabeth is married to a temple priest. In their old age they had a baby, and although Zechariah didn't talk about it much at first, he now insists an angel told him his son would be...

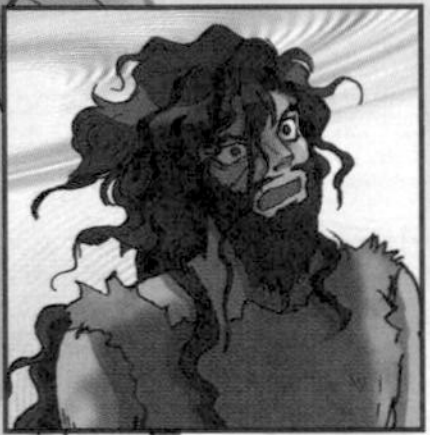

John the Baptizer

John is a "Nazirite" – a person who takes a holy vow to never cut his hair or drink wine. His warnings to the people to clean up their lives prepare the way for Yeshuah but get him in trouble with Herod Antipas.

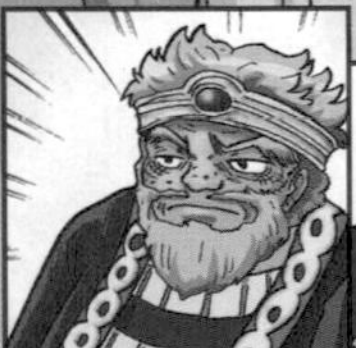

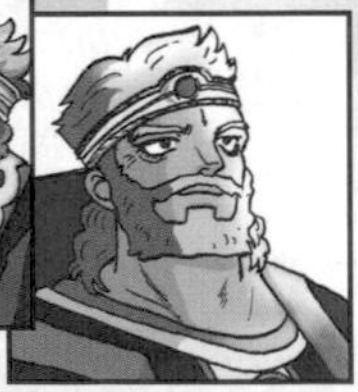

The Two Herods

King Herod the Great governs Judea at the time of Yeshuah's birth. His insecurity about being replaced by Messiah leads him to commit a hideous massacre. His son, Herod Antipas, is responsible for horrible crimes as well.

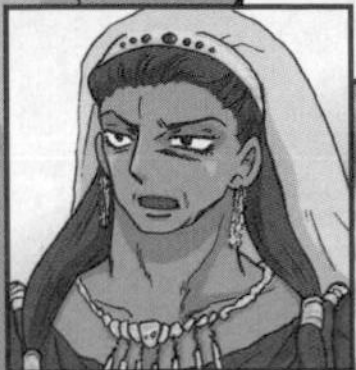

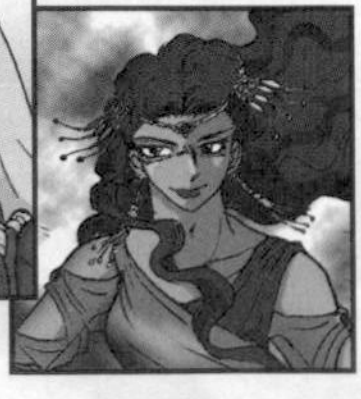

Herodias

Herodias is the wife of Herod Antipas. She hates John the Baptizer because he has denounced her perverse marriage. She uses her beautiful daughter to gain revenge!

Nicodemus

A member of the ruling council who believes Yeshuah really is Messiah ... but who is too frightened to share that opinion with anyone else, especially after Yeshuah tells him what it will really take to enter the Kingdom!

Pharisees & Scribes

These men are interpreters and teachers of the ancient texts and are well-known for their strict observance of tradition. They constantly oppose Yeshuah, because they think he is intent on breaking those very laws and customs. However, they are frustrated that they seem to find themselves on the losing side of every debate!

Zacchaeus

Zacchaeus is a tax collector in Jericho. His authority to collect taxes for the Empire – including whatever "extra" he can skim off the top for himself – has made him very wealthy. He is disliked for his profession and disrespected because he's very, very short.

the Women

These volunteers and supporters from Galilee help Yeshuah and his followers financially and practically. Mary of Magdala is one of these women. Others in the group include Joanna, the wife of Chuza, who manages King Herod's household, and Susanna.

Martha, Mary, and Lazarus

Lazarus is one of Yeshuah's best friends, and Martha and Mary are his sisters. They all live in Bethany, and when Yeshuah travels to Jerusalem he usually stays at their house. When there is a serious illness in the family, they call for Yeshuah and are devastated when he doesn't arrive in time!

Pontius Pilate

Pontius Pilate is the Empire's "prefect" or lower military governor for the areas of Judea, Samaria, and Idumaea. He is widely known for his arrogance and serious lack of empathy for other cultures and their differences, but he is receptive to the advice of his wife.

THE TWELVE

These are the handpicked followers of Yeshuah who are given power to heal sicknesses, bring the dead back to life, and overcome demonic forces!

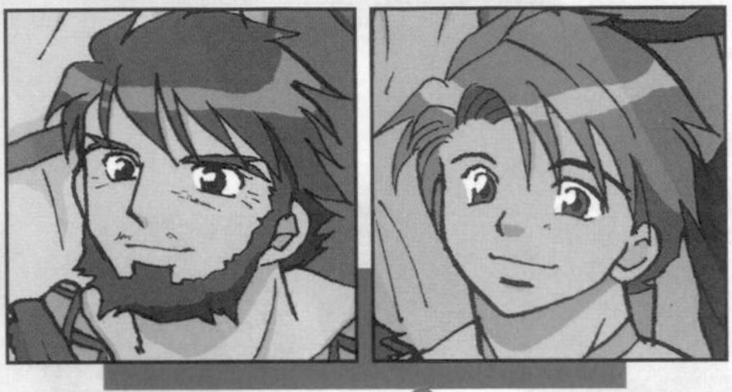

Peter (Simon) & Andrew

These brothers live as fishermen on Lake Galilee and are the first to become followers. Andrew, the younger brother, has also followed John the Baptizer. When Andrew first introduces Simon to Yeshuah, Simon gets a new name... Peter ("the Rock"). But will this Rock crumble when the going gets tough?

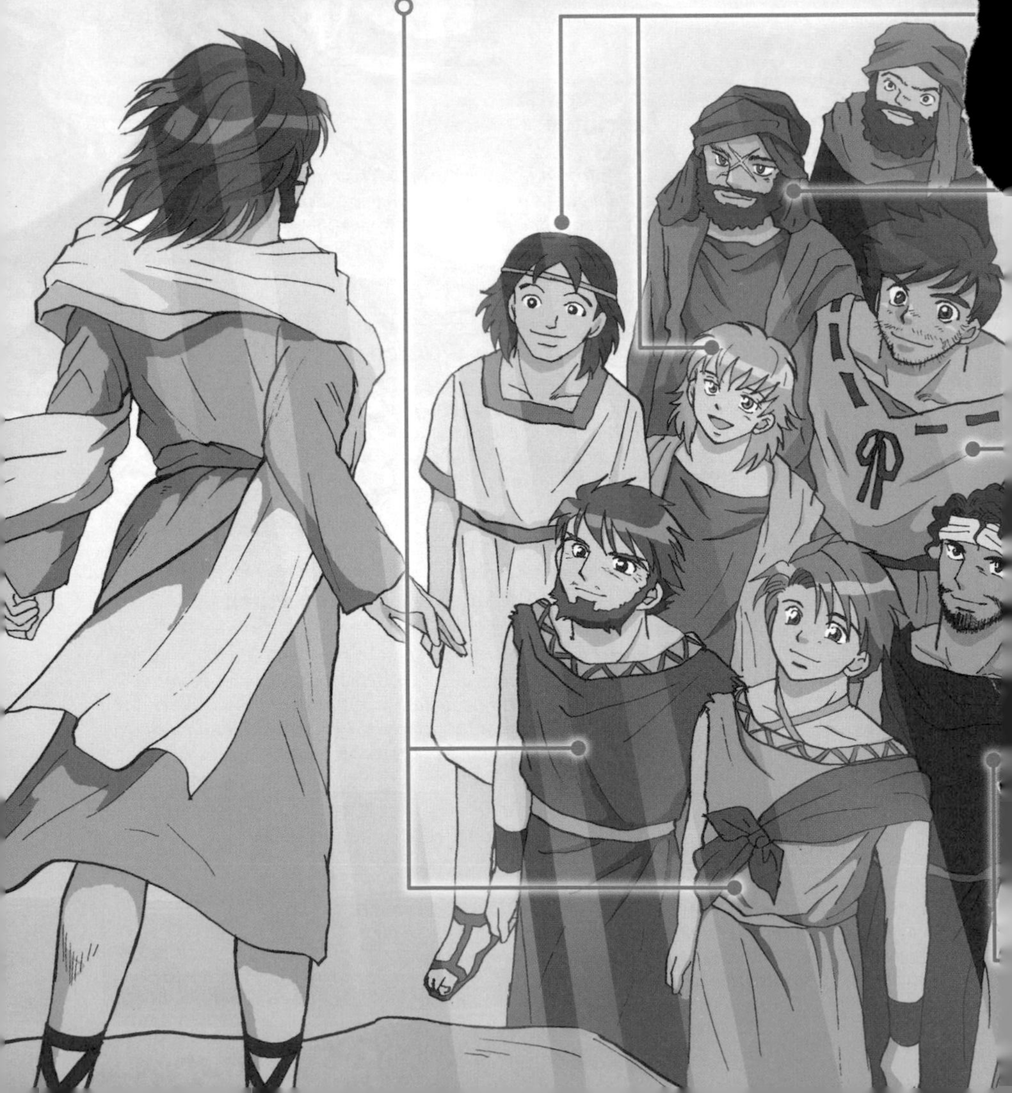

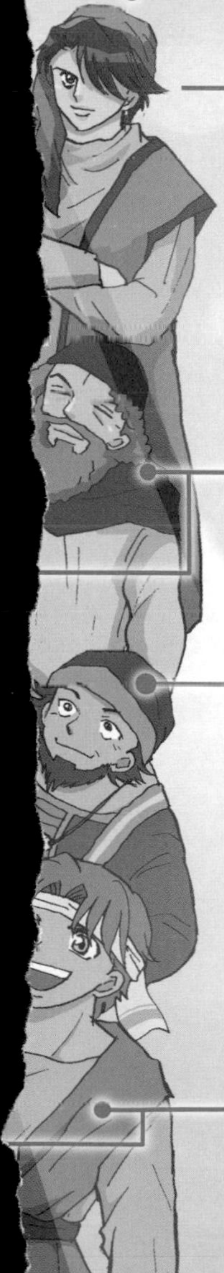

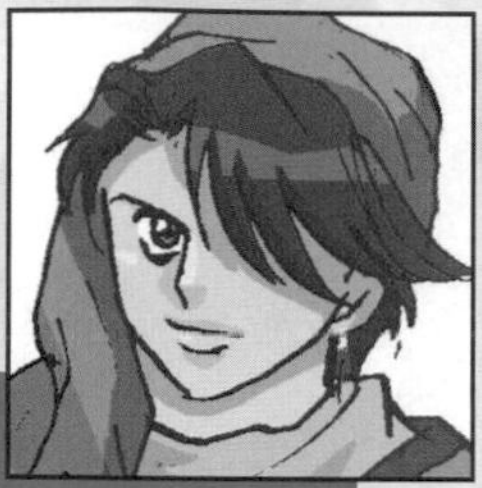

Judas Iscariot

Judas is the disiciple in charge of the group's finances. Beyond that, little is certain about him. Does his second name indicate he's one of the Sicarii, the "knife man" sect of the Zealots who seek to overthrow the Empire ... or merely that he's from the small Judean town of Kerioth? Nobody seems to be sure, and the thoughts of this quiet but intense disciple are known only to himself ... and Yeshuah!

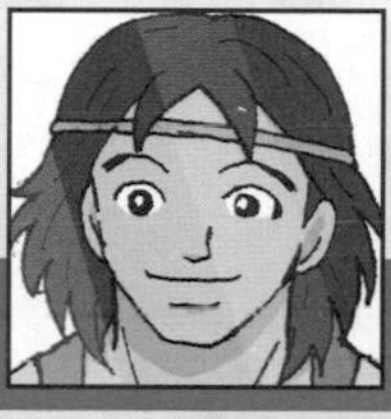

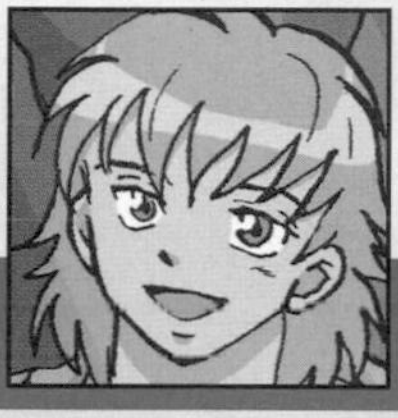

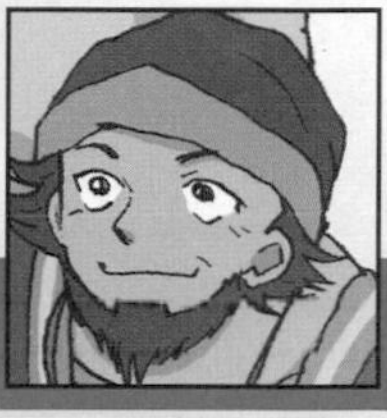

Philip

This disciple has an obsession with numbers... but has he counted the cost of following a controversial Messiah?

Nathanael Bartholomew

Philip's close friend Nathanael is a devout scholar ... one whose book knowledge could cause him to miss the big picture!

Matthew

Only Yeshuah would dare make a hated tax collector part of his group ... and he even knows Matthew will one day write a "tell all" book about him!

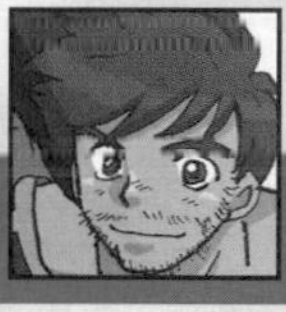

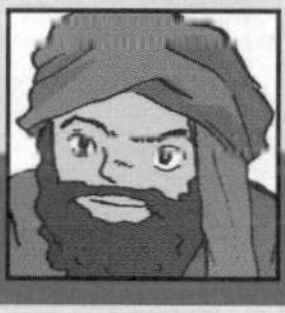

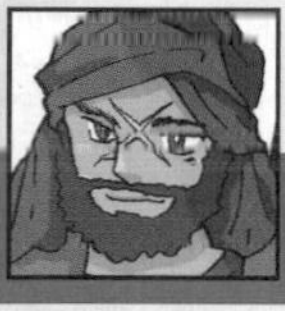

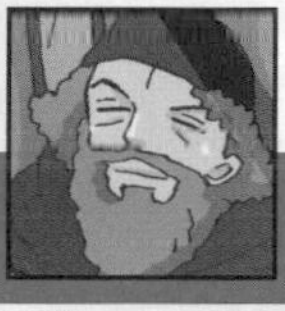

Thomas the Twin · *Thaddaeus (Jude)* · *Simon the Zealot* · *James, son of Alphaeus*

These four are also numbered among Yeshuah's Twelve. Thomas is a sincere "I'll-believe-it-when-I-see-it" realist. Thaddaeus (also called Jude), Simon (known as "the Zealot" because of his extreme political views), and James (referred to as "son of Alphaeus" or "James the Less") do not enjoy the same high profile as the others, but nobody should doubt their loyalty to Yeshuah ...or should they?

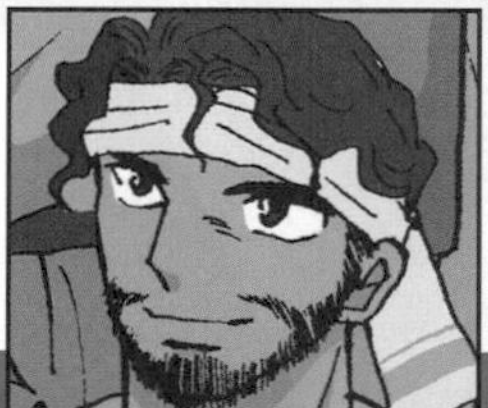

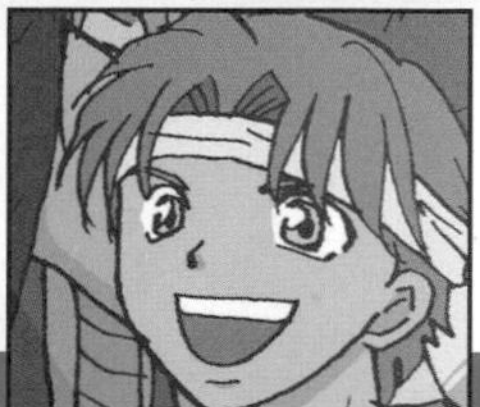

James & John, the sons of Zebedee

James and his younger brother John are also fishermen. With Peter, they enjoy the closest relationship with Yeshuah, who calls them "Sons of Thunder" for their passion and enthusiasm. Yet there is some tension in the group because John may be Yeshuah's favorite. Will petty rivalry and jealousy break the Twelve apart?